Also by Bernard Smith

FORCES IN AMERICAN CRITICISM

*A Study in the History of American
Literary Thought*

Edited by Mr. Smith, with Malcolm Cowley

BOOKS THAT CHANGED OUR MINDS

THE DEMOCRATIC SPIRIT

THE
DEMOCRATIC
SPIRIT

*A Collection of American Writings
from the Earliest Times to the Present Day*

EDITED, WITH AN INTRODUCTION, BY

BERNARD SMITH

SECOND EDITION, REVISED

❖❖❖❖❖❖❖❖❖❖❖❖❖❖❖❖❖❖❖❖❖❖❖❖❖❖❖❖❖❖❖

NEW YORK: ALFRED · A · KNOPF

1 9 4 3

To my wife
FRANCES NEWMARK SMITH
who helped to make this book
by her interest in it
and by her ardent collaboration
in research

PREFACE

TO THE SECOND EDITION

✢

THE FIRST EDITION of this work was prepared in the winter of 1940 and
the spring of '41. It was completed almost immediately after the Nazi
invasion of Russia. The impulse to prepare it originated, naturally, in
the war, or perhaps I should say in the tensions it created. And yet I
felt at the time that the war had no place in the volume, first because
to many Americans — perhaps to most — the war was still a remote affair, and secondly because the war had not yet inspired any significant
expressions of the democratic spirit. The book ended, then, logically
I think, with a good deal of material reflecting the democratic tendencies which arose from the great crisis of the 1930's and with some
which reflected American reaction to the rise of European fascism.

This second edition is being prepared in the summer of 1943, when
there is no phase of our thinking or feeling that is not conditioned by
the fact that we are at war. The crisis of the 1930's is history now, although its results — in literature, politics, law, and the very structure
of our state — will surround us for a long time to come. At the moment
we are troubled by questions concerning the domestic effects of our
military effort, our place in the peace to come, our relations with the
rest of the world, our attitude toward backward and colonial peoples.
Some people think they can add up all these questions and arrive at a
phrase: our war aims. That seems to me to be a naïve simplification.
What we are really concerned with are the fundamental questions of
democracy: questions of power, of the attitude of ruling groups toward
the masses they rule, of the aspirations of those masses and the degree
to which the realization of those aspirations will be facilitated or im-
peded by various kinds of ambitions and vested interests.

That such are the real questions of this stage of the war is proved
by the new material which concludes the present edition — the speeches

i

by President Roosevelt, Wendell L. Willkie, and Henry A. Wallace. They are, I think, the most important and most eloquent expressions of the democratic spirit that America has produced in this period, and they deal with nothing more or less than those questions of power and peoples' aspirations to which I have referred.

This edition differs from the first principally, then, in containing selections which are directly inspired by the war and in omitting a considerable number which were inspired by the crisis of the 1930's. That crisis is amply represented here, but it no longer dominates the concluding section of the book. The other major change in the work is the inclusion of material which should have been included in the first edition and which I regretted having omitted as soon as it was published. In addition, a few minor errors have been corrected and a few biographical sketches brought up to date.

In the Introduction to this volume I say: " Democracy is a very simple principle, and those who speculate about its meaning are those who are not quite willing to accept it. The dictionary defines it as ' the rule of the people.' Not much more need be said about it." It is interesting that several critics of the original edition quarreled with those remarks. One tried to convert democracy into a synonym for liberty (which he apparently regarded as freedom to accumulate wealth!). Another suggested that the proper concern of an American is not democracy but republicanism. A third hinted that the real problem about democracy is how to limit it. It is difficult to believe that democracy would have become the basic political force of the modern world if republican movements had not succeeded; and it is inconceivable that without liberty there can be any true or lasting democracy. But still it should be clear that democracy is much more than either republicanism or liberty (and that liberty is not worth dying for if all it means is respect for commercial success).

A reviewer complained that many of the contemporary selections are critical of certain aspects of American life. He thought there should be more selections in praise of our achievements. I can only say again what I said to him: " The literature of democracy, from its beginnings to the present, has been a literature of protest against inertia, complacency, greed, and intolerance. The democratic tradition is a tradition of struggle and action. It is not a tradition of smug self-congratulation."

There were complaints about the fact that a few of the contemporary writers here represented are partisans of socialism or communism. I can only repeat what I said in the Introduction: " It is not the purpose of this volume to argue for or against any specific democratic sentiment or theory, but rather to argue for the democratic spirit itself. No matter what one's own beliefs may be, however, one must agree that the socialist movement, in all its variations and developments, has been part of the democratic movement. No one can conceive of modern democracy without equalitarian and collectivist strains. . . . The ' left ' has helped to broaden and extend democracy in America." And to that I will add that one's disagreement with a writer's political program or his solutions of economic problems should not blind one to the worth or value of a specific example of his art.

In short, nothing that has been said to date about my remarks on the subject of democracy has persuaded me to alter those remarks in any particular whatever. I have been confirmed in my opinion that the fight for democracy is constant, must never be relaxed, must be prepared to face philosophical legerdemain and must assume that opposition will be found in influential and respectable quarters.

I hope that disposes of the complaint that Alexander Hamilton is not represented in this volume. I am charmed by the simple-mindedness of the critic who assumes that because Hamilton is not here I am not aware of how great a man Hamilton was or how great were his contributions to the formation of the American state. What I am actually not aware of is any significant contribution by him to the democratic spirit.

Nothing has changed — yet. The struggle for democracy continues in the heat of the war. It will continue after the war. It may become more intense after the war; it may even become desperate. The war is being fought on several levels: there is a war for power, there is a war for security, there is a war for democracy and justice to nations. It may be that we shall not win all of these wars at the same time. It may be that what need there has been for the words in this volume will not be lessened but enhanced by the conclusion of hostilities.

CONTENTS

A starred title denotes a selection from a larger work of the same title.

CONTENTS

CONTENTS

WALT WHITMAN (1819–1892)

DAVID R. LOCKE (1833–1888)

CONTENTS

xviii

CONTENTS

Contents

INTRODUCTION

✧

THE WORDS men fight and die for are the coins of politics, where by much usage they are soiled and by much manipulating debased. That has evidently been the fate of the word " democracy." It has come to mean whatever anyone wants it to mean.

For example: soon after the word " fascism " became widely known, there were some who said that our people could be persuaded to accept fascism if it were disguised as a democratic movement. Fortunately, they have not had the satisfaction of seeing their prophecies fulfilled, but they have certainly seen some rather weird distortions of the democratic idea advanced as measures for the defense of democracy. Sentiments born of bigotry, race prejudice, and private interest have been advocated, more than once, as expressions of this country's magnificent tradition of freedom and equality.

There are some who say that the present debasement of the word would not have been possible if our people actually believed in democracy. On the contrary, it is because the mass of Americans believe in it that those who would destroy or limit it must corrupt it by specious arguments and appeals to primitive fears. There are also some who say that no one knows what democracy really is — offering as proof of their contention the fact that there exists a variety of interpretations. Such reasoning creates the perfect mental climate for denials of democratic rights, because, obviously, if no one knows what it means, how can anyone say that a given idea, or project, or law, is or is not democratic? No doubt among the questioning philosophers are many who are sincerely puzzled, but their sincerity merely suggests that they are almost as little moved by the democratic ideal as those who have special ambitions.

For, after all, democracy is a very simple principle, and those who speculate about its meaning are those who are not quite willing to accept it. The dictionary defines it as " the rule of the people." Not much more need be said about it. To speak of the people is to refer to the majority of the population — and the majority is composed of men and women in modest circumstances and of all races and faiths. A significant factor in our history has been the effort, on the one hand, of minority groups to prevent the people from ruling, and, on the other hand, of the people to express their will and to have it applied rationally. The people's desire to rule has been simply a desire for greater opportunities to get more of the good things of life — food, shelter, leisure, education, security, pleasure. Occasionally their will has been deliberately thwarted; usually they have been misinformed as to what their will should be and how they should attempt to satisfy it. The people are in general inadequately educated and have little experience in philosophical and political reasoning, and so it is possible to misinform, divert, and delude them. But not forever and not about everything. They learn. The proof is the fact that they have bettered their material circumstances and acquired self-respect, and in the process of doing so they have constantly enlarged and enforced the application of such doctrines as equality before the law, universal suffrage, free public education, limitation of economic privilege, religious and racial tolerance, and so on — for those are the social conditions that are favorable to the progress of the people.

That, in sum, is the history of democracy. In that history writers have had an important role — all kinds of writers: poets, essayists, storytellers, journalists, preachers, politicians, lawyers. Their role has been not merely to express the people's will, but to formulate it. In other words, while often they do no more than set down eloquently what the community is vaguely feeling and thinking, quite as often they predict what the community will feel and think in the future. Why they have had such a role is a problem in itself, and one we are not directly concerned with here. There are many reasons, both social and psychological. All we need do here is to note the fact that the writer (with many notable exceptions!) has had an inspirational and prophetic role in the democratic era — a fact so obvious that it is seldom noted. The writer had a quite different role in the classical and feudal ages. Perhaps one can indicate his position in modern history just by pointing out that the invention of printing and the spread of literacy coincide with the beginnings of the rise of democracy.

To record the democratic movement in America, to show how it has found expression, and to illustrate its development, I have therefore thought it sufficient to gather together the truly influential and characteristic works of the democratic writers of this country. The latter phrase alludes to most of the writers of genuine stature that we have produced. We possess an aristocratic literary tradition too, but even though it includes several of our most distinguished writers, it is a minor tradition.

A general history of democracy would, of course, be very much larger than its history in America. The democratic idea did not originate here and its development here has been constantly influenced by developments elsewhere. But surely some of its brightest moments, some of its noblest heroes and heroines, and some of its finest expressions have occurred in the United States. For this was the first country that sought to create a state based on the democratic idea, and in this country there were fewer obstacles, fewer hostile traditions and institutions than in any other country in the world. Here the democratic idea has been an integral element in the national psychology, an unavoidable element in the national conduct, from the very beginning. Men have been freer here to speak and write what they have thought, and the people have accordingly been more alert and more determined.

The motive for the creation of this volume should be obvious. In these days, when we are one of the few peoples that can still cherish democracy, it behooves us to recollect our peculiar tradition and to review its growth so that we may know exactly what it is and not be led into believing it is something else. Here is a noble heritage. We must know it well if we are not to lose it. There are always forces at work to deprive us of it.

2

The selections speak for themselves, and I hope their authors are adequately "placed" by the prefatory biographical notes. It may be useful, however, to suggest briefly the background against which they should be viewed — the stream of social history from which they grew.

Our first settlers were mainly Protestants of English descent, and the Protestant elements continued to predominate when other national groups began to arrive — Scotch, Dutch, German, Scandinavian. A sure foundation for a democratic state was thus laid, for in the Protestant faiths were the sources of that respect and sympathy for the commoner which is the essence of democracy.

They were seldom, at first, aware of it. Indeed, our early settlers were often as bigoted as the established churches they were fleeing. But they could not escape the implications of their origins and creeds. They wanted Bibles available for everyone, they wanted everyone to read the Bible. Therefore, willy-nilly, they believed in the intelligence of the average man, in his capacity for understanding God's word, in the value of his conscience.

Moreover, they were largely drawn from the middle and lower classes, and they came here not just to worship freely, but to better themselves. They wanted land to cultivate and opportunities to trade, which meant that they wanted to be rid of the restrictions imposed upon them in the Old World. Therefore they wanted physical as well as religious freedom. In the end they wanted a free market — a community in which there was competition in production and selling — and out of that desire came the belief that there ought to be equality of opportunity.

The above is a generalized statement of the situation, and consequently subject to all sorts of qualifications. Actually, there were enormous differences between the Protestant sects. Many of the Puritans in Massachusetts were contemptuous of the mass of men and believed that only the " elect " (the elite) were worth bothering about — and the " elect " were usually the governing officials, the clergy, and the rich. In Virginia the planters established the Anglican Church and instituted a set of laws that were quite as " Puritanic " as those of Massachusetts. But the Quakers were here too, and they were comparatively tolerant and democratic; and there were also men and women who had certain " primitive Christian " beliefs in which little importance was attributed to professional clergymen and much emphasis was placed on Everyman's personal relations with his Maker — beliefs which held that anyone could achieve salvation. In addition, there were soon frontier settlements, out of the reach of churches and governments, where the most democratic religious sentiments prevailed, where the equality of all men in the eyes of God was assumed.

Naturally, in the frontier settlements the mere conditions of living encouraged democratic ideas; indeed, there tended to exist an equality in fact as well as in idea. On this subject many have written eloquently since 1893, when Frederick Jackson Turner first called the attention of American scholars to the significance of the frontier in American history. What has not, perhaps, been written about sufficiently is that social conditions in the towns along the Atlantic seaboard also encouraged the growth of democracy. For as the original settlements were increasingly populated, classes of small farmers, small merchants, independent artisans, and mechanics came into being, and they found that their interests were not always identical with those of the great merchants and the aristocratic landowners. A series of struggles began which have continued to this day. We know those struggles, in their later versions, as agrarian reform movements, the organization of workingmen into labor unions, the fight against "trusts" and monopolies, and the legislative drive to regulate competition. All of these campaigns had their seeds in the early days of the nation, for within any given settled area, at any given moment, the main sources of wealth were controlled by relatively few men, and it was therefore always necessary to find new ways to widen the field of opportunity and to establish the minimum human rights of those who had little property and no social status.

The form of the problem has changed continuously, and with each change there has been progress. The first problem was to secure religious tolerance, for without it the community could not maintain internal peace and the dissenting individual could not enjoy civil equality. Tolerance was not easily won. The need for it was superbly stated by Roger Williams; its philosophy was clearly formulated by Jefferson and Madison; it was bitterly fought for by later immigrant groups, such as the Irish Catholics and the eastern European Jews; yet even now, even in this country, it must constantly be defended.

The next great problem was to free America from the oppressive laws and trade practices of England — a goal in which rich and poor, merchants, farmers, and mechanics, North and South, were united. In the course of this struggle the basic doctrines of political equality and liberty were defined once and forever. Then after the Revolution the wants of the debt-ridden "little man," especially of the landless, had to be considered. Soon, with the coming of industrialism, there were labor contests. Above every other problem in the early nineteenth century, however, was the slavery issue. So long as slavery existed, democracy could hardly exist in the South and it could grow only with difficulty in the North.

Once chattel slavery was abolished, industrialism was triumphant, and in its boom period, despite its manifold blessings, it created the unspeakable conditions that surrounded what has come to be known as wage-slavery. Attacks upon these conditions were made on two fronts: directly by means of trade unions, and indirectly in the legislative halls — and victories were won on both fronts. At the same time a new agrarian movement boiled, when the farmers of the Middle West protested wrathfully against the hardships they were suffering because of the practices of wheat speculators, railroads, and mortgage-holding banks. The small manufacturer and store-keeper rose to protest against the controls exercised by the giant corporations which united to stifle competition and to maintain prices which would guarantee their own profits. These problems and the movements they created are with us today, in more complex forms than previously, and in new relations towards each other and towards the government.

A century ago, in the Mexican War, the nation was disturbed by the issue of imperialism. The question had to be faced: could democracy flourish at home while war and exploitation were visited upon other peoples? There was never really any doubt about the moral answer, but the pressures of an expanding economy were stronger than moral values. The Spanish-American War proved that, even though the idealists were convincing. The American people have never condoned imperialism; on the contrary, they have fiercely condemned it at the very moment when they were being pushed into it. The issue arose again in the First World War, and it is a matter of record that our government stated, when we went into the war, that we had no territorial ambitions. This was not simply propaganda directed at the peoples of Europe; it was a statement to the people of America to persuade them that they were not being shipped abroad to oppress weaker nations. Nevertheless, the United States *has* engaged in imperialistic ventures — and some of the most passionate, some of the most biting, pieces written in our history have been protests against imperialism. James Russell Lowell, Charles Eliot Norton, Mark Twain, William Vaughn Moody, and Finley Peter Dunne are only a few of the many distinguished writers who have raised their voices to that effect.

In the course of these various movements, campaigns, and contests a number of Americans decided that they could not attain their democratic ends under our traditional economic system. That is to say, they decided that in a competitive economy true freedom, plenty, peace, and social equality could not be obtained. They sought, therefore, to create a collective economy — in a word, socialism. A hundred different kinds of socialism have been advocated in America; scores of sects, parties, orders, and communities dedicated to the building of a socialist society have arisen, died, and been reborn during the past century. Those who believe that socialist ideas are "alien" — importations by foreigners from distant lands — have failed to define their terms. How many of our ideas are not importations? We can point to very few significant political doctrines, hardly one philosophy of government, that did not originate, in some form, elsewhere. So, too, with socialism. But if the notion exists that it is a *recent* importation, the notion is wholly erroneous. We had socialists among us soon after the Republic was founded. Material conditions, in certain sections of the population, favored the rise of collectivist movements.

It is not the purpose of this volume to argue for or against any specific democratic sentiment or theory, but rather to argue for the democratic spirit itself. No matter what one's own political beliefs may be, however, one must agree that the socialist movement, in all its variations and developments, has been part of the democratic movement. No one can conceive of modern democracy without equalitarian and collectivist strains. It is a commonplace of political thought, for example, that the radical proposals of yesterday are the laws of today. Our statute books are full of laws that not long ago were denounced as dangerous and subversive. The "left" has helped to broaden and extend democracy in America.

This brings us to considerations that are not essentially economic — to moral considerations. Ideas of justice, of social decency and humanity, are inherent in American idealism. Politics and economics determined the time and character of the war that freed the slaves, but a moral judgment preceded the war, and that moral judgment inspired the great denunciations of slavery. Neither Samuel Sewall nor John Woolman spoke for Northern manufacturers when they said that slavery was wrong. They spoke from a religious conviction, and the nonreligious men who agreed with them did so on the basis of a concept of justice. And slavery was not the only issue that moved men to take a position according to their ideas of right and wrong without reference to political and material interests; suffrage for women was another — and still others were the issues that derived from imperialism, war, and religious and racial tolerance. Even the most material problems — such as wage scales and free schools — were not decided by a clear-cut contest between the "haves" and the "have-nots"; large numbers of "haves" have consistently aligned themselves with the "have-nots" out of purely humanitarian impulses.

It is interesting also to note that the weight of sentiment and opinion which tends to settle one problem often tends to settle others. When, for instance, the people accepted the principles of religious tolerance and political equality, they inferentially accepted the principle that racial discrimination is obnoxious. It would be naïve to suppose that race hatreds and prejudices do not exist in the United States, but there are few men who would dare openly to defend them. Vicious practices survive, at times flourish, but the principle is not a matter of public debate. Equal treatment is the official policy of this country, and the mass of the people approve of it.

As the reader goes through this volume, he may wonder whether there has actually been any progress, for there are certain basic ideas and emotions that recur again and again. It would seem that the same battles are always being fought, the same points of view always being argued. In one sense, that is true. Nothing has been eternally settled; the great goals are still ahead of us. But progress has most certainly been made. When a battle is re-fought, it occurs on a different level from any previous time; when a viewpoint is re-argued, whatever is decided is vitally different from any previous decision. For the environment in which the debate takes place is new and the implications of the viewpoint therefore equally new. Nor is the environment the only thing that has changed. We know that a number of principles have been sufficiently established so that the overwhelming majority of the people tacitly obey them. Hence when such a principle is re-argued, it is really a new interpretation or a new application of it that is the subject of the argument.

Consider the crucial debates and contests of our own period, and especially of the 1930's. We had economic and social crises before in our history, but never such a crisis. We had writings before which spoke for the poor, the degraded, the beaten, the faithless, but never such a mass of writing that was so bitter and so critical. What happened was that the American people — most of the people — began to conceive of democracy in terms quite unlike any they had ever thought of before. They began to think of economic democracy as indispensable to liberty, and thus they began to look at themselves, at each other, and at their government in new ways. No idea that had never previously occurred to the mind of man, no viewpoint unknown in American thought, suddenly appeared. But where a hundred had once conceived of liberty as a matter of decent living and collective effort *as well as* freedom from restraint, now a thousand did so. As a result, our political life was transformed and our literature revolutionized. Now, at last, our fiction and drama were inspired by the kind of critical idealism which had once been found almost exclusively in the poem and the essay.

That is progress. In that sense we have steadily progressed for two centuries, and whoever has eyes to see and a heart to feel knows that we are still progressing and that the American people are determined to continue to do so. It is not any specific plan or law or campaign that matters at this time, but rather the democratic spirit itself. It is that above all that has been attacked, criticized, and perverted. Yet it has survived. Proof? The people of America have dignity and they are ready to fight for their rights, their liberties, and their needs. A nation of which that can be said is a nation in which the democratic spirit is alive.

EDITORIAL NOTE

✴

IN COLLECTING THE WORKS which comprise this volume, I have interpreted "writings" broadly: there are speeches and sermons as well as actual writings; there are examples of journalism and public documents as well as philosophical essays, stories, and poems. I have tried to effect a useful compromise between works that were important only at the time they appeared and works of permanent interest and value, and the emphasis is upon the latter category. I have sought to represent every major aspect of the democratic movement.

It would be absurd to suppose that this volume is a comprehensive anthology of American literature — firstly because there are other sides to our literature than the single side represented here, and secondly because there is much here that cannot be regarded as literature. And yet I believe that the volume as a whole expresses our literature in some ways that are not expressed by many systematic anthologies. I for one would rather see Americans read Wise and Mayhew than Wigglesworth and Mather; rather Emerson's "The Young American" than his essays on "compensation" and the "over-soul"; rather Whittier's "Clerical Oppressors" than his "Barbara Frietchie"; and I cannot understand why Parker should be neglected while Oliver Wendell Holmes is read.

As to method, since this volume is intended for the general reader rather than for professional scholars, and since enjoyment in reading is the aim, I have thought it wise to modernize the style of my selections from seventeenth- and early eighteenth-century writings. That is to say, I have frequently altered spelling, punctuation, and grammar to conform with present-day usage. The date in brackets at the end of each selection is the year — so far as I have been able to determine it — in which the work first appeared (whether in printed form or as a speech or sermon).

No anthology can be presented without an apology for omissions. I thought it advisable to select substantial works rather than fragments, and to represent writers of genuine stature or great influence by several titles rather than one or two. Hence, to keep this volume within reasonable space limits, I had to omit a number of men whom I should have liked to include. I know very well that another editor could prepare just as interesting a volume with a quite different table of contents. I do not regret that fact. It is one of the glories of American literature that it is so rich in works that reflect or express the democratic spirit.

For the final list of selections I am alone responsible, but I want to record here my gratitude for the good advice given me by Professor Newton Arvin, Van Wyck Brooks, Dr. Henry Seidel Canby, Dorothy Canfield Fisher, and Professor Arthur M. Schlesinger.

THE DEMOCRATIC SPIRIT

THE MAYFLOWER
COMPACT

IN SEPTEMBER 1620 the *Mayflower* sailed from Plymouth, England, with one hundred and two passengers bound for the "northern parts of Virginia," where they intended to settle under the jurisdiction of the Virginia Company. Thirty-five of the passengers were members of the Leyden congregation — the group of Separatists (or Pilgrims) who had left England to set up their own church in Holland and had afterwards decided that they could better their conditions in America. The other sixty-seven passengers were from London. Some of the latter were of the same character as the Leyden immigrants; others were merely adventurers. On November 6 they sighted land far to the north of the region named in their patent. They attempted to sail southward, but encountered dangerous waters and finally resolved to enter any safe near-by harbor. On November 21 they cast anchor at Provincetown, Cape Cod, subsequently moving on to Plymouth, Massachusetts.

When it became known on board ship that the company would settle outside the boundary of Virginia, some of the passengers boasted, according to Bradford's *History of Plymouth Plantation,* that they "would use their own liberty" and would recognize no government. The leaders of the company then realized that they would have to create a government whose edicts the majority of their members would be willing to enforce. Before landing they therefore drew up the celebrated Compact upon which their community would be based. It was signed by forty-one adult males, including John Carver, William Bradford, Stephen Hopkins, William Brewster, Miles Standish, John Alden, and Edward Winslow. The signers did not intend to create a new form of constitution; they had no strong democratic inclinations; they were ordinary Englishmen, most of them of the lower orders, loyal to their King, materially ambitious, and radical only in their desire to maintain their own unorthodox form of religious worship. But circumstances forced them to establish a democracy, for the Compact was clearly a democratic document, asserting as it did the will of the responsible majority, who claimed the right to adopt and administer laws deemed necessary by them. The Mayflower Compact was thus the first seed of democracy planted on American soil. The Pilgrims themselves later modified their democratic methods, but the seed had taken root. Their secular covenant, which resembled their church covenant, became a precedent for other companies of immigrants and other towns. Hence the origin of the democratic idea in America may be traced to this brief Compact. It follows in full:

I N the name of God, amen, we whose names are underwritten, the loyal subjects of our dread sovereign lord King James, by the grace of God, of Great Britain, France, and Ireland, King, Defender of the Faith, etc., having undertaken for the glory of God, and advancement of the Christian faith, and the honor of our King and country, a voyage to plant the first colony in the northern parts of Virginia, do by these presents, solemnly and mutually in the presence of God and one another, covenant and combine ourselves together into a civil body politic, for our better ordering and preservation, and furtherance of the ends aforesaid; and by virtue hereof do enact, constitute, and frame such just and equal laws, ordinances, acts, constitutions, and offices, from time to time, as shall be thought most meet and covenient for the general good of the colony; unto which we promise all due submission and obedience. In witness whereof we have hereunto subscribed our names at Cape Cod the eleventh of November, in the reign of our sovereign lord King James of England, France, and Ireland, the eighteenth and of Scotland, the fifty-fourth. *Anno Domini,* 1620.

ROGER WILLIAMS

[1603?–1683]

HE CAME from the class that was responsible for the rising tide of political and religious liberalism: his father was a well-to-do merchant in London. Through the interest of Sir Edward Coke, the jurist, he obtained scholarships at Charterhouse and Pembroke College, Cambridge, receiving his B.A. in 1627. Two years later he took holy orders. Meanwhile he became acquainted with the Puritan party and allied himself with it. In 1631 he arrived in New England. He quickly discovered that the Massachusetts government was as bigoted and illiberal as the English. He refused a call to Boston Church, tried Plymouth, finally settled in Salem. In a short time he achieved notoriety as a "dangerous agitator." He demanded that the New England churches separate themselves completely from the Church of England; he denounced English imperialism and claimed that the King had no title to American land and that the colonists had only to deal with the Indians; he argued that the magistrates had no power to punish persons for their religious opinions. In 1635 a sentence of banishment was passed upon him, and the following year, when he was about to be arrested, he fled to what is now Rhode Island, where he founded Providence. There he set up the most democratic government in America. He spent the rest of his life fighting for religious freedom, maintaining friendly relations with the Indians, and defending Rhode Island against the encroachments of the Puritan oligarchs, who feared that his colony would infect their own people with ideas of liberty and democracy. His two most famous books, from which excerpts follow, were masterpieces of invective and argument against religious persecution.

from

THE BLOODY TENENT OF PERSECUTION
FOR CAUSE OF CONSCIENCE

PREFACE

First, that the blood of so many hundred thousand souls of Protestants and Papists, spilt in the wars of present and former ages for their respective consciences, is not required nor accepted by Jesus Christ the Prince of Peace.

Secondly, pregnant scriptures and arguments are throughout the work proposed against the doctrine of persecution for the cause of conscience.

Thirdly, satisfactory answers are given to scriptures and objections produced by Mr. Calvin, Beza, Mr. Cotton, and the ministers of the New England churches, and others former and later, tending to prove the doctrine of persecution for cause of conscience.

Fourth, the doctrine of persecution for cause of conscience is proved guilty of all the blood of the souls crying for vengeance under the altar.

Fifthly, all civil states with their officers of justice in their respective constitutions and administrations are proved essentially civil, and therefore not judges, governors, or defenders of the spiritual or Christian state and worship.

Sixthly, it is the will and command of God that (since the coming of his Son the Lord Jesus) a permission of the most Paganish, Jewish, Turkish, or Antichristian consciences and worships be granted to all men in all nations and countries: and they are only to be fought against with that sword which is only (in soul matters) able to conquer: to wit, the sword of God's spirit, the word of God.

Seventhly, the state of the land of Israel, the kings and people thereof, in peace and war, is proved figurative and ceremonial, and no pattern nor precedent for any kingdom or civil state in the world to follow.

Eighthly, God requireth not a uniformity of religion to be enacted and enforced in any civil state; which enforced uniformity (sooner or later) is the great occasion of civil war, ravishing of conscience, persecution of Christ Jesus in his servants, and of the hypocrisy and destruction of millions of souls.

Ninthly, in holding an enforced uniformity of religion in a civil state,

6

we must necessarily disclaim our desires and hopes of the Jews' conversion to Christ.

Tenthly, an enforced uniformity of religion throughout a nation or civil state confounds the civil and religious, denies the principles of Christianity and civility, and that Jesus Christ is come in the flesh.

Eleventhly, the permission of other consciences and worships than a state professeth only can (according to God) procure a firm and lasting peace (good assurance being taken according to the wisdom of the civil state for uniformity of civil obedience from all sorts).

Twelfthly, lastly, true civility and Christianity may both flourish in a state or kingdom, notwithstanding the permission of divers and contrary consciences, either of Jew or Gentile.

TO EVERY COURTEOUS READER

While I plead the cause of truth and innocence against the bloody doctrine of persecution for cause of conscience, I judge it not unfit to give alarm to myself and all men to prepare to be persecuted or hunted for cause of conscience.

Whether thou standest charged with 10 or but 2 talents, if thou huntest any for cause of conscience, how canst thou say thou followest the Lamb of God, who so abhorred that practice?

If Paul, if Jesus Christ were present here at London, and the question were proposed what religion would they approve of, the Papists, Prelatists, Presbyterians, Independents, etc., would each say: of mine, of mine.

But put the second question: if one of the several sorts should by major vote attain the sword of steel, what weapons doth Christ Jesus authorize them to fight with in his cause? Do not all men hate the persecutor, and every conscience, true or false, complain of cruelty, tyranny, etc.?

Two mountains of crying guilt lie heavy upon the backs of all that name the name of Christ in the eyes of Jews, Turks, and Pagans.

First, the blasphemies of their idolatrous inventions, superstitions, and most unchristian conversations.

Secondly, the bloody irreligious and inhumane oppressions and destructions under the mask or veil of the name of Christ, etc.

Oh, how like is the jealous Jehovah, the consuming fire, to end these present slaughters in a greater slaughter of the holy witnesses (Rev. ii).

7

Six years' preaching of so much truth of Christ (as that time afforded in K. Edward's days) kindles the flames of Q. Mary's bloody persecutions.

Who can now but expect that after so many scores of years preaching and professing of more truth, and amongst so many great contentions amongst the very best of Protestants, a fiery furnace should be heat, and who sees not now the fires kindling?

I confess I have little hopes, till those flames are over, that this discourse against the doctrine of persecution for cause of conscience should pass current (I say not amongst the wolves and lions, but even amongst the sheep of Christ themselves), yet *liberavi animam meam,* I have not hid within my breast my soul's belief: and although sleeping on the bed either of the pleasures or profits of sin, thou thinkest thy conscience bound to smite at him that dares to waken thee? Yet in the midst of all these civil and spiritual wars I hope we shall agree in these particulars.

First, however the proud (upon the advantage of a higher earth or ground) o'erlook the poor and cry out: schismatics, heretics, etc., shall blasphemers and seducers scape unpunished? Etc. Yet there is a sorer punishment in the Gospel for despising of Christ than Moses, even when the despiser of Moses was put to death without mercy (Heb. x. 28, 29). He that believeth not shall be damned (Mark xvi. 16).

Secondly, whatever worship, ministry, ministration, the best and purest are practiced without faith and true persuasion that they are the true institutions of God, they are sin, sinful worships, ministries, etc. And however in civil things we may be servants unto men, yet in divine and spiritual things the poorest peasant must disdain the service of the highest prince: Be ye not the servants of men (I Cor. xiv).

Thirdly, without search and trial no man attains this faith and right persuasion (I Thess. v). Try all things.

In vain have English parliaments permitted English Bibles in the poorest English houses, and the simplest man or woman to search the Scriptures, if yet against their soul's persuasion from the Scripture they should be forced (as if they lived in Spain or Rome itself without the sight of a Bible) to believe as the church believes.

Fourthly, having tried, we must hold fast (I Thess. v) upon the loss of a crown (Rev. iii. 11); we must not let go for all the fleabitings of the present afflictions, etc.; having bought truth dear, we must not sell it cheap, not the least grain of it for the whole world, no,

8

not for the saving of souls, though our own most precious; least of all for the bitter sweetening of a little vanishing pleasure.

For a little puff of credit and reputation from the changeable breath of uncertain sons of men.

For the broken bags of riches on eagles' wings, for a dream of these, any or all of these which on our death-bed vanish and leave tormenting stings behind them: oh, how much better is it from the love of truth, from the love of the Father of lights, from whence it comes, from the love of the son of God, who is the Way and the Truth, to say as he (John xviii. 37)! For this end was I born, and for this end came I into the world, that I might bear witness to the truth.

[*1644*]

from

THE BLOODY TENENT YET MORE BLOODY

I must proclaim before the Most Holy God, angels, and men that . . . this [persecution for cause of conscience] is a foul, a black, and a bloody tenent.

A tenent of high blasphemy against the God of Peace, the God of Order, who hath of one blood made all mankind, to dwell upon the face of the earth, now all confounded and destroyed in their civil beings and subsistences by mutual flames of war from their several respective religions and consciences.

A tenent warring against the Prince of Peace, Christ Jesus, denying his appearance and coming in the flesh to put an end to and abolish the shadows of that ceremonial and typical land of Canaan.

A tenent fighting against the sweet end of his coming, which was not to destroy men's lives for their religions, but to save them by the meek and peaceable invitations and persuasions of his peaceable wisdom's maidens.

A tenent foully charging his wisdom, faithfulness, and love, in so poorly providing such magistrates and civil powers all the world over as might effect so great a charge pretended to be committed to them.

A tenent lamentably guilty of his most precious blood, shed in the blood of so many hundred thousand of his poor servants by the civil

9

powers of the world, pretending to suppress blasphemies, heresies, idolatries, superstition, etc.

A tenent fighting with the spirit of love, holiness, and meekness, by kindling fiery spirits or false zeal and fury, when yet such spirits know not of what spirit they are.

A tenent fighting with those mighty angels who stand up for the peace of the saints against Persia, Greece, etc., and so consequently all other nations who, fighting for their several religions and against the truth, leave no room for such as fear and love the Lord on the earth.

A tenent against which the blessed souls under the altar cry aloud for vengeance, this tenent having cut their throats, torn our their hearts, and poured forth their blood in all ages, as the only heretics and blasphemers in the world.

A tenent which no uncleanness, no adultery, incest, sodomy, or bestiality can equal, this ravishing and forcing (explicitly or implicity) the very souls and consciences of all the nations and inhabitants of the world.

A tenent that puts out the very eye of all true faith, which cannot but be as free and voluntary as any virgin in the world, in refusing or embracing any spiritual offer or object.

A tenent loathsome and ugly (in the eyes of the God of Heaven, and serious sons of men) I say, loathsome with the palpable filths of gross dissimulation and hypocrisy; thousands of peoples and whole nations compelled by this tenent to put on the foul vizard of religious hypocrisy for fear of laws, losses, and punishments, and for the keeping and hoping for of favor, liberty, worldly commodity, etc.

A tenent woefully guilty of hardening all false and deluded consciences (of whatsoever sect, faction, heresy, or idolatry, though never so horrid and blasphemous) by cruelties and violences practiced against them, all false teachers and their followers (ordinarily) contracting a brawny and steely hardness from their sufferings for their consciences.

A tenent that shuts and bars out the gracious prophecies and promises and discoveries of the most glorious Sun of Righteousness, Christ Jesus; that burns up the Holy Scriptures, and forbids them, upon the point, to be read in English, or that any trial or search or truly free disquisition be made by them; when the most able, diligent, and conscionable readers must pluck forth their own eyes and be forced to read by the (whichsoever predominant) clergy's spectacles.

A tenent that seals up the spiritual graves of all men, Jews and Gentiles, and consequently stands guilty of the damnation of all men, since no preachers nor trumpets of Christ himself may call them out but such as the several and respective nations of the world themselves allow of.

A tenent that fights against the common principles of all civility, and in the very civil being and combinations of men in nations, cities, etc., by commixing (explicitly or implicitly) a spiritual and civil state together, and so confounding and overthrowing the purity and strength of both.

A tenent that kindles the devouring flames of combustions and wars in most nations of the world, and (if God were not infinitely gracious) had almost ruined the English, French, and Scotch and Irish, and many other nations, German, Polish, Hungarian, Bohemian, etc.

A tenent that bows down the backs and necks of all civil states and magistrates, kings and emperors, under the proud feet of that man and monster of sin and pride the pope, and all popish and proud clergymen, rendering such laics and seculars (as they call them) but slavish executioners (upon the point) of their most imperious synodical decrees and sentences.

A tenent that renders the highest civil magistrates and ministers of justice (the fathers and gods of their countries) either odious or lamentably grievous unto the very best subjects by either clapping or keeping on the iron yokes of cruelest oppression. No yoke or bondage comparably so grievous as that upon the soul's neck of men's religion and consciences.

A tenent all besprinkled with the bloody murders, stabs, poisonings, pistolings, powder-plots, etc., against many famous kings, princes, and states, either actually performed or attempted, in France, England, Scotland, Low Countries, and other nations.

A tenent all red and bloody with those most barbarous and tiger-like massacres of so many thousand and ten thousands formerly in France and other parts, and so lately and so horribly in Ireland; of which, whatever causes be assigned, this chiefly will be found the true; and while this continues (to wit, violence against conscience), this bloody issue sooner or later must break forth again (except God wonderfully stop it) in Ireland and other places too.

A tenent that stunts the growth and flourishing of the most likely and hopefulest commonweals and countries, while consciences the best and the best-deserving subjects are forced to fly (by enforced or voluntary banishment) from their native countries; the lamentable proof whereof England hath felt in the flight of so many worthy English into the Low Countries and New England, and from New England into Old again and other foreign parts.

A tenent whose gross partiality denies the principles of common justice, while men weigh out to the consciences of all others that which they judge not fit nor right to be weighed out to their own, since the persecutor's rule is to take and persecute all consciences, only himself must not be touched.

A tenent that is but Machiavellism, and makes a religion but a cloak or stalking-horse to policy and private ends of Jeroboam's crown, and the priest's benefice, etc.

A tenent that corrupts and spoils the very civil honesty and natural conscience of a nation, since conscience to God, violated, proves (without repentance) ever after a very jade, a drug, loose and unconscionable in all converse with men.

Lastly, a tenent in England most unseasonable, as pouring oil upon those flames which the high wisdom of the Parliament, by easing the yokes on men's consciences) had begun to quench.

[1652]

BACON'S "MAN"

POLITICAL and social struggles began early in the history of America. In 1676 a revolt broke out in Virginia against the administration of Governor Berkeley. This brutal English aristocrat, who boasted that his territory had neither schools nor newspapers, lacked even the saving grace of competence. For while all the British rulers were interested solely in the profits to be got out of their colonies, some of them knew at least how to keep the colonists peaceful. Berkeley not only exploited the common people (especially the poorer planters on the frontier), but also failed to give them police protection. When he refused to help the frontier settlements put down an Indian uprising, the rebellion began. At its head was Nathaniel Bacon, Cambridge University graduate, who had openly sympathized with the people ever since he had arrived in Virginia. The rebels intended to force social and economic reforms as well as to clear out the hostile Indians. They were winning both fights until Bacon's sudden death from fever, whereupon Berkeley drowned the rebellion in blood. The epitaph which follows is the finest poem that came out of America during the first century of English rule. No one knows anything about its author except that he proclaimed himself " Bacon's man." It has been suggested, therefore, that he was Bacon's servant. This seems unlikely. He was probably one of Bacon's followers — one of the poor planters who participated in the rebellion. His elegy was not merely a tribute to a heroic leader, but a quite eloquent expression of the struggle for freedom and justice. It was another of the seeds planted on American soil in the seventeenth century from which our libertarian and democratic traditions were to grow.

BACON'S EPITAPH MADE BY HIS MAN

Death, why so cruel? What! No other way
To manifest thy spleen, but thus to slay
Our hopes of safety, liberty, our all,
Which, through thy tyranny, with him must fall
To its late chaos? Had thy rigid force
Been dealt by retail, and not thus in gross,
Grief had been silent. Now we must complain,

13

Since thou, in him, hast more than thousand slain,
Whose lives and safeties did so much depend
On him their life, with him their lives must end.
    If't be a sin to think Death bribed can be
We must be guilty; say it was bribery
Guided the fatal shaft, Virginia's foes,
To whom for secret crimes just vengeance owes
Deserved plagues, dreading their just desert,
Corrupted Death by Paracelsian art,
Him to destroy, whose well tried courage such,
Their heartless hearts, nor arms nor strength could touch.
    Who now must heal those wounds or stop that blood
The Heathen made, and drew into a flood?
Who is it must plead our cause? Nor trump nor drum
Nor Deputations; these, alas! are dumb
And cannot speak. Our arms (though ne'er so strong)
Will want the aid of his commanding tongue,
Which conquered more that Cæsar.
                    He o'erthrew
Only the outward frame; this could subdue
The rugged works of nature. Souls replete
With dull chill cold, he'd animate with heat
Drawn forth of reason's limbec. In a word,
Mars and Minerva both in him concurred
For arts, for arms, whose pen and sword alike
As Cato's did, may admiration strike
Into his foes; while they confess withal
It was their guilt styled him a criminal.
Only this difference does from truth proceed:
They in the guilt, he in the name must bleed.
While none shall dare his obsequies to sing
In deserved measures: until time shall bring
Truth crowned with freedom, and from danger free
To sound his praises to posterity.
    Here let him rest; while we this truth report
He's gone from hence unto a higher Court
To plead his cause, where he by this doth know
Whether to Cæsar he was friend, or foe.

[1676]

14

SAMUEL SEWALL

[1652–1730]

BORN in England, he was nine years old when his family brought him to Boston, where he was reared and prepared for Harvard. In 1673, two years after his graduation, he was appointed tutor at the college. Not long afterwards, however, he married a very rich young lady. From then on he was a man of substance and leisure, dividing his time between his mercantile interests, public affairs, and literature. He held several judicial posts, was a deputy to the General Court, managed the colony's printing press, was a commissioner of the Society for the Propagation of the Gospel in New England. In 1692 he was made a member of the commission formed to try the cases of witchcraft at Salem and he took part in the decisions that resulted in the execution of nineteen persons. But Sewall repented, and he was the only one of the judges to confess publicly that he had been mistaken. In 1697 he stood up in church while a minister read his confession of error and guilt. It was a characteristic act of courage. Three years later he published his tract *The Selling of Joseph,* which was probably the first published attack on slavery in America. His courage and liberalism were also evident in his judicial career and in his enlightened attitude toward the Indians. Sewall is best known today for his diary, which affords an interesting picture of Puritan life and thought.

THE SELLING OF JOSEPH

A MEMORIAL

Forasmuch as liberty is in real value next unto life, none ought to part with it themselves, or deprive others of it, but upon most mature consideration.

The numerousness of slaves at this day in the province, and the uneasiness of them under their slavery, hath put many upon thinking whether the foundation of it be firmly and well laid, so as to sustain

15

the vast weight that is built upon it. It is most certain that all men, as they are the sons of Adam, are coheirs, and have equal right unto liberty and all other outward comforts of life. GOD hath given the earth [with all its commodities] unto the sons of Adam (Ps. cxv. 16). And hath made of one blood, all nations of men, for to dwell on all the face of the earth, and hath determined the times before appointed, and the bounds of their habitation, that they should seek the Lord. Forasmuch, then, as we are of the offspring of God, etc. (Acts xvii. 26, 27, 29). Now, although the title given by the last Adam doth infinitely better men's estates respecting God and themselves, and grants them a most beneficial and inviolable lease under the broad seal of Heaven, who were before only tenants at will, yet through the indulgence of God to our first parents after the Fall, the outward estate of all and every of their children remains the same, as to one another. So that originally, and naturally, there is no such thing as slavery. Joseph was rightfully no more a slave to his brethren than they were to him; and they had no more authority to sell him than they had to slay him. And if they had nothing to do to sell him, the Ishmaelites bargaining with them, and paying down twenty pieces of silver, could not make a title. Neither could Potiphar have any better interest in him than the Ishmaelites had (Gen. xxxvii. 20, 27, 28). For he that shall in this case plead alteration of property seems to have forfeited a great part of his own claim to humanity. There is no proportion between twenty pieces of silver and liberty. The commodity itself is the claimer. If Arabian gold be imported in any quantities, most are afraid to meddle with it, though they might have it at easy rates; lest if it should have been wrongfully taken from the owners, it should kindle a fire to the consumption of their whole estate. 'Tis pity there should be more caution used in buying a horse, or a little lifeless dust, than there is in purchasing men and women, whenas they are the offspring of God, and their liberty is *auro pretiosior omni*.

And seeing God hath said: *He that stealeth a man and selleth him, or if he be found in his hand, he shall surely be put to death* (Exod. xxi. 16) this Law being of everlasting equity, wherein man-stealing is ranked amongst the most atrocious of capital crimes, what louder cry can there be made of that celebrated warning: *Caveat emptor!*

And all things considered, it would conduce more to the welfare of the province to have white servants for a term of years than to have slaves for life. Few can endure to hear of a Negro's being made free;

16

and indeed they can seldom use their freedom well; yet their continual aspiring after their forbidden liberty renders them unwilling servants. And there is such a disparity in their conditions, color, and hair that they can never embody with us, and grow up into orderly families, to the peopling of the land; but still remain in our body politic as a kind of extravasate blood. As many Negro men as there are among us, so many empty places there are in our train bands, and the places taken up of men that might make husbands for our daughters. And the sons and daughters of New England would become more like Jacob and Rachel if this slavery were thrust quite out of doors. Moreover it is too well known what temptations masters are under to connive at the fornication of their slaves, lest they should be obliged to find them wives or pay their fines. It seems to be practically pleaded that they might be lawless; 'tis thought much of that the law should have satisfaction for their thefts and other immoralities; by which means, *Holiness to the Lord* is more rarely engraven upon this sort of servitude. It is likewise most lamentable to think how in taking Negroes out of Africa and selling of them here, that which God has joined together, men do boldly rend asunder; men from their country, husbands from their wives, parents from their children. How horrible is the uncleanness, mortality, if not murder that the ships are guilty of that bring great crowds of these miserable men and women. Methinks, when we are bemoaning the barbarous usage of our friends and kinsfolk in Africa, it might not be unseasonable to inquire whether we are not culpable in forcing the Africans to become slaves amongst ourselves. And it may be a question whether all the benefit received by Negro slaves will balance the account of cash laid out upon them, and for the redemption of our own enslaved friends out of Africa, besides all the persons and estates that have perished there.

Obj. 1. *These blackamoors are of the posterity of Cham, and therefore are under the curse of slavery* (Gen. ix. 25, 26, 27).

Answ. Of all offices, one would not beg this: viz., uncalled for, to be an executioner of the vindictive wrath of God, the extent and duration of which is to us uncertain. If this ever was a commission, how do we know but that it is long since out of date? Many have found it to their cost that a prophetical denunciation of judgment against a person or people would not warrant them to inflict that evil. If it would, Hazael might justify himself in all he did against his master and the Israelites, from II Kings viii. 10, 12.

17

But it is possible that by cursory reading, this text may have been mistaken. For Canaan is the person cursed three times over, without the mentioning of Cham. Good expositors suppose the curse entailed on him, and that this prophecy was accomplished in the extirpation of the Canaanites and in the servitude of the Gibeonites. *Vide pareum.* Whereas the blackamoors are not descended of Canaan, but of Cush (Ps. lxviii. 31). *Princes shall come out of Egypt* [Mizraim]; *Ethiopia* [Cush] *shall soon stretch out her hands unto God.* Under which names all Africa may be comprehended; and their promised conversion ought to be prayed for (Jer. xiii. 23). *Can the Ethiopian change his skin?* This shows that black men are the posterity of Cush, who time out of mind have been distinguished by their color. And for want of the true, Ovid assigns a fabulous cause of it: *Sanguine tum credunt in corpora summa vocato Æthiopum populos nigrum traxisse colorem* (*Metamorph.* lib. 2).

Obj. 2. *The Nigers are brought out of a pagan country, into places where the Gospel is preached.*

Answ. Evil must not be done that good may come of it. The extraordinary and comprehensive benefit accruing to the church of God, and to Joseph personally, did not rectify his brethren's sale of him.

Obj. 3. *The Africans have wars one with another; our ships bring lawful captives taken in those wars.*

Answ. For aught is known, their wars are much such as were between Jacob's sons and their brother Joseph. If they be between town and town, provincial, or national, every war is upon one side unjust. An unlawful war can't make lawful captives. And by receiving, we are in danger to promote and partake in their barbarous cruelties. I am sure, if some gentlemen should go down to the Brewsters to take the air, and fish, and a stronger party from Hull should surprise them, and sell them for slaves to a ship outward bound, they would think themselves unjustly dealt with, both by sellers and buyers. And yet 'tis to be feared we have no other kind of title to our Nigers. *Therefore all things whatsoever ye would that men should do to you, do ye even so to them: for this is the law and the prophets* (Matt. vii. 12).

Obj. 4. *Abraham had servants bought with his money, and born in his house.*

Answ. Until the circumstances of Abraham's purchase be recorded, no argument can be drawn from it. In the mean time charity obliges us to conclude that he knew it was lawful and good.

It is observable that the Israelites were strictly forbidden the buying or selling one another for slaves (Lev. xxv. 39, 46; Jer. xxxiv. 8, 22).
And God gaged his blessing in lieu of any loss they might conceit
they suffered thereby (Deut. xv. 18). And since the partition wall is
broken down, inordinate self-love should likewise be demolished.
God expects that Christians should be of a more ingenuous and benign
frame of spirit. Christians should carry it to all the world, as the
Israelites were to carry it one towards another. And for men ob-
stinately to persist in holding their neighbors and brethren under the
rigor of perpetual bondage seems to be no proper way of gaining assurance that God has given them spiritual freedom. Our blessed
Saviour has altered the measures of the ancient love-song and set it
to a most excellent new tune, which all ought to be ambitious of learning (Matt. v. 43, 44; John xiii. 34). These Ethiopians, as black as they
are, seeing they are the sons and daughters of the first Adam, the
brethren and sisters of the last Adam, and the offspring of God, they
ought to be treated with a respect agreeable.

*Servitus perfecta voluntaria, inter Christianum et Christianum, ex
parte servi patientis sæpe est licita, quia est necessaria: sed ex parte
domini agentis, et procurando et exercendo, vix potest esse licita: quia
non convenit regulæ illi generali: Quæcunque volueritis ut factant vobis
homines, ita et vos facite eis* (Matt. viii. 12).

*Perfecta servitus pænæ, non potest jure locum habere, nisi ex delicto
gravi quod ultimatum supplicium aliquo modo meretur: quia Libertas
ex naturali æstimatione proxime accedit ad vitam ipsam, et eidem a
multis præferri solet.* (Ames: Cas. Consc., Lib. 5, Cap. 23, Thes. 2, 3).

[*1700*]

JOHN WISE

[1652–1725]

THE SON of an indentured servant, he was born in Roxbury, Massachusetts, attended the free school of that city, and then studied theology at Harvard, from which he was graduated in 1673. He preached in several villages before settling down as minister of a small church in the Ipswich township, where he remained until his death. Every time he appeared in a public role, it was in order to attack tyranny and aristocracy and to champion the cause of the common people. He supported the movement for paper money, petitioned the General Court to reverse the Salem witchcraft convictions, and fought magnificently in behalf of democracy in church and state. At the beginning of the eighteenth century there was a movement to put all the Congregationalist churches under the supervision of associations of clergymen, thus depriving the members of the individual churches of their traditional right to govern themselves in certain important particulars. Wise reacted vehemently. In 1710 he published *The Churches Quarrel Espoused,* a pamphlet in which he exposed the reactionary character of the clerical movement. Then, in 1717, he issued his *Vindication of the Government of New England Churches,* in which he wrote with great passion and force, and with fine logic, of the desirability of democracy and the dangers and injustices of aristocratic governments.

---

from

A VINDICATION OF THE GOVERNMENT
OF NEW ENGLAND CHURCHES

I shall disclose several principles of natural knowledge, plainly discovering the law of nature, or the true sentiments of natural reason, with respect to man's being and government. And in this essay I shall peculiarly confine the discourse to two heads: viz.

I. Of the natural (in distinction to the civil), and then,

II. Of the civil being of man. And I shall principally take Baron Puffendorff for my chief guide and spokesman.

I. I shall consider man in a state of natural being, as a free-born subject under the crown of Heaven, and owing homage to none but God himself. It is certain civil government in general is a very admirable result of Providence, and an incomparable benefit to mankind, yet must needs be acknowledged to be the effect of human free-compacts and not of divine institution; it is the produce of man's reason, of human and rational combinations, and not from any direct orders of infinite wisdom, in any positive law wherein is drawn up this or that scheme of civil government. Government (says the Lord Warrington) is necessary — in that no society of men can subsist without it; and that particular form of government is necessary which best suits the temper and inclination of a people. Nothing can be God's ordinance but what he has particularly declared to be such; there is no particular form of civil government described in God's Word, neither does nature prompt it. The government of the Jews was changed five times. Government is not formed by nature, as other births or productions; if it were, it would be the same in all countries, because nature keeps the same method, in the same thing, in all climates. If a commonwealth be changed into a monarchy, is it nature that forms and brings forth the monarch? Or if a royal family be wholly extinct (as in Noah's case, being not heir apparent from descent from Adam) is it nature that must go to work (with the king bees, who themselves alone preserve the royal race in that empire) to breed a monarch before the people can have a king or a government set over them? And thus we must leave kings to resolve which is their best title to their crowns, whether natural right, or the constitution of government settled by human compacts, under the direction and conduct of reason. But to proceed under the head of a state of natural being, I shall more distinctly explain the state of human nature in its original capacity, as man is placed on earth by his Maker, and clothed with many investitures and immunities which properly belong to man separately considered. As:

1. The prime immunity in man's state is that he is most properly the subject of the law of nature. He is the favorite animal on earth, in that this part of God's image: viz., Reason, is congenate with his nature, wherein by a law immutable, enstamped upon his frame, God

has provided a rule for men in all their actions, obliging each one to the performance of that which is right, not only as to justice, but likewise as to all other moral virtues, the which is nothing but the dictate of right reason founded in the soul of man. . . . That which is to be drawn from man's reason, flowing from the true current of that faculty, when unperverted, may be said to be the law of nature, on which account the Holy Scriptures declare it written on men's hearts. For being endowed with a soul, you may know from yourself how and what you ought to act (Rom. ii. 14): *These having not a law are a law to themselves.* So that the meaning is, when we acknowledge the law of nature to be the dictate of right reason, we must mean that the understanding of man is endowed with such a power as to be able from the contemplation of human condition to discover a necessity of living agreeably with this law. . . . If a man anyways doubts whether what he is going to do to another man to be agreeable to the law of nature, then let him suppose himself to be in that other man's room, and by this rule effectually executed. A man must be a very dull scholar to nature not to make proficiency in the knowledge of her laws. But more particularly in pursuing our condition for the discovery of the law of nature, this is very obvious to view: viz.,

1. A principle of self-love and self-preservation is very predominant in every man's being.

2. A sociable disposition.

3. An affection or love to mankind in general. And to give such sentiments the force of a law, we must suppose a God who takes care of all mankind and has thus obliged each one as a subject of higher principles of being than mere instincts. For that all law, properly considered, supposes a capable subject and a superior power; and the law of God, which is binding, is published by the dictates of right reason as other ways: therefore, says Plutarch, *To follow God and obey reason is the same thing.* But moreover that God has established the law of nature as the general rule of government is further illustrable from the many sanctions in Providence, and from the peace and guilt of conscience in them that either obey, or violate the law of nature. But, moreover, the foundation of the law of nature with relation to government may be thus discovered: *scil.,* Man is a creature extremely desirous of his own preservation; of himself he is plainly exposed to many wants, unable to secure his own safety and maintenance without the assistance of his fellows; and he is also able of returning kindness by the furtherance of mutual good; but yet man is often found to be malicious, insolent, and easily provoked, and as powerful in effecting mischief as he is ready in designing it. Now, that such a creature may be preserved, it is necessary that he be sociable; that is, that he be capable and disposed to unite himself to those of his own species, and to regulate himself towards them, that they may have no fair reason to do him harm, but rather incline to promote his interests, and secure his rights and concerns. This, then, is a fundamental law of nature, that every man as far as in him lies, do maintain a sociableness with others, agreeable with the main end and disposition of human nature in general. For this is very apparent, that reason and society render man the most potent of all creatures. And finally, from the principles of sociableness, it follows as a fundamental law of nature that man is not so wedded to his own interest, but that he can make the common good the mark of his aim; and hence he becomes capacitated to enter into a civil state by the law of nature; for without his property in nature: viz., sociableness, which is for cementing of parts, every government would soon molder and dissolve.

2. The second great immunity of man is an original liberty enstamped upon his rational nature. He that intrudes upon this liberty violates the law of nature. In this discourse I shall waive the consideration of man's moral turpitude, but shall view him physically as a creature which God has made and furnished essentially with many ennobling immunities, which render him the most august animal in the world, and still, whatever has happened since his creation, he remains at the upper end of nature, and as such is a creature of a very noble character. For as to his dominion, the whole frame of the lower part of the universe is devoted to his use and at his command; and his liberty under the conduct of right reason is equal with his trust. Which liberty may be briefly considered, internally as to his mind, and externally as to his person.

1. The internal native liberty of man's nature in general implies a faculty of doing or omitting things according to the direction of his judgment. But in a more special meaning, this liberty does not consist in a loose and ungovernable freedom, or in an unbounded license of acting. Such license is disagreeing with the condition and

dignity of man and would make man of a lower and meaner constitution than brute creatures, who in all their liberties are kept under a
better and more rational government by their instincts. Therefore,
as Plutarch says, *Those persons only who live in obedience to reason
are worthy to be accounted free; they alone live as they will,* who have
learned what they ought to will. So that the true natural liberty of man,
such as really and truly agrees to him, must be understood as he is
guided and restrained by the ties of reason and laws of nature; all
the rest is brutal, if not worse.

2. Man's external personal, natural liberty, antecedent to all
human parts or alliances, must also be considered. And so every man
must be conceived to be perfectly in his own power and disposal, and
not to be controlled by the authority of any other. And thus every
man must be acknowledged equal to every man, since all subjection
and all command are equally banished on both sides; and considering
all men thus at liberty, every man has a prerogative to judge for himself: viz., what shall be most for his behoof, happiness, and well-being.

3. The third capital immunity belonging to man's nature is an
equality amongst men, which is not to be denied by the law of nature
till man has resigned himself with all his rights for the sake of a civil
state, and then his personal liberty and equality is to be cherished and
preserved to the highest degree as will consist with all just distinctions
amongst men of honor and shall be agreeable with the public good.
For man has a high valuation of himself, and the passion seems to
lay its first foundation, not in pride, but really in the high and admirable frame and constitution of human nature. The word *man,* says my
author, is thought to carry somewhat of dignity in its sound; and we
commonly make use of this as the most proper and prevailing argument against a rude insulter: viz., *I am not a beast or a dog, but am a
man as well as yourself.* Since then human nature agrees equally with
all persons; and since no one can live a sociable life with another that
does not own or respect him as a man, it follows as a command of the
law of nature that every man esteem and treat another as one who is
naturally his equal, or who is a man as well as he. There be many
popular or plausible reasons that greatly illustrate this equality: viz.,
that we all derive our being from one stock, the same common father
of human race. On this consideration Boethius checks the pride of the
insulting nobility.

> *Quid genus et proavos strepitis?*
> *Si primordia vestra,*
> *Auteremque Deum spectas,*
> *Nullus degener extat*
> *Nisi vitiis pejora fovens,*
> *Proprium deserat ortum.*

> *Fondly our first descent we boast;*
> *If whence at first our breath we drew,*
> *The common springs of life we view,*
> *The airy notion soon is lost.*

> *The Almighty made us equal all;*
> *But he that slavishly complies*
> *To do the drudgery of vice,*
> *Denies his high original.*

And also that our bodies are composed of matter, frail, brittle, and liable to be destroyed by thousand accidents; we all owe our existence to the same method of propagation. The noblest mortal in his entrance on to the stage of life is not distinguished by any pomp or of passage from the lowest of mankind; and our life hastens to the same general mark: death observes no ceremony, but knocks as loud at the barriers of the court as at the door of the cottage. This equality being admitted bears a great force in maintaining peace and friendship amongst men. For that he who would use the assistance of others in promoting his own advantage ought as freely to be at their service when they want his help on the like occasions. *One good turn requires another* is the common proverb, for otherwise he must need esteem others unequal to himself who constantly demands their aid and as constantly denies his own. And whoever is of this insolent temper cannot but highly displease those about him and soon give occasion of the breach of the common peace. It was a manly reproof which Caractacus gave the Romans: *Num si vos omnibus,* etc. What! because you desire to be masters of all men, does it follow therefore that all men should desire to be your slaves, for that it is a command of nature's law that no man that has not obtained a particular and special right shall arrogate to himself a larger share than his fellows, but shall admit others to equal privileges with himself. So that the principle of equality in a natural state is peculiarly transgressed by pride, which is when a man without sufficient reason prefers himself to others. And though as Hensius paraphrases upon Aristotle's *Politics* to this purpose: viz., *Nothing is more suitable to nature than that those who excel in understanding and prudence should rule and control those who are less happy in those advantages,* etc., yet we must note that there is room for an answer: *scil.,* that it would be the greatest absurdity to believe that nature actually invests the wise with a sovereignty over the weak; or with a right of forcing them against their wills; for that no sovereignty can be established unless some human deed or covenant precede; nor does natural fitness for government make a man presently governor over another; for that, as Ulpian says, *by a natural right all men are born free;* and nature having set all men upon a level and made them equals, no servitude or subjection can be conceived without inequality; and this cannot be made without usurpation or force in others, or voluntary compliance in those who resign their freedom and give away their degree of natural being. And thus we come:

II. To consider man in a civil state of being; wherein we shall observe the great difference between a natural and political state; for in the latter state many great disproportions appear, or at least many obvious distinctions are soon made amongst men; which doctrine is to be laid open under a few heads.

1. Every man considered in a natural state must be allowed to be free and at his own dispose; yet to suit man's inclinations to society, and in a peculiar manner to gratify the necessity he is in of public rule and order, he is impelled to enter into a civil community, and divests himself of his natural freedom, and puts himself under government; which amongst other things comprehends the power of life and death over him, together with authority to enjoin him some things to which he has an utter aversion, and to prohibit him other things, for which he may have as strong an inclination; so that he may be often, under this authority, obliged to sacrifice his private for the public good. So that though man is inclined to society, yet he is driven to a combination by great necessity. For that the true and leading cause of forming governments, and yielding up natural liberty, and throwing man's equality into a common pile to be new cast by the rules of fellowship, was really and truly to guard themselves against the injuries men were

26

liable to interchangeably; for none so good to man as man, and yet none a greater enemy, So that:

2. The first human subject and original of civil power is the people. For as they have a power every man over himself in a natural state, so upon a combination they can and do bequeath this power unto others, and settle it according as their united discretion shall determine. For that this is very plain, that when the subject of sovereign power is quite extinct, that power returns to the people again. And when they are free, they may set up what species of government they please; or if they rather incline to it, they may subside into a state of natural being if it be plainly for the best. . . .

3. The formal reason of government is the will of a community, yielded up and surrendered to some other subject, either of one particular person or more, conveyed in the following manner.

Let us conceive in our mind a multitude of men, all naturally free and equal, going about voluntarily to erect themselves into a new commonwealth. Now, their condition being such, to bring themselves into a politic body, they must needs enter into divers covenants.

1. They must interchangeably each man covenant to join one lasting society, that they may be capable to concert the measures of their safety, by a public vote. .

2. A vote or decree must then nextly pass to set up some particular species of government over them. And if they are joined in their first compact upon absolute terms to stand to the decision of the first vote concerning the species of government, then all are bound by the majority to acquiesce in that particular form thereby settled, though their own private opinion incline them to some other model.

3. After a decree has specified the particular form of government, then there will be need of a new government, whereby those on whom sovereignty is conferred engage to take care of the common peace and welfare. And the subjects, on the other hand, to yield them faithful obedience. In which covenant is included that submission and union of wills by which a state may be conceived to be but one person. So that the most proper definition of a civil state is this: viz., A civil state is a compound moral person whose will (united by those covenants before passed) is the will of all; to the end it may use and apply the strength and riches of private persons towards maintaining the common peace, security, and well-being of all. . . .

The forms of a regular state are three only, which forms arise from the proper and particular subject in which the supreme power resides. As:

1. A democracy, which is when the sovereign power is lodged in a council consisting of all the members, and where every member has the privilege of a vote. This form of government appears in the greatest part of the world to have been the most ancient. For that reason seems to show it to be most probable that when men (being originally in a condition of natural freedom and equality) had thoughts of joining in a civil body, they would without question be inclined to administer their common affairs by their common judgment, and so must necessarily to gratify that inclination establish a democracy; neither can it be rationally imagined that fathers of families being yet free and independent should in a moment or little time take off their long delight in governing their own affairs, and devolve all upon some single sovereign commander; for that it seems to have been thought more equitable that what belonged to all should be managed by all, when all had entered by compact into one community. . . .

A democracy is then erected when a number of free persons do assemble together in order to enter into a covenant for uniting themselves in a body; and such a preparative assembly hath some appearance already of a democracy; it is a democracy in embryo properly in this respect: that every man hath the privilege freely to deliver his opinion concerning the common affairs. Yet he who dissents from the vote of the majority is not in the least obliged by what they determine, till by a second covenant a popular form be actually established; for not before then can we call it a democratical government: viz., till the right of determining all matters relating to the public safety is actually placed in a general assembly of the whole people; or by their own compact and mutual agreement determine themselves the proper subject for the exercise of sovereign power. . . .

2. The second species of regular government is an aristocracy; and this is said then to be constituted when the people or assembly united by a first covenant, and having thereby cast themselves into the first rudiments of a state, do then by common decree devolve the sovereign power on a council consisting of some select members; and these, having accepted of the designation, are then properly invested with sovereign command; and then an aristocracy is formed.

3. The third species of a regular government is a monarchy, which

is settled when the sovereign power is conferred on some one worthy
person. It differs from the former because a monarch who is but one
person in natural as well as in moral account, and so is furnished with
an immediate power of exercising sovereign command in all instances
of government; but the forenamed must needs have particular time
and place assigned; but the power and authority is equal in each. . . .

[The author now discussed the evils of monarchical and aristocratic
church governments, and then proceeded to democracy, as follows:]

A democracy. This is a form of government which the light of nature does highly value, and often directs to as most agreeable to the
just and natural prerogatives of human beings. This was of great account in the early times of the world. And not only so, but upon the
experience of several thousand years, after the world had been tumbled
and tossed from one species of government to another, at a great expense of blood and treasure, many of the wise nations of the world have
sheltered themselves under it again; or at least have blendished and
balanced their governments with it.

It is certainly a great truth: *scil.*, that man's original liberty after it is
resigned (yet under due restrictions) ought to be cherished in all wise
governments; or otherwise a man in making himself a subject, he alters
himself from a freeman into a slave, which to do is repugnant to the
law of nature. Also the natural equality of men amongst men must be
duly favored; in that government was never established by God or
nature to give one man a prerogative to insult over another; therefore
in a civil as well as in a natural state of being, a just equality is to be
indulged so far as that every man is bound to honor every man, which
is agreeable both with nature and religion (I Pet. ii. 17): *Honor all
men.* — The end of all good government is to cultivate humanity, and
promote the happiness of all, and the good of every man in all his
rights, his life, liberty, estate, honor, etc., without injury or abuse done
to any. Then certainly it cannot easily be thought that a company of
men that shall enter into a voluntary compact to hold all power in their
own hands, thereby to use and improve their united force, wisdom,
riches, and strength for the common and particular good of every member, as is the nature of a democracy; I say it cannot be that this sort of
constitution will so readily furnish those in government with an appetite or disposition to prey upon each other, or embezzle the common
stock, as some particular persons may be apt to do when set off, and

29

entrusted with the same power. And moreover this appears very natural that when the aforesaid government or power settled in all, when they have elected certain capable persons to minister in their affairs, and the said ministers remain accountable to the assembly, these officers must needs be under the influence of many wise cautions from their own thoughts (as well as under confinement by their commission) in their whole administration; and from thence it must needs follow that they will be more apt and inclined to steer right for the main point, viz., the peculiar good and benefit of the whole and every particular member fairly and sincerely. And why may not these stand for very rational pleas in church order?

For certainly if Christ has settled any form of power in his church he has done it for his church's safety, and for the benefit of every member; then he must needs be presumed to have made choice of that government as should least expose his people to hazard, either from the fraud or arbitrary measures of particular men. And it is as plain as daylight there is no species of government like a democracy to attain this end. There is but about two steps from an aristocracy to a monarchy, and from thence but one to a tyranny; an able standing force, and an ill nature, *ipso facto*, turns an absolute monarch into a tyrant; this is obvious among the Roman Cæsars, and through the world. And all these direful transmutations are easier in church affairs (from the different qualities of things) than in civil states. For what is it that cunning and learned men can't make the world swallow as an article of their creed if they are once invested with an uncontrollable power, and are to be the standing orators to mankind in matters of faith and obedience?

[1717]

JONATHAN MAYHEW

[1720–1766]

HIS FATHER, Experience Mayhew, was a famous missionary to the Indians of Martha's Vineyard. Jonathan followed his father into the ministry, but *his* mission was of a wholly different kind. From the time he was graduated from Harvard, in 1744, until his death, he was known as a liberal and agitator in both theology and politics. It is reported that when he became pastor of the West Church in Boston, only two ministers were willing to attend his ordination. As early as 1755 he anticipated the Unitarian theory. He upheld the doctrine of free will, defended the right of private judgment, decried all attempts to introduce an American episcopate. In the political sphere he was equally radical: he fought for civil liberties, stirred up sentiment against the Stamp Act, agitated for the colonies to combine in defense of liberty. His friends were such men as Sam Adams, Josiah Quincy, and James Otis. In short, with Mayhew we reach the Revolutionary era, for he was its prophet in the pulpit. His best known sermon, the *Discourse Concerning Unlimited Submission and Non-Resistance to Higher Powers*, was a brilliant denunciation of tyranny and an affirmation of the right to disobey a government which is unreasonable and unchristian.

---

from

A DISCOURSE CONCERNING UNLIMITED SUB-MISSION AND NON–RESISTANCE TO THE HIGHER POWERS

It is hoped that few will think the subject . . . an improper one to be discoursed on in the pulpit, under a notion that this is preaching politics instead of Christ. However, to remove all prejudices of this sort, I beg it may be remembered that " all scripture is profitable for doctrine, for reproof, for correction, for instruction in righteousness." Why, then, should not those parts of scripture which relate to civil

31

government be examined and explained from the desk as well as others? Obedience to the civil magistrate is a Christian duty; and if so, why should not the nature, grounds, and extent of it be considered in a Christian assembly? Besides, if it be said that it is out of character for a Christian minister to meddle with such a subject, this censure will at last fall upon the holy apostles. They write upon it in their epistles to Christian churches; and surely it cannot be deemed either criminal or impertinent to attempt an explanation of their doctrine.

It was the near approach of the thirtieth of January [the anniversary of the beheading of Charles I] that turned my thoughts to this subject: on which solemnity the slavish doctrine of passive obedience and non-resistance is often warmly asserted; and the dissenters from the Established Church represented not only as schismatics (with more of triumph than of truth, and of choler than Christianity), but also as persons of seditious, traitorous, and rebellious principles. God be thanked, one may, in any part of the British dominions, speak freely (if a decent regard be paid to those in authority) both of government and religion; and even give some broad hints that he is engaged on the side of liberty, the Bible and Common Sense, in opposition to Tyranny, Priestcraft and Non-Sense, without being in danger either of the Bastille or the Inquisition: — though there will always be *some* interested politicians, contracted bigots, and hypocritical zealots for a party, to take offense at such freedoms. *Their* censure is praise; *their* praise is infamy — A spirit of domination is always to be guarded against both in church and state, even in times of the greatest security, such as the present is amongst us, at least as to the latter. Those nations who are now groaning under the iron scepter of tyranny were once free. So they might, probably, have remained, by a seasonable caution against despotic measures. Civil tyranny is usually small in its beginning, like "the drop of a bucket," till at length, like a mighty torrent, or the raging waves of the sea, it bears down all before it and deluges whole countries and empires. Thus it is as to ecclesiastical tyranny also — the most cruel, intolerable and impious of any. From small beginnings, "it exalts itself above all that is called God and that is worshipped." People have no security against being unmercifully priest-ridden, but by keeping all imperious bishops, and other clergymen who love to "lord it over God's heritage," from getting their foot into the stirrup at all. Let them be once fairly mounted, and their "beasts, the laity," may prance and flounce about to no purpose: And they will, at length, be so jaded and hacked by these reverend jockeys that they will not even have spirits enough to complain that their backs are galled; or, like Balaam's ass, to "rebuke the madness of the prophet."

. . . Tyranny brings ignorance and brutality along with it. It degrades men from their just rank into the class of brutes. It damps their spirits. It suppresses arts. It extinguishes every spark of noble ardor and generosity in the breasts of those who are enslaved by it. It makes naturally strong and great minds feeble and little; and triumphs over the ruins of virtue and humanity. This is true of tyranny in every shape. There can be nothing great or good where its influence reaches. For which reason it becomes every friend to truth and human kind, every lover of God and the Christian religion, to bear a part in opposing this hateful monster. It was a desire to contribute a mite towards carrying on a war against this common enemy that produced the following discourse. And if it serve in any measure to keep up a spirit of civil and religious liberty amongst us, my end is answered. — There are virtuous and candid men in all sects; all such are to be esteemed: There are also vicious men and bigots in all sects; and all such ought to be despised.

[Dr. Mayhew then proceeded to discuss Paul's admonition: "Let every soul be subject unto the higher powers. For there is no power but of God: the powers that be are ordained of God. Whosoever therefore resisteth the power, resisteth the ordinance of God. . . . Render therefore to all their dues: tribute to whom tribute is due; custom to whom custom; fear to whom fear; honor to whom honor." He maintained that this passage is not to be taken literally — that certain qualifications and conditions are implied in it. Resistance to tyranny and oppression, he concluded, is not contrary to scripture. Then followed this stirring argument:]

If we calmly consider the nature of the thing itself, nothing can well be imagined more directly contrary to common sense than to suppose that millions of people should be subjected to the arbitrary, precarious pleasure of one single man (who has *naturally* no superiority over them in point of authority), so that their estates, and everything that is valuable in life, and even their lives also, shall be absolutely at his disposal, if he happens to be wanton and capricious enough to demand them. What unprejudiced man can think that God made *all* to be thus subservient to the lawless pleasure and frenzy of *one,* so that it shall always be a sin to resist him! Nothing but the most plain and express revelation from heaven could make a sober impartial man believe such a monstrous, unaccountable doctrine, and, indeed, the thing itself appears so shocking — so out of all proportion — that it may be questioned whether all the miracles that ever were wrought could make it credible that this doctrine really came from God. At present there is not the least syllable in scripture which gives any countenance to it. The hereditary, indefeasible, divine right of kings, and the doctrine of non-resistance, which is built upon the supposition of such a right, are altogether as fabulous and chimerical as transubstantiation or any of the most absurd reveries of ancient or modern visionaries. These notions are fetched neither from divine revelation nor human reason; and if they are derived from neither of those sources, it is not much matter from whence they come, or whither they go. Only it is a pity that such doctrines should be propagated in society to raise factions and rebellions, as we see they have, in fact, been both in the last and in the present reign.

But then, if unlimited submission and passive obedience to the higher powers, in all possible cases, be not a duty, it will be asked: "How far are we obliged to submit? If we may innocently disobey and resist in some cases, why not in all? Where shall we stop? What is the measure of our duty? This doctrine tends to the total dissolution of civil government, and to introduce such scenes of wild anarchy and confusion as are more fatal to society than the worst of tyranny."

After this manner some men object; and, indeed, this is the most plausible thing that can be said in favor of such an absolute submission as they plead for. But the worst (or rather the best) of it is that there is very little strength or solidity in it. For similar difficulties may be raised with respect to almost every duty of natural and revealed religion. — To instance only in two, both of which are near akin, and indeed exactly parallel, to the case before us. It is unquestionably the duty of children to submit to their parents; and of servants to their masters. But no one asserts that it is their duty to obey and submit to them in all supposable cases, or universally a sin to resist them. Now does this tend to subvert the just authority of parents and masters? Or to introduce confusion and anarchy into private families? No. How then does the same principle tend to unhinge the government of that larger family, the body politic? We know, in general, that children and servants are obliged to obey their parents and masters respectively. We know also, with equal certainty, that they are not obliged to submit to them in all things, without exception, but may, in some cases, reasonably, and therefore innocently, resist them. These principles are acknowledged upon all hands, whatever difficulty there may be in fixing the exact limits of submission. Now, there is at least as much difficulty in stating the measure of duty in these two cases as in the case of rulers and subjects. So that this is really no objection, at least no reasonable one, against resistance to the higher powers; or, if it is one, it will hold equally against resistance in the other cases mentioned. — It is indeed true that turbulent, vicious-minded men may take occasion from this principle that their rulers may, in some cases, be lawfully resisted, to raise factions and disturbances in the state, and to make resistance where resistance is needless and therefore sinful. But is it not equally true that children and servants of turbulent, vicious minds may take occasion from this principle that parents and masters may in some cases be lawfully resisted, to resist when resistance is unnecessary, and therefore criminal? Is the principle in either case false in itself merely because it may be abused, and applied to legitimate disobedience and resistance in those instances to which it ought not to be applied? According to this way of arguing, there will be no true principles in the world; for there are none but what may be wrested and perverted to serve bad purposes, either through the weakness or wickedness of men.[1]

---

[1] We may very safely assert these two things in general, without undermining government: One is that no civil rulers are to be obeyed when they enjoin things that are inconsistent with the commands of God; all such disobedience is lawful and glorious; particularly if persons refuse to comply with any legal establishment of religion because it is a gross perversion and corruption (as to doctrine, worship, and discipline) of a pure and divine religion, brought from heaven to earth by the Son of God (the only King and Head of the Christian church) and propagated through the world by His inspired apostles. All commands running counter to the declared will of the supreme legislator of heaven and earth are null and void; and therefore disobedience to them is a duty, not a crime. . . . Another thing that may be asserted with equal truth and safety is that no government is to be submitted to at the expense of that which is the sole end of all government — the common good and safety of society. Because to submit in this case, if it should ever happen, would evidently be to set up the means as more valuable and above the end: than which there cannot be a greater solecism and contradiction. The only reason of the institution of civil government, and the only rational ground of submission to it, is the common safety and utility. If therefore, in any case, the common safety and utility would not be promoted by submission to government, but the contrary, there is no ground or motive for obedience and submission, but for the contrary.

Whoever considers the nature of civil government must, indeed, be sensible

A people really oppressed to a great degree by their sovereign cannot well be insensible when they are so oppressed. And such a people (if I may allude to an ancient fable) have, like the Hesperian fruit, a dragon for their protector and guardian: nor would they have any

that a great degree of implicit confidence must unavoidably be placed in those that bear rule; this is implied in the very notion of authority's being originally a trust committed by the people to those who are vested with it, as all just and righteous authority is; all besides is mere lawless force and usurpation; neither God nor nature having given any man a right of dominion over any society independently of that society's approbation and consent to be governed by him. — Now, as all men are fallible, it cannot be supposed that the public affairs of any state should be always administered in the best manner possible, even by persons of the greatest wisdom and integrity. Nor is it sufficient to legitimate disobedience to the higher powers that they are not so administered; or that they are, in some instances, very ill-managed; for upon this principle it is scarcely supposable that any government at all could be supported or subsist. Such a principle manifestly tends to the dissolution of government, and to throw all things into confusion and anarchy. — But it is equally evident, upon the other hand, that those in authority may abuse their trust and power to such a degree that neither the law of reason nor of religion requires that any obedience or submission should be paid to them; but, on the contrary, that they should be totally discarded, and the authority which they were before vested with transferred to others, who may exercise it more to those good purposes for which it is given. — Nor is this principle, that resistance to the higher powers is in some extraordinary cases justifiable, so liable to abuse as many persons seem to apprehend it. For although there will be always some petulant, querulous men in every state — men of factious, turbulent, and carping dispositions — glad to lay hold of any trifle to justify and legitimate their caballing against their rulers, and other seditious practices; yet there are, comparatively speaking, but a few men of this contemptible character: It does not appear but that mankind, in general, have a disposition to be as submissive and passive and tame under government as they ought to be. — Witness a great, if not the greatest, part of the known world, who are now groaning, but not murmuring, under the heavy yoke of tyranny! While those who govern do it with any tolerable degree of moderation and justice and in any good measure act up to their office and character by being public benefactors, the people will generally be easy and peaceable and be rather inclined to flatter and adore than to insult and resist them. Nor was there ever any general complaint against any administration which lasted long but what there was good reason for. Till people find themselves greatly abused and oppressed by their governors, they are not apt to complain; and whenever they do, in fact, find themselves thus abused and oppressed, they must be stupid not to complain. To say that subjects in general are not proper judges when their governors oppress them and play the tyrant and when they defend their rights, administer justice impartially, and promote the public welfare, is as great treason as ever man uttered: — 'tis treason, not against one single man, but the state — against the whole body politic — 'tis treason against mankind — 'tis treason against common sense — 'tis treason against God. And this impious principle lays the foundation for justifying all the tyranny and oppression that ever any prince was guilty of. The people know for what end they set up and maintain their governors; and they are the proper judges when they execute their trust as they ought to do it — when their prince exercises an equitable and paternal authority over them — when from a prince and common father he exalts himself into a tyrant — when from subjects and children he degrades them into the class of slaves — plunders them, makes them his prey, and unnaturally sports himself with their lives and fortunes.

reason to mourn, if some Hercules should appear to dispatch him — for a nation thus abused to arise unanimously, and to resist their prince, even to the dethroning him, is not criminal, but a reasonable way of vindicating their liberties and just rights; it is making use of the means, and the only means, which God has put into their power for mutual and self-defense. And it would be highly criminal in them not to make use of this means. It would be stupid tameness and unaccountable folly for whole nations to suffer one unreasonable, ambitious, and cruel man to wanton and riot in their misery. And in such a case it would, of the two, be more rational to suppose that they that did *not* resist, than that they who did, would receive to themselves damnation.

[*1750*]

JOHN WOOLMAN

[1720–1772]

WOOLMAN was the perfect Quaker, and that is almost like saying that he was saintly. He was born in New Jersey of a fairly prosperous rural family and spent his youth working on his father's farm and studying at a neighborhood Quaker school. In his early twenties he became a tailor's apprentice, eventually setting up his own shop in the village of Mount Holly. Although his formal education was limited, he studied by himself and was able at various times to secure employment teaching school, surveying, and drawing up wills and bills of sale. He managed also to secure some good land of his own. But his real vocation was preaching. He felt the " call " at the age of twenty-three and from then on he labored in the service of his faith, journeying through the South, the middle colonies, and New England, speaking at Quaker meetings, and investigating the conditions of the exploited and oppressed classes. He had a mystical but none the less profound and abiding love of mankind, and out of that love came his tireless efforts in behalf of social and racial justice. He preached humility and plain living to the rich and strove incessantly to end slavery, to rectify the white man's treatment of the Indian, to secure land for the landless, to lower rents for the poor, to shorten the working hours of the toiler — in brief, to persuade men to obey the golden rule. He wrote essays on Negro slavery, on labor and poverty, and on " the true harmony of mankind." But the best thing he wrote was his *Journal*, first published two years after his death. He died in England of the smallpox while working among the poor of Yorkshire.

---

from

THE JOURNAL OF JOHN WOOLMAN

I looked upon the works of God in this visible creation, and an awfulness covered me. My heart was tender and often contrite, and universal love to my fellow creatures increased in me. This will be understood by such as have trodden in the same path. Some glances of real beauty may be seen in their faces who dwell in true meekness. There is a harmony in the sound of that voice to which divine love gives utterance, and some appearance of right order in their temper and conduct whose passions are regulated; yet these do not fully show forth that inward life to those who have not felt it; this white stone and new name is only known rightly by such as receive it.

Now, though I had been thus strengthened to bear the cross, I still found myself in great danger, having many weaknesses attending me, and strong temptations to wrestle with; in the feeling whereof I frequently withdrew into private places, and often with tears besought the Lord to help me, and his gracious ear was open to my cry.

All this time I lived with my parents, and wrought on the plantation; and having had schooling pretty well for a planter, I used to improve myself in winter evenings, and other leisure times. Being now in the twenty-first year of my age, with my father's consent I engaged with a man, in much business as a shopkeeper and baker, to tend shop and keep books. At home I had lived retired; and now having a prospect of being much in the way of company, I felt frequent and fervent cries in my heart to God, the Father of Mercies, that he would preserve me from all taint and corruption; that, in this more public employment, I might serve him, my gracious Redeemer, in that humility and self-denial which I had in a small degree exercised in a more private life. . . .

My employer, though now a retailer of goods, was by trade a tailor, and kept a servant-man at that business; and I began to think about learning the trade, expecting that if I should settle I might by this trade and a little retailing of goods get a living in a plain way, without the load of great business. I mentioned it to my employer, and we soon agreed on terms, and when I had leisure from the affairs of merchandise I worked with his man. I believed the hand of Providence pointed out this business for me, and I was taught to be content with it, though I felt at times a disposition that would have sought for something greater; but through the revelation of Jesus Christ I had seen the happiness of humility, and there was an earnest desire in me to enter deeply into it; at times this desire arose to a degree of fervent supplication wherein my soul was so environed with heavenly light and consolation that things were made easy to me which had been otherwise.

My employer, having a Negro woman, sold her, and desired me to write a bill of sale, the man being waiting who bought her. The thing was sudden; and though I felt uneasy at the thought of writing an instrument of slavery for one of my fellow creatures, yet I remembered that I was hired by the year, that it was my master who directed me to do it, and that it was an elderly man, a member of our Society, who bought her; so through weakness I gave way and wrote it; but at the executing of it I was so afflicted in my mind that I said before my master and the Friend that I believed slave-keeping to be a practice inconsistent with the Christian religion. This, in some degree, abated my uneasiness; yet as often as I reflected seriously upon it I thought I should have been clearer if I had desired to be excused from it, as a thing against my conscience; for such it was. Some time after this a young man of our Society spoke to me to write a conveyance of a slave to him, he having lately taken a Negro into his house. I told him I was not easy to write it; for, though many of our meeting and in other places kept slaves, I still believed the practice was not right, and desired to be excused from the writing. I spoke to him in goodwill; and he told me that keeping slaves was not altogether agreeable to his mind; but that the slave being a gift made to his wife he had accepted her. . . .

[On a visit to the South] when I ate, drank, and lodged free-cost with people who lived in ease on the hard labor of their slaves I felt uneasy; and as my mind was inward to the Lord, I found this uneasiness return upon me, at times, through the whole visit. Where the masters bore a good share of the burden, and lived frugally, so that their servants were well provided for, and their labor moderate, I felt more easy; but where they lived in a costly way, and laid heavy burdens on their slaves, my exercise was often great, and I frequently had conversation with them in private concerning it. Secondly, this trade of importing slaves from their native country being much encouraged amongst them, and the white people and their children so generally living without much labor, was frequently the subject of my serious thoughts. I saw in these Southern provinces so many vices and corruptions, increased by this trade and this way of life, that it appeared to me as a dark gloominess hanging over the land; and though now many willingly run into it, yet in future the consequence will be grievous to posterity. I express it as it hath appeared to me, not once, nor twice, but as a matter fixed on my mind. . . .

A person at some distance lying sick, his brother came to me to write his will. I knew he had slaves, and, asking his brother, was told he intended to leave them as slaves to his children. As writing is a profitable employ, and as offending sober people was disagreeable to my inclination, I was straitened in my mind; but as I looked to the Lord, he inclined my heart to his testimony. I told the man that I believed the practice of continuing slavery to this people was not right, and that I had a scruple in my mind against doing writings of that kind; that though many in our Society kept them as slaves, still I was not easy to be concerned in it, and desired to be excused from going to write the will. I spake to him in the fear of the Lord, and he made no reply to what I said, but went away; he also had some concerns in the practice, and I thought he was displeased with me. In this case I had fresh confirmation that acting contrary to present outward interest, from a motive of divine love and in regard to truth and righteousness, and thereby incurring the resentments of people, opens the way to a treasure better than silver, and to a friendship exceeding the friendship of men. . . .

From the time of my entering Maryland I have been much under sorrow, which of late so increased upon me that my mind was almost overwhelmed, and I may say with the Psalmist: "In my distress I called upon the Lord, and cried to my God," who, in infinite goodness, looked upon my affliction, and in my private retirement sent the Comforter for my relief, for which I humbly bless his holy name.

The sense I had of the state of the churches brought a weight of distress upon me. The gold to me appeared dim, and the fine gold changed, and though this is the case too generally, yet the sense of it in these parts hath in a particular manner borne heavy upon me. It appeared to me that through the prevailing of the spirit of this world the minds of many were brought to an inward desolation, and instead of the spirit of meekness, gentleness, and heavenly wisdom, which are the necessary companions of the true sheep of Christ, a spirit of fierceness and the love of dominion too generally prevailed. From small beginnings in error great buildings by degrees are raised, and from one age to another are more and more strengthened by the general concurrence of the people; and as men obtain reputation by their profession of the truth, their virtues are mentioned as arguments in favor of general error; and those of less note, to justify themselves, say such and such good men did the like. By what other steps could the

41

people of Judah arise to that height in wickedness as to give just ground for the Prophet Isaiah to declare, in the name of the Lord, "that none calleth for justice, nor any pleadeth for truth" (Isa. lix. 4), or for the Almighty to call upon the great city of Jerusalem just before the Babylonish captivity: "If ye can find a man, if there be any who executeth judgment, that seeketh the truth, and I will pardon it"? (Jer. v. 1.)

The prophet of a way being open to the same degeneracy, in some parts of this newly settled land of America, in respect to our conduct towards the Negroes, hath deeply bowed my mind in this journey. . . .

In my youth I was used to hard labor, and though I was middling healthy, yet my nature was not fitted to endure so much as many others. Being often weary, I was prepared to sympathize with those whose circumstances in life, as free men, required constant labor to answer the demands of their creditors, as well as with others under oppression. In the uneasiness of body which I have many times felt by too much labor, not as a forced but a voluntary oppression, I have often been excited to think on the original cause of that oppression which is imposed on many in the world. The latter part of the time wherein I labored on our plantation, my heart, through the fresh visitations of heavenly love, being often tender, and my leisure time being frequently spent in reading the life and doctrines of our blessed Redeemer, the account of the sufferings of martyrs, and the history of the first rise of our Society, a belief was gradually settled in my mind that if such as had great estates generally lived in that humility and plainness which belong to a Christian life, and laid much easier rents and interests on their lands and moneys, and thus led the way to a right use of things, so great a number of people might be employed in things useful that labor both for men and other creatures would need to be no more than an agreeable employ, and divers branches of business, which serve chiefly to please the natural inclinations of our minds, and which at present seem necessary to circulate that wealth which some gather, might, in this way of pure wisdom, be discontinued. As I have thus considered these things, a query at times hath arisen: Do I, in all my proceedings, keep to that use of things which is agreeable to universal righteousness? And then there hath some degree of sadness at times come over me because I accustomed myself to some things which have occasioned more labor than I believe divine wisdom intended for us.

From my early acquaintance with truth I have often felt an inward distress, occasioned by the striving of a spirit in me against the operation of the heavenly principle; and in this state I have been affected with a sense of my own wretchedness, and in a mourning condition have felt earnest longings for that divine help which brings the soul into true liberty. Sometimes, on retiring into private places, the spirit of supplication hath been given me, and under a heavenly covering I have asked my gracious Father to give me a heart in all things resigned to the direction of his wisdom; in uttering language like this, the thought of my wearing hats and garments dyed with a dye hurtful to them has made lasting impression on me.

In visiting people of note in the Society who had slaves, and laboring with them in brotherly love on that account, I have seen, and the sight has affected me, that a conformity to some customs distinguishable from pure wisdom has entangled many, and that the desire of gain to support these customs has greatly opposed the work of truth. Sometimes when the prospect of the work before me has been such that in bowedness of spirit I have been drawn into retired places, and have besought the Lord with tears that he would take me wholly under his direction and show me the way in which I ought to walk, it hath revived with strength of conviction that if I would be his faithful servant I must in all things attend to his wisdom and be teachable, and so cease from all customs contrary thereto, however used among religious people.

As he is the perfection of power, of wisdom, and of goodness, so I believe he hath provided that so much labor shall be necessary for men's support in this world as would, being rightly divided, be a suitable employment of their time; and that we cannot go into superfluities, or grasp after wealth in a way contrary to his wisdom, without having connection with some degree of oppression, and with that spirit which leads to self-exaltation and strife, and which frequently brings calamities on countries by parties contending about their claims.

Being thus fully convinced, and feeling an increasing desire to live in the spirit of peace, I have often been sorrowfully affected with thinking on the unquiet spirit in which wars are generally carried on, and with the miseries of many of my fellow creatures engaged therein;

43

some suddenly destroyed; some wounded, and after much pain remaining cripples; some deprived of all their outward substance and reduced to want; and some carried into captivity.

Having for many years felt love in my heart towards the natives of this land who dwell far back in the wilderness, whose ancestors were formerly the owners and possessors of the land where we dwell, and who for a small consideration assigned their inheritance to us, and being at Philadelphia in the 8th month, 1761, on a visit to some Friends who had slaves, I fell in company with some of those natives who lived on the east branch of the river Susquehanna, at an Indian town called Wehaloosing, two hundred miles from Philadelphia. In conversation with them by an interpreter, as also by observations on their countenances and conduct, I believed some of them were measurably acquainted with that divine power which subjects the rough and froward will of the creature. At times I felt inward drawings towards a visit to that place, which I mentioned to none except my dear wife until it came to some ripeness. In the winter of 1762 I laid my prospects before my friends at our monthly and quarterly and afterwards at our general spring meeting; and having the unity of Friends, and being thoughtful about an Indian pilot, there came a man and three women from a little beyond that town to Philadelphia on business. Being informed thereof by letter, I met them in town in the 5th month, 1763; and after some conversation, finding they were sober people, I, with the concurrence of Friends in that place, agreed to join them as companions in their return. . . .

I took leave of my family and neighbors in much bowedness of spirit and went to our monthly meeting at Burlington. After taking leave of Friends there, I crossed the river, accompanied by my friends Israel and John Pemberton; and parting the next morning with Israel, John bore me company to Samuel Foulk's, where I met the before-mentioned Indians; and we were glad to see each other. Here my friend Benjamin Parvin met me, and proposed joining me as a companion — we had before exchanged some letters on the subject — and now I had a sharp trial on his account; for, as the journey appeared perilous, I thought if he went chiefly to bear me company, and we should be taken captive, my having been the means of drawing him into these difficulties would add to my own afflictions; so I told him my mind freely, and let him know that I was resigned to go alone; but after all, if he really believed it to be his duty to go on, I believed his company would be very comfortable to me. It was, indeed, a time of deep exercise, and Benjamin appeared to be so fastened to the visit that he could not be easy to leave me; so we went on, accompanied by our friends John Pemberton and William Lightfoot of Pikeland. We lodged at Bethlehem, and there parting with John, William and we went forward on the 9th of the sixth month, and got lodging on the floor of a house about five miles from Fort Allen. Here we parted with William, and at this place we met with an Indian trader lately come from Wyoming. In conversation with him, I perceived that many white people often sell rum to the Indians, which I believe is a great evil. In the first place, they are thereby deprived of the use of reason, and, their spirits being violently agitated, quarrels often arise which end in mischief, and the bitterness and resentment occasioned thereby are frequently of long continuance. Again, their skins and furs, gotten through much fatigue and hard travels in hunting, with which they intended to buy clothing, they often sell at a low rate for more rum, when they become intoxicated; and afterward, when they suffer for want of the necessaries of life, are angry with those who, for the sake of gain, took advantage of their weakness. Their chiefs have often complained of this in their treaties with the English. Where cunning people pass counterfeits and impose on others that which is good for nothing, it is considered as wickedness; but for the sake of gain to sell that which we know does people harm, and which often works their ruin, manifests a hardened and corrupt heart, and is an evil which demands the care of all true lovers of virtue to suppress. While my mind this evening was thus employed, I also remembered that the people on the frontiers, among whom this evil is too common, are often poor; and that they venture to the outside of a colony in order to live more independently of the wealthy, who often set high rents on their land. I was renewedly confirmed in a belief that if all our inhabitants lived according to sound wisdom, laboring to promote universal love and righteousness, and ceased from every inordinate desire after wealth, and from all customs which are tinctured with luxury, the way would be easy for our inhabitants, though they might be much more numerous than at present, to live comfortably on honest employments, without the temptation they are so often under of being drawn into schemes to make settlements on lands which have not been purchased of the Indians, or of applying to that wicked practice of selling rum to them. . . .

45

We crossed the western branch of Delaware, called the Great Lehie, near Fort Allen. The water being high, we went over in a canoe. Here we met an Indian, had friendly conversation with him, and gave him some biscuit; and he, having killed a deer, gave some of it to the Indians with us. After traveling some miles, we met several Indian men and women with a cow and horse and some household goods, who were lately come from their dwelling at Wyoming and were going to settle at another place. We made them some small presents, and, as some of them understood English, I told them my motive for coming into their country, with which they appeared satisfied. One of our guides talking awhile with an ancient woman concerning us, the poor old woman came to my companion and me and took her leave of us with an appearance of sincere affection. We pitched our tent near the banks of the same river, having labored hard in crossing some of those mountains called the Blue Ridge. The roughness of the stones and the cavities between them, with the steepness of the hills, made it appear dangerous. But we were preserved in safety, through the kindness of him whose works in these mountainous deserts appeared awful, and towards whom my heart was turned during this day's travel.

Near our tent, on the sides of large trees peeled for that purpose, were various representations of men going to and returning from the wars, and of some being killed in battle. This was a path heretofore used by warriors, and as I walked about viewing those Indian histories, which were painted mostly in red or black, and thinking on the innumerable afflictions which the proud, fierce spirit produceth in the world, also on the toils and fatigues of warriors in traveling over mountains and deserts; on their miseries and distresses when far from home and wounded by their enemies; of their bruises and great weariness in chasing one another over the rocks and mountains; of the restless, unquiet state of mind of those who live in this spirit, and of the hatred which mutually grows up in the minds of their children — the desire to cherish the spirit of love and peace among these people arose very fresh in me. This was the first night that we lodged in the woods, and being wet with traveling in the rain, as were also our blankets, the ground, our tent, and the bushes under which we purposed to lay, all looked discouraging; but I believed that it was the Lord who had thus far brought me forward, and that he would dispose of me as he saw good, and so I felt easy. We kindled a fire, with our tent open to it, then laid some bushes next the ground and put our blankets upon them for our bed, and, lying down, got some sleep. In the morning, feeling a little unwell, I went into the river; the water was cold, but soon after I felt fresh and well. About eight o'clock we set forward and crossed a high mountain supposed to be upward of four miles over, the north side being the steepest. About noon we were overtaken by one of the Moravian brethren going to Wehaloosing, and an Indian man with him who could talk English; and we being together while our horses ate grass had some friendly conversation; but they, traveling faster than we, soon left us. This Moravian, I understood, had this spring spent some time at Wehaloosing and was invited by some of the Indians to come again.

Twelfth of sixth month being the first of the week and a rainy day, we continued in our tent, and I was led to think on the nature of the exercise which hath attended me. Love was the first motion, and thence a concern arose to spend some time with the Indians, that I might feel and understand their life and the spirit they live in, if haply I might receive some instruction from them, or they might be in any degree helped forward by my following the leadings of truth among them; and as it pleased the Lord to make way for my going at a time when the troubles of war were increasing, and when, by reason of much wet weather, traveling was more difficult than usual at that season, I looked upon it as a more favorable opportunity to season my mind, and to bring me into a nearer sympathy with them. As mine eye was to the great Father of Mercies, humbly desiring to learn his will concerning me, I was made quiet and content.

Having been some time under a religious concern to prepare for crossing the seas, in order to visit Friends in the northern parts of England, and more particularly in Yorkshire, after consideration I thought it expedient to inform Friends of it at our monthly meeting at Burlington, who, having unity with me therein, gave me a certificate. I afterwards communicated the same to our quarterly meeting, and they likewise certified their concurrence. Some time after, at the general spring meeting of ministers and elders, I thought it my duty to acquaint them with the religious exercise which attended my mind; and they likewise signified their unity therewith by a certificate, dated the 24th of third month, 1772, directed to Friends in Great Britain.

In the fourth month following I thought the time was come for me to make some inquiry for a suitable conveyance; and as my concern was principally towards the northern parts of England, it seemed most proper to go in a vessel bound to Liverpool or Whitehaven. While I was at Philadelphia deliberating on this subject I was informed that my beloved friend Samuel Emlen, junior, intended to go to London, and had taken a passage for himself in the cabin of the ship called the *Mary and Elizabeth*, of which James Sparks was master, and John Head, of the city of Philadelphia, one of the owners; and feeling a draught in my mind towards the steerage of the same ship, I went first and opened to Samuel the feeling I had concerning it.

My beloved friend wept when I spake to him, and appeared glad that I had thoughts of going in the vessel with him, though my prospect was toward the steerage; and he offering to go with me, we went on board, first into the cabin — a commodious room — and then into the steerage, where we sat down on a chest, the sailors being busy about us. The owner of the ship also came and sat down with us. My mind was turned towards Christ, the heavenly Counsellor, and feeling at this time my own will subjected, my heart was contrite before him. A motion was made by the owner to go and sit in the cabin, as a place more retired; but I felt easy to leave the ship, and, making no agreement as to a passage in her, told the owner if I took a passage in the ship I believed it would be in the steerage; but did not say much as to my exercise in that case.

After I went to my lodgings, and the case was a little known in town, a Friend laid before me the great inconvenience attending a passage in the steerage, which for a time appeared very discouraging to me.

I soon after went to bed, and my mind was under a deep exercise before the Lord, whose helping hand was manifested to me as I slept that night, and his love strengthened my heart. In the morning I went with two Friends on board the vessel again, and after a short time spent therein, I went with Samuel Emlen to the house of the owner, to whom, in the hearing of Samuel only, I opened my exercise in relation to a scruple I felt with regard to a passage in the cabin, in substance as follows: —

" That on the outside of that part of the ship where the cabin was I observed sundry sorts of carved work and imagery; that in the cabin I observed some superfluity of workmanship of several sorts; and that according to the ways of men's reckoning, the sum of money to be paid for a passage in that apartment has some relation to the expense of furnishing it to please the minds of such as give way to a conformity to this world; and that in this, as in other cases, the moneys received from the passengers are calculated to defray the cost of these superfluities, as well as the other expenses of their passage. I therefore felt a scruple with regard to paying my money to be applied to such purposes."

As my mind was now opened, I told the owner that I had, at several times in my travels, seen great oppressions on this continent, at which my heart had been much affected and brought into a feeling of the state of the sufferers; and having many times been engaged in the fear and love of God to labor with those under whom the oppressed have been borne down and afflicted, I have often perceived that with a view to get riches and to provide estates for children, that they may live conformably to the customs and honors of this world, many are entangled in the spirit of oppression, and the exercise of my soul had been such that I could not find peace in joining in anything which I saw was against that wisdom which is pure. . . .

As my lodging in the steerage, now near a week, hath afforded me sundry opportunities of seeing, hearing, and feeling with respect to the life and spirit of many poor sailors, an exercise of soul hath attended me in regard to placing out children and youth where they may be likely to be exampled and instructed in the pure fear of the Lord.

Being much among the seamen I have, from a motion of love, taken sundry opportunities with one of them at a time, and have in free conversation labored to turn their minds towards the fear of the Lord. This day we had a meeting in the cabin, where my heart was contrite under a feeling of divine love.

I believe a communication with different parts of the world by sea is at times consistent with the will of our heavenly Father, and to educate some youth in the practice of sailing I believe may be right; but how lamentable is the present corruption of the world! How impure are the channels through which trade is conducted! How great is the danger to which poor lads are exposed when placed on shipboard to learn the art of sailing! Five lads training up for the seas were on board this ship. Two of them were brought up in our Society, and the other, by name James Naylor, is a member, to whose father James Naylor mentioned in Sewel's history appears to have been uncle. I often feel a tenderness of heart towards these poor lads, and at times look at them as though they were my children according to the flesh.

Oh, that all may take heed and beware of covetousness! Oh, that all may learn of Christ, who was meek and lowly of heart. Then in faithfully following him he will teach us to be content with food and raiment without respect to the customs or honors of this world. Men thus redeemed will feel a tender concern for their fellow creatures, and a desire that those in the lowest stations may be assisted and encouraged, and where owners of ships attain to the perfect law of liberty and are doers of the Word, these will be blessed in their deeds.

A ship at sea commonly sails all night, and the seamen take their watches four hours at a time. Rising to work in the night, it is not commonly pleasant in any case, but in dark rainy nights it is very disagreeable, even though each man were furnished with all conveniences. If, after having been on deck several hours in the night, they come down into the steerage soaking wet, and are so closely stowed that proper convenience for change of garments is not easily come at, but for want of proper room their wet garments are thrown in heaps, and sometimes, through much crowding, are trodden under foot in going to their lodgings and getting out of them, and it is difficult at times for each to find his own. Here are trials for the poor sailors.

Now, as I have been with them in my lodge, my heart hath often yearned for them, and tender desires have been raised in me that all owners and masters of vessels may dwell in the love of God and therein act uprightly, and by seeking less for gain and looking carefully to their ways they may earnestly labor to remove all cause of provocation from the poor seamen, so that they may neither fret nor use excess of strong drink; for, indeed, the poor creatures, in the wet and cold, seem to apply at times to strong drink to supply the want of other convenience. Great reformation is wanting in the world, and the necessity of it among those who do business on great waters hath at this time been abundantly opened before me.

In a time of sickness, a little more than two years and a half ago, I was brought so near the gates of death that I forgot my name. Being then desirous to know who I was, I saw a mass of matter of a dull gloomy color between the south and the east, and was informed that this mass was human beings in as great misery as they could be and live, and that I was mixed with them, and that henceforth I might not consider myself as a distinct or separate being. In this state I remained several hours. I then heard a soft melodious voice, more pure and harmonious than any I had heard with my ears before; I believed it was the voice of an angel who spake to the other angels; the words were: "John Woolman is dead." I soon remembered that I was once John Woolman, and being assured that I was alive in the body, I greatly wondered what that heavenly voice could mean. I believed beyond doubting that it was the voice of an holy angel, but as yet it was a mystery to me.

I was then carried in spirit to the mines where poor oppressed people were digging rich treasures for those called Christians, and heard them blaspheme the name of Christ, at which I was grieved, for his name to me was precious. I was then informed that these heathens were told that those who oppressed them were the followers of Christ, and they said among themselves: "If Christ directed them to use us in this sort, then Christ is a cruel tyrant."

All this time the song of the angel remained a mystery; and in the morning, my dear wife and some others coming to my bedside, I asked them if they knew who I was, and they, telling me I was John Woolman, thought I was light-headed, for I told them not what the angel said, nor was I disposed to talk much to anyone, but was very desirous to get so deep that I might understand this mystery.

My tongue was often so dry that I could not speak till I had moved it about and gathered some moisture, and as I lay still for a time I at length felt a divine power prepare my mouth that I could speak, and I then said: "I am crucified with Christ, nevertheless I live; yet not I, but Christ liveth in me. And the life which I now live in the flesh I live by the faith of the Son of God, who loved me and gave himself for me." Then the mystery was opened and I perceived there was joy in heaven over a sinner who had repented, and that the language: "John Woolman is dead," meant no more than the death of my own will.

My natural understanding now returned as before. . . .

[1774]

JAMES OTIS

[1725–1783]

OTIS was not really a democrat and he was almost consistently opposed to direct action against England. Yet he greatly furthered the rise of revolutionary sentiment and he developed some of the ideas that finally led to the establishment of a political democracy. More than once in history men have started movements they could not stop. He was born in West Barnstable, Massachusetts, the son of a lawyer, the grandson of a judge. Graduated from Harvard in 1743, he followed the family profession and studied law. After his admission to the bar he moved to Boston and soon afterwards married the daughter of a well-to-do merchant. He was a restless, ambitious man, studied assiduously, and became known as a legal authority. In addition, he was a classical scholar and an expert in political theory. In 1754 he acted as King's attorney and subsequently was appointed advocate general of the vice-admiralty court in Boston. In 1760 the English government undertook to enforce the Sugar Act, whereupon the customs collectors applied to the superior court for writs of assistance. It was Otis's duty to argue for the writs. Instead he resigned his office and argued for the merchants. The basis of his argument was that natural law is superior to acts of Parliament, and this was the doctrine that the political agitators of the period from then on employed to justify the break with England. Immediately after the case was decided against Otis, he was elected to the General Court. As the quarrel with the King's governors intensified, he became increasingly active and vehement in defense of the Americans. He began to publish the brilliant pamphlets which are now ranked among the great polemical writings: *A Vindication of the Conduct of the House of Representatives,* analyzing the rights of free-born Englishmen; *The Rights of the British Colonies Asserted and Proved,* elaborating and applying the theory of natural law; and others in which he denounced " taxation without representation." In 1769 he got into a brawl with some of the King's officers and was struck on the head. That ended his career. He fell ill, was for a time insane, began to drink heavily, and finally retired to a quiet, secluded life.

from

A VINDICATION OF THE CONDUCT OF THE HOUSE OF REPRESENTATIVES

Let us now . . . review the passage which . . . has been represented as seditious, rebellious, and traitorous. . . . The house assert that " it would be of little consequence to the people whether they were subject to George or Louis, the King of Great Britain or the French King, if both were arbitrary, as both would be, if both could levy taxes without parliament."

The first question that would occur to a philosopher, if any question could be made about it, would be whether the position were true. But truth being of little importance with most modern politicians, we shall touch lightly upon that topic, and proceed to inquiries of a more interesting nature.

That arbitrary government implies the worst of temporal evils, or at least the continual danger of them, is certain. That a man would be pretty equally subjected to these evils under every arbitrary government is clear. That I should die very soon after my head should be cut off, whether by a saber or a broadsword, whether chopped off to gratify a tyrant by the Christian name of Tom, Dick, or Harry is evident. That the name of the tyrant would be of no more avail to save my life than the name of the executioner needs no proof. It is therefore manifestly of no importance what a prince's Christian name is if he be arbitrary, any more, indeed, than if he were not arbitrary. So the whole amount of this dangerous proposition may at least in one view be reduced to this: viz., It is of little importance what a king's Christian name is. It is indeed of importance that a king, a governor, and all other good Christians should have a Christian name, but whether Edward, Francis, or William is of none that I can discern. It being a rule to put the most mild and favorable construction upon words that they can possibly bear, it will follow that this proposition is a very harmless one, that cannot by any means tend to prejudice His Majesty's person, crown, dignity, or cause, all which I deem equally sacred with His Excellency.

If this proposition will bear an hundred different constructions, they must all be admitted before any that imports any bad meaning, much more a treasonable one.

It is conceived the house intended nothing disrespectful of His Majesty, his government or governor in those words. It would be very injurious to insinuate this of a house that upon all occasions had distinguished itself by a truly loyal spirit, and which spirit possesses at least nine hundred and ninety-nine in a thousand of their constituents throughout the province. One good-natured construction at least seems to be implied in the assertion, and that pretty strongly: viz., that in the present situation of Great Britain and France it is of vast importance to be a Briton rather than a Frenchman, as the French King is an arbitrary despotic prince, but the King of Great Britain is not so *de jure, de facto,* nor by inclination; a greater difference on this side the grave cannot be found than that which subsists between British subjects and the slaves of tyranny.

Perhaps it may be objected that there is some difference even between arbitrary princes in this respect at least, that some are more rigorous than others. It is granted, but then let it be remembered that the life of man is as a vapor that soon vanisheth away, and we know not who may come after him, a wise man or a fool; though the chances before and since Solomon have ever been in favor of the latter. Therefore it is said of little consequence. Had it been *no* instead of *little,* the clause upon the most rigid stricture might have been found barely exceptionable.

Some fine gentlemen have charged the expression as indelicate. This is a capital impeachment in politics, and therefore demands our most serious attention. The idea of delicacy in the creed of some politicians implies that an inferior should at the peril of all that is near and dear to him (i.e., his interest) avoid every the least trifle that can offend his superior. Does my superior want my estate? I must give it him, and that with a good grace, which is appearing and if possible being really obliged to him that he will condescend to take it. The reason is evident; it might give him some little pain or uneasiness to see me whimpering — much more, openly complaining — at the loss of a little glittering dirt. I must according to this system not only endeavor to acquire myself, but impress upon all around me a reverence and passive obedience to the sentiments of my superior, little short of adoration. Is the superior in contemplation a king, I must consider him as God's vicegerent, clothed with unlimited power, his will the supreme law, and not accountable for his actions, let them be what they may, to any tribunal upon earth. Is the superior a plantation governor? he must be viewed not only as the most excellent representation of majesty, but as a viceroy in his department, and *quoad* provincial administration, to all intents and purposes vested with all the prerogatives that were ever exercised by the most absolute prince in Great Britain.

The votaries of this sect are all monopolizers of offices, peculators, informers, and generally the seekers of all kinds. It is better, say they, " to give up anything and everything quietly than contend with a superior, who by his prerogative can do, and (as the vulgar express it) right or wrong, will have whatever he pleases." For you must know that according to some of the most refined and fashionable systems of modern politics, the ideas of right and wrong, and all the moral virtues, are to be considered only as the vagaries of a weak or distempered imagination in the possessor, and of no use in the world but for the skillful politician to convert to his own purposes of power and profit.

[*1762*]

---

from

THE RIGHTS OF THE BRITISH COLONIES
ASSERTED AND PROVED

Let the origin of government be placed where it may, the end of it is manifestly the good of *the whole. Salus populi suprema lex esto* is the law of nature, and part of that grand charter given the human race (though too many of them are afraid to assert it) by the only monarch in the universe who has a clear and indisputable right to *absolute* power; because he is the *only* One who is *omniscient* as well as *omnipotent.*

It is evidently contrary to the first principles of reason that supreme *unlimited* power should be in the hands of *one* man. It is the greatest " idolatry, begotten by flattery, on the body of pride," that could induce one to think that a single mortal should be able to hold so great a power, if ever so well inclined. Hence the origin of deifying princes: It was from the trick of gulling the vulgar into a belief that their tyrants were omniscient; and that it was therefore right that they should be considered as omnipotent. Hence the *Dii majorum et minorum gentium;* the great, the monarchical, the little, provincial subordinate and subaltern gods, demigods, and semi-demigods, ancient and modern. Thus deities of all kinds were multiplied and increased in abundance; for every devil incarnate who could enslave a people acquired a title to divinity; and thus the " rabble of the skies " was made up of locusts and caterpillars; lions, tigers, and harpies; and other devourers translated from plaguing the earth! [1]

The end of the government being the good of mankind points out its great duties: It is above all things to provide for the security, the quiet, and happy enjoyment of life, liberty, and property. There is no one act which a government can have a right to make that does not tend to the advancement of the security, tranquillity, and prosperity of the people. If life, liberty, and property could be enjoyed in as great perfection in solitude as in society, there would be no need of government. But the experience of ages has proved that such is the nature of man, a weak, imperfect being, that the valuable ends of life cannot be obtained without the union and assistance of many. Hence 'tis clear that men cannot live apart or independent of each other: in solitude men would perish; and yet they cannot live together without contests. These contests require some arbitrator to determine them. The necessity of a common, indifferent, and impartial judge makes all men seek one; though few find him in the sovereign power of their respective states or anywhere else in subordination to it.

Government is founded *immediately* on the necessities of human nature, and *ultimately* on the will of God, the author of nature, who has not left it to men in general to choose whether they will be members of society or not, but at the hazard of their senses if not of their lives. Yet it is left to every man as he comes of age to choose *what society* he will continue to belong to. Nay, if one has a mind to turn hermit, and after he has been born, nursed, and brought up in the arms of society, and acquired the habits and passions of social life, is willing to run the risk of starving alone, which is generally most unavoidable in a state of hermitage, who shall hinder him? I know of no human law, founded on the law of nature, to refrain him from separating himself from all the species if he can find it in his heart to leave

---

[1] Kingcraft and priestcraft have fell out so often, that 'tis a wonder this grand and ancient alliance is not broken off forever. Happy for mankind will it be when such a separation shall take place.

them; unless it should be said it is against the great law of self-preservation; but of this every man will think himself his own judge.

The few hermits and misanthropes that have ever existed show that those states are unnatural. If we were to take out from them those who have made great worldly gain of their godly hermitage, and those who have been under the madness of enthusiasm, or disappointed hopes in their ambitious projects, for the detriment of mankind, perhaps there might not be left ten from Adam to this day.

The form of government is by nature and by right so far left to the individuals of each society that they may alter it from a simple democracy or government of all over all to any other form they please. Such alteration may and ought to be made by express compact; but how seldom this right has been asserted, history will abundantly show. For once that it has been fairly settled by compact, fraud, force, or accident have determined it an hundred times. As the people have gained upon tyrants, these have been obliged to relax, only till a fairer opportunity has put it in their power to encroach again.

But if every prince since Nimrod has been a tyrant, it would not prove a right to tyrannize. There can be no prescription old enough to supersede the law of nature, and the grant of God Almighty, who has given to all men a natural right to be free, and they have it ordinarily in their power to make themselves so, if they please. . . .

In order to form an idea of the natural rights of the colonists, I presume it will be granted that they are men, the common children of the same Creator with their brethren of Great Britain. Nature has placed all such in a state of equality and perfect freedom, to act within the bounds of the laws of nature and reason without consulting the will or regarding the humor, the passions or whims of any other man, unless they are formed into a society or body politic. This it must be confessed is rather an abstract way of considering men than agreeable to the real and general course of nature. The truth is, as has been shown, men come into the world and into society at the same instant. But this hinders not but that the natural and original rights of each individual may be illustrated and explained in this way better than in any other. We see here by the way a probability that this abstract consideration of men, which has its use in reasoning on the principles of government, has insensibly led some of the greatest men to imagine some real general state of nature agreeable to this abstract conception,

57

antecedent to and independent of society. This is certainly not the case in general, for most men become members of society from their birth, though separate independent states are really in the condition of perfect freedom and equality with regard to each other; and so are any number of individuals who separate themselves from a society of which they have formerly been members, for ill treatment or other good cause, with express design to found another. If in such case there is a real interval between the separation and the new conjunction, during such interval the individuals are as much detached, and under the law of nature only, as would be two men who should chance to meet on a desolate island.

The colonists are by the law of nature free-born, as indeed all men are, white or black. No better reasons can be given for enslaving those of any color than such as Baron Montesquieu has humorously given as the foundation of that cruel slavery exercised over the poor Ethiopians, which threatens one day to reduce both Europe and America to the ignorance and barbarity of the darkest ages. Does it follow that 'tis right to enslave a man because he is black? Will short curled hair like wool, instead of Christian hair, as 'tis called by those whose hearts are as hard as the nether millstone, help the argument? Can any logical inference in favor of slavery be drawn from a flat nose, a long or a short face? Nothing better can be said in favor of a trade that is the most shocking violation of the law of nature, has a direct tendency to diminish the idea of the inestimable value of liberty, and makes every dealer in it a tyrant, from the director of an African company to the petty chapman in needles and pins on the unhappy coast. It is a clear truth that those who every day barter away other men's liberty will soon care little for their own. To this cause must be imputed that ferocity, cruelty, and brutal barbarity that has long marked the general character of the sugar-islanders. They can in general form no idea of government but that which in person, or by an overseer, the joint and several proper representative of a Creole [1] and of the D–1, is exercised over ten thousands of their fellow men, born with the same right to freedom and the sweet enjoyments of liberty and life as their unrelenting taskmasters, the overseers and planters.

Is it to be wondered at if, when people of the stamp of a Creolian

---

[1] Those in England who borrow the terms of the Spaniards, as well as their notions of government, apply this term to all Americans of European extract; but the Northern colonists apply it only to the Islanders and others of such extract, under the Torrid Zone.

planter get into power, they will not stick for a little present gain at making their own posterity, white as well as black, worse slaves if possible than those already mentioned?

There is nothing more evident, says Mr. Locke, than "that creatures of the same species and rank promiscuously born to all the same advantages of nature, and the use of the same faculties, should also be equal one among another, without subordination and subjection, unless the master of them all should by any manifest declaration of his will set one above another, and confer on him by an evident and clear appointment an undoubted right to dominion and sovereignty." "The natural liberty of man is to be free from any superior power on earth, and not to be under the will or legislative authority of man, but only to have the law of nature for his rule." This is the liberty of independent states; this is the liberty of every man out of society, and who has a mind to live so; which liberty is only abridged in certain instances, not lost to those who are born or voluntarily enter into society; this gift of God cannot be annihilated.

The colonists, being men, have a right to be considered as equally entitled to all the rights of nature with the Europeans, and they are not to be restrained in the exercise of any of these rights but for the evident good of the whole community.

By being or becoming members of society, they have not renounced their natural liberty in any greater degree than other good citizens, and if 'tis taken from them without their consent, they are so far enslaved. . . .

1. *To govern by stated laws.*

2. *Those laws should have no other end ultimately but the good of the people.*

3. *Taxes are not to be laid on the people but by their consent in person or by deputation.*

4. *Their whole power is not transferable.*

These are the first principles of law and justice, and the great barriers of a free state, and of the British Constitution in particular. I ask, I want no more. — Now let it be shown how 'tis reconcilable with these principles, or to many other fundamental maxims of the British Constitution, as well as the natural and civil rights which by the laws of their country all British subjects are entitled to as their best inheritance and birthright, that all the Northern colonies, who are without one representative in the House of Commons, should be taxed by the British Parliament.

That the colonists, black and white, born here are free-born British subjects, and entitled to all the essential civil rights of such, is a truth not only manifest from the provincial charters, from the principles of the common law, and acts of Parliament, but from the British Constitution, which was re-established at the Revolution, with a professed design to secure the liberties of all the subjects to all generations.

In the 12 and 13 of Wm. cited above, the liberties of the subject are spoken of as their best birthrights. — No one ever dreamt, surely, that these liberties were confined to the realm. At that rate, no British subjects in the dominions could, without a manifest contradiction, be declared entitled to all the privileges of subjects born within the realm, to all intents and purposes, which are rightly given foreigners, by Parliament, after residing seven years. These expressions of Parliament, as well as of the charters, must be vain and empty sounds unless we are allowed the essential rights of our fellow subjects in Great Britain.

Now, can there be any liberty where property is taken away without consent? Can it with any color of truth, justice, or equity be affirmed that the Northern colonies are represented in Parliament? Has this whole continent of near three thousand miles in length, and in which and his other American dominions His Majesty has, or very soon will have, some millions of as good, loyal, and useful subjects, white and black, as any in the three kingdoms, the election of one member of the House of Commons?

Is there the least difference, as to the consent of the colonists, whether taxes and impositions are laid on their trade and other property by the crown alone or by the Parliament? As it is agreed on all hands the crown alone cannot impose them, we should be justifiable in refusing to pay them, but must and ought to yield obedience to an act of Parliament, though erroneous till repealed.

I can see no reason to doubt but that the imposition of taxes, whether on trade, or on land, or houses, or ships, on real or personal, fixed, or floating property, in the colonies, is absolutely irreconcilable with the rights of the colonists, as British subjects, and as men. I say men, for in a state of nature no man can take my property from me without my consent. If he does, he deprives me of my liberty and makes me a slave. If such a proceeding is a breach of the law of nature, no law of society can make it just. — The very act of taxing, exercised over those who are not represented, appears to me to be depriving them of one of their most essential rights as freemen; and if continued, seems to be in effect an entire disfranchisement of every civil right. For what one civil right is worth a rush after a man's property is subject to be taken from him at pleasure, without his consent? If a man is not his own assessor in person or by deputy, his liberty is gone, or lays entirely at the mercy of others.

I think I have heard it said that when the Dutch are asked why they enslave their colonies, their answer is that the liberty of Dutchmen is confined to Holland, and that it was never intended for provincials in America, or anywhere else. A sentiment this very worthy of modern Dutchmen; but if their brave and worthy ancestors had entertained such narrow ideas of liberty, seven poor and distressed provinces would never have asserted their rights against the whole Spanish monarchy, of which the present is but a shadow. It is to be hoped none of our fellow subjects of Britain, great or small, have borrowed this Dutch maxim of plantation politics; if they have, they had better return it from whence it came; indeed they had. Modern Dutch or French maxims of state never will suit with a British Constitution. . . .

I have waited years in hopes to see some one friend of the colonies pleading in public for them. I have waited in vain. One privilege is taken away after another, and where we shall be landed, God knows, and I trust will protect and provide for us even should we be driven and persecuted into a more western wilderness, on the score of liberty, civil and religious, as many of our ancestors were to these once inhospitable shores of America. I had formed great expectations from a gentleman who published his first volume in quarto on the rights of the colonies two years since; but, as he foresaw, the state of his health and affairs have prevented his further progress. The misfortune is, gentlemen in America, the best qualified in every respect to state the rights of the colonists, have reasons that prevent them from engaging. Some of them have good ones. There are many infinitely better able to serve this cause than I pretend to be; but from indolence, from timidity, or by necessary engagements, they are prevented. There has been a most profound and I think shameful silence, till it seems almost too late to assert our indisputable rights as men and as citizens. What must posterity think of us! The trade of the whole continent taxed by Parliament, stamps and other internal duties and taxes, as they are called, talked of, and not one petition to the King and Parliament for relief.

I cannot but observe here that if the Parliament have an equitable right to tax our trade, 'tis indisputable that they have as good an one to tax the lands, and everything else. The taxing trade furnishes one reason why the other should be taxed, or else the burdens of the province will be unequally borne, upon a supposition that a tax on trade is not a tax on the whole. But take it either way, there is no foundation for the distinction some make in England between an internal and an external tax on the colonies. By the first is meant a tax on trade, by the latter a tax on land and the things on it. A tax on trade is either a tax of every man in the province, or 'tis not. If 'tis not a tax on the whole, 'tis unequal and unjust, that a heavy burden should be laid on the trade of the colonies, to maintain an army of soldiers, custom-house officers, and fleets of guard-ships; all which the incomes of both trade and land would not furnish means to support so lately as the last war, when all was at stake, and the colonies were reimbursed in part by Parliament. How can it be supposed that all of a sudden the trade of the colonies alone can bear all this terrible burden? The late acquisitions in America, as glorious as they have been, and as beneficial as they are to Great Britain, are only a security to these colonies against the ravages of the French and Indians. Our trade upon the whole is not, I believe, benefited by them one groat. All the time the French islands were in our hands, the fine sugars, etc., were all shipped home. None, as I have been informed, were allowed to be brought to the colonies. They were too delicious a morsel for a North American palate. If it be said that a tax on the trade of the colonies is an equal and just tax on the whole of the inhabitants, what then becomes of the notable distinction between external and internal taxes? Why may not the parliament lay stamps, land taxes, establish tithes to the Church of England, and so indefinitely? I know of no bounds. . . .

[*1764*]

SAMUEL ADAMS

[1722–1803]

In his own day he was called an " incendiary," and only a short time ago a presumably scholarly historian called him an " excitable demagogue." Both remarks tend to confirm Professor Parrington's opinion that " he was probably the most thoroughgoing democrat of his generation." For Adams not only believed " that the sovereign people have a right to change their fundamental law . . . whenever they desire," but also that one should appeal *directly* to the people to do the changing. That was his own procedure when he became convinced that the colonies should separate from England, and as a result of his inflammatory manifestoes, articles, letters, and pamphlets he did more than any other man to prepare the masses for the Revolution. His sole reward was his place in American history, for he was a ne'er-do-well before the Revolution and not much better off after it.

But he had not been born into poverty. His father was a socially prominent landlord and merchant, a deacon and justice of the peace in Boston. Samuel was educated at Harvard and for a short time studied law. On his father's death he inherited considerable property, but mismanaged his affairs and lost everything. Simultaneously, however, as a member of an important political club he was displaying a talent for politics. He was appointed tax-collector of the Town of Boston — and promptly got into trouble by misappropriating the funds he collected. He would certainly have ended his life in disgrace if the conflict with England had not suddenly engaged him. Because of his known abilities, he was selected, in 1764, to write the instructions of the town to its representatives in the General Court. He produced a startling document: he attacked the Stamp Act, suggested the principle of " No taxation without representation," and hinted at a union of the colonies. He became famous instantly and a new career was opened to him. The following year he again drafted revolutionary instructions to the town's representatives, and then wrote the resolutions of the House of Representatives in which he formulated some of the principles of the Declaration of Independence. From then on he was apparently inexhaustible, as a steady stream of fiery articles poured from his pen. With the outbreak of the Revolution his work was done; he played a minor role during its course and afterwards confined himself to local activities, eventually being elected Governor of his state. As a spokesman for the little merchants against the aristocracy

63

he was a typical eighteenth-century democrat. It is significant that he fought Shays' Rebellion: the best of his thought was political, not economic. Two of the pieces that follow are good examples of his agitational writing, while the third states completely his general outlook.

[ON RESISTANCE TO TYRANNY]

I believe that no people ever yet groaned under the heavy yoke of slavery but when they deserved it. This may be called a severe censure upon by far the greatest part of the nations in the world who are involved in the misery of servitude; but however they may be thought by some to deserve commiseration, the censure is just. Zwinglius, one of the first reformers, in his friendly admonition to the Republic of the Switzers, discourses much of his countrymen's throwing off the yoke: He says that they who lie under oppression deserve what they suffer, and a great deal more; and he bids them perish with their oppressors. The truth is, all might be free if they valued freedom, and defended it as they ought. Is it possible that millions could be enslaved by a few, which is a notorious fact, if all possessed the independent spirit of Brutus, who, to his immortal honor, expelled the proud tyrant of Rome and his "royal and rebellious race"? If therefore a people will not be free, if they have not virtue enough to maintain their liberty against a presumptuous invader, they deserve no pity and are to be treated with contempt and ignominy. Had not Cæsar seen that Rome was ready to stoop, he would not have dared to make himself the master of that once brave people. He was indeed, as a great writer observes, a smooth and subtle tyrant, who led them *gently* into slavery; "and on his brow, o'er daring vice deluding virtue smiled." By pretending to be the people's greatest friend, he gained the ascendancy over them; by beguiling arts, hypocrisy, and flattery, which are even more fatal than the sword, he obtained that supreme power which his ambitious soul had long thirsted for. The people were finally prevailed upon to consent to their own ruin: by the force of persuasion, or rather by cajoling arts and tricks always made use of by men who have ambitious views, they enacted their *Lex Regia;* whereby *Quod placuit principi legis habuit vigorem;* that is, *the will and pleasure of the*

Prince had the force of law. His minions had taken infinite pains to paint to their imaginations the godlike virtues of Cæsar: they first persuaded them to believe that he was a deity, and then to sacrifice to him those rights and liberties which their ancestors had so long maintained, with unexampled bravery, and with blood and treasure. By this act they fixed a precedent fatal to all posterity: the Roman people afterwards, influenced no doubt by this pernicious example, renewed it to his successors, not at the end of every ten years, but for life. They transferred all their right and power to Charles the Great: *In eum transtulit omne suum jus et potestatem.* Thus they voluntarily and ignominiously surrendered their own liberty, and exchanged a free constitution for a *tyranny!*

It is not my design at present to form the comparison between the state of this country now and that of the Roman Empire in those dregs of time; or between the disposition of Cæsar and that of ——. The comparison, I confess, would not in all parts hold good: the tyrant of Rome, to do him justice, had learning, courage, and great abilities. It behooves us, however, to awake and advert to the danger we are in. The tragedy of American Freedom, it is to be feared, is nearly completed: a tyranny seems to be at the very door. It is to little purpose, then, to go about coolly to rehearse the gradual steps that have been taken, the means that have been used, and the instruments employed, to encompass the ruin of the public liberty; we know them and we detest them. But what will this avail if we have not courage and resolution to prevent the completion of their system?

Our enemies would fain have us lie down on the bed of sloth and security and persuade ourselves that there is no danger: they are daily administering the opiate with multiplied arts and delusions; and I am sorry to observe that the gilded pill is so alluring to some who call themselves the friends of Liberty. But is there no danger when the very foundations of our civil constitution tremble? — When an attempt was first made to disturb the cornerstone of the fabric, we were universally and justly alarmed; and can we be cool spectators when we see it already removed from its place? With what resentment and indignation did we first receive the intelligence of a design to make us tributary, not to natural enemies, but, infinitely more humiliating, to fellow subjects? And yet with unparalleled insolence we are told to be *quiet,* when we see that very money which is torn from us by lawless force made use of still further to oppress us — to feed and pamper a set of infamous wretches, who swarm like the locusts of Egypt; and some of them expect to revel in wealth and riot on the spoils of our country. — Is it a time for us to *sleep* when our free government is essentially changed, and a new one is forming upon a quite different system? A government without the least dependence upon the people: a government under the absolute control of a minister of state, upon whose sovereign dictates is to depend not only the time when, and the place where, the legislative assembly shall sit, but whether it shall sit at all; and if it is allowed to meet, it shall be liable immediately to be thrown out of existence if in any one point it fails in obedience to his arbitrary mandates. Have we not already seen specimens of what we are to expect under such a government in the instructions which Mr. Hutchinson has received, and which he has publicly avowed, and declared he is bound to obey? — By one, he is to refuse his assent to a tax-bill unless the Commissioners of the Customs and other favorites are exempted; and if these may be freed from taxes by the order of a minister, may not all his tools and drudges, or any others who are subservient to his designs, expect the same indulgence? By another he is to forbid to pass a grant of the assembly to any agent but one to whose election he has given his consent; which is in effect to put it out of our power to take the necessary and *legal* steps for the redress of those grievances which we suffer by the arts and machinations of ministers, and their minions here. What difference is there between the present state of this province, which in course will be the deplorable state of all America, and that of Rome under the law before mentioned? The difference is only this, that *they* gave their formal consent to the change, which *we* have not yet done. But let us be upon our guard against even a *negative* submission; for agreeable to the sentiments of a celebrated writer, who thoroughly understood his subject, if we are voluntarily silent, as the conspirators would have us to be, it will be considered as an approbation of the change. " By the fundamental laws of England, the two houses of Parliament, in concert with the King, exercise the legislative power; but if the two houses should be so infatuated as to resolve to suppress their powers and invest the King with the full and absolute government, certainly the nation would not suffer it." And if a minister shall usurp the supreme and absolute government of America and set up his instructions as laws in the colonies, and their Governors shall be so weak or so wicked as for the sake of keeping their places to be made the instruments in putting them in execution, who will presume to say that the people have not a right, or that *it is not their indispensable duty to God and their country, by all rational means in their power,* to RESIST THEM? . . .

The liberties of our country, the freedom of our civil constitution, are worth defending at all hazards; and it is our duty to defend them against all attacks. We have received them as a fair inheritance from our worthy ancestors: they purchased them for us with toil and danger and expense of treasure and blood, and transmitted them to us with care and diligence. It will bring an everlasting mark of infamy on the present generation, enlightened as it is, if we should suffer them to be wrested from us by violence without a struggle, or be cheated out of them by the artifices of false and designing men. Of the latter we are in most danger at present; let us therefore be aware of it. Let us contemplate our forefathers and posterity, and resolve to maintain the rights bequeathed to us from the former, for the sake of the latter. — Instead of sitting down satisfied with the efforts we have already made, *which is the wish of our enemies,* the necessity of the times, more than ever, calls for our utmost circumspection, deliberation, fortitude, and perseverance. Let us remember that " if we suffer tamely a lawless attack upon our liberty, we encourage it, and involve others in our doom." It is a very serious consideration, which should deeply impress our minds, that *millions yet unborn may be the miserable sharers in the event.*

[*1771*]

[ON THE HUMILIATION OF AMERICANS]

I think it necessary the public should be informed that His Excellency Thomas Hutchinson, Esq., Governor of this province, has lately received a warrant from the Lords of the Treasury in England for the sum of twenty-two hundred and fifty pounds sterling for his services for one year and a half, being at the rate of fifteen hundred sterling or two thousand L.M. per ann. — The payment is to be made out of the commissioners' chest, wherein are reposited the treasures that are daily collected, though perhaps insensibly, from the earnings and industry of the honest yeomen, merchants, and tradesmen of this continent, against their consent; and if his friends speak the truth, against *his own private* judgment. — This treasure is to be appropriated according to the act of Parliament so justly and loudly complained of by Americans, for the support of civil government, the payment of the charges of the administration of justice, and the defense of the colonies: and it may hereafter be made use of for the support of standing armies and ships of war; episcopates and their numerous ecclesiastical retinue; pensioners, placemen, and other jobbers for an abandoned and shameless ministry; hirelings, pimps, parasites, panders, prostitutes and whores. — His Excellency had repeatedly refused to accept the usual salary out of the treasury of this province, which leads us to think that his eminent patron the Earl of Hillsborough, or his most respected friend Sir Francis Bernard, who is ever at His Lordship's elbow, had given him *certain* information that this *honorable* stipend would be allowed to him. — Whether he thought the generous grant of a thousand sterling, annually made to his predecessors, and offered to him by the assembly, not adequate to his important services to the province in supporting and vindicating its charter and constitutional rights and liberties; or whether he was forbid by instruction from His Lordship to receive it, which is probable from his own words, "I could not consistent with my duty to the King"; or lastly, and which is still more probable, whether he was ambitious of being, beyond any of his predecessors, a Governor independent of the free grants of the assembly, which is no doubt reconcilable with His Excellency's idea of a *constitutional* governor of a free people, are matters problematical. — Adulating priestlings and others, who have sounded his high praises in the newspapers and in the church of God, as well as in other solemn assemblies, may perhaps echo the fallacious reasoning from one of his public speeches: "The people will not blame (him) for being willing to avoid burdening them with his support, by the increase of the tax upon their polls and estates," since it is now "provided for another way." In all ages the *supercilious* part of the clergy have adored the Great Man and shown a thorough contempt of the understanding of the people. But the people, and a great part, I hope, of the clergy of this enlightened country, have understanding enough to know that a governor independent of the people for his support as well as his political being is in fact a *master;* and may be, and probably, such is the nature of uncontrollable power, soon will be a *tyrant.* It will be recorded by the faithful historian, for the information of posterity, that the first American Pensioner — the first *independent Governor* of this province — was, not a stranger, but one "born and educated" in it — not an ANDROSS or a RANDOLPH; but that cordial friend to our civil constitution — that main pillar of the religion and the learning of this country, the man upon whom she has (I will not say wantonly) heaped all the honors she had to bestow — HUTCHINSON!! — We are told that the justices of the superior court are also to receive fixed salaries out of this American revenue! — "Is it possible to form an idea of slavery more complete, more miserable, more disgraceful than that of a people where justice is administered, government exercised, and a standing army maintained at the expense of the people, and yet without the least dependence upon them? If we can find no relief from this infamous situation" — I repeat it: "*If we can find no relief from this infamous situation,* let the ministry who have stripped us of our property and liberty deprive us of our understanding too; that unconscious of what we have been or are, and ungoaded by tormenting reflections, we may tamely bow down our necks, with all the stupid serenity of servitude, to any drudgery which our lords and masters may please to command." — I appeal to the common sense of mankind. To what a state of misery and infamy must a people be reduced! To have a governor by the sole appointment of the crown; under the absolute control of a weak and arbitrary minister, to whose dictates he is to yield an unlimited obedience or forfeit his political existence; while he is to be supported at the expense of the people, by virtue of an authority claimed by *strangers,* to oblige them to contribute for him such an annual stipend, however unbounded, as the crown shall be advised to order! If this be not a state of despotism, what is? Could such a governor, by all the arts of persuasion, prevail upon a people to be quiet and contented under such a mode of government, his noble patron might spare himself the trouble of getting their Charter vacated by a formal decision of Parliament or in the tedious process of law. — Whenever the relentless enemies of America shall have completed their system, which they are still, though more silently, pursuing, by subtle arts, deep dissimulation, and manners calculated to deceive, our condition will then be more humiliating and miserable, and perhaps more inextricable too, than that of the people of England in the infamous reigns of the Stuarts, which blacken the pages of history; when

" Oppression stalk'd at large and pour'd abroad
Her unrelenting train; informers — spies —
Hateful projectors of aggrieving schemes
To sell the starving many to the few,
And drain a thousand ways th' exhausted land.
. . . And on the venal bench
Instead of Justice, Party held the scale,
And Violence the sword."

[*1771*]

THE RIGHTS OF THE COLONISTS

Among the natural rights of the colonists are these: first, a right to *life;* secondly to *liberty;* thirdly to *property;* together with the right to support and defend them in the best manner they can. — Those are evident branches of, rather than deductions from, the duty of self-preservation, commonly called the first law of nature.

All men have a right to remain in a state of nature as long as they please; and in case of intolerable oppression, civil or religious, to leave the society they belong to and enter into another.

When men enter into society, it is by voluntary consent; and they have a right to demand and insist upon the performance of such conditions and previous limitations as form an equitable *original compact.*

Every natural right not expressly given up or from the nature of a social compact necessarily ceded remains.

All positive and civil laws should conform as far as possible to the law of natural reason and equity.

As neither reason requires nor religion permits the contrary, every man living in or out of a state of civil society has a right peaceably and quietly to worship God according to the dictates of his conscience.

" Just and true liberty, equal and impartial liberty " in matters spiritual and temporal, is a thing that all men are clearly entitled to, by the eternal and immutable laws of God and nature, as well as by the law of nations, and all well-grounded municipal laws, which must have their foundation in the former.

70

In regard to religion, mutual toleration in the different professions thereof is what all good and candid minds in all ages have ever practiced, and both by precept and example inculcated on mankind; and it is now generally agreed among Christians that this spirit of toleration in the fullest extent consistent with the being of civil society "is the chief characteristical mark of the true church" and in so much that Mr. Locke has asserted, and proved beyond the possibility of contradiction on any solid ground, that such toleration ought to be extended to all whose doctrines are not subversive of society. The only sects which he thinks ought to be and which by all wise laws are excluded from such toleration are those who teach doctrines subversive of the civil government under which they live. The Roman Catholics or Papists are excluded by reason of such doctrines as these: that princes excommunicated may be deposed, and those they call heretics may be destroyed without mercy; besides their recognizing the pope in so absolute a manner, in subversion of government, by introducing as far as possible into the states under whose protection they enjoy life, liberty, and property that solecism in politics, *Imperium in imperio*, leading directly to the worse anarchy and confusion, civil discord, war and bloodshed.

The natural liberty of men by entering into society is abridged or restrained so far only as is necessary for the great end of society, the best good of the whole.

In the state of nature every man is, under God, judge and sole judge of his own rights and the injuries done him. By entering into society he agrees to an arbiter or indifferent judge between him and his neighbors; but he no more renounces his original right than by taking a cause out of the ordinary course of law and leaving the decision to referees or indifferent arbitrations. In the last case he must pay the referees for time and trouble; he should be also willing to pay his just quota for the support of government, the law and constitution, the end of which is to furnish indifferent and impartial judges in all cases that may happen, whether civil, ecclesiastical, marine, or military.

"The natural liberty of man is to be free from any superior power on earth, and not to be under the will or legislative authority of man; but only to have the law of nature for his rule."

In the state of nature men may, as the patriarchs did, employ hired servants for the defense of their lives, liberty, and property; and they should pay them reasonable wages. Government was instituted for the purposes of common defense; and those who hold the reins of government have an equitable natural right to an honorable support from the same principle "that the laborer is worthy of his hire"; but then the same community which they serve ought to be assessors of their pay: governors have no right to seek what they please; by this, instead of being content with the station assigned them, that of honorable servants of the society, they would soon become absolute masters, despots, and tyrants. Hence, as a private man has a right to say what wages he will give in his private affairs, so has a community to determine what they will give and grant of their substance for the administration of public affairs. And in both cases more are ready generally to offer their service at the proposed and stipulated price than are able and willing to perform their duty.

In short, it is the greatest absurdity to suppose it in the power of one or any number of men at the entering into society to renounce their essential natural rights, or the means of preserving those rights when the great end of civil government from the very nature of its institution is for the support, protection, and defense of those very rights, the principal of which, as is before observed, are life, liberty, and property. If men through fear, fraud, or mistake should *in terms* renounce and give up any essential natural right, the eternal law of reason and the great end of society would absolutely vacate such renunciation; the right to freedom being *the gift* of God Almighty, it is not in the power of man to alienate this gift and voluntarily become a slave.

2nd. *The Rights of the Colonists as Christians.*

These may be best understood by reading, and carefully studying, the institutes of the great Lawgiver and head of the Christian Church, which are to be found closely written and promulgated in the New Testament.

By the act of the British Parliament commonly called the Toleration Act, every subject in England except papists and etc. was restored to, and re-established in, his natural right to worship God according to the dictates of his own conscience. And by the Charter of this province it is granted, ordained, and established (that it is declared as an original right) that there shall be liberty of conscience allowed in the worship of God to all Christians except papists inhabiting or which shall inhabit or be resident within said province or territory. Magna

Charta itself is in substance but a constrained declaration, or proclamation, and promulgation in the name of King, Lords, and Commons
of the sense the latter had of their original inherent, indefeasible natural rights, as also those of free citizens equally perdurable with the
other. That great author, that great jurist, and even that court writer
Mr. Justice Blackstone holds that this recognition was justly obtained
of King John sword in hand; and peradventure it must be one day
sword in hand again rescued and preserved from total destruction and
oblivion.

3rd. *The Rights of the Colonists as Subjects.*

A commonwealth or state is a body politic or civil society of men
united together to promote their mutual safety and prosperity by
means of their union.

The *absolute rights* of Englishmen, and all freemen in or out of civil
society, are principally: *personal security, personal liberty,* and *private
property.*

All persons born in the British American colonies are by the laws
of God and nature, and by the common law of England, exclusive of
all charters from the crown, well entitled, and by the acts of the British
Parliament are declared to be entitled to all the natural essential, inherent, and inseparable rights, liberties, and privileges of subjects born
in Great Britain or within the realm. Among those rights are the following, which no men or body of men, consistently with their own
rights as men and citizens or members of society, can for themselves
give up or take away from others:

First, "the first fundamental positive law of all commonwealths or
states is the establishing the legislative power; as the first fundamental
natural law also, which is to govern even the legislative power itself, is
the preservation of the society." [1]

Secondly, the legislative has no right to absolute arbitrary power
over the lives and fortunes of the people; nor can mortals assume a
prerogative, not only too high for men, but for angels, and therefore
reserved for the exercise of the Deity alone.

"The legislative cannot justly *assume* to itself a power to rule by
extempore arbitrary decrees; but it is bound to see that justice is dispensed, and that the rights of the subjects be decided by promulgated,
standing, and known laws and authorized *independent judges*"; that

---

[1] Locke.

is, independent as far as possible of prince or people. "*There shall be one rule of justice for rich and poor; for the favorite in court and the countryman at the plough.*" [1]

Thirdly, the supreme power cannot justly take from any man any part of his property without his consent, in person or by his representative.

These are some of the first principles of natural law and justice, and the great barriers of all free states, and of the British Constitution in particular. It is utterly irreconcilable to these principles, and to many other fundamental maxims of the common law, common sense, and reason, that a British House of Commons should have a right, at pleasure, to give and grant the property of the colonists. That these colonists are well entitled to all the essential rights, liberties, and privileges of men and freemen born in Britain is manifest, not only from the colony Charter, in general, but acts of the British Parliament. The statute of the 13th of George 2.c.7. naturalizes even foreigners after seven years' residence. The words of the Massachusetts Charter are these: "And further our will and pleasure is, and we do hereby for us, our heirs and successors, grant, establish, and ordain, that all and every of the subjects of us, our heirs and successors which shall go to and inhabit within our said province or territory and every of their children which shall happen to be born there, or on the seas in going thither, or returning from thence shall have and enjoy all liberties and immunities of free and natural subjects within any of the dominions of us, our heirs and successors, to all intents, constructions, and purposes whatsoever as if they and every of them were born within this our realm of England." Now, what liberty can there be where property is taken away without consent? Can it be said with any color of truth and justice that this continent of three thousand miles in length, and of a breadth as yet unexplored, in which, however, it's supposed there are five millions of people, has the least voice, vote, or influence in the decisions of the British Parliament? Have they, all together, any more right or power to return a single member to that House of Commons, who have not inadvertently but deliberately assumed a power to dispose of their lives, liberties, and properties, than to choose an emperor of China! Had the colonists a right to return members to the British Parliament, it would only be hurtful, as from their local situation and circumstances it is impossible they should be ever truly and properly

[1] Locke.

represented there. The inhabitants of this country in all probability in a few years will be more numerous than those of Great Britain and Ireland together; yet it is absurdly expected by the promoters of the present measures that these, with their posterity to all generations, should be easy while their property shall be disposed of by a House of Commons at three thousand miles distant from them, and who cannot be supposed to have the least care or concern for their real interest; who have not only no natural care for their interest, but must be *in effect* bribed against it, as every burden they lay on the colonists is so much saved or gained to themselves. Hitherto many of the colonists have been free from quit rents; but if the breath of a British House of Commons can originate an act for taking away all our money, our lands will go next or be subject to rack rents from haughty and relentless landlords who will ride at ease, while we are trodden in the dirt. The colonists have been branded with the odious names of traitors and rebels, only for complaining of their grievances. How long such treatment will or ought to be borne is submitted.

[1772]

JOHN ADAMS

[1735–1826]

SECOND PRESIDENT of the United States, father of the seventh President, and grandfather of the American Minister to England during the Civil War, he made the name of Adams one of the most important in American history. He was the first of the line to enter law and politics. Before him the Adamses had been prosperous farmers in Braintree, Massachusetts. After being graduated from Harvard in 1755, he studied law and was admitted to the bar three years later. He began to build up a law practice, became interested in Boston affairs, contributed articles on current problems to the local newspapers. In 1765 he published " A Dissertation on the Canon and Feudal Law." This work was distinguished by scholarship, forceful and eloquent prose, and a thoroughly liberal viewpoint, expressing the advanced middle-class thought of the day. Although reluctant to accept a complete break with England and antagonistic to mass action, he did not hesitate to take the American side, and when the Revolution came, he joined the revolutionaries. Except for short periods, he was thereafter consistently active in the affairs of his state and nation — until the end of his term as President. Then he isolated himself from the public, which had come to dislike him. For Adams had developed into a conservative, a defender of property rights and champion of aristocracy, at a time when the tide was in favor of democracy. He had had a troubled presidency, principally because of the treacherous and greedy conduct of his associates. Jefferson's presidency was at hand and Jacksonism was already in the air. It is interesting that some of the writings of the testy aristocrat Adams paved the way for them.

---

from

DISSERTATION ON THE CANON AND THE

FEUDAL LAW

" Ignorance and inconsideration are the two great causes of the ruin of mankind." This is an observation of Dr. Tillotson, with relation to the interest of his fellow men in a future and immortal state. But it is of equal truth and importance if applied to the happiness of men in society, on this side the grave. In the earliest ages of the world, absolute monarchy seems to have been the universal form of government. Kings, and a few of their great counselors and captains, exercised a cruel tyranny over the people, who held a rank in the scale of intelligence, in those days, but little higher than the camels and elephants that carried them and their engines to war.

By what causes it was brought to pass that the people in the Middle Ages became more intelligent in general would not, perhaps, be possible in these days to discover. But the fact is certain; and wherever a general knowledge and sensibility have prevailed among the people, arbitrary government and every kind of oppression have lessened and disappeared in proportion. Man has certainly an exalted soul; and the same principle in human nature — that aspiring, noble principle founded in benevolence, and cherished by knowledge; I mean the love of power, which has been so often the cause of slavery — has, whenever freedom has existed, been the cause of freedom. If it is this principle that has always prompted the princes and nobles of the earth by every species of fraud and violence to shake off all the limitations of their power, it is the same that has always stimulated the common people to aspire at independency, and to endeavor at confining the power of the great within the limits of equity and reason.

The poor people, it is true, have been much less successful than the great. They have seldom found either leisure or opportunity to form a union and exert their strength; ignorant as they were of arts and letters, they have seldom been able to frame and support a regular opposition. This, however, has been known by the great to be the temper of mankind; and they have accordingly labored, in all ages, to wrest from the populace, as they are contemptuously called, the knowledge of their rights and wrongs, and the power to assert the former or redress the latter. I say RIGHTS, for such they have, undoubtedly, antecedent to all earthly government — *rights* that cannot be repealed or restrained by human laws — *rights* derived from the great Legislator of the universe.

Since the promulgation of Christianity, the two greatest systems of tyranny that have sprung from this original are the canon and the feudal law. The desire of dominion, that great principle by which we have attempted to account for so much good and so much evil, is, when properly restrained, a very useful and noble movement in the human mind. But when such restraints are taken off, it becomes an encroaching, grasping, restless, and ungovernable power. Numberless have been the systems of iniquity contrived by the great for the gratification of this passion in themselves; but in none of them were they ever more successful than in the invention and establishment of the canon and the feudal law.

By the former of these, the most refined, sublime, extensive, and astonishing constitution of policy that ever was conceived by the mind of man was framed by the Romish clergy for the aggrandizement of their own order. All the epithets I have here given to the Romish policy are just, and will be allowed to be so when it is considered that they even persuaded mankind to believe, faithfully and undoubtingly, that God Almighty had entrusted them with the keys of heaven, whose gates they might open and close at pleasure; with a power of dispensation over all the rules and obligations of morality; with authority to license all sorts of sins and crimes; with a power of deposing princes and absolving subjects from allegiance; with a power of procuring or withholding the rain of heaven and the beams of the sun; with the management of earthquakes, pestilence, and famine; nay, with the mysterious, awful, incomprehensible power of creating out of bread and wine the flesh and blood of God himself. All these opinions they were enabled to spread and rivet among the people by reducing their minds to a state of sordid ignorance and staring timidity, and by infusing into them a religious horror of letters and knowledge. Thus was human nature chained fast for ages in a cruel, shameful, and deplorable servitude to him and his subordinate tyrants, who, it was foretold, would exalt himself above all that was called God and that was worshipped.

In the latter we find another system, similar in many respects to the former; which, although it was originally formed, perhaps, for the necessary defense of a barbarous people against the inroads and invasions of her neighboring nations, yet for the same purposes of tyranny, cruelty, and lust which had dictated the canon law, it was soon adopted by almost all the princes of Europe and wrought into the constitutions of their government. It was originally a code of laws for a vast army in a perpetual encampment. The general was invested with the sovereign propriety of all the lands within the territory. Of him, as his servants and vassals, the first rank of his great officers held the lands; and in the same manner the other subordinate officers held of them; and all ranks and degrees held their lands by a variety of duties and services, all tending to bind the chains the faster on every

order of mankind. In this manner the common people were held together in herds and clans in a state of servile dependence on their
lords, bound, even by the tenure of their lands, to follow them, whenever they commanded, to their wars, and in a state of total ignorance
of everything divine and human excepting the use of arms and the
culture of their lands.

But another event still more calamitous to human liberty was a
wicked confederacy between the two systems of tyranny above described. It seems to have been even stipulated between them that the
temporal grandees should contribute everything in their power to
maintain the ascendancy of the priesthood, and that the spiritual
grandees in their turn should employ their ascendancy over the consciences of the people, in impressing on their minds a blind, implicit
obedience to civil magistracy.

Thus, as long as this confederacy lasted and the people were held in
ignorance, liberty, and, with her, knowledge and virtue too, seem to
have deserted the earth, and one age of darkness succeeded another,
till God in his benign providence raised up the champions who began
and conducted the Reformation. From the time of the Reformation
to the first settlement of America, knowledge gradually spread in Europe, but especially in England; and in proportion as that increased
and spread among the people, ecclesiastical and civil tyranny, which
I use as synonymous expressions for the canon and feudal laws, seem
to have lost their strength and weight. The people grew more and
more sensible of the wrong that was done them by these systems, more
and more impatient under it, and determined at all hazards to rid themselves of it; till at last, under the execrable race of the Stuarts, the struggle between the people and the confederacy aforesaid of temporal and
spiritual tyranny became formidable, violent, and bloody.

It was this great struggle that peopled America. It was not religion
alone, as is commonly supposed; but it was a love of universal liberty,
and a hatred, a dread, a horror, of the infernal confederacy before described, that projected, conducted, and accomplished the settlement
of America.

It was a resolution formed by a sensible people — I mean the Puritans — almost in despair. They had become intelligent in general, and
many of them learned. . . . They saw clearly that of all the nonsense
and delusion which had ever passed through the mind of man, none
had ever been more extravagant than the notions of absolutions, in-

79

delible characters, uninterrupted successions, and the rest of those fantastical ideas, derived from the canon law, which had thrown such a glare of mystery, sanctity, reverence, and right reverend eminence and holiness around the idea of a priest as no mortal could deserve, and as always must, from the constitution of human nature, be dangerous in society. For this reason they demolished the whole system of diocesan episcopacy; and, deriding, as all reasonable and impartial men must do, the ridiculous fancies of sanctified effluvia from episcopal fingers, they established sacerdotal ordination on the foundation of the Bible and common sense. This conduct at once imposed an obligation on the whole body of the clergy to industry, virtue, piety, and learning, and rendered that whole body infinitely more independent of the civil powers, in all respects, than they could be where they were formed into a scale of subordination, from a pope down to priests and friars and confessors — necessarily and essentially a sordid, stupid, and wretched herd — or than they could be in any other country where an archbishop held the place of a universal bishop, and the vicars and curates that of the ignorant, dependent, miserable rabble aforesaid — and infinitely more sensible and learned than they could be in either. . . . The adventurers so often mentioned had an utter contempt of all that dark ribaldry of hereditary, indefeasible right — the Lord's anointed — and the divine, miraculous original of government, with which the priesthood had enveloped the feudal monarch in clouds and mysteries, and from whence they had deduced the most mischievous of all doctrines, that of passive obedience and non-resistance. They knew that government was a plain, simple, intelligible thing, founded in nature and reason, and quite comprehensible by common sense. They detested all the base services and servile dependencies of the feudal system. They knew that no such unworthy dependencies took place in the ancient seats of liberty, the republics of Greece and Rome; and they thought all such slavish subordinations were equally inconsistent with the constitution of human nature and that religious liberty with which Jesus had made them free. This was certainly the opinion they had formed; and they were far from being singular or extravagant in thinking so. . . .

They were convinced, by their knowledge of human nature, derived from history and their own experience, that nothing could preserve their posterity from the encroachments of the two systems of tyranny, in opposition to which, as has been observed already, they erected their government in church and state, but knowledge diffused generally through the whole body of the people. Their civil and religious principles, therefore, conspired to prompt them to use every measure and take every precaution in their power to propagate and perpetuate knowledge. For this purpose they laid very early the foundations of colleges and invested them with ample privileges and emoluments; and it is remarkable that they have left among their posterity so universal an affection and veneration for those seminaries, and for liberal education, that the meanest of the people contribute cheerfully to the support and maintenance of them every year, and that nothing is more generally popular than projections for the honor, reputation, and advantage of those seats of learning. But the wisdom and benevolence of our fathers rested not here. They made an early provision by law that every town consisting of so many families should be always furnished with a grammar school. They made it a crime for such a town to be destitute of a grammar schoolmaster for a few months, and subjected it to a heavy penalty. So that the education of all ranks of people was made the care and expense of the public, in a manner that I believe has been unknown to any other people ancient or modern. . . .

It is true, there has been among us a party for some years, consisting chiefly not of the descendants of the first settlers of this country, but of high churchmen and high statesmen imported since, who affect to censure this provision for the education of our youth as a needless expense, and an imposition upon the rich in favor of the poor, and as an institution productive of idleness and vain speculation among the people, whose time and attention, it is said, ought to be devoted to labor, and not to public affairs or to examination into the conduct of their superiors. And certain officers of the crown, and certain other missionaries of ignorance, foppery, servility, and slavery, have been most inclined to countenance and increase the same party. Be it remembered, however, that liberty must at all hazards be supported. We have a right to it, derived from our Maker. But if we had not, our fathers have earned and bought it for us, at the expense of their ease, their estates, their pleasure, and their blood. And liberty cannot be preserved without a general knowledge among the people, who have a right, from the frame of their nature, to knowledge, as their great Creator, who does nothing in vain, has given them understandings, and a desire to know; but besides this, they have a right, an indisputable, unalienable, indefeasible, divine right to that most dreaded and envied kind of knowledge; I mean, of the characters and conduct of their rulers. Rulers are no more than attorneys, agents, and trustees, for the people; and if the cause, the interest and trust, is insidiously betrayed, or wantonly trifled away, the people have a right to revoke the authority that they themselves have deputed, and to constitute abler and better agents, attorneys, and trustees. And the preservation of the means of knowledge among the lowest ranks is of more importance to the public than all the property of all the rich men in the country. It is even of more consequence to the rich themselves, and to their posterity. The only question is whether it is a public emolument; and if it is, the rich ought undoubtedly to contribute, in the same proportion as to all other public burdens — that is, in proportion to their wealth, which is secured by public expenses. But none of the means of information are more sacred, or have been cherished with more tenderness and care by the settlers of America, than the press. Care has been taken that the art of printing should be encouraged, and that it should be easy and cheap and safe for any person to communicate his thoughts to the public. And you, Messieurs printers,[1] whatever the tyrants of the earth may say of your paper, have done important service to your country by your readiness and freedom in publishing the speculations of the curious. The stale, impudent insinuations of slander and sedition with which the gormandizers of power have endeavored to discredit your paper are so much the more to your honor; for the jaws of power are always opened to devour, and her arm is always stretched out, if possible, to destroy the freedom of thinking, speaking, and writing. And if the public interest, liberty, and happiness have been in danger from the ambition or avarice of any great man, whatever may be his politeness, address, learning, ingenuity, and, in other respects, integrity and humanity, you have done yourselves honor and your country service by publishing and pointing out that avarice and ambition. These vices are so much the more dangerous and pernicious for the virtues with which they may be accompanied in the same character, and with so much the more watchful jealousy to be guarded against.

" Curse on such virtues, they've undone their country."

. Be not intimidated, therefore, by any terrors, from publishing with the utmost freedom whatever can be warranted by the laws of your

---

[1] Edies and Gill, printers of the *Boston Gazette* [in which this work first appeared].

country; nor suffer yourselves to be wheedled out of your liberty by any pretenses of politeness, delicacy, or decency. These, as they are often used, are but three different names for hypocrisy, chicanery, and cowardice. Much less, I presume, will you be discouraged by any pretenses that malignants on this side the water will represent your paper as factious and seditious, or that the great on the other side the water will take offense at them. . . .

Let us dare to read, think, speak, and write. Let every order and degree among the people rouse their attention and animate their resolution. Let them all become attentive to the grounds and principles of government, ecclesiastical and civil. Let us study the law of nature; search into the spirit of the British Constitution; read the histories of ancient ages; contemplate the great examples of Greece and Rome; set before us the conduct of our own British ancestors, who have defended for us the inherent rights of mankind against foreign and domestic tyrants and usurpers, against arbitrary kings and cruel priests; in short, against the gates of earth and hell. Let us read and recollect and impress upon our souls the views and ends of our own more immediate forefathers in exchanging their native country for a dreary, inhospitable wilderness. Let us examine into the nature of that power, and the cruelty of that oppression, which drove them from their homes. Recollect their amazing fortitude, their bitter sufferings — the hunger, the nakedness, the cold, which they patiently endured — the severe labors of clearing their grounds, building their houses, raising their provisions, amidst dangers from wild beasts and savage men, before they had time or money or materials for commerce. Recollect the civil and religious principles and hopes and expectations which constantly supported and carried them through all hardships with patience and resignation. Let us recollect it was liberty, the hope of liberty for themselves and us and ours, which conquered all discouragements, dangers, and trials. In such researches as these let us all in our several departments cheerfully engage — but especially the proper patrons and supporters of law, learning, and religion!

Let the pulpit resound with the doctrines and sentiments of religious liberty. Let us hear the danger of thraldom to our consciences from ignorance, extreme poverty, and dependence; in short, from civil and political slavery. Let us see delineated before us the true map of man. Let us hear the dignity of his nature, and the noble rank he holds among the works of God — that consenting to slavery is a sacrilegious breach of trust, as offensive in the sight of God as it is derogatory from our own honor or interest or happiness — and that God Almighty has promulgated from heaven liberty, peace, and goodwill to man!

Let the bar proclaim "the laws, the rights, the generous plan of power" delivered down from remote antiquity — inform the world of the mighty struggles and numberless sacrifices made by our ancestors in defense of freedom. Let it be known that original rights, conditions of original contracts, coequal with prerogative and coeval with government; that many of our rights are inherent and essential, agreed on as maxims and established as preliminaries, even before a parliament existed. Let them search for the foundations of British laws and government in the frame of human nature, in the constitution of the intellectual and moral world. There let us see that truth, liberty, justice, and benevolence are its everlasting basis; and if these could be removed, the superstructure is overthrown of course.

Let the colleges join their harmony in the same delightful concert. Let every declamation turn upon the beauty of liberty and virtue, and the deformity, turpitude, and malignity of slavery and vice. Let the public disputations become researches into the grounds and nature and ends of government, and the means of preserving the good and demolishing the evil. Let the dialogues, and all the exercises, become the instruments of impressing on the tender mind, and of spreading and distributing far and wide, the ideas of right and the sensations of freedom.

In a word, let every sluice of knowledge be opened and set a-flowing. The encroachments upon liberty in the reigns of the first James and the first Charles, by turning the general attention of learned men to government, are said to have produced the greatest number of consummate statesmen which has ever been seen in any age or nation. The Brookes, Hampdens, Vanes, Seldens, Miltons, Nedhams, Harringtons, Nevilles, Sidneys, Lockes, are all said to have owed their eminence in political knowledge to the tyrannies of those reigns. The prospect now before us in America ought in the same manner to engage the attention of every man of learning to matters of power and of right, that we may be neither led nor driven blindfold to irretrievable destruction. Nothing less than this seems to have been meditated for us, by somebody or other in Great Britain. There seems to be a direct and formal design on foot to enslave all America. This, however, must be done by degrees. The first step that is intended seems to be an entire subversion of the whole system of our fathers, by the introduction of the canon and feudal law into America. The canon and feudal systems, though greatly mutilated in England, are not yet destroyed. Like the temples and palaces in which the great contrivers of them once worshipped and inhabited, they exist in ruins; and much of the domineering spirit of them still remains. The designs and labors of a certain society to introduce the former of them into America have been well exposed to the public. . . . These are not the vapors of a melancholy mind, nor the effusions of envy, disappointed ambition, nor of a spirit of opposition to government, but the emanations of a heart that burns for its country's welfare. No one of any feeling, born and educated in this once happy country, can consider the numerous distresses, the gross indignities, the barbarous ignorance, the haughty usurpations, that we have reason to fear are meditating for ourselves, our children, our neighbors — in short, for all our countrymen and all their posterity — without the utmost agonies of heart and many tears.

[*1765*]

PATRICK HENRY

[1736–1799]

HIS FATHER was an Aberdeen Scot, his mother of Yorkshire descent. They had little money, but they were intelligent, hard-working, and independent. They were one of the upland families — the settlers in western Virginia who would democratize the colony and wrest political power from the feudal lords of the tidewater. Patrick was a poor student at school, and so at fifteen was sent to work as a store clerk. Later he opened a store in partnership with his father, but soon failed. He tried farming, failed at that, and then once again ventured unsuccessfully into store-keeping. He finally decided to study law, and in 1760 he was admitted to the bar. In 1763 he argued a case against the clergy which involved the rights of the colonists to self-rule. The jury, made up of farmers, brought in a verdict favorable to Henry. He was a notable figure from then on — and always, during this period, on the side of the plain people. In 1765 he was elected a member of the House of Burgesses. A brilliant orator, he soon acquired enormous influence. He became a member of Virginia's Revolutionary Convention and of the Continental Congress and was elected first Governor of the state. After the Revolution he developed into a conservative and fought against his erstwhile allies, Jefferson and Madison. He was neither the first nor the last man to turn against a revolution he had helped to start. Henry lives in American history — and in our literature — for one speech: it was delivered in March 1775 to the Virginia Convention when the aristocrats opposed the organization of a company of militia to act against British tyranny. There is little in modern oratory to compare with it, and its peroration is still the libertarian's slogan.

[LIBERTY OR DEATH]

Mr. President, it is natural to men to indulge in the illusions of hope. We are apt to shut our eyes against a painful truth — and listen to the song of that siren, till she transforms us into beasts. Is this the part of wise men, engaged in a great and arduous struggle for liberty? Are we disposed to be of the number of those who, having eyes, see not, and having ears, hear not, the things which so nearly concern their temporal salvation? For my part, whatever anguish of spirit it may cost, I am willing to know the whole truth; to know the worst and to provide for it.

I have but one lamp by which my feet are guided, and that is the lamp of experience. I know of no way of judging of the future but by the past. And judging by the past, I wish to know what there has been in the conduct of the British ministry for the last ten years to justify those hopes with which gentlemen have been pleased to solace themselves and the house? Is it that insidious smile with which our petition has been lately received? Trust it not, sir; it will prove a snare to your feet. Suffer not yourself to be betrayed with a kiss. Ask yourself how this gracious reception of our petition comports with those warlike preparations which cover our waters and darken our land. Are fleets and armies necessary to a work of love and reconciliation? Have we shown ourselves so unwilling to be reconciled that force must be called in to win back our love? Let us not deceive ourselves, sir. These are the implements of war and subjugation — the last arguments to which kings resort. I ask gentlemen, sir, what means this martial array if its purpose be not to force us to submission? Can gentlemen assign any other possible motive for it? Has Great Britain any enemy in this quarter of the world, to call for this accumulation of navies and armies? No, sir, she has none. They are meant for us: they can be meant for no other. They are sent over to bind and rivet upon us those chains which the British ministry have been so long forging. And what have we to oppose to them? Shall we try argument? Sir, we have been trying that for the last ten years. Have we anything new to offer upon the subject? Nothing. We have the subject up in every light of which it is capable; but it has been all in vain. Shall we resort to entreaty and humble supplication? What terms shall we find which have not been already exhausted? Let us not, I beseech you, sir, deceive ourselves longer. Sir, we have done everything that could be done to avert the storm which is now coming on. We have petitioned — we have remonstrated — we have supplicated — we have prostrated ourselves before the throne, and have implored its interposition to arrest the tyrannical hands of the ministry and Parliament. Our petitions have been slighted; our remonstrances have produced additional violence and insult; our supplications have been disregarded; and we have been spurned with contempt from the foot of the throne. In vain, after these things, may we indulge the fond hope of peace and reconciliation. There is no longer any room for hope. If we wish to be free — if we mean to preserve inviolate those inestimable privileges for which we have been so long contending — if we mean not basely to abandon the noble struggle in which we have been so long engaged, and which we have pledged ourselves never to abandon until the glorious object of our contest shall be obtained — we must fight! — I repeat it, sir, we must fight; an appeal to arms and to the God of Hosts is all that is left us!

They tell us, sir, that we are weak — unable to cope with so formidable an adversary. But when shall we be stronger? Will it be the next week or the next year? Will it be when we are totally disarmed, and when a British guard shall be stationed in every house? Shall we gather strength by irresolution and inaction? Shall we acquire the means of effectual resistance by lying supinely on our backs and hugging the delusive phantom of hope, until our enemy shall have bound us hand and foot? Sir, we are not weak, if we make a proper use of those forces which the God of nature hath placed in our power. Three millions of people armed in the holy cause of liberty, and in such a country as that which we possess, are invincible by any force which our enemy can send against us. Besides, sir, we shall not fight our battles alone. There is a just God who presides over the destinies of nations, and who will raise up friends to fight our battles for us. The battle, sir, is not to the strong alone; it is to the vigilant, the active, the brave. Besides, sir, we have no election. If we were base enough to desire it, it is now too late to retire from the contest. There is no retreat but in submission and slavery! Our chains are forged. Their clanking may be heard on the plains of Boston! The war is inevitable — and let it come!! I repeat it sir, let it come!!!

It is vain, sir, to extenuate the matter. Gentlemen may cry, Peace, peace, peace — but there is no peace. The war is actually begun! The next gale that sweeps from the north will bring to our ears the clash of resounding arms! Our brethren are already in the field! Why stand we here idle? What is it that gentlemen wish? What would they have? Is life so dear, or peace so sweet, as to be purchased at the price of chains and slavery? Forbid it, Almighty God! I know not what course others may take; but as for me, give me liberty, or give me death!

[1775]

THOMAS JEFFERSON

[1743–1826]

THE JEFFERSONS were of yeoman stock, apparently of Welsh descent. Certainly they were a modest family living in the uplands of Virginia — geographically as well as socially far removed from the tidewater aristocracy. But Thomas's father, a surveyor and magistrate, had the good fortune to marry a Randolph, so Thomas was born into the " nobility " and was reared in comfortable circumstances. His permanent home, however, was his father's plantation on the frontier of the colony, and there Thomas came into contact with, and learned to love, the independent, democratically minded small farmers of German, Irish, and Welsh origin who were antagonistic to the aristocrats. To these people he was faithful all his life.

He was graduated from William and Mary College in 1762, studied law, was admitted to the bar in 1767. Two years later he was elected to the House of Burgesses, of which he continued to be a member until 1775. During this time he became completely identified with the anti-British movement, was friendly with the revolutionary Patrick Henry, and wrote a spirited defense of the rights of the colonists. He was elected in 1775 to the Continental Congress and the following year, because of his known gifts as a writer, was appointed to the committee formed to draw up a declaration of independence. The other members were Benjamin Franklin, John Adams, Roger Sherman, and Robert Livingston. The Declaration as we know it today was almost entirely the work of Jefferson. His fellows on the committee made some changes in his draft, and additional changes (chiefly cuts) were made after the draft was reported to Congress. When the Declaration was finally accepted, Jefferson returned to Virginia to work for local reforms. He was associated with Madison in the fight for religious freedom; he wrote a bill to achieve that end, which was presented in 1779 but not passed until 1786. He fought for general public education, tried to establish a public library, successfully modernized the landholding and inheritance laws — in short, did everything possible to rid Virginia of its feudal traditions. He was elected Governor of the state, was appointed Minister to France, became Secretary of State under Washington, Vice-President and then President of the United States, and at last first Rector of the University of Virginia. Throughout his political career he was consistently the champion of the small man, struggling against privilege, wealth, and tyranny. Defender of the French Revolution and friend of Tom Paine, he became — and has remained — a hero of every democratic and libertarian movement American has had. He cannot be regarded as an original thinker, but there was no subject on which he did not have advanced views — and he expressed them well and upheld them courageously.

His masterpiece is, of course, the Declaration of Independence. Ever since he wrote it attempts have been made to prove that he did not mean what he said. But the people have taken his magnificent words at their face value; and so long as those words are taken seriously by this country, democracy will be secure. When he substituted the phrase "pursuit of happiness" for the usual word "property," a revolution in social thought was accomplished. The text of the Declaration used here is the one reported to Congress.

DECLARATION OF INDEPENDENCE

A Declaration by the Representatives of the UNITED STATES OF AMERICA in General Congress assembled.

When in the course of human events it becomes necessary for one people to dissolve the political bands which have connected them with another and to assume among the powers of the earth the separate and equal station to which the laws of nature and of nature's God entitle them, a decent respect to the opinions of mankind requires that they should declare the causes which impel them to the separation.

We hold these truths to be self-evident: that all men are created equal; that they are endowed by their Creator with inherent and inalienable rights; that among these are life, liberty, and the pursuit of happiness; that to secure these rights governments are instituted among men, deriving their just powers from the consent of the governed; that whenever any form of government becomes destructive of these ends, it is the right of the people to alter or to abolish it, and to institute new government, laying its foundation on such principles and organizing its powers in such form as to them shall seem most likely to effect their happiness. Prudence indeed will dictate that governments long established should not be changed for light and transient causes; and accordingly all experience hath shown that mankind are more disposed to suffer while evils are sufferable than to right themselves by abolishing the forms to which they are accustomed. But when a long train of abuses and usurpations, begun at a distinguished period and pursuing invariably the same object, evinces a design to reduce them under absolute despotism, it is their right, it is their duty, to throw off such government and to provide new guards for their future security. Such has been the patient sufferance of these colonies, and such is now the necessity which constrains them to expunge their former systems of government. The history of the present King of Great Britain is a history of unremitting injuries and usurpations, among which appears no solitary fact to contradict the uniform tenor of the rest; but all having in direct object the establishment of an absolute tyranny over these states. To prove this let facts be submitted to a candid world, for the truth of which we pledge a faith yet unsullied by falsehood.

He has refused his assent to laws the most wholesome and necessary for the public good:

He has forbidden his governors to pass laws of immediate and pressing importance, unless suspended in their operation till his assent should be obtained, and when so suspended, he has utterly neglected to attend to them.

He has refused to pass other laws for the accommodation of large districts of people unless those people would relinquish the right of representation in the legislature, a right inestimable to them, and formidable to tyrants only.

He has called together legislative bodies at places unusual, uncomfortable, and distant from the depository of the public records, for the sole purpose of fatiguing them into compliance with his measures.

He has dissolved representative houses repeatedly and continually for opposing with manly firmness his invasions on the right of the people.

He has refused for a long time after such dissolutions to cause others to be elected whereby the legislative powers incapable of annihilation have returned to the people at large for their exercise, the state remaining in the meantime exposed to all the dangers of invasion from without and convulsions within.

He has endeavored to prevent the population of these states, for that purpose obstructing the laws for naturalization of foreigners, refusing to pass others to encourage their migrations hither, and raising the conditions of new appropriations of lands.

He has suffered the administration of justice totally to cease in some of these states, refusing his assent to laws for establishing judiciary powers.

He has made judges dependent on his will alone, for the tenure of their offices and the amount and payment of their salaries.

91

He has erected a multitude of new offices by a self-assumed power and sent hither swarms of officers to harass our people and eat out their substance.

He has kept among us, in times of peace, standing armies and ships of war without the consent of our legislatures.

He has affected to render the military independent of and superior to the civil power.

He has combined with others to subject us to a jurisdiction foreign to our constitutions and unacknowledged by our laws, giving his assent to their acts of pretended legislation, for quartering large bodies of armed troops among us; for protecting them by a mock trial from punishment for any murders which they should commit on the inhabitants of these states; for cutting off our trade with all parts of the world; for imposing taxes on us without our consent; for depriving us in many cases of the benefits of trial by jury; for transporting us beyond seas to be tried for pretended offenses; for abolishing the free system of English laws in a neighboring province, establishing therein an arbitrary government and enlarging its boundaries so as to render it at once an example and fit instrument for introducing the same absolute rule into these colonies; for taking away our charters, abolishing our most valuable laws, and fundamentally the forms of our governments; for suspending our own legislatures and declaring themselves invested with power to legislate for us in all cases whatsoever.

He has abdicated government here, withdrawing his governors, and declaring us out of his allegiance and protection.

He has plundered our seas, ravaged our coasts, burnt our towns, and destroyed the lives of our people.

He is at this time transporting large armies of foreign mercenaries to complete the works of death, desolation, and tyranny already begun, with circumstances of cruelty and perfidy unworthy the head of a civilized nation.

He has endeavored to bring on the inhabitants of our frontiers the merciless Indian savages, whose known rule of warfare is an undistinguished destruction of all ages, sexes, and conditions of existence.

He has incited treasonable insurrections of our fellow citizens, with the allurements of forfeiture and confiscation of our property.

He has constrained others, taken captive on the high seas, to bear arms against their country, to become the executioners of their friends and brethren, or to fall themselves by their hands.

92

He has waged cruel war against human nature itself, violating its most sacred rights of life and liberty in the persons of distant people, who never offended him, captivating and carrying them into slavery in another hemisphere, or to incur miserable death in their transportation thither. This piratical warfare, the opprobrium of infidel powers, is the warfare of the Christian King of Great Britain. Determined to keep open a market where men should be bought and sold, he has prostituted his negative for suppressing every legislative attempt to prohibit or to restrain this execrable commerce; and that this assemblage of horrors might want no fact of distinguished dye, he is now exciting those very people to rise in arms among us, and to purchase that liberty of which he has deprived them by murdering the people upon whom he also obtruded them; thus paying off former crime committed against the liberties of one people with crimes which he urged them to commit against the lives of another.

In every stage of these oppressions we have petitioned for redress in the most humble terms; our repeated petitions have been answered only by repeated injuries. A prince whose character is thus marked by every act which may define a tyrant is unfit to be the ruler of a people who mean to be free. Future ages will scarce believe that the hardiness of one man adventured, within the short compass of twelve years only, to build a foundation so broad and undisguised for tyranny over a people fostered and fixed in principles of freedom.

Nor have we been wanting in attentions to our British brethren. We have warned them from time to time of attempts by their legislature to extend an unwarrantable jurisdiction over these our states. We have reminded them of the circumstances of our emigration and settlement here, no one of which could warrant so strange a pretension: that these were effected at the expense of our own blood and treasure, unassisted by the wealth or strength of Great Britain; that in constituting indeed our several forms of government, we had adopted a common king, thereby laying a foundation for perpetual league and amity with them; but that submission to their Parliament was no part of our constitution nor ever in idea, if history be credited; and we have appealed to their native justice and magnanimity, as well as to the ties of our common kindred, to disavow these usurpations which were likely to interrupt our connection and correspondence. They too have been deaf to the voice of justice and of consanguinity, and when occasions have been given them, by the regular course of their laws, of removing from their councils the disturbers of our harmony, they have by their free elections re-established them in power. At this very time they are permitting their chief magistrate to send over not only soldiers of our own blood, but Scotch and other foreign mercenaries, to invade and destroy us. These facts have given the last stab to agonizing affections, and manly spirit bids us to renounce forever these unfeeling brethren. We must endeavor to forget our former love for them, to hold them as we hold the rest of mankind enemies in war, in peace friends.

We might have been a free and a great people together; but a communication of grandeur and of freedom, it seems, is below their dignity. Be it so, since they will have it: the road to happiness and to glory is open to us too; we will climb it apart from them, and acquiesce in the necessity which denounces our eternal separation!

We therefore, the representatives of the United States in General Congress assembled in the name and by authority of the good people of these states, reject and renounce all allegiance and subjection to the kings of Great Britain and all others who may hereafter claim by, through, or under them; we utterly dissolve all political connection which may heretofore have subsisted between us and the people or Parliament of Great Britain; and finally we do assert and declare these colonies to be free and independent, and that as free and independent states they have full power to levy war, conclude peace, contract alliances, establish commerce, and to do all other acts and things which independent states may of right do. And for the support of this declaration we mutually pledge to each other our lives, our fortunes, and our sacred honor.

[*1776*]

A BILL FOR ESTABLISHING RELIGIOUS FREEDOM

SECTION I. Well aware that the opinions and belief of men depend not on their own will, but follow involuntarily the evidence proposed to their minds; that Almighty God hath created the mind free, and manifested his supreme will that free it shall remain by making it altogether insusceptible of restraint; that all attempts to influence it by temporal punishments, or burthens, or by civil incapacitations, tend only to beget habits of hypocrisy and meanness, and are a departure from the plan of the holy author of our religion, who being lord both of body and mind, yet chose not to propagate it by coercions on either, as was in his almighty power to do, but to exalt it by its influence on reason alone; that the impious presumption of legislature and ruler, civil as well as ecclesiastical, who, being themselves but fallible and uninspired men, have assumed dominion over the faith of others, setting up their own opinions and modes of thinking as the only true and infallible, and as such endeavoring to impose them on others, hath established and maintained false religions over the greatest part of the world and through all time: that to compel a man to furnish contributions of money for the propagation of opinions which he disbelieves and abhors is sinful and tyrannical; that even the forcing him to support this or that teacher of his own religious persuasion is depriving him of the comfortable liberty of giving his contributions to the particular pastor whose morals he would make his pattern and whose powers he feels most persuasive to righteousness, and is withdrawing from the ministry those temporary rewards which, proceeding from an approbation of their personal conduct, are an additional incitement to earnest and unremitting labors for the instruction of mankind; that our civil rights have no dependence on our religious opinions, any more than our opinions in physics or geometry; and therefore the proscribing any citizen as unworthy the public confidence by laying upon him an incapacity of being called to offices of trust or emolument, unless he profess or renounce this or that religious opinion, is depriving him injudiciously of those privileges and advantages to which, in common with his fellow citizens, he has a natural right; that it tends also to corrupt the principles of that very religion it is meant to encourage, by bribing with a monopoly of worldly honors and emoluments those who will externally profess and conform to it; that though indeed these are criminals who do not withstand such temptation, yet neither are those innocent who lay the bait in their way; that the opinions of men are not the object of civil government, nor under its jurisdiction; that to suffer the civil magistrate to intrude his powers into the field of opinion and to restrain the profession or propagation of principles on supposition of their ill tendency is a dangerous fallacy, which at once destroys all religious liberty, because he being of course judge of that tendency will make his opinions the rule of judgment and approve or condemn the sentiments of others only as they shall square with or suffer from his own; that it is time enough for the rightful purposes of civil government for its officers to interfere when principles break out into overt acts against peace and good order; and finally, that truth is great and will prevail if left to herself; that she is the proper and sufficient antagonist to error, and has nothing to fear from the conflict unless by human interposition disarmed of her natural weapons, free argument and debate; errors ceasing to be dangerous when it is permitted freely to contradict them.

SECTION II. We the General Assembly of Virginia do enact that no man shall be compelled to frequent or support any religious worship, place, or ministry whatsoever, nor shall be enforced, restrained, molested, or burthened in his body or goods, or shall otherwise suffer, on account of his religious opinions or beliefs; but that all men shall be free to profess, and by argument to maintain, their opinions in matters of religion, and that the same shall in no wise diminish, enlarge, or affect their civil capacities.

SECTION III. And though we well know that this Assembly, elected by the people for their ordinary purposes of legislation only, have no power to restrain the acts of succeeding Assemblies, constituted with powers equal to our own, and that therefore to declare this act to be irrevocable would be of no effect in law; yet we are free to declare, and do declare, that the rights hereby asserted are of the natural rights of mankind, and that if any act shall be hereafter passed to repeal the present or to narrow its operations, such act will be an infringement of natural right.

[*1779*]

---

from

LETTER TO JOHN ADAMS
[ON ARISTOCRACY]

I agree with you that there is a natural aristocracy among men. The grounds of this are virtue and talents. Formerly, bodily powers gave place among the aristoi. But since the invention of gunpowder has armed the weak as well as the strong with missile death, bodily strength, like beauty, good humor, politeness, and other accomplishments, has become but an auxiliary ground for distinction. There is also an artificial aristocracy, founded on wealth and birth, without either virtue or talents; for with these it would belong to the first class. The natural aristocracy I consider as the most precious gift of nature, for the instruction, the trusts, and government of society. And, indeed, it would have been inconsistent in creation to have formed man for the social state and not to have provided virtue and wisdom enough to manage the concerns of the society. May we not even say that that form of government is the best which provides the most effectually for a pure selection of these natural aristoi into the offices of government? The artificial aristocracy is a mischievous ingredient in government, and provision should be made to prevent its ascendancy. On the question what is the best provision, you and I differ; but we differ as rational friends, using the free exercise of our own reason, and mutually indulging its errors. You think it best to put the pseudo-aristoi into a separate chamber of legislation, where they may be hindered from doing mischief by their co-ordinate branches, and where, also, they may be a protection to wealth against the agrarian and plundering enterprises of the majority of the people. I think that to give them power in order to prevent them from doing mischief is arming them for it, and increasing instead of remedying the evil. For if the co-ordinate branches can arrest their action, so may they that of the co-ordinates. Mischief may be done negatively as well as positively. Of this, a cabal in the Senate of the United States has furnished many proofs. Nor do I believe them necessary to protect the wealthy; because enough of these will find their way into every branch of the legislation to protect themselves. From fifteen to twenty legislatures of our own, in action for thirty years past, have proved that no fears of an equalization of property are to be apprehended from them. I think the best remedy is exactly that provided by all our constitutions, to leave to the citizens the free election and separation of the aristoi from the pseudo-aristoi, of the wheat from the chaff. In general they will elect the really good and wise. In some instances wealth may corrupt and birth blind them; but not in sufficient degree to endanger the society.

It is probable that our difference of opinion may, in some measure, be produced by a difference of character in those among whom we live. From what I have seen of Massachusetts and Connecticut myself, and still more from what I have heard, and the character given of the former by yourself, who know them so much better, there seems to be in those two states a traditionary reverence for certain families, which has rendered the offices of the government nearly hereditary in those families. I presume that from an early period of your history members of those families, happening to possess virtue and talents, have honestly exercised them for the good of the people, and by their services have endeared their names to them. In coupling Connecticut with you, I mean it politically only, not morally. For having made the Bible the common law of their land, they seemed to have modeled their morality on the story of Jacob and Laban. But although this hereditary succession to office with you may, in some degree, be founded in real family merit, yet in a much higher degree it has proceeded from your strict alliance of church and state. These families are canonized in the eyes of the people on common principles; "you tickle me, and I will tickle you." In Virginia we have nothing of this. Our clergy, before the Revolution, having been secured against rivalship by fixed salaries, did not give themselves the trouble of acquiring influence over the people. Of wealth, there were great accumulations in particular families, handed down from generation to generation, under the English law of entails. But the only object of ambition for the wealthy was a seat in the King's Council. All their court then was paid to the crown and its creatures; and they Philipized in all collisions between the King and the people. Hence they were unpopular; and that unpopularity continues attached to their names. A Randolph, a Carter, or a Burwell must have great personal superiority over a common competitor to be elected by the people even at this day. At the first session of our legislature after the Declaration of Independence we passed a law abolishing entails. And this was followed by one abolishing the privilege of primogeniture, and dividing the lands of intestates equally among all their children or other representatives. These laws, drawn by myself, laid the ax to the foot of pseudo-aristocracy. And had another which I prepared been adopted by the legislature, our work would have been complete. It was a bill for the more general diffusion of learning. This proposed to divide every county into wards of five or six miles square, like your townships; to establish in each ward a free school for reading, writing, and common arithmetic; to provide for the annual selection of the best subjects from these schools, who might receive, at the public expense, a higher degree of education at a district school; and from these district schools to select a certain number of the most promising subjects to be completed at an university, where all the useful sciences should be taught. Worth and genius would thus have been sought out from every condition of life and completely prepared by education for defeating the competition of wealth and birth for public trusts. My proposition had for a further object to impart to these wards those portions of self-government for which they are best qualified, by confiding to them the care of their poor, their roads, police, elections, the nomination of jurors, administration of justice in small cases, elementary exercises of militia; in short, to have made them little republics, with a warden at the head of each, for all those concerns which, being under their eye, they would better manage than the larger republics of the county or state. A general call of ward meetings by their wardens on the same day through the state would at any time produce the genuine sense of the people on any required point, and would enable the state to act in mass, as your people have so often done and with so much effect by their town meetings. The law for religious freedom, which made a part of this system, having put down the aristocracy of the clergy and restored to the citizen the freedom of the mind, and those of entails and descents nurturing an equality of condition among them, this on education would have raised the mass of the people to the high ground of moral respectability necessary to their own safety and to orderly government; and would have completed the great object of qualifying them to select the veritable aristoi for the trusts of government, to the exclusion of the pseudolists. . . . Although this law has not yet been acted on but in a small and inefficient degree, it is still considered as before the legislature, with other bills of the revised code not yet taken up, and I have great hope that some patriotic spirit will, at a favorable moment, call it up and make it the keynote of the arch of our government.

[1813]

LETTER TO EDWARD COLES
[ON SLAVERY]

Dear Sir, — Your favor of July 31 was duly received, and was read with peculiar pleasure. The sentiments breathed through the whole do honor to both the head and heart of the writer. Mine on the subject of slavery of Negroes have long since been in possession of the public, and time has only served to give them stronger root. The love of justice and the love of country plead equally the cause of these people, and it is a moral reproach to us that they should have pleaded it so long in vain, and should have produced not a single effort, nay, I fear not much serious willingness to relieve them and ourselves from our present condition of moral and political reprobation. From those of the former generation who were in the fullness of age when I came into public life, which was while our controversy with England was on paper only, I soon saw that nothing was to be hoped. Nursed and educated in the daily habit of seeing the degraded condition, both bodily and mental, of those unfortunate beings, not reflecting that that degradation was very much the work of themselves and their fathers, few minds have yet doubted but that they were as legitimate subjects of property as their horses and cattle. The quiet and monotonous course of colonial life has been disturbed by no alarm, and little reflection on the value of liberty. And when alarm was taken at an enterprise on their own, it was not easy to carry them to the whole length of the principles which they invoked for themselves. In the first or second session of the legislature after I became a member, I drew to this subject the attention of Col. Bland, one of the oldest, ablest, and most respected members, and he undertook to move for certain moderate extensions of the protection of the laws to these people. I seconded his motion, and as a younger member, was more spared in the debate; but he was denounced as an enemy of his country, and was treated with the grossest indecorum. From an early stage of our Revolution other and more distant duties were assigned to me, so that from that time till my return from Europe in 1789, and I may say till I returned to reside at home in 1809, I had little opportunity of knowing the progress of public sentiment here on this subject. I had always hoped that the younger generation, receiving their early impressions after the flame of liberty had been kindled in every breast, and had become as it were the vital spirit of every American, that the generous temperament of youth, analogous to the motion of their blood, and above the suggestions of avarice, would have sympathized with oppression wherever found, and proved their love of liberty beyond their own share of it. But my intercourse with them since my return has not been sufficient to ascertain that they had made towards this point the progress I had hoped. Your solitary but welcome voice is the first which has brought this sound to my ear; and I have considered the general silence which prevails on this subject as indicating an apathy unfavorable to every hope. Yet the hour of emancipation is advancing, in the march of time. It will come; and whether brought on by the generous energy of our own minds, or by the bloody process of St. Domingo, excited and conducted by the power of our present enemy, if once stationed permanently within our country, and offering asylum and arms to the oppressed, is a leaf of our history not yet turned over. As to the method by which this difficult work is to be effected, if permitted to be done by ourselves, I have seen no proposition so expedient on the whole as that of emancipation of those born after a given day, and of their education and expatriation after a given age. This would give time for a gradual extinction of that species of labor and substitution of another, and lessen the severity of the shock which an operation so fundamental cannot fail to produce. For men probably of any color, but of this color we know, brought from their infancy without necessity for thought or forecast, are by their habits rendered as incapable as children of taking care of themselves, and are extinguished promptly wherever industry is necessary for raising young. In the meantime they are pests in society by their idleness and the depredations to which this leads them. Their amalgamation with the other color produces a degradation to which no lover of his country, no lover of excellence in the human character, can innocently consent. I am sensible of the partialities with which you have looked towards me as the person who should undertake this salutary but arduous work. But this, my dear sir, is like bidding old Priam to buckle the armor of Hector " *trementibus æquo humeris et inutile ferruncingi.*" No, I have overlived the generation with which mutual labors and perils begat mutual confidence and influence. This enterprise is for the young; for those who can follow it up, and bear it through to its consummation. It shall have all my prayers and these are the only weapons of an old man. But in the meantime are you right in abandoning this property, and your country with it? I think not. My opinion has ever been that, until more can be done for them, we should endeavor, with those whom fortune has thrown on our hands, to feed and clothe them well, protect them from all ill usage, require such reasonable labor only as is performed voluntarily by freemen, and be led by no repugnancies to abdicate them and our duties to them. The laws do not permit us to turn them loose, if that were for their good; and to commute them for other property is to commit them to those whose usage of them we cannot control. I hope then, my dear sir, you will reconcile yourself to your country and its unfortunate condition; that you will not lessen its stock of sound disposition by withdrawing your portion from the mass. That, on the contrary, you will come forward in the public councils, become the missionary of this doctrine truly Christian; insinuate and inculcate it softly but steadily, through the medium of writing and conversation; associate others in your labors, and when the phalanx is formed, bring on and press the proposition perseveringly until its accomplishment. It is an encouraging observation that no good measure was ever proposed which, if duly pursued, failed to prevail in the end. We have proof of this in the history of the endeavors in the English Parliament to suppress that very trade which brought this evil on us. And you will be supported by the religious precept, "be not weary in well-doing." That your success may be as speedy and complete as it will be of honorable and immortal consolation to yourself, I shall as fervently and sincerely pray as I assure you of my great friendship and respect.

[*1814*]

JAMES MADISON

[1751–1836]

HE WAS born in Virginia of a landowning family. After studying under local tutors, he entered the College of New Jersey (now Princeton), where he made an excellent record as a student of history and government. After receiving his B.A. in 1771, he stayed on at Princeton for another year, then went home to a period of inactivity. Soon, however, he became interested in the colonies' conflict with England and in the struggle for religious tolerance. In 1776 he was elected to the Virginia Convention, becoming a member of the committee formed to write a state constitution. Here he distinguished himself by his efforts to legalize absolute freedom in religion. From then on he was almost consistently prominent in the affairs of the young nation — as a member of the Continental Congress, member of the Virginia House of Delegates, Congressman from Virginia, Secretary of State under Jefferson, and fourth President of the United States. His greatest work was undoubtedly his part in *The Federalist* — a series of essays written in collaboration with Alexander Hamilton and John Jay and published in several New York newspapers to persuade Americans to accept the newly formulated federal Constitution. In these essays he argued strongly for the protection of property interests against the attacks of the majority, but he subsequently became an enemy of Hamilton and an ally of Jefferson in the struggle for civil rights. The latter phase of his thinking is not widely enough known, and the aspect of it that concerns religion is here represented. In 1785 an attempt was made in Virginia to tax the people to support " teachers of the Christian religion." Madison wrote *A Memorial and Remonstrance* which led to the passage of Jefferson's bill establishing religious freedom. It paved the way for other such bills and even influenced European governments, for it said well everything that needed to be said on the subject.

A MEMORIAL AND REMONSTRANCE

To the Honorable the General Assembly of the Commonwealth of Virginia:

We, the subscribers, citizens of the said commonwealth, having taken into serious consideration a bill printed by order of the last session of General Assembly, entitled "A Bill establishing a provision for Teachers of the Christian Religion," and conceiving that the same, if finally armed with the sanctions of a law, will be a dangerous abuse of power, are bound as faithful members of a free state to remonstrate against it, and to declare the reasons by which we are determined. We remonstrate against the said bill —

1. Because we hold it for a fundamental and undeniable truth "that religion, or the duty which we owe to our Creator, and the manner of discharging it, can be directed only by reason and conviction, not by force or violence." The religion, then, of every man must be left to the conviction and conscience of every man; and it is the right of every man to exercise it as these may dictate. This right is in its nature an unalienable right.   It is unalienable because the opinions of men, depending only on the evidence contemplated by their own minds, cannot follow the dictates of other men. It is unalienable, also, because what is here a right towards men is a duty towards the Creator. It is the duty of every man to render to the Creator such homage, and such only, as he believes to be acceptable to him. This duty is precedent, both in order of time and in degree of obligation, to the claims of civil society. Before any man can be considered as a member of civil society, he must be considered as a subject of the Governor of the universe; and if a member of civil society who enters into any subordinate association must always do it with a reservation of his duty to the general authority, much more must every man who becomes a member of any particular civil society do it with a saving of his allegiance to the Universal Sovereign. We maintain, therefore, that in matters of religion no man's right is abridged by the institution of civil society, and that religion is wholly exempt from its cognizance. True it is that no other rule exists by which any question which may divide a society can be ultimately determined than the will of the majority; but it is also true that the majority may trespass on the rights of the minority.

2. Because, if religion be exempt from the authority of the society at large, still less can it be subject to that of the legislative body. The latter are but the creatures and vicegerents of the former. Their jurisdiction is both derivative and limited. It is limited with regard to the co-ordinate departments; more necessarily is it limited with regard to the constituents. The preservation of a free government requires, not merely that the metes and bounds which separate each department of power be invariably maintained, but more especially that neither of them be suffered to overleap the great barrier which defends the rights of the people. The rulers who are guilty of such an encroachment exceed the commission from which they derive their authority, and are tyrants. The people who submit to it are governed by laws made neither by themselves nor by an authority derived from them, and are slaves.

3. Because it is proper to take alarm at the first experiment on our liberties. We hold this prudent jealousy to be the first duty of citizens, and one of the noblest characteristics of the late Revolution. The freedom of America did not wait till usurped power had strengthened itself by exercise and entangled the question in precedents. They saw all the consequences in the principle, and they avoided the consequences by denying the principle. We revere this lesson too much soon to forget it. Who does not see that the same authority which can establish Christianity in exclusion of all other religions may establish, with the same ease, any particular sect of Christians in exclusion of all other sects? that the same authority which can force a citizen to contribute threepence only of his property for the support of any one establishment may force him to conform to any other establishment in all cases whatsoever?

4. Because the bill violates that equality which ought to be the basis of every law, and which is more indispensable in proportion as the validity or expediency of any law is more liable to be impeached. "If all men are by nature equally free and independent," all men are to be considered as entering into society on equal conditions; as relinquishing no more, and therefore retaining no less, one than another, of their natural rights. Above all, are they to be considered as retaining an "*equal* title to the free exercise of religion according to the dictates of conscience." Whilst we assert for ourselves a freedom to embrace, to profess, and to observe the religion which we believe to be of divine origin, we cannot deny an equal freedom to them whose

minds have not yet yielded to the evidence which has convinced us. If this freedom be abused, it is an offense against God, not against man. To God, therefore, not to man, must an account of it be rendered. As the bill violates equality by subjecting some peculiar burdens, so it violates the same principle by granting to others peculiar exemptions. Are the Quakers and Menonists the only sects who think a compulsive support of their religions unnecessary and unwarrantable? Can their piety alone be entrusted with the care of public worship? Ought their religions to be endowed above all others with extraordinary privileges, by which proselytes may be enticed from all others? We think too favorably of the justice and good sense of these denominations to believe that they either covet pre-eminences over their fellow citizens or that they will be seduced by them from the common opposition to the measure.

5. Because the bill implies either that the civil magistrate is a competent judge of religious truths or that he may employ religion as an engine of civil policy. The first is an arrogant pretension, falsified by the contradictory opinions of rulers in all ages and throughout the world; the second, an unhallowed perversion of the means of salvation.

6. Because the establishment proposed by the bill is not requisite for the support of the Christian religion. To say that it is is a contradiction to the Christian religion itself, for every page of it disavows a dependence on the powers of this world. It is a contradiction to fact, for it is known that this religion both existed and flourished, not only without the support of human laws, but in spite of every opposition from them; and not only during the period of miraculous aid, but long after it had been left to its own evidence and the ordinary care of providence. Nay, it is a contradiction in terms; for a religion not invented by human policy must have pre-existed and been supported before it was established by human policy. It is, moreover, to weaken in those who profess this religion a pious confidence in its innate excellence and the patronage of its Author; and to foster in those who still reject it a suspicion that its friends are too conscious of its fallacies to trust it to its own merits.

7. Because experience witnesseth that ecclesiastical establishments, instead of maintaining the purity and efficacy of religion, have had a contrary operation. During almost fifteen centuries has the legal establishment of Christianity been on trial. What have been its fruits?

More or less, in all places, pride and indolence in the clergy; ignorance and servility in the laity; in both, superstition, bigotry, and persecution. Inquire of the teachers of Christianity for the ages in which it appeared in its greatest luster; those of every sect point to the ages prior to its incorporation with civil policy. Propose a restoration of this primitive state in which its teachers depended on the voluntary rewards of their flocks, many of them predict its downfall. On which side ought their testimony to have greatest weight, when for or when against their interest?

8. Because the establishment in question is not necessary for the support of civil government. If it be urged as necessary for the support of civil government only as it is a means of supporting religion, and it be not necessary for the latter purpose, it cannot be necessary for the former. If religion be not within the cognizance of civil government, how can its legal establishment be necessary to civil government? What influence, in fact, have ecclesiastical establishments had on civil society? In some instances they have been seen to erect a spiritual tyranny on the ruins of the civil authority; in many instances they have been seen upholding the thrones of political tyranny; in no instance have they been seen the guardians of the liberties of the people. Rulers who wished to subvert the public liberty may have found an established clergy convenient auxiliaries. A just government, instituted to secure and perpetuate it, needs them not. Such a government will be best supported by protecting every citizen in the enjoyment of his religion with the same equal hand which protects his person and his property; by neither invading the equal rights of any sect, nor suffering any sect to invade those of another.

9. Because the proposed establishment is a departure from that generous policy which, offering an asylum to the persecuted and oppressed of every nation and religion, promised a luster to our country, and an accession to the number of its citizens. What a melancholy mark is the bill of sudden degeneracy! Instead of holding forth an asylum to the persecuted, it is itself a signal of persecution. It degrades from the equal rank of citizens all those whose opinions in religion do not bend to those of the legislative authority. Distant as it may be in its present form from the Inquisition, it differs from it only in degree. The one is the first step, the other the last, in the career of intolerance. The magnanimous sufferer under this cruel scourge in foreign regions must view the bill as a beacon on our coast warning him to seek some other

haven, where liberty and philanthropy, in their due extent, may offer a more certain repose from his troubles.

10. Because it will have a like tendency to banish our citizens. The allurements presented by other situations are every day thinning their number. To superadd a fresh motive to emigration by revoking the liberty which they now enjoy would be the same species of folly which has dishonored and depopulated flourishing kingdoms.

11. Because it will destroy that moderation and harmony which the forbearance of our laws to intermeddle with religion has produced among its several sects. Torrents of blood have been spilt in the Old World in consequence of vain attempts of the secular arm to extinguish religious discord by proscribing all differences in religious opinion. Time has at length revealed the true remedy. Every relaxation of narrow and rigorous policy, wherever it has been tried, has been found to assuage the disease. The American theater has exhibited proofs that equal and complete liberty, if it does not wholly eradicate it, sufficiently destroys its malignant influence on the health and prosperity of the state. If, with the salutary effects of this system under our own eyes, we begin to contract the bounds of religious freedom, we know no name which will too severely reproach our folly. At least, let warning be taken at the first fruits of the threatened innovation. The very appearance of the bill has transformed " that Christian forbearance, love, and charity " which of late mutually prevailed, into animosities and jealousies which may not soon be appeased. What mischiefs may not be dreaded, should this enemy to the public quiet be armed with the force of a law?

12. Because the policy of the bill is adverse to the diffusion of the light of Christianity. The first wish of those who enjoy this precious gift ought to be that it may be imparted to the whole race of mankind. Compare the number of those who have as yet received it with the number still remaining under the dominion of false religions, and how small is the former! Does the policy of the bill tend to lessen the disproportion? No; it at once discourages those who are strangers to the light of revelation from coming into the region of it, and countenances by example the nations who continue in darkness in shutting out those who might convey it to them. Instead of leveling, as far as possible, every obstacle to the victorious progress of truth, the bill, with an ignoble and unchristian timidity, would circumscribe it with a wall of defense against the encroachments of error.

13. Because attempts to enforce, by legal sanctions, acts obnoxious to so great a proportion of citizens tend to enervate the laws in general, and to slacken the bands of society. If it be difficult to execute any law which is not generally deemed necessary or salutary, what must be the case where it is deemed invalid and dangerous? And what may be the effect of so striking an example of impotency in the government on its general authority?

14. Because a measure of such singular magnitude and delicacy ought not to be imposed without the clearest evidence that it is called for by a majority of citizens; and no satisfactory method is yet proposed by which the voice of the majority in this case may be determined, or its influence secured. "The people of the respective counties are, indeed, requested to signify their opinion respecting the adoption of the bill to the next session of the Assembly." But the representation must be made equal before the voice either of the representatives or of the counties will be that of the people. Our hope is that neither of the former will, after due consideration, espouse the dangerous principle of the bill. Should the event disappoint us, it will still leave us in full confidence that a fair appeal to the latter will reverse the sentence against our liberties.

15. Because, finally, " the equal right of every citizen to the free exercise of his religion, according to the dictates of conscience," is held by the same tenure with all our other rights. If we recur to its origin, it is equally the gift of nature; if we weigh its importance, it cannot be less dear to us; if we consult the Declaration of those rights " which pertain to the good people of Virginia as the basis and foundation of government," it is enumerated with equal solemnity, or rather with studied emphasis. Either, then, we must say that the will of the legislature is the only measure of their authority, and that in the plenitude of that authority they may sweep away all our fundamental rights, or that they are bound to leave this particular right untouched and sacred. Either we must say that they may control the freedom of the press, may abolish the trial by jury, may swallow up the executive and judiciary powers of the state; nay, that they may despoil us of our very right of suffrage, and erect themselves into an independent and hereditary Assembly; or we must say that they have no authority to enact into a law the bill under consideration.

We, the subscribers, say that the General Assembly of this commonwealth have no such authority. And in order that no effort may be omitted on our part against so dangerous an usurpation, we oppose to it this remonstrance; earnestly praying, as we are in duty bound, that the Supreme Lawgiver of the Universe, by illuminating those to whom it is addressed, may, on the one hand, turn their councils from every act which would affront his holy prerogative or violate the trust committed to them; and, on the other, guide them into every measure which may be worthy of his blessing, redound to their own praise, and establish more firmly the liberties, the prosperity, and the happiness of the commonwealth.

[*1785*]

THOMAS PAINE

[1737–1809]

HE WAS thirty-seven when he arrived in America — an obscure English Quaker, virtually penniless, self-educated. "It was the cause of America that made me an author," he said. For, a year after he landed in Philadelphia, a battle was fought at Lexington, and Paine was inspired to join the revolutionaries. He wrote his pamphlet *Common Sense* to prove that independence and a republican government were necessary and feasible. The pamphlet was an enormous success. At the end of that year, 1776, he published an article called *The Crisis*, which opened with the magnificent lines: "These are the times that try men's souls. The summer soldier and the sunshine patriot will, in this crisis, shrink from the service of their country; but he that stands it *now*, deserves the love and thanks of man and woman." It was read to Washington's troops before the battle of Trenton. Paine wrote other numbers of the *Crisis* at critical moments during the war. At the end of the war he retired to a farm for several years. In 1787 he went to England on business and two years later, after the fall of the Bastille, to Paris to take part in the French Revolution. When Edmund Burke denounced the Revolution, Paine replied with another famous work, *Rights of Man*. Subsequently, when the French were planning a new constitution, he wrote a *Dissertation on First Principles of Government*, which is a simple but forceful summary of his political views. Finally he published his views on religion: a two-part work, *The Age of Reason* (1794–6), expressing a deistic philosophy. He returned to America in 1802 and lived out his remaining years in poverty and an atmosphere of hostility.

Slaveholders hated him because he was an abolitionist, the wealthy and aristocratic because he was a democrat, the churchmen because he was unorthodox. Their attacks blackened his name and reputation; and for a long time he was revered only by the obscure, the rebellious, the generally unrespectable. But in recent years he has regained his position as one of the greatest of our libertarians, one of the noblest of our humanitarians. No man will remain forever unhonored who could say: "He that would make his own liberty secure must guard even his enemy from oppression; for if he violates this duty, he establishes a precedent that will reach to himself." And of himself: "My country is the world, and my religion is to do good."

from

RIGHTS OF MAN

[ON THE RIGHTS OF THE LIVING]

Among the incivilities by which nations or individuals provoke and irritate each other, Mr. Burke's pamphlet on the French Revolution is an extraordinary instance. Neither the people of France nor the National Assembly were troubling themselves about the affairs of England or the English Parliament; and why Mr. Burke should commence an unprovoked attack upon them, both in Parliament and in public, is a conduct that cannot be pardoned on the score of manners, nor justified on that of policy.

There is scarcely an epithet of abuse to be found in the English language with which Mr. Burke has not loaded the French nation and the National Assembly. Everything which rancor, prejudice, ignorance, or knowledge could suggest are poured forth in the copious fury of near four hundred pages. In the strain and on the plan Mr. Burke was writing, he might have wrote on to as many thousand. When the tongue or the pen is let loose in a frenzy of passion, it is the man and not the subject that becomes exhausted.

Hitherto Mr. Burke has been mistaken and disappointed in the opinions he has formed on the affairs of France; but such is the ingenuity of his hope, or the malignancy of his despair, that it furnishes him with new pretenses to go on. There was a time when it was impossible to make Mr. Burke believe there would be any revolution in France. His opinion then was that the French had neither spirit to undertake it nor fortitude to support it; and now that there is one, he seeks an escape by condemning it.

Not sufficiently content with abusing the National Assembly, a great part of his work is taken up with abusing Dr. Price (one of the best-hearted men that exist) and the two societies in England known by the name of the Revolution and the Constitutional societies.

Dr. Price had preached a sermon on the 4th of November 1789, being the anniversary of what is called in England the Revolution, which took place in 1688. Mr. Burke, speaking of this sermon, says: "the political divine proceeds dogmatically to assert that, by the principles of the Revolution, the people of England have acquired three fundamental rights.

" 1st, To choose our own governors.

" 2nd, To cashier them for misconduct.

" 3rd, To frame a government for ourselves."

Dr. Price does not say that the right to do these things exists in this or in that person, or in this or in that description of persons, but that it exists in the *whole* — that it is a right resident in the nation. Mr. Burke, on the contrary, denies that such a right exists in the nation, either in whole or in part, or that it exists anywhere; and what is still more strange and marvelous, he says that " the people of England utterly disclaim such right, and that they will resist the practical assertion of it with their lives and fortunes." That men will take up arms and spend their lives and fortunes *not* to maintain their rights, but to maintain that they have *not* rights is an entire new species of discovery, and suited to the paradoxical genius of Mr. Burke.

The method which Mr. Burke takes to prove that the people of England have no such rights, and that such rights do not exist in the nation, either in whole or in part, or anywhere at all, is of the same marvelous and monstrous kind with what he has already said, for his arguments are that the persons or the generation of persons in whom they did exist are dead, and with them the right is dead also. To prove this, he quotes a declaration made by Parliament about a hundred years ago, to William and Mary, in these words: " The Lords spiritual and temporal, and Commons, do, in the name of the people aforesaid — (meaning the people of England then living) — most humbly and faithfully *submit* themselves, their *heirs* and *posterity* FOREVER " — He also quotes a clause of another act of Parliament made in the same reign, the terms of which, he says, " bind us — (meaning the people of that day) — our *heirs* and our *posterity*, to *them,* their *heirs* and *posterity* to the end of time."

Mr. Burke considers his point sufficiently established by producing those clauses, which he enforces by saying that they exclude the right of the nation *forever;* and not yet content with making such declarations repeated over and over again, he further says " that if the people of England possessed such a right before the Revolution " (which he acknowledges to have been the case, not only in England, but throughout Europe at an early period) " yet that the *English nation* did, at the time of the Revolution, most solemnly renounce and abdicate it, for themselves, and *for all their posterity forever."*

As Mr. Burke occasionally applies the poison drawn from his horrid principles (if it is not a profanation to call them by the name of principles) not only to the English nation, but to the French Revolution and the National Assembly, and charges that august, illuminated, and illuminating body of men with the epithet of *usurpers,* I shall, *sans cérémonie,* place another system of principles in opposition to his.

The English Parliament of 1688 did a certain thing which for themselves and their constitutents they had a right to do, and which appeared right should be done; but, in addition to this right, which they possessed by delegation, *they set up another right by assumption,* that of binding and controlling posterity to the end of time. The case, therefore, divides itself into two parts; the right which they possessed by delegation and the right which they set up by assumption. The first is admitted; but with respect to the second, I reply: —

There never did nor never can exist a parliament, or any description of men, or any generation of men, in any country, possessed of the right or the power of binding or controlling posterity to the " end of time," or of commanding forever how the world shall be governed, or who shall govern it; and therefore all such clauses, acts, or declarations, by which the makers of them attempt to do what they have neither the right nor the power to do, nor the power to execute, are in themselves null and void. Every age and generation must be as free to act for itself, *in all cases,* as the ages and generations which preceded it. The vanity and presumption of governing beyond the grave is the most ridiculous and insolent of all tyrannies. Man has no property in man; neither has any generation a property in the generations which are to follow. The Parliament or the people of 1688, or of any other period, had no more right to dispose of the people of the present day, or to bind or to control them *in any shape whatever,* than the Parliament or the people of the present day have to dispose of, bind, or control those who are to live a hundred or a thousand years hence. Every generation is and must be competent to all the purposes which its occasions require. It is the living and not the dead that are to be accommodated. When man ceases to be, his powers and his wants cease with him; and having no longer any participation in the concerns of this world, he has no longer any authority in directing who shall be its governors, or how its government shall be organized, or how administered.

I am not contending for, nor against, any form of government, nor for nor against any party, here or elsewhere. That which a whole nation chooses to do, it has a right to do. Mr. Burke denies it. Where then does the right exist? I am contending for the right of the *living* and against their being willed away, and controlled and contracted for, by the manuscript-assumed authority of the dead over the rights and freedom of the living. There was a time when kings disposed of their crowns by will upon their death-beds, and consigned the people like beasts of the field to whatever successor they appointed. This is now so exploded as scarcely to be remembered, and so monstrous as hardly to be believed; but the parliamentary clauses upon which Mr. Burke builds his political church are of the same nature.

The laws of every country must be analogous to some common principle. In England no parent or master, nor all the authority of Parliament, omnipotent as it has called itself, can bind or control the personal freedom even of an individual beyond the age of twenty-one years: on what ground of right then could the Parliament of 1688, or any other parliament, bind all posterity forever?

Those who have quitted the world and those who are not arrived yet in it are as remote from each other as the utmost stretch of mortal imagination can conceive; what possible obligation, then, can exist between them, what rule or principle can be laid down, that two nonentities, the one out of existence and the other not in, and who never can meet in this world, that the one should control the other to the end of time?

[ON RELIGION]

Toleration is not the *opposite* of intoleration, but is the *counterfeit* of it. Both are despotisms. The one assumes to itself the right of withholding liberty of conscience, and the other of granting it. . . . But toleration may be viewed in a much stronger light. Man worships not himself but his Maker; and the liberty of conscience which he claims is not for the service of himself, but of his God. In this case, therefore, we must necessarily have the associated idea of two beings: the *mortal* who renders the worship, and the *immortal being* who is worshipped. Toleration, therefore, places itself not between man and man, nor between church and church, nor between one denomination of religion and another, but between God and man; between the being who worships and the being who is worshipped; and by the same act of assumed authority by which it tolerates man to pay his worship, it presumptuously and blasphemously sets up itself to tolerate the Almighty to receive it.

Were a bill brought into Parliament entitled: "An act to tolerate or grant liberty to the Almighty to receive the worship of a Jew or a Turk," or "to prohibit the Almighty from receiving it," all men would startle, and call it blasphemy. There would be an uproar. The presumption of toleration in religious matters would then present itself unmasked; but the presumption is not the less because the name of "man" only appears to those laws, for the associated idea of the *worshipper* and the *worshipped* cannot be separated. Who, then, art thou, vain dust and ashes! by whatever name thou art called, whether a king, a bishop, a church, or a state, a parliament or anything else, that obtrudest thine insignificance between the soul of man and his Maker? Mind thine own concerns. If he believeth not as thou believest, it is a proof that thou believest not as he believeth, and there is no earthly power can determine between you.

With respect to what are called denominations of religion, if everyone is left to judge of his own religion, there is no such thing as a religion that is wrong; but if they are to judge of each other's religion, there is no such thing as a religion that is right; and therefore all the world is right, or all the world is wrong. But with respect to religion itself, without regard to names, and as directing itself from the universal family of mankind to the divine object of all adoration, it is man bringing to his Maker the fruits of his heart; and though these fruits may differ from each other like the fruits of the earth, the grateful tribute of everyone is accepted.

A bishop of Durham, or a bishop of Winchester, or the archbishop who heads the dukes, will not refuse a tithe-sheaf of wheat because it is not a cock of hay; nor a cock of hay because it is not a sheaf of wheat; nor a pig because it is neither the one nor the other: but these same persons, under the figure of an established church, will not permit their Maker to receive the varied tithes of man's devotion.

One of the continual choruses of Mr. Burke's book is "church and state"; he does not mean some one particular church, or some one particular state, but any church and state; and he uses the term as a general figure to hold forth the political doctrine of always uniting the church with the state in every country, and he censures the National Assembly for not having done this in France. Let us bestow a few thoughts on this subject.

All religions are, in their nature, mild and benign, and united with principles of morality. They could not have made proselytes at first by professing anything that was vicious, cruel, persecuting, or immoral. Like everything else, they had their beginning; and they proceeded by persuasion, exhortation, and example. How then is it that they lose their native mildness, and become morose and intolerant?

It proceeds from the connection which Mr. Burke recommends. By engendering the church with the state, a sort of mule animal, capable only of destroying, and not of breeding up, is produced, called *the church established by law*. It is a stranger, even from its birth, to any parent mother on which it is begotten, and whom in time it kicks out and destroys.

The Inquisition in Spain does not proceed from the religion originally professed, but from this mule animal, engendered between the church and the state. The burnings in Smithfield proceeded from the same heterogeneous production; and it was the regeneration of this strange animal in England afterwards that renewed rancor and irreligion among the inhabitants, and that drove the people called Quakers and Dissenters to America. Persecution is not an original feature in *any* religion; but is always the strongly marked feature of all law-religions, or religions established by law. Take away the law-establishment, and every religion reassumes its original benignity. In America, a Catholic priest is a good citizen, a good character, and a good neighbor; an Episcopalian minister is of the same description: and this proceeds independent of men, from there being no law-establishment in America.

If also we view this matter in a temporal sense, we shall see the ill effects it has had on the prosperity of nations. The union of church and state has impoverished Spain. — The revoking the Edict of Nantes drove the silk manufacture from that country into England; and church and state are now driving the cotton manufacture from England to America and France. Let then Mr. Burke continue to preach his antipolitical doctrine of church and state. It will do some good. The National Assembly will not follow his advice, but will benefit by his folly. It was by observing the ill effects of it in England that America has been warned against it; and it is by experiencing them in France that the National Assembly have abolished it, and, like America, has established *universal right of conscience, and universal right of citizenship.* . . .

Throughout this work, various and numerous as the subjects are which I have taken up and investigated, there is only a single paragraph upon religion: viz., " *that every religion is good that teaches man to be good.*"

I have carefully avoided to enlarge upon the subject, because I am inclined to believe that what is called the present ministry wish to see contentions about religion kept up to prevent the nation turning its attention to subjects of government. It is as if they were to say: "*look that way, or any way but this.*"

But as religion is very improperly made a political machine, and the reality of it is thereby destroyed, I will conclude this work with stating in what light religion appears to me.

If we suppose a large family of children who, on any particular day, or particular occasion, made it a custom to present to their parents some token of their affection and gratitude, each of them would make a different offering, and most probably in a different manner. Some would pay their congratulations in themes of verse and prose, by some little devices, as their genius dictated, or according to what they thought would please; and, perhaps, the least of all, not able to do any of those things, would ramble into the garden or the field and gather what it thought the prettiest flower it could find, though perhaps it might be but a single weed. The parents would be more gratified by such a variety than if the whole of them had acted on a concerted plan and each had made exactly the same offering. This would have the cold appearance of contrivance, or the harsh one of control. But of all unwelcome things, nothing would more afflict the parent than to know that the whole of them had afterwards gotten together by the ears, boys and girls, fighting, reviling, and abusing each other about which was the best or the worst present.

Why may we not suppose that the great Father of all is pleased with variety of devotion; and that the greatest offense we can act is that by which we seek to torment and render each other miserable? For my own part, I am fully satisfied that what I am now doing, with an endeavor to conciliate mankind, to render their condition happy, to unite nations that have hitherto been enemies, and to extirpate the horrid practice of war, and break the chains of slavery and oppression, is acceptable in his sight, and being the best service I can perform, I act it cheerfully.

[ON THE AMERICAN REVOLUTION]

What Archimedes said of the mechanical powers may be applied to reason and liberty: " Had we," said he, " a place to stand upon, we might raise the world."

The Revolution in America presented in politics what was only theory in mechanics. So deeply rooted were all the governments of the Old World, and so effectually had the tyranny and the antiquity of habit established itself over the mind, that no beginning could be made in Asia, Africa, or Europe to reform the political condition of man. Freedom had been hunted round the globe: reason was considered as rebellion; and the slavery of fear had made men afraid to think.

But such is the irresistible nature of truth that all it asks, and all it wants, is the liberty of appearing. The sun needs no inscription to distinguish him from darkness, and no sooner did the American governments display themselves to the world than despotism felt a shock, and man began to contemplate redress.

The independence of America, considered merely as a separation from England, would have been a matter but of little importance had it not been accompanied by a revolution in the principles and practice of government. She made a stand, not for herself only, but for the world, and looked beyond the advantages which *she* could receive. Even the Hessian, though hired to fight against her, may live to bless his defeat; and England, condemning the viciousness of its government, rejoice in its miscarriage.

As America was the only spot in the political world where the principles of universal reformation could begin, so also was it the best in the natural world. An assemblage of circumstances conspired, not only to give birth, but to add gigantic maturity to its principles. The scene which that country presents to the eye of the spectator has something in it which generates and enlarges great ideas. Nature appears to him in magnitude. The mighty objects he beholds act upon the mind by enlarging it, and he partakes of the greatness he contemplates. Its first settlers were emigrants from different European nations, and of diversified professions of religion, retiring from the governmental persecutions of the Old World, and meeting in the New, not as enemies, but as brothers. The wants which necessarily accompany the cultivation of a wilderness produced among them a state of society which countries long harassed by the quarrels and intrigues of governments had neglected to cherish. In such a situation man becomes what he ought to be. He sees his species, not with the inhuman idea of a natural enemy, but as kindred; and the example shows to the artificial world that man must go back to nature for information.

From the rapid progress which America makes in every species of improvement, it is rational to conclude that if the governments of Asia, Africa, and Europe had begun on a principle similar to that of America, or had they not been very early corrupted therefrom, those countries must by this time have been in a far superior condition to what they are. Age after age has passed away for no other purpose than to behold their wretchedness. Could we suppose a spectator who knew nothing of the world, and who was put into it merely to make his observations, he would take a great part of the Old World to be new, just struggling with the difficulties and hardships of an infant settlement. He could not suppose that the hordes of miserable poor with which old countries abound could be any other than those who had not yet been able to provide for themselves. Little would he think they were the consequence of what in such countries is called government.

If, from the more wretched parts of the Old World, we look at those which are in an advanced state of improvement, we still find the greedy hand of government thrusting itself into every corner and crevice of industry, and grasping the spoil of the multitude. Invention is continually exercised to furnish new pretenses for revenue and taxation. It watches prosperity as its prey, and permits none to escape without a tribute.

As revolutions have begun (and as the probability is always greater against a thing beginning than of proceeding after it has begun), it is natural to expect that other revolutions will follow. The amazing and still increasing expenses with which old governments are conducted, the numerous wars they engage in or provoke, the embarrassments they throw in the way of universal civilization and commerce, and the oppression and usurpation acted at home, have wearied out the patience and exhausted the property of the world. In such a situation, and with such examples already existing, revolutions are to be looked for.

They are become subjects of universal conversation, and may be considered as the order of the day.

If systems of government can be introduced less expensive, and more productive of general happiness, than those which have existed, all attempts to oppose their progress will in the end prove fruitless. Reason, like time, will make its own way, and prejudice will fall in the combat with interest. If universal peace, harmony, civilization, and commerce are ever to be the happy lot of man, it cannot be accomplished but by a revolution in the present system of governments. All the monarchical governments are military. War is their trade; plunder and revenue their objects. While such governments continue, peace has not the absolute security of a day. What is the history of all monarchical governments but a disgustful picture of human wretchedness, and the accidental respite of a few years' repose? Wearied with war, and tired with human butchery, they sat down to rest and called it peace. This certainly is not the condition that heaven intended for man; and if this be monarchy, well might monarchy be reckoned among the sins of the Jews.

The revolutions which formerly took place in the world had nothing in them that interested the bulk of mankind. They extended only to a change of persons and measures, but not of principles, and rose or fell among the common transactions of the moment. What we now behold may not improperly be called a "*counter revolution.*" Conquest and tyranny, at some early period, dispossessed man of his rights, and he is now recovering them. And as the tide of human affairs has its ebb and flow in directions contrary to each other, so also is it in this. Government founded on a *moral theory, on a system of universal peace, on the indefeasible, hereditary rights of man,* is now revolving from west to east by a stronger impulse than the government of the sword revolved from east to west. It interests not particular individuals but nations in its progress, and promises a new era to the human race.

[1791–2]

121

from

DISSERTATION ON FIRST PRINCIPLES OF GOVERNMENT

In contemplating government by election and representation, we amuse not ourselves in inquiring when or how, or by what right, it began. Its origin is ever in view. Man is himself the origin and the evidence of the right. It appertains to him in right of his existence, and his person is the title deed.

The true and only true basis of representative government is equality of rights. Every man has a right to one vote, and no more, in the choice of representatives. The rich have no more right to exclude the poor from the right of voting, or of electing and being elected, than the poor have to exclude the rich; and whenever it is attempted, or proposed, on either side, it is a question of force and not of right. Who is he that would exclude another? That other has a right to exclude him.

That which is now called aristocracy implies an inequality of rights; but who are the persons that have a right to establish this inequality? Will the rich exclude themselves? No. Will the poor exclude themselves? No. By what right then can any be excluded? It would be a question if any man or class of men have a right to exclude themselves; but, be this as it may, they cannot have the right to exclude another. The poor will not delegate such a right to the rich, nor the rich to the poor, and to assume it is not only to assume arbitrary power, but to assume a right to commit robbery. Personal rights, of which the right of voting for representatives is one, are a species of property of the most sacred kind: and he that would employ his pecuniary property, or presume upon the influence it gives him, to dispossess or rob another of his property rights uses that pecuniary property as he would use firearms, and merits to have it taken from him.

Inequality of rights is created by a combination in one part of the community to exclude another part from its rights. Whenever it be made an article of a constitution, or a law, that the right of voting, or of electing and being elected, shall appertain exclusively to persons possessing a certain quantity of property, be it little or much, it is a combination of the persons possessing that quantity to exclude those who do not possess the same quantity. It is investing themselves with powers as a self-created part of society, to the exclusion of the rest.

It is always to be taken for granted that those who oppose an equality of rights never mean the exclusion should take place on themselves; and in this view of the case, pardoning the vanity of the thing, aristocracy is a subject of laughter. This self-soothing vanity is encouraged by another idea not less selfish, which is that the opposers conceive they are playing a safe game, in which there is a chance to gain and none to lose; that at any rate the doctrine of equality includes *them,* and that if they cannot get more rights than those whom they oppose and would exclude, they shall not have less. This opinion has already been fatal to thousands, who, not contented with *equal rights,* have sought more till they lost all, and experienced in themselves the degrading *inequality* they endeavored to fix upon others.

In any view of the case it is dangerous and impolitic, sometimes ridiculous, and always unjust, to make property the criterion of the right of voting. If the sum or value of the property upon which the right is to take place be considerable, it will exclude a majority of the people, and unite them in a common interest against the government and against those who support it; and as the power is always with the majority, they can overturn such a government and its supporters whenever they please.

If, in order to avoid this danger, a small quantity of property be fixed as the criterion of the right, it exhibits liberty in disgrace, by putting it in competition with accident and insignificance. When a brood-mare shall fortunately produce a foal or a mule that, by being worth the sum in question, shall convey to its owner the right of voting, or by its death take it from him, in whom does the origin of such a right exist? Is it in the man or in the mule? When we consider how many ways property may be acquired without merit, and lost without a crime, we ought to spurn the idea of making it a criterion of rights.

But the offensive part of the case is that this exclusion from the right of voting implies a stigma on the moral character of the persons excluded; and this is what no part of the community has a right to pronounce upon another part. No external circumstance can justify it: wealth is no proof of moral character; nor poverty of the want of it. On the contrary, wealth is often the presumptive evidence of dishonesty; and poverty the negative evidence of innocence. If therefore property, whether little or much, be made a criterion, the means by which that property has been acquired ought to be made a criterion also.

The only ground upon which exclusion from the right of voting is consistent with justice would be to inflict it as a punishment for a certain time upon those who should propose to take away that right from others. The right of voting for representatives is the primary right by which other rights are protected. To take away this right is to reduce a man to slavery, for slavery consists in being subject to the will of another, and he that has not a vote in the election of representatives is in this case. The proposal therefore to disfranchise any class of men is as criminal as the proposal to take away property. When we speak of right, we ought always to unite with it the idea of duties: rights become duties by reciprocity. The right which I enjoy becomes my duty to guarantee it to another, and he to me; and those who violate the duty justly incur a forfeiture of the right.

In a political view of the case, the strength and permanent security of government is in proportion to the number of people interested in supporting it. The true policy therefore is to interest the whole by an equality of rights, for the danger arises from exclusions. It is possible to exclude men from the right of voting, but it is impossible to exclude them from the right of rebelling against that exclusion; and when all other rights are taken away, the right of rebellion is made perfect.

While men could be persuaded they had no rights, or that rights appertained only to a certain class of men, or that government was a thing existing in right of itself, it was not difficult to govern them authoritatively. The ignorance in which they were held, and the superstition in which they were instructed, furnished the means of doing it. But when the ignorance is gone, and the superstition with it; when they perceive the imposition that has been acted upon them; when they reflect that the cultivator and the manufacturer are the primary means of all the wealth that exists in the world, beyond what nature spontaneously produces; when they begin to feel their consequence by their usefulness, and their right as members of society, it is then no longer possible to govern them as before. The fraud once detected cannot be reacted. To attempt it is to provoke derision, or invite destruction.

That property will ever be unequal is certain. Industry, superiority of talents, dexterity of management, extreme frugality, fortunate opportunities, or the opposite, or the means of those things, will ever produce that effect, without having recourse to the harsh, ill-sounding names of avarice and oppression; and besides this, there are some men who, though they do not despise wealth, will not stoop to the drudgery or the means of acquiring it, nor will be troubled with it beyond their wants or their independence; whilst in others there is an avidity to obtain it by every means not punishable; it makes the sole business of their lives, and they follow it as a religion. All that is required with respect to property is to obtain it honestly, and not employ it criminally; but it is always criminally employed when it is made a criterion for exclusive rights.

In institutions that are purely pecuniary, such as that of a bank or a commercial company, the rights of the members composing that company are wholly created by the property they invest therein; and no other rights are represented in the government of that company than what arise out of that property; neither has that government cognizance of *anything but property.*

But the case is totally different with respect to the institution of civil government, organized on the system of representation. Such a government has cognizance of *everything,* and of *every man* as a member of the national society, whether he has property or not; and, therefore, the principle requires that *every man,* and *every kind of right,* be represented, of which the right to acquire and to hold property is but one, and that not of the most essential kind. The protection of a man's person is more sacred than the protection of property; and besides this, the faculty of performing any kind of work or services by which he acquires a livelihood, or maintaining his family, is of the nature of property. It is property to him; he has acquired it; and it is as much the object of his protection as exterior property, possessed without that faculty, can be the object of protection in another person.

I have always believed that the best security for property, be it much or little, is to remove from every part of the community, as far as can possibly be done, every cause of complaint, and every motive to violence; and this can only be done by an equality of rights. When rights are secure, property is secure in consequence. But when property is made a pretense for unequal or exclusive rights, it weakens the right to hold the property, and provokes indignation and tumult; for it is unnatural to believe that property can be secure under the guarantee of a society injured in its rights by the influence of that property.

Next to the injustice and ill policy of making property a pretense for exclusive rights is the unaccountable absurdity of giving to mere *sound* the idea of property, and annexing to it certain rights; for what else is a title but sound? Nature is often giving to the world some extraordinary men who arrive at fame by merit and universal consent, such as Aristotle, Socrates, Plato, etc. They were truly great or noble. But when government sets up a manufactory of nobles, it is as absurd as if she undertook to manufacture wise men. Her nobles are all counterfeits.

This waxwork order has assumed the name of aristocracy; and the disgrace of it would be lessened if it could be considered only as childish imbecility. We pardon foppery because of its insignificance, and on the same ground we might pardon the foppery of titles. But the origin of aristocracy was worse than foppery. It was robbery. The first aristocrats in all countries were brigands. Those of later times, sycophants.

It is very well known that in England (and the same will be found in other countries) the great landed estates now held in descent were plundered from the quiet inhabitants at the Conquest. The possibility did not exist of acquiring such estates honestly. If it be asked how they could have been acquired, no answer but that of robbery can be given. That they were not acquired by trade, by commerce, by manufactures, by agriculture, or by any reputable employment is certain. How then were they acquired? Blush, aristocracy, to hear your origin, for your progenitors were thieves. They were the Robespierres and the Jacobins of that day. When they had committed the robbery, they endeavored to lose the disgrace of it by sinking their real names under fictitious ones, which they called titles. It is ever the practice of felons to act in this manner. They never pass by their real names.

As property, honestly obtained, is best secured by an equality of rights, so ill-gotten property depends for protection on a monopoly of rights. He who has robbed another of his property will next endeavor to disarm him of his rights, to secure that property; for when the robber becomes the legislator he believes himself secure. That part of the government of England that is called the House of Lords was originally composed of persons who had committed the robberies of which I have been speaking. It was an association for the protection of the property they had stolen.

But besides the criminality of the origin of aristocracy, it has an injurious effect on the moral and physical character of man. Like slavery it debilitates the human faculties; for as the mind bowed down by slavery loses in silence its elastic powers, so, in the contrary extreme, when it is buoyed up by folly, it becomes incapable of exerting them, and dwindles into imbecility. It is impossible that a mind employed upon ribands and titles can ever be great. The childishness of the objects consumes the man.

It is at all times necessary, and more particularly so during the progress of a revolution, and until right ideas confirm themselves by habit, that we frequently refresh our patriotism by reference to first principles. It is by tracing things to their origin that we learn to understand them; and it is by keeping that line and that origin always in view that we never forget them.

An inquiry into the origin of rights will demonstrate to us that *rights* are not *gifts* from one man to another, nor from one class of men to another; for who is he who could be the first giver; or by what principle, or on what authority, could he possess the right of giving? A declaration of rights is not a creation of them, nor a donation of them. It is a manifest of the principle by which they exist, followed by a detail of what the rights are; for every civil right has a natural right for its foundation, and it includes the principle of a reciprocal guarantee of those rights from man to man. As, therefore, it is impossible to discover any origin of rights otherwise than in the origin of man, it consequently follows that rights appertain to man in right of his existence only, and must therefore be equal to every man. The principle of an *equality of rights* is clear simple. Every man can understand it, and it is by understanding his rights that he learns his duties; for where the rights of men are equal, every man must finally see the necessity of protecting the rights of others as the most effectual security for his own. But if, in the formation of a constitution, we depart from the principle of equal rights, or attempt any modification of it, we plunge into a labyrinth of difficulties from which there is no way out but by retreating. Where are we to stop? Or by what principle are we to find out the point to stop at, that shall discriminate between men of the same country, part of whom shall be free, and the rest not? If property is to be made the criterion, it is a total departure from every moral principle of liberty, because it is attaching rights to mere matter, and making man the agent of that matter. It is, moreover, holding up property as an apple of discord, and not only exciting but justifying war against it; for I maintain the principle that when property is used as an instrument to take away the rights of those who may happen not to possess property, it is used to an unlawful purpose, as firearms would be in a similar case.

In a state of nature all men are equal in rights, but they are not equal in power; the weak cannot protect themselves against the strong. This being the case, the institution of civil society is for the purpose of making an equalization of powers that shall be parallel to, and a guarantee of, the equality of rights. The laws of a country, when properly constructed, apply to this purpose. Every man takes the arm of the law for his protection as more effectual than his own; and therefore every man has an equal right in the formation of the government, and of the laws by which he is to be governed and judged.

[1795]

PHILIP FRENEAU

[1752–1832]

Son of a wealthy New York merchant, reared in an atmosphere of culture and learning, educated at Princeton, where he was a classmate of James Madison, Freneau was apparently destined to enjoy a privileged position and a prejudiced philosophy. Instead he became one of the great rebels of his age. He had already revealed a strong nationalist bias — his commencement poem, written in 1771 in collaboration with H. H. Brackenridge, was entitled "The Rising Glory of America" — when the American Revolution broke out. Like Paine, whom he greatly admired, he was inspired to active partisanship. His hatred of monarchical England was strengthened by an unfortunate personal experience: during the war he went on a cruise to the West Indies; on the return voyage the British captured the ship and evidently treated the prisoners brutally. He recorded the experience in a long poem called "The British Prison Ship" (1781). Freneau became the chief poet-propagandist of our Revolution and continued to espouse its principles long after hostilities had ceased. A friend of Jefferson and enemy of Hamilton, it goes without saying that he defended the French Revolution just as ardently as our own. Not a great poet, only occasionally even a good one, he was certainly one of the few in the early days of the republic who aroused to vigorous life the democratic spirit of the people. He wrote verse on almost all of the traditional subjects of romanticism, but the Revolution was his favorite subject and the one that earned him distinction and fame.

---

from

TO THE AMERICANS

If to control the cunning of a knave,
Freedom respect, and scorn the name of slave;
If to protest against a tyrant's laws,
And arm for vengeance in a rightful cause,
Be deemed Rebellion — 'tis a harmless thing:
This bugbear name, like death, has lost its sting.
[1775]

from

A PICTURE OF THE TIMES

Still round the world triumphant Discord flies,
Still angry kings to bloody contest rise;
Hosts bright with steel, in dreadful order plac'd,
And ships contending on the watery waste;
Distracting demons every breast engage,
Unwearied nations glow with mutual rage;
Still to the charge the routed Briton turns,
The war still rages and the battle burns;
See man with man in deadly combat join,
See the black navy form the flaming line;
Death smiles alike at battles lost or won —
Art does for him what Nature would have done.
Can scenes like these delight the human breast? —
Who sees with joy humanity distress'd;
Such tragic scenes fierce passion might prolong,
But slighted Reason says they must be wrong.
Curs'd be the day, how bright soe'er it shin'd,
That first made kings the masters of mankind;
And curs'd the wretch who first with regal pride
Their equal rights to equal men deni'd.
But curs'd o'er all who first to slav'ry broke
Submissive bow'd and own'd a monarch's yoke,
Their servile souls his arrogance ador'd
And basely own'd a brother for a lord;
Hence wrath and blood, and feuds and wars began,
And man turned monster to his fellow man. . . .
[*1782*]

ON THE FOURTEENTH OF JULY [1]

Bright day, that did to France restore
What priests and kings had seiz'd away,
That bade her generous sons disdain

---

[1] Bastille Day.

The fetters that their fathers wore,
The titled slave, a tyrant's sway,
That ne'er shall curse her soil again!

Bright day! a partner in thy joy,
Columbia hails the rising sun,
She feels her toils, her blood repaid,
When fiercely frantic to destroy
(Proud of the laurels he had won),
The Briton, here, unsheath'd his blade.

By traitors driven to ruin's brink
Fair freedom dreads united knaves,
The world must fall if she must bleed; —
And yet, by heaven! I'm proud to think
The world was ne'er subdued by slaves —
Nor shall the hireling herd succeed.

Boy! fill the generous goblet high;
Success to France, shall be the toast:
The fall of kings the fates foredoom,
The crown decays, its splendors die;
And they, who were a nation's boast,
Sink, and expire in endless gloom.

Thou, stranger, from a distant shore,[1]
Where fetter'd men their rights avow,
Why on this joyous day so sad?
Louis insults with chains no more, —
Then why thus wear a clouded brow,
When every manly heart is glad?

Some passing days and rolling years
May see the wrath of kings display'd,
Their wars to prop the tarnish'd crown;
But orphans' groans, and widows' tears,
And justice lifts her shining blade
To bring the tottering bauble down.
[1792]

---

[1] Addressed to the Aristocrats from Hispaniola.

TO A REPUBLICAN

WITH MR. PAINE'S *Rights of Man*

Thus briefly sketch'd the sacred Rights of Man,
How inconsistent with the Royal Plan!
Which for itself exclusive honor craves,
Where some are masters born, and millions slaves.
With what contempt must every eye look down
On that base, childish bauble call'd a crown,
The gilded bait that lures the crowd to come,
Bow down their necks, and meet a slavish doom;
The source of half the miseries men endure,
The quack that kills them, while it seems to cure.
   Rous'd by the Reason of his manly page,
Once more shall Paine a listening world engage:
From Reason's source, a bold reform he brings,
In raising up mankind, he pulls down kings,
Who, source of discord, patrons of all wrong,
On blood and murder have been fed too long:
Hid from the world, and tutor'd to be base,
The curse, the scourge, the ruin of our race,
Theirs was the task, a dull designing few,
To shackle beings that they scarcely knew,
Who made this globe the residence of slaves,
And built their thrones on systems form'd by knaves —
Advance, bright years, to work their final fall,
And haste the period that shall crush them all.
   Who that has read and scann'd the historic page
But glows, at every line, with kindling rage,
To see by them the rights of men aspers'd,
Freedom restrain'd, and Nature's law revers'd,
Man rank'd with beasts, by monarchs will'd away,
And bound young fools or madmen to obey:
Now driven to wars, and now oppress'd at home,
Compell'd in crowds o'er distant seas to roam,
From India's climes the plundered prize to bring

To glad the strumpet, or to glut the king?
  Columbia, hail! immortal be thy reign:
Without a king, we till the smiling plain;
Without a king, we trace the unbounded sea,
And traffic round the globe, through each degree;
Each foreign clime our honor'd flag reveres,
Which asks no monarch, to support the Stars:
Without a king, the Laws maintain their sway,
While honor bids each generous heart obey.
Be ours the task the ambitious to restrain,
And this great lesson teach — that kings are vain;
That warring realms to certain ruin haste,
That kings subsist by war, and wars are waste:
So shall our nation, form'd on Virtue's plan,
Remain the guardian of the Rights of Man,
A vast Republic, fam'd through every clime,
Without a king, to see the end of time.

[1795]

from

REFLECTIONS

Left to himself, wherever man is found,
In peace he aims to walk life's little round;
In peace to sail, in peace to till the soil,
Nor force false grandeur from a brother's toil.
All but the base, designing, scheming few,
Who seize on nations with a robber's view,
With crowns and scepters awe his dazzled eye,
And priests that hold the artillery of the sky;
These, these, with armies, navies, potent grown,
Impoverish man and bid the nations groan.
These with pretended balances of states
Keep worlds at variance, breed eternal hates,
Make man the poor base slave of low design,

Degrade his nature to its last decline,
Shed hell's worse blots on his exalted race,
And make them poor and mean, to make them base.

Shall views like these assail our happy land,
Where embryo monarchs thirst for wide command,
Shall a whole nation's strength and fair renown
Be sacrific'd, to prop a tottering throne,
That, ages past, the world's great curse has stood,
Has throve on plunder, and been fed on blood? —
Americans! will you control such views?
Speak — for you must — you have no hour to lose.
[*1815*]

MICHEL–GUILLAUME JEAN
DE CRÈVECŒUR

[1735–1813]

CRÈVECŒUR was born of an upper-class family in Normandy, France. He was hardly twenty when he left Europe to seek adventure in the New World. He explored the Great Lakes and Ohio River regions and fought in Canada, under General Montcalm, in the French and Indian Wars. In 1759 he landed in New York City to begin a decade of wandering through New York and Pennsylvania. Eventually he became an American citizen, and in 1769 he married and settled down on his farm in Orange County, New York. During the next decade he wrote an unusually interesting series of essays on the life, manners, and problems of the rural population of America. They were published in London in 1782 under the title of *Letters from an American Farmer*. (He had returned to his fatherland in 1780 and did not again visit America until 1783.) He became the French consul at New York, then in 1790 left to spend the rest of his life in France. Some unpublished papers, which were presumably suppressed fragments of his *Letters,* were discovered in 1922 and published three years later as *Sketches of Eighteenth Century America*. Upon these works depends his reputation — and it has proved to be a lasting one. He was a fine reporter of rural life, for he was at once honest and sympathetic. Although he sided with England during the Revolution, he was certainly appreciative of the character of the farmer in a frontier democracy — as the following well-known section from his *Letters* proves.

from

LETTERS FROM AN AMERICAN FARMER

WHAT IS AN AMERICAN

I wish I could be acquainted with the feelings and thoughts which must agitate the heart and present themselves to the mind of an enlightened Englishman when he first lands on this continent. He must greatly rejoice that he lived at a time to see this fair country discovered and settled; he must necessarily feel a share of national pride when he views the chain of settlements which embellishes these extended shores. When he says to himself, this is the work of my countrymen, who, when convulsed by factions, afflicted by a variety of miseries and wants, restless and impatient, took refuge here. They brought along with them their national genius, to which they principally owe what liberty they enjoy, and what substance they possess. Here he sees the industry of his native country displayed in a new manner, and traces in their works the embryos of all the arts, sciences, and ingenuity which flourish in Europe. Here he beholds fair cities, substantial villages, extensive fields, an immense country filled with decent houses, good roads, orchards, meadows, and bridges, where an hundred years ago all was wild, woody, and uncultivated! What a train of pleasing ideas this fair spectacle must suggest; it is a prospect which must inspire a good citizen with the most heartfelt pleasure. The difficulty consists in the manner of viewing so extensive a scene. He is arrived on a new continent; a modern society offers itself to his contemplation, different from what he had hitherto seen. It is not composed, as in Europe, of great lords who possess everything, and of a herd of people who have nothing. Here are no aristocratical families, no courts, no kings, no bishops, no ecclesiastical dominion, no invisible power giving to a few a very visible one; no great manufacturers employing thousands, no great refinements of luxury. The rich and the poor are not so far removed from each other as they are in Europe. Some few towns excepted, we are all tillers of the earth, from Nova Scotia to West Florida. We are a people of cultivators, scattered over an immense territory, communicating with each other by means of good roads and navigable rivers, united by the silken bands of mild government, all respecting the laws, without dreading their power, because they are equitable. We are all animated with the spirit of an industry which is unfettered and unrestrained, because each person works for himself. If he travels through our rural districts he views not the hostile castle, and the haughty mansion, contrasted with the clay-built hut and miserable cabin, where cattle and men help to keep each other warm, and dwell in meanness, smoke, and indigence. A pleasing uniformity of decent competence appears throughout our habitations. The meanest of our log houses is a dry and comfortable habitation. Lawyer or merchant are the fairest titles our towns afford; that of a farmer is the only appellation of the rural inhabitants of our country. It must take some time ere he can reconcile himself to our dictionary, which is but short in words of dignity and names of honor. There, on a Sunday, he sees a congregation of respectable farmers and their wives, all clad in neat homespun, well mounted, or riding in their own humble wagons. There is not among them an esquire, saving the unlettered magistrate. There he sees a parson as simple as his flock, a farmer who does not riot on the labor of others. We have no princes, for whom we toil, starve, and bleed: we are the most perfect society now existing in the world. Here man is free as he ought to be; nor is this pleasing equality so transitory as many others are. Many ages will not see the shores of our great lakes replenished with inland nations, nor the unknown bounds of North America entirely peopled. Who can tell how far it extends? Who can tell the millions of men whom it will feed and contain? for no European foot has as yet traveled half the extent of this mighty continent!

The next wish of this traveler will be to know whence came all these people? They are a mixture of English, Scotch, Irish, French, Dutch, Germans, and Swedes. From this promiscuous breed, that race now called Americans have arisen. The eastern provinces must indeed be excepted, as being the unmixed descendants of Englishmen. I have heard many wish that they had been more intermixed also; for my part, I am no wisher, and think it much better as it has happened. They exhibit a most conspicuous figure in this great and variegated picture; they too enter for a great share in the pleasing perspective displayed in these thirteen provinces. I know it is fashionable to reflect on them, but I respect them for what they have done; for the accuracy and wisdom with which they have settled their territory; for the decency of their manners; for their early love of letters; their ancient college, the first in this hemisphere; for their industry, which to me, who am but a farmer, is the criterion of everything. There never was a people, situated as they are, who with so ungrateful a soil have done more in so short a time. Do you think that the monarchical ingredients which are more prevalent in other governments have purged them from all foul stains? Their histories assert the contrary.

In this great American asylum, the poor of Europe have by some means met together, and in consequence of various causes; to what purpose should they ask one another what countrymen they are? Alas, two thirds of them had no country. Can a wretch who wanders about, who works and starves, whose life is a continual scene of sore affliction or pinching penury; can that man call England or any other kingdom his country? A country that had no bread for him, whose fields procured him no harvest, who met with nothing but the frowns of the rich, the severity of the laws, with jails and punishments; who owned not a single foot of the extensive surface of this planet? No! urged by a variety of motives, here they came. Everything has tended to regenerate them; new laws, a new mode of living, a new social system; here they are become men: in Europe they were as so many useless plants, wanting vegetative mold, and refreshing showers; they withered, and were mowed down by want, hunger, and war; but now by the power of transplantation, like all other plants they have taken root and flourished! Formerly they were not numbered in any civil lists of their country, except in those of the poor; here they rank as citizens. By what invisible power has this surprising metamorphosis been performed? By that of the laws and that of their industry. The laws, the indulgent laws, protect them as they arrive, stamping on them the symbol of adoption; they receive ample rewards for their labors; these accumulated rewards procure them lands; those lands confer on them the title of freemen, and to that title every benefit is affixed which men can possibly require. This is the great operation daily performed by our laws. From whence proceed these laws? From our government. Whence the government? It is derived from the original genius and strong desire of the people ratified and confirmed by the crown. . . .

What attachment can a poor European emigrant have for a country where he had nothing? The knowledge of the language, the love of a few kindred as poor as himself, were the only cords that tied him: his country is now that which gives him land, bread, protection, and consequence: *Ubi panis ibi patria*, is the motto of all emigrants. What then is the American, this new man? He is either an European, or the descendant of an European, hence that strange mixture of blood, which you will find in no other country. I could point out to you a family whose grandfather was an Englishman, whose wife was Dutch, whose son married a French woman, and whose present four sons have now four wives of different nations. *He* is an American, who, leaving behind him all his ancient prejudices and manners, receives new ones from the new mode of life he has embraced, the new government he obeys, and the new rank he holds. He becomes an American by being received in the broad lap of our great *Alma Mater*. Here individuals of all nations are melted into a new race of men, whose labors and posterity will one day cause great changes in the world. Americans are the western pilgrims, who are carrying along with them that great mass of arts, sciences, vigor, and industry which began long since in the east; they will finish the great circle. The Americans were once scattered all over Europe; here they are incorporated into one of the finest systems of population which has ever appeared, and which will hereafter become distinct by the power of the different climates they inhabit. The American ought therefore to love this country much better than that wherein either he or his forefathers were born. Here the rewards of his industry follow with equal steps the progress of his labor; his labor is founded on the basis of nature, *self-interest;* can it want a stronger allurement? Wives and children, who before in vain demanded of him a morsel of bread, now, fat and frolicsome, gladly help their father to clear those fields whence exuberant crops are to arise to feed and to clothe them all; without any part being claimed, either by a despotic prince, a rich abbot, or a mighty lord. Here religion demands but little of him; a small voluntary salary to the minister, and gratitude to God; can he refuse these? The American is a new man, who acts upon new principles; he must therefore entertain new ideas, and form new opinions. From involuntary idleness, servile dependence, penury, and useless labor, he has passed to toils of a very different nature, rewarded by ample subsistence. — This is an American. . . .

Men are like plants; the goodness and flavor of the fruit proceeds from the peculiar soil and exposition in which they grow. We are nothing but what we derive from the air we breathe, the climate we inhabit, the government we obey, the system of religion we profess, and the nature of our employment. Here you will find but few crimes; these have acquired as yet no root among us. I wish I were able to trace all my ideas; if my ignorance prevents me from describing them properly, I hope I shall be able to delineate a few of the outlines, which are all I propose.

Those who live near the sea feed more on fish than on flesh, and often encounter that boisterous element. This renders them more bold and enterprising; this leads them to neglect the confined occupations of the land. They see and converse with a variety of people; their intercourse with mankind becomes extensive. The sea inspires them with a love of traffic, a desire of transporting produce from one place to another; and leads them to a variety of resources which supply the place of labor. Those who inhabit the middle settlements, by far the most numerous, must be very different; the simple cultivation of the earth purifies them, but the indulgences of the government, the soft remonstrances of religion, the rank of independent freeholders, must necessarily inspire them with sentiments, very little known in Europe among people of the same class. What do I say? Europe has no such class of men; the early knowledge they acquire, the early bargains they make, give them a great degree of sagacity. As freemen they will be litigious; pride and obstinacy are often the cause of lawsuits; the nature of our laws and governments may be another. As citizens it is easy to imagine that they will carefully read the newspapers, enter into every political disquisition, freely blame or censure governors and others. As farmers they will be careful and anxious to get as much as they can, because what they get is their own. As northern men they will love the cheerful cup. As Christians, religion curbs them not in their opinions; the general indulgence leaves everyone to think for themselves in spiritual matters; the laws inspect our actions, our thoughts are left to God. Industry, good living, selfishness, litigiousness, country politics, the pride of freemen, religious indifference, are their characteristics. If you recede still farther from the sea, you will come into more modern settlements; they exhibit the same strong lineaments, in a ruder appearance. Religion seems to have still less influence, and their manners are less improved.

Now we arrive near the great woods, near the last inhabited districts; there men seem to be placed still farther beyond the reach of government, which in some measure leaves them to themselves. How can it pervade every corner? As they were driven there by misfortunes, necessity of beginnings, desire of acquiring large tracts of land, idleness, frequent want of economy, ancient debts; the reunion of such people does not afford a very pleasing spectacle. When discord, want of unity and friendship; when either drunkenness or idleness prevail in such remote districts; contention, inactivity, and wretchedness must ensue. There are not the same remedies to these evils as in a long established community. The few magistrates they have are in general little better than the rest; they are often in a perfect state of war; that of man against man, sometimes decided by blows, sometimes by means of the law; that of man against every wild inhabitant of these venerable woods, of which they are come to dispossess them. There men appear to be no better than carnivorous animals of a superior rank, living on the flesh of wild animals when they can catch them, and when they are not able, they subsist on grain. He who would wish to see America in its proper light, and have a true idea of its feeble beginnings and barbarous rudiments, must visit our extended line of frontiers where the last settlers dwell, and where he may see the first labors of settlement, the mode of clearing the earth, in all their different appearances; where men are wholly left dependent on their native tempers, and on the spur of uncertain industry, which often fails when not sanctified by the efficacy of a few moral rules. There, remote from the power of example, and check of shame, many families exhibit the most hideous parts of our society. They are a kind of forlorn hope, preceding by ten or twelve years the most respectable army of veterans, which come after them. In that space, prosperity will polish some, vice and the law will drive off the rest, who uniting again with others like themselves will recede still farther; making room for more industrious people, who will finish their improvements, convert the log house into a convenient habitation, and rejoicing that the first heavy labors are finished, will change in a few years that hitherto barbarous country into a fine fertile, well-regulated district. Such is our progress, such is the march of the Europeans toward the interior parts of this continent. In all societies there are off-casts; this impure part serves as our precursors or pioneers; my father himself was one of that class, but he came upon honest principles, and was therefore one of the few who held fast; by good conduct and temperance, he transmitted to me his fair inheritance, when not above one in fourteen of his contemporaries had the same good fortune. . . .

I must tell you that there is something in the proximity of the woods which is very singular. It is with men as it is with the plants and animals that grow and live in the forests; they are entirely different from those that live in the plains. I will candidly tell you all my thoughts, but you are not to expect that I shall advance any reasons. By living in or near the woods, their actions are regulated by the wildness of the neighborhood. The deer often come to eat their grain, the wolves to destroy their sheep, the bears to kill their hogs, the foxes to catch their poultry. This surrounding hostility immediately puts the gun into their hands; they watch these animals, they kill some; and thus by defending their property, they soon become professed hunters; this is the progress; once hunters, farewell to the plow. The chase renders them ferocious, gloomy, and unsociable; a hunter wants no neighbor, he rather hates them, because he dreads the competition. In a little time their success in the woods makes them neglect their tillage. They trust to the natural fecundity of the earth, and therefore do little; carelessness in fencing often exposes what little they sow to destruction; they are not at home to watch; in order therefore to make up the deficiency, they go oftener to the woods. That new mode of life brings along with it a new set of manners, which I cannot easily describe. These new manners, being grafted on the old stock, produce a strange sort of lawless profligacy, the impressions of which are indelible. The manners of the Indian natives are respectable compared with this European medley. Their wives and children live in sloth and inactivity; and having no proper pursuits, you may judge what education the latter receive. Their tender minds have nothing else to contemplate but the example of their parents; like them they grow up a mongrel breed, half civilized, half savage, except nature stamps on them some constitutional propensities. That rich, that voluptuous sentiment is gone that struck them so forcibly; the possession of their freeholds no longer conveys to their minds the same pleasure and pride. To all these reasons you must add their lonely situation, and you cannot imagine what an effect on manners the great distances they live from each other has! Consider one of the last settlements in its first view: of what is it composed? Europeans who have not that sufficient share of knowledge they ought to have in order to prosper; people who have suddenly passed from oppression, dread of government, and fear of laws into the unlimited freedom of the woods. This sudden change must have a very great effect on most men, and on that class particularly. . . .

Thus have I faintly and imperfectly endeavored to trace our society from the sea to our woods! Yet you must not imagine that every person who moves back acts upon the same principles, or falls into the same degeneracy. Many families carry with them all their decency of conduct, purity of morals, and respect of religion; but these are scarce, the power of example is sometimes irresistible. Even among these back-settlers, their depravity is greater or less according to what nation or province they belong. Were I to adduce proofs of this, I might be accused of partiality. If there happens to be some rich intervals, some fertile bottoms, in those remote districts, the people will there prefer tilling the land to hunting, and will attach themselves to it; but even on these fertile spots you may plainly perceive the inhabitants to acquire a great degree of rusticity and selfishness.

It is in consequence of this straggling situation, and the astonishing power it has on manners, that the back-settlers of both the Carolinas, Virginia, and many other parts have been long a set of lawless people; it has been even dangerous to travel among them. Government can do nothing in so extensive a country; better it should wink at these irregularities than that it should use means inconsistent with its usual mildness. Time will efface those stains: in proportion as the great body of population approaches them they will reform, and become polished and subordinate. Whatever has been said of the four New England provinces, no such degeneracy of manners has ever tarnished their annals; their back-settlers have been kept within the bounds of decency and government, by means of wise laws, and by the influence of religion. What a detestable idea such people must have given to the natives of the Europeans! They trade with them, the worst of people are permitted to do that which none but persons of the best characters should be employed in. They get drunk with them, and often defraud the Indians. Their avarice, removed from the eyes of their superiors, knows no bounds; and aided by a little superiority of knowledge, these traders deceive them, and even sometimes shed blood. Hence those shocking violations, those sudden devastations which have so often stained our frontiers, when hundreds of innocent people have been sacrificed for the crimes of a few. It was in consequence of such behavior that the Indians took the hatchet against the Virginians in 1774. Thus are our first steps trod, thus are our first trees felled, in general, by the most vicious of our people; and thus the path is opened for the arrival of a second and better class, the true American freeholders; the most respectable set of people in this part of the world: respectable for their industry, their happy independence, the great share of freedom they possess, the good regulation of their families, and for extending the trade and the dominion of our mother country.

Europe contains hardly any other distinctions but lords and tenants; this fair country alone is settled by freeholders, the possessors of the soil they cultivate, members of the government they obey, and the framers of their own laws, by means of their representatives.

[*1782*]

BENJAMIN FRANKLIN

[1706–1794]

HE WAS decidedly a commoner: the Franklins had been farmers, smiths, and dyers; his father was a "tallow-chandler and sope-boiler." The family was large — Benjamin was the fifteenth of seventeen children — and so there was no question about his receiving a higher education. At the age of ten, after two years at grammar school, he was apprenticed to his father and two years later to his brother, a printer. Printing was the trade he loved and at which he became a master and to which he devoted a large part of his life. At seventeen, after quarreling with his brother, he quit Boston and journeyed to Philadelphia. Every schoolboy is familiar with the story of how he walked up Market Street, past his future wife's home, with a loaf of bread under each arm, and with the story of how he became, through his industry, thrift, and shrewdness, a successful printer and publisher. To improve himself, materially and culturally, was his dominant passion; it was a short step from that to a passion for improving others. This he manifested in two ways: by writing a series of maxims advising the reader how to behave so as to get on in the world — which he published from 1733 to 1758 in his *Poor Richard's Almanac;* secondly, by becoming very active in civic affairs — working for libraries, hospitals, schools, and scientific research. In the latter sphere he earned great distinction through his practical inventions and his work in electricity. His civic interests led inevitably to wider activities. He acted for Pennsylvania in colonial questions and subsequently for the country as a whole. He was a member of the Continental Congress, of the committee that drafted the Declaration of Independence, of the commission that negotiated peace with England, and of the Constitutional Convention. From 1776 to 1785 he lived in France as a representative (virtually an ambassador) of his country.

Franklin was not a professional writer. His greatest and longest work was his autobiography, which he did not originally intend to publish. Most of his periodical pieces were very short. He was an indefatigable correspondent, however, and out of his letters and little articles a definite character emerges: a man of simplicity, directness, and candor; a practical, worldly-wise man, seldom given to philosophizing or to poetic rapture; a decent, generous, unpretentious man who disliked foppishness, snobbery, and conspicuous waste — in short, the middle-class American business man in an age when such a man was democratic, progressive, and creative.

from

INFORMATION TO THOSE WHO WOULD
REMOVE TO AMERICA

Many persons in Europe having by letters expressed to the writer of this, who is well acquainted with North America, their desire of transporting and establishing themselves in that country, but who appear to have formed, through ignorance, mistaken ideas and expectations of what is to be obtained there, he thinks it may be useful, and prevent inconvenient, expensive, and fruitless removals and voyages of improper persons, if he gives some clearer and truer notions of that part of the world than appear to have hitherto prevailed.

He finds it is imagined by numbers that the inhabitants of North America are rich, capable of rewarding, and disposed to reward, all sorts of ingenuity; that they are at the same time ignorant of all the sciences, and, consequently, that strangers possessing talents in the belles-lettres, fine arts, etc., must be highly esteemed, and so well paid as to become easily rich themselves; that there are also abundance of profitable offices to be disposed of, which the natives are not qualified to fill; and that, having few persons of family among them, strangers of birth must be greatly respected, and of course easily obtain the best of those offices, which will make all their fortunes; that the governments too, to encourage emigration from Europe, not only pay the expense of personal transportation, but give lands gratis to strangers, with Negroes to work for them, utensils of husbandry, and stocks of cattle. These are all wild imaginations; and those who go to America with expectations founded upon them will surely find themselves disappointed.

The truth is that though there are in that country few people so miserable as the poor of Europe, there are also very few that in Europe would be called rich; it is rather a general happy mediocrity that prevails. There are few great proprietors of the soil, and few tenants; most people cultivate their own lands, or follow some handicraft or merchandise; very few rich enough to live idly upon their rents or incomes, or to pay the highest prices given in Europe for painting, statues, architecture, and the other works of art that are more curious than useful. Hence the natural geniuses that have arisen in America with such talents have uniformly quitted that country for Europe, where they can be more suitably rewarded. It is true that letters and mathematical knowledge are in esteem there, but they are at the same time more common than is apprehended; there being already existing nine colleges or universities: viz., four in New England, and one in each of the provinces of New York, New Jersey, Pennsylvania, Maryland, and Virginia, all furnished with learned professors; besides a number of smaller academies. These educate many of their youth in the languages, and those sciences that qualify men for the professions of divinity, law, or physic. Strangers indeed are by no means excluded from exercising those professions; and the quick increase of inhabitants everywhere gives them a chance of employ, which they have in common with the natives. Of civil officers or employments, there are few; no superfluous ones, as in Europe; and it is a rule established in some of the states that no office should be so profitable as to make it desirable. The thirty-sixth article of the Constitution of Pennsylvania runs expressly in these words: "As every freeman, to preserve his independence (if he has not a sufficient estate), ought to have some profession, calling, trade, or farm, whereby he may honestly subsist, there can be no necessity for, nor use in, establishing offices of profit, the usual effects of which are dependence and servility unbecoming freemen, in the possessors and expectants; faction, contention, corruption, and disorder among the people. Wherefore, whenever an office, through increase of fees or otherwise, becomes so profitable as to occasion many to apply for it, the profits ought to be lessened by the legislature."

These ideas prevailing more or less in all the United States, it cannot be worth any man's while, who has a means of living at home, to expatriate himself in hopes of obtaining a profitable civil office in America; and, as to military offices, they are at an end with the war, the armies being disbanded. Much less is it advisable for a person to go thither who has no other quality to recommend him but his birth. In Europe it has indeed its value; but it is a commodity that cannot be carried to a worse market than that of America, where people do not inquire concerning a stranger: *What is he?* but: *What can he do?* If he has any useful art, he is welcome; and if he exercises it, and behaves well, he will be respected by all that know him; but a mere man of quality, who on that account wants to live upon the public, by some office or salary, will be despised and disregarded. The husbandman is in honor there, and even the mechanic, because their employments are useful. The people have a saying that God Almighty is himself a mechanic, the greatest in the universe; and he is respected and admired more for the variety, ingenuity, and utility of his handiwork than for the antiquity of his family. They are pleased with the observation of a Negro, and frequently mention it, that *Boccarora* (meaning the white man) *make de black man workee, make de horse workee, make de ox workee, make eberyting workee; only de hog. He, de hog, no workee; he eat, he drink, he walk about, he go to sleep when he please, he live like a gempleman.* According to these opinions of the Americans, one of them would think himself more obliged to a genealogist who could prove for him that his ancestors and relations for ten generations had been plowmen, smiths, carpenters, turners, weavers, tanners, or even shoemakers, and consequently that they were useful members of society, than if he could only prove that they were gentlemen, doing nothing of value, but living idly on the labor of others, mere *fruges consumere nati,* and otherwise *good for nothing,* till by their death their estates, like the carcass of the Negro's gentleman hog, come to be *cut up.*

With regard to encouragements for strangers from government, they are really only what are derived from good laws and liberty. Strangers are welcome, because there is room enough for them all, and therefore the old inhabitants are not jealous of them; the laws protect them sufficiently, so that they have no need of the patronage of great men; and everyone will enjoy securely the profits of his industry. But, if he does not bring a fortune with him, he must work and be industrious to live. One or two years' residence gives him all the rights of a citizen; but the government does not, at present, whatever it may have done in former times, hire people to become settlers, by paying their passages, giving land, Negroes, utensils, stock, or any other kind of emolument whatsoever. In short, America is the land of labor, and by no means what the English call *Lubberland,* and the French *Pays de Cocagne,* where the streets are said to be paved with half-peck loaves, the houses tiled with pancakes, and where the fowls fly about ready roasted, crying: *Come eat me!*

[1782]

LETTER TO SARAH FRANKLIN BACHE
[ON HEREDITARY NOBILITY]

Passy, 26 January, 1784

My dear child: — Your care in sending me the newspapers is very agreeable to me. I received by Captain Barney those relating to the *Cincinnati*. My opinion of the institution cannot be of much importance. I only wonder that, when the united wisdom of our nation had, in the Articles of Confederation, manifested their dislike of establishing ranks of nobility, by authority either of the Congress or of any particular state, a number of private persons should think proper to distinguish themselves and their posterity from their fellow citizens, and form an order of *hereditary knights,* in direct opposition to the solemnly declared sense of their country! I imagine it must be likewise contrary to the good sense of most of those drawn into it by the persuasion of its projectors, who have been too much struck with the ribands and crosses they have seen hanging to the buttonholes of foreign officers. And I suppose those who disapprove of it have not hitherto given it much opposition, from a principle somewhat like that of your good mother, relating to punctilious persons, who are always exacting little observances of respect: that, "*if people can be pleased with small matters, it is a pity but they should have them.*"

In this view, perhaps, I should not myself, if my advice had been asked, have objected to their wearing their ribands and badges themselves according to their fancy, though I certainly should to the entailing it as an honor on their posterity. For honor, worthily obtained (as that, for example, of our officers), is in its nature a *personal* thing, and incommunicable to any but those who had some share in obtaining it. Thus among the Chinese, the most ancient and from long experience the wisest of nations, honor does not *descend,* but *ascends.* If a man, from his learning, his wisdom, or his valor, is promoted by the Emperor to the rank of Mandarin, his parents are immediately entitled to all the same ceremonies of respect from the people that are established as due to the Mandarin himself; on the supposition that it must have been owing to the education, instruction, and good example afforded him by his parents that he was rendered capable of serving the public.

This *ascending* honor is therefore useful to the state, as it encourages parents to give their children a good and virtuous education. But the *descending honor,* to a posterity who could have no share in obtaining it, is not only groundless and absurd, but often hurtful to that posterity, since it is apt to make them proud, disdaining to be employed in useful arts, and thence falling into poverty, and all the meannesses, servility, and wretchedness attending it; which is the present case with much of what is called the *noblesse* in Europe. Or if, to keep up the dignity of the family, estates are entailed entire on the eldest male heir, another pest to industry and improvement of the country is introduced, which will be followed by all the odious mixture of pride, and beggary, and idleness, that have half depopulated and *decultivated* Spain; occasioning continual extinction of families by the discouragements of marriage and neglect in the improvement of estates.

I wish, therefore, that the Cincinnati, if they must go on with their project, would direct the badges of their order to be worn by their fathers and mothers, instead of handing them down to their children. It would also be a kind of obedience of the fourth commandment, in which God enjoins us to *honor* our father and mother, but has nowhere directed us to honor our children. And certainly no mode of honoring those immediate authors of our being can be more effectual than that of doing praiseworthy actions, which reflect honor on those who gave us our education; or more becoming than that of manifesting, by some public expression or token, that it is to their instruction and example we ascribe the merit of those actions.

But the absurdity of *descending honors* is not a mere matter of philosophical opinion; it is capable of mathematical demonstration. A man's son, for instance, is but half of his family, the other half belonging to the family of his wife. His son, too, marrying into another family, his share in the grandson is but a fourth; in the great-grandson, by the same process, it is but an eighth; in the next generation a sixteenth; the next a thirty-second; the next a sixty-fourth; the next an hundred and twenty-eighth; the next a two hundred and fifty-sixth; and the next a five hundred and twelfth. Thus in nine generations, which will not require more than three hundred years (no very great antiquity for a family), our present Chevalier of the Order of Cincinnatus' share in the then existing knight will be but a five hundred and twelfth part, which, allowing the present certain fidelity of American wives to be ensured down through all those nine generations, is so small a consideration that methinks no reasonable man would hazard for the sake of it the disagreeable consequences of the jealousy, envy, and ill will of his countrymen.

Let us go back with our calculation from this young noble, the five hundred and twelfth part of the present knight, through his nine generations, till we return to the year of the institution. He must have had a father and a mother, they are two; each of them had a father and a mother, they are four. Those of the next preceding generation will be eight, the next sixteen, the next thirty-two, the next sixty-four, the next one hundred and twenty-eight, the next two hundred and fifty-six, and the ninth in this retrocession five hundred and twelve, who must be now existing, and all contribute their proportion of this future *Chevalier de Cincinnatus*. These, with the rest, make together as follows:

$$
\begin{array}{r}
2 \\
4 \\
8 \\
16 \\
32 \\
64 \\
128 \\
256 \\
512 \\
\hline
\text{Total} \ldots\ldots \ 1{,}022
\end{array}
$$

One thousand and twenty-two men and women, contributors to the formation of one knight. And if we are to have a thousand of these future knights, there must be now and hereafter existing one million and twenty-two thousand fathers and mothers who are to contribute to their production, unless a part of the number are employed in making more knights than one. Let us strike off, then, the twenty-two thousand, on the supposition of this double employ, and then consider whether, after a reasonable estimation of the number of rogues, and fools, and scoundrels, and prostitutes that are mixed with, and help to make up, necessarily their million of predecessors, posterity will have much reason to boast of the noble blood of the then existing set of Chevaliers of Cincinnatus. The future genealogists, too, of these Chevaliers, in proving the lineal descent of their honor through so many generations (even supposing honor capable in its nature of descending), will only prove the small share of this honor which can be justly claimed by any one of them, since the above simple process in arithmetic makes it quite plain and clear that, in proportion as the antiquity of the family shall augment, the right to the honor of the ancestor will diminish; and a few generations more would reduce it to something so small as to be very near an absolute nullity. I hope, therefore, that the Order will drop this part of their project, and content themselves, as the Knights of the Garter, Bath, Thistle, St. Louis, and other Orders of Europe do, with a life enjoyment of their little badge and riband, and let the distinction die with those who have merited it. This, I imagine, will give no offense. For my own part, I shall think it a convenience, when I go into a company where there may be faces unknown to me, if I discover, by this badge, the persons who merit some particular expression of my respect; and it will save modest virtue the trouble of calling for our regard by awkward roundabout intimations of having been heretofore employed as officers in the Continental service.

The gentleman who made the voyage to France to provide the ribands and medals has executed his commission. To me they seem tolerably done; but all such things are criticized. Some find fault with the Latin, as wanting classical elegance and correctness; and, since our nine universities were not able to furnish better Latin, it was a pity, they say, that the mottoes had not been in English. Others object to the title, as not properly assumable by any but General Washington, and a few others, who served without pay. Others object to the *bald eagle* as looking too much like a *dindon,* or turkey. For my own part, I wish the bald eagle had not been chosen as the representative of our country; he is a bird of bad moral character; he does not get his living honestly; you may have seen him perched on some dead tree, where, too lazy to fish for himself, he watches the labor of the fishing-hawk; and, when that diligent bird has at length taken a fish, and is bearing it to his nest for the support of his mate and young ones, the bald eagle pursues him and takes it from him. With all this injustice he is never in good case; but, like those among men who live by sharping and robbing, he is generally poor, and often very lousy. Besides, he is a rank coward; the little king-bird, not bigger than a sparrow, attacks him boldly and drives him out of the district. He is therefore by no means a proper emblem for the brave and honest Cincinnati of

151

America, who have driven all the *king-birds* from our country; though exactly fit for that order of knights which the French call *Chevaliers d'Industrie.*

I am, on this account, not displeased that the figure is not known as a bald eagle, but looks more like a turkey. For, in truth, the turkey is in comparison a much more respectable bird, and withal a true original native of America. Eagles have been found in all countries, but the turkey was peculiar to ours; the first of the species seen in Europe being brought to France by the Jesuits from Canada, and served up at the wedding table of Charles the Ninth. He is, besides (though a little vain and silly, it is true, but not the worst emblem for that), a bird of courage, and would not hesitate to attack a grenadier of the British Guards who should presume to invade his farm yard with a *red* coat on.

I shall not enter into the criticisms made upon their Latin. The gallant officers of America may not have the merit of being great scholars, but they undoubtedly merit much, as brave soldiers, from their country, which should therefore not leave them merely to *fame* for their "*virtutis premium*," which is one of their Latin mottoes. Their "*esto perpetua*," another, is an excellent wish, if they meant it for their country; bad, if intended for their Order. The States should not only restore to them the *omnia* of their first motto,[1] which many of them have left and lost, but pay them justly, and reward them generously. They should not be suffered to remain, with all their new-created chivalry, *entirely* in the situation of the gentleman in the story, which their *omnia reliquit* reminds me of. You know everything makes me recollect some story. He had built a very fine house, and thereby much impaired his fortune. He had a pride, however, in showing it to his acquaintance. One of them, after viewing it all, remarked a motto over the door: "$\overline{\text{OIA}}$ VANITAS." "What," says he, "is the meaning of this $\overline{\text{OIA}}$? It is a word I don't understand." "I will tell you," said the gentleman, "I had a mind to have the motto cut on a piece of smooth marble, but there was not room for it between the ornaments, to be put in characters large enough to read. I therefore made use of a contraction anciently very common in Latin manuscripts, whereby the *m's* and *n's* in words are omitted, and the omission noted by a line above, which you may see there; so that the word is *omnia*, OMNIA VANITAS." "Oh," said his friend, "I now comprehend the meaning

---

[1] "*Omnia reliquit servare Rempublicam.*"

of your motto: it relates to your edifice; and signifies that, if you have abridged your *omnia*, you have, nevertheless, left your VANITAS legible at full length." I am, as ever, your affectionate father,

B. Franklin

[1784]

ON THE SLAVE TRADE

To the Editor of the Federal Gazette:

Sir: — Reading last night in your excellent paper the speech of Mr. Jackson in Congress against their meddling with the affairs of slavery, or attempting to mend the condition of the slaves, it put me in mind of a similar one made about one hundred years since by Sidi Mehemet Ibrahim, a member of the Divan of Algiers, which may be seen in Martin's account of his consulship, anno 1687. It was against granting the petition of the sect called *Erika*, or Purists, who prayed for the abolition of piracy and slavery as being unjust. Mr. Jackson does not quote it; perhaps he has not seen it. If, therefore, some of its reasonings are to be found in his eloquent speech, it may only show that men's interests and intellects operate and are operated on with surprising similarity in all countries and climates, whenever they are under similar circumstances. The African's speech, as translated, is as follows:

Allah Bismillah, etc. God is great, and Mahomet is his Prophet.

Have these *Erika* considered the consequences of granting their petition? If we cease our cruises against the Christians, how shall we be furnished with the commodities their countries produce, and which are so necessary for us? If we forbear to make slaves of their people, who in this hot climate are to cultivate our lands? Who are to perform the common labors of our city, and in our families? Must we not then be our own slaves? And is there not more compassion and more favor due to us as Mussulmen than to these Christian dogs? We have now above fifty thousand slaves in and near Algiers. This number, if not kept up by fresh supplies, will soon diminish and be gradually annihilated. If we then cease taking and plundering the infidel ships, and making slaves of the seamen and passengers, our lands will become of no value for want of cultivation; the rents of houses in the city will sink one half; and the revenue of government arising from its share of prizes be totally destroyed! And for what? To gratify the whims of a whimsical sect, who would have us not only forbear making more slaves, but even manumit those we have.

But who is to indemnify their masters for the loss? Will the state do it? Is our treasury sufficient? Will the *Erika* do it? Can they do it? Or would they, to do what they think justice to the slaves, do a greater injustice to the owners? And if we set our slaves free, what is to be done with them? Few of them will return to their countries; they know too well the greater hardships they must there be subject to; they will not embrace holy religion; they will not adopt our manners; our people will not pollute themselves by intermarrying with them. Must we maintain them as beggars in our streets, or suffer our properties to be the prey of their pillage? For men accustomed to slavery will not work for a livelihood when not compelled. And what is there so pitiable in their present condition? Were they not slaves in their own countries?

Are not Spain, Portugal, France, and the Italian states governed by despots, who hold all their subjects in slavery, without exception? Even England treats its sailors as slaves; for they are, whenever the government pleases, seized, and confined in ships of war, condemned not only to work, but to fight, for small wages, or a mere subsistence, not better than our slaves are allowed by us. Is their condition then made worse by their falling into our hands? No; they have only exchanged one slavery for another, and I may say a better; for here they are brought into a land where the sun of Islamism gives forth its light, and shines in full splendor, and they have an opportunity of making themselves acquainted with the true doctrine, and thereby saving their immortal souls. Those who remain at home have not that happiness. Sending the slaves home then would be sending them out of light into darkness.

I repeat the question: What is to be done with them? I have heard it suggested that they may be planted in the wilderness, where there is plenty of land for them to subsist on, and where they may flourish as a free state; but they are, I doubt, too little disposed to labor without compulsion, as well as to ignorant to establish a good government, and the wild Arabs would soon molest and destroy or again enslave them. While serving us, we take care to provide them with everything, and they are treated with humanity. The laborers in their own country are, as I am well informed, worse fed, lodged, and clothed. The condition of most of them is therefore already mended, and requires no further improvement. Here their lives are in safety. They are not liable to be impressed for soldiers, and forced to cut one another's Christian throats, as in the wars of their own countries. If some of the religious mad bigots, who now tease us with their silly petitions, have in a fit of blind zeal freed their slaves, it was not generosity, it was not humanity, that moved them to the action; it was the conscious burthen of a load of sins, and a hope, from the supposed merits of so good a work, to be excused from damnation.

How grossly are they mistaken to suppose slavery to be disallowed by the Alcoran! Are not the two precepts, to quote no more: " Master, treat your slaves with kindness; Slaves, serve your masters with cheerfulness and fidelity," clear proofs to the contrary? Nor can the plundering of infidels be in that sacred book forbidden, since it is well known from it that God has given the world, and all that it contains, to his faithful Mussulmen, who are to enjoy it of right as fast as they conquer it. Let us then hear no more of this detestable proposition, the manumission of Christian slaves, the adoption of which would, by depreciating our lands and houses, and thereby depriving so many good citizens of their properties, create universal discontent, and provoke insurrections, to the endangering of government and producing general confusion. I have therefore no doubt but this wise council will prefer the comfort and happiness of a whole nation of true believers to the whim of a few *Erika,* and dismiss their petition.

The result was, as Martin tells us, that the Divan came to this resolution: " The doctrine that plundering and enslaving the Christians is unjust is at best *problematical;* but that it is the interest of this state to continue the practice is clear; therefore let the petition be rejected."

And it was rejected accordingly.

And since like motives are apt to produce in the minds of men like opinions and resolutions, may we not, Mr. Brown, venture to predict, from this account, that the petitions to the Parliament of England for abolishing the slave trade, to say nothing of other legislatures, and the debates upon them will have a similar conclusion? I am, sir, your constant reader and humble servant,

HISTORICUS

[1790]

JOEL BARLOW

[1754-1812]

BORN in Redding, Connecticut, of a prosperous line of farmers, he was educated at Yale and became a school-teacher, business man, lawyer, student of
military problems, entrepreneur of real estate, and finally a poet and diplomat.
He first won fame through an epic poem caller *The Vision of Columbus*,
published in 1787. He extended his reputation through his association with
the " Hartford Wits," a group of Tory satirists. In 1788 he sailed for Europe,
and then his true character began to form. All his Federalist and upper-class
prejudices disappeared as he made such friends as Priestley and Tom Paine
and observed the course of the French Revolution. He evolved into a vigorous democrat and libertarian, published his *Advice to the Privileged
Orders*, was prosecuted by the British government, fled to Paris, where he
wrote in favor of the Revolution, and at last stood, unsuccessfully, for election to the Convention as deputy from Savoy. In 1795 he was appointed
American consul to Algiers. Then followed ten years of important diplomatic activity. In 1805 he returned to America. Two years later he published *The Columbiad*, an expansion and revision of his epic poem, which is
notable for its democratic patriotism but not for any æsthetic merit. In 1811
he returned to Europe on a diplomatic mission, and while in Poland, where
he was to meet Napoleon, he fell ill and died. An engaging person, energetic,
courageous, living richly and colorfully, he nevertheless produced little of
permanent interest. Of that little, his *Advice* is probably the most interesting
item, for many of his admonitions to the privileged are still pertinent.

---

from

ADVICE TO THE PRIVILEGED ORDERS

Among those whose anxieties arise only from interest, the inquiry
is how their privileges or their professions are to be affected by the
new order of things [following the French Revolution]. These form
a class of men respectable both for their numbers and their sensibility;
it is our duty to attend to their case. I sincerely hope to administer
some consolation to them in the course of this essay. And though I

have a better opinion of their philanthropy than political opponents generally entertain of each other, yet I do not altogether rely upon their presumed sympathy with their fellow citizens, and their supposed willingness to sacrifice to the public good; but I hope to convince them that the establishment of general liberty will be less injurious to those who now live by abuses than is commonly imagined; that protected industry will produce effects far more astonishing than have ever been calculated; that the increase of enjoyments will be such as to ameliorate the condition of every human creature.

To persuade this class of mankind that it is neither their duty nor their interest to endeavor to perpetuate the ancient forms of government would be a high and holy office; it would be the greatest act of charity to them, as it might teach them to avoid a danger that is otherwise unavoidable; it would preclude the occasion of the people's indulging what is sometimes called a ferocious disposition, which is apt to grow upon the revenge of injuries, and render them less harmonious in their new station of citizens; it would prevent the civil wars which might attend the insurrections of the people where there should be a great want of unanimity — for we are not to expect in every country that mildness and dignity which have uniformly characterized the French, even in their most tumultuous movements; it would remove every obstacle and every danger that may seem to attend that rational system of public felicity to which the nations of Europe are moving with rapid strides, and which in prospect is so consoling to the enlightened friends of humanity.

To induce the men who now govern the world to adopt these ideas is the duty of those who now possess them. I confess the task at first view appears more than Herculean; it will be thought an object from which the eloquence of the closest must shrink in despair, and which prudence would leave to the more powerful argument of events. But I believe at the same time that some success may be expected; that though the harvest be great, the laborers may not be few; that prejudice and interest cannot always be relied on to garrison the mind against the assaults of truth. This belief, ill-grounded as it may appear, is sufficient to animate me in the cause; and to the venerable host of republican writers who have preceded me in the discussions occasioned by the French Revolution, this belief is my only apology for offering to join the fraternity, and for thus practically declaring my opinion that they have not exhausted the subject.

157

The very powerful weapons, the force of reason and the force of numbers, are in the hands of the political reformers. While the use of the first brings into action the second, and ensures its co-operation, it remains a sacred duty, imposed on them by the God of reason, to wield with dexterity this mild and beneficent weapon before recurring to the use of the other; which, though legitimate, may be less harmless; though infallible in operation, may be less glorious in victory.

The tyrannies of the world, whatever be the appellation of the government under which they are exercised, are all aristocratical tyrannies. An ordinance to plunder and murder, whether it culminate from the Vatican, or steal silently forth from the Harem; whether it come clothed in the *certain science* of a Bed of Justice, or in the legal solemnities of a bench of lawyers; whether it be purchased by the caresses of a woman, or the treasures of a nation — never confines its effects to the benefit of a single individual; it goes to enrich the whole combination of conspirators, whose business it is to dupe and to govern the nation. It carries its own bribery with itself through all its progress and connections — in its origination, in its enaction, in its vindication, in its execution; it is a fertilizing stream, that waters and vivifies its happy plants in the numerous channels of its communication. Ministers and secretaries, commanders of armies, contractors, collectors and tide-waiters, intendants, judges and lawyers, — whoever is permitted to drink of the salutary stream — are all interested in removing the obstructions and in praising the fountain from whence it flows.

The state of human nature requires that this should be the case. Among beings so nearly equal in power and capacity as men of the same community are, it is impossible that a solitary tyrant should exist. Laws that are designed to operate unequally on society must offer an exclusive interest to a considerable portion of its members, to ensure their execution upon the rest. Hence has arisen the necessity of that strange complication in the governing power which has made of politics an inexplicable science; hence the reason for arming one class of our fellow creatures with the weapons of bodily destruction, and another with the mysterious artillery of the vengeance of heaven; hence the cause of what in England is called the independence of the judges, and what on the Continent has created a judiciary nobility, a set of men who purchase the privilege of being the professional enemies of the people, of selling their decisions to the rich, and of distributing individual oppression; hence the source of those Draconian codes of criminal jurisprudence which enshrine the idol property in a bloody sanctuary, and teach the modern European that his life is of less value than the shoes on his feet; hence the positive discouragements laid upon agriculture, manufactures, commerce, and every method improving the condition of men; for it is to be observed that in every country the shackles imposed upon industry are in proportion to the degree of general despotism that reigns in the government. This arises not only from the greater debility and want of enterprise in the people, but from the superior necessity that such governments are under to prevent their subjects from acquiring that ease and information by which they could discern the evil and apply the remedy.

To the same fruitful source of calamities we are to trace that perversity of reason which, in governments where men are permitted to discuss political subjects, has given rise to those perpetual shifts of sophistry by which they vindicate the prerogative of kings. In one age it is the *right of conquest,* in another *the divine right,* then it comes to be a *compact between king and people,* and last of all it is said to be founded on general convenience, *the good of the whole community.* In England these several arguments have all had their day; though it is astonishing that the two former could ever have been the subjects of rational debate: the first is the logic of the musket, and the second of the chalice; the one was buried at Runnymede on the signature of Magna Charta, the other took its flight to the Continent with James the Second. The compact of king and people has lain dormant the greater part of the present century; till it was roused from slumber by the French Revolution, and came into the service of Mr. Burke.

Hasty men discover their errors when it is too late. It had certainly been much more consistent with the temperament of that writer's mind, and quite as serviceable to his cause, to have recalled the fugitive claim of the divine right of kings. It would have given a mystic force to his declamation, afforded him many new epithets, and furnished subjects perfectly accordant with the copious charges of sacrilege, atheism, murders, assassinations, rapes, and plunders with which his three volumes abound. He then could not have disappointed his friends by his total want of argument, as he now does in his two first essays; for on such a subject no argument could be expected; and in his third, where it is patiently attempted, he would have avoided the necessity of showing that he has none, by giving a different title to his book; for the "appeal," instead of being "from the new to the old Whigs," would have been *from the new Whigs to the old Tories;* and he might as well have appealed to Cæsar; he could have found at this day no court to take cognizance of his cause.

But the great advantage of this mode of handling the subject would have been that it could have provoked no answers; the gauntlet might have been thrown, without a champion to have taken it up; and the last solitary admirer of chivalry have retired in negative triumph from the field.

Mr. Burke, however, in his defense of royalty, does not rely on this argument of the compact. Whether it be that he is conscious of its futility, or that in his rage he forgets that he has used it, he is perpetually recurring to the last ground that has yet been heard of, on which we are called upon to consider kings even as a tolerable nuisance, and to support the existing forms of government: this ground is *the general good of the community.* It is said to be dangerous to pull down systems that are already formed, or even to attempt to improve them; and it is likewise said that, were they peaceably destroyed, and we had society to build up anew, it would be best to create hereditary kings, hereditary orders, and exclusive privileges.

These are sober opinions, uniting a class of reasoners too numerous and too respectable to be treated with contempt. I believe, however, that their number is every day diminishing, and I believe the example which France will soon be obliged to exhibit to the world on this subject will induce every man to reject them who is not personally and exclusively in their support.

[*1792*]

GEORGE NICHOLAS

[1754?–1799]

In 1798 the government was in the hands of the Federalist Party, which is to say the mercantile, moneyed party. At that time we were on the verge of war with France. Congress took advantage of the war hysteria to pass three of the most offensive acts in American legislative history: a Naturalization Act which required fourteen years of residence before aliens could obtain citizenship, in the meantime placing them under surveillance; an Alien Act which gave President Adams the power to banish aliens whom he considered dangerous to peace; and a Sedition Act which made it a crime to speak or write against the President or Congress with intent to " defame . . . or to bring them into contempt or disrepute." The last of these acts clearly violated the Bill of Rights; the constitutionality of the others was dubious. In any case, these acts were undemocratic and illiberal. The masses of the people hated them, and two states, Kentucky and Virginia, formally denounced them. The Kentucky Resolves were written by Jefferson.

George Nicholas's letter attacking the acts and defending the Kentucky Resolves is a fine expression of the libertarian spirit of the frontier — for Kentucky was then the frontier. It is pure Jeffersonism, which, a generation later, evolved into Jacksonism. It is here reprinted because it is pertinent to our own times: we had such sedition laws in 1918 and we may have them again. Moreover, we are witnessing a new wave of antagonism toward foreigners. Nicholas's words still apply. He himself was not important: he was an officer in the Revolutionary army, a politician in Virginia, a pioneer and land-speculator in Kentucky.

---

from

LETTER FROM GEORGE NICHOLAS, OF KENTUCKY, TO HIS FRIEND, IN VIRGINIA

My dear Sir,
 . . . having shown me that part of your letter to him which respects our politics and myself, I have prevailed on him to lend me the letter, that I might have it in my power to answer it. I am induced to do this

as well from a desire to remove the unjust impressions and representations which have been received by, and made to, our fellow citizens, of our views and designs; as from a wish that by making our real sentiments public, an opportunity may be afforded of detecting the errors on which they are founded, if they really are erroneous.

Before I enter on this subject, let me request your calm and deliberate consideration of what I shall advance. Opinions and reasoning which are in opposition to what we think right ourselves are often condemned and rejected too hastily; but this is not the way to remove error; full and dispassionate investigation is the only means of arriving at truth, and the real patriot can have no other object in his political inquiries.

The warmth of my own passions, the improper influence which I am conscious that they too often have over my own judgment, and the peculiar tendency which I feel that they possess to lead the mind astray in its attempts to form a just opinion as to our present political questions, all conspire to make me urge this request on my friend, whose good opinion I wish to preserve, whose unintentional errors I wish to see corrected, and whose well-known patriotism I wish to rouse, before that period shall arrive when a conviction of the most important truths will come too late; and when the remembrance that it was not felt earlier will be attended with the most heartfelt concern and sorrow. If after having devoted the prime of your life to the establishment of the liberty of your country; if after having shed your blood in its defense; if after seeing yourself surrounded with children and grandchildren, for whose sakes you have voluntarily submitted to all the ills necessarily attendant on revolutions and wars; what will be your feelings in the decline of life if you should see that liberty destroyed? I know you so well as to be satisfied that nothing could add to the bitterness of such a situation but the recollection that you had by an improper and unlimited confidence even undesignedly contributed to it. Pause then, my friend, and think deliberately and dispassionately, and do not let any improper conduct in a foreign nation, to which your attention is artfully turned on one side, blind you to the imminent danger which hangs over the liberties of your country on the other. At the time you are calling out Arm, arm, against the foreign foe, who you say threatens the independence of our country, do not shut your eyes to domestic violations of our Constitution and our liberties. What will it avail us if we can preserve our independence as a nation, nay, if we can even raise our country to the highest pitch of national glory, provided we at the same time lose our own liberties? If France is at this time subjected at home to the military despotism which is said to reign there, will the conquests achieved by her arms, and the glory which surrounds her, compensate the people of that country in the smallest degree for their lost liberties? Can the power and consequences of tyrants ever alleviate the miseries of their slaves? If they cannot, we ought to consider it as a truth of the most important nature — that independence abroad is of no real value unless it is accompanied with liberty at home.

The preamble to our Constitution declares that the securing this liberty was the great and primary consideration which induced the people of America to form that Constitution: "We the people of the United States, in order to form a more perfect union, establish justice, ensure domestic tranquillity, provide for the common defense, promote the general welfare, *and secure the blessings of liberty to ourselves and our posterity,* do ordain and establish this Constitution for the United States of America."

My feelings have forced from me these observations. I will now answer your letter. . . .

If those state laws [with respect to naturalization and the rights of aliens] are examined, it will be found that every security which is given to a natural-born citizen for the enjoyment of his privileges is also given to all alien friends for the enjoyment of theirs; and that those laws were so far from intending to deprive persons in their situation of any privilege which would prevent them from having as full and as fair trials as natural-born citizens were entitled to, that they have in certain cases allowed them to claim privileges in our courts (such as that their jury should consist of half foreigners) which were allowed to no other persons; and the federal Constitution also declares that in *all* criminal prosecutions the accused shall enjoy the right to a speedy and public trial by jury; and that the trial of *all* crimes shall be by jury. We find in these clauses no terms of restriction which can confine their operation, or the privileges they were intended to grant, to any particular persons; on the contrary, the expressions used in the Constitution are as general as they could have been, such as: *no* person, in *all* criminal prosecutions, *all* crimes, etc.

Suppose an alien who had resided here many years, under the protection of the state laws, and in the enjoyment of the privileges given him by those laws, without having been naturalized under the law of the United States, was to be prosecuted for treason; would he be tried by a jury? Certainly he would. If so, it would be because the law directs that this shall be the case; for there can be but one legal mode of trial, no discretionary power having been vested in any court to prescribe or alter the mode which shall be pursued. If this is the legal mode of trial, it is the privilege of the alien to have it followed, and in a prosecution for treason he could not be legally deprived of it. And if this would be his privilege in a prosecution for treason, although he had never been naturalized, the Constitution secures it to him equally in all other cases where accusations are brought against him; because it declares that, " in *all* criminal prosecutions, the *accused* shall enjoy the right to a speedy and public *trial, by an impartial jury,* of the state and district wherein the crime shall have been committed; which district shall have been previously ascertained by law; and *to be informed* of the nature and cause of the accusation; *to be confronted* with the witnesses against him; *to have compulsory process* for obtaining witnesses in his favor; and *to have the assistance of counsel for his defense."*

Considering this punishment of banishment as a novelty in our law, it is for that reason also unconstitutional; because the Constitution declares that " cruel and *unusual* punishments shall not be inflicted." And although this law directs this punishment to be inflicted on alien friends only, if the principle is once admitted to be a constitutional one, it will soon be extended to natives also; and then the best of our patriots would, under new-fangled charges of sedition, be sent to Botany Bay, to lament the general downfall of liberty, with the British patriots who have been already exiled there, under sentences given on similar charges. . . .

The advocates of this bill give it great merit because it declares that in every prosecution founded on it the defendant shall be at liberty " to give in evidence, in his defense, the truth of the matter contained in the publication charged as a libel." I can never acknowledge the justice of a thief who restores to a man he has robbed a part only of what he has taken from him; but, if I understand this bill, this clause is so far from restoring anything which had been before taken away that it adds mockery to oppression. In some cases, the privilege of giving the truth of the charge in evidence, on a prosecution for a libel, would be important; if, for instance, A was to publish in writing that B was a horse-thief, and had stolen his horse; if A was indicted for this as a libel, it would be of great importance, and a complete justification to him, if B was really guilty of the charge, to be allowed to give the truth of it in evidence. But in the prosecutions contemplated and authorized by this act, this would, in ninety-nine cases out of an hundred, be no privilege at all. This act declares that "if any person shall publish any false, scandalous, or malicious writing against either house of the Congress of the United States, or the President of the United States, with intent to defame or bring them or either of them into contempt or disrepute, or to excite against them or either of them the hatred of the good people of the United States, that he shall be punished by fine and imprisonment." Now, it must be obvious that very few charges that will be brought against either house of Congress or the President will be founded on a single or a simple fact which will be capable of being proved by testimony, as might be done in the case already put, of a charge brought against a man for stealing a horse.

All political writings contain not only facts, but also reasoning and deductions drawn from those facts; and the object of the writer must generally be illustrated by the reasoning and deductions drawn from the facts, and not from the facts themselves: and the libel, if it is one, will consist generally in what is contained in that reasoning and those deductions, and not in the facts. But evidence can be given only of the truth of facts, and no testimony can be brought to prove the truth of the opinions stated as arising out of those facts. The consequence therefore must be either that A will be found guilty of the charge brought against him, because he does not prove the truth of that which is incapable of being proved; or that he will be found guilty or acquitted, according to the political sentiments of his jury: upon the same charge, a jury of republicans would acquit him — a jury of aristocrats would condemn him — A would be acquitted today, and B condemned tomorrow, for the same publication. Can this be right; if it is not, does it not prove unquestionably that this pretended privilege is a delusion only? I will illustrate this reasoning by two examples; suppose A was to publish in writing that the President had by his writings declared his approbation and esteem of monarchical governments; and his disapprobation of and dislike to republican principles; and was to argue from thence that he was unworthy of the confidence of a people living under and attached to a republican government; and was also to assert that the sedition bill was a violation of the Constitution in a very plain instance; and was then to argue that all who had been concerned in the passing of it had violated that Constitution, and by doing so had also violated their oaths, by which they were bound to support that Constitution. If A was tried for this publication, he might prove by the President's writings and the sedition bill that what he said as to them was true; but how could he prove that the inferences that he drew from them — that the President was unworthy of public confidence, and that all concerned in passing the sedition bill had wilfully violated the Constitution and their oaths — was true also? Neither could be proved by testimony, and yet as a freeman A had a right to form this opinion; and the opinion itself being founded on facts, he had a right to communicate it to his fellow citizens, to prevent them from placing an improper confidence a second time in these men. But for this opinion A would be either applauded or condemned by a jury, according to their private political sentiments. This law then in the first place declares it to be an offense to publish a writing the truth of which is from its nature incapable of being proved; and then graciously adds that before you are convicted of this offense, you may, if you please, make an attempt to prove the truth of the charge, although that attempt, when made, must be ineffectual because it is to do a thing which is impossible to be done. If the writer's condemnation or acquittal is to depend on the political opinion of a jury collected in a country rent into political factions, and selected by an officer under the absolute influence and control of his prosecutors and enemies, will it not put a total stop to all political writings but those in favor of the measures of government; and how long will even the shadow of liberty remain after the door of information is by that means effectually barred against the body of the people?

So far from its being right to abridge the freedom of speech or of the press when it is exercised to censure the measures of government, it is the only time when it is necessary to protect either of them. As long as the speaker or writer approves of their measures, he may not only proceed with safety, but he will be thanked and paid for it. If he praises handsomely, he will be taken into favor — if he deifies the object of his flattery, he will confess that he has " melted his heart." It is said that a pleasing song has been paid for with an office; that many have been given as rewards for addresses: and that more than one have been taken from those who refused to become addressers.

What has been said must prove that the liberty of the press ought to be left where the Constitution has placed it, without any power in Congress to abridge it; that if they can abridge it, they will destroy it; and that whenever that falls, all our liberties must fall with it. I cannot close this part of the subject better than by copying what was said respecting it by our late envoys; their expressions on this occasion are so just and forcible as to give real cause to lament that their abilities *are not oftener exerted* in illustrating and enforcing republican principles. They say "the genius of the Constitution and the opinions of the people of the United States cannot be overruled by those who administer the government. Among those principles deemed sacred in America; among those sacred rights considered as forming the bulwark of their liberty, which the government contemplates with *awful reverence,* and would approach only with the most *cautious circumspection,* there is none of which the importance is more deeply impressed on the public mind than the liberty of the press. That this liberty is often carried to excess, that it has sometimes degenerated to licentiousness, is seen and lamented; but the remedy has not yet been discovered. Perhaps it is an evil inseparable from the good with which it is allied: perhaps it is a shoot which cannot be stripped from the stalk *without wounding vitally the plant from which it is torn.*" . . .

You say: "you know I love Nicholas. I really am most seriously concerned for him; assure him from a friend that loves him most sincerely, he is in danger. At any event, let him not oppose the execution of the laws. A watchful eye is kept upon him, and there are not wanting those in your country who will readily take advantage of his indiscretions. Once more, give my warmest respects and affection to Nicholas. Entreat him to be cautious. Government will exercise all its energy. If he goes beyond certain lengths, he is lost. How could he use arguments to a most tumultuous mob 'that they could not pay their taxes; and that because our ships were beehives, French hornets must be permitted to eat them up'; and not hear him answered? Oh, fie! It was rude — uncivil — but a true emblem of Kentucky manners!"

If we were *now* slaves, it might be improper for anyone to tell his brother slaves that they could not bear the burdens which their masters had imposed upon them. But as we are not *yet* fixed in that condition, it certainly must be right in a freeman who believes that the imposing these burdens, and the other measures which accompany them, will bring his country into a state of servitude to warn his fellow citizens against giving their consent to such measures. . . .

Get better information, my friend, of the kind of men who composed that meeting which you call " a most tumultuous mob "; when you do, I am certain that you will find that *you* never saw a meeting the members of which possessed as much understanding, wealth, and public virtue as those men did who attended that meeting. You will also find that you were misinformed when you were told that " they refused to hear me answered." The fact is I was answered twice, by a gentleman of very considerable abilities. It is also true that the meeting refused to hear another person, who attempted to speak to them on that side of the question; but that proceeded from personal objections to the man. How does it happen, when the Constitution declares that " the people have a right to assemble peaceably to petition for a redress of grievances "; when Congress by publishing the communications from our envoys appealed to the people as to their subject matter: when addresses have not only been received, but encouraged, from every part of America; and when the President has declared that " there is a peculiar propriety in the people's expressing their sentiments on the present occasion "; that our meeting held for that purpose should be denominated a mob? Does the propriety or illegality of such a meeting depend on their sentiments, so as to make it a regular, legal assembly when it applauds — but a mob when it censures the measures of the government? If this is the law, it puts the privilege of holding " peaceable assemblies " on the same just and republican footing that our rulers now want to place " the freedom of the press ": that they may both be exercised to *approve,* but never to *condemn* public measures.

If our manners are not as polished as those of the more civilized people in your part of America, you should excuse it — and attribute it in part to our want of opportunities of attending levees, visiting placemen, and associating with *supple* courtiers and office-hunters. When men associate with none but their equals, they will not acquire that refinement of manners which is generally met with about courts; but they will retain what is a thousand times more valuable — a greater proportion of republican veracity and independence. But if, from our situation, we can give you no aid in the article of manners, that same situation will enable us to do you a more essential service. We will preserve and keep alive for you and ourselves that sacred fire of liberty which once blazed so brilliantly throughout America, but which appears to be now entirely extinguished in the Eastern states; which the greatest efforts are making to destroy in the middle states; and which will require all the exertions of its friends and votaries to preserve it alive in the Southern states.

Your expressions of esteem and friendship for me give me great pleasure, and the more so because neither distance nor length of time has been able to diminish, in the smallest degree, the sincere respect and affection which I have long entertained for you. It is not one of the smallest complaints that I have to make against our rulers that they have acted in such a manner as to divide in sentiments men equally honest, and all anxiously wishing for the liberty and happiness of their country. That political conduct cannot be right which causes a conscientious difference of opinion between friends, brothers, father and son. But as that difference in sentiment does really exist, no man can honorably or virtuously sacrifice his opinion to that of his nearest connection; all that remains is that we should each of us suppose that it is more than possible that he errs in his opinions; and not suffer any difference in sentiment to change his esteem or affection for another who has an equal right to think for himself, and who has honestly exercised his judgment in forming his opinion.

Although I consider your fears for me as proceeding from your friendship, and therefore thank you for suggesting them, I view them as unnecessary; I have none such for myself. As long as my country continues free, I care not who watches me; I wish all my thoughts, words, and deeds, so far as they concern the public, to be known. He who has no political objects but the happiness and liberty of his country need not fear having them exposed to the eyes of the world. And if the time has come when that liberty is to be terminated, I have lived long enough. Indeed, I have lived too long; for if that is to be the case, it would have been better that I should have died before I became the father of eleven children; and before I had instilled into them republican principles, which must add greatly to their wretchedness if they are now to be slaves. I can suffer nothing by my conduct in the first event; and although my sufferings may be greater for a time in the second, they will also be of shorter duration; and if those sufferings should be one means of opening the eyes of my countrymen, so as to cause a destruction of the tyranny which inflicted them, it would be a sufficient consolation to me, even in the moment of execution and death.

The result of my thoughts on this subject is, I have lived too long as a freeman ever to act *well* the part of a slave; my conduct has been such as to give me no just cause to fear anything from law and justice; and I know not how to shape that conduct so as to escape punishment from lawless power; I will therefore continue to pursue that line of conduct which my conscience tells me is right; and then, happen whatever may, I shall carry with me self-approbation and the applause of the wise and the virtuous. As I have no improper views, there is no danger of my " going beyond certain lengths "; indeed, from my knowledge of myself, and from the obstacles which I find in my way, I am more afraid that, my constancy failing me, I shall stop short of what my duty as a father and a citizen ought to stimulate me to than that I should go beyond that line of conduct which they would make it proper for me to pursue.

When I began this letter, I intended it for your sight only; but after I had reflected that the reasoning contained in yours was that of the aristocratical party, dressed up in your energetic language; and that the misrepresentations which had reached you of *our* views, language, and conduct had also been made to thousands besides you; I determined to publish my answer to that reasoning, and my corrections of those unjust statements. If by doing so I can be in any manner instrumental in removing the improper impressions caused by either of them, it will make me happy; if nothing that I have said can produce that effect, I shall still retain the pleasing consolation which arises from the reflection that I have done my duty.

Let the event be what it may, be assured that I shall always continue to be

Your affectionate friend,

George Nicholas

[1798]

CHARLES BROCKDEN BROWN

[1771–1810]

IN THE history of American literature Brown occupies a minor but interesting position. He was our first professional man of letters, and he was one of the first to inject a democratic and liberal spirit into purely belletristic writing. Born in Philadelphia of a merchant family, he was quite well educated according to the standards of the time, but never attended a college. At sixteen he was apprenticed to a lawyer. He had become an omnivorous and passionate reader, however, and he pursued his literary interests even while studying law. Finally, in 1793, he quit the law office for good, to devote himself to authorship. Soon he revealed radical sentiments. He admired and studied William Godwin, the English radical who had been greatly influenced by French revolutionary thought. Brown's point of view could therefore be described as a kind of left-wing Jeffersonism. His first book was *Alcuin*, a dialogue on the rights of women, which put forth some remarkable progressive ideas. It had little perceptible influence, yet is important as an indication of the liberalism of that period. Then followed such Godwinian novels as *Wieland* (1798), *Arthur Mervyn* (1799–1800), *Ormond* (1799), *Edgar Huntly* (1799), and others. In later years he edited several magazines, to which he contributed some essays and considerable literary criticism. (He found, in the end, that he had to supplement his income by occasional forays into commerce.) Brown was far from being a first-rate writer, but he was courageous, independent, willing to experiment — a true pioneer in letters.

---

from

ALCUIN

A DIALOGUE

If I understand you rightly (said the lady), you are of opinion that the sexes are essentially equal.

It appears to me (answered I), that human beings are molded by the circumstances in which they are placed. In this they are all alike. The differences that flow from the sexual distinction are as nothing in the balance.

And yet women are often reminded that none of their sex are to be found among the formers of states, and the instructors of mankind — that Pythagoras, Lycurgus, and Socrates, Newton, and Locke were not women.

True; nor were they mountain savages, nor helots, nor shoemakers. You might as well expect a Laplander to write Greek spontaneously, and without instruction, as that anyone should be wise or skillful without suitable opportunities. I humbly presume one has a better chance of becoming an astronomer by gazing at the stars through a telescope than in eternally plying the needle or snapping the scissors. To settle a bill of fare, to lard a pig, to compose a pudding, to carve a goose, are tasks that do not, in any remarkable degree, tend to instill the love or facilitate the acquisition of literature and science. Nay, I do not form prodigious expectations even of one who reads a novel or comedy once a month, or chants once a day to her harpsichord the hunter's foolish invocation to Phœbus or Cynthia. Women are generally superficial and ignorant because they are generally cooks and sempstresses. Men are the slaves of habit. It is doubtful whether the career of the species will ever terminate in knowledge. Certain it is, they began in ignorance. Habit has given permanence to errors which ignorance had previously rendered universal. They are prompt to confound things which are really distinct; and to persevere in a path to which they have been accustomed. Hence it is that certain employments have been exclusively assigned to women, and that their sex is supposed to disqualify them for any other. Women are defective. They are seldom or never metaphysicians, chemists, or lawgivers. Why? Because they are sempstresses and cooks. This is unavoidable. Such is the unalterable constitution of human nature. They cannot read who never saw an alphabet. They who know no tool but the needle cannot be skillful at the pen.

Yes (said the lady); of all forms of injustice, that is the most egregious which makes the circumstance of sex a reason for excluding one half of mankind from all those paths which lead to usefulness and honor.

Without doubt (returned I) there is abundance of injustice in the sentence; yet it is possible to misapprehend and to overrate the injury that flows from the established order of things. If a certain part of every community must be condemned to servile and mechanical professions, it matters not of what sex they may be. If the benefits of leisure and science be, of necessity, the portion of a few, why should we be anxious to which sex the preference is given? The evil lies in so much of human capacity being thus fettered and perverted. This allotment is sad. Perhaps it is unnecessary. Perhaps that precept of justice is practicable which requires that each man should take his share of the labor, and enjoy his portion of the rest: that the tasks now assigned to a few might be divided among the whole; and what now degenerates into ceaseless and brutalizing toil might, by an equitable distribution, be changed into agreeable and useful exercise. Perhaps this inequality is incurable. In either case it is to be lamented, and, as far as possible, mitigated. Now, the question of what sex either of those classes may be composed is of no importance. Though we must admit the claims of the female sex to an equality with the other, we cannot allow them to be superior. The state of the ignorant, servile, and laborious is entitled to compassion and relief; not because they are women, nor because they are men; but simply because they are rational. — Among savage nations the women are slaves. They till the ground, and cook the victuals. Such is the condition of half of the community — deplorable, without doubt; but it would be neither more nor less so if the sexes were equally distributed through each class.

But the burthen is unequal (said Mrs. Carter), since the strength of the females is less.

What matters it (returned I) whether my strength be much or little if I am tasked to the amount of it, and no more; and no task can go beyond?

But nature (said the lady) has subjected us to peculiar infirmities and hardships. In consideration of what we suffer as mothers and nurses, I think we ought to be exempted from the same proportion of labor.

It is hard (said I) to determine what is the amount of your pains as mothers and nurses. Have not ease and luxury a tendency to increase that amount? Is not the sustenance of infant offspring in every view a privilege? Of all changes in their condition, that which should transfer to men the task of nurturing the innocence and helplessness of infancy would, I should imagine, be to mothers the least acceptable.

I do not complain of this province. It is not, however, exempt from danger and trouble. It makes a large demand upon our time and attention. Ought not this to be considered in the distribution of tasks and duties?

Certainly. I was afraid you would imagine that too much regard had been paid to it; that the circle of female pursuits had been too much contracted on this account.

I, indeed (rejoined the lady), think it by far too much contracted. But I cannot give the authors of our institutions credit for any such motives. On the contrary, I think we have the highest reason to complain of our exclusion from many professions which might afford us, in common with men, the means of subsistence and independence. . . .

Nothing has been more injurious than the separation of the sexes [said the lady]. They associate in childhood without restraint; but the period quickly arrives when they are obliged to take different paths. Ideas, maxims, and pursuits wholly opposite engross their attention. Different systems of morality, different languages, or, at least, the same words with a different set of meanings are adopted. All intercourse between them is fettered and embarrassed. On one side, all is reserve and artifice. On the other, adulation and affected humility. The same end must be compassed by opposite means. The man must affect a disproportionable ardor; while the woman must counterfeit indifference and aversion. Her tongue has no office but to belie the sentiments of her heart, and the dictates of her understanding.

By marriage she loses all right to separate property. The will of her husband is the criterion of all her duties. All merit is comprised in unlimited obedience. She must not expostulate or rebel. In all contests with him, she must hope to prevail by blandishments and tears; not by appeals to justice and addresses to reason. She will be most applauded when she smiles with most perseverance on her oppressor, and when, with the undistinguishing attachment of a dog, no caprice or cruelty shall be able to estrange her affection.

Surely, madam, this picture is exaggerated. You derive it from some other source than your own experience, or even your own observation.

No; I believe the picture to be generally exact. No doubt there are exceptions. I believe myself to be one. I think myself exempt from the grosser defects of women; but by no means free from the influence of a mistaken education. But why should you think the picture exaggerated? Man is the strongest. This is the reason why, in the earliest stage of society, the females are slaves. The tendency of rational improvement is to equalize conditions; to abolish all distinctions but those that are founded in truth and reason; to limit the reign of brute force, and uncontrollable accidents. Women have unquestionably benefited by the progress that has hitherto taken place. If I look abroad, I may see reason to congratulate myself on being born in this age and country. Women, that are nowhere totally exempt from servitude, nowhere admitted to their true rank in society, may yet be subject to different degrees or kinds of servitude. Perhaps there is no country in the world where the yoke is lighter than here. But this persuasion, though, in one view, it may afford us consolation, ought not to blind us to our true condition, or weaken our efforts to remove the evils that still oppress us. It is manifest that we are hardly and unjustly treated. The natives of the most distant regions do not less resemble each other than the male and female of the same tribe, in consequence of the different discipline to which they are subject. Now, this is palpably absurd. Men and women are partakers of the same nature. They are rational beings; and, as such, the same principles of truth and equity must be applicable to both.

To this I replied: Certainly, madam; but it is obvious to inquire to which of the sexes the distinction is most favorable. In some respects, different paths are allotted to them, but I am apt to suspect that of the woman to be strewed with fewest thorns; to be beset with fewest asperities; and to lead, if not absolutely in conformity to truth and equity, yet with fewest deviations from it. There are evils incident to your condition as women. As human beings, we all lie under considerable disadvantages; but it is of an unequal lot that you complain. The institutions of society have injuriously and capriciously distinguished you. True it is, laws, which have commonly been male births, have treated you unjustly; but it has been with that species of injustice that has given birth to nobles and kings. They have distinguished you by irrational and undeserved indulgences. They have exempted you from a thousand toils and cares. Their tenderness has secluded you from tumult and noise; your persons are sacred from profane violences; your eyes from ghastly spectacles; your ears from a thousand discords, by which ours are incessantly invaded. Yours are the peacefulest recesses of the mansion; your hours glide along in sportive chat, in harmless recreation, or voluptuous indolence; or in labor so light as scarcely to be termed encroachments on the reign of contemplation. Your industry delights in the graceful and minute; it enlarges the empire of the senses, and improves the flexibility of the fibers. The art of the needle, by the luster of its hues and the delicacy of its touches, is able to mimic all the forms of nature, and portray all the images of fancy; and the needle but prepares the hand for doing wonders on the harp; for conjuring up the " piano " to melt and the " forte " to astound us.

This (cried the lady) is a very partial description. It can apply only to the opulent, and but to few of them. Meanwhile, how shall we estimate the hardships of the lower class? You have only pronounced a panegyric on indolence and luxury. Eminent virtue and true happiness are not to be found in this element.

True (returned I). I have only attempted to justify the male sex from the charge of cruelty. Ease and luxury are pernicious. Kings and nobles, the rich and the idle, enjoy no genuine content. Their lot is hard enough; but still it is better than brutal ignorance and unintermitted toil; than nakedness and hunger. There must be one condition of society that approaches nearer than any other to the standard of rectitude and happiness. For this it is our duty to search; and, having found it, endeavor to reduce every other condition to this desirable mean. It is useful, meanwhile, to ascertain the relative importance of different conditions; and since deplorable evils are annexed to every state, to discover in what respects, and in what degree, one is more or less eligible than another. Half of the community are females. Let the whole community be divided into classes; and let us inquire whether the wives, and daughters, and single women, of each class, be not placed in a more favorable situation than the husbands, sons, and single men, of the same class. Our answer will surely be in the affirmative.

There is (said the lady) but one important question relative to this subject. Are women as high in the scale of social felicity and usefulness as they may and ought to be?

To this (said I) there can be but one answer: No. At present they are only higher on that scale than the men. You will observe, madam, I speak only of that state of society which we enjoy. If you had excluded sex from the question, I must have made the same answer. Human beings, it is to be hoped, are destined to a better condition on this stage, or some other, than is now allotted them. . . .

Pray, madam, permit me to . . . repeat my question — " Are you a federalist? "

And let me (replied she) repeat my answer — What have I, as a woman, to do with politics? Even the government of our country, which is said to be the freest in the world, passes over women as if they were not. We are excluded from all political rights without the least ceremony. Law-makers thought as little of comprehending us in their code of liberty as if we were pigs, or sheep. That females are exceptions to their general maxims perhaps never occurred to them. If it did, the idea was quietly discarded, without leaving behind the slightest consciousness of inconsistency or injustice. If to uphold and defend, as far as woman's little power extends, the Constitution, against violence; if to prefer a scheme of union and confederacy, to war and dissension, entitle me to that name, I may justly be styled a federalist. But if that title be incompatible with a belief that, in many particulars, this Constitution is unjust and absurd, I certainly cannot pretend to it. But how should it be otherwise? While I am conscious of being an intelligent and moral being; while I see myself denied, in so many cases, the exercise of my own discretion; incapable of separate property; subject, in all periods of my life, to the will of another, on whose bounty I am made to depend for food, raiment, and shelter; when I see myself, in my relation to society, regarded merely as a beast, or an insect; passed over, in the distribution of public duties, as absolutely nothing, by those who disdain to assign the least apology for their injustice — what though politicians say I am nothing, it is impossible I should assent to their opinion, as long as I am conscious of willing and moving. If they generously admit me into the class of existence, but affirm that I exist for no purpose but the convenience of the more dignified sex; that I am not to be entrusted with the government of myself; that to foresee, to deliberate and decide, belongs to others, while all my duties resolve themselves into this precept: "listen and obey"; it is not for me to smile at their tyranny, or receive, as my gospel, a code built upon such atrocious maxims. No, I am no federalist.

You are, at least (said I), a severe and uncommon censor. You assign most extraordinary reasons for your political heresy. You have many companions in your aversion to the government, but, I suspect, are wholly singular in your motives. There are few, even among your own sex, who reason in this manner.

Very probably; thoughtless and servile creatures! but that is not wonderful. All despotism subsists by virtue of the errors and supineness of its slaves. If their discernment was clear, their persons would be free. Brute strength has no part in the government of multitudes: they are bound in the fetters of opinion.

The maxims of constitution-makers sound well. All power is derived from the people. Liberty is everyone's birthright. Since all cannot govern or deliberate individually, it is just that they should elect their representatives. That everyone should possess, indirectly, and through the medium of his representatives, a voice in the public councils; and should yield to no will but that of an actual or virtual majority. Plausible and specious maxims! but fallacious. What avails it to be told by anyone that he is an advocate for liberty? We must first know what he means by the word. We shall generally find that he intends only freedom to himself, and subjection to all others. Suppose I place myself where I can conveniently mark the proceedings at a general election: " All," says the code, " are free. Liberty is the immediate gift of the Creator to all mankind, and is unalienable. Those that are subject to the laws should possess a share in their enaction. This privilege can be exercised, consistently with the maintenance of social order, in a large society only in the choice of deputies." A person advances with his ticket. " Pray," says the officer, " are you twenty-one years of age? " — " No." — " Then I cannot receive your vote; you are no citizen." Disconcerted and abashed, he retires. A second assumes his place. " How long," says the officer, " have you been an inhabitant of this state? " — " Nineteen months and a few days." — " None has a right to vote who has not completed two years' residence." A third approaches, who is rejected because his name is not found in the catalogue of taxables. At length room is made for a fourth person. " Man," cries the magistrate, " is your skin black or white? " — " Black." — " What, a sooty slave dare to usurp the rights of freemen? " The way being now clear, I venture to approach. " I am not a minor," say I to myself. " I was born in the state, and cannot, therefore, be stigmatized as a foreigner. I pay taxes, for I have no father or husband to pay them for me. Luckily my complexion is white. Surely my vote will be received. But no, I am a woman. Neither short residence, nor poverty, nor age, nor color, nor sex exempt from the jurisdiction of the laws." " True," says the magistrate; " but they deprive you from bearing any part in their formation." " So I perceive, but I cannot perceive the justice of your pretentions to equality and liberty when those principles are thus openly and grossly violated."

If a stranger question me concerning the nature of our government,

I answer that in this happy climate all men are free: the people are the source of all authority; from them it flows, and to them, in due season, it returns. But in what (says my friend) does this unrivaled and precious freedom consist? Not (say I) in every man's governing himself, literally and individually; that is impossible. Not in the control of an actual majority; they are by much too numerous to deliberate commodiously, or decide expeditiously. No, our liberty consists in the choice of our governors: all, as reason requires, have a part in this choice, yet not without a few exceptions; for, in the first place, all females are excepted. They, indeed, compose one half of the community; but, no matter, women cannot possibly have any rights. Secondly, those whom the feudal law calls minors, because they could not lift a shield, or manage a pike, are excepted. They comprehend one half of the remainder. Thirdly, the poor. These vary in number, but are sure to increase with the increase of luxury and opulence, and to promote these is well known to be the aim of all wise governors. Fourthly, those who have not been two years in the land; and, lastly, slaves. It has been sagely decreed that none but freemen shall enjoy this privilege, and that all men are free but those that are slaves. When all these are sifted out, a majority of the remainder are entitled to elect our governor; provided, however, the candidate possess certain qualifications, which you will excuse me from enumerating. I am tired of explaining this charming system of equality and independence. Let the black, the young, the poor, and the stranger support their own claims. I am a woman. As such, I cannot celebrate the equity of that scheme of government which classes me with dogs and swine.

[*1798*]

JAMES K. PAULDING

[1778–1860]

EARLY last century the United States fought an acrimonious literary war with England. The young Republic had become an object of curiosity to Englishmen, and many of them traveled here and returned to write supercilious, sneering accounts of what they had seen. On the whole, their attacks expressed the attitude of snobs toward a pioneering democracy. American writers took up the challenge and returned blow for blow — sometimes angrily, sometimes humorously. Of the latter mood, Paulding's *John Bull in America* is one of the best examples. Not only did it effectively burlesque the ignorant, prejudiced, upper-class British traveler, but also the Tory quarterlies which specialized in defaming America.

Paulding was born in Putnam County, New York, of a patriot Dutch family in reduced circumstances. He had little schooling, went to work at eighteen, but had serious literary interests which were encouraged by his friendship with Washington Irving. With Irving he published a periodical, *Salmagundi,* in 1807–8. In 1812 he published *The Diverting History of John Bull and Brother Jonathan,* a comic history of the Revolution. Then came several attacks on England and defenses of America, all of which, but especially *John Bull in America,* were popular. His reward was an appointment as navy agent for New York and then as Secretary of the Navy under Van Buren. The rewards were incidental, however. He was a true liberal who wrote out of felt sentiments.

---

from

JOHN BULL IN AMERICA

Previous to my departure for the western Paradise of Liberty, my impressions with regard to the country were, upon the whole, rather of a favourable character. It is true, I did not believe a word of the inflated accounts given by certain French revolutionary travellers, such as Brissot, Chastellux, and others; much less in those of Birkbeck, Miss

Wright, Captain Hall, and the rest of the radical fry. I was too con-
versant with the Quarterly Review to be led astray by these Utopian
romancers, and felt pretty well satisfied that the institutions of the
country were altogether barbarous. I also fully believed that the people
were a bundling, gouging, drinking, spitting, impious race, without
either morals, literature, religion, or refinement; and that the turbulent
spirit of democracy was altogether incompatible with any state of
society becoming a civilized nation. Being thus convinced that their
situation was, for the present, deplorable, and in the future entirely
hopeless, unless they presently relieved themselves from the cumbrous
load of liberty under which they groaned, I fell into a sort of compassion for them, such as we feel for condemned criminals, having no
hope of respite, and no claim to benefit of clergy.

Under this impression, and with a determination to look to the
favourable side of the subject on all occasions; to be pleased with
everything I saw, and to make a reasonable allowance for the faults
orginating in their unhappy situation, I left England. I can safely lay
my hand on my heart and declare to the world that I was, and still
am, as free from prejudices against any nation whatever as any English
traveller who has ever visited this country.

Being fully aware of the superiority of British ships and British
sailors, I declined the advice of certain merchants at Liverpool, to
embark in one of the line of American packets, and took passage on
board the British brig Wellington, for Boston, as my business was
principally in New Orleans, and I wished to arrive at the nearest port.
I did not like to go directly for New Orleans, being apprehensive of
the yellow fever, which rages there all the year round, with such viru-
lence that the people all die off there regularly once in two years. Our
passage was long and tedious, so much so that the packet in which I
was advised to sail from Liverpool arrived at Boston four weeks before the Wellington. But this I am assured was owing more to good
fortune than to any superiority either in the ship or sailors over those
of the mistress of the seas. I passed my time both pleasantly and
profitably in reading the Quarterly.

On the seventieth day from losing sight of Old England, we made
land at Cape Hatteras, which forms the eastern point of Boston Bay,
which we entered just before sunset; and being favoured with a fine
fair wind from the north, came up to the wharf in about two hours from
entering the Capes. Coming up, we saw the famous sea-serpent, but

he was nothing to those I had frequently seen in the Serpentine, so called from its abounding in these articles. Being very anxious to go on shore, I desired one of the sailors to call a hack, which very soon arriving, I ordered the fellow to drive me to the best hotel in the place; accordingly he put me down at the Mansion House hotel, kept by William Renshaw, a place of great reputation throughout the United States. The fellow charged me a quarter of a dollar, which is twice as much as I should have paid in London! Being determined not to be imposed upon, I appealed to the landlord, who assured me it was all right; so I paid him, after giving himself and his horses a hearty malediction.

The landlord, civilly enough, considering the country I was in, desired to know if I wished to have a room for the night. I answered him in the affirmative, and begged, as a particular favour, that he would put me into one with not more than six beds in it. He seemed a little surprised, but assured me my wishes should be gratified. I was accordingly shown into a neat room enough, with a single bed. Ay, ay, thought I, this landlord knows how to distinguish his guests — but my wonder subsided when the waiter, who I was surprised to find was a white man, told me his master was an Englishman.

Soon after I was called down to supper, where I found twenty or thirty persons, all perfect strangers to me, and who, seeing I was a stranger I suppose, paid me those little civilities which, to one who knows the world, are always sufficient to put him on his guard. Accordingly I declined them all, and answered the questions put to me rather short, insomuch that a person who I took to be a naval officer seemed inclined to quarrel with me. Nothing indeed can be more disgusting to a stranger than these civilities from people one does not know; and nothing gave me a more unfavourable impression of the rude manners of these republicans than the freedom with which they chatted about their private affairs, and joked each other before me, a perfect stranger. It displayed a want of — tact — a familiarity so different from the conduct of people in similar circumstances in London that I retired to my room in disgust. I afterwards learned that the naval officer threatened to " lick " me, as he called it, for my surly ill manners, as he was pleased to denominate my gentlemanly reserve.

I retired to rest, and found my bed tolerable enough; but the American goose feathers are by no means as soft as those of London. In the morning I went down to breakfast, determined to keep these forward gentry at a distance. But it did not appear to be necessary, as none of these rude boors took the least notice of me, and if I wanted anything, I was obliged to call the waiter to bring it to me, for no one offered to hand it about the table; I was exceedingly disgusted at this Gothic want of politeness, which, however, was nothing strange, considering the vulgar habits of equality which prevail in this republic; so I called for a coach, with an air of importance, and rode round the city, with a view of seeing into the character and habits of the people.

The first thing that struck me was the vast disproportion of negroes, in the streets and everywhere else. I may affirm, with perfect veracity, that nearly one half the inhabitants of Boston are black. Each of these poor creatures has a white man always standing over him, with a large club about the thickness of a man's arm, with which he beats the poor slave for his amusement. I assure you I have seen, I may say, a thousand instances of this kind of a morning. There is hardly a slave here that has not his head covered with scars, and bound up with a handkerchief; and almost every step you take, you perceive the stains of blood upon the pavement, which, I am assured by Governor Hancock himself, is that of the negroes. I have seen a lady of the first distinction here walking the Mall, as it is called, with a stout black fellow behind her, and occasionally amusing herself with turning round and scratching his face till it was covered with blood. This *Mall* is a place of about half an acre, covered with dust, with a few rotten elms, and a puddle in the centre. Even the little children here are initiated into human blood almost as soon as they are able to walk; and the common amusement of young persons is to stick pins in their black attendants, while every boy has a little negro, of about his own age, to torture for his pastime.

The blacks here, as I was assured by his excellency the Governor, whose name is Hancock, have but one meal a day, which is principally potatoes, and fare little better than the miserable Irish or English peasantry at home. The Governor told me a story of a man who tied his black servant naked to a stake, in one of the neighbouring canebrakes, near the city, which abound with a race of mosquitoes that bite through a boot. Here he was left one night, in the month of December, which is a spring month in this climate, and the next morning was found stone dead, without a drop of blood in his body. I asked if this brutal tyrant was not brought to justice. The Governor shrugged up his shoulders and replied that he was now a member of Congress!

To an Englishman, who is only accustomed to see white men in a state of slavery and want, it is shocking to see black ones in a similar situation. My heart bled with sympathy for the wrongs of this injured race, and I could not sufficiently admire the philanthropy of the members of the Holy Alliance, who have lately displayed such a laudable compassion for the blacks.

Next to the continual recurrence of these disgusting exhibitions of cruelty, the most common objects seen in the streets of Boston are drunken men, women, and children. I was assured by the Mayor, Mr. Phillips, one of the most charitable and philanthropic men in the State of Maine, that on an average, every third person was drunk every day, by nine o'clock in the morning. The women, however, don't get fuddled, he tells me, till after they have cleared the breakfast table, and put the room to rights, when they set to and make merry with the young children, not one in a hundred of whom ever see the inside of a school, or a church. The consequences of this mode of life are that the whole of the people exhibit a ruddy complexion, and what appears at first sight to be a strong muscular figure; but on a closer examination the roses will be found to be nothing more than what is called grog-blossoms, and the muscular appearance only bloated intemperance.

Ignorance is the natural result of a want of knowledge, as the Quarterly says. Consequently, where children never go to school, it is not probable that learning will flourish. Accordingly, nothing can equal the barbarous ignorance of both the children and grown-up persons in this republican city. I happened to be at the house of a judge of one of the courts, and was astonished to find, on my giving his son, a boy of about twelve years old, a book to read, that he could not comprehend a single word! The poor mother, who was, I suppose, a little mortified on account of my being a stranger (they don't mind these things among themselves), patted the booby on the back, and assured me the poor boy was *so* bashful! Most of the justices of the peace here make their mark instead of signing their names to warrants, etc., and what is difficult to believe, many of the clerks in the banks can't write their names. I never saw a school while in Boston. There is a college, to be sure, but I was assured the professors did not quite understand English. The Rev. Cotton Mather, one of the most enlightened and popular preachers here, has written a book called the Magnalia, in which he gives a variety of witch stories, such as would be laughed at, even among the Indians, but which they all believe here, as if it were

Holy Writ. The work is just come out, and affords apt illustration of the state of the human intellect on this side of the Atlantic.

Religion is, if possible, in a worse state than literature, manners, or morals. There is not a single church in Boston, nor any religious exercises on Sunday, except in a few *school rooms*, by the Methodists and other fanatics. I am assured it is the custom all over New England, as well as in the states of Newburyport and Pasquotank, to spend the Sabbath like every other day in the week, except that they put on clean clothes, a thing never thought of, even among the most fashionable ladies, except on that occasion.

Boston is a terrible place for fevers and agues. Every one of the inhabitants, except the slaves, is afflicted with them in the spring and autumn, as sure as the leaves appear in the former, and fall in the latter. The consequence is that they look like so many ghosts, without flesh or blood, and if you go into the shops, you may hear the money jingling in the pockets of the shop-keepers, by the mere force of habit, even if the poor man should happen, at that moment, to be free from the ague; or "shake," as they call it.

Besides this, they have earthquakes and inundations, three times a week if not more. After the earthquake generally comes an inundation, which destroys all the crops for hundreds of miles around, and covers the country so that the tops of trees and chimneys just appear above the water. This is succeeded by a fog so thick that many persons are lost in the streets of Boston and wander about several days, without being able to find any of the houses. This is the origin of the phrase "I guess," so universal in New England; for these fogs are so common that one half the time people are obliged to "guess" at what they are about. Hence, too, the half pint of whiskey which every man takes in the morning the first thing he does after getting up is called an anti-fogmatic.

These are the principal things I observed in my morning's ride. At dinner the naval officer took occasion to make himself most indecently merry, with certain sarcasms on the stupid, surly self-importance which *some* people attempted to pass off for real dignity and high breeding. The rudeness of republicanism, indeed, is obvious to the most superficial observer from the first moment a man sets foot in this country of beastly equality. After dinner a person who had been troubling me with his attentions, since my arrival, offered to carry me to the Athenæum, a great literary institution, where they read newspapers, and talk politics, which they mistake for literature. I must not forget to observe that nothing can be worse than the taste of these people, which is perfectly barbarous, except their genius, which is perfectly barren. Nothing is read here but newspapers, almanacs, dying-speeches, ghost stories, and the like. Their greatest scholar is Noah Webster, who compiled a spelling-book, and their greatest poet the author of Yankee Doodle. The utmost effort of republican genius is to write an additional stanza to this famous song, which, in consequence of these perpetual contributions, is, by this time, almost as long as a certain Persian poem, which, if I recollect right, consisted of one hundred and twenty thousand verses.

I brought letters to some of the principal magnificoes here, but did not deliver them. I like the dinners and old wine of these vulgarians, but really it is paying too much for them to be obliged to listen to their vulgar hemp, cotton, tobacco, and nankeen speculations, without being allowed the privilege of laughing, or even yawning in their stupid faces. Then one is obliged to drink wine with madam, be civil to her dowdy daughters, who " guess they have no occasion for dancing " — and what is the climax of horrors, retire from the dinner-table to the drawing-room, to hear miss break the sixth commandment in the matter of half a dozen sonatas, and two dozen of Moore's Melodies.

By the time I had sojourned a single day in the land of promise, I began to be mortally ennuyé. I inquired of the waiter if there was any thing in the *fancy* way going on. He replied there were plenty of fancy stores in Court Street! — I asked if there was likely to be a mob soon, as I had heard these republicans amused themselves in that way. He replied that mobs never happened in Boston. Any executions? No — " My G–d," exclaimed I in despair, " what a dull place! " I devoted the evening to packing up, and after supper, being desirous to make an impression on these bumpkin demos, called out loudly to the waiter, in my best Corinthian tone — " Waiter! — you infernal waiter! " " Here, sir." " Waiter, bring a boot-jack and pair of slippers." " Waiter — you infernal waiter," replied a voice which I took for an echo. " Here, sir! " said the waiter. " Waiter, bring me two boot-jacks, and two pair of slippers." On looking around I perceived the echo was my old enemy, the naval officer. Being determined, however, to take no notice of such a low fellow, I again called out — " Waiter, bring a candle into my chamber, and a warming pan to warm my bed." — " Waiter, bring two candles, and two warming pans, into my chamber. I shall sleep in two beds tonight," cried echo. I gave him a look of withering contempt and walked out of the room, leaving behind me a horse laugh, which, as I judged, proceeded from these illiterate cyclops. Before I went to bed I looked over the fifty-eighth number of the Quarterly to refresh my memory.

[*1825*]

TIMOTHY FLINT

[1780–1840]

He was born in North Reading, Massachusetts, of a family of farmers and clergymen. He was destined for the ministry, and after attending Phillips Academy and Harvard, he studied theology for two years. In 1802 he was ordained. Financial difficulties, ill health, and differences with his congregation led him, in 1814, to enter missionary work. The following year he went west on behalf of the Presbyterian Church. For a whole decade he traveled up and down the Mississippi Valley — from Ohio to Louisiana. He was an alert and observant man, interested in the people among whom he journeyed, and devoted to his work. He was moved to describe his experiences in a series of letters to a cousin in Salem, the first being dated October 1824 and the last September 1825. They were put together and published in book form in 1826. The result was the liveliest and most vivid, and probably the most reliable, picture of the Middle Western frontier that any American produced in that period. Flint was certainly not typical of the pioneers — he was much better educated and more "refined" than the vast majority — yet he was an authentic voice of the West. For he understood the region, liked it, and sympathized with its people. Presumably a Federalist, he was nevertheless hostile to industrialism and partial to small farmers; a Calvinist, he nevertheless shared the optimism and "boom" spirit of the pioneers. In the excerpt printed here, the reader will find Flint defending the poor and uncouth Westerners against the sneers of the cultured and snobbish East. The democratic individualism of the region had infected him.

from

RECOLLECTIONS OF THE LAST
TEN YEARS

The people in the Atlantic states have not yet recovered from the horror inspired by the term "backwoodsman." This prejudice is particularly strong in New England, and is more or less felt from Maine to

Georgia. When I first visited this country, I had my full share, and my family by far too much for their comfort. In approaching the country, I heard a thousand stories of gougings, and robberies, and shooting down with the rifle. I have travelled in these regions thousands of miles under all circumstances of exposure and danger. I have travelled alone, or in company only with such as needed protection, instead of being able to impart it; and this too, in many instances, where I was not known as a minister, or where such knowledge would have had no influence in protecting me. I never have carried the slightest weapon of defence. I scarcely remember to have experienced anything that resembled insult, or to have felt myself in danger from the people. I have often seen men that had lost an eye. Instances of murder, numerous and horrible in their circumstances, have occurred in my vicinity. But they were such lawless rencounters as terminate in murder everywhere, and in which the drunkenness, brutality, and violence were mutual. They were catastrophes in which quiet and sober men would be in no danger of being involved. When we look round these immense regions, and consider that I have been in settlements three hundred miles from any court of justice, when we look at the position of the men, and the state of things, the wonder is that so few outrages and murders occur. The gentlemen of the towns, even here, speak often with a certain contempt and horror of the backwoodsmen. I have read, and not without feelings of pain, the bitter representations of the learned and virtuous Dr. Dwight, in speaking of them. He represents these vast regions as a grand reservoir for the scum of the Atlantic states. He characterizes in the mass the emigrants from New England as discontented coblers, too proud, too much in debt, too unprincipled, too much puffed up with self-conceit, too strongly impressed that their fancied talents could not find scope in their own country, to stay there. It is true there are worthless people here, and the most so, it must be confessed, are from New England. It is true there are gamblers, and gougers, and outlaws; but there are fewer of them than from the nature of things, and the character of the age and the world, we ought to expect. But it is unworthy of the excellent man in question so to designate this people in the mass. The backwoodsman of the west, as I have seen him, is generally an amiable and virtuous man. His general motive for coming here is to be a freeholder, to have plenty of rich land, and to be able to settle his children about him. It is a most virtuous motive. And notwithstanding all that Dr. Dwight and Talleyrand have said to the contrary, I fully believe that nine in ten of the emigrants have come here with no other motive. You find, in truth, that he has vices and barbarisms, peculiar to his situation. His manners are rough. He wears, it may be, a long beard. He has a great quantity of bear or deer skins wrought into his household establishment, his furniture, and dress. He carries a knife, or a dirk in his bosom, and when in the woods has a rifle on his back, and a pack of dogs at his heels. An Atlantic stranger, transferred directly from one of our cities to his door, would recoil from a rencounter with him. But remember that his rifle and his dogs are among his chief means of support and profit. Remember that all his first days here were passed in dread of the savages. Remember that he still encounters them, still meets bears and panthers. Enter his door, and tell him you are benighted, and wish the shelter of his cabin for the night. The welcome is indeed seemingly ungracious: " I reckon you can stay," or " I suppose we must let you stay." But this apparent ungraciousness is the harbinger of every kindness that he can bestow, and every comfort that his cabin can afford. Good coffee, corn bread and butter, venison, pork, wild and tame fowls are set before you. His wife, timid, silent, reserved, but constantly attentive to your comfort, does not sit at the table with you, but like the wives of the patriarchs stands and attends on you. You are shown to the best bed which the house can offer. When this kind of hospitality has been afforded you as long as you choose to stay, and when you depart, and speak about your bill, you are most commonly told with some slight mark of resentment, that they do not keep tavern. Even the flaxen-headed urchins will turn away from your money.

In all my extensive intercourse with these people, I do not recollect but one instance of positive rudeness and inhospitality. It was on the waters of the Cuivre of the upper Mississippi; and from a man to whom I had presented Bibles, who had received the hospitalities of my house, who had invited me into his settlement to preach. I turned away indignantly from a cold and reluctant reception here, made my way from the house of this man, — who was a German and comparatively rich, — through deep and dark forests, and amidst the concerts of wolves howling on the neighbouring hills. Providentially, about midnight, I heard the barking dogs at a distance, made my way to the cabin of a very poor man, who arose at midnight, took me in, provided supper, and gave me a most cordial reception.

With this single exception, I have found the backwoodsmen to be such as I have described; a hardy, adventurous, hospitable, rough, but sincere and upright race of people. I have received so many kindnesses from them that it becomes me always to preserve a grateful and affectionate remembrance of them. If we were to try them by the standard of New England customs and opinions, that is to say, the customs of a people under entirely different circumstances, there would be many things in the picture that would strike us offensively. They care little about ministers, and think less about paying them. They are averse to all, even the most necessary restraints. They are destitute of the forms and observances of society and religion; but they are sincere and kind without professions, and have a coarse, but substantial morality, which is often rendered more striking by the immediate contrast of the graceful bows, civility, and professions of their French Catholic neighbours, who have the observances of society and the forms of worship, with often but a scanty modicum of the blunt truth and uprightness of their unpolished neighbours.

We may justly remark, that man is everywhere a dissatisfied and complaining animal; and if he had a particle of unchanged humanity in him, would find reasons for complaining and repining in paradise. It is to be observed that most of the causes of dissatisfaction and disquietude are in the mind and in the imagination, are unreal, and may be overcome by that effort, equally called for by common sense, philosophy, and religion, which is made to vanquish all sorrow but that which is unavoidable and incurable. In my view, after all the evils of the condition of an immigrant are considered, there is a great balance of real and actual advantages in his favour. There is much in that real and genuine American independence, which is possessed by an industrious and frugal planter in a great degree. A Missouri planter, with a moderate force and a good plantation, can be as independent as it is fit that we should be. He can raise the materials for manufacturing his own clothing. He has the greatest abundance of everything within himself; an abundance in all the articles, except those which have been enumerated, as not naturally congenial to the climate, of which a northern farmer has no idea. One of my immediate neighbours, on the prairie below St. Charles, had a hired white man, a negro, and two sons large enough to begin to help him. He had an hundred acres enclosed. He raised, the year that I came away, two thousand four hundred bushels of corn, eight hundred bushels of wheat, and other articles in proportion, and the number of cattle and hogs that he might raise was indefinite; for the pasturage and hay were as sufficient for a thousand cattle as for twenty. If the summer be hot, the autumns are longer and far more beautiful, and the winters much milder and drier, than at the North, and the snow seldom falls more than six inches. Owing to the dryness and levelness of the country, the roads are good, and passing is always easy and practicable. Any person able and disposed to labour is forever freed from the apprehension of poverty; and let philosophers in their bitter irony pronounce as many eulogies as they may on poverty, it is a bitter evil, and all its fruits are bitter. We need not travel these wilds in order to understand what a blessing it is to be freed forever from the apprehension of this evil. Even here there are sick, and there is little sympathy; no poor laws, no resource but in the charity of a people not remarkable for their feeling.

Thence it results that there are the more inducements to form families, and those ties which are the cause that while one is sick the rest are bound for his nursing and sustenance. A father can settle his children about him. They need not be "hewers of wood and drawers of water." A vigorous and active young man needs but two years of personal labour to have a farm ready for the support of a small family. There is less need of labour for actual support. The soil is free from stones, loose and mellow, and needs no manure, and it is very abundant in the productions natural to it, the principal of which are corn, fruits, and wheat. The calculation is commonly made that two days in a week contribute as much to support here as the whole week at the North. Plenty of hay can be cut in the prairies to answer for working cattle and horses in the periods when the season is too severe, and where the rushes and pea-vines are eaten out, and, in the more southern districts, the cane, so as to require the cattle to be fed.

The objection commonly made is that this ease of subsistence fosters idleness. But it is equally true that this depends entirely on the person, and a man of good principles and habits will find useful and happy employment for all that time which the wants of actual subsistence do not require. The orchards, if the fruit be not so highly flavoured, are much easier created; the fruits are fairer and more abundant. The smaller fruits, plums, peaches, quinces, and the fruit-bearing shrubs, are indigenous, and are raised with great facility. If the garden is inferior in some respects, it is superior in others, as in the size of the taprooted vegetables, especially beets, parsnips, carrots, and radishes. I have seen one of the latter perfectly fair, taper, and of a fine colour, as large as a man's leg, and weighing seven pounds. The fields are made at once, and are the second year in their highest state of productiveness. For sickness, more can be done in this country by way of preventive than by way of remedy. Every family ought to have a good author upon domestic medicine, if such can be found, and a medicine chest. People who take this precaution suffer, perhaps, as little from sickness here as elsewhere. For, as I have remarked in another place, the disorders are more manageable than at the North. With respect to society, all that the emigrant has to do is to bridle his tongue and his temper, cultivate good feelings and kind affections, and meet every advance of his neighbours with an honest disposition to reorganize in the deserts, — where they have met from distant regions and countries, — an harmonious and affectionate interchange of mutual kind offices.

As it respects that nationality which forms so striking a feature in the people of the western country, men of education and enlargement of mind are every day operating upon the community to lay aside their prejudices, such as judging of men by their country, or being prepossessed for or against them on account of the place of their birth. One of the first things that a man who is capable of learning anything in this country learns is the folly of selecting his associates according to their country, or of having his friends and companions of the same country with himself. He sees good and bad, promiscuously, from all countries, and soon learns to try and weigh men by their character, and not by the place of birth. During the ten years of my acquaintance with the country, I have discovered these feelings lessening in every place. Educated men and women are alike, and have many feelings and thoughts in common, come from what country they may. The time will come and is rapidly approaching when all local partialities will be merged in the pride of being a citizen of our great and free country, a country which is destined shortly to make a most distinguished figure among the nations.

For myself, the western country is endeared to me by a thousand recollections. Its beautiful scenery has left traces in my memory which will never be effaced. The hospitality of its inhabitants to me, and to those who are most dear to me, has marked on my heart deep impressions of gratitude. I hail the anticipation that in a century to come it will be a great and populous country, as great in a moral point of view as it is at present rich in natural resource and beauty.

[1826]

JAMES FENIMORE COOPER

[1789–1851]

BORN of a wealthy, landed family and raised on the great Cooper estate in western New York, he was trained to live the enviable life of a Tory squire. Needless to say, he was disposed to accept the aristocratic attitudes of his class. A challenge by his wife led him to try his hand at writing fiction, and thus he discovered his genius and an outlet for his abundant energies. In his Leather-Stocking Tales he was obviously sympathetic to the commoners who were penetrating the wilderness, but he romanticized them, while in many ways revealing the viewpoint of an aristocrat. In 1826 he went abroad, traveled throughout the Continent, and did not return to America until 1833. During his absence he lost touch with his people, wrote about them more romantically than ever, yet allowed his upper-class bias to be strengthened by his cosmopolitan contacts. On his return he looked at the bumptiousness, loudness, and vulgarity of his country with new eyes. Manners had come to mean too much to him. He became a vehement critic of almost everything his neighbors cherished. But no matter how critical he was of democracy, he believed in it. His *The American Democrat* was a complete statement of his views. In it he wrote disparagingly of America's manners, but defended its institutions. The following two chapters from his work show us that by this time the basic principles of political democracy were taken for granted even by those who believed in the rule of gentlemen.

---

from
THE AMERICAN DEMOCRAT

ON LIBERTY

Liberty, like equality, is a word more used than understood. Perfect and absolute liberty is as incompatible with the existence of society as equality of condition. It is impracticable in a state of nature even, since, without the protection of the law, the strong would oppress and enslave the weak. We are then to understand by liberty merely such a state of the social compact as permits the members of a community to lay no more restraints on themselves than are required by their real necessities, and obvious interests. To this definition may be added that it is a requisite of liberty that the body of a nation should retain the power to modify its institutions, as circumstances shall require.

The natural disposition of all men being to enjoy a perfect freedom of action, it is a common error to suppose that the nation which possesses the mildest laws, or laws that impose the least personal re- straints, is the freest. This opinion is untenable, since the power that concedes this freedom of action can recall it. Unless it is lodged in the body of the community itself, there is, therefore, no pledge for the con- tinuance of such a liberty. A familiar, supposititious case will render this truth more obvious.

A slave holder in Virginia is the master of two slaves: to one he grants his liberty, with the means to go to a town in a free state. The other accompanies his old associate clandestinely. In this town, they engage their services voluntarily, to a common master, who assigns to them equal shares in the same labor, paying them the same wages. In time, the master learns their situation, but, being an indulgent man, he al- lows the slave to retain his present situation. In all material things, these brothers are equal; they labor together, receive the same wages, and eat of the same food. Yet one is bond, and the other free, since it is in the power of the master, or of his heir, or of his assignee, at any time, to reclaim the services of the one who was not legally manumitted, and reduce him again to the condition of slavery. One of these brothers is the master of his own acts, while the other, though temporarily en- joying the same privileges, holds them subject to the will of a superior.

This is an all important distinction in the consideration of political liberty, since the circumstances of no two countries are precisely the same, and all municipal regulations ought to have direct reference to the actual condition of a community. It follows that no country can properly be deemed free unless the body of the nation possess, in the last resort, the legal power to frame its laws according to its wants. This power must also abide in the nation, or it becomes merely an historical fact, for he that was once free is not necessarily free always, any more than he that was once happy is to consider himself happy in perpetuity.

This definition of liberty is new to the world, for a government founded on such principles is a novelty. Hitherto, a nation has been deemed free whose people were possessed of a certain amount of franchises, without any reference to the general repository of power. Such a nation may not be absolutely enslaved, but it can scarcely be considered in possession of an affirmative political liberty, since it is not the master of its own fortunes.

Having settled what is the foundation of liberty, it remains to be seen by what process a people can exercise this authority over themselves. The usual course is to refer all matters of choice to the decision of majorities. The common axiom of democracies, however, which says that "the majority must rule," is to be received with many limitations. Were the majority of a country to rule without restraint, it is probable as much injustice and oppression would follow as are found under the dominion of one. It belongs to the nature of men to arrange themselves in parties, to lose sight of truth and justice in partizanship and prejudice, to mistake their own impulses for that which is proper, and to do wrong because they are indisposed to seek the right. Were it wise to trust power, unreservedly, to majorities, all fundamental and controlling laws would be unnecessary, since they might, as occasion required, emanate from the will of numbers. Constitutions would be useless.

The majority rules in prescribed cases, and in no other. It elects to office, it enacts ordinary laws, subject however to the restrictions of the constitution, and it decides most of the questions that arise in the primitive meetings of the people; questions that do not usually effect any of the principal interests of life.

The majority does not rule in settling fundamental laws, under the constitution; or when it does rule in such cases, it is with particular checks produced by time and new combinations; it does not pass judgment in trials at law, or under impeachment, and it is impotent in many matters touching vested rights. In the state of New York, the majority is impotent in granting corporations, and in appropriating money for local purposes.

Though majorities often decide wrong, it is believed that they are less liable to do so than minorities. There can be no question that the educated and affluent classes of a country are more capable of coming to wise and intelligent decisions in affairs of state than the mass of a population. Their wealth and leisure afford them opportunities for observation and comparison, while their general information and greater knowledge of character enable them to judge more accurately of men and measures. That these opportunities are not properly used is owing to the unceasing desire of men to turn their advantages to their own particular benefit, and to their passions. All history proves, when power is the sole possession of a few, that it is perverted to their sole advantage, the public suffering in order that their rulers may prosper. The same nature which imposes the necessity of governments at all seems to point out the expediency of confiding its control, in the last resort, to the body of the nation, as the only lasting protection against gross abuses.

We do not adopt the popular polity because it is perfect, but because it is less imperfect than any other. As man, by his nature, is liable to err, it is vain to expect an infallible whole that is composed of fallible parts. The government that emanates from a single will, supposing that will to be pure, enlightened, impartial, just and consistent, would be the best in the world, were it attainable for men. Such is the government of the universe, the result of which is perfect harmony. As no man is without spot in his justice, as no man has infinite wisdom, or infinite mercy, we are driven to take refuge in the opposite extreme, or in a government of many.

It is common for the advocates of monarchy and aristocracy to deride the opinion of the mass, as no more than the impulses of ignorance and prejudices. While experience unhappily shows that this charge has too much truth, it also shows that the educated and few form no exemption to the common rule of humanity. The most intelligent men of every country in which there is liberty of thought and action, yielding to their interests or their passions, are always found taking the opposite extremes of contested questions, thus triumphantly refuting an arrogant proposition, that of the exclusive fitness of the few to govern, by an unanswerable fact. The minority of a country is never known to agree, except in its efforts to reduce and oppress the majority. Were this not so, parties would be unknown in all countries but democracies, whereas the factions of aristocracies have been among the fiercest and least governable of any recorded in history.

Although real political liberty can have but one character, that of a popular base, the world contains many modifications of governments that are, more or less, worthy to be termed free. In most of these states, however, the liberties of the mass are of the negative character of franchises, which franchises are not power of themselves, but merely an exemption from the abuses of power. Perhaps no state exists in which the people either by usage, or by direct concessions from the source of authority, do not possess some of these franchises; for, if there is no such thing, in practice, as perfect and absolute liberty, neither is there any such thing, in practice, as total and unmitigated slavery. In the one case, nature has rendered man incapable of enjoying freedom without restraint, and in the other, incapable of submitting, entirely with resistance, to oppression. The harshest despots are compelled to acknowledge the immutable principles of their eternal justice, affecting necessity and the love of right, for their most ruthless deeds. . . .

ADVANTAGES OF A DEMOCRACY

The principal advantage of a democracy is a general elevation in the character of the people. If few are raised to a very great height, few are depressed very low. As a consequence, the average of society is much more respectable than under any other form of government. The vulgar charge that the tendency of democracies is to levelling, meaning to drag all down to the level of the lowest, is singularly untrue, its real tendency being to elevate the depressed to a condition not unworthy of their manhood. In the absence of privileged orders, entails and distinctions, devised permanently to separate men into social castes, it is true none are great but those who become so by their acts, but confining the remark to the upper classes of society, it would be much more true to say that democracy refuses to lend itself to unnatural and arbitrary distinctions than to accuse it of a tendency to level those who have a just claim to be elevated. A denial of a favor is not an invasion of a right.

Democracies are exempt from the military charges, both pecuniary and personal, that become necessary in governments in which the majority are subjects, since no force is required to repress those who, under other systems, are dangerous to the state, by their greater physical power.

As the success of democracies is mainly dependent on the intelligence of the people, the means of preserving the government are precisely those which most conduce to the happiness and social progress of man. Hence we find the state endeavoring to raise its citizens in the scale of being, the certain means of laying the broadest foundation of national prosperity. If the arts are advanced in aristocracies, through the taste of patrons, in democracies, though of slower growth, they will prosper as a consequence of general information; or as a super-structure reared on a wider and more solid foundation.

Democracies being, as nearly as possible, founded in natural justice, little violence is done to the sense of right by the institutions, and men have less occasion than usual to resort to fallacies and false principles in cultivating the faculties. As a consequence, common sense is more encouraged, and the community is apt to entertain juster notions of all moral truths than under systems that are necessarily sophisticated. Society is thus a gainer in the greatest element of happiness, or in the right perception of the different relations between men and things.

Democracies being established for the common interests, and the public agents being held in constant check by the people, their general tendency is to serve the whole community, and not small portions of it, as is the case in narrow governments. It is as rational to suppose that a hungry man will first help his neighbor to bread, when master of his own acts, as to suppose that any but those who feel themselves to be truly public servants will first bethink themselves of the public when in situations of public trust. In a government of one, that one and his parasites will be the first and best served; in a government of a few, the few; and in a government of many, the many. Thus the general tendency of democratical institutions is to equalize advantages, and to spread its blessings over the entire surface of society.

Democracies, other things being equal, are the cheapest form of government, since little money is lavished in representation, and they who have to pay the taxes have also, directly or indirectly, a voice in imposing them.

Democracies are less liable to popular tumults than any other polities, because the people, having legal means in their power to redress wrongs, have little inducement to employ any other. The man who can right himself by a vote will seldom resort to a musket. Grievances, moreover, are less frequent, the most corrupt representatives of a democratic constituency generally standing in awe of its censure.

As men in bodies usually defer to the right, unless acting under erroneous impressions, or excited by sudden resentments, democracies pay more respect to abstract justice, in the management of their foreign concerns, than either aristocracies or monarchies, an appeal always lying against abuses, or violations of principle, to a popular sentiment, that, in the end, seldom fails to decide in favor of truth.

199

In democracies, with a due allowance for the workings of personal selfishness, it is usually a motive with those in places of trust to consult the interests of the mass, there being little doubt that in this system the entire community has more regard paid to its wants and wishes than in either of the two others.

[*1836*]

WILLIAM CULLEN BRYANT

[1794–1878]

HIS FATHER and grandfather were country doctors, his previous ancestors small farmers. He was born in a village in western Massachusetts, prepared for college at home, spent just one year at Williams, and then was trained for the law in the offices of local attorneys. In 1815 he was admitted to the bar and for ten years thereafter he practiced his profession. But his real interest was literature. When he was twelve years old he had started writing poetry. When he was seventeen he had composed a first draft of his justly famous long poem on death, " Thanatopsis." At nineteen he had written " To a Waterfowl." In 1817 his father gave these poems to the editors of the *North American Review*. When they were published Bryant was securely established as a poet. A small collection of his verses was published in 1821, and then he was universally recognized as the finest poet America had produced up to that time. In 1825 he was called to an editorial position in New York. He was only too glad to forsake the law — forever. The following year he joined the staff of the New York *Evening Post* and three years later he became its editor and subsequently its chief owner. From that time on he wrote little poetry. Together with his associates, he made the *Post* the foremost liberal newspaper in the country, standing consistently for social justice and political progress. While he was less radical than his assistant, William Leggett, or even his son-in-law, Parke Godwin, he was nevertheless in the vanguard of the democratic movement. He defended labor unions and fought for abolition. Two of his typical editorials on these subjects follow. Included also are several of his poems, expressing his democratic sentiments. While they are not his greatest poems, they are among the best he wrote after the early masterpieces named above.

HYMN OF THE WALDENSES

Hear, Father, hear thy faint afflicted flock,
Cry to thee, from the desert and the rock;
While those who seek to slay thy children hold

Blasphemous worship under roofs of gold;
And the broad goodly lands, with pleasant airs
That nurse the grape and wave the grain, are theirs.

Yet better were this mountain wilderness,
And this wild life of danger and distress —
Watchings by night and perilous flight by day,
And meetings in the depths of earth to pray —
Better, far better, than to kneel with them,
And pay the impious rite thy laws condemn.

Thou, Lord, dost hold the thunder; the firm land
Tosses in billows when it feels thy hand;
Thou dashest nation against nation, then
Stillest the angry world to peace again.
Oh, touch their stony hearts who hunt thy sons —
The murderers of our wives and little ones.

Yet, mighty God, yet shall thy frown look forth
Unveiled, and terribly shall shake the earth.
Then the foul power of priestly sin and all
Its long-upheld idolatries shall fall.
Thou shalt raise up the trampled and oppressed,
And thy delivered saints shall dwell in rest.
[*1824*]

THE BATTLE-FIELD

Once this soft turf, this rivulet's sands,
    Were trampled by a hurrying crowd,
And fiery hearts and armèd hands
    Encountered in the battle-cloud.

Ah! never shall the land forget
    How gushed the life-blood of her brave —

Gushed, warm with hope and courage yet,
　Upon the soil they fought to save.

Now all is calm, and fresh, and still;
　Alone the chirp of flitting bird,
And talk of children on the hill,
　And bell of wandering kine, are heard.

No solemn host goes trailing by
　The black-mouthed gun and staggering wain;
Men start not at the battle-cry,
　Oh, be it never heard again!

Soon rested those who fought; but thou
　Who minglest in the harder strife
For truths which men receive not now,
　Thy warfare only ends with life.

A friendless warfare! lingering long
　Through weary day and weary year;
A wild and many-weaponed throng
　Hang on thy front, and flank, and rear.

Yet nerve thy spirit to the proof,
　And blench not at thy chosen lot,
The timid good may stand aloof,
　The sage may frown — yet faint thou not.

Nor heed the shaft too surely cast,
　The foul and hissing bolt of scorn;
For with thy side shall dwell, at last,
　The victory of endurance born.

Truth, crushed to earth, shall rise again;
　Th' eternal years of God are hers;
But Error, wounded, writhes in pain,
　And dies among his worshippers.

Yea, though thou lie upon the dust,
　When they who helped thee flee in fear,

Die full of hope and manly trust,
  Like those who fell in battle here.

Another hand thy sword shall wield,
  Another hand the standard wave,
Till from the trumpet's mouth is pealed
  The blast of triumph o'er thy grave.
[*1837*]

THE ANTIQUITY OF FREEDOM

Here are old trees, tall oaks, and gnarlèd pines,
That stream with gray-green mosses; here the ground
Was never trenched by spade, and flowers spring up
Unsown, and die ungathered. It is sweet
To linger here, among the flitting birds
And leaping squirrels, wandering brooks, and winds
That shake the leaves, and scatter, as they pass,
A fragrance from the cedars, thickly set
With pale-blue berries. In these peaceful shades —
Peaceful, unpruned, immeasurably old —
My thoughts go up the long dim path of years,
Back to the earliest days of liberty.

O Freedom! thou art not, as poets dream,
A fair young girl, with light and delicate limbs,
And wavy tresses gushing from the cap
With which the Roman master crowned his slave
When he took off the gyves. A bearded man,
Armed to the teeth, art thou; one mailèd hand
Grasps the broad shield, and one the sword; thy brow,
Glorious in beauty though it be, is scarred
With tokens of old wars; thy massive limbs
Are strong with struggling. Power at thee has launched
His bolts, and with his lightnings smitten thee;

They could not quench the life thou hast from heaven;
Merciless Power has dug thy dungeon deep,
And his swart armorers, by a thousand fires,
Have forged thy chain; yet, while he deems thee bound
The links are shivered, and the prison-walls
Fall outward; terribly thou springest forth,
As springs the flame above a burning pile,
And shoutest to the nations, who return
Thy shoutings, while the pale oppressor flies.

Thy birthright was not given by human hands:
Thou wert twin-born with man. In pleasant fields,
While yet our race was few, thou sat'st with him,
To tend the quiet flock and watch the stars,
And teach the reed to utter simple airs.
Thou by his side, amid the tangled wood,
Didst war upon the panther and the wolf,
His only foes; and thou with him didst draw
The earliest furrow on the mountain-side,
Soft with the deluge. Tyranny himself,
Thy enemy, although of reverend look,
Hoary with many years, and far obeyed,
Is later born than thou; and as he meets
The grave defiance of thine elder eye,
The usurper trembles in his fastnesses.

Thou shalt wax stronger with the lapse of years,
But he shall fade into a feebler age —
Feebler, yet subtler. He shall weave his snares,
And spring them on thy careless steps, and clap
His withered hands, and from their ambush call
His hordes to fall upon thee. He shall send
Quaint maskers, wearing fair and gallant forms
To catch thy gaze, and uttering graceful words
To charm thy ear; while his sly imps, by stealth,
Twine round thee threads of steel, light thread on thread,
That grow to fetters; or bind down thy arms
With chains concealed in chaplets. Oh! not yet
Mayst thou unbrace thy corslet, nor lay by

Thy sword; nor yet, O Freedom! close thy lids
In slumber; for thine enemy never sleeps,
And thou must watch and combat till the day
Of the new earth and heaven. But wouldst thou rest
Awhile from tumult and the frauds of men,
These old and friendly solitudes invite
Thy visit. They, while yet the forest trees
Were young upon the unviolated earth,
And yet the moss-stains on the rock were new,
Beheld thy glorious childhood, and rejoiced.

[*1842*]

"OH MOTHER OF A MIGHTY RACE"

Oh mother of a mighty race,
Yet lovely in thy youthful grace!
The elder dames, thy haughty peers,
Admire and hate thy blooming years.
　　With words of shame
And taunts of scorn they join thy name.

For on thy cheeks the glow is spread
That tints thy morning hills with red;
Thy step — the wild deer's rustling feet
Within thy woods are not more fleet;
　　Thy hopeful eye
Is bright as thine own sunny sky.

Ay, let them rail — those haughty ones,
While safe thou dwellest with thy sons.
They do not know how loved thou art,
How many a fond and fearless heart
　　Would rise to throw
Its life between thee and the foe.

206

They know not, in their hate and pride,
What virtues with thy children bide;
How true, how good, thy graceful maids
Make bright, like flowers, the valley shades;
    What generous men
Spring, like thine oaks, by hill and glen.

What cordial welcomes greet the guest
By thy lone rivers of the West;
How faith is kept, and truth revered,
And man is loved, and God is feared,
    In woodland homes,
And where the ocean border foams.

There's freedom at thy gates and rest
For Earth's down-trodden and opprest,
A shelter for the hunted head,
For the starved laborer toil and bread.
    Power, at thy bounds,
Stops and calls back his baffled hounds.

Oh, fair young mother! on thy brow
Shall sit a nobler grace than now.
Deep in the brightness of thy skies
The thronging years in glory rise,
    And, as they fleet,
Drop strength and riches at thy feet.

Thine eye, with every coming hour,
Shall brighten, and thy form shall tower;
And when thy sisters, elder born,
Would brand thy name with words of scorn,
    Before thine eye,
Upon their lips the taunt shall die.
[*1847*]

from

THE DEATH OF SLAVERY

O thou great Wrong, that, through the slow-paced years,
  Didst hold thy millions fettered, and didst wield
  The scourge that drove the laborer to the field,
And turn a stony gaze on human tears,
    Thy cruel reign is o'er;
    Thy bondmen crouch no more
In terror at the menace of thine eye;
  For He who marks the bounds of guilty power,
Long-suffering, hath heard the captive's cry,
  And touched his shackles at the appointed hour,
And lo! they fall, and he whose limbs they galled
Stands in his native manhood, disenthralled.

A shout of joy from the redeemed is sent;
  Ten thousand hamlets swell the hymn of thanks;
  Our rivers roll exulting, and their banks
Send up hosannas to the firmament!
    Fields where the bondman's toil
    No more shall trench the soil,
Seem now to bask in a serener day;
  The meadow-birds sing sweeter, and the airs
Of heaven with more caressing softness play,
  Welcoming man to liberty like theirs.
A glory clothes the land from sea to sea,
For the great land and all its coasts are free.

[*1866*]

---

from

[THE RIGHT OF WORKMEN TO STRIKE]

  Sentence was passed on Saturday on the twenty "men who had determined not to work." The punishment selected, on due consideration, by the judge, was that officers appointed for the purpose should immediately demand from each of the delinquents a sum of money which was named in the sentence of the court. The amount demanded would not have fallen short of the savings of many years. Either the offenders had not parted with these savings, or their brother workmen raised the ransom money for them on the spot. The fine was paid over as required. All is now well; justice has been satisfied. But if the expenses of their families had anticipated the law, and left nothing in their hands, or if friends had not been ready to buy the freedom of their comrades, they would have been sent to prison, and there they would have stayed, until their wives and children, besides earning their own bread, had saved enough to redeem the captives from their cells. Such has been their punishment. What was their offence? They had committed the crime of unanimously declining to go to work at the wages offered to them by their masters. They had said to one another, " Let us come out from the meanness and misery of our caste. Let us begin to do what every order more privileged and more honoured is doing every day. By the means which we believe to be the best let us raise ourselves and our families above the humbleness of our condition. We may be wrong, but we cannot help believing that we might do much if we were true brothers to each other, and would resolve not to sell the only thing which is our own, the cunning of our hands, for less than it is worth." What other things they may have done is nothing to the purpose: it was for this they were condemned; it is for this they are to endure the penalty of the law.

We call upon a candid and generous community to mark that the punishment inflicted upon these twenty "men who had determined not to work" is not directed against the offense of conspiring to prevent others by force from working at low wages, but expressly against the offence of settling by pre-concert the compensation which they thought they were entitled to obtain. It is certainly superfluous to repeat that this journal would be the very last to oppose a law levelled at any attempt to molest the labourer who chooses to work for less than the prices settled by the union. We have said, and to cut off cavil, we say it now again, that a conspiracy to deter, by threats of violence, a fellow workman from arranging his own terms with his employers is a conspiracy to commit a felony — a conspiracy which, being a crime against liberty, we should be the first to condemn — a conspiracy which no strike should, for its own sake countenance for a moment — a conspiracy already punishable by the statute, and far easier to reach than the one of which " the twenty " stood accused; but a conspiracy, we must add, that has not a single feature in common with the base and barbarous prohibition under which the offenders were indicted and condemned.

They were condemned because they had determined not to work for the wages that were offered them! Can anything be imagined more abhorrent to every sentiment of generosity or justice than the law which arms the rich with the legal right to fix, by assize, the wages of the poor? If this is not SLAVERY, we have forgotten its definition. Strike the right of associating for the sale of labour from the privileges of a freeman, and you may as well at once bind him to a master, or ascribe him to the soil. If it be not in the colour of his skin, and in the poor franchise of naming his own terms in a contract for his work, what advantage has the labourer of the north over the bondman of the south? Punish by human laws a " determination not to work," make it penal by any other penalty than idleness inflicts, and it matters little whether the task-masters be one or many, an individual or an order, the hateful scheme of slavery will have gained a foothold in the land. And then the meanness of this law, which visits with its malice those who cling to it for protection, and shelters with all its fences those who are raised above its threats. A late solicitation for its aid against employers is treated with derision and contempt, but the moment the " masters " invoked its intervention, it came down from its high place with most indecent haste, and has now discharged its fury upon the naked heads of wretches so forlorn that their worst faults multiply their titles to a liberty which they must learn to win from livelier sensibilities than the barren benevolence of Wealth, or the tardy magnanimity of Power.

Since the above was written we have read the report of Judge Edwards's address on sentencing the journeymen. It will be found in another part of this paper. We see in this address an apparent disposition to mix up the question of *combination*, which is a lawful act, with that of *violence*, which is allowed on all hands to be unlawful. We repeat — that it was for the simple act of combining not to work under a certain rate of wages, and not for a disturbance of the peace, that the twenty journeymen were indicted, tried, convicted and punished. It was expressly so stated in Judge Edwards's charge to the jury which brought in the verdict of guilty; and whoever will look at the address made by him in pronouncing the sentence will find that he still maintains and repeats, in various forms of expression, the doctrine that combinations to demand a fixed rate of wages are unlawful and punishable. This tyrannical doctrine we affirm to be a forced construction of the statute against conspiracies injurious to commerce — a construction which the makers of the law, we are sure, never contemplated. We are now told, however, that it will be insisted upon and enforced — let it be so — it is the very method by which either the courts of justice will be compelled to recede from their mistaken and arbitrary construction, or the legislature will interpose to declare that such is not the law. Carry it into effect impartially and without respect of persons, and there will not be people enough left without the penitentiaries to furnish subsistence to those who are confined within them.

"Self-created societies," says Judge Edwards, "are unknown to the constitution and laws, and will not be permitted to rear their crest and extend their baneful influence over any portion of the community." If there is any sense in this passage it means that self-created societies are unlawful, and must be put down by the courts. Down then with every literary, every religious, and every charitable association not incorporated! What nonsense is this! Self-created societies *are* known to the constitution and laws, for they are not prohibited, and the laws which allow them will, if justly administered, protect them. But suppose in charity that the reporter has put his absurdity into the mouth of Judge Edwards, and that he meant only those self-created societies which have an effect upon trade and commerce. Gather up then and sweep to the penitentiary all those who are confederated to carry on any business or trade in concert, by fixed rules, and see how many men you would leave at large in this city. The members of every partnership in the place will come under the penalties of the law, and not only these, but every person pursuing any occupation whatever who governs himself by a mutual understanding with others that follow the same occupation. . . .

[1836]

[THE DEATH OF LOVEJOY]

We have received by this morning's mail a slip from the Missouri Argus, printed at St. Louis, containing intelligence which has filled us with surprise and horror. A mob, in making an attack upon an abolition press established at Alton, in Illinois, murdered two persons, wounded several others, and triumphing over the objects of their fury by this atrocious violence, destroyed the press which these men had defended at the cost of their blood and their lives.

We give the slip from the Missouri Argus as we received it, but we cannot forbear expressing in the strongest language our condemnation of the manner in which it speaks of this bloody event. The right to discuss freely and openly, by speech, by the pen, by the press, all political questions, and to examine and animadvert upon all political institutions, is a right so clear and certain, so interwoven with our other liberties, so necessary, in fact, to their existence, that without it we must fall at once into despotism or anarchy. To say that he who holds unpopular opinions must hold them at the peril of his life, and that, if he expresses them in public, he has only himself to blame if they who disagree with him should rise and put him to death, is to strike at all rights, all liberties, all protection of law, and to justify or extenuate all crimes.

We regard not this as a question connected with the abolition of slavery in the South, but as a question vital to the liberties of the entire Union. We may have different opinions concerning the propriety of the measures which the abolitionists desire to recommend, but we marvel and we deplore that any difference can exist as to the freedom of discussion. We are astonished that even a single journal can be found so forgetful of its own rights, to say nothing of its duties to the community, as to countenance, even indirectly, the idea of muzzling the press by the fear of violence.

For our own part we approve, we applaud, we would consecrate, if we could, to universal honor, the conduct of those who bled in this gallant defence of the freedom of the press. Whether they erred or not in their opinions, they did not err in the conviction of their right as citizens of a democratic government to express them, nor did they err in defending this right with an obstinacy which yielded only to death and the uttermost violence. With these remarks we lay before our readers the brief narrative with which we are furnished of this bloody outrage.

Office of the Missouri Argus,
St. Louis, Nov. 9, 1837.

MOB AT ALTON, ILLINOIS

THE REV. P. E. LOVEJOY KILLED, AND HIS ABOLITION PRESS DESTROYED!!

The infatuated editor of the Alton Observer has at length fallen a victim to his obstinacy in the cause of the Abolitionists. Disregarding the known and expressed sentiments of a large portion of the citizens of Alton, in relation to his incendiary publications, and, as it would seem, bent upon his own destruction, he formed the determination to establish another press for the propagation of the odious and disorganizing principles of Tappan and his eastern confederates. But his temerity has received an awful retribution from the hands of an infuriated and lawless mob. — The following particulars of the tragical outrage is [*sic*] contained in a postscript to the Alton Telegraph of the 8th inst.:

LAMENTABLE OCCURRENCE. — It is with the deepest regret that we stop the press in order to state that, at a late hour last night, an attack was made by a large number of persons on the warehouse of Messrs. Godfrey, Gilman & Co., for the purpose of destroying a press intended for the revival of the Alton Observer, which, shocking to relate, resulted in the death of two individuals — the Rev. E. P. LOVEJOY, late editor of the Observer, and a man named —— Bishop. Seven others were wounded, two severely, and the others slightly. We can add no more at this time than that the assailants succeeded in effecting their object.

[*1837*]

WILLIAM LEGGETT

[1801–1839]

HE WAS born and brought up in New York City, but at the age of eighteen moved with his parents to Illinois, where he lived a pioneer's life. A few years later he joined the navy as a midshipman. In 1826 he surrendered his commission after being court-martialed for dueling with another officer. He then decided to enter journalism in his native city: he published verse, stories, and sketches and for a short time issued a weekly of his own. In 1829 he became assistant editor of the *Evening Post*, which was then edited and partly owned by William Cullen Bryant. Leggett quickly developed into an extreme Jacksonian. Applauded by Bryant's son-in-law, Parke Godwin, he helped to make the *Post* an outstandingly progressive paper. While Bryant was sympathetic, he was not enough so to suit Leggett, so the latter quit the *Post* and went to other papers where no restraints were placed upon him. He was an abolitionist, a free-trader, favored broad suffrage, advocated direct taxation, denounced state banks as privileged monopolies, and upheld the right of workmen to combine into trade unions. In all of these particulars he was clearly a democrat, but in the last he was more: like Bryant, whom he may have influenced, he was far ahead of his time, for respectable people were then almost unanimous in attacking unionism. Leggett was certainly one of the most courageous, but also one of the ablest, of our early nineteenth-century journalists: his collected editorials, two of which follow, can still be read with interest.

RICH AND POOR

The rich perceive, acknowledge, and act upon a common interest, and why not the poor? Yet the moment the latter are called upon to combine for the preservation of their rights, forsooth the community is in danger! Property is no longer secure, and life in jeopardy. This cant has descended to us from those times when the poor and labouring classes had no stake in the community, and no rights except such

214

as they could acquire by force. But the times have changed, though the cant remains the same. The scrip nobility of this Republic have adopted towards the free people of this Republic the same language which the Feudal Barons and the despots who contested with them the power of oppressing the people used towards their serfs and villains, as they were opprobiously called.

These would-be lordlings of the Paper Dynasty cannot or will not perceive that there is some difference in the situation and feelings of the people of the United States and those of the despotic governments of Europe. They forget that at this moment our people, we mean emphatically the class which labours with its own hands, is in possession of a greater portion of the property and intelligence of this country, ay, ten times over, than all the creatures of the paper credit system put together. This property is indeed more widely and equally distributed among the people than among the phantoms of the paper system, and so much the better. And as to their intelligence, let any man talk with them, and if he does not learn something it is his own fault. They are as well acquainted with the rights of person and property, and have as just a regard for them, as the most illustrious lordling of the scrip nobility. And why should they not? Who and what are the great majority of the wealthy people of this city — we may say of this country? Are they not (we say it not in disparagement, but in high commendation), are they not men who began the world comparatively poor with ordinary education and ordinary means? And what should make them so much wiser than their neighbors? Is it because they live in better style, ride in carriages, and have more money — or at least more credit than their poorer neighbors? Does a man become wiser, stronger, or more virtuous and patriotic because he has a fine house over his head? Does he love his country the better because he has a French cook, and a box at the opera? Or does he grow more learned, logical and profound by intense study of the day-book, ledger, bills of exchange, bank promises, and notes of hand?

Of all the countries on the face of the earth, or that ever existed on the face of the earth, this is the one where the claims of wealth and aristocracy are the most unfounded, absurd and ridiculous. With no claim to hereditary distinctions; with no exclusive rights except what they derive from monopolies, and no power of perpetuating their estates in their posterity, the assumption of aristocratic airs and claims is supremely ridiculous. To-morrow they themselves may be beggars for aught they know, or at all events their children may become so. Their posterity in the second generation will have to begin the world again, and work for a living as did their forefathers. And yet the moment a man becomes rich among us, he sets up for wisdom — he despises the poor and ignorant — he sets up for patriotism: he is your only man who has a stake in the community, and therefore the only one who ought to have a voice in the state. What folly is this? And how contemptible his presumption? He is not a whit wiser, better or more patriotic than when he commenced the world, a waggon driver. Nay, not half so patriotic, for he would see his country disgraced a thousand times rather than see one fall of the stocks, unless perhaps he had been speculating on such a contingency. To him a victory is only of consequence as it raises, and a defeat only to be lamented as it depresses a loan. His soul is wrapped up in a certificate of scrip, or a Bank note. Witness the conduct of these pure patriots, during the late war, when they, at least a large proportion of them, not only withheld all their support from the Government, but used all their influence to prevent others from giving their assistance. Yet these are the people who alone have a stake in the community, and of course exclusively monopolized patriotism.

But let us ask what and where is the danger of a combination of the labouring classes in vindication of their political principles, or in defence of their menaced rights? Have they not the right to act in concert, when their opponents act in concert? Nay, is it not their bounden duty to combine against the only enemy they have to fear as yet in this free country, monopoly and a great paper system that grinds them to the dust? Truly this is strange republican doctrine, and this is a strange republican country, where men cannot unite in one common effort, in one common cause, without rousing the cry of danger to the rights of person and property. Is not this a government of the people, founded on the rights of the people, and instituted for the express object of guarding them against the encroachments and usurpations of power? And if they are not permitted the possession of common interest; the exercise of a common feeling; if they cannot combine to resist, by constitutional means, these encroachments; to what purpose were they declared free to exercise the right of suffrage in the choice of rulers, and the making of laws?

And what we ask is the power against which the people, not only of this country, but of almost all Europe, are called upon to array themselves, and the encroachment on their rights, they are summoned to resist? Is it not emphatically the power of monopoly, and the encroachment of corporate privileges of every kind, which the cupidity of the rich engenders to the injury of the poor?

It was to guard against the encroachments of power, the insatiate ambition of wealth that this government was instituted, by the people themselves. But the objects which call for the peculiar jealousy and watchfulness of the people are not now what they once were. The cautions of the early writers in favour of the liberties of mankind have in some measure become obsolete and inapplicable. We are menaced by our old enemies, avarice and ambition, under a new name and form. The tyrant is changed from a steel-clad feudal baron, or a minor despot, at the head of thousands of ruffian followers, to a mighty civil gentleman, who comes mincing and bowing to the people with a quill behind his ear, at the head of countless millions of magnificent *promises*. He promises to make everybody rich; he promises to pave cities with gold; and he promises to pay. In short he is made up of promises. He will do wonders, such as never were seen or heard of, provided the people will only allow him to make his promises equal to silver and gold, and human labour, and grant him the exclusive benefits of all the great blessings he intends to confer on them. He is the sly, selfish, grasping and insatiable tyrant the people are now to guard against. A CONCENTRATED MONEY POWER; a usurper in the disguise of a benefactor; an agent exercising privileges which his principal never possessed; an impostor who, while he affects to wear chains, is placed above those who are free; a chartered libertine, that pretends to be manacled only that he may the more safely pick our pockets, and lord it over our rights. This is the enemy we are now to encounter and overcome, before we can expect to enjoy the substantial realities of freedom.

[*1834*]

ASSOCIATED EFFORT

Some days ago, we observed in one of the newpapers a paragraph stating that a meeting of mechanics and labourers was about to be held in this city for the purpose of adopting measures of concerted or combined action against the practice, which we have reason to believe exists to a very great extent, of paying them in the uncurrent notes of distant or suspected banks. No such meeting, however, as far as we can learn, has yet been held. We hope it soon will be; for the object is a good one, and there is no other way of resisting the rapacious and extortionate custom of employers paying their journeymen and laborers in depreciated paper half so effectual as combination.

There are some journalists who affect to entertain great horror of combinations, considering them as utterly adverse to the principles of free trade; and it is frequently recommended to make them penal by law. Our notions of free trade were acquired in a different school, and dispose us to leave men entirely at liberty to effect a proper object either by concerted or individual action. The character of combinations, in our view, depends entirely upon the intrinsic character of the end which is aimed at. In the subject under consideration, the end proposed is good beyond all possibility of question. There is high warrant for saying that the *labourer is worthy of his hire;* but the employer, who takes advantage of his necessities and defencelessness to pay him in a depreciated substitute for money, does not give him his hire; he does not perform his engagement with him; he filches from the poor man a part of his hard-earned wages, and is guilty of a miserable fraud. Who shall say that this sneaking species of extortion ought not to be prevented? Who will say that separate individual action is adequate to that end? There is no one who will make so rash an assertion.

The only effectual mode of doing away with the evil is by attacking it with the great instrument of the rights of the poor — *associated effort.* There is but one bulwark behind which mechanics and labourers may safely rally to oppose a common enemy, who, if they ventured singly into the field against him, would cut them to pieces: that bulwark is the *Principle of Combination.* We would advise them to take refuge behind it only in extreme cases, because in their collisions with their employers, as in those between nations, the manifold evils of a siege are experienced, more or less, by both parties, and are therefore to be incurred only in extreme emergencies.

But the evil of being habitually paid in a depreciated substitute for money; of being daily cheated out of a portion of the just fruits of honest toil; of having a slice continually clipped from the hard-earned crust; is one of great moment, and is worthy of such an effort as we propose.

[*1836*]

RICHARD HENRY DANA

[1815–1882]

HE CAME from one of the leading families of Massachusetts. His father, also named Richard Henry, was an able literary essayist and an independent aristocrat. Richard Henry the younger was born and brought up in Cambridge. He entered Harvard in 1831, but left after two years because of illness and eye trouble. To recover his health he sailed as a common seaman on the brig *Pilgrim* on a voyage round Cape Horn. When he returned to Boston, two years later, he was robust and vigorous. He re-entered Harvard and was graduated at the head of his class in 1837. He then turned to the study of the law, but at the same time began to write his reminiscences of adventure on the high sea. In 1840, the year in which he was admitted to the bar, he published his *Two Years before the Mast*. An exciting and colorful narrative, it was also a strong plea for justice for the sailor. Dana had achieved the extraordinary feat of writing about life on a ship from the point of view of the forecastle. There have been many such books since then; there had been few previously. The sailor had been completely at the mercy of the officers and had lived and worked under degrading conditions. Dana's book helped to prepare public opinion for the legislative and trade-union drives which eventually improved the sailor's lot. (Ten years later, in his narrative *White-Jacket*, Herman Melville exposed the shocking treatment of the seamen on a man-of-war.) Dana's sympathy for the underdog was subsequently manifested in his work for the anti-slavery movement. From 1861 to 1866 he was U. S. Attorney for Massachusetts. He died of pneumonia in Rome while pursuing his studies in international law.

---

from

TWO YEARS BEFORE THE MAST

[THE FLOGGING]

For several days the captain seemed very much out of humor. Nothing went right or fast enough for him. He quarrelled with the cook, and threatened to flog him for throwing wood on deck; and had a dispute with the mate about reeving a Spanish burton; the mate saying that he was right, and had been taught how to do it by a man *who was a sailor!* This the captain took in dudgeon, and they were at swords' points at once. But his displeasure was chiefly turned against a large, heavy-moulded fellow from the Middle States, who was called Sam. This man hesitated in his speech, and was rather slow in his motions, but was a pretty good sailor, and always seemed to do his best; but the captain took a dislike to him, thought he was surly, and lazy; and " if you once give a dog a bad name " — as the sailor-phrase is — " he may as well jump overboard." The captain found fault with everything this man did, and hazed him for dropping a marlin-spike from the main-yard, where he was at work. This, of course, was an accident, but it was set down against him. The captain was on board all day Friday, and everything went on hard and disagreeably. " The more you drive a man, the less he will do," was as true with us as with any other people. We worked late Friday night, and were turned-to early Saturday morning. About ten o'clock the captain ordered our new officer, Russell, who by this time had become thoroughly disliked by all the crew, to get the gig ready to take him ashore. John, the Swede, was sitting in the boat alongside, and Russell and myself were standing by the main hatchway, waiting for the captain, who was down in the hold, where the crew were at work, when he heard his voice raised in violent dispute with somebody, whether it was with the mate, or one of the crew, I could not tell; and then came blows and scuffling. I ran to the side and beckoned to John, who came up, and we leaned down the hatchway; and though we could see no one, yet we knew that the captain had the advantage, for his voice was loud and clear —

" You see your condition! You see your condition! Will you ever give me any more of your *jaw*? " No answer; and then came wrestling and heaving, as though the man was trying to turn him. " You may as well keep still, for I have got you," said the captain. Then came the question, " Will you ever give me any more of your jaw? "

" I never gave you any, sir," said Sam; for it was his voice that we heard, though low and half choked.

" That's not what I ask you. Will you ever be impudent to me again? "

" I never have been, sir," said Sam.

" Answer my question, or I'll make a spread eagle of you! I'll flog you."

" I'm no negro slave," said Sam.

"Then I'll make you one," said the captain; and he came to the hatchway, and sprang on deck, threw off his coat, and rolling up his sleeves, called out to the mate — "Seize that man up, Mr. A——! Seize him up! Make a spread eagle of him! I'll teach you all who is master aboard!"

The crew and officers followed the captain up the hatchway, and after repeated orders the mate laid hold of Sam, who made no resistance, and carried him to the gangway.

"What are you going to flog that man for, sir?" said John, the Swede, to the captain.

Upon hearing this, the captain turned upon him, but knowing him to be quick and resolute, he ordered the steward to bring the irons, and calling upon Russell to help him, went up to John.

"Let me alone," said John. "I'm willing to be put in irons. You need not use any force"; and putting out his hands, the captain slipped the irons on, and sent him aft to the quarter-deck. Sam by this time was *seized up*, as it is called, that is, placed against the shrouds, with his wrists made fast to the shrouds, his jacket off, and his back exposed. The captain stood on the break of the deck, a few feet from him, and a little raised, so as to have a good swing at him, and held in his hand the bight of a thick, strong rope. The officers stood round, and the crew grouped together in the waist. All these preparations made me feel sick and almost faint, angry and excited as I was. A man — a human being, made in God's likeness — fastened up and flogged like a beast! A man, too, whom I had lived with and eaten with for months, and knew almost as well as a brother. The first and almost uncontrollable impulse was resistance. But what was to be done? The time for it had gone by. The two best men were fast, and there were only two beside myself, and a small boy of ten or twelve years of age. And then there were (beside the captain) three officers, steward, agent, and clerk. But beside the numbers, what is there for sailors to do? If they resist, it is mutiny; and if they succeed, and take the vessel, it is piracy. If they ever yield again, their punishment must come; and if they do not yield, they are pirates for life. If a sailor resist his commander, he resists the law, and piracy or submission are his only alternatives. Bad as it was, it must be borne. It is what a sailor ships for. Swinging the rope over his head, and bending his body so as to give it full force, the captain brought it down upon the poor fellow's back. Once, twice, — six times. "Will you ever give me any more of your jaw?" The man writhed with pain, but said not a word. Three times more. This was too much, and he muttered something which I could not hear; this brought as many more as the man could stand; when the captain ordered him to be cut down, and to go forward.

"Now for you," said the captain, making up to John and taking his irons off. As soon as he was loose, he ran forward to the forecastle. "Bring that man aft," shouted the captain. The second mate, who had been a shipmate of John's, stood still in the waist, and the mate walked slowly forward; but our third officer, anxious to show his zeal, sprang forward over the windlass, and laid hold of John; but he soon threw him from him. At this moment I would have given worlds for the power to help the poor fellow; but it was all in vain. The captain stood on the quarter-deck, bare-headed, his eyes flashing with rage, and his face as red as blood, swinging the rope, and calling out to his officers, "Drag him aft! — Lay hold of him! I'll *sweeten* him!" etc. The mate now went forward and told John quietly to go aft; and he, seeing resistance in vain, threw the blackguard third mate from him; said he would go aft of himself; that they should not drag him; and went up to the gangway and held out his hands; but as soon as the captain began to make him fast, the indignity was too much, and he began to resist; but the mate and Russell holding him, he was soon seized up. When he was made fast, he turned to the captain, who stood turning up his sleeves and getting ready for the blow, and asked him what he was to be flogged for. "Have I ever refused my duty, sir? Have you ever known me to hang back, or to be insolent, or not to know my work?"

"No," said the captain, "it is not that that I flog you for; I flog you for your interference — for asking questions."

"Can't a man ask a question here without being flogged?"

"No," shouted the captain; "nobody shall open his mouth aboard this vessel, but myself"; and he began laying the blows upon his back, swinging half round between each blow, to give it full effect. As he went on, his passion increased, and he danced about the deck, calling out as he swung the rope, — "If you want to know what I flog you for, I'll tell you. It's because I like to do it! — because I like to do it! — It suits me! That's what I do it for!"

The man writhed under the pain, until he could endure it no longer, when he called out, with an exclamation more common among foreigners than with us — "Oh, Jesus Christ! Oh, Jesus Christ!"

"Don't call on Jesus Christ," shouted the captain; "*he can't help you. Call on Captain T——*. He's the man! He can help you! Jesus Christ can't help you now!"

At these words, which I never shall forget, my blood ran cold. I could look on no longer. Disgusted, sick, and horror-struck, I turned away and leaned over the rail, and looked down into the water. A few rapid thoughts of my own situation, and of the prospect of future revenge, crossed my mind; but the falling of the blows and the cries of the man called me back at once. At length they ceased, and turning round, I found that the mate, at a signal from the captain, had cut him down. Almost doubled up with pain, the man walked slowly forward, and went down into the forecastle. Every one else stood still at his post, while the captain, swelling with rage and with the importance of his achievement, walked the quarter-deck, and at each turn, as he came forward, calling out to us, — "You see your condition! You see where I've got you all, and you know what to expect!" — "You've been mistaken in me — you didn't know what I was! Now you know what I am!" — "I'll make you toe the mark, every soul of you, or I'll flog you all, fore and aft, from the boy up!" — "You've got a driver over you! Yes, a *slave-driver — a negro-driver!* I'll see who'll tell me he isn't a negro slave!" With this and the like matter, equally calculated to quiet us, and to allay any apprehensions of future trouble, he entertained us for about ten minutes, when he went below. Soon after, John came aft, with his bare back covered with stripes and wales in every direction, and dreadfully swollen, and asked the steward to ask the captain to let him have some salve, or balsam, to put upon it. "No," said the captain, who heard him from below; "tell him to put his shirt on; that's the best thing for him; and pull me ashore in the boat. Nobody is going to lay-up on board this vessel." He then called to Mr. Russell to take those two men and two others in the boat, and pull him ashore. I went for one. The two men could hardly bend their backs, and the captain called to them to "give way," "give way!" but finding they did their best, he let them alone. The agent was in the stern sheets, but during the whole pull — a league or more — not a word was spoken. We landed; the captain, agent, and officer went up to the house, and left us with the boat. I, and the man with me, stayed near the boat, while John and Sam walked slowly away, and sat down on the rocks. They talked some time together, but at length separated, each sitting alone. I had some fears of John. He was a foreigner, and violently tempered, and under suffering; and he had his knife with him, and the captain was to come down alone to the boat. But nothing happened; and we went quietly on board. The captain was probably armed, and if either of them had lifted a hand against him, they would have had nothing before them but flight, and starvation in the woods of California, or capture by the soldiers and Indian blood-hounds, whom the offer of twenty dollars would have set upon them.

After the day's work was done, we went down into the forecastle, and ate our plain supper; but not a word was spoken. It was Saturday night; but there was no song — no " sweethearts and wives." A gloom was over everything. The two men lay in their berths, groaning with pain, and we all turned in, but for myself, not to sleep. A sound coming now and then from the berths of the two men showed that they were awake, as awake they must have been, for they could hardly lie in one posture a moment; the dim, swinging lamp of the forecastle shed its light over the dark hole in which we lived; and many and various reflections and purposes coursed through my mind. I thought of our situation, living under a tyranny; of the character of the country we were in; of the length of the voyage, and of the uncertainty attending our return to America; and then, if we should return, of the prospect of obtaining justice and satisfaction for these poor men; and vowed that if God should ever give me the means, I would do something to redress the grievances and relieve the sufferings of that poor class of beings, of whom I then was one.

[*1840*]

JOHN GREENLEAF WHITTIER

[1807–1892]

THE AVERAGE American thinks of Whittier as the author of " Snow-Bound,"
" Barbara Frietchie," and " The Barefoot Boy." But it was not merely for
such poetry that Whittier was known in his own day. In the quarter-century
before the Civil War he was *the* anti-slavery poet of America — the prophet
of the abolitionists, the scourge of the compromising clergy, the champion of
law-breakers on behalf of freedom. William Lloyd Garrison was the man
who turned him in that direction. In 1826 Whittier's first poem was published in a newspaper which was then edited by Garrison. The latter visited
the young poet and found a Quaker farm-boy who had been given little
schooling and whose interest in verse was objected to by a stern and pious
father. Garrison befriended and encouraged him. The result we know: his
profoundly religious impulses acquired a valid outlet in the crusade for
liberty and racial equality. After the Civil War he retired from public life
and, to the disappointment of many, ignored the newer political and social
movements. In fact, he proved to be extremely conservative regarding labor
questions. In this period he wrote some of his popular hymns, nature poems,
and narratives. Today, however, there are critics who believe that his anti-
slavery poems, as a group, form the most valuable and significant section of
his total work.

STANZAS FOR THE TIMES

*The " Times " referred to were those evil times of the pro-slavery meeting
in Faneuil Hall, August 21, 1835, in which a demand was made for the suppression of free speech, lest it should endanger the foundation of commercial
society.*

> Is this the land our fathers loved,
>   The freedom which they toiled to win?
> Is this the soil whereon they moved?

226

Are these the graves they slumber in?
Are we the sons by whom are borne
The mantles which the dead have worn?

And shall we crouch above these graves,
    With craven soul and fettered lip?
Yoke in with marked and branded slaves,
    And tremble at the driver's whip?
Bend to the earth our pliant knees,
And speak but as our masters please?

Shall outraged Nature cease to feel?
    Shall Mercy's tears no longer flow?
Shall ruffian threats of cord and steel,
    The dungeon's gloom, the assassin's blow,
Turn back the spirit roused to save
The Truth, our Country, and the slave?

Of human skulls that shrine was made,
    Round which the priests of Mexico
Before their loathsome idol prayed;
    Is Freedom's altar fashioned so?
And must we yield to Freedom's God,
As offering meet, the negro's blood?

Shall tongue be mute, when deeds are wrought
    Which well might shame extremest hell?
Shall freemen lock the indignant thought?
    Shall Pity's bosom cease to swell?
Shall Honor bleed? — shall Truth succumb?
Shall pen, and press, and soul be dumb?

No; by each spot of haunted ground,
    Where Freedom weeps her children's fall;
By Plymouth's rock, and Bunker's mound;
    By Griswold's stained and shattered wall;
By Warren's ghost, by Langdon's shade;
By all the memories of our dead!

By their enlarging souls, which burst
　　The bands and fetters round them set;
By the free Pilgrim spirit nursed
　　Within our inmost bosoms, yet,
By all above, around, below,
Be ours the indignant answer, — No!

No; guided by our country's laws,
　　For truth, and right, and suffering man,
Be ours to strive in Freedom's cause,
　　As Christians may, as freemen can!
Still pouring on unwilling ears
That truth oppression only fears.

What! shall we guard our neighbor still,
　　While woman shrieks beneath his rod,
And while he tramples down at will
　　The image of a common God?
Shall watch and ward be round him set,
Of Northern nerve and bayonet?

And shall we know and share with him
　　The danger and the growing shame?
And see our Freedom's light grow dim,
　　Which should have filled the world with flame?
And, writhing, feel, where'er we turn,
A world's reproach around us burn?

Is't not enough that this is borne?
　　And asks our haughty neighbor more?
Must fetters which his slaves have worn
　　Clank round the Yankee farmer's door?
Must he be told, beside his plough,
What he must speak, and when, and how?

Must he be told his freedom stands
　　On Slavery's dark foundations strong;
On breaking hearts and fettered hands,
　　On robbery, and crime, and wrong?

That all his fathers taught is vain, —
That Freedom's emblem is the chain?

Its life, its soul, from slavery drawn!
   False, foul, profane! Go, teach as well
Of holy Truth from Falsehood born!
   Of Heaven refreshed by airs from Hell!
Of Virtue in the arms of Vice!
Of Demons planting Paradise!

Rail on, then, brethren of the South,
   Ye shall not hear the truth the less;
No seal is on the Yankee's mouth,
   No fetter on the Yankee's press!
From our Green Mountains to the sea,
One voice shall thunder, We are free!

[1835]

CLERICAL OPPRESSORS

In the report of the celebrated pro-slavery meeting in Charleston, S. C., on the 4th of the ninth month, 1835, published in the Courier *of that city, it is stated: " The clergy of all denominations attended in a body, lending their sanction to the proceedings, and adding by their presence to the impressive character of the scene! "*

Just God! and these are they
Who minister at thine altar, God of Right!
Men who their hands with prayer and blessing lay
   On Israel's Ark of light!

What! preach and kidnap men?
Give thanks, and rob thy own afflicted poor?
Talk of thy glorious liberty, and then
   Bolt hard the captive's door?

What! servants of thy own
Merciful Son, who came to seek and save
The homeless and the outcast, fettering down
   The tasked and plundered slave!

Pilate and Herod, friends!
Chief priests and rulers, as of old, combine!
Just God and holy! is that church, which lends
   Strength to the spoiler, thine?

Paid hypocrites, who turn
Judgment aside, and rob the Holy Book
Of those high words of truth which search and burn
   In warning and rebuke;

Feed fat, ye locusts, feed!
And, in your tasselled pulpits, thank the Lord
That, from the toiling bondman's utter need,
   Ye pile your own full board.

How long, O Lord! how long
Shall such a priesthood barter truth away,
And in Thy name, for robbery and wrong
   At Thy own altars pray?

Is not Thy hand stretched forth
Visibly in the heavens, to awe and smite?
Shall not the living God of all the earth,
   And heaven above, do right?

Woe, then, to all who grind
Their brethren of a common Father down!
To all who plunder from the immortal mind
   Its bright and glorious crown!

Woe to the priesthood! woe
To those whose hire is with the price of blood;
Perverting, darkening, changing, as they go,
   The searching truths of God!

Their glory and their might
Shall perish; and their very names shall be
Vile before all the people, in the light
Of a world's liberty.

Oh, speed the moment on
When Wrong shall cease, and Liberty and Love
And Truth and Right throughout the earth be known
As in their home above.

[*1836*]

MASSACHUSETTS TO VIRGINIA

Written on reading an account of the proceedings of the citizens of Norfolk, Va., in reference to George Latimer, the alleged fugitive slave, who was seized in Boston without warrant at the request of James B. Grey, of Norfolk, claiming to be his master. The case caused great excitement North and South, and led to the presentation of a petition to Congress, signed by more than fifty thousand citizens of Massachusetts, calling for such laws and proposed amendments to the Constitution as should relieve the Commonwealth from all further participation in the crime of oppression. George Latimer himself was finally given free papers for the sum of four hundred dollars.

The blast from Freedom's Northern hills, upon its Southern way,
Bears greeting to Virginia from Massachusetts Bay:
No word of haughty challenging, nor battle bugle's peal,
Nor steady tread of marching files, nor clang of horsemen's steel.

No trains of deep-mouthed cannon along our highways go;
Around our silent arsenals untrodden lies the snow;
And to the land-breeze of our ports, upon their errands far,
A thousand sails of commerce swell, but none are spread for war.

We hear thy threats, Virginia! thy stormy words and high
Swell harshly on the Southern winds which melt along our sky;
Yet not one brown, hard hand forgoes its honest labor here,
No hewer of our mountain oaks suspends his axe in fear.

Wild are the waves which lash the reefs along St. George's bank;
Cold on the shores of Labrador the fog lies white and dank;
Through storm, and wave, and blinding mist, stout are the hearts
    which man
The fishing-smacks of Marblehead, the seaboats of Cape Ann.

The cold north light and wintry sun glare on their icy forms,
Bent grimly o'er their straining lines or wrestling with the storms;
Free as the winds they drive before, rough as the waves they roam,
They laugh to scorn the slaver's threat against their rocky home.

What means the Old Dominion? Hath she forgot the day
When o'er her conquered valleys swept the Briton's steel array?
How side by side, with sons of hers, the Massachusetts men
Encountered Tarleton's charge of fire, and stout Cornwallis, then?

Forgets she how the Bay State, in answer to the call
Of her old House of Burgesses, spoke out from Faneuil Hall?
When, echoing back her Henry's cry, came pulsing on each breath
Of Northern winds the thrilling sounds of " Liberty or Death! "

What asks the Old Dominion? If now her sons have proved
False to their fathers' memory, false to the faith they loved;
If she can scoff at Freedom, and its great charter spurn,
Must we of Massachusetts from truth and duty turn?

We hunt your bondmen, flying from Slavery's hateful hell;
Our voices, at your bidding, take up the bloodhound's yell;
We gather, at your summons, above our fathers' graves,
From Freedom's holy altar-horns to tear your wretched slaves!

Thank God! not yet so vilely can Massachusetts bow;
The spirit of her early time is with her even now;
Dream not because her Pilgrim blood moves slow and calm and cool,
She thus can stoop her chainless neck, a sister's slave and tool!

All that a sister State should do, all that a free State may,
Heart, hand, and purse we proffer, as in our early day;

But that one dark loathsome burden ye must stagger with alone,
And reap the bitter harvest which ye yourselves have sown!

Hold, while ye may, your struggling slaves, and burden God's free air
With woman's shriek beneath the lash, and manhood's wild despair;
Cling closer to the " cleaving curse " that writes upon your plains
The blasting of Almighty wrath against a land of chains.

Still shame your gallant ancestry, the cavaliers of old,
By watching round the shambles where human flesh is sold;
Gloat o'er the new-born child, and count his market value, when
The maddened mother's cry of woe shall pierce the slaver's den!

Lower than plummet soundeth, sink the Virginia name;
Plant, if ye will, your fathers' graves with rankest weeds of shame;
Be, if ye will, the scandal of God's fair universe;
We wash our hands forever of your sin and shame and curse.

A voice from lips whereon the coal from Freedom's shrine hath been,
Thrilled, as but yesterday, the hearts of Berkshire's mountain men:
The echoes of that solemn voice are sadly lingering still
In all our sunny valleys, on every windswept hill.

And when the prowling man-thief came hunting for his prey
Beneath the very shadow of Bunker's shaft of gray,
How, through the free lips of the son, the father's warning spoke;
How, from its bonds of trade and sect, the Pilgrim city broke!

A hundred thousand right arms were lifted up on high,
A hundred thousand voices sent back their loud reply;
Through the thronged towns of Essex the startling summons rang,
And up from bench and loom and wheel her young mechanics sprang!

The voice of free, broad Middlesex, of thousands as of one,
The shaft of Bunker calling to that of Lexington;
From Norfolk's ancient villages, from Plymouth's rocky bound
To where Nantucket feels the arms of ocean close her round;

From rich and rural Worcester, where through the calm repose
Of cultured vales and fringing woods the gentle Nashua flows,

To where Wachusett's wintry blasts the mountain larches stir,
Swelled up to Heaven the thrilling cry of " God save Latimer! "

And sandy Barnstable rose up, wet with the salt sea spray;
And Bristol sent her answering shout down Narragansett Bay!
Along the broad Connecticut old Hampden felt the thrill,
And the cheer of Hampshire's woodmen swept down from Holyoke Hill.

The voice of Massachusetts! Of her free sons and daughters,
Deep calling unto deep aloud, the sound of many waters!
Against the burden of that voice what tyrant power shall stand?
No fetters in the Bay State! No slave upon her land!

Look to it well, Virginians! In calmness we have borne,
In answer to our faith and trust, your insult and your scorn;
You've spurned our kindest counsels; you've hunted for our lives;
And shaken round our hearths and homes your manacles and gyves!

We wage no war, we lift no arm, we fling no torch within
The fire-damps of the quaking mine beneath your soil of sin;
We leave ye with your bondmen, to wrestle, while ye can,
With the strong upward tendencies and godlike soul of man!

But for us and for our children, the vow which we have given
For freedom and humanity is registered in heaven;
No slave-hunt in our borders, — no pirate on our strand!
No fetters in the Bay State, — no slave upon our land!

[*1843*]

THE PEACE OF EUROPE

" Great peace in Europe! Order reigns
From Tiber's hills to Danube's plains! "
So say her kings and priests; so say
The lying prophets of our day.

Go lay to earth a listening ear;
The tramp of measured marches hear;
The rolling of the cannon's wheel,
The shotted musket's murderous peal,
The night alarm, the sentry's call,
The quick-eared spy in hut and hall!
From Polar sea and tropic fen
The dying-groans of exiled men!
The bolted cell, the galley's chains,
The scaffold smoking with its stains!
Order, the hush of brooding slaves!
Peace, in the dungeon-vaults and graves!

O Fisher! of the world-wide net,
With meshes in all waters set,
Whose fabled keys of heaven and hell
Bolt hard the patriot's prison-cell,
And open wide the banquet-hall,
Where kings and priests hold carnival!
Weak vassal tricked in royal guise,
Boy Kaiser with thy lip of lies;
Base gambler for Napoleon's crown,
Barnacle on his dead renown!
Thou, Bourbon Neapolitan,
Crowned scandal, loathed of God and man;
And thou, fell Spider of the North!
Stretching thy giant feelers forth,
Within whose web the freedom dies
Of nations eaten up like flies!
Speak, Prince and Kaiser, Priest and Czar!
If this be Peace, pray what is War?

White Angel of the Lord! unmeet
That soil accursed for thy pure feet.
Never in Slavery's desert flows
The fountain of thy charmed repose;
No tyrant's hand thy chaplet weaves
Of lilies and of olive-leaves;
Not with the wicked shalt thou dwell,

235

Thus saith the Eternal Oracle;
Thy home is with the pure and free!
Stern herald of thy better day,
Before thee, to prepare thy way,
The Baptist Shade of Liberty,
Gray, scarred and hairy-robed, must press
With bleeding feet the wilderness!
Oh that its voice might pierce the ear
Of princes, trembling while they hear
A cry as of the Hebrew seer:
Repent! God's kingdom draweth near!

[*1852*]

FOR RIGHTEOUSNESS' SAKE

Inscribed to friends under arrest for treason against the slave power. [*Originally entitled* Lines.]

The age is dull and mean. Men creep,
    Not walk; with blood too pale and tame
    To pay the debt they owe to shame;
Buy cheap, sell dear; eat, drink, and sleep
    Down-pillowed, deaf to moaning want;
Pay tithes for soul-insurance; keep
    Six days to Mammon, one to Cant.

In such a time, give thanks to God
    That somewhat of the holy rage
    With which the prophets in their age
On all its decent seemings trod,
    Has set your feet upon the lie
That man and ox and soul and clod
    Are market stock to sell and buy!

The hot words from your lips, my own,
    To caution trained, might not repeat;

236

But if some tares among the wheat
Of generous thought and deed were sown,
　　No common wrong provoked your zeal;
The silken gauntlet that is thrown
　　In such a quarrel rings like steel.

The brave old strife the fathers saw
　　For Freedom calls for men again
　　Like those who battled not in vain
For England's Charter, Alfred's law;
　　And right of speech and trial just
Wage in your name their ancient war
　　With venal courts and perjured trust.

God's ways seem dark, but, soon or late,
　　They touch the shining hills of day;
　　The evil cannot brook delay,
The good can well afford to wait.
　　Give ermined knaves their hour of crime;
Ye have the future grand and great,
　　The safe appeal of Truth to Time!

[*1855*]

---

from

THE PROCLAMATION

President Lincoln's proclamation of emancipation was issued January 1, 1863.

O dark, sad millions, patiently and dumb
Waiting for God, your hour at last has come,
　　And freedom's song
Breaks the long silence of your night of wrong!

Arise and flee! shake off the vile restraint
Of ages; but, like Ballymena's saint,
　　The oppressor spare,
Heap only on his head the coals of prayer.

237

Go forth, like him! like him return again,
To bless the land whereon in bitter pain
   Ye toiled at first,
And heal with freedom what your slavery cursed.
[*1863*]

WILLIAM ELLERY CHANNING

[1780–1842]

His BACKGROUND was eminently respectable: he was born in Newport, Rhode Island, of a well-placed, comfortably prosperous family, brought up in a federalist atmosphere, and educated at Harvard. He studied theology, was ordained in 1803, and became minister of the Federal Street Church in Boston. Who could have anticipated that he would go over to the " Jacobins "? He began his leftward swing by allying himself with the recently emerged group called the Unitarians — not because he was worried about the idea of the Trinity, but because he loathed the Calvinistic concept of man as essentially wicked. His belief in the innate goodness of man led him to the humanitarian movements. It goes without saying that he was opposed to slavery. More than that, he attacked wage slavery, favored wide public education, became a leader of the anti-war and temperance groups. His gentle and generous spirit was well expressed in his essays and sermons. Eventually he became the foremost representative of the Unitarians, and as such he influenced Emerson, Longfellow, Lowell, and many others who were rebelling against Calvinism and creating a social and literary philosophy defending the natural dignity and value of the individual human being. Thus he was one of the ideological forerunners of romanticism. His essay " Honor Due to All Men " reveals how " he breathed into theology a humane spirit." The essay " On the Elevation of the Laboring Classes " is worth recalling not only because it is a noble utterance, but because it is typical of the newly aroused interest in the life of the masses.

---

from

HONOR DUE TO ALL MEN

Among the many and inestimable blessings of Christianity, I regard as not the least the new sentiment with which it teaches man to look upon his fellow-beings; the new interest which it awakens in us towards everything human; the new importance which it gives to the soul; the new relation which it establishes between man and man. In this respect it began a mighty revolution, which has been silently spreading itself through society, and which, I believe, is not to stop until new ties shall have taken the place of those which have hitherto, in the main, connected the human race. Christianity has as yet but begun its work of reformation. Under its influences a new order of society is advancing, surely though slowly; and this beneficent change it is to accomplish in no small measure by revealing to men their own nature, and teaching them to " honor all " who partake it.

As yet Christianity has done little, compared with what it is to do, in establishing the true bond of union between man and man. The old bonds of society still continue in a great degree. They are instinct, interest, force. The true tie, which is mutual respect, calling forth mutual, growing, never-failing acts of love, is as yet little known. A new revelation, if I may so speak, remains to be made; or rather, the truths of the old revelation in regard to the greatness of human nature are to be brought out from obscurity and neglect. The soul is to be regarded with a religious reverence hitherto unfelt; and the solemn claims of every being to whom this divine principle is imparted are to be established on the ruins of those pernicious principles, both in church and state, which have so long divided mankind into the classes of the abject many and the self-exalting few. . . .

It may be said that Christianity has done much to awaken benevolence, and that it has taught men to call one another brethren. Yes, to *call* one another so; but has it as yet given the true feeling of brotherhood? We undoubtedly feel ourselves to be all of one race, and this is well. We trace ourselves up to one pair, and feel the same blood flowing in our veins. But do we understand our spiritual brotherhood? Do we feel ourselves to be derived from one Heavenly Parent, in whose image we are all made, and whose perfection we may constantly approach? Do we feel that there is one divine life in our own and in all souls? This seems to me the only true bond of man to man. Here is a tie more sacred, more enduring, than all the ties of this earth. Is it felt, and do we in consequence truly honor one another?

Sometimes, indeed, we see men giving sincere, profound, and almost unmeasured respect to their fellow-creatures; but to whom? To great men; to men distinguished by a broad line from the multitude; to men pre-eminent by genius, force of character, daring effort, high station, brilliant success. To such honor is given; but this is not to " honor all men "; and the homage paid to such is generally unfriendly to that

Christian estimate of human beings for which I am now pleading. The great are honored at the expense of their race. They absorb and concentrate the world's admiration, and their less gifted fellow-beings are thrown by their brightness into a deeper shade, and passed over with a colder contempt. Now I have no desire to derogate from the honor paid to great men, but I say, Let them not rise by the depression of the multitude. I say that great men, justly regarded, exalt our estimate of the human race, and bind us to the multitude of men more closely; and when they are not so regarded, when they are converted into idols, when they serve to wean our interest from ordinary men, they corrupt us, they sever the sacred bond of humanity which should attach us to all, and our characters become vitiated by our very admiration of greatness. The true view of great men is that they are only examples and manifestations of our common nature, showing what belongs to all souls, though unfolded as yet only in a few. The light which shines from them is, after all, but a faint revelation of the power which is treasured up in every human being. They are not prodigies, not miracles, but natural developments of the human soul. They are indeed as men among children, but the children have a principle of growth which leads to manhood.

That great men and the multitude of minds are of one family is apparent, I think, in the admiration which the great inspire into the multitude. A sincere, enlightened admiration always springs from something congenial in him who feels it with him who inspires it. He that can understand and delight in greatness was created to partake of it; the germ is in him; and sometimes this admiration, in what we deem inferior minds, discovers a nobler spirit than belongs to the great man who awakens it; for sometimes the great man is so absorbed in his own greatness as to admire no other; and I should not hesitate to say that a common mind, which is yet capable of a generous admiration, is destined to rise higher than the man of eminent capacities, who can enjoy no power or excellence but his own. When I hear of great men, I wish not to separate them from their race, but to blend them with it. I esteem it no small benefit of the philosophy of mind that it teaches us that the elements of the greatest thoughts of the man of genius exist in his humbler brethren, and that the faculties which the scientific exert in the profoundest discoveries are precisely the same with those which common men employ in the daily labors of life.

To show the grounds on which the obligation to honor all men rests,

I might take a minute survey of that human nature which is common to all, and set forth its claims to reverence. But, leaving this wide range, I observe that there is one principle of the soul which makes all men essentially equal, which places all on a level as to means of happiness, which may place in the first rank of human beings those who are the most depressed in worldly condition, and which therefore gives the most depressed a title to interest and respect. I refer to the sense of duty, to the power of discerning and doing right, to the moral and religious principle, to the inward monitor which speaks in the name of God, to the capacity of virtue or excellence. This is the great gift of God. We can conceive no greater. In seraph and archangel we can conceive no higher energy than the power of virtue, or the power of forming themselves after the will and moral perfections of God. This power breaks down all barriers between the seraph and the lowest human being; it makes them brethren. Whoever has derived from God this perception and capacity of rectitude has a bond of union with the spiritual world stronger than all the ties of nature. He possesses a principle which, if he is faithful to it, must carry him forward forever, and insures to him the improvement and happiness of the highest order of beings.

It is this moral power which makes all men essentially equal, which annihilates all the distinctions of this world. Through this, the ignorant and the poor may become the greatest of the race; for the greatest is he who is most true to the principle of duty. It is not improbable that the noblest human beings are to be found in the least favored conditions of society, among those whose names are never uttered beyond the narrow circle in which they toil and suffer, who have but "two mites" to give away, who have perhaps not even that, but who "desire to be fed with the crumbs which fall from the rich man's table"; for in this class may be found those who have withstood the severest temptation, who have practised the most arduous duties, who have confided in God under the heaviest trials, who have been most wronged and have forgiven most; and these are the great, the exalted. It matters nothing what the particular duties are to which the individual is called, — how minute or obscure in their outward form. Greatness in God's sight lies, not in the extent of the sphere which is filled, or of the effect which is produced, but altogether in the power of virtue in the soul, in the energy with which God's will is chosen, with which trial is borne, and goodness loved and pursued. . . .

From these brief views of human nature and of Christianity, you will see the grounds of the solemn obligation of honoring all men, of attaching infinite importance to human nature, and of respecting it, even in its present infant, feeble, tottering state. This sentiment of honor or respect for human beings strikes me more and more as essential to the Christian character. I conceive that a more thorough understanding and a more faithful culture of this would do very much to carry forward the church and the world. In truth, I attach to this sentiment such importance that I measure by its progress the progress of society. I judge of public events very much by their bearing on this. I estimate political revolutions chiefly by their tendency to exalt men's conceptions of their nature, and to inspire them with respect for one another's claims. The present stupendous movements in Europe naturally suggest, and almost force upon me, this illustration of the importance which I have given to the sentiment enjoined in our text. Allow me to detain you a few moments on this topic.

What is it, then, I ask, which makes the present revolutionary movement abroad so interesting? I answer that I see in it the principle of respect for human nature and for the human race developing itself more powerfully, and this to me constitutes its chief interest. I see in it proofs, indications, that the mind is awakening to a consciousness of what it is, and of what it is made for. In this movement I see man becoming to himself a higher object. I see him attaining to the conviction of the equal and indestructible rights of every human being. I see the dawning of that great principle that the individual is not made to be the instrument of others, but to govern himself by an inward law, and to advance towards his proper perfection; that he belongs to himself and to God, and to no human superior. I know, indeed, that, in the present state of the world, these conceptions are exceedingly unsettled and obscure; and, in truth, little effort has hitherto been made to place them in a clear light, and to give them a definite and practical form in men's minds. The multitude know not with any distinctness what they want. Imagination, unschooled by reason and experience, dazzles them with bright but baseless visions. They are driven onward with a perilous violence, by a vague consciousness of not having found their element; by a vague yet noble faith in a higher good than they have attained; by impatience under restraints which they feel to be degrading. In this violence, however, there is nothing strange, nor ought it to discourage us. It is, I believe, universally true that great principles, in

243

their first development, manifest themselves irregularly. It is so in religion. In history we often see religion, especially after long depression, breaking out in vehemence and enthusiasm, sometimes stirring up bloody conflicts, and through struggles establishing a calmer empire over society. In like manner, political history shows us that men's consciousness of their rights and essential equality has at first developed itself passionately. Still the consciousness is a noble one, and the presage of a better social state.

Am I asked what I hope from the present revolutionary movements in Europe? I answer that I hope a good which includes all others, and which almost hides all others from my view. I hope the subversion of institutions by which the true bond between man and man has been more or less dissolved, by which the will of one or a few has broken down the will, the heart, the conscience of the many; and I hope that, in the place of these, are to grow up institutions which will express, cherish, and spread far and wide a just respect for human nature, which will strengthen in men a consciousness of their powers, duties, and rights, which will train the individual to moral and religious independence, which will propose as their end the elevation of all orders of the community, and which will give full scope to the best minds in this work of general improvement. I do not say that I expect it to be suddenly realized. The sun which is to bring on a brighter day is rising in thick and threatening clouds. Perhaps the minds of men were never more unquiet than at the present moment. Still I do not despair. That a higher order of ideas or principles is beginning to be unfolded; that a wider philanthropy is beginning to triumph over the distinctions of ranks and nations; that a new feeling of what is due to the ignorant, poor, and depraved has sprung up; that the right of every human being to such an education as shall call forth his best faculties and train him more and more to control himself is recognized as it never was before; and that government is more and more regarded as intended not to elevate the few but to guard the rights of all; that these great revolutions in principle have commenced and are spreading, who can deny? and to me they are prophetic of any improved condition of human nature and human affairs. — O, that this melioration might be accomplished without blood! As a Christian, I feel a misgiving when I rejoice in any good, however great, for which this fearful price has been paid. In truth, a good so won is necessarily imperfect and generally transient. War may subvert a despotism, but seldom builds up better institutions. Even when joined, as in our own history, with high principles, it inflames and leaves behind it passions which make liberty a feverish conflict of jealous parties, and which expose a people to the tyranny of faction under the forms of freedom. Few things impair men's reverence for human nature more than war; and did I not see other and holier influences than the sword working out the regeneration of the race, I should indeed despair.

[*1832*]

from

ON THE ELEVATION OF THE
LABORING CLASSES

A very common [prejudice] is that the many are not to be called to think, study, improve their minds, because a privileged few are intended by God to do their thinking for them. "Providence," it is said, "raises up superior minds, whose office it is to discover truth for the rest of the race. Thinking and manual toil are not meant to go together. The division of labor is a great law of nature. One man is to serve society by his head, another by his hands. Let each class keep to its proper work." These doctrines I protest against. I deny to any individual or class this monopoly of thought. Who among men can show God's commission to think for his brethren, to shape passively the intellect of the mass, to stamp his own image on them as if they were wax? As well might a few claim a monopoly of light and air, of seeing and breathing, as of thought. Is not the intellect as universal a gift as the organs of sight and respiration? Is not truth as freely spread abroad as the atmosphere or the sun's rays? Can we imagine that God's highest gifts of intelligence, imagination, and moral power were bestowed to provide only for animal wants? to be denied the natural means of growth, which is action? to be starved by drudgery? Were the mass of men made to be monsters? to grow only in a few organs and faculties, and to pine away and shrivel in others? or were they made to put forth all the powers of men, especially the best and most distinguishing? No man, not the lowest, is all hands, all bones and muscles. The mind is more essential to human nature, and more enduring, than the limbs; and was this made to lie dead? Is not thought the right and duty of all? Is not truth alike precious to all? Is not truth the natural aliment of the mind, as plainly as the wholesome grain is of the body? Is not the mind adapted to thought, as plainly as the eye to light, the ear to sound? Who dares to withhold it from its natural action, its natural element and joy? Undoubtedly some men are more gifted than others, and are marked out for more studious lives. But the work of such men is not to do others' thinking for them, but to help them to think more vigorously and effectually. Great minds are to make others great. Their superiority is to be used, not to break the multitude to intellectual vassalage, not to establish over them a spiritual tyranny, but to rouse them from lethargy, and to aid them to judge for themselves. The light and life which spring up in one soul are to be spread far and wide. Of all treasons against humanity, there is no one worse than his who employs great intellectual force to keep down the intellect of his less favored brother.

It is sometimes urged by those who consider the multitude as not intended to think, that at best they can learn but little, and that this is likely to harm rather than to do them good. "A little learning," we are told, "is a dangerous thing." "Shallow draughts" of knowledge are worse than ignorance. The mass of the people, it is said, can go to the bottom of nothing; and the result of stimulating them to thought will be the formation of a dangerous set of half-thinkers. To this argument I reply, first, that it has the inconvenience of proving too much; for, if valid, it shows that none of any class ought to think. For who, I would ask, can go to the bottom of anything? Whose "learning" is not "little"? Whose "draughts" of knowledge are not "shallow"? Who of us has fathomed the depths of a single product of nature or a single event in history? Who of us is not baffled by the mysteries in a grain of sand? How contracted the range of the widest intellect! But is our knowledge, because so little, of no worth? Are we to despise the lessons which are taught us in this nook of creation, in this narrow round of human experience, because an infinite universe stretches around us, which we have no means of exploring, and in which the earth, and sun, and planets, dwindle to a point? We should remember that the known, however little it may be, is in harmony with the boundless unknown, and a step towards it. We should remember, too, that the gravest truths may be gathered from a very narrow compass of information. God is revealed in his smallest work as truly as in his greatest. The principles of human nature may be studied better in a family than in the history of the world. The finite is a manifestation of the infinite. The great ideas of which I have formerly spoken are within the reach of every man who thirsts for truth, and seeks it with singleness of mind. I will only add that the laboring class are not now condemned to draughts of knowledge so shallow as to merit scorn. Many of them know more of the outward world than all the philosophers of antiquity; and Christianity has opened to them mysteries of the spiritual world which kings and prophets were not privileged to understand. And are they, then, to be doomed to spiritual inaction, as incapable of useful thought?

It is sometimes said that the multitude may think on the common business of life, but not on higher subjects, and especially on religion. This, it is said, must be received on authority; on this, men in general can form no judgment of their own. But this is the last subject on which the individual should be willing to surrender himself to others' dictation. In nothing has he so strong an interest. In nothing is it so important that his mind and heart should be alive and engaged. In nothing has he readier means of judging for himself. In nothing, as history shows, is he more likely to be led astray by such as assume the office of thinking for him. Religion is a subject open to all minds. Its great truths have their foundation in the soul itself, and their proofs surround us on all sides. God has not shut up the evidence of his being in a few books, written in a foreign language, and locked up in the libraries of colleges and philosophers; but has written his name on the heavens and on the earth, and even on the minutest animal and plant; and his word, taught by Jesus Christ, was not given to scribes and lawyers, but taught to the poor, to the mass of men, on mountains, in streets, and on the seashore. Let me not be told that the multitude do actually receive religion on authority, or on the word of others. I reply that a faith so received seems to me of little worth. The precious, the living, the effectual part of a poor man's faith is that of which he sees the reasonableness and excellence; that which approves itself to his intelligence, his conscience, his heart; that which answers to deep wants in his own soul, and of which he has the witness in his own inward and outward experience. All other parts of his belief, those which he takes on blind trust, and in which he sees no marks of truth and divinity, do him little or no good. Too often they do him harm, by perplexing his simple reason, by substituting the fictions and artificial systems of theologians for the plain precepts of love, and justice, and humility, and filial trust in God. As long as it was supposed that religion is to benefit the world by laying restraints, awakening fears, and acting as a part of the system of police, so long it was natural to rely on authority and tradition as the means of its propagation; so long it was desirable to stifle thought and inquiry on the subject. But now that we have learned that the true office of religion is to awaken pure and lofty sentiments, and to unite man to God by rational homage and enlightened love, there is something monstrous in placing religion beyond the thought and the study of the mass of the human race.

I proceed to another prejudice. It is objected that the distinction of ranks is essential to social order, and that this will be swept away by calling forth energy of thought in all men. This objection, indeed, though exceedingly insisted on in Europe, has nearly died out here; but still enough of it lingers among us to deserve consideration. I reply, then, that it is a libel on social order to suppose that it requires for its support the reduction of the multitude of human beings to ignorance and servility; and that it is a libel on the Creator to suppose that He requires, as the foundation of communities, the systematic depression of the majority of his intelligent offspring. The supposition is too grossly unreasonable, too monstrous, to require labored refutations. I see no need of ranks, either for social order or for any other purpose. A great variety of pursuits and conditions is indeed to be desired. Men ought to follow their genius, and to put forth their powers in every useful and lawful way. I do not ask for a monotonous world. We are far too monotonous now. The vassalage of fashion, which is a part of rank, prevents continually the free expansion of men's powers. Let us have the greatest diversity of occupations. But this does not imply that there is a need of splitting society into castes or ranks, or that a certain number should arrogate superiority, and stand apart from the rest of men as a separate race. Men may work in different departments of life, and yet recognize their brotherly relation, and honor one another, and hold friendly communion with one another. Undoubtedly, men will prefer as friends and common associates those with whom they sympathize most. But this is not to form a rank or caste. For example, the intelligent seek out the intelligent; the pious, those who reverence God. But suppose the intellectual and the religious to cut themselves off by some broad, visible distinction from the rest of society, to form a clan of their own, to refuse admission into their houses to people of inferior knowledge and virtue, and to diminish as far as possible the occasions of intercourse with them; would not society rise up, as one man, against this arrogant exclusiveness? And if intelligence and piety may not be the foundations of a caste, on what ground shall they who have no distinction but wealth, superior costume, richer equipages, finer houses, draw lines around themselves and constitute themselves a higher class? That some should be richer than others is natural, and is necessary, and could only be prevented by gross violations of right. Leave men to the free use of their powers, and some will accumulate more than their neighbors. But to be prosperous is not to be superior, and should form no barrier between men. Wealth ought not to secure to the prosperous the slightest consideration. The only distinctions which should be recognized are those of the soul, of strong principle, of incorruptible integrity, of usefulness, of cultivated intellect, of fidelity in seeking for truth. A man, in proportion as he has these claims, should be honored and welcomed everywhere. I see not why such a man, however coarsely if neatly dressed, should not be a respected guest in the most splendid mansions, and at the most brilliant meetings. A man is worth infinitely more than the saloons, and the costumes, and the show of the universe. He was made to tread all these beneath his feet. What an insult to humanity is the present deference to dress and upholstery, as if silk-worms, and looms, and scissors, and needles could produce something nobler than a man! Every good man should protest against a caste founded on outward prosperity, because it exalts the outward above the inward, the material above the spiritual; because it springs from and cherishes a contemptible pride in superficial and transitory distinctions; because it alienates man from his brother, breaks the tie of common humanity, and breeds jealousy, scorn, and mutual ill-will. Can this be needed to social order?

It is true that in countries where the mass of the people are ignorant and servile, the existence of a higher and a worshipped rank tends to keep them from outrage. It infuses a sentiment of awe, which prevents more or less the need of force and punishment. But it is worthy of remark that the means of keeping order in one state of society may become the chief excitement of discontent and disorder in another, and this is peculiarly true of aristocracy or high rank. In rude ages this keeps the people down; but when the people by degrees have risen to some consciousness of their rights and essential equality with the rest of the race, the awe of rank naturally subsides, and passes into suspicion, jealousy, and sense of injury, and a disposition to resist. The very institution which once restrained, now provokes. Through this process the Old World is now passing. The strange illusion that a man because he wears a garter or a riband, or was born to a title, belongs to another race is fading away; and society must pass through a series of revolutions, silent or bloody, until a more natural order takes the place of distinctions which grew originally out of force. Thus, aristocracy, instead of giving order to society, now convulses it. So impossible is it for arbitrary human ordinations permanently to degrade human nature, or subvert the principles of justice and freedom.

[*1840*]

WILLIAM LLOYD GARRISON

[1805–1879]

HE WAS born in Newburyport, Massachusetts. His father, a sea-captain, was a drunkard who deserted his family before William was three. He had little schooling and at thirteen was apprenticed to a local newspaper-printer. When his apprenticeship of seven years was over, he became the editor of another Newburyport newspaper. From then on he spent his life mainly as a periodical-publisher and editor. But soon his profession had a moral purpose; he was still in his early twenties when he joined the abolitionists and proceeded to devote himself to the Negro cause with a passion and zeal unequaled in that fervent movement. In 1831 he founded a weekly magazine which he called the *Liberator*. He published it for exactly thirty-five years, and throughout that period it was the most vehement and uncompromising, as well as the most famous, organ of the abolitionists. An arrogant and hot-tempered man, he made enemies even among his fellow reformers; yet his integrity and courage were never questioned and his inspiration was felt by many. No danger daunted him. The state of Georgia offered five thousand dollars for his arrest and conviction, but he did not slacken his activities. In 1835 a mob in Boston put a rope around his neck and dragged him through the streets of the city, but after a few weeks he returned to carry on his work. Garrison's unfortunate childhood had made him a good deal of a " blue-nose ": he was a prohibitionist.and attacked the use of tobacco. He was also a rather gullible man: he was taken in by phrenologists and clairvoyants. But there were other causes he was right about — he fought for woman's rights and against imprisonment for debt — and on the main cause, abolition, he never had to yield. There is a kind of intolerance that is magnificent, and the pieces that follow are examples of it.

COMMENCEMENT OF THE LIBERATOR

In the month of August, I issued proposals for publishing " THE LIBERATOR " in Washington city; but the enterprise, though hailed approvingly in different sections of the country, was palsied by public indifference. Since that time, the removal of the " Genius of Universal

251

Emancipation " to the Seat of Government has rendered less imperious the establishment of a similar periodical in that quarter.

During my recent tour for the purpose of exciting the minds of the people by a series of discourses on the subject of slavery, every place that I visited gave fresh evidence of the fact that a greater revolution in public sentiment was to be effected in the free States — and particularly in New England — than at the South. I found contempt more bitter, opposition more active, detraction more relentless, prejudice more stubborn, and apathy more frozen than among slave-owners themselves. Of course, there were individual exceptions to the contrary. This state of things afflicted, but did not dishearten me. I determined, at every hazard, to lift up the standard of emancipation in the eyes of the nation, within sight of Bunker Hill, and in the birth-place of liberty. That standard is now unfurled; and long may it float, unhurt by the spoliations of time or the missiles of a desperate foe; yea, till every chain be broken, and every bondman set free! Let Southern oppressors tremble; let their secret abettors tremble; let their Northern apologists tremble; let all the enemies of the persecuted blacks tremble.

Assenting to the " self-evident truths " maintained in the American Declaration of Independence, "that all men are created equal, and endowed by their Creator with certain inalienable rights — among which are life, liberty, and the pursuit of happiness," I shall strenuously contend for the immediate enfranchisement of our slave population. In Park Street Church, on the Fourth of July, 1829, in an address on slavery, I unreflectingly assented to the popular but pernicious doctrine of gradual abolition. I seize this opportunity to make a full and unequivocal recantation, and thus publicly to ask pardon of my God, of my country, and of my brethren, the poor slaves, for having uttered a sentiment so full of timidity, injustice and absurdity. A similar recantation, from my pen, was published in the " Genius of Universal Emancipation," at Baltimore, in September, 1829. My conscience is now satisfied.

I am aware that many object to the severity of my language; but is there not cause for severity? I will be as harsh as truth, and as uncompromising as justice. On this subject I do not wish to think, or speak, or write, with moderation. No! no! Tell a man whose house is on fire to give a moderate alarm; tell him to moderately rescue his wife from the hands of the ravisher; tell the mother to gradually extricate her babe from the fire into which it his fallen; but urge me not to use moderation in a cause like the present! I am in earnest. I will not equivocate — I will not excuse — I will not retreat a single inch — AND I WILL BE HEARD. The apathy of the people is enough to make every statue leap from its pedestal, and to hasten the resurrection of the dead.

It is pretended that I am retarding the cause of emancipation by the coarseness of my invective, and the precipitancy of my measures. The charge is not true. On this question, my influence, humble as it is, is felt at this moment to a considerable extent, and shall be felt in coming years — not perniciously, but beneficially — not as a curse, but as a blessing; and POSTERITY WILL BEAR TESTIMONY THAT I WAS RIGHT. I desire to thank God that he enables me to disregard " the fear of man which bringeth a snare," and to speak his truth in its simplicity and power. And here I close with this fresh dedication: —

> " Oppression! I have seen thee, face to face,
> And met thy cruel eye and cloudy brow;
> But thy soul-withering glance I fear not now —
> For dread to prouder feelings doth give place,
> Of deep abhorrence! Scorning the disgrace
> Of slavish knees that at thy footstool bow,
> I also kneel — but with far other vow
> Do hail thee and thy herd of hirelings base: —
> I swear, while life-blood warms my throbbing veins,
> Still to oppose and thwart, with heart and hand,
> Thy brutalizing sway — till Afric's chains
> Are burst, and Freedom rules the rescued land;
> Trampling Oppression and his iron rod: —
> Such is the vow I take — so help me, God! "
> [*1831*]

NO COMPROMISE WITH SLAVERY

Cost what it may, every slave on the American soil must be liberated from his chains. Nothing is to be put in competition, on the score of value, with the price of his liberty; for whatever conflicts with the rights of man must be evil, and therefore intrinsically worthless. Are we to be intimidated from defending his cause by the fear of consequences? Is it, then, safe to do wrong? Has a just God so ordered it that the strong may oppress the weak, the rich defraud the poor, the merciless torture the innocent, not only without guilt, but with benefit to mankind? Is there no similitude between the seed that is sown and the harvest which it brings forth? Have cause and effect ceased to retain an indissoluble connection with each other? On such a plea, what crime may not be committed with impunity? what deed of villainy may not demand exemption from rebuke? what system of depravity may not claim protection against the assaults of virtue?

Let not those who say that the path of obedience is a dangerous one claim to believe in the living and true God. They deny his omniscience, omnipresence, omnipotence. It is his will that the bands of wickedness should be loosed, the heavy burdens of tyranny undone, the oppressed set free. They reject it as absurd, impracticable, dangerous. It is his promise that the results of emancipation shall be noon-day light for darkness, health for disease, fertility for barrenness, prosperity like a spring of water whose waters fail not, the building up of old waste places, the restoring of paths to dwell in, the glory of the Lord for a reward, and his guidance continually! They affirm that the promise is worthless, and to disregard it is a duty. They exalt the Spirit of Evil above all that is called God, and raise an Ephesian clamor against those who will not fall down and worship it. Yet they put on the garb of religion; they extol faith, hope, charity; they build and dedicate temples of worship, in the name of Christ; they profess to be the disciples of Him who came to proclaim liberty to the captives, and the opening of the prison to them that are bound. Unblushing hypocrites! think not, by your pious dissembling, to hide your iniquity from the pure in heart, or to " circumvent God "! Impious contemner of Divine wisdom and goodness! from your companionship, the spirits of the free shrink with horror!

For more than two centuries, slavery has polluted the American soil. It has grown with the growth, and strengthened with the strength of the republic. Its victims have multiplied, from a single cargo of stolen Africans, to three millions of native-born inhabitants. In our colonial state, it was deemed compatible with loyalty to the mother country. In our revolutionary struggle for independence, it exchanged the sceptre of monarchy for the star-spangled banner of republicanism, under the folds of which it has found ample encouragement and protection. From the days of the Puritans down to the present time, it has been sanctified by the religion, and upheld by the patriotism of the nation. From the adoption of the American Constitution, it has declared war and made peace, instituted and destroyed national banks and tariffs, controlled the army and navy, prescribed the policy of the government, ruled in both houses of Congress, occupied the Presidential chair, governed the political parties, distributed offices of trust and emolument among its worshippers, fettered Northern industry and enterprise, and trampled liberty of speech and of conscience in the dust.

It has exercised absolute mastery over the American Church. In her skirts is found " the blood of the souls of the poor innocents." With the Bible in their hands, her priesthood have attempted to prove that slavery came down from God out of heaven. They have become slaveowners and dealers in human flesh. They have justified robbery, adultery, barbarity, man-stealing and murder, on a frightful scale. They have been among the foremost to crush the sacred cause of emancipation, to cover its advocates with infamy, to oppose the purification of the Church. They have become possessors of the flock, whom they slay, " and hold themselves not guilty; and they that sell them say, Blessed be the Lord, for I am rich: and their own shepherds pity them not."

If slavery be thus entwined around the civil, social, and pecuniary interests of the republic — if the religious sects and political parties are banded together for its safety from internal revolt and external opposition — if the people, awed by its power and corrupted by its influence, are basely bending their knees at its footstool — is it wonderful that Church and State are shaken to their foundations by the rallying cry of Liberty, "To the rescue! " in behalf of imbruted humanity? Or should it be accounted marvellous that they who have sternly resolved to effect the utter overthrow of this frightful usurpation are subjected to persecution, reproach, loss of character, and the hazard of life? Constituting the " forlorn hope " in the struggling cause of freedom, they must be prepared to meet all the vicissitudes of the conflict, and to make whatever sacrifices may be needed to achieve the victory. Hereafter, when the song of jubilee shall be sung by those for whose deliverance they toiled so devotedly, their deeds and their memories shall be covered with a halo of glory, and held in grateful remembrance by enfranchised millions.

Slavery must be overthrown. No matter how numerous the difficul-

ties, how formidable the obstacles, how strong the foes to be vanquished — slavery must cease to pollute the land. No matter whether
the event be near or remote, whether the taskmaster willingly or un-
willingly relinquish his arbitrary power, whether by a peaceful or a
bloody process — slavery must die. No matter, though, to effect it,
every party should be torn by dissensions, every sect dashed into fragments, the national compact dissolved, the land filled with the horrors
of a civil and a servile war — still, slavery must be buried in the grave
of infamy, beyond the possibility of a resurrection. If the State cannot
survive the anti-slavery agitation, then let the State perish. If the
Church must be cast down by the strugglings of Humanity to be free,
then let the Church fall, and its fragments be scattered to the four
winds of heaven, never more to curse the earth. If the American Union
cannot be maintained, except by immolating human freedom on the
altar of tyranny, then let the American Union be consumed by a living
thunderbolt, and no tear be shed over its ashes. If the Republic must
be blotted out from the roll of nations, by proclaiming liberty to the
captives, then let the Republic sink beneath the waves of oblivion,
and a shout of joy, louder than the voice of many waters, fill the universe at its extinction.

Against this declaration, none but traitors and tyrants will raise an
outcry. It is the mandate of Heaven, and the voice of God. It has righteousness for its foundation, reason for its authority, and truth for its
support. It is not vindictive but merciful, not violent but pacific, not
destructive but preservative. It is simply asserting the supremacy of
right over wrong, of liberty over slavery, of God over man. It is only
raising the standard of rectitude from the dust, and placing it on the
eternal throne.

The Party or Sect that will suffer by the triumph of justice cannot
exist with safety to mankind. The State that cannot tolerate universal
freedom must be despotic; and no valid reason can be given why despotism should not at once be hurled to the dust. The Church that is
endangered by the proclamation of eternal truth, and that trades in
slaves and souls of men, is " the habitation of devils, and the hold of
every foul spirit, and a cage of every unclean and hateful bird; therefore shall her plagues come in one day, death, and mourning, and
famine; and she shall be utterly burned with fire; for strong is the
Lord God who judgeth her." The Union that can be perpetuated only
by enslaving a portion of the people is " a covenant with death, and an

agreement with hell," and destined to be broken in pieces as a potter's vessel. When judgment is laid to the line, and righteousness to the plummet, the hail shall sweep away the refuge of lies, and the waters shall overflow the hiding-place. The Republic that depends for its stability on making war against the government of God and the rights of man, though it exalt itself as the eagle, and set its nest among the stars, shall be cast into the bottomless deep, and the loss of it shall be a gain to the world.

There must be no compromise with slavery — none whatever. Nothing is gained, everything is lost, by subordinating principle to expediency. The spirit of freedom must be inexorable in its demand for the instant release of all who are sighing in bondage, nor abate one jot or tittle of its righteous claims. By one remorseless grasp, the rights of humanity have been taken away; and by one strong blow, the iron hand of usurpation must be made to relinquish its hold. The apologist for oppression becomes himself the oppressor. To palliate crime is to be guilty of its perpetration. To ask for a postponement of the case, till a more convenient season, is to call for a suspension of the moral law, and to assume that it is right to do wrong, under present circumstances. Talk not of other questions to be settled, of other interests to be secured, of other objects to be attained, before the slave can have his fetters broken. Nothing can take precedence of the question of liberty. No interest is so momentous as that which involves " the life of the soul "; no object so glorious as the restoration of a man to himself. It is idle to talk of human concerns where there are not human beings. Slavery annihilates manhood, and puts down in its crimson ledger as chattels personal those who are created in the image of God. Hence, it tramples under foot whatever pertains to human safety, human prosperity, human happiness. Hence, too, its overthrow is the primary object to be sought, in order to secure private advantage and promote the public weal.

In the present struggle, the test of character is as infallible as it is simple. He that is with the slaveholder is against the slave: he that is with the slave is against the slaveholder. He that thinks, speaks, acts, on the subject of slavery, in accordance with the feelings and wishes of the tyrant, does everything to perpetuate the thralldom of his victims. When was it ever known for tyranny to devise and execute effective measures for its own overthrow? Or for the oppressor and the oppressed to be agreed on the great question of equal rights? Who talks of occupying neutral ground between these hostile parties? of reconciling them, by prolonging the sufferings of the one, and the cruelty of the other? of mutually satisfying them as to the means and the plan by which the rod and the chain shall be broken? I tell such vain babbler, or crafty hypocrite, that he is acting the part of a fool or a knave. Impossibilities are impossibilities; and to propose their adoption, as the only rational methods by which to dethrone injustice, is an insult to human intelligence. Slavery cannot be conquered by flattery or stratagem. Its dying throes will convulse the land and sea.

Abolitionists! friends of liberty! remember that the foe with whom you are in conflict is full " of all deceivableness or unrighteousness," and will resort to every artifice to make you quit the field. Put on the whole armor of God; so shall you be invulnerable and invincible; so shall no weapon against you prosper. The war admits of no parley. No flag of truce must be sent or received by you; you must neither give nor take any quarters. As Samuel hewed Agag in pieces, so, with the battle-ax of Truth, you must cleave Slavery to the ground, and give its carcass to the fowls of the air. May Heaven reinspire your hearts, give new vigor to your arms, direct your blows aright, fill the breast of the enemy with dismay, and grant you a splendid victory!

[1852?]

HENRY WADSWORTH LONGFELLOW

[1807–1882]

DESCENDED from Pilgrim families, from judges, lawyers, and men of property, Longfellow was born in Portland, Maine, educated at private schools and Bowdoin College, and sent abroad to study languages and literature. He returned to Bowdoin in 1829 to accept a professorship. In 1835 he left for another year in Europe to prepare for a professorship at Harvard, and in 1836 settled down in Cambridge at the famous Craigie House, which was to be his home until his death. He held his chair at Harvard only until 1854; thereafter he devoted himself entirely to his writing. Long before this he had won popularity and critical esteem for his poems. In the end, thanks to " Evangeline," " Hiawatha," " The Courtship of Miles Standish," and such shorter pieces as " The Village Blacksmith," " The Wreck of the Hesperus," " The Psalm of Life," and " Excelsior," he became and has remained the most popular of American poets. At their best, his poems are sentimental, benign, mild in expression, easy to recite — which explains their vogue. At their worst, they are sugary, didactic, full of trite symbolism and imagery — which explains why serious critics are contemptuous of them. He is the poet of simple people and of children. A decent, kindly man who stood for homely virtues, he sought to inculcate " goodness " in his readers, and that " goodness " consisted not only in genteel behavior and domestic morality, but also hatred of slavery, of intolerance, and of war. These sentiments are here represented.

THE WARNING

Beware! The Israelite of old, who tore
    The lion in his path, — when, poor and blind,
He saw the blessed light of heaven no more,
    Shorn of his noble strength and forced to grind

In prison, and at last led forth to be
A pander to Philistine revelry, —

Upon the pillars of the temple laid
   His desperate hands, and in its overthrow
Destroyed himself, and with him those who made
   A cruel mockery of his sightless woe;
The poor, blind Slave, the scoff and jest of all,
Expired, and thousands perished in the fall!

There is a poor, blind Samson in this land,
   Shorn of his strength, and bound in bonds of steel,
Who may, in some grim revel, raise his hand,
   And shake the pillars of this Commonweal,
Till the vast Temple of our liberties
A shapeless mass of wreck and rubbish lies.
[*1842*]

THE ARSENAL AT SPRINGFIELD

This is the Arsenal. From floor to ceiling,
   Like a huge organ, rise the burnished arms;
But from their silent pipes no anthem pealing
   Startles the villages with strange alarms.

Ah! what a sound will arise, how wild and dreary,
   When the death-angel touches those swift keys
What loud lament and dismal Miserere
   Will mingle with their awful symphonies!

I hear even now the infinite fierce chorus,
   The cries of agony, the endless groan,
Which, through the ages that have gone before us,
   In long reverberations reach our own.

On helm and harness rings the Saxon hammer,
   Through Cimbric forests roars the Norseman's song,
And loud, amid the universal clamor,
   O'er distant deserts sounds the Tartar gong.

I hear the Florentine, who from his palace
   Wheels out his battle-bell with dreadful din,
And Aztec priests upon their teocallis
   Beat the wild war-drums made of serpent's skin;

The tumult of each sacked and burning village;
   The shout that every prayer for mercy drowns;
The soldiers' revels in the midst of pillage;
   The wail of famine in beleaguered towns;

The bursting shell, the gateway wrenched asunder,
   The rattling musketry, the clashing blade;
And ever and anon, in tones of thunder,
   The diapason of the cannonade.

Is it, O man, with such discordant noises,
   With such accursed instruments as these,
Thou drownest Nature's sweet and kindly voices,
   And jarrest the celestial harmonies?

Were half the power that fills the world with terror,
   Were half the wealth bestowed on camps and courts,
Given to redeem the human mind from error,
   There were no need of arsenals nor forts:

The warrior's name would be a name abhorrèd!
   And every nation, that should lift again
Its hand against a brother, on its forehead
   Would wear forevermore the curse of Cain!

Down the dark future, through long generations,
   The echoing sounds grow fainter and then cease;
And like a bell, with solemn, sweet vibrations,
   I hear once more the voice of Christ say, " Peace! "

Peace! and no longer from its brazen portals
    The blast of War's great organ shakes the skies!
But beautiful as songs of the immortals,
    The holy melodies of love arise.

[*1844*]

THE JEWISH CEMETERY AT NEWPORT

How strange it seems! These Hebrews in their graves,
    Close by the street of this fair seaport town,
Silent beside the never-silent waves,
    At rest in all this moving up and down!

The trees are white with dust, that o'er their sleep
    Wave their broad curtains in the south wind's breath.
While underneath such leafy tents they keep
    The long, mysterious Exodus of Death.

And these sepulchral stones, so old and brown,
    That pave with level flags their burial-place,
Seem like the tablets of the Law, thrown down
    And broken by Moses at the mountain's base.

The very names recorded here are strange,
    Of foreign accent, and of different climes;
Alvares and Rivera interchange
    With Abraham and Jacob of old times.

" Blessed be God! for He created Death! "
    The mourners said, " and Death is rest and peace ";
Then added, in the certainty of faith,
    " And giveth life that never more shall cease."

Closed are the portals of their Synagogue,
    No Psalms of David now the silence break,

No Rabbi reads the ancient Decalogue
    In the grand dialect the Prophets spake.

Gone are the living, but the dead remain,
    And not neglected; for a hand unseen,
Scattering its bounty, like a summer rain,
    Still keeps their graves and their remembrance green.

How came they here? What burst of Christian hate,
    What persecution, merciless and blind,
Drove o'er the sea — that desert desolate —
    These Ishmaels and Hagars of mankind?

They lived in narrow streets and lanes obscure,
    Ghetto and Judenstrass, in mirk and mire;
Taught in the school of patience to endure
    The life of anguish and the death of fire.

All their lives long, with the unleavened bread
    And bitter herbs of exile and its fears,
The wasting famine of the heart they fed,
    And slaked its thirst with marah of their tears.

Anathema maranatha! was the cry
    That rang from town to town, from street to street:
At every gate the accursed Mordecai
    Was mocked and jeered, and spurned by Christian feet.

Pride and humiliation hand in hand
    Walked with them through the world where'er they went;
Trampled and beaten were they as the sand,
    And yet unshaken as the continent.

For in the background figures vague and vast
    Of patriarchs and of prophets rose sublime,
And all the great traditions of the Past
    They saw reflected in the coming time.

And thus forever with reverted look
    The mystic volume of the world they read,

Spelling it backward, like a Hebrew book,
Till life became a legend of the Dead.

But ah! what once has been shall be no more!
The groaning earth in travail and in pain
Brings forth its races, but does not restore,
And the dead nations never rise again.

[*1852*]

RALPH WALDO EMERSON

[1803–1882]

ON HIS father's side he came from a long line of clergymen; on his mother's, from a mercantile family. His father, William Emerson, was minister of the First Church of Boston and editor of one of the best of our early literary magazines, the *Monthly Anthology*. In brief, it was a well-established and cultured family. Ralph Waldo was born in Boston and attended the Boston Latin School and Harvard College, from which he was graduated in 1821. He taught school for four years, then returned to Cambridge to enter the Divinity School. From 1829 to 1832 he was a minister in the Second Church of Boston, resigning because of his doubts concerning matters of ritual. He preached as a sort of free-lance minister for some years afterwards, but from 1834 on, his major interest was writing, with lecturing as a parallel occupation. In 1836 he published his first book, *Nature*, which contained the seeds of most of his later philosophical essays. In 1837 he was the Phi Beta Kappa orator at Harvard, delivering " The American Scholar," which Oliver Wendell Holmes called " our intellectual Declaration of Independence." In 1841 he published his first volume of *Essays*. He was now the involuntary spokesman of the transcendentalist movement, for while he did not wholly align himself with the mystics who founded Brook Farm and published that strange and invigorating magazine the *Dial*, he was nevertheless sympathetic to them, shared their primary ideas, and expressed those ideas better than anyone else did.

The transcendentalist philosophy was an assertion of man's nearness to God – of his innate ability to communicate directly with God and therefore to interpret nature and the universe without anyone's intercession; hence it was an expression of belief in the inherent value and potential goodness of the individual human being. Such a system of thought could not be anything but libertarian and democratic; it could not help being indignant about the degradation of masses of men and women caused by the industrial revolution; and it *had* to be opposed to opportunistic and materialistic tendencies. Transcendentalism was the kernel of Emerson's thought – as of Thoreau's, Parker's, Margaret Fuller's, Brownson's, and others'. In Emerson's case, perhaps more than in any other writer's, there were conflicting ideas. He, too, was infected by the temper of the times. But in the last analysis he was on the side of the common man, against the ruthlessness of a boom economy; and in the essays here reprinted we find some of the finest and most moving expressions of the democratic spirit that America has ever produced.

Among Emerson's various later volumes, the following are the best known: *Representative Men* (1850), *English Traits* (1856), *Society and Solitude* (1870). He also published some remarkable poems. He died in Concord, Massachusetts, where he had lived since 1834.

from

THE AMERICAN SCHOLAR

Historically, there is thought to be a difference in the ideas which predominate over successive epochs, and there are data for marking the genius of the Classic, of the Romantic, and now of the Reflective or Philosophical age. With the views I have intimated of the oneness or the identity of the mind through all individuals, I do not much dwell on these differences. In fact, I believe each individual passes through all three. The boy is a Greek; the youth, romantic; the adult, reflective. I deny not, however, that a revolution in the leading idea may be distinctly enough traced.

Our age is bewailed as the age of Introversion. Must that needs be evil? We, it seems, are critical; we are embarrassed with second thoughts; we cannot enjoy anything for hankering to know whereof the pleasure consists; we are lined with eyes; we see with our feet; the time is infected with Hamlet's unhappiness, —

"Sicklied o'er with the pale cast of thought."

It is so bad then? Sight is the last thing to be pitied. Would we be blind? Do we fear lest we should outsee nature and God, and drink truth dry? I look upon the discontent of the literary class as a mere announcement of the fact that they find themselves not in the state of mind of their fathers, and regret the coming state as untried; as a boy dreads the water before he has learned that he can swim. If there is any period one would desire to be born in, is it not the age of Revolution; when the old and the new stand side by side and admit of being compared; when the energies of all men are searched by fear and by hope; when the historic glories of the old can be compensated by the rich possibilities of the new era? This time, like all times, is a very good one, if we but know what to do with it.

I read with some joy of the auspicious signs of the coming days, as they glimmer already through poetry and art, through philosophy and science, through church and state.

One of these signs is the fact that the same movement which affected the elevation of what was called the lowest class in the state assumed in literature a very marked and as benign an aspect. Instead of the sublime and beautiful, the near, the low, the common, was explored and poetized. That which had been negligently trodden under foot by those who were harnessing and provisioning themselves for long journeys into far countries is suddenly found to be richer than all foreign parts. The literature of the poor, the feelings of the child, the philosophy of the street, the meaning of household life, are the topics of the time. It is a great stride. It is a sign — is it not? — of new vigor when the extremities are made active, when currents of warm life run into the hands and the feet. I ask not for the great, the remote, the romantic; what is doing in Italy or Arabia; what is Greek art, or Provençal minstrelsy; I embrace the common, I explore and sit at the feet of the familiar, the low. Give me insight into today, and you may have the antique and future worlds. What would we really know the meaning of? The meal in the firkin; the milk in the pan; the ballad in the street; the news of the boat; the glance of the eye; the form and the gait of the body; — show me the ultimate reason of these matters; show me the sublime presence of the highest spiritual cause lurking, as always it does lurk, in these suburbs and extremities of nature; let me see every trifle bristling with the polarity that ranges it instantly on an eternal law; and the shop, the plough, and the ledger referred to the like cause by which light undulates and poets sing; — and the world lies no longer a dull miscellany and lumber-room, but has form and order; there is no trifle, there is no puzzle, but one design unites and animates the farthest pinnacle and the lowest trench.

This idea has inspired the genius of Goldsmith, Burns, Cowper, and, in a newer time, of Goethe, Wordsworth, and Carlyle. This idea they have differently followed and with various success. In contrast with their writing, the style of Pope, of Johnson, of Gibbon, looks cold and pedantic. This writing is blood-warm. Man is surprised to find that things near are not less beautiful and wondrous than things remote. The near explains the far. The drop is a small ocean. A man is related to all nature. This perception of the worth of the vulgar is fruitful in discoveries. Goethe, in this very thing the most modern of the moderns, has shown us, as none ever did, the genius of the ancients.

There is one man of genius who has done much for this philosophy of life, whose literary value has never yet been rightly estimated; — I mean Emanuel Swedenborg. The most imaginative of men, yet writing with the precision of a mathematician, he endeavored to engraft a purely philosophical Ethics on the popular Christianity of his time. Such an attempt of course must have difficulty which no genius could surmount. But he saw and showed the connection between nature and the affections of the soul. He pierced the emblematic or spiritual character of the visible, audible, tangible world. Especially did his shade-loving muse hover over and interpret the lower parts of nature; he showed the mysterious bond that allies moral evil to the foul material forms, and has given in epical parables a theory of insanity, of beasts, of unclean and fearful things.

Another sign of our times, also marked by an analogous political movement, is the new importance given to the single person. Everything that tends to insulate the individual, — to surround him with barriers of natural respect, so that each man shall feel the world is his, and man shall treat with man as a sovereign state with a sovereign state, — tends to true union as well as greatness. "I learned," said the melancholy Pestalozzi, "that no man in God's wide earth is either willing or able to help any other man." Help must come from the bosom alone. The scholar is that man who must take up into himself all the ability of the time, all the contributions of the past, all the hopes of the future. He must be an university of knowledges. If there be one lesson more than another which should pierce his ear, it is, The world is nothing, the man is all; in yourself is the law of all nature, and you know not yet how a globule of sap ascends; in yourself slumbers the whole of Reason; it is for you to know all; it is for you to dare all. . . . . This confidence in the unsearched might of man belongs, by all motives, by all prophecy, by all preparation, to the American scholar. We have listened too long to the courtly muses of Europe. The spirit of the American freeman is already suspected to be timid, imitative, tame. Public and private avarice make the air we breathe thick and fat. The scholar is decent, indolent, complaisant. See already the tragic consequence. The mind of this country, taught to aim at low objects, eats upon itself. There is no work for any but the decorous and the complaisant. Young men of the fairest promise, who begin life upon our shores, inflated by the mountain winds, shined upon by all the stars of God, find the earth below not in unison with these, but are hindered from action by the disgust which the principles on which business is managed inspire, and turn drudges, or die of disgust, some of them suicides. What is the remedy? They did not yet see, and thousands of young men as hopeful now crowding to the barriers for the career do not yet see, that if the single man plant himself indomitably on his instincts, and there abide, the huge world will come round to him. Patience, — patience; with the shades of all the good and great for company; and for solace the perspective of your own infinite life; and for work the study and the communication of principles, the making those instincts prevalent, the conversion of the world. Is it not the chief disgrace in the world, not to be an unit; — not to be reckoned one character; — not to yield that peculiar fruit which each man was created to bear, but to be reckoned in the gross, in the hundred, or the thousand, of the party, the section, to which we belong; and our opinion predicted geographically, as the north, or the south? Not so, brothers and friends — please God, ours shall not be so. We will walk on our own feet; we will work with our own hands; we will speak our own minds. The study of letters shall be no longer a name for pity, for doubt, and for sensual indulgence. The dread of man and the love of man shall be a wall of defense and a wreath of joy around all. A nation of men will for the first time exist, because each believes himself inspired by the Divine Soul which also inspires all men.

[*1837*]

from

MAN THE REFORMER

In the history of the world the doctrine of Reform had never such scope as at the present hour. Lutherans, Herrnhuters, Jesuits, Monks, Quakers, Knox, Wesley, Swedenborg, Bentham, in their accusations of society, all respected something, — church or state, literature or history, domestic usages, the market town, the dinner table, coined money. But now all these and all things else hear the trumpet, and must rush to judgment, — Christianity, the laws, commerce, schools, the farm, the laboratory; and not a kingdom, town, statute, rite, calling, man, or woman, but is threatened by the new spirit.

What if some of the objections whereby our institutions are assailed are extreme and speculative, and the reformers tend to idealism? That only shows the extravagance of the abuses which have
driven the mind into the opposite extreme. It is when your facts and
persons grow unreal and fantastic by too much falsehood that the
scholar flies for refuge to the world of ideas, and aims to recruit and
replenish nature from that source. Let ideas establish their legitimate
sway again in society, let life be fair and poetic, and the scholars will
gladly be lovers, citizens, and philanthropists.

It will afford no security from the new ideas that the old nations,
the laws of centuries, the property and institutions of a hundred cities,
are built on other foundations. The demon of reform has a secret door
into the heart of every lawmaker, of every inhabitant of every city.
The fact that a new thought and hope have dawned in your breast
should apprize you that in the same hour a new light broke in upon
a thousand private hearts. That secret which you would fain keep, —
as soon as you go abroad, lo! there is one standing on the doorstep
to tell you the same. There is not the most bronzed and sharpened
money-catcher who does not, to your consternation almost, quail and
shake the moment he hears a question prompted by the new ideas.
We thought he had some semblance of ground to stand upon, that
such as he at least would die hard; but he trembles and flees. Then the
scholar says, " Cities and coaches shall never impose on me again; for
behold every solitary dream of mine is rushing to fulfilment. That
fancy I had, and hesitated to utter because you would laugh, — the
broker, the attorney, the market-man are saying the same thing. Had
I waited a day longer to speak, I had been too late. Behold, State
Street thinks, and Wall Street doubts, and begins to prophesy! "

It cannot be wondered at that this general inquest into abuses should
arise in the bosom of society, when one considers the practical impediments that stand in the way of virtuous young men. The young man,
on entering life, finds the way to lucrative employments blocked with
abuses. The ways of trade are grown selfish to the borders of theft, and
supple to the borders (if not beyond the borders) of fraud. The employments of commerce are not intrinsically unfit for a man, or less
genial to his faculties; but these are now in their general course so
vitiated by derelictions and abuses at which all connive that it requires
more vigor and resources than can be expected of every young man
to right himself in them; he is lost in them; he cannot move hand or

foot in them. Has he genius and virtue? the less does he find them
fit for him to grow in, and if he would thrive in them, he must sacrifice
all the brilliant dreams of boyhood and youth as dreams; he must forget the prayers of his childhood and must take on him the harness
of routine and obsequiousness. If not so minded, nothing is left him
but to begin the world anew, as he does who puts the spade into the
ground for food. We are all implicated of course in this charge; it is
only necessary to ask a few questions as to the progress of the articles
of commerce from the fields where they grew, to our houses, to become
aware that we eat and drink and wear perjury and fraud in a hundred commodities. . . .

I do not charge the merchant or the manufacturer. The sins of our
trade belong to no class, to no individual. One plucks, one distributes,
one eats. Everybody partakes, everybody confesses, — with cap and
knee volunteers his confession, yet none feels himself accountable.
He did not create the abuse; he cannot alter it. What is he? an obscure
private person who must get his bread. That is the vice, — that no one
feels himself called to act for man, but only as a fraction of man. It
happens therefore that all such ingenuous souls as feel within themselves the irrepressible strivings of a noble aim, who by the law of
their nature must act simply, find these ways of trade unfit for them,
and they come forth from it. Such cases are becoming more numerous
every year.

But by coming out of trade you have not cleared yourself. The
trail of the serpent reaches into all the lucrative professions and practices of man. Each has its own wrongs. Each finds a tender and very
intelligent conscience a disqualification for success. Each requires of
the practitioner a certain shutting of the eyes, a certain dapperness
and compliance, an acceptance of customs, a sequestration from the
sentiments of generosity and love, a compromise of private opinion and
lofty integrity. Nay, the evil custom reaches into the whole institution of property, until our laws which establish and protect it seem
not to be the issue of love and reason, but of selfishness. Suppose a man
is so unhappy as to be born a saint, with keen perceptions but with the
conscience and love of an angel, and he is to get his living in the world;
he finds himself excluded from all lucrative works; he has no farm,
and he cannot get one; for to earn money enough to buy one requires
a sort of concentration toward money, which is the selling himself for
a number of years, and to him the present hour is as sacred and in-

violable as any future hour. Of course, whilst another man has no land, my title to mine, your title to yours, is at once vitiated. Inextricable seem to be the twinings and tendrils of this evil, and we all involve ourselves in it the deeper by forming connections, by wives and children, by benefits and debts. . . .

I do not wish to be absurd and pedantic in reform. I do not wish to push my criticism on the state of things around me to that extravagant mark that shall compel me to suicide, or to an absolute isolation from the advantages of civil society. If we suddenly plant our foot and say, — I will neither eat nor drink nor wear nor touch any food or fabric which I do not know to be innocent, or deal with any person whose whole manner of life is not clear and rational, we shall stand still. Whose is so? Not mine; not thine; not his. But I think we must clear ourselves each one by the interrogation whether we have earned our bread today by the hearty contribution of our energies to the common benefit; and we must not cease to *tend* to the correction of flagrant wrongs, by laying one stone aright every day.

But the idea which now begins to agitate society has a wider scope than our daily employments, our households, and the institutions of property. We are to revise the whole of our social structure, the State, the school, religion, marriage, trade, science, and explore their foundations in our own nature; we are to see that the world not only fitted the former men, but fits us, and to clear ourselves of every usage which has not its roots in our own mind. What is a man born for but to be a Reformer, a Remaker of what man has made; a renouncer of lies; a restorer of truth and good, imitating that great Nature which embosoms us all, and which sleeps no moment on an old past, but every hour repairs herself, yielding us every morning a new day, and with every pulsation a new life? Let him renounce everything which is not true to him, and put all his practices back on their first thoughts, and do nothing for which he has not the whole world for his reason. If there are inconveniences and what is called ruin in the way, because we have so enervated and maimed ourselves, yet it would be like dying of perfumes to sink in the effort to re-attach the deeds of every day to the holy and mysterious recesses of life.

The power which is at once spring and regulator in all efforts of reform is the conviction that there is an infinite worthiness in man, which will appear at the call of worth, and that all particular reforms are the removing of some impediment. Is it not the highest duty that man should be honored in us? I ought not to allow any man because he has broad lands to feel that he is rich in my presence. I ought to make him feel that I can do without his riches, that I cannot be bought, — neither by comfort, neither by pride, — and though I be utterly penniless, and receiving bread from him, that he is the poor man beside me. And if, at the same time, a woman or a child discovers a sentiment of piety, or a juster way of thinking than mine, I ought to confess it by my respect and obedience, though it go to alter my whole way of life.

The Americans have many virtues, but they have not Faith and Hope. I know no two words whose meaning is more lost sight of. We use these words as if they were as obsolete as Selah and Amen. And yet they have the broadest meaning, and the most cogent application to Boston in this year. The Americans have little faith. They rely on the power of a dollar; they are deaf to a sentiment. They think you may talk the north wind down as easily as raise society; and no class more faithless than the scholars or intellectual men. Now if I talk with a sincere wise man, and my friend, with a poet, with a conscientious youth who is still under the dominion of his own wild thoughts, and not yet harnessed in the team of society to drag with us all in the ruts of custom, I see at once how paltry is all this generation of unbelievers, and what a house of cards their institutions are, and I see what one brave man, what one great thought executed might effect. I see that the reason of the distrust of the practical man in all theory is his inability to perceive the means whereby we work. Look, he says, at the tools with which this world of yours is to be built. As we cannot make a planet, with atmosphere, rivers, and forests, by means of the best carpenters' or engineers' tools, with chemist's laboratory and smith's forge to boot, — so neither can we ever construct that heavenly society you prate of out of foolish, sick, selfish men and women, such as we know them to be. But the believer not only beholds his heaven to be possible, but already to begin to exist, — not by the men or materials the statesman uses, but by men transfigured and raised above themselves by the power of principles. To principles something else is possible that transcends all the power of expedients.

Every great and commanding moment in the annals of the world is the triumph of some enthusiasm. The victories of the Arabs after Mahomet, who, in a few years, from a small and mean beginning, established a larger empire than that of Rome, is an example. They did they knew not what. The naked Derar, horsed on an idea, was found an overmatch for a troop of Roman cavalry. The women fought like men, and conquered the Roman men. They were miserably equipped, miserably fed. They were Temperance troops. There was neither brandy nor flesh needed to feed them. They conquered Asia, and Africa, and Spain, on barley. The Caliph Omar's walking-stick struck more terror into those who saw it than another man's sword. His diet was barley bread; his sauce was salt; and oftentimes by way of abstinence he ate his bread without salt. His drink was water. His palace was built of mud; and when he left Medina to go to the conquest of Jerusalem, he rode on a red camel, with a wooden platter hanging at his saddle, with a bottle of water and two sacks, one holding barley and the other dried fruits.

But there will dawn ere long on our politics, on our modes of living, a nobler morning than that Arabian faith, in the sentiment of love. This is the one remedy for all ills, the panacea of nature. We must be lovers, and at once the impossible becomes possible. Our age and history, for these thousand years, has not been the history of kindness, but of selfishness. Our distrust is very expensive. The money we spend for courts and prisons is very ill laid out. We make, by distrust, the thief, and burglar, and incendiary, and by our court and jail we keep him so. An acceptance of the sentiment of love throughout Christendom for a season would bring the felon and the outcast to our side in tears, with the devotion of his faculties to our service. See this wide society of laboring men and women. We allow ourselves to be served by them, we live apart from them, and meet them without a salute in the streets. We do not greet their talents, nor rejoice in their good fortune, nor foster their hopes, nor in the assembly of the people vote for what is dear to them. Thus we enact the part of the selfish noble and king from the foundation of the world. See, this tree always bears one fruit. In every household, the peace of a pair is poisoned by the malice, slyness, indolence, and alienation of domestics. Let any two matrons meet, and observe how soon their conversation turns on the troubles from their " *help*," as our phrase is. In every knot of laborers the rich man does not feel himself among his friends, — and at the polls he finds them arrayed in a mass in distinct opposition to him. We complain that the politics of masses of the people are controlled by designing men, and led in opposition to manifest justice and the common weal, and to their own interests. But the people do not wish to be represented or ruled by the ignorant and base. They only vote for these because they were asked with the voice and semblance of kindness. They will not vote for them long. They inevitably prefer wit and probity. To use an Egyptian metaphor, it is not their will for any long time "to raise the nails of wild beasts, and to depress the heads of the sacred birds." Let our affection flow out to our fellows; it would operate in a day the greatest of all revolutions. It is better to work on institutions by the sun than by the wind. The State must consider the poor man, and all voices must speak for him. Every child that is born must have a just chance for his bread. Let the amelioration in our laws of property proceed from the concession of the rich, not from the grasping of the poor. Let us begin by habitual imparting. Let us understand that the equitable rule is that no one should take more than his share, let him be ever so rich. Let me feel that I am to be a lover. I am to see to it that the world is the better for me, and to find my reward in the act. Love would put a new face on this weary old world in which we dwell as pagans and enemies too long, and it would warm the heart to see how fast the vain diplomacy of statesmen, the impotence of armies, and navies, and lines of defence, would be superseded by this unarmed child. Love will creep where it cannot go, will accomplish that by imperceptible methods, — being its own lever, fulcrum, and power, — which force could never achieve. Have you not seen in the woods, in a late autumn morning, a poor fungus of mushroom, — a plant without any solidity, nay, that seemed nothing but a soft mush or jelly, — by its constant, total, and inconceivably gentle pushing, manage to break its way up through the frosty ground, and actually to lift a hard crust on its head? It is the symbol of the power of kindness. The virtue of this principle in human society in application to great interests is absolute and forgotten. Once or twice in history it has been tried in illustrious instances, with signal success. This great, overgrown, dead Christendom of ours still keeps alive at least the name of a lover of mankind. But one day all men will be lovers; and every calamity will be dissolved in the universal sunshine.

Will you suffer me to add one trait more to this portrait of man the reformer? The mediator between the spiritual and the actual world should have a great prospective prudence. An Arabian poet describes his hero by saying,

> Sunshine was he
> In the winter day;
> And in the midsummer
> Coolness and shade.

He who would help himself and others should not be a subject of irregular and interrupted impulses of virtue, but a continent, persisting, immovable person, — such as we have seen a few scattered up and down in time for the blessing of the world; men who have in the gravity of their nature a quality which answers to the fly-wheel in a mill, which distributes the motion equably over all the wheels and hinders it from falling unequally and suddenly in destructive shocks. It is better that joy should be spread over all the day in the form of strength than it should be concentrated into ecstasies, full of danger and followed by reactions. There is a sublime prudence which is the very highest that we know of man, which, believing in a vast future, — sure of more to come than is yet seen, — postpones always the present hour to the whole life; postpones talent to genius, and special results to character. As the merchant gladly takes money from his income to add to his capital, so is the great man very willing to lose particular powers and talents so that he gain in the elevation of his life. The opening of the spiritual sense disposes men ever to greater sacrifices, to leave their signal talents, their best means and skill of procuring a present success, their power and their fame, — to cast all things behind, in the insatiable thirst for divine communications. A purer fame, a greater power rewards the sacrifice. It is the conversion of our harvest into seed. As the farmer casts into the ground the finest ears of his grain, the time will come when we too shall hold nothing back, but shall eagerly convert more than we now possess into means and powers, when we shall be willing to sow the sun and the moon for seeds.

[*1841*]

from

THE YOUNG AMERICAN

We cannot look on the freedom of this country, in connexion with its youth, without a presentiment that here shall laws and institutions exist on some scale of proportion to the majesty of nature. To men legislating for the area betwix the two oceans, betwixt the snows and the tropics, somewhat of the gravity of nature will infuse itself into the code. A heterogeneous population crowding on all ships from all corners of the world to the great gates of North America, namely Boston, New York, and New Orleans, and thence proceeding inward to the prairie and the mountains, and quickly contributing their private thought to the public opinion, their toll to the treasury, and their vote to the election, it cannot be doubted that the legislation of this country should become more catholic and cosmopolitan than that of any other. It seems so easy for America to inspire and express the most expansive and humane spirit; new-born, free, healthful, strong, the land of the laborer, of the democrat, of the philanthropist, of the believer, of the saint, she should speak for the human race. It is the country of the Future. From Washington, proverbially "the city of magnificent distances," through all its cities, states, and territories, it is a country of beginnings, of projects, of designs, of expectations.

Gentlemen, there is a sublime and friendly Destiny by which the human race is guided, — the race never dying, the individual never spared, — to results affecting masses and ages. Men are narrow and selfish, but the Genius or Destiny is not narrow, but beneficent. It is not discovered in their calculated and voluntary activity, but in what befalls, with or without their design. Only what is inevitable interests us, and it turns out that love and good are inevitable, and in the course of things. That Genius has infused itself into nature. It indicates itself by a small excess of good, a small balance in brute facts always favourable to the side of reason. All the facts in any part of nature shall be tabulated and the results shall indicate the same security and benefit; so slight as to be hardly observable, and yet it is there. . . .

The history of commerce is the record of this beneficent tendency. The patriarchal form of government readily becomes despotic, as each person may see in his own family. Fathers wish to be fathers of the minds of their children, and behold with impatience a new character and way of thinking presuming to show itself in their own son or daughter. This feeling, which all their love and pride in the powers of their children cannot subdue, becomes petulance and tyranny when the head of the clan, the emperor of an empire, deals with the same difference of opinion in his subjects. Difference of opinion is the one crime which kings never forgive. An empire is an immense egotism. "I am the State," said the French Louis. When a French ambassador mentioned to Paul of Russia that a man of consequence in St. Petersburg was interesting himself in some manner, the Czar interrupted him, — "There is no man of consequence in this empire but he with whom I am actually speaking; and so long only as I am speaking to him is he of any consequence." And the Emperor Nicholas is reported to have said to his council, "The age is embarrassed with new opinions; rely on me, gentlemen, I shall oppose an iron will to the progress of liberal opinions."

It is easy to see that this patriarchal or family management gets to be rather troublesome to all but the papa; the sceptre comes to be a crow-bar. And this unpleasant egotism, Feudalism opposes and finally destroys. The king is compelled to call in the aid of his brothers and cousins and remote relations, to help him keep his overgrown house in order; and this club of noblemen always come at last to have a will of their own; they combine to brave the sovereign, and call in the aid of the people. Each chief attaches as many followers as he can, by kindness, maintenance, and gifts; and as long as war lasts, the nobles, who must be soldiers, rule very well. But when peace comes, the nobles prove very whimsical and uncomfortable masters; their frolics turn out to be insulting and degrading to the commoner. Feudalism grew to be a bandit and brigand.

Meantime Trade had begun to appear: Trade, a plant which grows wherever there is peace, as soon as there is peace, and as long as there is peace. The luxury and necessity of the noble fostered it. And as quickly as men go to foreign parts in ships or caravans, a new order of things springs up; new command takes place, new servants and new masters. Their information, their wealth, their correspondence, have made them quite other men than left their native shore. *They* are nobles now, and by another patent than the king's. Feudalism had been good, had broken the power of the kings, and had some good traits of its own; but it had grown mischievous, it was time for it to die, and as they say of dying people, all its faults came out. Trade was the strong man that broke it down and raised a new and unknown power in its place. It is a new agent in the world, and one of great function; it is a very intellectual force. This displaces physical strength, and installs computation, combination, information, science, in its room. It calls out all force of a certain kind that slumbered in the former dynasties. It is now in the midst of its career. Feudalism is not ended yet. Our governments still partake largely of that element. Trade goes to make the governments insignificant, and to bring every kind of faculty of every individual that can in any manner serve any person, *on sale*. Instead of a huge Army and Navy and Executive Department, it converts Government into an Intelligence-Office, where every man may find what he wishes to buy, and expose what he has to sell; not only produce and manufactures, but art, skill, and intellectual and moral values. This is the good and this the evil of trade, that it would put everything into market; talent, beauty, virtue, and man himself.

The philosopher and lover of man have much harm to say of trade; but the historian will see that trade was the principle of Liberty; that trade planted America and destroyed Feudalism; that it makes peace and keeps peace, and it will abolish slavery. We complain of its oppression of the poor, and of its building up a new aristocracy on the ruins of the aristocracy it destroys. But the aristocracy of trade has no permanence, is not entailed, was the result of toil and talent, the result of merit of some kind, and is continually falling, like the waves of the sea, before new claims of the same sort. Trade is an instrument in the hands of that friendly Power which works for us in our own despite. We design it thus and thus; it turns out otherwise and far better. This beneficent tendency, omnipotent without violence, exists and works. Every line of history inspires a confidence that we shall not go far wrong; that things mend. That is the moral of all we learn, that it warrants Hope, the prolific mother of reforms. Our part is plainly not to throw ourselves across the track, to block improvement and sit till we are stone, but to watch the uprise of successive mornings and to conspire with the new works of new days. Government has been a fossil; it should be a plant. I conceive that the office of statute law should be to express and not to impede the mind of mankind. New thoughts, new things. Trade was one instrument, but Trade is also but for a time, and must give way to somewhat broader and better, whose signs are already dawning in the sky.

I pass to speak of the signs of that which is the sequel of trade.

In consequence of the revolution in the state of society wrought by trade, Government in our times is beginning to wear a clumsy and cumbrous appearance. We have already seen our way to shorter methods. The time is full of good signs. Some of them shall ripen to fruit. All this beneficent socialism is a friendly omen, and the swelling cry of voices for the education of the people indicates that Government has other offices than those of banker and executioner. Witness the new movements in the civilized world, the Communism of France, Germany, and Switzerland; the Trades' Unions, the English League against the Corn Laws; and the whole *Industrial Statistics*, so called. In Paris, the blouse, the badge of the operative, has begun to make 'its appearance in the *salons*. Witness too the spectacle of three Communities which have within a very short time sprung up within this Commonwealth, besides several others undertaken by citizens of Massachusetts within the territory of other States. These proceeded from a variety of motives, from an impatience of many usages in common life, from a wish for greater freedom than the manners and opinions of society permitted, but in great part from a feeling that the true offices of the State, the State had let fall to the ground; that in the scramble of parties for the public purse, the main duties of government were omitted, — the duty to instruct the ignorant, to supply the poor with work and with good guidance. These communists preferred the agricultural life as the most favorable condition for human culture; but they thought that the farm, as we manage it, did not satisfy the right ambition of man. The farmer, after sacrificing pleasure, taste, freedom, thought, love, to his work, turns out often a bankrupt, like the merchant. This result might well seem astounding. All this drudgery, from cock-crowing to starlight, for all these years, to end in mortgages and the auctioneer's flag, and removing from bad to worse. It is time to have the thing looked into, and with a sifting criticism ascertain who is the fool. It seemed a great deal worse, because the farmer is living in the same town with men who pretend to know exactly what he wants. On one side is agricultural chemistry, coolly exposing the nonsense of our spendthrift agriculture and ruinous expense of manures, and offering, by means of a teaspoonful of artificial guano, to turn a sandbank into corn; and on the other, the farmer, not only eager for the information, but with bad crops and in debt and bankruptcy, for want of it. Here are Etzlers and mechanical projectors, who, with the Fourierists, undoubtingly affirm that the smallest union would make every man rich; — and, on the other side, a multitude of poor men and women seeking work, and who cannot find enough to pay their board. The science is confident, and surely the poverty is real. If any means could be found to bring these two together!

This was one design of the projectors of the Associations which are now making their first feeble experiments. They were founded in love and in labor. They proposed, as you know, that all men should take a part in the manual toil, and proposed to amend the condition of men by substituting harmonious for hostile industry. It was a noble thought of Fourier, which gives a favorable idea of his system, to distinguish in his Phalanx a class as the Sacred Band, by whom whatever duties were disagreeable and likely to be omitted were to be assumed.

At least an economical success seemed certain for the enterprise, and that agricultural association must, sooner or later, fix the price of bread, and drive single farmers into association in self-defence; as the great commercial and manufacturing companies had already done. The Community is only the continuation of the same movement which made the joint-stock companies for manufactures, mining, insurance, banking, and so forth. It has turned out cheaper to make calico by companies; and it is proposed to plant corn and to bake bread by companies.

Undoubtedly, abundant mistakes will be made by these first adventurers, which will draw ridicule on their schemes. I think for example that they exaggerate the importance of a favorite project of theirs, that of paying talent and labor at one rate, paying all sorts of service at one rate, say ten cents the hour. They have paid it so; but not an instant would a dime remain a dime. In one hand it became an eagle as it fell, and in another hand a copper cent. For the whole value of the dime is in knowing what to do with it. One man buys with it a land-title of an Indian, and makes his posterity princes; or buys corn enough to feed the world; or pen, ink, and paper, or a painter's brush, by which he can communicate himself to the human race as if he were fire; and the other buys barley candy. Money is of no value; it cannot spend itself. All depends on the skill of the spender. Whether to the objection almost universally felt by such women in the community as were mothers, to an associate life, to a common table, and a common nursery, etc., setting a higher value on the private family, with poverty, than on an association with wealth, will not prove insuperable, remains to be determined.

But the Communities aimed at a higher success in securing to all their members an equal and thorough education. And on the whole one may say that aims so generous and so forced on them by the times, will not be relinquished, even if these attempts fail, but will be prosecuted until they succeed.

This is the value of the Communities; not what they have done, but the revolution which they indicate as on the way. Yes, Government must educate the poor man. Look across the country from any hill-side around us and the landscape seems to crave Government. The actual differences of men must be acknowledged, and met with love and wisdom. These rising grounds which command the champaign below seem to ask for lords, true lords, *land*lords, who understand the land and its uses and the applicabilities of men, and whose government would be what it should, namely mediation between want and supply. . . .

How can our young men complain of the poverty of things in New England and not feel that poverty as a demand on their charity to make New England rich? Where is he who seeing a thousand men useless and unhappy, and making the whole region forlorn by their inaction, and conscious himself of possessing the faculty they want, does not hear his call to go and be their king?

We must have kings, and we must have nobles. Nature provides such in every society, — only let us have the real instead of the titular. Let us have our leading and our inspiration from the best. In every society some men are born to rule and some to advise. Let the powers be well directed, directed by love, and they would everywhere be greeted with joy and honor. The chief is the chief all the world over, only not his cap and his plume. It is only their dislike of the pretender which makes men sometimes unjust to the accomplished man. If society were transparent, the noble would everywhere be gladly received and accredited, and would not be asked for his day's work, but would be felt as benefit, inasmuch as he was noble. That were his duty and stint, — to keep himself pure and purifying, the leaven of his nation. I think I see the place and duties for a nobleman in every society; but it is not to drink wine and ride in a fine coach, but to guide and adorn life for the multitude by forethought, by elegant studies, by perseverance, self-devotion, and the remembrance of the humble old friend, by making his life secretly beautiful.

I call upon you, young man, to obey your heart and be the nobility of this land. In every age of the world there has been a leading nation, one of a more generous sentiment, whose eminent citizens were willing to stand for the interests of general justice and humanity, at the risk of being called, by the men of the moment, chimerical and fantastic. Which should be that nation but these States? Which should lead that movement, if not New England? Who should lead the leaders, but the Young American? The people, and the world, are now suffering from the want of religion and honor in its public mind. In America, out-of-doors all seems a market; in-doors an air-tight stove of conventionalism. Everybody who comes into our houses savors of these habits; the men, of the market; the women, of the custom. I find no expression in our state papers or legislative debate, in our lyceums or churches, especially in our newspapers, of a high national feeling, no lofty counsels that rightfully stir the blood. I speak of those organs which can be presumed to speak a popular sense. They recommend conventional virtues, whatever will earn and preserve property; always the capitalist; the college, the church, the hospital, the theatre, the hotel, the road, the ship of the capitalist, — whatever goes to secure, adorn, enlarge these is good; what jeopardizes any of these is damnable. The " opposition " papers, so called, are on the same side. They attack the great capitalist, but with the aim to make a capitalist of the poor man. The opposition is against those who have money, from those who wish to have money. But who announces to us in journal, or in pulpit, or in the street, the secret of heroism? . . .

The timidity of our public opinion is our disease, or, shall I say, the publicness of opinion, the absence of private opinion. Good nature is plentiful, but we want justice, with heart of steel, to fight down the proud. The private mind has the access to the totality of goodness and truth that it may be a balance to a corrupt society; and to stand for the private verdict against popular clamor is the office of the noble. If a humane measure is propounded in behalf of the slave, or of the Irishman, or the Catholic, or for the succor of the poor; that sentiment, that project, will have the homage of the hero. That is his nobility, his oath of knighthood, to succor the helpless and oppressed; always to throw himself on the side of weakness, of youth, of hope; on the liberal, on the expansive side, never on the defensive, the conserving, the timorous, the lock-and-bolt system. More than our good-will we may not be able to give. We have our own affairs, our own genius, which chains each to his proper work. We cannot give our life to the cause of the debtor, of the slave, or the pauper, as another is doing; but to one thing we are bound, not to blaspheme the sentiment and the work of that man, not to throw stumbling-blocks in the way of abolitionist, the philanthropist; as the organs of influence and opinion are swift to do. It is for us to confide in the beneficent Supreme Power, and not to rely on our money, and on the state because it is the guard of money. At this moment the terror of old people and of vicious people is lest the Union of these states be destroyed: as if the Union had any other real basis than the good pleasure of a majority of the citizens to be united. But the wise and just man will always feel that he stands on his own feet; that he imparts strength to the State, not receives security from it; and that if all went down, he and such as he would quite easily combine in a new and better constitution. Every great and memorable community has consisted of formidable individuals, who, like the Roman or the Spartan, lent his own spirit to the State and made it great. Yet only by the supernatural is a man strong; nothing is so weak as an egotist. Nothing is mightier than we, when we are vehicles of a truth before which the State and the individual are alike ephemeral.

Gentlemen, the development of our American internal resources, the extension to the utmost of the commercial system, and the appearance of new moral causes which are to modify the State are given an aspect of greatness to the Future, which the imagination fears to open. One thing is plain for all men of common sense and common conscience, that here, here in America, is the home of man. After all the deductions which are to be made for our pitiful politics, which stake every gravest national question on the silly die whether James or whether Robert shall sit in the chair and hold the purse; after all the deduction is made for our frivolities and insanities, there still remains an organic simplicity and liberty, which, when it loses its balance, redresses itself presently, which offers opportunity to the human mind not known in any other region.

It is true, the public mind wants self-respect. We are full of vanity, of which the most signal proof is our sensitiveness to foreign and especially English censure. One cause of this is our immense reading, and that reading chiefly confined to the productions of the English press. It is also true that to imaginative persons in this country there is somewhat bare and bald in our short history and unsettled wilderness. They ask, who would live in a new country that can live in an old? and it is not strange that our youths and maidens should burn to see the picturesque extremes of an antiquated country. But it is one thing to visit the Pyramids, and another to wish to live there. Would they like tithes to the clergy, and sevenths to the government, and Horse-Guards, and licensed press, and grief when a child is born, and threatening, starved weavers, and pauperism now constituting one thirteenth of the population? Instead of the open future expanding here before the eye of every boy to vastness, would they like the closing in of the future to a narrow slit of sky, and that fast contracting to be no future? One thing for instance, the beauties of aristocracy, we commend to study of the travelling American. The English, the most conservative people this side of India, are not sensible of the restraint, but an American would seriously resent it. The aristocracy, incorporated by law and education, degrades life for the unprivileged classes. It is a questionable compensation to the embittered feeling of a proud commoner, the reflection that a fop, who, by the magic of title, paralyzes his arm and plucks from him half the graces and rights of a man, is himself also an aspirant excluded with the same ruthlessness from higher circles, since there is no end to the wheels within wheels of this spiral heaven. Something may be pardoned to the spirit of loyalty when it becomes fantastic; and something to the imagination, for the baldest life is symbolic. Philip II. of Spain rated his ambassador for neglecting serious affairs in Italy, while he debated some point of honor with the French ambassador; "You have left a business of importance for a ceremony." The ambassador replied, "Your Majesty's self is but a ceremony." In the East, where the religious sentiment comes in to the support of the aristocracy, and in the Romish church also, there is a grain of sweetness in the tyranny; but in England, the fact seems to me intolerable, what is commonly affirmed, that such is the transcendent honor accorded to wealth and birth that no man of letters, be his eminence what it may, is received into the best society, except as a lion and a show. The English have many virtues, many advantages and the proudest history of the world; but they need all and more than all the resources of the past to indemnify a heroic gentleman in that country for the mortifications prepared for him by the system of society, and which seem to impose the alternative to resist or to avoid it. That there are mitigations and practical alleviations to this rigor is not an excuse for the rule. Commanding worth and personal power must sit crowned in all companies, nor will extraordinary persons be slighted or affronted in any company of civilized men. But the system is an invasion of the sentiment of justice and the native rights of men, which, however, decorated, must lessen the value of English citizenship. It is for Englishmen to consider, not for us; we only say, Let us live in America, too thankful for our want of feudal institutions. Our houses and towns are like mosses and lichens, so slight and new; but youth is a fault of which we shall daily mend. This land too is as old as the Flood, and wants no ornament or privilege which nature could bestow. Here stars, here woods, here hills, here animals, here men abound, and the vast tendencies concur of a new order. If only the men are employed in conspiring with the designs of the Spirit who led us hither and is leading us still, we shall quickly enough advance out of all hearing of others' censures, out of all regrets of our own, into a new and more excellent social state than history has recorded.

[*1844*]

from

CIVILIZATION

If there be a country which cannot stand any one of these tests, — a country where knowledge cannot be diffused without perils of mob law and statute law; where speech is not free; where the post-office is violated, mail-bags opened and letters tampered with; where public debts and private debts outside of the State are repudiated; where liberty is attacked in the primary institution of social life; where the position of the white woman is injuriously affected by the outlawry of the black woman; where the arts, such as they have, are all imported, having no indigenous life; where the laborer is not secured in the earnings of his own hands; where suffrage is not free or equal; — that country is, in all these respects, not civil, but barbarous; and no advantages of soil, climate or coast can resist these suicidal mischiefs.

Morality and all the incidents of morality are essential; as, justice to the citizen, and personal liberty. Montesquieu says: "Countries are well cultivated, not as they are fertile, but as they are free"; and the remark holds not less but more true of the culture of men than of the tillage of land. And the highest proof of civility is that the whole public action of the State is directed on securing the greatest good of the greatest number.

[*1862*]

ODE

Inscribed to W. H. Channing

Though loath to grieve
The evil time's sole patriot,
I cannot leave
My honied thought
For the priest's cant,
Or statesman's rant.

If I refuse
My study for their politique,
Which at the best is trick,
The angry Muse
Puts confusion in my brain.

But who is he that prates
Of the culture of mankind,
Of better arts and life?
Go, blindworm, go,
Behold the famous States
Harrying Mexico
With rifle and with knife!

Or who, with accent bolder,
Dare praise the freedom-loving mountaineer?
I found by thee, O rushing Contoocook!

And in thy valleys, Agiochook!
The jackals of the negro-holder.

The God who made New Hampshire
Taunted the lofty land
With little men; —
Small bat and wren
House in the oak: —
If earth-fire cleave
The upheaved land, and bury the folk,
The southern crocodile would grieve.
Virtue palters; Right is hence;
Freedom praised, but hid;
Funeral eloquence
Rattles the coffin-lid.

What boots thy zeal,
O glowing friend,
That would indignant rend
The northland from the south?
Wherefore? to what good end?
Boston Bay and Bunker Hill
Would serve things still; —
Things are of the snake.

The horseman serves the horse,
The neatherd serves the neat,
The merchant serves the purse,
The eater serves his meat;
'Tis the day of the chattel,
Web to weave, and corn to grind;
Things are in the saddle,
And ride mankind.

There are two laws discrete,
Not reconciled, —
Law for man, and law for thing;
The last builds town and fleet,
But it runs wild,
And doth the man unking.

'Tis fit the forest fall,
The steep be graded,
The mountain tunnelled,
The sand shaded,
The orchard planted,
The glebe tilled,
The prairie granted,
The steamer built.

Let man serve law for man;
Live for friendship, live for love,
For truth's and harmony's behoof;
The state many follow how it can,
As Olympus follows Jove.

Yet do not I implore
The wrinkled shopman to my sounding woods,
Nor bid the unwilling senator
Ask votes of thrushes in the solitudes.
Every one to his chosen work; —
Foolish hands may mix and mar;
Wise and sure the issues are.
Round they roll till dark is light,
Sex to sex, and even to odd; —
The over-god
Who marries Right to Might,
Who peoples, unpeoples, —
He who exterminates
Races by stronger races,
Black by white faces, —
Knows to bring honey
Out of the lion;
Grafts gentlest scion
On pirate and Turk.

The Cossack eats Poland,
Like stolen fruit;
Her last noble is ruined,
Her last poet mute:

Straight, into double band
The victors divide;
Half for freedom strike and stand; —
The astonished Muse finds thousands at her side.
[*1847*]

VOLUNTARIES

I

Low and mournful be the strain,
Haughty thought be far from me;
Tones of penitence and pain,
Moanings of the tropic sea;
Low and tender in the cell
Where a captive sits in chains,
Crooning ditties treasured well
From his Afric's torrid plains.
Sole estate his sire bequeathed, —
Hapless sire to hapless son, —
Was the wailing song he breathed,
And his chain when life was done.

What his fault, or what his crime?
Or what ill planet crossed his prime?
Heart too soft and will too weak
To front the fate that crouches near, —
Dove beneath the vulture's beak; —
Will song dissuade the thirsty spear?
Dragged from his mother's arms and breast,
Displaced, disfurnished here,
His wistful toil to do his best
Chilled by a ribald jeer.
Great men in the Senate sate,

Sage and hero, side by side,
Building for their sons the State,
Which they shall rule with pride.
They forbore to break the chain
Which bound the dusky tribe,
Checked by the owners' fierce disdain,
Lured by " Union " as the bribe.
Destiny sat by, and said,
" Pang for pang your seed shall pay,
Hide in false peace your coward head,
I bring round the harvest day."

II

Freedom all winged expands,
Nor perches in a narrow place;
Her broad van seeks unplanted lands;
She loves a poor and virtuous race.
Clinging to a colder zone
Whose dark sky sheds the snowflake down,
The snowflake is her banner's star,
Her stripes the boreal streamers are.
Long she loved the Northman well;
Now the iron age is done,
She will not refuse to dwell
With the offspring of the Sun;
Foundling of the desert far,
Where palms plume, siroccos blaze,
He roves unhurt the burning ways
In climates of the summer star.
He has avenues to God
Hid from men of Northern brain,
Far beholding, without cloud,
What these with slowest steps attain.
If once the generous chief arrive
To lead him willing to be led,
For freedom he will strike and strive,
And drain his heart till he be dead.

III

In an age of fops and toys,
Wanting wisdom, void of right,
Who shall nerve heroic boys
To hazard all in Freedom's fight, —
Break sharply off their jolly games,
Forsake their comrades gay
And quit proud homes and youthful dames
For famine, toil and fray?
Yet on the nimble air benign
Speed nimbler messages,
That waft the breath of grace divine
To hearts in sloth and ease.
So nigh is grandeur to our dust,
So near is God to man,
When Duty whispers low, *Thou must,*
The youth replies, *I can.*

IV

O, well for the fortunate soul
Which Music's wings infold,
Stealing away the memory
Of sorrows new and old!
Yet happier he whose inward sight,
Stayed on his subtile thought,
Shuts his sense on toys of time,
To vacant bosoms brought.
But best befriended of the God
He who, in evil times,
Warned by an inward voice,
Heeds not the darkness and the dread,
Biding by his rule and choice,
Feeling only the fiery thread
Leading over heroic ground,
Walled with mortal terror round,
To the aim which him allures,
And the sweet heaven his deed secures

Peril around, all else appalling,
Cannon in front and leaden rain
Him duty through the clarion calling
To the van called not in vain.

Stainless soldier on the walls,
Knowing this, — and knows no more, —
Whoever fights, whoever falls,
Justice conquers evermore,
Justice after as before, —
And he who battles on her side,
God, though he were ten times slain,
Crowns him victor glorified,
Victor over death and pain.

v

Blooms the laurel which belongs
To the valiant chief who fights;
I see the wreath, I hear the songs
Lauding the Eternal Rights,
Victors over daily wrongs:
Awful victors, they misguide
Whom they will destroy,
And their coming triumph hide
In our downfall, or our joy:
They reach no term, they never sleep,
In equal strength through space abide;
Though, feigning dwarfs, they crouch and creep,
The strong they slay, the swift outstride:
Fate's grass grows rank in valley clods,
And rankly on the castled steep, —
Speak it firmly, these are gods,
All are ghosts beside.

[1863]

MARGARET FULLER

[1810–1850]

ONE of the truly remarkable women America has produced, her colorful personality and rather spectacular life have obscured her actual accomplishments. At a very early age she revealed great abilities as a scholar, whereupon her father — an educated and ambitious man, state Senator in Massachusetts — encouraged her to become a monster of erudition. The result was, of course, that the sensitive, precocious girl became a somewhat hysterical woman. Hardly prepossessing in appearance, she was an easy object of irony. Nevertheless, she was accepted in the transcendentalist community on equal terms with its illustrious male members: Emerson, Alcott, Thoreau, George Ripley, and the others. Miss Fuller very quickly became our foremost champion of women's rights. She was not merely a feminist, however. Her demands for the liberation and equality of women were part of her entire system of thought, which was that of a radical democrat. Her general point of view is evident in her provocative literary criticism — of which she wrote a great deal for Horace Greeley's paper, the *New York Tribune* — quite as much as in her philosophical and social writings. Her style was not felicitous: it was heavy, full of the vague transcendentalist phraseology of the day; but her ideas and emotions came through well enough. In 1846 she went on a visit to Europe. In Rome she met the Marquese d'Ossoli and joined him in the republican movement led by Mazzini. She married Ossoli, became a mother, yet continued her political work. When the revolt collapsed she sailed for America. The ship bearing the Ossolis was wrecked off Fire Island, New York, on July 19, 1850. She perished with her husband and child.

POETS OF THE PEOPLE

There are two ways of considering Poems, or the products of literature in general. We may tolerate only what is excellent, and demand that whatever is consigned to print for the benefit of the human race should exhibit fruits perfect in shape, colour, and flavour, enclosing kernels of permanent value.

Those who demand this will be content only with the Iliads and Odysseys of the mind's endeavour. — They can feed nowhere but at rich men's tables; in the wildest recess of nature roots and berries will not content them. They say, " If you can thus satiate your appetite it is degrading; we, the highly refined in taste and the tissue of the mind, can nowhere be appeased, unless by golden apples, served up on silver dishes."

But, on the other hand, literature may be regarded as the great mutual system of interpretation between all kinds and classes of men. It is an epistolary correspondence between brethren of one family, subject to many and wide separations, and anxious to remain in spiritual presence one of another. These letters may be written by the prisoner in soot and water, illustrated by rude sketches in charcoal; — by nature's nobleman, free to use his inheritance, in letters of gold, with the fair margin filled with exquisite miniatures; — to the true man each will have value, *first*, in proportion to the degree of its revelation as to the life of the human soul, *second*, in proportion to the perfection of form in which that revelation is expressed.

In like manner are there two modes of criticism. One which tries, by the highest standard of literary perfection the critic is capable of conceiving, each work which comes in his way; rejecting all that it is possible to reject, and reserving for toleration only what is capable of standing the severest test. It crushes to earth without mercy all the humble buds of Phantasy, all the plants that, though green and fruitful, are also a prey to insects, or have suffered by death. It weeds well the garden, and cannot believe that the weed in its native soil may be a pretty, graceful plant.

There is another mode which enters into the natural history of every thing that breathes and lives, which believes no impulse to be entirely in vain, which scrutinizes circumstances, motive and object before it condemns, and believes there is a beauty in each natural form, if its law and purpose be understood. It does not consider a literature merely as the garden of the nation, but as the growth of the entire region, with all its variety of mountain, forest, pasture, and tillage lands. Those who observe in this spirit will often experience, from some humble offering to the Muses, the delight felt by the naturalist in the grasses and lichens of some otherwise barren spot. These are the earliest and humblest efforts of nature, but to a discerning eye they indicate the entire range of her energies.

These two schools have each their dangers. The first tends to hyper-criticism and pedantry, to a cold restriction on the unstudied action of a large and flowing life. In demanding that the stream should always flow transparent over golden sands, it tends to repress its careless majesty, its vigour, and its fertilizing power.

The other shares the usual perils of the genial and affectionate; it tends to indiscriminate indulgence and a leveling of the beautiful with what is merely tolerable. For indeed the vines need judicious pruning if they are to bring us the ruby wine.

In the golden age to which we are ever looking forward, these two tendencies will be harmonized. The highest sense of fulfilled excellence will be found to consist with the largest appreciation of every sign of life. The eye of man is fitted to range all around no less than to be lifted on high.

Meanwhile the spirit of the time, which is certainly seeking, though by many and strange ways, the greatest happiness for the greatest number, by discoveries which facilitate mental no less than bodily communication, till soon it will be almost as easy to get your thought printed or engraved on a thousand leaves as to drop it from the pen on one, and by the simultaneous bubbling up of rills of thought in a thousand hitherto obscure and silent places, declares that the genial and generous tendency shall have the lead, at least for the present.

We are not ourselves at all concerned, lest excellent expression should cease because the power of speech to some extent becomes more general. The larger the wave and the more fish it sweeps along, the likelier that some fine ones should enrich the net. It has always been so. The great efforts of art belong to artistic regions, where the boys in the street draw sketches on the wall and torment melodies on rude flutes; shoals of sonneteers follow in the wake of the great poet. The electricity which flashes with the thunderbolts of Jove must first pervade the whole atmosphere.

[1845]

from

WOMAN IN THE NINETEENTH CENTURY

It should be remarked that, as the principle of liberty is better understood, and more nobly interpreted, a broader protest is made in behalf of woman. As men become aware that few men have had a fair chance, they are inclined to say that no women have had a fair chance. The French Revolution, that strangely disguised angel, bore witness in favour of woman, but interpreted her claims no less ignorantly than those of man. Its idea of happiness did not rise beyond outward enjoyment, unobstructed by the tyranny of others. The title it gave was citoyen, citoyenne, and it is not unimportant to woman that even this species of equality was awarded her. Before, she could be condemned to perish on the scaffold for treason, not as a citizen, but as a subject. The right with which this title then invested a human being was that of bloodshed and license. The Goddess of liberty was impure. As we read the poem addressed to her not long since, by Béranger, we can scarcely refrain from tears as painful as the tears of blood that flowed when "such crimes were committed in her name." Yes! man, born to purify and animate the unintelligent and the cold, can, in his madness, degrade and pollute no less the fair and the chaste. Yet truth was prophesied in the ravings of that hideous fever, caused by long ignorance and abuse. Europe is conning a valued lesson from the blood-stained page. The same tendencies, farther unfolded, will bear good fruit in this country.

Yet, by men in this country, as by the Jews, when Moses was leading them to the promised land, everything has been done that inherited depravity could do, to hinder the promise of heaven from its fulfilment. The cross here, as elsewhere, has been planted only to be blasphemed by cruelty and fraud. The name of the Prince of Peace has been profaned by all kinds of injustice toward the Gentile whom he said he came to save. But I need not speak of what has been done towards the red man, the black man. Those deeds are the scoff of the world; and they have been accompanied by such pious words that the gentlest would not dare to intercede with "Father, forgive them, for they know not what they do."

Here, as elsewhere, the gain of creation consists always in the growth of individual minds, which live and aspire, as flowers bloom and birds sing, in the midst of morasses; and in the continual development of that thought, the thought of human destiny, which is given to eternity adequately to express, and which ages of failure only seemingly impede. Only seemingly, and whatever seems to the contrary, this country is as surely destined to elucidate a great moral law as Europe was to promote the mental culture of man.

Though the national independence be blurred by the servility of individuals, though freedom and equality have been proclaimed only to leave room for a monstrous display of slave-dealing and slave-keeping; though the free American so often feels himself free, like the Roman, only to pamper his appetites and his indolence through the misery of his fellow-beings, still it is not in vain that the verbal statement has been made, "All men are born free and equal." There it stands, a golden certainty wherewith to encourage the good, to shame the bad. The new world may be called clearly to perceive that it incurs the utmost penalty if it reject or oppress the sorrowful brother. And, if men are deaf, the angels hear. But men cannot be deaf.

It is inevitable that an external freedom, an independence of the encroachments of other men, such as has been achieved for the nation, should be so also for every member of it. That which has once been clearly conceived in the intelligence cannot fail, sooner or later, to be acted out. It has become a law as irrevocable as that of the Medes in their ancient dominion; men will privately sin against it, but the law, as expressed by a leading mind of the age,

> " *Tutti fatti a sembianza d'un Solo,*
> *Figil tutti d'un solo riscatto,*
> *In qual'ora, in qual parte del suolo,*
> *Tras corriamo quest'aura vital,*
> *Siam fratelli, siam stretti ad un patto:*
> *Maladetto colui che lo infrange,*
> *Che s'innalza sul fiacco che piange*
> *Che contrista uno spirto immortal.*" [1]

> " All made in the likeness of the One,
> All children of one ransom,
> In whatever hour, in whatever part of the soil,
> We draw this vital air,

[1] Manzoni.

298

> We are brothers; we must be bound by one compact,
>   Accursed he who infringes it,
> Who raises himself upon the weak who weep,
>   Who saddens an immortal spirit."

This law cannot fail of universal recognition. Accursed be he who willingly saddens an immortal spirit, doomed to infamy in latter, wiser ages, doomed in future stages of his own being to deadly penance, only short of death. Accursed be he who sins in ignorance, if that ignorance be caused by sloth. . . .

It is not the transient breath of poetic incense that women want; each can receive that from a lover. It is not life-long sway; it needs but to become a coquette, a shrew, or a good cook to be sure of that. It is not money, nor notoriety, nor the badges of authority that men have appropriated to themselves. If demands, made in their behalf, lay stress on any of these particulars, those who make them have not searched deeply into the need. It is for that which at once includes these and precludes them; which would not be forbidden power, lest there be temptation to steal and misuse it; which would not have the mind perverted by flattery from a worthiness of esteem. It is for that which is the birthright of every being capable to receive it — the freedom, the religious, the intelligent freedom of the universe, to use its means; to learn its secret as far as nature has enabled them, with God alone for their guide and their judge.

Ye cannot believe it, men; but the only reason why women ever assume what is more appropriate to you is because you prevent them from finding out what is fit for themselves. Were they free, were they wise fully to develop the strength and beauty of woman, they would never wish to be men, or man-like. The well-instructed moon flies not from her orbit to seize on the glories of her partner. No; for she knows that one law rules, one heaven contains, one universe replies to them alike. It is with women as with the slave —

> "*Vor dem Sklaven, wenn er die Kette bricht,*
>   *Vor dem frein Menschen erzittert nicht.*"

Tremble not before the free man, but before the slave who has chains to break.

[*1843–55*]

ORESTES A. BROWNSON

[1803–1876]

HE WAS born in Stockbridge, Vermont, and raised in extreme poverty by a widowed mother, until she gave up the struggle and left him to the charity of a neighbor. He grew up on a small farm where he had no opportunities to acquire a formal education. But he read avidly and continuously, particularly in philosophy and religion. At nineteen he turned toward the Presbyterian Church, then left it because of its severe doctrines. In 1826 he was ordained as a Universalist minister. Eventually this church also dissatisfied him, as his theological and social opinions grew more and more unorthodox. He associated himself with the utopian socialists, Robert Dale Owen and Fanny Wright, and participated in the launching of a Workingmen's Party. In 1832 he entered the Unitarian Church, in 1836 organized his own church for the workingmen of Boston. He was now definitely and publicly opposed to all the established churches and sects. In 1838 he founded the *Boston Quarterly Review,* in which he published some of the most radical essays of that literarily radical period. He wrote of the class struggle, attacked wealth, predicted revolution, denounced formal religion. He was certainly the most "left" of the transcendentalist and Brook Farm groups. After six years of writing for this journal and its successors, he suddenly announced his conversion to Catholicism. Naturally, his social views changed completely after that, and his later writings were devoted chiefly to answering the enemies of the Catholic Church.

---

from

THE LABORING CLASSES

[A REVIEW OF THOMAS CARLYLE'S "CHARTISM"]

Chartism, properly speaking, is no local or temporary phenomenon. Its germ may be found in every nation in Christendom; indeed wherever man has approximated a state of civilization, wherever there is inequality in social condition, and in the distribution of the products of industry. And where does not this inequality obtain? Where is the spot on earth, in which the actual producer of wealth is not one of the lower class, shut out from what are looked upon as the main advantages of the social state?

Mr. Carlyle, though he gives us few facts, yet shows us that the condition of the workingmen in England is deplorable, and every day growing worse. It has already become intolerable, and hence the outbreak of the Chartists. Chartism is the protest of the working classes against the injustice of the present social organization of the British community, and a loud demand for a new organization which shall respect the rights and well-being of the laborer.

The movements of the Chartists have excited considerable alarm in the higher classes of English society, and some hope in the friends of Humanity among ourselves. We do not feel competent to speak with any decision on the extent or importance of these movements. If our voice could reach the Chartists we would bid them be bold and determined; we would bid them persevere even unto death; for their cause is that of justice, and in fighting for it they will be fighting the battles of God and man. But we look for no important results from their movements. We have little faith in a John Bull mob. It will bluster, and swagger, and threaten much; but give it plenty of porter and roast beef, and it will sink back to its kennel, as quiet and as harmless as a lamb. The lower classes in England have made many a move since the days of Wat Tyler for the betterment of their condition, but we cannot perceive that they have ever effected much. They are doubtless nearer the day of their emancipation than they were, but their actual condition is scarcely superior to what it was in the days of Richard the Second.

There is no country in Europe, in which the condition of the laboring classes seems to us so hopeless as in that of England. This is not owing to the fact that the aristocracy is less enlightened, more powerful, or more oppressive in England than elsewhere. The English laborer does not find his worst enemy in the nobility, but in the middling class. The middle class is much more numerous and powerful in England than in any other European country, and is of a higher character. It has always been powerful; for by means of the Norman Conquest it received large accessions from the old Saxon nobility. The Conquest established a new aristocracy, and degraded the old to the condition of Commoners. The superiority of the English Commons is, we suppose, chiefly owing to this fact.

The middle class is always a firm champion of equality when it concerns humbling a class above it; but it is its inveterate foe when it concerns elevating a class below it. Manfully have the British Commoners struggled against the old feudal aristocracy, and so successfully that they now constitute the dominant power in the state. To their struggles against the throne and the nobility is the English nation indebted for the liberty it so loudly boasts, and which, during the last half of the last century, so enraptured the friends of Humanity throughout Europe.

But this class has done nothing for the laboring population, the real *proletarii*. It has humbled the aristocracy; it has raised itself to dominion, and it is now conservative, — conservative in fact, whether it call itself Whig or Radical. From its near relation to the workingmen, its kindred pursuits with them, it is altogether more hostile to them than the nobility ever were or ever can be. This was seen in the conduct of England towards the French Revolution. So long as that Revolution was in the hands of the middle class, and threatened merely to humble monarchy and nobility, the English nation applauded it; but as soon as it descended to the mass of the people, and promised to elevate the laboring classes, so soon as the starving workingman began to flatter himself, that there was to be a Revolution for him too as well as for his employer, the English nation armed itself and poured out its blood and treasure to suppress it. Everybody knows that Great Britain, boasting of her freedom and of her love of freedom, was the life and soul of the opposition to the French Revolution; and on her head almost alone should fall the curses of Humanity for the sad failure of that glorious uprising of the people in behalf of their imprescriptible and inalienable rights. Yet it was not the English monarchy, nor the English nobility, that was alone in fault. Monarchy and nobility would have been powerless, had they not had with them the great body of the English Commoners. England fought in the ranks, nay, at the head of the allies, not for monarchy, not for nobility, nor yet for religion; but for trade and manufactures, for her middle class, against the rights and well-being of the workingman; and her strength and efficiency consisted in the strength and efficiency of this class.

Now this middle class, which was strong enough to defeat nearly all the practical benefit of the French Revolution, is the natural enemy of the Chartists. It will unite with the monarchy and nobility against them; and spare neither blood nor treasure to defeat them. Our despair for the poor Chartists arises from the number and power of the middle class. We dread for them neither monarchy nor nobility. Nor should they. Their only real enemy is in the employer. In all countries is it the same. The only enemy of the laborer is your employer, whether appearing in the shape of the master mechanic, or in the owner of a factory. A Duke of Wellington is much more likely to vindicate the rights of labor than an Abbot Lawrence, although the latter may be a very kind-hearted man, and liberal citizen, as we always find Blackwood's Magazine more true to the interests of the poor than we do the Edinburgh Review, or even the London and Westminster.

Mr. Carlyle, contrary to his wont, in the pamphlet we have named, commends two projects for the relief of the workingmen, which he finds others have suggested, — universal education, and general emigration. Universal education we shall not be thought likely to depreciate; but we confess that we are unable to see in it that sovereign remedy for the evils of the social state as it is which some of our friends do, or say they do. We have little faith in the power of education to elevate a people compelled to labor from twelve to sixteen hours a day, and to experience for no mean portion of the time a paucity of even the necessaries of life, let alone its comforts. Give your starving boy a breakfast before you send him to school, and your tattered beggar a cloak before you attempt his moral and intellectual elevation. A swarm of naked and starving urchins crowded into a schoolroom will make little proficiency in the "Humanities." Indeed, it seems to us most bitter mockery for the well-dressed and well-fed to send the schoolmaster and priest to the wretched hovels of squalid poverty, — a mockery at which devils may laugh, but over which angels must weep. Educate the working classes of England; and what then? Will they require less food and less clothing when educated than they do now? Will they be more contented or more happy in their condition? For God's sake beware how you kindle within them the intellectual spark, and make them aware that they too are men, with powers of thought and feeling which ally them by the bonds of brotherhood to their betters. If you will doom them to the external condition of brutes, do in common charity keep their minds and hearts brutish. Render them as insensible as possible, that they may feel the less acutely their degradation, and see the less clearly the monstrous injustice which is done them.

General emigration can at best afford only a temporary relief, for the colony will soon become an empire, and reproduce all the injustice and wretchedness of the mother country. Nor is general emigration necessary. England, if she would be just, could support a larger population than she now numbers. The evil is not from over-population, but from the unequal repartition of the fruits of industry. She suffers from over-production . . . because her workmen produce not for themselves but for their employers. What then is the remedy? As it concerns England, we shall leave the English statesman to answer. Be it what it may, it will not be obtained without war and bloodshed. It will be found only at the end of one of the longest and severest struggles the human race has ever been engaged in, only by that most dreaded of all wars, the war of the poor against the rich, a war which, however long it may be delayed, will come, and come with all its horrors. The day of vengeance is sure; for the world after all is under the dominion of a Just Providence.

No one can observe the signs of the times with much care without perceiving that a crisis as to the relation of wealth and labor is approaching. It is useless to shut our eyes to the fact, and like the ostrich fancy ourselves secure because we have so concealed our heads that we see not the danger. We or our children will have to meet this crisis. The old war between the King and the Barons is well-nigh ended, and so is that between the Barons and the Merchants and Manufacturers, — landed capital and commercial capital. The business man has become the peer of my Lord. And now commences the new struggle between the operative and his employer, between wealth and labor. Every day does this struggle extend further and wax stronger and fiercer; what or when the end will be, God only knows.

In this coming contest there is a deeper question at issue than is commonly imagined; a question which is but remotely touched in your controversies about United States Banks and Sub Treasuries, chartered Banking and free Banking, free trade and corporations, although these controversies may be paving the way for it to come up. We have discovered no presentiment of it in any king's or queen's speech, nor in any president's message. It is embraced in no popular political creed of the day, whether christened Whig or Tory, *Juste-milieu* or Democratic. No popular senator, or deputy, or peer seems to have any glimpse of it; but it is working in the hearts of the million, is struggling to shape itself, and one day it will be uttered, and in thunder tones. Well will it be for him who, on that day, shall be found ready to answer it.

[*1840*]

THEODORE PARKER

[1810–1860]

SON OF a poor farmer and mechanic, he could afford little schooling. He was brilliant and ambitious, however, and so he studied at home — in Lexington, Massachusetts — and at seventeen became a school-teacher. Harvard was too expensive for him, but his ability was recognized and he was allowed to take the examinations. Then he worked his way through the Divinity School and in 1837 was ordained a minister. Within a few years he was a center of controversy in the Unitarian Church. Deeply influenced by Channing, he was the inevitable heir to the latter's intellectual position. A friend of Emerson, Alcott, and Wendell Phillips, he turned toward transcendentalism and various progressive social and political movements. Of course, his own background and struggles made him sympathetic with the unfortunate and oppressed. He became an uncompromising abolitionist; he was one of the secret committee that aided John Brown's raid on Harper's Ferry. His fiery sermons and essays on slavery were famous, and equally famous and very little less fiery were his preachings on economic injustice. Lincoln evidently derived from him the formula: " government of the people, by the people, for the people," and others derived ideas on social relations which are still agitating our community.

from

THOUGHTS ON LABOUR

There are some who count labour a curse and a punishment. They regard the necessity of work as the greatest evil brought on us by the " Fall "; as a curse that will cling to our last sand. Many submit to this yoke, and toil, and save, in hope to leave their posterity out of the reach of this primitive curse!

Others, still more foolish, regard it as a disgrace. Young men, — the children of honest parents, who living by their manly and toil-hardened hands, bear up the burthen of the world on their shoulders, and eat with thankful hearts their daily bread, won in the sweat of their face, — are ashamed of their fathers' occupation, and forsaking the plough, the chisel, or the forge, seek a livelihood in what is sometimes named a more respectable and genteel vocation; that is, in a calling which demands less of the hands than their fathers' hardy craft, and quite often less of the head likewise; for that imbecility which drives men to those callings has its seat mostly in a higher region than the hands. Affianced damsels beg their lovers to discover (or invent) some ancestor in buckram who did not work. The Sophomore in a small college is ashamed of his father who wears a blue frock, and his dusty brother who toils with the saw and the axe. These men, after they have wiped off the dirt and the soot of their early life, sometimes become arrant coxcombs, and standing like the head of Hermes without hands, having only a mouth, make faces at such as continue to serve the state by plain handiwork. . . .

It were to be wished that this notion of labour being disgraceful was confined to vain young men, and giddy maidens of idle habits and weak heads, for then it would be looked upon as one of the diseases of early life, which we know must come, and rejoice when our young friends have happily passed through it, knowing it is one of " the ills that flesh is heir to," but is not very grievous, and comes but once in the lifetime. This aversion to labour, this notion that it is a curse and a disgrace, this selfish desire to escape from the general and natural lot of man, is the sacramental sin of " the better class " in our great cities. The children of the poor pray to be rid of work; and what son of a rich man learns a trade, or tills the soil with his own hands? Many men look on the ability to be idle as the most desirable and honourable ability. They glory in being the mouth that consumes, not the hand that works. Yet one would suppose a man of useless hands and idle head, in the midst of God's world, where each thing works for all, in the midst of the toil and sweat of the human race, must needs make an apology for his sloth, and would ask pardon for violating the common law, and withdrawing his neck from the general yoke of humanity. Still more does he need an apology if he is active only in getting into his hands the result of others' work. But it is not so. The man who is rich enough to be idle, values himself on his leisure; and what is worse, others value him for it. Active men must make a shamefaced excuse for being busy, and working men for their toil, as if business and toil were not the duty of all, and the support of the world. In certain countries men are divided horizontally into two classes, the men who WORK and the men who RULE, and the latter despise the employment of the former as mean and degrading. It is the slave's duty to plough, said a Heathen poet, and a freeman's business to enjoy at leisure the fruit of that ploughing. This same foolish notion finds favour with many here. It is a remnant of those barbarous times when all labour was performed by serfs and bondsmen, and exemption from toil was the exclusive sign of the free-born. But this notion, that labour is disgraceful, conflicts as sharply with our political institutions as it does with common sense, and the law God has writ on man. An old author, centuries before Christ, was so far enlightened on this point as to see the true dignity of manual work, and to say, " God is well pleased with honest works; he suffers the labouring man, who ploughs the earth by night and day, to call his life most noble. If he is good and true, he offers continual sacrifice to God, and is not so lustrous in his dress as in his heart."

Manual labour is a blessing and a dignity. But to state the case on its least favourable issue, admit it were both a disgrace and a curse, would a true man desire to escape it for himself, and leave the curse to fall on other men? Certainly not. The generous soldier fronts death, and charges in the cannon's mouth; it is the coward who lingers behind. If labour were hateful, as the proud would have us believe, then they who bear its burthens, and feed and clothe the human race, and fetch and carry for them, should be honoured as those have always been who defend society in war. If it be glorious, as the world fancies, to repel a human foe, how much more is he to be honoured who stands up when Want comes upon us, like an armed man, and puts him to rout! One would fancy the world was mad when it bowed in reverence to those who by superior cunning possessed themselves of the earnings of others, while it made wide the mouth and drew out the tongue at such as do the world's work. " Without these," said an ancient, " cannot a city be inhabited, but they shall not be sought for in public council, nor sit high in the congregation "; and those few men and women who are misnamed the World, in their wisdom have confirmed the saying. Thus they honour those who sit in idleness and ease; they extol such as defend a state with arms, or those who collect in their hands the result of Asiatic or American industry; but pass by with contempt the men who rear corn and cattle, and weave and spin, and fish and build for the whole human race. Yet if the state of labour were so hard and disgraceful as some fancy, the sluggard in fine raiment, and that trim figure which, like the lilies in the Scripture, neither toils nor spins, and is yet clothed in more glory than Solomon, would both bow down before colliers and farmers, and bless them as the benefactors of the race. Christianity has gone still farther, and makes a man's greatness consist in the amount of service he renders to the world. Certainly he is the most honourable who, by his head or his hand, does the greatest and best work for his race. The noblest soul the world ever saw appeared not in the ranks of the indolent; but "took on him the form of a servant," and when he washed his disciples' feet, meant something not very generally understood, perhaps, in the nineteenth century.

Now, manual labour, though an unavoidable duty, though designed as a blessing, and naturally both a pleasure and a dignity, is often abused, till, by its terrible excess, it becomes really a punishment and a curse. It is only a proper amount of work that is a blessing. Too much of it wears out the body before its time; cripples the mind, debases the soul, blunts the senses, and chills the affections. It makes a man a spinning-jenny, or a ploughing-machine, and not "a being of a large discourse, that looks before and after." He ceases to be a man, and becomes a thing.

In a rational and natural state of society, — that is, one in which every man went forward towards the true end he was designed to reach; towards perfection in the use of all his senses; towards perfection in wisdom, virtue, affection, and religion, — labour would never interfere with the culture of what is best in each man. His daily business would be a school to aid in developing the whole man, body and soul, because he would then do what nature fitted him to do. Then his business would be really his calling. The diversity of gifts is quite equal to the diversity of work to be done. There is some one thing which each man can do with pleasure, and better than any other man; because he was born to do it. Then all men would labour, each at his proper vocation, and an excellent farmer would not be spoiled to make a poor lawyer, a blundering physician, or a preacher who puts the world asleep. Then a small body of men would not be pampered in indolence, to grow up into gouty worthlessness, and die of inertia; nor would the large part of men be worn down as now by excessive toil before half their life is spent. They would not be so severely tasked as to have no time to read, think, and converse. When he walked abroad, the labouring man would not be forced to catch mere transient glimpses of the flowers by the way-side, or the stars over his head, as the dogs, it is said, drink the waters of the Nile, running while they drink, afraid the crocodiles should seize them if they stop. When he looked from his window at the landscape, Distress need not stare at him from every bush. He would then have leisure to cultivate his mind and heart no less than to do the world's work.

[*1841*]

from

THE STATE OF THE NATION

A Sermon Preached on Thanksgiving Day, November 28, 1850

Now in public opinion and in the laws of the United States, there are two distinct political ideas. I shall call one the Democratic, and the other the Despotic idea. Neither is wholly sectional; both chiefly so. Each is composed of several simpler ideas. Each has enacted laws and established institutions. This is the democratic idea: that all men are endowed by their Creator with certain natural rights, which only the possessor can alienate; that all men are equal in these rights; that amongst them is the right to life, liberty, and the pursuit of happiness; that the business of the government is to preserve for every man all of these rights until he alienates them.

This democratic idea is founded in human nature, and comes from the nature of God, who made human nature. To carry it out politically is to execute justice, which is the will of God. This idea, in its realization, leads to a democracy, a government of all, for all, by all. Such a government aims to give every man all his natural rights; it desires to have political power in all hands, property in all hands, wisdom in all heads, goodness in all hearts, religion in all souls. I mean the religion that makes a man self-respectful, earnest, and faithful to the infinite God, that disposes him to give all men their rights, and to claim his own rights at all times; the religion which is piety within you, and goodness in the manifestation. Such a government has laws, and the aim thereof is to give justice to all men; it has officers to execute these laws, for the sake of justice. Such a government founds schools for all; looks after those most who are most in need; defends and protects the feeblest as well as the richest and most powerful. The state is for the individual, and for all the individuals, and so it reverences justice, where the rights of all, and the interests of all, exactly balance. It demands free speech; everything is open to examination, discussion, "agitation," if you will. Thought is to be free, speech to be free, work to be free, and worship to be free. Such is the democratic idea, and such the State which it attempts to found.

The despotic idea is just the opposite: — That all men are *not* endowed by the Creator with certain natural rights which only the possessor can alienate, but that one man has a natural right to overcome and make use of some other men for his advantage and their hurt; that all men are *not* equal in their rights; that all men have *not* a natural right to life, liberty, and the pursuit of happiness; that government is *not* instituted to preserve these natural rights for all.

This idea is founded on the excess of human passions, and it represents the compromise between a man's idleness and his appetite. It is not based on facts eternal in human nature, but on facts transient in human nature. It does not aim to do justice to all, but injustice to some; to take from one man what he ought not to lose, and give to another what he ought not to get.

This leads to aristocracy in various forms, to the government of all by means of a part and for the sake of a part. In this state of things political power must be in few hands; property in few hands; wisdom in few heads; goodness in few hearts, and religion in few souls. I mean the religion which leads a man to respect himself and his fellow-men; to be earnest, and to trust in the infinite God; to demand his rights of other men and to give their rights to them.

Neither the democratic nor the despotic idea is fully made real anywhere in the world. There is no perfect democracy, nor perfect aristocracy. There are democrats in every actual aristocracy; despots in every actual democracy. But in the Northern States the democratic idea prevails extensively and chiefly, and we have made attempts at establishing a democratic government. In the Southern States the despotic idea prevails extensively and chiefly, and they have made attempts to establish an aristocratic government. In an aristocracy there are two classes: the people to be governed, and the governing class, the nobility which is to govern. This nobility may be moveable, and depend on wealth; or immoveable, and depend on birth. In the Southern States the nobility is immoveable, and depends on colour. . . .

Men seek to spread their sentiments and ideas. The democratic idea tries to spread; the despotic idea tries to spread. For a long time the nation held these two ideas in its bosom, not fully conscious of either of them. Both came here in a state of infancy, so to say, with our fathers; the democratic idea very dimly understood; the despotic idea not fully carried out, yet it did a great mischief in the State and church. In the Declaration of Independence, writ by a young man, only the democratic idea appears, and that idea never got so distinctly stated before. But mark you, and see the confusion in men's minds. That democratic idea was thus distinctly stated by a man who was a slave-holder almost all his life; and unless public rumour has been unusually false, he has left some of his own offspring under the influence of the despotic and not the democratic idea; slaves and not free men.

In the Constitution of the United States these two ideas appear. It was thought for a long time they were not incompatible; it was thought the great American party might recognize both, and a compromise was made between the two. It was thought each might go about its own work and let the other alone; that the hawk and the hen might dwell happily together in the same coop, each lay her own eggs, and rear her own brood, and neither put a claw upon the other.

In the meantime each founded institutions after its kind; in the Northern States, democratic institutions; in the Southern, aristocratic. What once lay latent in the mind of the nation has now become patent. The thinking part of the nation sees the difference between the two. Some men are beginning to see that the two are completely incompatible, and cannot be good friends. Others are asking us to shut our eyes and not see it, and they think that so long as our eyes are shut, all things will go on peacefully. Such is the wisdom of the ostrich.

At first the trouble coming from this source was a very little cloud, far away on the horizon, not bigger than a man's hand. It seemed so in 1804, when the brave senator from Massachusetts, a Hartford Convention Federalist, a name that calls the blood to some rather pale cheeks nowadays, proposed to alter the Constitution of the United States, and cut off the North from all responsibility for slavery. It was a little cloud not bigger than a man's hand; now it is a great cloud which covers the whole hemisphere of heaven, and threatens to shut out the day.

In the last session of Congress, ten months long, the great matter was the contest between the two ideas. All the newspapers rung with the battle. Even the pulpits now and then alluded to it; forgetting their decency, that they must preach "only religion," which has not the least to do with politics and the welfare of the State.

Each idea has its allies, and it is worth while to run our eye over the armies and see what they amount to. The idea of despotism has for its allies: —

1. The slaveholders of the South with their dependents; and the servile class who take their ideas from the prominent men about them. This servile class is more numerous at the South than even at the North.

2. It has almost all the distinguished politicians of the North and South; the distinguished great politicians in the Congress of the nation, and the distinguished little politicians in the Congress of the several states.

3. It has likewise the greater portion of the wealthy and educated men in many large towns of the North; with their dependents and the servile men who take their opinions from the prominent class about them. And here, I am sorry to say, I must reckon the greater portion of the prominent and wealthy clergy, the clergy in the large cities. Once this class of men were masters of the rich and educated; and very terrible masters they were in Madrid and in Rome. Now their successors are doing penance for those old sins. "It is a long lane," they say, "which has no turn," and the clerical has had a very short and complete turn. When I say the majority of the clergy in prominent situations in the large cities are to be numbered among the allies of the despotic idea, and are a part of the great pro-slavery army, I know there are some noble and honourable exceptions, men who do not fear the face of gold, but reverence the face of God.

Then on the side of the democratic idea there are: —

1. The great mass of the people at the North; farmers, mechanics, and the humbler clergy. This does not appear so at first sight, because these men have not much confidence in themselves, and require to be shaken many times before they are thoroughly waked up.

2. Besides that, there are a few politicians at the North who are on this side; some distinguished ones in Congress, some less distinguished ones in the various legislatures of the North.

3. Next there are men, North and South, who look at the great causes of the welfare of nations, and make up their minds historically, from the facts of human history, against despotism. Then there are such

312

as study the great principles of justice and truth, and judge from human nature, and decide against despotism. And then such as look at the law of God, and believe Christianity is sense and not nonsense; that Christianity is the ideal for earnest men, not a pretence for a frivolous hypocrite. Some of these men are at the South; the greater number are in the North; and here again you see the difference between the son of the Planter and the son of the Puritan.

Here are the allies, the threefold armies of Despotism on the one side, and of Democracy on the other.

Now it is not possible for these two ideas to continue to live in peace. For a long time each knew not the other, and they were quiet. The men who clearly knew the despotic idea thought, in 1787, it would die " of a rapid consumption ": they said so; but the culture of cotton has healed its deadly wound, at least for the present. After the brief state of quiet, there came a state of armed neutrality. They were hostile, but under bonds to keep the peace. Each bit his thumb, but neither dared say he bit it at the other. Now the neutrality is over; attempts are made to compromise, to compose the difficulty. Various peace measures were introduced to the Senate last summer; but they all turned out war measures, every one of them. Now there is a trial of strength between the two. Which shall recede? which be extended? Freedom or Slavery? That is the question; refuse to look at it as we will, — refrain or refrain not from " political agitation," that is the question. . . .

Of the final issue I have no doubt; but no man can tell what shall come to pass in the meantime. We see that political parties in the State are snapped asunder: whether the national party shall not be broken up, no man can say. In 1750, on the 28th day of November, no man in Old England or New England could tell what 1780 would bring forth. No man, North or South, can tell to-day what 1880 will bring to pass. He must be a bold man who declares to the nation that no new political machinery shall be introduced, in the next thirty years, to our national mill. We know not what a day shall bring forth, but we know that God is on the side of right and justice, and that they will prevail so long as God is God. . . .

It is not possible to suppress the idea of freedom, or for ever hold down its institutions. But it is possible to destroy a State; a political party with geographical bounds may easily be rent asunder. It is not impossible to shiver this American Union. But how? What clove asunder the great British party, one nation once in America and England? Did not our fathers love their fatherland? Ay. They called it home, and were loyal with abundant fealty; there was no lack of piety for home. It was the attempt to make old English injustice New England law! Who did it, — the British people? Never. Their hand did no such sacrilege! It was the merchants of London, with the " Navigation Act "; the politicians of Westminster with the " Stamp Act "; the tories of America, who did not die without issue, that for office and its gold would keep a king's unjust commands. It was they who drove our fathers into disunion against their will. Is here no lesson? We love law, all of us love it; but a true man loves it only as the Safeguard of the Rights of Man. If it destroys these rights, he spurns it with his feet. Is here no lesson? Look further, then.

Do you know how empires find their end? Yes, the great States eat up the little. As with fish, so with nations. Ay, but how do the great States come to an end? By their own injustice, and no other cause. They would make unrighteousness their law, and God wills not that it be so. Thus they fall; thus they die. Look at these ancient States, and queenliest queens of earth. There is Rome, the widow of two civilizations, — the Pagan and the Catholic. They both had her, and unto both she bore daughters and fair sons. But, the Niobe of Nations, she boasted that her children were holier and more fair then all the pure ideas of justice, truth, and love, the offspring of the eternal God. And now she sits there, transformed into stone, amid the ruins of her children's bones. At midnight I have heard the owl hoot in the colosseum and the forum, giving voice to desolation; and at mid-day I have seen the fox in the palace where Augustus gathered the wealth, the wit, the beauty, and the wisdom of a conquered world; and the fox and the owl interpreted to me the voice of many ages, which came to tell this age that though hand joined in hand, the wicked shall not prosper.

Come with me, my friends, a moment more, pass over this Golgotha of human history, treading reverent as you go, for our feet are on our mothers' grave, and our shoes defile our fathers' hallowed bones. Let us not talk of them; go further on, look and pass by. Come with me into the Inferno of the nations, with such poor guidance as my lamp can lend. Let us disquiet and bring up the awful shadows of empires buried long ago, and learn a lesson from the tomb.

Come, old Assyria, with the Ninevitish dove upon thy emerald crown! What laid thee low? " I fell by own injustice. Thereby Nineveh and Babylon came, with me, also, to the ground."

Oh, queenly Persia, flame of the nations, wherefore art thou so fallen, who troddest the people under thee, bridgedst the Hellespont with ships, and pouredst thy temple-wasting millions on the western world? " Because I trod the people under me, and bridged the Hellespont with ships, and poured my temple-wasting millions on the western world. I fell by own misdeeds."

Thou muse-like, Grecian queen, fairest of all thy classic sisterhood of States, enchanting yet the world with thy sweet witchery, speaking in art, and most seductive song, why liest thou there with beauteous yet dishonoured brow, reposing on thy broken harp? " I scorned the law of God; banished and poisoned wisest, justest men; I loved the loveliness of flesh, embalmed it in the Parian stone; I loved the loveliness of thought, and treasured that in more than Parian speech. But the beauty of justice, the loveliness of love, I trod them down to earth! Lo, therefore, have I become as those Barbarian States — as one of them! " . . .

" God save the Commonwealth! " proclaims the Governor. God will do his part, — doubt not of that. But you and I must help Him save the State. What can we do? Next Sunday I will ask you for your charity; to-day I ask a greater gift, more than the abundance of the rich, or the poor widow's long-remembered mite. I ask you for your justice. Give that to your native land. Do you not love your country? I know you do. Here are our homes and the graves of our fathers; the bones of our mothers are under the sod. The memory of past deeds is fresh with us; many a farmer's and mechanic's son inherits from his sires some cup of manna gathered in the wilderness, and kept in memory of our exodus; some stones from the Jordan, which our fathers passed over sorely bested and hunted after; some Aaron's rod, green and blossoming with fragrant memories of the day of small things, when the Lord led us — and all these attach us to our land, our native land. We love the great ideas of the North, the institutions which they founded, the righteous laws, the schools, the churches, too — do we not love all these? Ay. I know well you do. Then by all these, and more than all, by the dear love of God, let us swear that we will keep the justice of the Eternal Law. Then are we all safe. . . .

[1850]

HENRY DAVID THOREAU

[1817–1862]

HE WAS born in Concord, Massachusetts, and there he spent practically all of his life. The family had limited means — his father was a pencil-maker and store-keeper — but he was able to go through Harvard with the aid of a scholarship and by teaching school between terms. On being graduated, in 1837, he began teaching in the town school of Concord, but soon resigned because he objected to whipping the students. For several years thereafter he ran a private school in collaboration with his brother, closing it only when the brother fell ill. He went then to live with Ralph Waldo Emerson, working as a handy man but accepted in the household as a friend and equal. There he became acquainted with the transcendentalist group, was invited to contribute to the *Dial*, which he helped edit, and was encouraged to study and write. In 1843 he went to Staten Island to act as tutor in the home of William Emerson. After a year he returned to Concord and prepared to realize a dream he had long had. He built a hut on Walden Pond and lived there, alone and as simply as he could, for two years. Out of that experience came his masterpiece, *Walden* — a volume compounded of reflections on nature, observations about mankind, and commentaries on society and economics. In the summer of 1845 he was arrested and jailed (for one night) for refusing to pay a tax as a protest against slavery. This led to his famous essay "Civil Disobedience," which in our time has inspired the Hindu leader Ghandi. When he left Walden Pond he went to live in his father's house, taking up the family occupation of pencil-making. In addition he did some surveying — and almost anything else he was hired to do, becoming a handy man for the whole town. His deep love of nature found expression not only in local nature studies, but also in excursions to Cape Cod, Maine, and Canada, which he described meticulously in his journal. Out of this material some charming books were published posthumously. Thoreau avoided reform movements and disliked the public life, but twice he was stirred to impassioned action. The case of Anthony Burns, a fugitive slave arrested in Boston, led him to deliver a speech called "Slavery in Massachusetts" at an anti-slavery meeting in Framingham. The Harper's Ferry affair moved him to deliver "A Plea for Captain John Brown" at a church meeting which he called in Concord. These addresses are among his greatest writings as well as his most outspoken commentaries on government and society.

from

CIVIL DISOBEDIENCE

How does it become a man to behave toward this American government to-day? I answered that he cannot without disgrace be associated with it. I cannot for an instant recognize that political organization as *my* government which is the *slave's* government also.

All men recognize the right of revolution; that is, the right to refuse allegiance to, and to resist, the government, when its tyranny or its inefficiency are great and unendurable. But almost all say that such is not the case now. But such was the case, they think, in the Revolution of '75. If one were to tell me that this was a bad government because it taxed certain foreign commodities brought to its ports, it is most probable that I should not make an ado about it, for I can do without them. All machines have their friction; and possibly this does enough good to counterbalance the evil. At any rate, it is a great evil to make a stir about it. But when the friction comes to have its machine, and oppression and robbery are organized, I say, let us not have such a machine any longer. In other words, when a sixth of the population of a nation which has undertaken to be the refuge of liberty are slaves, and a whole country is unjustly overrun and conquered by a foreign army, and subjected to military law, I think that it is not too soon for honest men to rebel and revolutionize. What makes this duty the more urgent is the fact that the country so overrun is not our own, but ours is the invading army.

Paley, a common authority with many on moral questions, in his chapter on the "Duty of Submission to Civil Government," resolves all civil obligations into expediency; and he proceeds to say "that so long as the interest of the whole society requires it, that is, so long as the established government cannot be resisted or changed without public inconvenience, it is the will of God that the established government be obeyed, and no longer. . . . This principle being admitted, the justice of every particular case of resistance is reduced to a computation of the quantity of the danger and grievance on the one side, and of the probability and expense of redressing it on the other." Of this, he says, every man shall judge for himself. But Paley appears never to have contemplated those cases to which the rule of expediency does not apply, in which a people, as well as an individual, must do justice, cost what it may. If I have unjustly wrested a plank from a drowning man, I must restore it to him though I drown myself. This, according to Paley, would be inconvenient. But he that would save his life, in such a case, shall lose it. This people must cease to hold slaves, and to make war on Mexico, though it cost them their existence as a people.

In their practice, nations agree with Paley; but does any one think that Massachusetts does exactly what is right at the present crisis?

> "A drab of state, a cloth-o'-silver slut,
>   To have her train borne up, and her soul trail in the dirt."

Practically speaking, the opponents to a reform in Massachusetts are not a hundred thousand politicians at the South, but a hundred thousand merchants and farmers here, who are more interested in commerce and agriculture than they are in humanity, and are not prepared to do justice to the slave and to Mexico, *cost what it may.* I quarrel not with far-off foes, but with those who, near at home, coöperate with, and do the bidding of, those far away, and without whom the latter would be harmless. We are accustomed to say that the mass of men are unprepared; but improvement is slow, because the few are not materially wiser or better than the many. It is not so important that many should be as good as you as that there be some absolute goodness somewhere; for that will leaven the whole lump. There are thousands who are *in opinion* opposed to slavery and to the war, who yet in effect do nothing to put an end to them; who, esteeming themselves children of Washington and Franklin, sit down with their hands in their pockets, and say that they know not what to do, and do nothing; who even postpone the question of freedom to the question of free-trade, and quietly read the prices-current along with the latest advices from Mexico, after dinner, and, it may be, fall asleep over them both. What is the price-current of an honest man and patriot to-day? They hesitate, and they regret, and sometimes they petition; but they do nothing in earnest and with effect. They will wait, well disposed, for others to remedy the evil, that they may no longer have it to regret. At most, they give only a cheap vote, and a feeble countenance and God-speed, to the right, as it goes by them. There are nine hundred and ninety-nine patrons of virtue to one virtuous man. But it is easier to deal with the real possessor of a thing than with the temporary guardian of it.

318

All voting is a sort of gaming, like checkers or backgammon, with a slight moral tinge to it, a playing with right and wrong, with moral questions; and betting naturally accompanies it. The character of the voters is not staked. I cast my vote, perchance, as I think right; but I am not vitally concerned that that right should prevail. I am willing to leave it to the majority. Its obligation, therefore, never exceeds that of expediency. Even voting *for the right* is *doing* nothing for it. It is only expressing to men feebly your desire that it should prevail. A wise man will not leave the right to the mercy of chance, nor wish it to prevail through the power of the majority. There is but little virtue in the action of masses of men. When the majority shall at length vote for the abolition of slavery, it will be because they are indifferent to slavery, or because there is but little slavery left to be abolished by their vote. *They* will then be the only slaves. Only *his* vote can hasten the abolition of slavery who asserts his own freedom by his vote. . . .

It is not a man's duty, as a matter of course, to devote himself to the eradication of any, even the most enormous wrong; he may still properly have other concerns to engage him; but it is his duty, at least, to wash his hands of it, and, if he gives it no thought longer, not to give it practically his support. If I devote myself to other pursuits and contemplations, I must first see, at least, that I do not pursue them sitting upon another man's shoulders. I must get off him first, that he may pursue his contemplations too. See what gross inconsistency is tolerated. I have heard some of my townsmen say, "I should like to have them order me out to help put down an insurrection of the slaves, or to march to Mexico; — see if I would go"; and yet these very men have each, directly by their allegiance, and so indirectly, at least, by their money, furnished a substitute. The soldier is applauded who refuses to serve in an unjust war by those who do not refuse to sustain the unjust government which makes the war; is applauded by those whose own act and authority he disregards and sets at naught; as if the state were penitent to that degree that it hired one to scourge it while it sinned, but not to that degree that it left off sinning for a moment. Thus, under the name of Order and Civil Government, we are all made at last to pay homage to and support our own meanness. After the first blush of sin comes its indifference; and from immoral it becomes, as it were, *un*moral, and not quite unnecessary to that life which we have made.

319

The broadest and most prevalent error requires the most disinterested virtue to sustain it. The slight reproach to which the virtue of patriotism is commonly liable, the noble are most likely to incur. Those who, while they disapprove of the character and measures of a government, yield to it their allegiance and support are undoubtedly its most conscientious supporters, and so frequently the most serious obstacles to reform. Some are petitioning the state to dissolve the Union, to disregard the requisitions of the President. Why do they not dissolve it themselves, — the union between themselves and the state, — and refuse to pay their quota into its treasury? Do not they stand in the same relation to the state that the state does to the Union? And have not the same reasons prevented the state from resisting the Union which have prevented them from resisting the state?

How can a man be satisfied to entertain an opinion merely, and enjoy *it*? Is there any enjoyment in it, if his opinion is that he is aggrieved? If you are cheated out of a single dollar by your neighbor, you do not rest satisfied with knowing that you are cheated, or with saying that you are cheated, or even with petitioning him to pay you your due; but you take effectual steps at once to obtain the full amount, and see that you are never cheated again. Action from principle, the perception and the performance of right, changes things and relations; it is essentially revolutionary, and does not consist wholly with anything which was. It not only divides states and churches, it divides families; ay, it divides the *individual*, separating the diabolical in him from the divine.

Unjust laws exist: shall we be content to obey them, or shall we endeavor to amend them, and obey them until we have succeeded, or shall we transgress them at once? Men generally, under such a government as this, think that they ought to wait until they have persuaded the majority to alter them. They think that, if they should resist, the remedy would be worse than the evil. But it is the fault of the government itself that the remedy *is* worse than the evil. *It* makes it worse. Why is it not more apt to anticipate and provide for reform? Why does it not cherish its wise minority? Why does it cry and resist before it is hurt? Why does it not encourage its citizens to be on the alert to point out its faults, and *do* better than it would have them? Why does it always crucify Christ, and excommunicate Copernicus and Luther, and pronounce Washington and Franklin rebels? . . .

Under a government which imprisons any unjustly, the true place for a just man is also a prison. The proper place to-day, the only place which Massachusetts has provided for her freer and less desponding spirits, is in her prisons, to be put out and locked out of the State by her own act, as they have already put themselves out by their principles. It is there that the fugitive slave, and the Mexican prisoner on parole, and the Indian come to plead the wrongs of his race should find them; on that separate, but more free and honorable ground, where the State places those who are not *with* her, but *against* her — the only house in a slave State in which a free man can abide with honor. If any think that their influence would be lost there, and their voices no longer afflict the ear of the State, that they would not be as an enemy within its walls, they do not know by how much truth is stronger than error, nor how much more eloquently and effectively he can combat injustice who has experienced a little in his own person. Cast your whole vote, not a strip of paper merely, but your whole influence. A minority is powerless while it conforms to the majority; it is not even a minority then; but it is irresistible when it clogs by its whole weight. If the alternative is to keep all just men in prison, or give up war and slavery, the State will not hesitate which to choose. If a thousand men were not to pay their tax-bills this year, that would not be a violent and bloody measure, as it would be to pay them, and enable the State to commit violence and shed innocent blood. This is, in fact, the definition of a peaceable revolution, if any such is possible. If the tax-gatherer, or any other public officer, asks me, as one has done, " But what shall I do? " my answer is, " If you really wish to do anything, resign your office." When the subject has refused allegiance, and the officer has resigned his office, then the revolution is accomplished. But even suppose blood should flow. Is there not a sort of blood shed when the conscience is wounded? Through this wound a man's real manhood and immortality flow out, and he bleeds to an everlasting death. I see this blood flowing now.

I have contemplated the imprisonment of the offender, rather than the seizure of his goods, — though both will serve the same purpose, — because they who assert the purest right, and consequently are most dangerous to a corrupt State, commonly have not spent much time in accumulating property. To such the State renders comparatively small service, and a slight tax is wont to appear exorbitant, particularly if they are obliged to earn it by special labor with their hands. If there were one who lived wholly without the use of money, the State itself would hesitate to demand it of him. But the rich man — not to make any invidious comparison — is always sold to the institution which makes him rich. Absolutely speaking, the more money, the less virtue; for money comes between a man and his objects, and obtains them for him; and it was certainly no great virtue to obtain it. It puts to rest many questions which he would otherwise be taxed to answer; while the only new question which it puts is the hard but superfluous one, how to spend it. Thus his moral ground is taken from under his feet. The opportunities of living are diminished in proportion as what are called the "means" are increased. The best thing a man can do for his culture when he is rich is to endeavor to carry out those schemes which he entertained when he was poor. Christ answered the Herodians according to their condition. "Show me the tribute-money," said he; — and one took a penny out his pocket; — if you use money which has the image of Cæsar on it and which he has made current and valuable, that is, *if you are men of the State,* and gladly enjoy the advantages of Cæsar's government, then pay him back some of his own when he demands it. "Render therefore to Cæsar that which is Cæsar's, and to God those things which are God's," — leaving them no wiser than before as to which was which; for they did not wish to know.

When I converse with the freest of my neighbors, I perceive that, whatever they may say about the magnitude and seriousness of the question, and their regard for the public tranquillity, the long and the short of the matter is that they cannot spare the protection of the existing government, and they dread the consequences to their property and families of disobedience to it. For my own part, I should not like to think that I ever rely on the protection of the State. But, if I deny the authority of the State when it presents its tax-bill, it will soon take and waste all my property, and so harass me and my children without end. This is hard. This makes it impossible for a man to live honestly, and at the same time comfortably, in outward respects. It will not be worth the while to accumulate property; that would be sure to go again. You must hire or squat somewhere, and raise but a small crop, and eat that soon. You must live within yourself, and depend upon yourself always tucked up and ready for a start, and not have many affairs. A man may grow rich in Turkey even, if he will be in all respects a good subject of the Turkish government. Confucius said " If a state is governed by the principles of reason, poverty and misery are subjects of shame; if a state is not governed by the principles of reason, riches and honors are the subjects of shame." No: until I want the protection of Massachusetts to be extended to me in some distant Southern port, where my liberty is endangered, or until I am bent solely on building up an estate at home by peaceful enterprise, I can afford to refuse allegiance to Massachusetts, and her right to my property and life. It costs me less in every sense to incur the penalty of disobedience to the State than it would to obey. I should feel as if I were worth less in that case.

Some years ago, the State met me in behalf of the Church, and commanded me to pay a certain sum toward the support of a clergyman whose preaching my father attended, but never I myself. " Pay," it said, " or be locked up in the jail." I declined to pay, but, unfortunately, another man saw fit to pay it. I did not see why the schoolmaster should be taxed to support the priest, and not the priest the schoolmaster; for I was not the State's schoolmaster, but I supported myself by voluntary subscription. I did not see why the lyceum should not present its tax-bill, and have the State to back its demand, as well as the Church. However, at the request of the selectmen, I condescended to make some such statement as this in writing: — " Know all men by these presents, that I, Henry Thoreau, do not wish to be regarded as a member of any incorporated society which I have not joined." This I gave to the town clerk; and he has it. The State, having thus learned that I did not wish to be regarded as a member of that church, has never made a like demand on me since; though it said that it must adhere to its original presumption that time. If I had known how to name them, I should then have signed off in detail from all the societies which I never signed on to; but I did not know where to find a complete list.

I have paid no poll-tax for six years. I was put into a jail once on this account, for one night; and, as I stood considering the walls of solid stone, two or three feet thick, the door of wood and iron, a foot thick, and the iron grating which strained the light, I could not help being struck with the foolishness of that institution which treated me as if I were mere flesh and blood and bones, to be locked up. I wondered that it should have concluded at length that this was the best use it could put me to, and had never thought to avail itself of my services in some way. I saw that, if there was a wall of stone between me and my townsmen, there was a still more difficult one to climb or break through before they could get to be as free as I was. I did not for a moment feel confined, and the walls seemed a great waste of stone and mortar. I felt as if I alone of all my townsmen had paid my tax. They plainly did not know how to treat me, but behaved like persons who are underbred. In every threat and in every compliment there was a blunder; for they thought that my chief desire was to stand the other side of that stone wall. I could not but smile to see how industriously they locked the door on my meditations, which followed them out again without let or hindrance, and *they* were really all that was dangerous. As they could not reach me, they had resolved to punish my body; just as boys, if they cannot come at some person against whom they have a spite, will abuse his dog. I saw that the State was half-witted, that it was timid as a lone woman with her silver spoons, and that it did not know its friends from its foes, and I lost all my remaining respect for it, and pitied it. . . .

The authority of government, even such as I am willing to submit to, — for I will cheerfully obey those who know and can do better than I, and in many things even those who neither know nor can do so well, — is still an impure one: to be strictly just, it must have the sanction and counsel of the governed. It can have no pure right over my person and property but what I concede to it. The progress from an absolute to a limited monarchy, from a limited monarchy to a democracy, is a progress toward a true respect for the individual. Even the Chinese philosopher was wise enough to regard the individual as the basis of the empire. Is a democracy, such as we know it, the last improvement possible in government? Is it not possible to take a step further towards recognizing and organizing the rights of man? There will never be a really free and enlightened State until the State comes to recognize the individual as a higher and independent power, from which all its own power and authority are derived, and treats him accordingly. I please myself with imagining a State at last which can afford to be just to all men, and to treat the individual with respect as a neighbor; which even would not think it inconsistent with its own repose if a few were to live aloof from it, not meddling with it, nor embraced by it, who fulfilled all the duties of neighbors and fellowmen. A State which bore this kind of fruit, and suffered it to drop off as fast as it ripened, would prepare the way for a still more perfect and glorious State, which also I have imagined, but not yet anywhere seen.

[*1849*]

from

SLAVERY IN MASSACHUSETTS

I wish my countrymen to consider that whatever the human law may be, neither an individual nor a nation can ever commit the least act of injustice against the obscurest individual without having to pay the penalty for it. A government which deliberately enacts injustice, and persists in it, will at length even become the laughing-stock of the world.

Much has been said about American slavery, but I think that we do not even yet realize what slavery is. If I were seriously to propose to Congress to make mankind into sausages, I have no doubt that most of the members would smile at my proposition, and if any believed me to be in earnest, they would think that I proposed something much worse than Congress had ever done. But if any of them will tell me that to make a man into a sausage would be much worse, — would be any worse, — than to make him into a slave, — than it was to enact the Fugitive Slave Law, — I will accuse him of foolishness, of intellectual incapacity, of making a distinction without a difference. The one is just as sensible a proposition as the other.

I hear a good deal said about trampling this law under foot. Why, one need not go out of his way to do that. This law rises not to the level of the head or the reason; its natural habitat is in the dirt. It was born and bred, and has its life, only in the dust and mire, on a level with the feet; and he who walks with freedom, and does not with Hindoo mercy avoid treading on every venomous reptile, will inevitably tread on it, and so trample it under foot, — and Webster, its maker, with it, like the dirt-bug and its ball.

Recent events will be valuable as a criticism on the administration of justice in our midst, or, rather, as showing what are the true resources of justice in any community. It has come to this, that the friends of liberty, the friends of the slave, have shuddered when they have understood that his fate was left to the legal tribunals of the country to be decided. Free men have no faith that justice will be awarded in such a case. The judge may decide this way or that; it is a kind of accident, at best. It is evident that he is not a competent authority in so important a case. It is no time, then, to be judging according to his precedents, but to establish a precedent for the future. I would much rather trust to the sentiment of the people. In their vote you would get something of some value, at least, however small; but in the other case, only the trammeled judgment of an individual, of no significance, be it which way it might.

It is to some extent fatal to the courts when the people are compelled to go behind them. I do not wish to believe that the courts were made for fair weather, and for very civil cases merely; but think of leaving it to any court in the land to decide whether more than three millions of people, in this case a sixth part of a nation, have a right to be free-men or not! But it has been left to the courts of *justice*, so called, — to the Supreme Court of the land, — and, as you all know, recognizing no authority but the Constitution, it has decided that the three millions are and shall continue to be slaves. Such judges as these are merely the inspectors of a pick-lock and murderer's tools, to tell him whether they are in working order or not, and there they think that their responsibility ends. There was a prior case on the docket, which they, as judges appointed by God, had no right to skip; which having been justly settled, they would have been saved from this humiliation. It was the case of the murderer himself.

The law will never make men free; it is men who have got to make the law free. They are the lovers of law and order who observe the law when the government breaks it. . . .

The majority of the men of the North, and of the South and East and West, are not men of principle. If they vote, they do not send men to Congress on errands of humanity; but while their brothers and sisters are being scourged and hung for loving liberty, while — I might here insert all that slavery implies and is — it is the mismanagement of wood and iron and stone and gold which concerns them. Do what you will, O Government, with my wife and children, my mother and brother, my father and sister, I will obey your commands to the letter.

It will indeed grieve me if you hurt them, if you deliver them to overseers to be hunted by hounds or to be whipped to death; but, nevertheless, I will peaceably pursue my chosen calling on this fair earth, until perchance, one day, when I have put on mourning for them dead, I shall have persuaded you to relent. Such is the attitude, such are the words of Massachusetts.

Rather than do thus, I need not say what match I would touch, what system endeavor to blow up; but as I love my life, I would side with the light, and let the dark earth roll from under me, calling my mother and my brother to follow.

I would remind my countrymen that they are to be men first, and Americans only at a late and convenient hour. No matter how valuable law may be to protect your property, even to keep soul and body together, if it do not keep you and humanity together.

I am sorry to say that I doubt if there is a judge in Massachusetts who is prepared to resign his office, and get his living innocently, whenever it is required of him to pass sentence under a law which is merely contrary to the law of God. I am compelled to see that they put themselves, or rather are by character, in this respect, exactly on a level with the marine who discharges his musket in any direction he is ordered to. They are just as much tools, and as little men. Certainly, they are not the more to be respected, because their master enslaves their understandings and consciences, instead of their bodies.

The judges and lawyers, — simply as such, I mean, — and all men of expediency, try this case by a very low and incompetent standard. They consider, not whether the Fugitive Slave Law is right, but whether it is what they call *constitutional*. Is virtue constitutional, or vice? Is equity constitutional, or iniquity? In important moral and vital questions, like this, it is just as impertinent to ask whether a law is constitutional or not, as to ask whether it is profitable or not. They persist in being the servants of the worst of men, and not the servants of humanity. The question is, not whether you or your grandfather, seventy years ago, did not enter into an agreement to serve the Devil, and that service is not accordingly now due; but whether you will not now, for once and at last, serve God, — in spite of your own past recreancy, or that of your ancestor, — by obeying that eternal and only just CONSTITUTION, which He, and not any Jefferson or Adams, has written in your being.

327

The amount of it is, if the majority vote the Devil to be God, the minority will live and behave accordingly, — and obey the successful candidate, trusting that, some time or other, by some Speaker's casting-vote, perhaps, they may reinstate God. This is the highest principle I can get out or invent for my neighbors. These men act as if they believed that they could safely slide down a hill a little way, — or a good way, — and would surely come to a place, by and by, where they could begin to slide up again. This is expediency, or choosing that course which offers the slightest obstacles to the feet, that is, a down-hill one. But there is no such thing as accomplishing a righteous re-form by the use of "expediency." There is no such thing as sliding up hill. In morals the only sliders are backsliders.

Thus we steadily worship Mammon, both school and state and church, and on the seventh day curse God with a tintamar from one end of the Union to the other.

Will mankind never learn that policy is not morality, — that it never secures any moral right, but considers merely what is expedient? chooses the available candidate, — who is invariably the Devil, — and what right have his constituents to be surprised because the Devil does not behave like an angel of light? What is wanted is men, not of policy, but of probity, — who recognize a higher law than the Constitution, or the decision of the majority. The fate of the country does not depend on how you vote at the polls, — the worst man is as strong as the best at that game; it does not depend on what kind of paper you drop into the ballot-box once a year, but on what kind of man you drop from your chamber into the street every morning.

What should concern Massachusetts is not the Nebraska Bill, nor the Fugitive Slave Bill, but her own slaveholding and servility. Let the State dissolve her union with the slaveholder. She may wriggle and hesitate, and ask leave to read the Constitution once more; but she can find no respectable law or precedent which sanctions the con-tinuance of such a union for an instant.

Let each inhabitant of the State dissolve his union with her, as long as she delays to do her duty.

The events of the past month teach me to distrust Fame. I see that she does not finely discriminate, but coarsely hurrahs. She con-siders not the simple heroism of an action, but only as it is connected with its apparent consequences. She praises till she is hoarse the easy exploit of the Boston tea party, but will be comparatively silent about the braver and more disinterestedly heroic attack on the Boston Court-House, simply because it was unsuccessful!

Covered with disgrace, the State has sat down coolly to try for their lives and liberties the men who attempted to do its duty for it. And this is called *justice!* They who have shown that they can behave particularly well may perchance be put under bonds for *their good behavior*. They whom truth requires at present to plead guilty are, of all the inhabitants of the State, preëminently innocent. While the Governor, and the Mayor, and countless officers of the Commonwealth are at large, the champions of liberty are imprisoned.

Only they are guiltless who commit the crime of contempt of such a court. It behooves every man to see that his influence is on the side of justice, and let the courts make their own characters. My sympathies in this case are wholly with the accused, and wholly against their accusers and judges. Justice is sweet and musical; but injustice is harsh and discordant. The judge still sits grinding at his organ, but it yields no music, and we hear only the sound of the handle. He believes that all the music resides in the handle, and the crowd toss him their coppers the same as before.

Do you suppose that that Massachusetts which is now doing these things, — which hesitates to crown these men, some of whose lawyers, and even judges, perchance, may be driven to take refuge in some poor quibble, that they may not wholly outrage their instinctive sense of justice, — do you suppose that she is anything but base and servile? that she is the champion of liberty?

Show me a free state, and a court truly of justice, and I will fight for them, if need be; but show me Massachusetts, and I refuse her my allegiance, and express contempt for her courts.

[*1854*]

---

from

A PLEA FOR CAPTAIN JOHN BROWN

I hear many condemn these men because they were so few. When were the good and the brave ever in a majority? Would you have had him wait till that time came? — till you and I came over to him? The very fact that he had no rabble or troop of hirelings about him would alone distinguish him from ordinary heroes. His company was small indeed, because few could be found worthy to pass muster. Each one who there laid down his life for the poor and oppressed was a picked man, culled out of many thousands, if not millions; apparently a man of principle, of rare courage, and devoted humanity; ready to sacrifice his life at any moment for the benefit of his fellow-man. It may be doubted if there were as many more their equals in these respects in all the country, — I speak of his followers only, — for their leader, no doubt, scoured the land far and wide, seeking to swell his troop. These alone were ready to step between the oppressor and the oppressed. Surely they were the very best men you could select to be hung. That was the greatest compliment which this country could pay them. They were ripe for her gallows. She has tried a long time, she has hung a good many, but never found the right one before.

When I think of him, and his six sons, and his son-in-law, not to enumerate the others, enlisted for this fight, proceeding coolly, reverently, humanely to work, for months if not years, sleeping and waking upon it, summering and wintering the thought, without expecting any reward but a good conscience, while almost all America stood ranked on the other side, — I say again that it affects me as a sublime spectacle. If he had had any journal advocating "*his cause,*" any organ, as the phrase is, monotonously and wearisomely playing the same old tune, and then passing round the hat, it would have been fatal to his efficiency. If he had acted in any way so as to be let alone by the government, he might have been suspected. It was the fact that the tyrant must give place to him, or he to the tyrant, that distinguished him from all the reformers of the day that I know.

It was his peculiar doctrine that a man has a perfect right to interfere by force with the slaveholder, in order to rescue the slave. I agree with him. They who are continually shocked by slavery have some right to be shocked by the violent death of the slaveholder, but no others. Such will be more shocked by his life than by his death. I shall not be forward to think him mistaken in his method who quickest succeeds to liberate the slave. I speak for the slave when I say that I prefer the philanthropy of Captain Brown to that philanthropy which neither shoots me nor liberates me. At any rate, I do not think it is quite sane for one to spend his whole life in talking or writing

330

about this matter, unless he is continuously inspired, and I have not done so. A man may have other affairs to attend to. I do not wish to kill nor to be killed, but I can foresee circumstances in which both these things would be by me unavoidable. We preserve the so-called peace of our community by deeds of petty violence every day. Look at the policeman's billy and handcuffs! Look at the jail! Look at the gallows! Look at the chaplain of the regiment! We are hoping only to live safely on the outskirts of *this* provisional army. So we defend ourselves and our hen-roosts, and maintain slavery. I know that the mass of my countrymen think that the only righteous use that can be made of Sharps rifles and revolvers is to fight duels with them, when we are insulted by other nations, or to hunt Indians, or shoot fugitive slaves with them, or the like. I think that for once the Sharps rifles and the revolvers were employed in a righteous cause. The tools were in the hands of one who could use them.

The same indignation that is said to have cleared the temple once will clear it again. The question is not about the weapon, but the spirit in which you use it. No man has appeared in America, as yet, who loved his fellow-man so well, and treated him so tenderly. He lived for him. He took up his life and he laid it down for him. What sort of violence is that which is encouraged, not by soldiers, but by peaceable citizens, not so much by laymen as by ministers of the Gospel, not so much by the fighting sects as by the Quakers, and not so much by Quaker men as by Quaker women?

This event advertises me that there is such a fact as death, — the possibility of a man's dying. It seems as if no man had ever died in America before; for in order to die you must first have lived. I don't believe in the hearses, and palls, and funerals that they have had. There was no death in the case, because there had been no life; they merely rotted or sloughed off, pretty much as they had rotted or sloughed along. No temple's veil was rent, only a hole dug somewhere. Let the dead bury their dead. The best of them fairly ran down like a clock. Franklin, — Washington, — they were let off without dying; they were merely missing one day. I hear a good many pretend that they are going to die; or that they have died, for aught that I know. Nonsense! I'll defy them to do it. They haven't got life enough in them. They'll deliquesce like fungi, and keep a hundred eulogists mopping the spot where they left off. Only half a dozen or so have died

331

since the world began. Do you think that you are going to die, sir? No! there's no hope for you. You haven't got your lesson yet. You've got to stay after school. We make a needless ado about capital punishment, — taking lives, when there is no life to take. *Memento mori!* We don't understand that sublime sentence which some worthy got sculptured on his gravestone once. We've interpreted it in a groveling and sniveling sense; we've wholly forgotten how to die.

But be sure you do die nevertheless. Do your work, and finish it. If you know how to begin, you will know when to end.

These men, in teaching us how to die, have at the same time taught us how to live. If this man's acts and words do not create a revival, it will be the severest possible satire on the acts and words that do. It is the best news that America has ever heard. It has already quickened the feeble pulse of the North, and infused more and more generous blood into her veins and heart than any number of years of what is called commercial and political prosperity could. How many a man who was lately contemplating suicide has now something to live for!

One writer says that Brown's peculiar monomania made him to be " dreaded by the Missourians as a supernatural being." Sure enough, a hero in the midst of us cowards is always so dreaded. He is just that thing. He shows himself superior to nature. He has a spark of divinity in him.

> " Unless above himself he can
> Erect himself, how poor a thing is man! "

Newspaper editors argue also that it is a proof of his *insanity* that he thought he was appointed to do this work which he did, — that he did not suspect himself for a moment! They talk as if it were impossible that a man could be " divinely appointed " in these days to do any work whatever; as if vows and religion were out of date as connected with any man's daily work; as if the agent to abolish slavery could only be somebody appointed by the President, or by some political party. They talk as if a man's death were a failure, and his continued life, be it of whatever character, were a success.

When I reflect to what a cause this man devoted himself, and how religiously, and then reflect to what cause his judges and all who condemn him so angrily and fluently devote themselves, I see that they are as far apart as the heavens and earth are asunder.

The amount of it is, our " *leading men* " are a harmless kind of folk, and they know *well enough* that *they* were not divinely appointed, but elected by the votes of their party.

Who is it whose safety requires that Captain Brown be hung? Is it indispensable to any Northern man? Is there no resource but to cast this man also to the Minotaur? If you do not wish it, say so distinctly. While these things are being done, beauty stands veiled and music is a screeching lie. Think of him, — of his rare qualities! — such a man as it takes ages to make, and ages to understand; no mock hero, nor the representative of any party. A man such as the sun may not rise upon again in this benighted land. To whose making went the costliest material, the finest adamant; sent to be the redeemer of those in captivity; and the only use to which you can put him is to hang him at the end of a rope! You who pretend to care for Christ crucified, consider what you are about to do to him who offered himself to be the saviour of four millions of men.

Any man knows when he is justified, and all the wits in the world cannot enlighten him on that point. The murderer always knows that he is justly punished; but when a government takes the life of a man without the consent of his conscience, it is an audacious government, and is taking a step towards its own dissolution. Is it not possible that an individual may be right and a government wrong? Are laws to be enforced simply because they were made? or declared by any number of men to be good, if they are *not* good? Is there any necessity for a man's being a tool to perform a deed of which his better nature disapproves? Is it the intention of lawmakers that *good* men shall be hung ever? Are judges to interpret the law according to the letter, and not the spirit? What right have *you* to enter into a compact with yourself that you *will* do thus or so, against the light within you? Is it for *you* to *make up* your mind, — to form any resolution whatever, — and not accept the convictions that are forced upon you, and which ever pass your understanding? I do not believe in lawyers, in that mode of attacking or defending a man, because you descend to meet the judge on his own ground, and, in cases of the highest importance, it is of no consequence whether a man breaks a human law or not. Let lawyers decide trivial cases. Business men may arrange that among themselves. If they were the interpreters of the everlasting laws which rightfully bind man, that would be another thing. A counterfeiting law-factory, standing half in a slave land and half in a free! What kind of laws for free men can you expect from that?

I am here to plead his cause with you. I plead not for his life, but for his character, — his immortal life; and so it becomes your cause wholly, and is not his in the least. Some eighteen hundred years ago Christ was crucified; this morning, perchance, Captain Brown was hung. These are the two ends of a chain which is not without its links. He is not Old Brown any longer; he is an angel of light.

I see now that it was necessary that the bravest and humanest man in all the country should be hung. Perhaps he saw it himself. I *almost fear* that I may yet hear of his deliverance, doubting if a prolonged life, if *any* life, can do as much good as his death.

"Misguided!" "Garrulous!" "Insane!" "Vindictive!" So ye write in your easy-chairs, and thus he wounded responds from the floor of the Armory, clear as a cloudless sky, true as the voice of nature is: "No man sent me here; it was my own prompting and that of my Maker. I acknowledge no master in human form."

And in what a sweet and noble strain he proceeds, addressing his captors, who stand over him: "I think, my friends, you are guilty of a great wrong against God and humanity, and it would be perfectly right for any one to interfere with you so far as to free those you willfully and wickedly hold in bondage."

And, referring to his movement: "It is, in my opinion, the greatest service a man can render to God."

"I pity the poor in bondage that have none to help them; that is why I am here; not to gratify any personal animosity, revenge, or vindictive spirit. It is my sympathy with the oppressed and the wronged, that are as good as you, and as precious in the sight of God."

You don't know your testament when you see it.

"I want you to understand that I respect the rights of the poorest and weakest of colored people, oppressed by the slave power, just as much as I do those of the most wealthy and powerful."

"I wish to say, furthermore, that you had better, all you people at the South, prepare yourselves for a settlement of that question that must come up for settlement sooner than you are prepared for it. The sooner you are prepared the better. You may dispose of me very easily. I am nearly disposed of now; but this question is still to be settled, — this negro question, I mean; the end of that is not yet."

I foresee the time when the painter will paint that scene, no longer going to Rome for a subject; the poet will sing it; the historian record it; and, with the Landing of the Pilgrims and the Declaration of In-

334

dependence, it will be the ornament of some future national gallery, when at least the present form of slavery shall be no more here. We shall then be at liberty to weep for Captain Brown. Then, and not till then, we will take our revenge.

[*1859*]

HERMAN MELVILLE

[1819–1891]

HIS FATHER was descended from a long line of Scottish aristocrats; his mother, a Gansevoort, was related to the leading Dutch families of New York. He got nothing from his connections but pride, however, for his father — a merchant in New York City, where Herman was born — went into bankruptcy and died when the boy was twelve. After some schooling at the Albany Academy, at the age of fifteen he became a bank clerk, then tried farming and school-teaching, and at last left home for good to ship as a cabin-boy. The experience excited him, and after an interval of teaching he again went to sea — this time on a whaler bound for the South Seas. Four years later he returned to America with some fascinating stories to tell. He had explored a jungle, lived among cannibals, worked and played in Tahiti, and spent a year as a seaman on an American naval vessel. These experiences provided him with the material for his best books — *Typee* (1846), *Omoo* (1847), *Mardi* (1849), *White-Jacket* (1850), *Moby Dick* (1851). The last of these is, of course, his greatest work — and one of the greatest of American novels. Some of his writings expressed his pleasure in the idyllic life of primitive peoples as contrasted with the cruelty and narrowness of our " civilized " commercial society; some of his writings expressed an unhappy search for a faith, a philosophy in which he could believe. Always he showed sympathy for, and respected the dignity of, simple uncorrupted men — whether South Sea Island savages, common sailors, or ordinary " little " people in a strangely malevolent world. Melville's early successes were not repeated. He suffered neglect and poverty and withdrew completely from literary society. His death was barely noticed. But in the 1920's there was a revival of interest in his work, and that interest will not die. The sketches reprinted here (originally published in *Harper's* magazine) reveal a side of him that should be better known.

POOR MAN'S PUDDING
AND RICH MAN'S CRUMBS

PICTURE FIRST

"You see," said poet Blandmour, enthusiastically — as some forty years ago we walked along the road in a soft, moist snowfall, toward the end of March — " you see, my friend, that the blessed almoner, Nature, is in all things beneficent; and not only so, but considerate in her charities, as any discreet human philanthropist might be. This snow, now, which seems so unseasonable, is in fact just what a poor husbandman needs. Rightly is this soft March snow, falling just before seed-time, rightly it is called ' Poor Man's Manure.' Distilling from kind heaven upon the soil, by a gentle penetration it nourishes every clod, ridge, and furrow. To the poor farmer it is as good as the rich farmer's farmyard enrichments. And the poor man has no trouble to spread it, while the rich man has to spread his."

"Perhaps so," said I, without equal enthusiasm, brushing some of the damp flakes from my chest. " It may be as you say, dear Blandmour. But tell me, how is it that the wind drives yonder drifts of ' Poor Man's Manure ' off poor Coulter's two-acre patch here, and piles it up yonder on rich Squire Teamster's twenty-acre field? "

" Ah! to be sure — yes — well; Coulter's field, I suppose, is sufficiently moist without further moistenings. Enough is as good as a feast, you know."

"Yes," replied I, " of this sort of damp fare," shaking another shower of the damp flakes from my person. " But tell me, this warm spring snow may answer very well, as you say; but how is it with the cold snows of the long, long winters here? "

" Why, do you not remember the words of the Psalmist? — ' The Lord giveth snow like wool '; meaning not only that snow is white as wool, but warm, too, as wool. For the only reason, as I take it, that wool is comfortable is because air is entangled, and therefore warmed among its fibres. Just so, then, take the temperature of a December field when covered with this snow-fleece, and you will no doubt find it several degrees above that of the air. So, you see, the winter's snow *itself* is beneficent; under the pretense of frost — a sort of gruff philanthropist — actually warming the earth, which afterward is to be fertilizingly moistened by these gentle flakes of March."

"I like to hear you talk, dear Blandmour; and, guided by your benevolent heart, can only wish to poor Coulter plenty of this 'Poor Man's Manure.'"

"But that is not all," said Blandmour, eagerly. "Did you never hear of the 'Poor Man's Eye-water'?"

"Never."

"Take this soft March snow, melt it, and bottle it. It keeps pure as alcohol. The very best thing in the world for weak eyes. I have a whole demijohn of it myself. But the poorest man, afflicted in his eyes, can freely help himself to this same all-bountiful remedy. Now, what a kind provision is that!"

"Then 'Poor Man's Manure' is 'Poor Man's Eye-water' too?"

"Exactly. And what could be more economically contrived? One thing answering two ends — ends so very distinct."

"Very distinct, indeed."

"Ah! that is your way. Making sport of earnest. But never mind. We have been talking of snow; but common rain-water — such as falls all the year round — is still more kindly. Not to speak of its known fertilizing quality as to fields, consider it in one of its minor lights. Pray, did you ever hear of a 'Poor Man's Egg'?"

"Never. What is that, now?"

"Why, in making some culinary preparations of meal and flour, where eggs are recommended in the receipt-book, a substitute for the eggs may be had in a cup of cold rain-water, which acts as leaven. And so a cup of cold rain-water thus used is called by housewives a 'Poor Man's Egg.' And many rich men's housekeepers sometimes use it."

"But only when they are out of hen's eggs, I presume, dear Blandmour. But your talk is — I sincerely say it — most agreeable to me. Talk on."

"Then there's 'Poor Man's Plaster' for wounds and other bodily harms; an alleviative and curative, compounded of simple, natural things; and so, being very cheap, is accessible to the poorest sufferers. Rich men often use 'Poor Man's Plaster.'"

"But not without the judicious advice of a fee'd physician, dear Blandmour."

"Doubtless, they first consult the physician; but that may be an unnecessary precaution."

"Perhaps so. I do not gainsay it. Go on."

"Well, then, did you ever eat of a 'Poor Man's Pudding'?"

338

"I never so much as heard of it before."

"Indeed! Well, now you shall eat of one; and you shall eat it, too, as made, unprompted, by a poor man's wife, and you shall eat it at a poor man's table, and in a poor man's house. Come now, and if after this eating, you do not say that a 'Poor Man's Pudding' is as relishable as a rich man's, I will give up the point altogether; which briefly is: that, through kind Nature, the poor, out of their very poverty, extract comfort."

Not to narrate any more of our conversations upon this subject (for we had several — I being at that time the guest of Blandmour in the country, for the benefit of my health), suffice it that acting upon Blandmour's hint, I introduced myself into Coulter's house on a wet Monday noon (for the snow had thawed), under the innocent pretense of craving a pedestrian's rest and refreshment for an hour or two.

I was greeted, not without much embarrassment — owing, I suppose to my dress — but still with unaffected and honest kindness. Dame Coulter was just leaving the wash-tub to get ready her one o'clock meal against her good man's return from a deep wood about a mile distant among the hills, where he was chopping by day's work — seventy-five cents per day and found himself. The washing being done outside the main building, under an infirm-looking old shed, the dame stood upon a half-rotten soaked board to protect her feet, as well as might be, from the penetrating damp of the bare ground; hence she looked pale and chill. But her paleness had still another and more secret cause — the paleness of a mother to be. A quiet, fathomless heart-trouble, too, couched beneath the mild, resigned blue of her soft and wife-like eye. But she smiled upon me, as apologizing for the unavoidable disorder of a Monday and a washing-day, and, conducting me into the kitchen, set me down in the best seat it had — an old-fashioned chair of an enfeebled constitution.

I thanked her; and sat rubbing my hands before the ineffectual low fire, and — unobservantly as I could — glancing now and then about the room, while the good woman, throwing on more sticks, said she was sorry the room was no warmer. Something more she said, too — not repiningly, however — of the fuel, as old and damp; picked-up sticks in Squire Teamster's forest, where her husband was chopping the sappy logs of the living tree for the Squire's fires. It needed not her remark, whatever it was, to convince me of the inferior quality of the sticks; some being quite mossy and toad-stooled with long lying bedded among the accumulated dead leaves of many autumns. They made a sad hissing, and vain spluttering enough.

"You must rest yourself here till dinner-time, at least," said the dame; "what I have you are heartily welcome to."

I thanked her again, and begged her not to heed my presence in the least, but go on with her usual affairs.

I was struck by the aspect of the room. The house was old, and constitutionally damp. The window-sills had beads of exuded dampness upon them. The shriveled sashes shook in their frames, and the green panes of glass were clouded with the long thaw. On some little errand the dame passed into an adjoining chamber, leaving the door partly open. The floor of that room was carpetless, as the kitchen's was. Nothing but bare necessaries were about me; and those not of the best sort. Not a print on the wall but an old volume of Doddridge lay on the smoked chimney-shelf.

"You must have walked a long way, sir; you sigh so with weariness."

"No, I am not nigh so weary as yourself, I dare say."

"Oh, but I am accustomed to that; *you* are not, I should think," and her soft, sad blue eye ran over my dress. "But I must sweep these shavings away; husband made him a new ax-helve this morning before sunrise, and I have been so busy washing that I have had no time to clear up. But now they are just the thing I want for the fire. They'd be much better though, were they not so green."

Now if Blandmour were here, thought I to myself, he would call those green shavings "Poor Man's Matches," or "Poor Man's Tinder," or some pleasant name of that sort.

"I do not know," said the good woman, turning round to me again — as she stirred among her pots on the smoky fire — "I do not know how you will like our pudding. It is only rice, milk, and salt boiled together."

"Ah, what they call 'Poor Man's Pudding,' I suppose you mean?"

A quick flush, half resentful, passed over her face.

"We do not call it so, sir," she said, and was silent.

Upbraiding myself for my inadvertence, I could not but again think to myself what Blandmour would have said, had he heard those words and seen that flush.

At last a slow, heavy footfall was heard; then a scraping at the door, and another voice said, "Come, wife; come, come — I must be back again in a jif — if you say I *must* take all my meals at home, you must be speedy; because the Squire — Good-day, sir," he exclaimed, now first catching sight of me as he entered the room. He turned toward his wife, inquiringly, and stood stock-still, while the moisture oozed from his patched boots to the floor.

"This gentleman stops here awhile to rest and refresh: he will take dinner with us, too. All will be ready now in a trice: so sit down on the bench, husband, and be patient, I pray. You see, sir," she continued, turning to me, "William there wants, of mornings, to carry a cold meal into the woods with him, to save the long one-o'clock walk across the fields to and fro. But I won't let him. A warm dinner is more than pay for the long walk."

"I don't know about that," said William, shaking his head. "I have often debated in my mind whether it really paid. There's not much odds, either way, between a wet walk after hard work, and a wet dinner before it. But I like to oblige a good wife like Martha. And you know, sir, that women will have their whimseys."

"I wish they all had as kind whimseys as your wife has," said I.

"Well, I've heard that some women ain't all maple-sugar; but content with dear Martha, I don't know much about others."

"You find rare wisdom in the woods," mused I.

"Now, husband, if you ain't too tired, just lend a hand to draw the table out."

"Nay," said I; "let him rest, and let me help."

"No," said William, rising.

"Sit still," said his wife to me.

The table set, in due time we all found ourselves with plates before us.

"You see what we have," said Coulter — "salt pork, rye-bread, and pudding. Let me help you. I got this pork of the Squire; some of his last year's pork, which he let me have on account. It isn't quite as sweet as this year's would be; but I find it hearty enough to work on, and that's all I eat for. Only let the rheumatiz and other sicknesses keep clear of me, and I ask no flavors or favors from any. But you don't eat of the pork!"

"I see," said the wife, gently and gravely, "that the gentleman knows the difference between this year's and last year's pork. But perhaps he will like the pudding."

I summoned up all my self-control, and smilingly assented to the proposition of the pudding, without by my looks casting any reflections upon the pork. But, to tell the truth, it was quite impossible for me (not being ravenous, but only a little hungry at that time) to eat of the latter. It had a yellowish crust all round it, and was rather rankish, I thought, to the taste. I observed, too, that the dame did not eat of it, though she suffered some to be put on her plate, and pretended to be busy with it when Coulter looked that way. But she ate of the rye-bread, and so did I.

" Now, then, for the pudding," said Coulter. " Quick, wife; the Squire sits in his sitting-room window, looking far out across the fields. His time-piece is true."

" He don't play the spy on you, does he? " said I.

" Oh, no! — I don't say that. He's a good enough man. He gives me work. But he's particular. Wife, help the gentleman. You see, sir, if I lose the Squire's work, what will become of — " and, with a look for which I honored humanity, with sly significance, he glanced toward his wife; then, a little changing his voice, instantly continued — " that fine horse I am going to buy? "

" I guess," said the dame, with a strange, subdued sort of inefficient pleasantry — " I guess that fine horse you sometimes so merrily dream of will long stay in the Squire's stall. But sometimes his man gives me a Sunday ride."

" A Sunday ride! " said I.

" You see," resumed Coulter, " wife loves to go to church; but the nighest is four miles off, over yon snowy hills. So she can't walk it; and I can't carry her in my arms, though I have carried her up-stairs before now. But, as she says, the Squire's man sometimes gives her a lift on the road; and for this cause it is that I speak of a horse I am going to have one of these fine sunny days. And already, before having it, I have christened it ' Martha.' But what am I about? Come, come, wife! The pudding! Help the gentleman, do! The Squire! the Squire! — think of the Squire! and help round the pudding. There, one — two — three mouthfuls must do me. Good-by, wife. Good-by, sir, I'm off."

And, snatching his soaked hat, the noble Poor Man hurriedly went out into the soak and the mire.

I suppose now, thinks I to myself, that Blandmour would poetically say, He goes to take a Poor Man's saunter.

" You have a fine husband," said I to the woman, as we were now left together.

" William loves me this day as on the wedding-day, sir. Some hasty words, but never a harsh one. I wish I were better and stronger for his sake. And, oh! sir, both for his sake and mine" (and the soft, blue, beautiful eyes turned into two well-springs), "how I wish little William and Martha lived — it is so lonely-like now. William named after him, and Martha for me."

When a companion's heart of itself overflows, the best one can do is to do nothing. I sat looking down on my as yet untasted pudding.

"You should have seen little William, sir. Such a bright, manly boy, only six years old — cold, cold now!"

Plunging my spoon into the pudding, I forced some into my mouth to stop it.

"And little Martha — Oh! sir, she was the beauty! Bitter, bitter! but needs must be borne!"

The mouthful of pudding now touched my palate, and touched it with a mouldy, briny taste. The rice, I knew, was of that damaged sort sold cheap; and the salt from the last year's pork barrel.

"Ah, sir, if those little ones yet to enter the world were the same little ones which so sadly have left it; returning friends, not strangers, strangers, always strangers! Yet does a mother soon learn to love them; for certain, sir, they come from where the others have gone. Don't you believe that, sir? Yes, I know all good people must. But, still, still — and I fear it is wicked, and very black-hearted, too — still, strive how I may to cheer me with thinking of reading Dr. Doddridge there — still, still does dark grief leak in, just like the rain through our roof. I am left so lonesome now; day after day, all the day long, dear William is gone; and all the damp day long grief drizzles and drizzles down on my soul. But I pray to God to forgive me for this; and for the rest, manage it as well as I may."

Bitter and mouldy is the "Poor Man's Pudding," groaned I to myself, half choked with but one little mouthful of it, which would hardly go down.

I could stay no longer to hear of sorrows for which the sincerest sympathies could give no adequate relief; of a fond persuasion, to which there could be furnished no further proof than already was had — a persuasion, too, of that sort which much speaking is sure more or less to mar; of causeless self-upbraidings, which no expostulations could have dispelled, I offered no pay for hospitalities gratuitous and honorable as those of a prince. I knew that such offerings would have been more than declined; charity resented.

The native American poor never lose their delicacy or pride; hence, though unreduced to the physical degradation of the European pauper, they yet suffer more in mind than the poor of any other people in the world. Those peculiar social sensibilities nourished by our peculiar political principles, while they enhance the true dignity of a prosperous American, do but minister to the added wretchedness of the unfortunate; first, by prohibiting their acceptance of what little random relief charity may offer; and, second, by furnishing them with the keenest appreciation of the smarting distinction between their ideal of universal equality and their grindstone experience of the practical misery and infamy of poverty — a misery and infamy which is, ever has been, and ever will be, precisely the same in India, England, and America.

Under pretense that my journey called me forthwith, I bade the dame good-by; shook her cold hand; looked my last into her blue, resigned eye, and went out into the wet. But cheerless as it was, and damp, damp, damp — the heavy atmosphere charged with all sorts of incipiencies — I yet became conscious, by the suddenness of the contrast, that the house air I had quitted was laden down with that peculiar deleterious quality, the height of which — insufferable to some visitants — will be found in a poorhouse ward.

This ill-ventilation in winter of the rooms of the poor — a thing, too, so stubbornly persisted in — is usually charged upon them as their disgraceful neglect of the most simple means to health. But the instinct of the poor is wiser than we think. The air which ventilates, likewise *cools*. And to any shiverer, ill-ventilated warmth is better than well-ventilated cold. Of all the preposterous assumptions of humanity over humanity, nothing exceeds most of the criticisms made on the habits of the poor by the well-housed, well-warmed, and well-fed.

"Blandmour," said I that evening, as after tea I sat on his comfortable sofa, before a blazing fire, with one of his two ruddy little children on my knee, "you are not what may rightly be called a rich man; you have a fair competence; no more. Is it not so? Well then, I do not include *you* when I say that if ever a rich man speaks prosperously to me of a Poor Man, I shall set it down as — I won't mention the word."

PICTURE SECOND

In the year 1814, during the summer following my first taste of the "Poor Man's Pudding," a sea-voyage was recommended to me by my physician. The Battle of Waterloo having closed the long drama of Napoleon's wars, many strangers were visiting Europe. I arrived in London at the time the victorious princes were there assembled enjoying the Arabian Nights' hospitalities of a grateful and gorgeous aristocracy, and the courtliest of gentlemen and kings — George the Prince Regent.

I had declined all letters but one to my banker. I wandered about for the best reception an adventurous traveler can have — the reception, I mean, which unsolicited chance and accident throw in his venturous way.

But I omit all else to recount one hour's hap under the lead of a very friendly man, whose acquaintance I made in the open street of Cheapside. He wore a uniform, and was some sort of a civic subordinate; I forget exactly what. He was off duty that day. His discourse was chiefly of the noble charities of London. He took me to two or three, and made admiring mention of many more.

" But," said he, as we turned into Cheapside again, " if you are at all curious about such things, let me take you — if it be not too late — to one of the most interesting of all — our Lord Mayor's Charities, sir; nay, the charities not only of a Lord Mayor, but I may truly say, in this one instance, of emperors, regents, and kings. You remember the event of yesterday? "

" That sad fire on the river-side, you mean, unhousing so many of the poor? "

" No. The grand Guildhall Banquet to the princes. Who can forget it? Sir, the dinner was served on nothing but solid silver and gold plate, worth at least £200,000 — that is, 1,000,000 of your dollars; while the mere expenditure of meats, wines, attendance and upholstery, etc., can not be footed under £25,000 — 120,000 dollars of your hard cash."

" But, surely, my friend, you do not call that charity — feeding kings at that rate? "

" No. The feast came first — yesterday; and the charity after — to-day. How else would you have it, where princes are concerned? But I think we shall be quite in time — come; here we are at King Street, and down there is Guildhall. Will you go? "

" Gladly, my good friend. Take me where you will. I come but to roam and see."

Avoiding the main entrance of the hall, which was barred, he took me through some private way, and we found ourselves in a rear blind-

345

walled place in the open air. I looked round amazed. The spot was grimy as a back-yard in the Five Points. It was packed with a mass of lean, famished, ferocious creatures, struggling and fighting for some mysterious precedency, and all holding soiled blue tickets in their hands.

"There is no other way," said my guide; "we can only get in with the crowd. Will you try it? I hope you have not on your drawing-room suit? What do you say? It will be well worth your sight. So noble a charity does not often offer. The one following the annual banquet of Lord Mayor's day — fine a charity as that certainly is — is not to be mentioned with what will be seen to-day. Is it, ay? "

As he spoke, a basement door in the distance was thrown open, and the squalid mass made a rush for the dark vault beyond.

I nodded to my guide, and sideways we joined in with the rest. Ere long we found our retreat cut off by the yelping crowd behind, and I could not but congratulate myself on having a civic as well as civil guide; one, too, whose uniform made evident his authority.

It was just the same as if I were pressed by a mob of cannibals on some pagan beach. The beings round me roared with famine. For in this mighty London misery but maddens. In the country it softens. As I gazed on the meagre, murderous pack, I thought of the blue eye of the gentle wife of poor Coulter. Some sort of curved, glittering steel thing (not a sword; I know not what it was), before worn in his belt, was now flourished overhead by my guide, menacing the creatures to forbear offering the stranger violence.

As we drove, slow and wedge-like, into the gloomy vault, the howls of the mass reverberated. I seemed seething in the Pit with the Lost. On and on, through the dark and damp, and then up a stone stairway to a wide portal; when, diffusing, the pestiferous mob poured in bright day between painted walls and beneath a painted dome. I thought of the anarchic sack of Versailles.

A few moments more and I stood bewildered among the beggars in the famous Guildhall.

Where I stood — where the thronged rabble stood, less than twelve hours before sat His Imperial Majesty, Alexander of Russia; His Royal Majesty, Frederick William, King of Prussia; His Royal Highness, George, Prince Regent of England; His world-renowned Grace, the Duke of Wellington; with a mob of magnificoes, made up of conquering field marshals, earls, counts, and innumerable other nobles of mark.

The walls swept to and fro, like the foliage of a forest with blazon-ings of conquerors' flags. Naught outside the hall was visible. No windows were within four-and-twenty feet of the floor. Cut off from all other sights, I was hemmed in by one splendid spectacle — splendid, I mean, everywhere but as the eye fell toward the floor. *That* was foul as a hovel's — as a kennel's; the naked boards being strewed with the smaller and more wasteful fragments of the feast, while the two long parallel lines, up and down the hall, of now unrobed, shabby, dirty pine tables were piled with less trampled wrecks. The dyed banners were in keeping with the last night's kings: the floor suited the beggars of to-day. The banners looked upon the floor as from his balcony Dives upon Lazarus. A line of liveried men kept back with their staves the impatient jam of the mob, who, otherwise, might have instantaneously converted the Charity into a Pillage. Another body of gowned and gilded officials distributed the broken meats — the cold victuals and crumbs of kings. One after another the beggars held up their dirty blue tickets, and were served with the plundered wreck of a pheasant, or the rim of a pasty — like the detached crown of an old hat — the solids and meats stolen out.

"What a noble charity," whispered my guide. "See that pasty now, snatched by that pale girl; I dare say the Emperor of Russia ate of that last night."

"Very probably," murmured I; "it looks as though some omnivorous emperor or other had had a finger in that pie."

"And see yon pheasant too — there — that one — the boy in the torn shirt has it now — look! The Prince Regent might have dined off that."

The two breasts were gouged ruthlessly out, exposing the bare bones, embellished with the untouched pinions and legs.

"Yes, who knows!" said my guide, "his Royal Highness the Prince Regent might have eaten of that identical pheasant."

"I don't doubt it," murmured I, "he is said to be uncommonly fond of the breast. But where is Napoleon's head in a charger? I should fancy that ought to have been the principal dish."

"You are merry. Sir, even Cossacks are charitable here in Guildhall. Look! the famous Platoff, the Hetman himself — (he was here last night with the rest) — no doubt he thrust a lance into yon pork-pie there. Look! the old shirtless man has it now. How he licks his chops over it, little thinking of or thanking the good, kind Cossack that left it him! Ah! another — a stouter has grabbed it. It falls; bless my soul! — the dish is quite empty — only a bit of the hacked crust."

"The Cossacks, my friend, are said to be immoderately fond of fat," observed I. "The Hetman was hardly so charitable as you thought."

"A noble charity, upon the whole, for all that. See, even Gog and Magog yonder, at the other end of the hall, fairly laugh out their delight at the scene."

"But don't you think, though," hinted I, "that the sculptor, whoever he was, carved the laugh too much into a grin — a sort of sardonical grin?"

"Well, that's as you take it, sir. But see — now I'd wager a guinea the Lord Mayor's lady dipped her golden spoon into yonder golden-hued jelly. See, the jelly-eyed old body has slipped it, in one broad gulp, down his throat."

"Peace to that jelly!" breathed I.

"What a generous, noble, magnanimous charity this is! unheard of in any country but England, which feeds her very beggars with golden-hued jellies."

"But not three times every day, my friend. And do you really think that jellies are the best sort of relief you can furnish to beggars? Would not plain beef and bread, with something to do, and be paid for, be better?"

"But plain beef and bread were not eaten here. Emperors, and prince-regents, and kings, and field marshals don't often dine on plain beef and bread. So the leavings are according. Tell me, can you expect that the crumbs of kings can be like the crumbs of squirrels?"

"*You!* I mean *you!* stand aside, or else be served and away! Here, take this pasty, and be thankful that you taste of the same dish with her Grace the Duchess of Devonshire. Graceless ragamuffin, do you hear?"

These words were bellowed at me through the din by a red-gowned official nigh the board.

"Surely he does not mean *me*," said I to my guide; "he has not confounded *me* with the rest."

"One is known by the company he keeps," smiled my guide. "See! not only stands your hat awry and bunged on your head, but your coat is fouled and torn. Nay," he cried to the red-gown, "this is an unfortunate friend; a simple spectator, I assure you."

348

"Ah! is that you, old lad?" responded the red-gown, in familiar recognition of my guide — a personal friend as it seemed; "well, convey your friend out forthwith. Mind the grand crash; it will soon be coming; hark! now! away with him!"

Too late. The last dish had been seized. The yet unglutted mob raised a fierce yell, which wafted the banners like a strong gust, and filled the air with a reek as from sewers. They surged against the tables, broke through all barriers, and billowed over the hall — their bare tossed arms like the dashed ribs of a wreck. It seemed to me as if a sudden impotent fury of fell envy possessed them. That one half-hour's peep at the mere remnants of the glories of the Banquets of Kings; the unsatisfying mouthfuls of disemboweled pasties, plundered pheasants, and half-sucked jellies, served to remind them of the intrinsic contempt of the alms. In this sudden mood, or whatever mysterious thing it was that now seized them, these Lazaruses seemed ready to spew up in repentant scorn the contumelious crumbs of Dives.

"This way, this way! stick like a bee to my back," intensely whispered my guide. "My friend there has answered my beck, and thrown open yon private door for us two. Wedge — wedge in — quick, there goes your bunged hat — never stop for your coat-tail — hit that man — strike him down! hold! jam! now! wrench along for your life! ha! here we breathe freely; thank God! You faint. Ho!"

"Never mind. This fresh air revives me."

I inhaled a few more breaths of it, and felt ready to proceed.

"And now conduct me, my good friend, by some front passage into Cheapside, forthwith. I must home."

"Not by the sidewalk though. Look at your dress. I must get a hack for you."

"Yes, I suppose so," said I, ruefully eyeing my tatters, and then glancing in envy at the close-buttoned coat and flat cap of my guide, which defied all tumblings and tearings.

"There, now, sir," said the honest fellow, as he put me into the hack, and tucked in me and my rags, "when you get back to your own country, you can say you have witnessed the greatest of all England's noble charities. Of course, you will make reasonable allowances for the unavoidable jam. Good-by. Mind, Jehu" — addressing the driver on the box — "this is a *gentleman* you carry. He is just from the Guildhall Charity, which accounts for his appearance. Go on now. London Tavern, Fleet Street, remember, is the place."

"Now, Heaven in its kind mercy save me from the noble charities of London," sighed I, as that night I lay bruised and battered on my bed; "and Heaven save me equally from the 'Poor Man's Pudding' and the 'Rich Man's Crumbs.'"

[1854]

JAMES RUSSELL LOWELL

[1819–1891]

THE LOWELL family was distinguished in business, law, and public affairs, but James Russell Lowell's father was a Unitarian clergyman and his mother was a sensitive, introspective woman much interested in spiritual problems. From them he probably derived his bookish inclinations. He went to Harvard College and the Harvard Law School, but never practiced his profession, for he turned immediately to belles-lettres. At this time he met and fell in love with Maria White, a charming and intelligent girl passionately devoted to the anti-slavery cause and other reform movements. Lowell, greatly influenced by her, adopted her interests and allied himself with the most progressive writers in New England. He married Miss White in 1844. Nine years later she died. Not for many years after that, however, did her influence upon him wane. He remained loyal to the anti-slavery cause, but in other respects reverted to his natural conservatism. His career confirmed the drift: he became a professor at Harvard, editor of the *Atlantic Monthly*, Minister to Spain and then Minister to the Court of St. James's. In the end he confessed to aristocratic sentiments. That is not to say, however, that he attacked the democratic forms. In 1884 he delivered an often quoted address on democracy which defined his position: it was not unlike Cooper's — he obviously favored the rule of gentlemen, shrank (more timidly than Cooper) from certain American vulgarities, but accepted the premises of political democracy. *The Biglow Papers* represent him in his most liberal phase — opposed not only to slavery, but to imperialism; and, in addition, militantly pacifist and almost equalitarian. By any standard, these poems in Yankee dialect are among his finest works. Perhaps his peak is the section on Lincoln from his " Commemoration Ode," here reprinted. Finally, there follow excerpts from his paper on the presidential election of 1860 in which he wrote eloquently on the effects of slavery upon a supposedly free people.

from

THE BIGLOW PAPERS

No. I

[EZ FER WAR]

Thrash away, you'll *hev* to rattle
  On them kittle-drums o' yourn, —
'Taint a knowin' kind o' cattle
  Thet is ketched with mouldy corn;
Put in stiff, you fifer feller,
  Let folks see how spry you be, —
Guess you'll toot till you are yeller
  'Fore you git ahold o' me!

Thet air flag's a leetle rotten,
  Hope it aint your Sunday's best; —
Fact! it takes a sight o' cotton
  To stuff out a soger's chest:
Sence we farmers hev to pay fer 't,
  Ef you must wear humps like these,
Sposin' you should try salt hay fer 't,
  It would du ez slick ez grease.

'T would n't suit them Southun fellers,
  They're a dreffle graspin' set,
We must ollers blow the bellers
  Wen they want their irons het;
May be it's all right ez preachin',
  But *my* narves it kind o' grates,
Wen I see the overreachin'
  O' them nigger-drivin' States.

Them thet rule us, them slave-traders,
  Haint they cut a thunderin' swarth
(Helped by Yankee renegaders),
  Thru the vartu o' the North!

352

We begin to think it's nater
    To take sarse an' not be riled; —
Who'd expect to see a tater
    All on eend at bein' biled?

Ez fer war, I call it murder, —
    There you hev it plain an' flat;
I don't want to go no furder
    Than my Testyment fer that;
God hez sed so plump an' fairly,
    It's ez long ez it is broad,
An' you've gut to git up airly
    Ef you want to take in God.

'Taint your eppyletts an' feathers
    Make the thing a grain more right;
'Taint afollerin' your bell-wethers
    Will excuse ye in His sight;
Ef you take a sword an' dror it,
    An' go stick a feller thru,
Guv'ment aint to answer for it,
    God'll send the bill to you.

Wut's the use o' meetin'-goin'
    Every Sabbath, wet or dry,
Ef it's right to go amowin'
    Feller-men like oats an' rye?
I dunno but wut it's pooty
    Trainin' round in bobtail coats, —
But it's curus Christian dooty
    This 'ere cuttin' folks's throats.

They make talk o' Freedom's airy
    Tell they're pupple in the face, —
It's a grand gret cemetary
    Fer the barthrights of our race;
They just want this Californy
    So's to lug new slave-states in
To abuse ye, an' to scorn ye,
    An' to plunder ye like sin.

353

Aint it cute to see a Yankee
  Take sech everlastin' pains,
All to git the Devil's thankee
  Helpin' on 'em weld their chains?
Wy, it's jest ez clear ez figgers,
  Clear ez one an' one make two,
Chaps thet make black slaves o' niggers
  Want to make wite slaves o' you.

Tell ye jest the eend I've come to
  Arter cipherin' plaguy smart,
An' it makes a handy sum, tu,
  Any gump could larn by heart;
Laborin' man an' laborin' woman
  Hev one glory an' one shame.
Ev'y thin' thet's done inhuman
  Injers all on 'em the same.

'Taint by turnin' out to hack folks
  You're agoin' to git your right,
Nor by lookin' down on black folks
  Coz you're put upon by wite;
Slavery aint o' nary color,
  'Taint the hide thet makes it wus,
All it keers fer in a feller
  'S jest to make him fill its pus.

Want to tackle *me* in, du ye?
  I expect you'll hev to wait;
Wen cold lead puts daylight thru ye
  You'll begin to kal'late;
S'pose the crows wun't fall to pickin'
  All the carkiss from your bones,
Coz you helped to give a lickin'
  To them poor half-Spanish drones?

Jest go home an' ask our Nancy
  Wether I'd be sech a goose
Ez to jine ye, — guess you'd fancy
  The etarnal bung wuz loose!

She wants me fer home consumption,
    Let alone the hay's to mow, —
Ef you're arter folks o' gumption,
    You've a darned long row to hoe.

Take them editors thet's crowin'
    Like a cockerel three months old, —
Don't ketch any on 'em goin',
    Though they *be* so blasted bold;
Ain't they a prime lot o' fellers?
    'Fore they think on 't guess they'll sprout
(Like a peach thet's got the yellers),
    With the meanness bustin' out.

Wal, go 'long to help 'em stealin'
    Bigger pens to cram with slaves,
Help the men thet's ollers dealin'
    Insults on your fathers' graves;
Help the strong to grind the feeble,
    Help the many agin the few,
Help the men thet call your people
    Witewashed slaves an' peddlin' crew!

Massachusetts, God forgive her,
    She's akneelin' with the rest,
She, thet ough' to ha' clung ferever
    In her grand old eagle-nest;
She thet ough' to stand so fearless
    Wile the wracks are round her hurled,
Holdin' up a beacon peerless
    To the oppressed of all the world!

Ha'n't they sold your colored seamen?
    Ha'n't they made your env'ys w'iz?
Wut'll make ye act like freemen?
    Wut'll git your dander riz?
Come, I'll tell ye wut I'm thinkin'
    Is our dooty in this fix,
They'd ha' done't ez quick ez winkin'
    In the days o' seventy-six.

Clang the bells in every steeple,
    Call all true men to disown
The tradoocers of our people,
    The enslavers o' their own;
Let our dear old Bay State proudly
    Put the trumpet to her mouth,
Let her ring this messidge loudly
    In the ears of all the South: —

" I'll return ye good fer evil
    Much ez we frail mortils can,
But I wun't go help the Devil
    Makin' man the cus o' man;
Call me coward, call me traiter,
    Jest ez suits your mean idees, —
Here I stand a tyrant-hater,
    An' the friend o' God an' Peace! "

Ef I'd *my* way I had ruther
    We should go to work an' part, —
They take one way, we take t' other, —
    Guess it wouldn't break my heart;
Man hed ough' to put asunder
    Them thet God has noways jined;
An' I shouldn't gretly wonder
    Ef there's thousands o' my mind.

[*1846*]

No. II

[SOGERIN' IN MEXICO]

This kind o' sogerin' aint a mite like our October trainin',
A chap could clear right out from there ef't only looked like rainin',
An' th' Cunnles, tu, could kiver up their shappoes with bandanners,
An' send the insines skootin' to the bar-room with their banners
(Fear o' gittin' on 'em spotted), an' a feller could cry quarter
Ef he fired away his ramrod arter tu much rum an' water.

Recollect wut fun we hed, you 'n' I an' Ezry Hollis,
Up there to Waltham plain last fall, along o' the Cornwallis?
This sort o' thing aint *jest* like thet, — I wish thet I wuz furder, —
Ninepunce a day fer killin' folks comes kind o' low fer murder.
(Wy I've worked out to slarterin' some fer Deacon Cephas Billins,
An' in the hardest times there wuz I ollers tetched ten shillins,)
There's sutthin' gits into my throat thet makes it hard to swaller,
It comes so nateral to think about a hempen collar;
It's glory, — but, in spite o' all my tryin' to git callous,
I feel a kind o' in a cart, aridin' to the gallus.
But wen it comes to *bein'* killed, — I tell ye I felt streaked
The fust time 't ever I found out wy baggonets wuz peaked;
Here's how it wuz: I started out to go to a fandango,
The sentinul he ups an' sez, "Thet's furder 'an you can go."
"None o' your sarse," sez I; sez he, "Stan' back!" "Aint you a buster?"
Sez I, "I'm up to all thet air, I guess I've ben to muster;
I know wy sentinuls air sot, you aint agoin' to eat us;
Caleb haint no monopoly to court the seenoreetas;
My folks to hum air full ez good ez hisn be, by golly!"
An' so ez I wuz goin' by, not thinkin' wut would folly,
The everlastin' cus he stuck his one-pronged pitchfork in me
An' made a hole right thru my close ez ef I wuz an in'my.

Wal, it beats all how big I felt hoorawin' in ole Funnel
Wen Mister Bolles he gin the sword to our Leftenant Cunnle,
(It's Mister Secondary Bolles, thet writ the prize peace essay;
Thet's why he didn't list himself along o' us, I dessay,)
An' Rantoul, tu, talked pooty loud, but don't put *his* foot in it,
Coz human life's so sacred that he's principled agin it, —
Though I myself can't rightly see it's any wus achokin' on 'em
Than puttin' bullets thru their lights, or with a bagnet pokin' on 'em;
How dreffle slick he reeled it off (like Blitz at our lyceum
Ahaulin' ribbins from his chops so quick you skeercely see 'em),
About the Anglo-Saxon race (an' saxons would be handy
To du the buryin' down here upon the Rio Grandy),
About our patriotic pas an' our star-spangled banner,
Our country's bird alookin' on an' singin' out hosanner,
An' how he (Mister B. himself) wuz happy for Ameriky, —

357

I felt, ez sister Patience sez, a leetle mite histericky.
I felt, I swon, ez though it wuz a dreffle kind o' privilege
Atrampin' round thru Boston streets among the gutter's drivelage;
I act'lly thought it wuz a treat to hear a little drummin',
An' it did bonyfidy seem millanyum wuz acomin'
Wen all on us got suits (darned like them wore in the state prison)
An' every feller felt ez though all Mexico wuz hisn.

This 'ere's about the meanest place a skunk could wal diskiver
(Saltillo's Mexican, I b'lieve, fer wut we call Salt-river);
The sort o' trash a feller gits to eat doos beat all nater,
I'd give a year's pay fer a smell o' one good blue-nose tater,
The country here thet Mister Bolles declared to be so charmin'
Throughout is swarmin' with the most alarmin' kind o' varmin'.
He talked about delishis froots, but then it wuz a wopper all,
The holl on 't's mud an' prickly pears, with here an' there a chapparal;
You see a feller peekin' out, an', fust you know, a lariat
Is round your throat an' you a copse, 'fore you can say, "Wut air
    ye at?"
You never see sech darned gret bugs (it may not be irrelevant
To say I've seen a *scarabæus pilularius* big ez a year-old elephant),
The rigiment come up one day in time to stop a red bug
From runnin' off with Cunnle Wright, — 't wuz jest a common *cimex
    lectularius.*

One night I started up on eend an' thought I wuz to hum agin,
I heern a horn, thinks I it's Sol the fisherman hez come agin,
His bellowses is sound enough, — ez I'm a livin' creeter,
I felt a thing go thru my leg, — 't wuz nothin' more 'n a skeeter!
Then there's the yaller fever, tu, they call it here el vomito, —
(Come, thet wun't du, you landcrab there, I tell ye to le' go my toe!
My gracious! it's a scorpion thet's took a shine to play with 't,
I darsn't skeer the tarnel thing fer fear he'd run away with 't).
Afore I come away from hum I hed a strong persuasion
Thet Mexicans worn't human beans, — an ourang-outang nation,
A sort o' folks a chap could kill an' never dream on 't arter,
No more'n a feller'd dream o' pigs thet he hed hed to slarter;
I'd an idee thet they were built arter the darkie fashion all,

An' kickin' colored folks about, you know, 's a kind o' national;
But wen I jined I worn't so wise ez thet air queen o' Sheby,
Fer, come to look at 'em, they aint much diff'rent from wut we be,
An' here we air ascrougin' 'em out o' thir own dominions,
Ashelterin' 'em, ez Caleb sez, under our eagle's pinions,
Wich means to take a feller up jest by the slack o' 's trowsis
An' walk him Spanish clean right out o' all his homes an' houses;
Wal, it doos seem a curus way, but then hooraw fer Jackson!
It must be right, fer Caleb sez it's reg'lar Anglo-saxon.
The Mex'cans don't fight fair, they say, they piz'n all the water,
An' du amazin' lots o' things thet isn't wut they ough' to;
Bein' they haint no lead, they make their bullets out o' copper
An' shoot the darned things at us, tu, wich Caleb sez aint proper;
He sez they'd ough' to stan' right up an' let us pop 'em fairly
(Guess wen he ketches 'em at thet he'll hev to git up airly),
Thet our nation's bigger'n theirn an' so its rights air bigger,
An' thet it's all to make 'em free thet we air pullin' trigger,
Thet Anglo-Saxondom's idee's abreakin' 'em to pieces,
An' thet idee 's thet every man doos jest wut he damn pleases;
Ef I don't make his meanin' clear, perhaps in some respex I can,
I know thet "every man" don't mean a nigger or a Mexican;
An' there's another thing I know, an' thet is, ef these creeturs,
Thet stick an Anglosaxon mask onto State-prison feeturs,
Should come to Jaalam Centre fer to argify an' spout on 't,
The gals 'ould count the silver spoons the minnit they cleared out on 't.

This goin' ware glory waits ye haint one agreeable feetur,
An' ef it worn't fer wakin' snakes, I'd home again short meter;
O, would n't I be off, quick time, ef 't worn't thet I wuz sartin
They'd let the daylight into me to pay me fer desartin!
I don't approve o' tellin' tales, but jest to you I may state
Our ossifers aint wut they wuz afore they left the Bay State;
Then it wuz "Mister Sawin, sir, you're middlin well now, be ye?
Step up an' take a nipper, sir; I'm dreffle glad to see ye";
But now it's "Ware's my eppylet? here, Sawin, step an' fetch it!
An' mind your eye, be thund'rin spry, or, damn ye, you shall ketch it!"
Wal, ez the Docter sez, some pork will bile so, but by mighty,
Ef I hed some on 'em to hum, I'd give 'em linkum vity,
I'd play the rogue's march on their hides an' other music follerin' —

But I must close my letter here, fer one on 'em's ahollerin',
These Anglosaxon ossifers, — wal, taint no use ajawin',
I'm safe enlisted fer the war,
Yourn,
BIRDOFREDUM SAWIN.

[1846]

No. VI

THE PIOUS EDITOR'S CREED

I du believe in Freedom's cause,
    Ez fur away ez Payris is;
I love to see her stick her claws
    In them infarnal Phayrisees;
It's wal enough agin a king
    To dror resolves an' triggers, —
But libbaty's a kind o' thing
    Thet don't agree with niggers.

I du believe the people want
    A tax on teas an' coffees,
Thet nothin' aint extravygunt, —
    Purvidin' I'm in office;
Fer I hev loved my country sence
    My eye-teeth filled their sockets,
An' Uncle Sam I reverence,
    Partic'larly his pockets.

I du believe in *any* plan
    O' levyin' the taxes,
Ez long ez, like a lumberman,
    I git jest wut I axes;
I go free-trade thru thick an' thin,
    Because it kind o' rouses
The folks to vote, — an' keeps us in
    Our quiet custom-houses.

I du believe it 's wise an' good
    To sen' out furrin missions,
Thet is, on sartin understood
    An' orthydox conditions; —

360

I mean nine thousan' dolls, per ann.,
    Nine thousan' more fer outfit,
An' me to recommend a man
    The place 'ould jest about fit.

I du believe in special ways
    O' prayin' an' convartin';
The bread comes back in many days,
    An' buttered, tu, fer sartin;
I mean in preyin' till one busts
    On wut the party chooses;
An' in convartin' public trusts
    To very privit uses.

I du believe hard coin the stuff
    Fer 'lectioneers to spout on;
The people 's ollers soft enough
    To make hard money out on;
Dear Uncle Sam pervides fer his,
    An' gives a good-sized junk to all, —
I don't care *how* hard money is,
    Ez long ez mine's paid punctooal.

I du believe with all my soul
    In the gret Press's freedom,
To pint the people to the goal
    An' in the traces lead 'em;
Palsied the arm thet forges yokes
    At my fat contracts squintin',
An' withered be the nose thet pokes
    Inter the gov'ment printin'!

I du believe thet I should give
    Wut's his'n unto Cæsar,
Fer it's by him I move an' live,
    From him my bread an' cheese air;
I du believe thet all o' me
    Doth bear his superscription, —
Will, conscience, honor, honesty,
    An' things o' thet description.

I du believe in prayer an' praise
    To him thet hez the grantin'
O' jobs, — in every thin' thet pays,
    But most of all in CANTIN';
This doth my cup with mercies fill,
    This lays all thought o' sin to rest, —
I *don't* believe in princerple,
    But O, I *du* in interest.

I du believe in bein' this
    Or thet, ez it may happen
One way or t' other hendiest is
    To ketch the people nappin';
It aint by princerples nor men
    My preudunt course is steadied, —
I scent wich pays the best, an' then
    Go into it baldheaded.

I du believe thet holdin' slaves
    Comes nat'ral to a Presidunt,
Let 'lone the rowdedow it saves
    To hev a wal-broke precedunt;
Fer any office, small or gret,
    I couldn't ax with no face,
'uthout I'd ben, thru dry an' wet,
    Th' unrizzest kind o' doughface.

I du believe wutever trash
    'll keep the people in blindness, —
Thet we the Mexicuns can thrash
    Right inter brotherly kindness,
Thet bombshells, grape, an' powder 'n' ball
    Air good-will's strongest magnets,
Thet peace, to make it stick at all, .
    Must be druv in with bagnets.

In short, I firmly du believe
    In Humbug generally,
Fer it's a thing thet I perceive
    To hev a solid vally;

This heth my faithful shepherd ben,
   In pasturs sweet heth led me,
  An' this'll keep the people green
   To feed ez they have fed me.

[*1847*]

from

ODE RECITED AT THE
HARVARD COMMEMORATION

Some day the soft Ideal that we wooed
Confronts us fiercely, foe-beset, pursued,
And cries reproachful: "Was it, then, my praise,
And not myself was loved? Prove now thy truth;
I claim of thee the promise of thy youth;
Give me thy life, or cower in empty phrase,
The victim of thy genius, not its mate!"
  Life may be given in many ways,
  And loyalty to Truth be sealed
As bravely in the closet as the field,
    So bountiful is Fate;
    But then to stand beside her,
    When craven churls deride her,
To front a lie in arms and not to yield,
    This shows, methinks, God's plan
    And measure of a stalwart man,
    Limbed like the old heroic breeds,
  Who stands self-poised on manhood's solid earth,
 Not forced to frame excuses for his birth
Fed from within with all the strength he needs.

Such was he, our Martyr-Chief,
  Whom late the Nation he had led,
   With ashes on her head,
Wept with the passion of an angry grief:

Forgive me, if from present things I turn
To speak what in my heart will beat and burn,
And hang my wreath on his world-honored urn,
    Nature, they say, doth dote,
    And cannot make a man
    Save on some worn-out plan,
    Repeating us by rote:
For him her Old-World moulds aside she threw,
    And, choosing sweet clay from the breast
    Of the unexhausted West,
With stuff untainted shaped a hero new,
Wise, steadfast in the strength of God, and true.
    How beautiful to see
Once more a shepherd of mankind indeed,
Who loved his charge, but never loved to lead;
One whose meek flock the people joyed to be,
    Not lured by any cheat of birth,
    But by his clear-grained human worth,
And brave old wisdom of sincerity!
    They knew that outward grace is dust;
    They could not choose but trust
In that sure-footed mind's unfaltering skill,
    And supple-tempered will
That bent like perfect steel to spring again and thrust.
    His was no lonely mountain-peak of mind,
    Thrusting to thin air o'er our cloudy bars,
    A sea-mark now, now lost in vapors blind;
    Broad prairie rather, genial, level-lined,
    Fruitful and friendly for all human kind,
Yet also nigh to heaven and loved of loftiest stars.
    Nothing of Europe here,
Or, then, of Europe fronting mornward still,
    Ere any names of Serf and Peer
    Could Nature's equal scheme deface
    And thwart her genial will;
    Here was a type of the true elder race,
And one of Plutarch's men talked with us face to face.
    I praise him not; it were too late;
And some innative weakness there must be

In him who condescends to victory
Such as the Present gives, and cannot wait,
    Safe in himself as in a fate.
        So always firmly he:
        He knew to bide his time,
        And can his fame abide,
Still patient in his simple faith sublime,
        Till the wise years decide.
    Great captains, with their guns and drums,
        Disturb our judgment for the hour,
        But at last silence comes;
These all are gone, and, standing like a tower,
    Our children shall behold his fame,
        The kindly-earnest, brave, foreseeing man,
Sagacious, patient, dreading praise, not blame,
    New birth of our new soil, the first American.

[1865]

from

THE ELECTION IN NOVEMBER

Whatever be the effect of slavery upon the States where it exists, there can be no doubt that its moral influence upon the North has been most disastrous. It has compelled our politicians into that first fatal compromise with their moral instincts and hereditary principles which makes all consequent ones easy; it has accustomed us to makeshifts instead of statesmanship, to subterfuge instead of policy, to party-platforms for opinions, and to a defiance of the public sentiment of the civilized world for patriotism. We have been asked to admit, first, that it was a necessary evil; then that it was a good both to master and slave; then that it was the corner-stone of free institutions; then that it was a system divinely instituted under the Old Law and sanctioned under the New. With a representation, three fifths of it based on the assumption that negroes are men, the South turns upon us and insists on our acknowledging that they are things. After compelling her Northern allies to pronounce the " free and equal " clause of the preamble to the Declaration of Independence (because it stood in the way of enslaving men) a manifest absurdity, she has declared, through the Supreme Court of the United States, that negroes are not men in the ordinary meaning of the word. To eat dirt is bad enough, but to find that we have eaten more than was necessary may chance to give us an indigestion. The slaveholding interest has gone on step by step, forcing concession after concession, till it needs but little to secure it forever in the political supremacy of the country. Yield to its latest demand, — let it mould the evil destiny of the Territories, — and the thing is done past recall. The next Presidential Election is to say *Yes* or *No*.

But we should not regard the mere question of political preponderancy as of vital consequence, did it not involve a continually increasing moral degradation on the part of the Non-slaveholding States, — for Free States they could not be called much longer. Sordid and materialistic views of the true value and objects of society and government are professed more and more openly by the leaders of popular outcry, — for it cannot be called public opinion. That side of human nature which it has been the object of all lawgivers and moralists to repress and subjugate is flattered and caressed; whatever is profitable is right; and already the slave-trade, as yielding a greater return on the capital invested than any other traffic, is lauded as the highest achievement of human reason and justice. Mr. Hammond has proclaimed the accession of King Cotton, but he seems to have forgotten that history is not without examples of kings who have lost their crowns through the folly and false security of their ministers. It is quite true that there is a large class of reasoners who would weigh all questions of right and wrong in the balance of trade; but we cannot bring ourselves to believe that it is a wise political economy which makes cotton by unmaking men, or a far-seeing statesmanship which looks on an immediate money-profit as a safe equivalent for a beggared public sentiment. We think Mr. Hammond even a little premature in proclaiming the new Pretender. The election of November may prove a Culloden. Whatever its result, it is to settle, for many years to come, the question whether the American idea is to govern this continent, whether the Occidental or the Oriental theory of society is to mould our future, whether we are to recede from principles which eighteen Christian centuries have been slowly establishing at the cost of so many saintly lives at the stake and so many heroic ones on the scaffold and the battle-field, in favor of some fancied assimilation to the household arrangements of Abraham, of which all that can be said with certainty is that they did not add to his domestic happiness.

We believe that this election is a turning-point in our history; for, although there are four candidates, there are really, as everybody knows, but two parties, and a single question that divides them. The supporters of Messrs. Bell and Everett have adopted as their platform the Constitution, the Union, and the enforcement of the Laws. This may be very convenient, but it is surely not very explicit. The cardinal question on which the whole policy of the country is to turn — a question, too, which this very election must decide in one way or the other — is the interpretation to be put upon certain clauses of the Constitution. All the other parties equally assert their loyalty to that instrument. Indeed, it is quite the fashion. The removers of all the ancient landmarks of our policy, the violators of thrice-pledged faith, the planners of new treachery to established compromises, all take refuge in the Constitution, —

> "Like thieves that in a hemp-plot lie,
> Secure against the hue and cry."

In the same way the first Bonaparte renewed his profession of faith in the Revolution at every convenient opportunity; and the second follows the precedent of his uncle, though the uninitiated fail to see any logical sequence from 1789 to 1815 or 1860. If Mr. Bell loves the Constitution, Mr. Breckenridge is equally fond; that Egeria of our statesmen could be "happy with either, were t'other dear charmer away." Mr. Douglas confides the secret of his passion to the unloquacious clams of Rhode Island, and the chief complaint made against Mr. Lincoln by his opponents is that he is *too* Constitutional.

Meanwhile, the only point in which voters are interested is, What do they mean by the Constitution? Mr. Breckenridge means the superiority of a certain exceptional species of property over all others; nay, over man himself. Mr. Douglas, with a different formula for expressing it, means practically the same thing. Both of them mean that Labor has no rights which Capital is bound to respect, — that there is no higher law than human interest and cupidity. Both of them represent not merely the narrow principles of a section, but the still narrower and more selfish ones of a caste. Both of them, to be sure, have convenient phrases to be juggled with before election, and which mean one thing or another, or neither one thing nor another, as a particular exigency may seem to require; but since both claim the regular Democratic nomination, we have little difficulty in divining what their course would be after the fourth of March, if they should chance to be elected. We know too well what regular Democracy is, to like either of the two faces which each shows by turns under the same hood. Everybody remembers Baron Grimm's story of the Parisian showman, who in 1789 exhibited the *royal* Bengal tiger under the new character of *national,* as more in harmony with the changed order of things. Could the animal have lived till 1848, he would probably have found himself offered to the discriminating public as the *democratic* and *social* ornament of the jungle. The Pro-slavery party of this country seeks the popular favor under even more frequent and incongruous aliases: it is now *national,* now *conservative,* now *constitutional;* here it represents Squatter-Sovereignty, and there the power of Congress over the Territories; but, under whatever name, its nature remains unchanged, and its instincts are none the less predatory and destructive. . . .

A great deal is said, to be sure, about the rights of the South; but has any such right been infringed? When a man invests money in any species of property, he assumes the risks to which it is liable. If he buy a house, it may be burned; if a ship, it may be wrecked; if a horse or an ox, it may die. Now the disadvantage of the Southern kind of property is — how shall we say it so as not to violate our Constitutional obligations? — that it is exceptional. When it leaves Virginia, it is a thing; when it arrives in Boston, it becomes a man, speaks human language, appeals to the justice of the same God whom we all acknowledge, weeps at the memory of wife and children left behind, — in short, hath the same organs and dimensions that a Christian hath — and is not distinguishable from ordinary Christians, except, perhaps, by a simpler and more earnest faith. There are people at the North who believe that, beside *meum* and *tuum,* there is also such a thing as *suum,* — who are old-fashioned enough, or weak enough, to have their feelings touched by these things, to think that human nature is older and more sacred than any claim of property whatever, and that it has rights at least as much to be respected as any hypothetical one of our Southern brethren. This, no doubt, makes it harder to recover a fugitive chattel; but the existence of human nature in a man here and there is surely one of those accidents to be counted on at least as often as fire, shipwreck, or the cattle-disease; and the man who chooses to put his money into these images of his Maker cut in ebony should be content to take the incident risks along with the advantages. We should be very sorry to deem this risk capable of diminution; for we think that the claims of a common manhood upon us should be at least as strong as those of Freemasonry, and that those whom the law of man turns away should find in the larger charity of the law of God and Nature a readier welcome and surer sanctuary. We shall continue to think the negro a man, and on Southern evidence, too, so long as he is counted in the population represented on the floor of Congress, — for three fifths of perfect manhood would be a high average even among white men; so long as he is hanged or worse, as an example and terror to others, — for we do not punish one animal for the moral improvement of the rest; so long as he is considered capable of religious instruction, — for we fancy the gorillas would make short work with a missionary; so long as there are fears of insurrection, — for we have never heard of a combined effort at revolt in a menagerie. Accordingly, we do not see how the particular right of whose infringement we hear so much is to be made safer by the election of Mr. Bell, Mr. Breckenridge, or Mr. Douglas, — there being quite as little chance that any of them would abolish human nature as that Mr. Lincoln would abolish slavery. The same generous instinct that leads some among us to sympathize with the sorrows of the bereaved master will always, we fear, influence others to take part with the rescued man.

But if our Constitutional Obligations, as we like to call our constitutional timidity or indifference, teach us that a particular divinity hedges the Domestic Institution, they do not require us to forget that we have institutions of our own, worth maintaining and extending, and not without a certain sacredness, whether we regard the traditions of the fathers or the faith of the children. It is high time that we should hear something of the rights of the Free States, and of the duties consequent upon them. We also have our prejudices to be respected, our theory of civilization, of what constitutes the safety of a state and insures its prosperity, to be applied wherever there is soil enough for a human being to stand on and thank God for making him a man. Is conservatism applicable only to property, and not to

369

justice, freedom, and public honor? Does it mean merely drifting with the current of evil times and pernicious counsels, and carefully nursing the ills we have, that they may, as their nature it is, grow worse?

To be told that we ought not to agitate the question of Slavery, when it is that which is forever agitating us, is like telling a man with the fever and ague on him to stop shaking, and he will be cured. The discussion of Slavery is said to be dangerous, but dangerous to what? The manufacturers of the Free States constitute a more numerous class than the slaveholders of the South: suppose they should claim an equal sanctity for the Protective System. Discussion is the very life of free institutions, and fruitful mother of all political and moral enlightenment, and yet the question of all questions must be tabooed. The Swiss guide enjoins silence in the region of avalanches, lest the mere vibration of the voice should dislodge the ruin clinging by frail roots of snow. But where is our avalanche to fall? It is to overwhelm the Union, we are told. The real danger to the Union will come when the encroachments of the Slave-Power and the concessions of the Trade-Power shall have made it a burden instead of a blessing. The real avalanche to be dreaded, — are we to expect it from the ever-gathering mass of ignorant brute force, with the irresponsibility of animals and the passions of men, which is one of the fatal necessities of slavery, or from the gradually increasing consciousness of the non-slaveholding population of the Slave States of the true cause of their material impoverishment and political inferiority? From one or the other source its ruinous forces will be fed, but in either event it is not the Union that will be imperilled, but the privileged Order who on every occasion of a thwarted whim have menaced its disruption, and who will then find in it their only safety.

We believe that the "irrepressible conflict" — for we accept Mr. Seward's much-denounced phrase in all the breadth of meaning he ever meant to give it — is to take place in the South itself; because the Slave System is one of those fearful blunders in political economy which are sure, sooner or later, to work their own retribution. The inevitable tendency of slavery is to concentrate in a few hands the soil, the capital, and the power of the countries where it exists, to reduce the non-slaveholding class to a continually lower and lower level of property, intelligence, and enterprise, — their increase in numbers adding much to the economical hardship of their position and nothing to their political weight in the community. There is no home-

encouragement of varied agriculture, — for the wants of a slave population are few in number and limited in kind; none of inland trade,
for that is developed only by communities where education induces
refinement, where facility of communication stimulates invention and
variety of enterprise, where newspapers make every man's improvement in tools, machinery, or culture of the soil an incitement to all,
and bring all the thinkers of the world to teach in the cheap university of the people. We do not, of course, mean to say that slaveholding
States may not and do not produce fine men; but they fail, by the
inherent vice of their constitution and its attendant consequences, to
create enlightened, powerful, and advancing communities of men,
which is the true object of all political organizations, and is essential
to the prolonged existence of all those whose life and spirit are derived directly from the people. Every man who has dispassionately
endeavored to enlighten himself in the matter cannot but see that,
for the many, the course of things in slaveholding States is substantially what we have described, a downward one, more or less rapid,
in civilization and in all those results of material prosperity which in
a free country show themselves in the general advancement for the
good of all, and give a real meaning to the word Commonwealth. No
matter how enormous the wealth centred in the hands of a few, it
has no longer the conservative force or the beneficent influence which
it exerts when equally distributed, — even loses more of both where
a system of absenteeism prevails so largely as in the South. In such
communities the seeds of an " irrepressible conflict " are surely if
slowly ripening, and signs are daily multiplying that the true peril to
their social organization is looked for, less in a revolt of the owned
labor than in an insurrection of intelligence in the labor that owns
itself and finds itself none the richer for it. To multiply such communities is to multiply weakness.

[*1860*]

FREDERICK DOUGLASS

[1817?–1895]

AMERICAN Negroes regard him as their race's greatest leader — and they are right. No man ever stated their case so forcefully and convincingly as he did. The son of an unknown white man and of a slave named Harriet Bailey (Douglass was the name he took when he won his freedom), he was born on a plantation in Talbot County, Maryland. He suffered from the usual hardships and indignities of a slave. His recalcitrance led to his being sent to Baltimore to work as a house-boy, but the death of his legal owner resulted in his being returned to the fields. A plan to escape was betrayed and he was jailed. Then he was again sent to Baltimore, and this time he was apprenticed to a shipyard, where he learned something about labor problems involving black and white relations. In 1838 he managed to escape to New York, married, and went on to New Bedford, Massachusetts, where he found work as a laborer. A reader of Garrison's periodical, the *Liberator*, he was moved to attend an abolitionist convention in 1841. Invited to speak, he made a deep impression and was immediately employed as an agent of the Massachusetts Anti-Slavery Society. He became one of the truly heroic figures of the abolitionist movement. He bore violence and insult with courage and determination and grew in mental stature. Douglass fought for more than mere emancipation; social and economic equality were his aims — and they are still the aims of the Negro. He published a newspaper, made many important speeches, and in 1845 published an autobiographical narrative which later became *My Bondage and My Freedom* (1855), and was finally expanded into a volume entitled *Life and Times of Frederick Douglass* (1881). His description of slavery is classic, his essential views of the Negro's status valid to this day.

---

from

MY BONDAGE AND MY FREEDOM

Established in my new home in Baltimore, I was not very long in perceiving that in picturing to myself what was to be my life there, my imagination had painted only the bright side; and that the reality had its dark shades as well as its light ones. . . .

Mrs. Sophia was naturally of an excellent disposition — kind, gentle, and cheerful. The supercilious contempt for the rights and feelings of others, and the petulance and bad humor which generally characterized slaveholding ladies, were all quite absent from her manner and bearing toward me.

She had never been a slaveholder — a thing then quite unusual at the South — but had depended almost entirely upon her own industry for a living. To this fact the dear lady no doubt owed the excellent preservation of her natural goodness of heart, for slavery could change a saint into a sinner, and an angel into a demon. I hardly knew how to behave towards " Miss Sophia," as I used to call Mrs. Hugh Auld. I could not approach her even as I had formerly approached Mrs. Thomas Auld. Why should I hang down my head, and speak with bated breath, when there was no pride to scorn me, no coldness to repel me, and no hatred to inspire me with fear? I therefore soon came to regard her as something more akin to a mother than a slaveholding mistress. So far from deeming it impudent in a slave to look her straight in the face, she seemed ever to say, "Look up, child; don't be afraid." The sailors belonging to the sloop esteemed it a great privilege to be the bearers of parcels or messages for her, for whenever they came, they were sure of a most kind and pleasant reception. If little Thomas was her son, and her most dearly loved child, she made me something like his half-brother in her affections. If dear Tommy was exalted to a place on his mother's knee, "Freddy" was honored by a place at the mother's side. Nor did the slave-boy lack the caressing strokes of her gentle hand, soothing him into the consciousness that, though motherless, he was not friendless. Mrs. Auld was not only kind-hearted, but remarkably pious; frequent in her attendance at public worship and much given to reading the Bible and to chanting hymns of praise when alone. Mr. Hugh was altogether a different character. He cared very little about religion; knew more of the world and was more a part of the world, than his wife. He doubtless set out to be, as the world goes, a respectable man and to get on by becoming a successful ship-builder, in that city of shipbuilding. This was his ambition, and it fully occupied him. I was of course of very little consequence to him, and when he smiled upon me, as he sometimes did, the smile was borrowed from his lovely wife, and like borrowed light, was transient, and vanished with the source whence it was derived. Though I must in truth characterize Master Hugh as a sour man of forbidding appearance, it is due to him to acknowledge that he was never cruel to me, according to the notion of cruelty in Maryland. During the first year or two, he left me almost exclusively to the management of his wife. She was my law-giver. In hands so tender as hers, and in the absence of the cruelties of the plantation, I became both physically and mentally much more sensitive, and a frown from my mistress caused me far more suffering than had Aunt Katy's hardest cuffs. Instead of the cold, damp floor of my old master's kitchen, I was on carpets; for the corn bag in winter, I had a good straw bed, well furnished with covers; for the coarse corn meal in the morning, I had good bread and mush occasionally; for my old tow-linen shirt, I had good clean clothes. I was really well off. My employment was to run errands, and to take care of Tommy; to prevent his getting in the way of carriages, and to keep him out of harm's way generally.

So for a time everything went well. I say for a time, because the fatal poison of irresponsible power, and the natural influence of slave customs, were not very long in making their impression on the gentle and loving disposition of my excellent mistress. She at first regarded me as a child, like any other. This was the natural and spontaneous thought; afterwards, when she came to consider me as property, our relations to each other were changed, but a nature so noble as hers could not instantly become perverted, and it took several years before the sweetness of her temper was wholly lost.

The frequent hearing of my mistress reading the Bible aloud, for she often read aloud when her husband was absent, awakened my curiosity in respect to this *mystery* of reading, and roused in me the desire to learn. Up to this time I had known nothing whatever of this wonderful art, and my ignorance and inexperience of what it could do for me, as well as my confidence in my mistress, emboldened me to ask her to teach me to read. With an unconsciousness and inexperience equal to my own, she readily consented, and in an incredible short time, by her kind assistance, I had mastered the alphabet and could spell words of three or four letters. My mistress seemed almost as proud of my progress as if I had been her own child, and supposing that her husband would be as well pleased, she made no secret of what she was doing for me. Indeed, she exultingly told him of the aptness of her pupil and of her intention to persevere, as she felt it her duty to do, in teaching me, at least, to read the Bible. And here arose the first dark cloud over my Baltimore prospects, the precursor of chilling blasts and drenching storms. Master Hugh was astounded beyond measure and, probably for the first time, proceeded to unfold to his wife the true philosophy of the slave system, and the peculiar rules necessary in the nature of the case to be observed in the management of human chattels. Of course he forbade her to give me any further instruction, telling her in the first place that to do so was unlawful, as it was also unsafe; "for," said he, "if you give a nigger an inch he will take an ell. Learning will spoil the best nigger in the world. If he learns to read the Bible it will forever unfit him to be a slave. He should know nothing but the will of his master, and learn to obey it. As to himself, learning will do him no good, but a great deal of harm, making him disconsolate and unhappy. If you teach him how to read, he'll want to know how to write, and this accomplished, he'll be running away with himself." Such was the tenor of Master Hugh's oracular exposition; and it must be confessed that he very clearly comprehended the nature and the requirements of the relation of master and slave. His discourse was the first decidedly anti-slavery lecture to which it had been my lot to listen. Mrs. Auld evidently felt the force of what he said, and, like an obedient wife, began to shape her course in the direction indicated by him. The effect of his words *on me* was neither slight nor transitory. His iron sentences, cold and harsh, sunk like heavy weights deep into my heart, and stirred up within me a rebellion not soon to be allayed.

This was a new and special revelation, dispelling a painful mystery against which my youthful understanding had struggled, and struggled in vain, to wit, the white man's power to perpetuate the enslavement of the black man. "Very well," thought I. "Knowledge unfits a child to be a slave." I instinctively assented to the proposition, and from that moment I understood the direct pathway from slavery to freedom. It was just what I needed, and it came to me at a time and from a source whence I least expected it. Of course I was greatly saddened at the thought of losing the assistance of my kind mistress, but the information so instantly derived, to some extent compensated me for the loss I had sustained in this direction. Wise as Mr. Auld was, he underrated my comprehension, and had little idea of the use to which I was capable of putting the impressive lesson he was giving to his wife. . . .

I lived in the family of Mr. Auld, at Baltimore, seven years, during which time, as the almanac makers say of the weather, my condition was variable. The most interesting feature of my history here was my learning, under somewhat marked disadvantages, to read and write. In attaining this knowledge I was compelled to resort to indirections by no means congenial to my nature, and which were really humiliating to my sense of candor and uprightness. My mistress, checked in her benevolent designs toward me, not only ceased instructing me herself, but set her face as a flint against my learning to read by any means. It is due to her to say, however, that she did not adopt this course in all its stringency at first. She either thought it unnecessary, or she lacked the depravity needed to make herself forget at once my human nature. She was, as I have said, naturally a kind and tender-hearted woman, and in the humanity of her heart and the simplicity of her mind, she set out, when I first went to live with her, to treat me as she supposed one human being ought to treat another.

Nature never intended that men and women should be either slaves or slaveholders, and nothing but rigid training long persisted in can perfect the character of the one or the other.

Mrs. Auld was singularly deficient in the qualities of a slaveholder. It was no easy matter for her to think or to feel that the curly-headed boy who stood by her side, and even leaned on her lap, who was loved by little Tommy, and who loved little Tommy in turn, sustained to her only the relation of a chattel. I was more than that; she felt me to be more than that. I could talk and sing; I could laugh and weep; I could reason and remember; I could love and hate. I was human, and she, dear lady, knew and felt me to be so. How could she then treat me as a brute, without a mighty struggle with all the noblest powers of her soul? That struggle came, and the will and power of the husband were victorious. Her noble soul was overcome, and he who wrought the wrong was injured in the fall no less than the rest of the household. When I went into that household, it was the abode of happiness and contentment. The wife and mistress there was a model of affection and tenderness. Her fervent piety and watchful uprightness made it impossible to see her without thinking and feeling that "that woman is a Christian." There was no sorrow nor suffering for which she had not a tear, and there was no innocent joy for which she had not a smile. She had bread for the hungry, clothes for the naked, and comfort for every mourner who came within her reach.

But slavery soon proved its ability to divest her of these excellent qualities, and her home of its early happiness. Conscience cannot stand much violence. Once thoroughly injured, who is he who can repair the damage? If it be broken toward the slave on Sunday, it will be toward the master on Monday. It cannot long endure such shocks. It must stand unharmed, or it does not stand at all. As my condition in the family waxed bad, that of the family waxed no better. The first step in the wrong direction was the violence done to nature and to conscience in arresting the benevolence that would have enlightened my young mind. In ceasing to instruct me, my mistress had to seek to justify herself *to* herself, and once consenting to take sides in such a debate, she was compelled to hold her position. One needs little knowledge of moral philosophy to see where she inevitably landed. She finally became even more violent in her opposition to my learning to read than was Mr. Auld himself. Nothing now appeared to make her more angry than seeing me, seated in some nook or corner, quietly reading a book or newspaper. She would rush at me with the utmost fury, and snatch the book or paper from my hand, with something of the wrath and consternation which a traitor might be supposed to feel on being discovered in a plot by some dangerous spy. The conviction once thoroughly established in her mind that education and slavery were incompatible with each other, I was most narrowly watched in all my movements. If I remained in a separate room from the family for any considerable length of time, I was sure to be suspected of having a book, and was at once called to give an account of myself. But this was too late: the first and never-to-be-retraced step had been taken. Teaching me the alphabet had been the " inch " given, I was now waiting only or the opportunity to " take the ell."

Filled with the determination to learn to read at any cost, I hit upon many expedients to accomplish that much desired end. The plan which I mainly adopted, and the one which was the most successful, was that of using as teachers my young white playmates, with whom I met on the streets. I used almost constantly to carry a copy of Webster's spelling-book in my pocket, and when sent of errands, or when play-time was allowed me, I would step aside with my young

377

friends and take a lesson in spelling. I am greatly indebted to these boys — Gustavus Dorgan, Joseph Bailey, Charles Farity, and William Cosdry.

Although slavery was a delicate subject and, in Maryland, very cautiously talked about among grown-up people, I frequently talked with the white boys about it, and that very freely. I would sometimes say to them, while seated on a curbstone or a cellar door, " I wish I could be free, as you will be when you get to be men." " You will be free, you know, as soon as you are twenty-one, and can go where you like, but I am a slave for life. Have I not as good a right to be free as you have? " Words like these, I observed, always troubled them; and I had no small satisfaction in drawing out from them, as I occasionally did, that fresh and bitter condemnation of slavery which ever springs from natures unseared and unperverted. Of all consciences, let me have those to deal with which have not been seared and bewildered with the cares and perplexities of life. I do not remember ever while I was in slavery to have met with a *boy* who defended the system, but I do remember many times when I was consoled by them, and by them encouraged to hope that something would yet occur by which I would be made free. Over and over again, they have told me that " they believed I had as good a right to be free as *they* had," and that " they did not believe God ever made any one to be a slave." It is easily seen that such little conversations with my playfellows had no tendency to weaken my love of liberty, nor to render me contented as a slave.

When I was about thirteen years old, and had succeeded in learning to read, every increase of knowledge, especially anything respecting the free states, was an additional weight to the almost intolerable burden of my thought — "*I am a slave for life.*" To my bondage I could see no end. It was a terrible reality, and I shall never be able to tell how sadly that thought chafed my young spirit. Fortunately or unfortunately, I had, by blacking boots for some gentlemen, earned a little money with which I purchased of Mr. Knight, on Thames street, what was then a very popular school book, viz., The Columbian Orator, for which I paid fifty cents. I was led to buy this book by hearing some little boys say that they were going to learn some pieces out of it for the exhibition. This volume was indeed a rich treasure, and, for a time, every opportunity afforded me was spent in diligently perusing it. Among much other interesting matter, that which I read again and again with unflagging satisfaction was a short dialogue between a master and his slave. The slave is represented as having been recaptured in a second attempt to run away; and the master opens the dialogue with an upbraiding speech, charging the slave with ingratitude, and demanding to know what he has to say in his own defense. Thus upbraided and thus called upon to reply, the slave rejoins that he knows how little anything that he can say will avail, seeing that he is completely in the hands of his owner; and with noble resolution, calmly says, " I submit to my fate." Touched by the slave's answer, the master insists upon his further speaking, and recapitulates the many acts of kindness which he has performed toward the slave, and tells him he is permitted to speak for himself. Thus invited, the quondam slave made a spirited defense of himself, and thereafter the whole argument for and against slavery is brought out. The master was vanquished at every turn in the argument, and, appreciating the fact, he generously and meekly emancipates the slave, with his best wishes for his prosperity.

It is unnecessary to say that a dialogue with such an origin and such an end, read by me when every nerve of my being was in revolt at my own condition as a slave, affected me most powerfully. I could not help feeling that the day might yet come when the well-directed answers made by the slave to the master, in this instance, would find a counterpart in my own experience. This, however, was not all the fanaticism which I found in the Columbian Orator. I met there one of Sheridan's mighty speeches on the subject of Catholic Emancipation, Lord Chatham's speech on the American War, and speeches by the great William Pitt, and by Fox. These were all choice documents to me, and I read them over and over again, with an interest ever increasing, because it was ever gaining in intelligence; for the more I read them the better I understood them. The reading of these speeches added much to my limited stock of language, and enabled me to give tongue to many interesting thoughts which had often flashed through my mind and died away for want of words in which to give them utterance. The mighty power and heart-searching directness of truth penetrating the heart of a slave-holder and compelling him to yield up his earthly interests to the claims of eternal justice, were finely illustrated in the dialogue, and from the speeches of Sheridan I got a bold and powerful denunciation of oppression and a most brilliant vindication of the rights of man.

Here was indeed a noble acquisition. If I had ever wavered under the consideration that the Almighty, in some way, had ordained slavery and willed my enslavement for His own glory, I wavered no longer. I had now penetrated to the secret of all slavery and of all oppression, and had ascertained their true foundation to be in the pride, the power and the avarice of man. With a book in my hand so redolent of the principles of liberty, and with a perception of my own human nature and of the facts of my past and present experience, I was equal to a contest with the religious advocates of slavery, whether white or black; for blindness in this matter was not confined to the white people. I have met, at the south, many good, religious colored people who were under the delusion that God required them to submit to slavery and to wear their chains with meekness and humility. I could entertain no such nonsense as this, and I quite lost my patience when I found a colored man weak enough to believe such stuff. Nevertheless, eager as I was to partake of the tree of knowledge, its fruits were bitter as well as sweet. " Slaveholders," thought I, "are only a band of successful robbers, who, leaving their own homes, went into Africa for the purpose of stealing and reducing my people to slavery." I loathed them as the meanest and the most wicked of men. And as I read, behold! the very discontent so graphically predicted by Master Hugh had already come upon me. I was no longer the light-hearted, gleesome boy, full of mirth and play, that I was when I landed in Baltimore. Light had penetrated the moral dungeon where I had lain, and I saw the bloody whip for my back and the iron chain for my feet, and my *good, kind* master was the author of my situation. The revelation haunted me, stung me, and made me gloomy and miserable. As I writhed under the sting and torment of this knowledge I almost envied my fellow slaves their stupid indifference. It opened my eyes to the horrible pit, and revealed the teeth of the frightful dragon that was ready to pounce upon me; but alas, it opened no way for my escape. I wished myself a beast, a bird, anything rather than a slave. I was wretched and gloomy beyond my ability to describe. This everlasting thinking distressed and tormented me; and yet there was no getting rid of this subject of my thoughts. Liberty, as the inestimable birthright of every man, converted every object into an asserter of this right. I heard it in every sound, and saw it in every object. It was ever present to torment me with a sense of my wretchedness. The more beautiful and charming were the smiles of nature, the more horrible and desolate was my condition. I saw nothing without seeing it, and I heard nothing without hearing it. I do not exaggerate when I say that it looked at me in every star, smiled in every calm, breathed in every wind and moved in every storm. I have no doubt that my state of mind had something to do with the change in treatment which my mistress adopted towards me. I can easily believe that my leaden, downcast, and disconsolate look was very offensive to her. Poor lady! She did not understand my trouble, and I could not tell her. Could I have made her acquainted with the real state of my mind and given her the reasons therefor, it might have been well for both of us. As it was, her abuse fell upon me like the blows of the false prophet upon his ass; she did not know that an angel stood in the way. Nature made us friends, but slavery had made us enemies. My interests were in a direction opposite to hers, and we both had our private thoughts and plans. She aimed to keep me ignorant, and I resolved to *know,* although knowledge only increased my misery. My feelings were not the result of any marked cruelty in the treatment I received; they sprung from the consideration of my being a slave at all. It was *slavery,* not its mere *incidents* that I hated. I had been cheated. I saw through the attempt to keep me in ignorance. I saw that slaveholders would have gladly made me believe that, in making a slave of me and in making slaves of others, they were merely acting under the authority of God, and I felt to them as to robbers and deceivers. The feeding and clothing me well could not atone for taking my liberty from me. The smiles of my mistress could not remove the deep sorrow that dwelt in my young bosom. Indeed, these came, in time, but to deepen my sorrow. She had changed, and the reader will see that I, too, had changed. We were both victims to the same overshadowing evil, *she* as mistress, I as slave. I will not censure her harshly.

[*1855*]

WENDELL PHILLIPS

[1811–1884]

EVERY now and then an aristocrat leaves his class and becomes a champion of the plain people. Wendell Phillips was that kind of maverick. He had every advantage: social position, wealth, appearance, attractive personality. Yet this Boston aristocrat was only a few years out of the Harvard Law School when he openly identified himself with the abolitionists. In 1837 he delivered his famous impromptu speech, at a meeting in Faneuil Hall, on the murder of Lovejoy, and soon afterwards he began to devote his time to the lyceum as an agitator for the Negroes and subsequently for other unpopular ideals, many of which have since been realized. He spoke and wrote in. behalf of woman's rights, penal reforms, prohibition, justice for the Indians, labor unions, economic and social equality. From a lieutenant of Garrison, he evolved into an independent crusader for every cause calculated to make this a juster, more humane world. In 1870 he ran for the governorship of Massachusetts on the Labor Reform and Prohibition tickets and received twenty thousand votes. He was a more scholarly man than Garrison, but no less impassioned and courageous. And like Garrison, while he participated in some futile and aberrant movements (such as prohibition), on the whole he was prophetically right.

THE MURDER OF LOVEJOY

On November 7, 1837, Rev. E. P. Lovejoy was shot by a mob at Alton, Illinois, while attempting to defend his printing press from destruction. When this was known in Boston, William Ellery Channing headed a petition to the Mayor and Aldermen, asking the use of Faneuil Hall for a public meeting. The request was refused. Dr. Channing then addressed a very impressive letter to his fellow-citizens, which resulted in a meeting of influential gentlemen at the Old Court Room. Resolutions, drawn by Hon. B. F. Hallett, were unanimously adopted, and measures taken to secure a much larger number of names to the petition. This call the Mayor and Aldermen obeyed.

The meeting was held on the 8th of December, and organized, with the Hon. Jonathan Phillips for Chairman.

Dr. Channing made a brief and eloquent address. Resolutions, drawn by him, were then read and offered by Mr. Hallett, and seconded in an able speech by George S. Hillard, Esq.

The Hon. James T. Austin, Attorney-General of the Commonwealth, followed in a speech of the utmost bitterness, styled by the Boston Atlas a few days after " most able and triumphant." He compared the slaves to a menagerie of wild beasts, and the rioters at Alton to the "orderly mob" which threw the tea overboard in 1773, — talked of the " conflict of laws" between Missouri and Illinois, — declared that Lovejoy was " presumptuous and imprudent," and " died as the fool dieth "; in direct and most insulting reference to Dr. Channing, he asserted that a clergyman with a gun in his hand, or one " mingling in the debates of a popular assembly, was marvellously out of place."

The speech of the Attorney-General produced great excitement throughout the Hall. Wendell Phillips, Esq., who had not expected to take part in the meeting, rose to reply. That portion of the assembly which sympathized with Mr. Austin now became so boisterous that Mr. Phillips had difficulty for a while in getting the attention of the audience.

MR. CHAIRMAN: — We have met for the freest discussion of these resolutions, and the events which gave rise to them. [Cries of " Question," " Hear him," " Go on," " No gagging," etc.] I hope I shall be permitted to express my surprise at the sentiments of the last speaker, — surprise not only at such sentiments from such a man, but at the applause they have received within these walls. A comparison has been drawn between the events of the Revolution and the tragedy at Alton. We have heard it asserted here, in Faneuil Hall, that Great Britain had a right to tax the Colonies, and we have heard the mob at Alton, the drunken murderers of Lovejoy, compared to those patriot fathers who threw the tea overboard! [Great applause.] Fellow-citizens, is this Faneuil Hall doctrine? [" No, no."] The mob at Alton were met to wrest from a citizen his just rights, — met to resist the laws. We have been told that our fathers did the same; and the glorious mantle of Revolutionary precedent has been thrown over the mobs of our day.

To make out their title to such defence, the gentleman says that the British Parliament had a *right* to tax these Colonies. It is manifest that, without this, his parallel falls to the ground; for Lovejoy had stationed himself within constitutional bulwarks. He was not only defending the freedom of the press, but he was under his own roof, in arms with the sanction of the civil authority. The men who assailed him went against and over the laws. The *mob,* as the gentleman terms it, — mob, forsooth! certainly we sons of the tea-spillers are a marvellously patient generation! — the "orderly mob" which assembled in the Old South to destroy the tea were met to resist, not the laws, but illegal exactions. Shame on the American who calls the tea-tax and stamp-act *laws!* Our fathers resisted, not the King's prerogative, but the King's usurpation. To find any other account, you must read our Revolutionary history upside down. Our State archives are loaded with arguments of John Adams to prove the taxes laid by the British Parliament unconstitutional, — beyond its power. It was not till this was made out that the men of New England rushed to arms. The arguments of the Council Chamber and the House of Representatives preceded and sanctioned the contest. To draw the conduct of our ancestors into a precedent for mobs, for a right to resist laws we ourselves have enacted, is an insult to their memory. The difference between the excitements of those days and our own, which the gentleman in kindness to the latter has overlooked, is simply this: the men of that day went for the right, as secured by the laws. They were the people rising to sustain the laws and constitution of the Province. The rioters of our day go for their own wills, right or wrong. Sir, when I heard the gentleman lay down principles which place the murderers of Alton side by side with Otis and Hancock, with Quincy and Adams, I thought those pictured lips [pointing to the portraits in the Hall] would have broken into voice to rebuke the recreant American, — the slanderer of the dead. [Great applause and counter applause.] The gentleman said that he should sink into insignificance if he dared to gainsay the principles of these resolutions. Sir, for the sentiments he has uttered, on soil consecrated by the prayers of Puritans and the blood of patriots, the earth should have yawned and swallowed him up.

[*Applause and hisses, with cries of "Take that back." The uproar became so great that for a long time no one could be heard. At length the Hon. William Sturgis came to Mr. Phillips's side at the front of the platform. He was met with cries of "Phillips or nobody," "Make him take back 'recreant,'" "He sha'n't go on till he takes it back." When it was understood that Mr. Sturgis meant to sustain, not to interrupt, Mr. Phillips, he was listened to, and said: "I did not come here to take any part in this discussion, nor do I intend to; but I do entreat you, fellow-citizens, by everything you hold sacred, — I conjure you by every association connected with this Hall, consecrated by our fathers to freedom of discussion, — that you listen to every man who addresses you in a decorous manner." Mr. Phillips resumed.]*

Fellow-citizens, I cannot take back my words. Surely the Attorney-General, so long and well known here, needs not the aid of your hisses against one so young as I am, — my voice never before heard within these walls!

Another ground has been taken to excuse the mob, and throw doubt and discredit on the conduct of Lovejoy and his associates. Allusion has been made to what lawyers understand very well, — the "conflict of laws." We are told that nothing but the Mississippi River rolls between St. Louis and Alton; and the conflict of laws somehow or other gives the citizens of the former a right to find fault with the defender of the press for publishing his opinions so near their limits. Will the gentleman venture that argument before lawyers? How the laws of the two States could be said to come into conflict in such circumstances I question whether any lawyer in this audience can explain or understand. No matter whether the line that divides one sovereign State from another be an imaginary one or ocean-wide, the moment you cross it the State you leave is blotted out of existence, so far as you are concerned. The Czar might as well claim to control the deliberations of Faneuil Hall, as the laws of Missouri demand reverence, or the shadow of obedience, from an inhabitant of Illinois.

I must find some fault with the statement which has been made of the events at Alton. It has been asked why Lovejoy and his friends did not appeal to the executive, — trust their defence to the police of the city. It has been hinted that, from hasty and ill-judged excitement, the men within the building provoked a quarrel, and that he fell in the course of it, one mob resisting another. Recollect, Sir, that they did act with the approbation and sanction of the Mayor. In strict truth, there was no executive to appeal to for protection. The Mayor acknowledged that he could not protect them. They asked him if it was lawful for them to defend themselves. He told them it was, and sanctioned their assembling in arms to do so. They were not, then a mob; they were not merely citizens defending their own property; they were in some sense the *posse comitatus,* adopted for the occasion into the police of the city, acting under the order of a magistrate. It was civil authority resisting lawless violence. Where, then, was the imprudence? Is the doctrine to be sustained here that it is *imprudent* for men to aid magistrates in executing the laws?

Men are continually asking each other, Had Lovejoy a right to resist? Sir, I protest against the question, instead of answering it. Lovejoy did not resist, in the sense they mean. He did not throw himself back on the natural right of self-defence. He did not cry anarchy, and let slip the dogs of civil war, careless of the horrors which would follow.

Sir, as I understand this affair, it was not an individual protecting his property; it was not one body of armed men resisting another, and making the streets of a peaceful city run blood with their contentions. It did not bring back the scenes in some old Italian cities, where family met family, and faction met faction, and mutually trampled the laws under foot. No; the men in that house were regularly *enrolled,* under the sanction of the Mayor. There being no militia in Alton, about seventy men were enrolled with the approbation of the Mayor. These relieved each other every other night. About thirty men were in arms on the night of the sixth, when the press was landed. The next evening, it was not thought necessary to summon more than half that number; among these was Lovejoy. It was, therefore, you perceive, Sir, the police of the city resisting rioters, — civil government breasting itself to the shock of lawless men.

Here is no question about the right of self-defence. It is in fact simply this: Has the civil magistrate a right to put down a riot?

Some persons seem to imagine that anarchy existed at Alton from the commencement of these disputes. Not at all. " No one of us," says an eyewitness and a comrade of Lovejoy, " has taken up arms during these disturbances but at the command of the Mayor." Anarchy did not settle down on that devoted city till Lovejoy breathed his last. Till then the law, represented in his person, sustained itself against its foes. When he fell, civil authority was trampled under foot. He had " planted himself on his constitutional rights," — appealed to the laws, — claimed the protection of the civil authority, — taken refuge under "the broad shield of the Constitution. When through that he was pierced and fell, he fell but one sufferer in a common catastrophe." He took refuge under the banner of liberty, — amid its folds; and when he fell, its glorious stars and stripes, the emblem of free institutions, around which cluster so many heart-stirring memories, were blotted out in the martyr's blood.

It has been stated, perhaps inadvertently, that Lovejoy or his comrades fired first. This is denied by those who have the best means of knowing. Guns were first fired by the mob. After being twice fired on, those within the building consulted together and deliberately returned the fire. But suppose they did fire first. They had a right so to do; not only the right which every citizen has to defend himself, but the further right which every civil officer has to resist violence. Even if Lovejoy fired the first gun, it would not lessen his claim to our sympathy, or destroy his title to be considered a martyr in defence of a free press. The question now is, Did he act within the Constitution and the laws? The men who fell in State Street on the 5th of March, 1770, did more than Lovejoy is charged with. They were the *first* assailants. Upon some slight quarrel they pelted the troops with every missile within reach. Did this bate one jot of the eulogy with which Hancock and Warren hallowed their memory, hailing them as the first martyrs in the cause of American liberty?

If, Sir, I had adopted what are called Peace principles, I might lament the circumstances of this case. But all you who believe, as I do, in the right and duty of magistrates to execute the laws join with me and brand as base hypocrisy the conduct of those who assemble year after year on the 4th of July to fight over the battles of the Revolution, and yet " damn with faint praise," or load with obloquy, the memory of this man, who shed his blood in defence of life, liberty, property, and the freedom of the press!

Throughout that terrible night I find nothing to regret but this, that within the limits of our country, civil authority should have been so prostrated as to oblige a citizen to arm in his own defence, and to arm in vain. The gentleman says Lovejoy was presumptuous and imprudent, — he " died as the fool dieth." And a reverend clergyman of the city [1] tells us that no citizen has a right to publish opinions disagree-

---

[1] See Rev. Hubbard Winslow's discourse on *Liberty!* in which he defines " republican liberty " to be " liberty to say and do what the *prevailing* voice and will of the brotherhood will allow and protect."

able to the community! If any mob follows such publication, on *him* rests its guilt! He must wait, forsooth, till the people come up to it and agree with him! This libel on liberty goes on to say that the want of right to speak as we think is an evil inseparable from republican institutions! If this be so, what are they worth? Welcome the despotism of the Sultan, where one knows what he may publish and what he may not, rather than the tyranny of this many-headed monster, the mob, where we know not what we may do or say, till some fellow-citizen has tried it, and paid for the lesson with his life. This clerical absurdity chooses as a check for the abuses of the press, not the *law*, but the dread of a mob. By so doing, it deprives not only the individual and the minority of their rights, but the majority also, since the expression of *their* opinion may sometimes provoke disturbance from the minority. A few men may make a mob as well as many. The majority, then, have no right, as Christian men, to utter their sentiments, if by any possibility it may lead to a mob! Shades of Hugh Peters and John Cotton, save us from such pulpits!

Imprudent to defend the liberty of the press! Why? Because the defence was unsuccessful? Does success gild crime into patriotism, and the want of it change heroic self-devotion to imprudence? Was Hampden imprudent when he drew the sword and threw away the scabbard? Yet he, judged by that single hour, was unsuccessful. After a short exile, the race he hated sat again upon the throne.

Imagine yourself present when the first news of Bunker Hill battle reached a New England town. The tale would have run thus: "The patriots are routed, — the redcoats victorious, — Warren lies dead upon the field." With what scorn would that *Tory* have been received who should have charged Warren with *imprudence!* who should have said that, bred a physician, he was "out of place" in that battle, and "died as the *fool dieth* "! [Great applause.] How would the intimation have been received that Warren and his associates should have waited a better time? But if success be indeed the only criterion of prudence, *Respice finem,* — wait till the end.

Presumptuous to assert the freedom of the press on American ground! Is the assertion of such freedom before the age? So much before the age as to leave one no right to make it because it displeases the community? Who invents this libel on his country? It is this very thing which entitles Lovejoy to greater praise. The disputed right which provoked the Revolution — taxation without representation — is far beneath that for which he died. [Here there was a strong and general expression of disapprobation.] One word, gentlemen. As much as *thought* is better than money, so much is the cause in which Lovejoy died nobler than a mere question of taxes. James Otis thundered in this Hall when the King did but touch his *pocket.* Imagine, if you can, his indignant eloquence, had England offered to put a gag upon his lips. [Great applause.]

The question that stirred the Revolution touched our civil interests. *This* concerns us not only as citizens, but as immortal beings. Wrapped up in its fate, saved or lost with it, are not only the voice of the states-man, but the instructions of the pulpit, and the progress of our faith.

The clergy " marvellously out of place " where free speech is battled for, — liberty of speech on national sins? Does the gentleman remem-ber that freedom to preach was first gained, dragging in its train free-dom to print? I thank the clergy here present, as I reverence their predecessors, who did not so far forget their country in their imme-diate profession as to deem it duty to separate themselves from the struggle of '76, — the Mayhews and Coopers, who remembered they were citizens before they were clergymen.

Mr. Chairman, from the bottom of my heart I thank that brave little band at Alton for resisting. We must remember that Lovejoy had fled from city to city, — suffered the destruction of three presses patiently. At length he took counsel with friends, men of character, of tried in-tegrity, of wide views, of Christian principle. They thought the crisis had come: it was full time to assert the laws. They saw around them, not a community like our own, of fixed habits, of character moulded and settled, but one " in the gristle, not yet hardened into the bone of manhood." The people there, children of our older States, seem to have forgotten the blood-tried principles of their fathers the moment they lost sight of our New England hills. Something was to be done to show them the priceless value of the freedom of the press, to bring back and set right their wandering and confused ideas. He and his advisers looked out on a community staggering like a drunken man, indifferent to their rights and confused in their feelings. Deaf to argument, haply they might be stunned into sobriety. They saw that of which we can-not judge, the *necessity* of resistance. Insulted law called for it. Public opinion, fast hastening on the downward course, must be arrested.

Does not the event show they judged rightly? Absorbed in a thou-sand trifles, how has the nation all at once come to a stand? Men begin, as in 1776 and 1640, to discuss principles, to weigh characters, to find out where they are. Haply we may awake before we are borne over the precipice.

I am glad, Sir, to see this crowded house. It is good for us to be here. When Liberty is in danger, Faneuil Hall has the right, it is her duty, to strike the key-note for these United States. I am glad, for one reason, that remarks such as those to which I have alluded have been uttered here. The passage of these resolutions, in spite of this opposition, led by the Attorney-General of the Commonwealth, will show more clearly, more decisively, the deep indignation with which Boston regards this outrage.

[*1837*]

from
WOMAN'S RIGHTS

I rejoice to see so large an audience gathered to consider this momentous subject. It was well described by Mrs. Rose as the most magnificent reform that has yet been launched upon the world. It is the first organized protest against the injustice which has brooded over the character and the destiny of one half of the human race. Nowhere else, under any circumstances, has a demand ever yet been made for the liberties of one whole half of our race. It is fitting that we should pause and consider so remarkable and significant a circumstance; that we should discuss the question involved with the seriousness and deliberation suitable to such an enterprise. It strikes, indeed, a great and vital blow at the whole social fabric of every nation; but this, to my mind, is no argument against it. The time has been when it was the duty of the reformer to show cause why he appeared to disturb the quiet of the world. But during the discussion of the many reforms that have been advocated, and which have more or less succeeded, one after another, — freedom of the lower classes, freedom of food, freedom of the press, freedom of thought, reform in penal legislation, and a thousand other matters, — it seems to me to have been proved conclusively that government commenced in usurpation and oppression; that liberty and civilization, at present, are nothing else than the fragments of rights which the scaffold and the stake have wrung from the strong hands of the usurpers. Every step of progress the world has made has been from scaffold to scaffold, and from stake to stake. It would hardly be exaggeration to say that all the great truths relating to society and government have been first heard in the solemn protests of martyred patriotism, or the loud cries of crushed and starving labor. The law has been always wrong. Government began in tyranny and force, began in the feudalism of the soldier and bigotry of the priest; and the ideas of justice and humanity have been fighting their way, like a thunder-storm, against the organized selfishness of human nature. And this is the last great protest against the wrong of ages. It is no argument to my mind, therefore, that the old social fabric of the past is against us.

Neither do I feel called upon to show what woman's proper sphere is. In every great reform, the majority have always said to the claimant, no matter what he claimed, " You are not fit for such a privilege." Luther asked of the Pope liberty for the masses to read the Bible. The reply was that it would not be safe to trust the common people with the word of God. " Let them try! " said the great reformer; and the history of three centuries of development and purity proclaims the result. They *have* tried; and look around you for the consequences. The lower classes in France claimed their civil rights, — the right to vote, and to direct representation in the government; but the rich and lettered classes, the men of cultivated intellects, cried out, " You cannot be made fit." The answer was, " Let us try." That France is not, as Spain, utterly crushed beneath the weight of a thousand years of misgovernment is the answer to those who doubt the ultimate success of this experiment.

Woman stands now at the same door. She says, " You tell me I have no intellect: give me a chance. You tell me I shall only embarrass politics: let me try." The only reply is the same stale argument that said to the Jews of Europe, " You are fit only to make money; you are not fit for the ranks of the army or the halls of Parliament." How cogent the eloquent appeal of Macaulay, — " What right have we to take this question for granted? Throw open the doors of this House of Commons, throw open the ranks of the imperial army, before you deny eloquence to the countrymen of Isaiah or valor to the descendants of the Maccabees." It is the same now with us. Throw open the doors of Congress, throw open those court-houses, throw wide open the doors of your colleges, and give to the sisters of the Motts and the Somervilles

391

the same opportunities for culture that men have, and let the result prove what their capacity and intellect really are. When, I say, woman has enjoyed, for as many centuries as we have, the aid of books, the discipline of life, and the stimulus of fame, it will be time to begin the discussion of these questions, — "What is the intellect of woman?" "Is it equal to that of man?" Till then, all such discussion is mere beating of the air.

While it is doubtless true that great minds, in many cases, make a way for themselves, spite of all obstacles, yet who knows how many Miltons have died "mute and inglorious"? However splendid the natural endowment, the discipline of life, after all, completes the miracle. The ability of Napoleon, — what was it? It grew out of the hope to be Cæsar or Marlborough, — out of Austerlitz and Jena, — out of his battle-fields, his throne, and all the great scenes of that eventful life. Open to woman the same scenes, immerse her in the same great interests and pursuits, and if twenty centuries shall not produce a woman Charlemagne or Napoleon, fair reasoning will then allow us to conclude that there is some distinctive peculiarity in the intellects of the sexes. Centuries alone can lay any fair basis for argument. I believe that, on this point, there is a shrinking consciousness of not being ready for the battle, on the part of *some* of the stronger sex, as they call themselves; a tacit confession of risk to this imagined superiority, if they consent to meet their sisters in the lecture-hall or the laboratory of science. My proof of it is this: that the mightiest intellects of the race, from Plato down to the present time, some of the rarest minds of Germany, France, and England, have successively yielded their assent to the fact that woman is, not perhaps identically, but equally, endowed with man in all intellectual capabilities. It is generally the second-rate men who doubt, — doubt, perhaps, because they fear a fair field: —

> "He either fears his fate too much,
> Or his deserts are small,
> Who fears to put it to the touch,
> To gain or lose it all."

But I wish especially to direct your attention to the precise principle which this movement undertakes to urge upon the community. We do not attempt to settle what shall be the profession, education, or employment of woman. We have not that presumption. What we ask is simply this, — what all other classes have asked before: Leave it to woman to choose for herself her profession, her education, and her sphere. We deny to any portion of the species the right to prescribe to any other portion its sphere, its education, or its rights. We deny the right of any individual to prescribe to any other individual his amount of education, or his rights. The sphere of each man, of each woman, of each individual, is that sphere which he can, with the highest exercise of his powers, perfectly fill. The highest act which the human being can do, that is the act which God designed him to do. All that woman asks through this movement is to be allowed to prove what she can do; to prove it by liberty of choice, by liberty of action, the only means by which it ever can be settled how much and what she can do. . . .

[1851]

---

from

THE FOUNDATION OF THE
LABOR MOVEMENT

We stand at an epoch when the nature of the government is undergoing a fundamental change. I have been speaking of machines, — whether we should operate through a Senate and President, or solely through a House. I have been speaking of the spindles and wheels. Below that lies the water-power. The water-power of Great Britain has been the wealth of thirty thousand landholders, — thirty thousand land-holding families, perhaps seven hundred thousand or a million voters. With us, the water-power is to be the ballots of ten millions of adult men and women, scattered through all classes, — rich and poor, educated and ignorant, prompt and conservative, radical and timid, all modes and kinds and qualities of mind. Well, that brings me to the form which this great advance of the people takes. It is the working masses that are really about to put their hands to the work of governing.

It is no accident, no caprice of an individual, no mere shout of the political arena, that heralds to-day the great Labor movement of the United States.

But in the mean time, over the horizon, looming at first and now almost touching its meridian, comes up another power, — I mean the power of wealth, the inordinate power of capital. Our fathers, when they prevented entail, when they provided for the distribution of estates, thought they had erected a bulwark against the money power that had killed Great Britain. They forgot that money could combine; that a moneyed corporation was like the papacy, — a succession of persons with a unity of purpose; that it never died; that it never by natural proclivity became imbecile. The grandson of a king is necessarily one third an idiot; but the third generation of a money corporation is wiser for the experience of predecessors, and preserves the same unity of purpose.

This great money power looms over the horizon at the very moment when, to every thoughtful man, the power of the masses concentrating in the House of Representatives is to become the sole omnipotence of the State. Naturally so ominous a conjecture provokes resistance; naturally a peril so immediate prompts the wealthy class of the community to combine for defence.

The land of England has ruled it for six hundred years. The corporations of America mean to rule it in the same way, and unless some power more radical than that of ordinary politics is found, will rule it inevitably. I confess that the only fear I have in regard to republican institutions is whether, in our day, any adequate remedy will be found for this incoming flood of the power of incorporated wealth. No statesman, no public man yet, has dared to defy it. Every man that has met it has been crushed to powder; and the only hope of any effectual grapple with it is in rousing the actual masses, whose interests permanently lie in an opposite direction, to grapple with this great force; for you know very well that our great cities are the radiating points from which go forth the great journalism, the culture, the education, the commercial influences, that make and shape the nation. The great cities are the arsenals of great wealth, where wealth manages everything its own way.

Now, gentlemen, to me the Labor movement means just this: It is the last noble protest of the American people against the power of incorporated wealth, seeking to do over again what the Whig aristocracy of Great Britain has successfully done for two hundred years. Thirty thousand families own Great Britain to-day; and if you multiply John

394

Bright by a hundred, and double his eloquence, it seems impossible that he should save England from a violent convulsion in the great grapple between such a power and the people who have determined to have their way.

Men blame us, the representatives of the working men of the nation, that we come into politics. The other day it was my good fortune to meet that distinguished Frenchman, Monsieur Coquerel; and he asked me what was the motto of the working-men of the United States. I said to him, " Short hours, better education, co-operation in the end, and in the mean time a political movement that will concentrate the thought of the country upon this thing."

Now, here I take issue with the best critic which the Labor movement has met: I refer to Rev. Samuel Johnson of Salem, one of the thinkers who has spread out before the people his objections to the Labor movement of this country. His first objection is that we will hurry into politics. Well, now, our answer to him, and to the score of other scholars who have been criticising us, is this: Gentlemen, we see the benefit of going into politics. If we had not rushed into politics, had not taken Massachusetts by the four corners and shaken her, you never would have written your criticisms. We rush into politics because politics is the safety-valve. We could discuss as well as you, if you would only give us bread and houses, fair pay and leisure, and opportunities to travel. We could sit and discuss the question for the next fifty years. It's a very easy thing to discuss, for a gentleman in his study, with no anxiety about to-morrow. Why, the ladies and gentlemen of the reign of Louis XV and Louis XVI, in France, seated in gilded saloons and on Persian carpets, surrounded with luxury, with the products of India, and the curious manufactures of ingenious Lyons and Rheims, discussed the rights of man, and balanced them in dainty phrases, and expressed them in such quaint generalizations that Jefferson borrowed the Declaration of Independence from their hands. There they sat, balancing and discussing sweetly, making out new theories, and daily erecting a splendid architecture of debate, till the angry crowd broke open the doors, and ended the discussion in blood. They waited too long, discussed about half a century too long. You see, discussion is very good when a man has bread to eat, and his children all portioned off, and his daughters married, and his house furnished and paid for, and his will made; but discussion is very bad when —

"Ye hear the children weeping, O my brothers!
Ere the sorrow comes with years ";

discussion is bad when a class bends under actual oppression. We want immediate action.

We would fain save this issue from an outbreak of actual violence. Therefore we go into politics.

Well, then, our critic goes on to say, "What do you call yourselves Labor party for? All men labor. Rufus Choate labors. Daniel Webster labors. Why do you confine your party to the men that work?" Well, now, we confine it because thus there is no mistake. Now, suppose you should take up a book presenting the condition of the laboring classes of Great Britain. Mr. Gladstone works harder than any other man there; Lord Brougham did more work than any other man there; Lord Palmerston, up to his eightieth year, worked hard as any man there. But if you were to take up a book on the working-men of Great Britain, do you think you would find the condition of Lord Brougham there? If you took up a book on the British laboring class, or how much they eat, what kind of houses they live in, etc., do you think you would find Gladstone's income, and the number of rooms he had in his house, and how many children he had had the last fifty years? So if an Englishman came here, and said, " I want to know something about your working-men. Please let me hear it from some of themselves. Whom shall I go to?" Would you send him to Daniel Webster or Rufus Choate? But Daniel Webster did as much work as any man of his day. Would you have him sent to Rufus Choate? But Rufus Choate was a hardworking man. John Marshall and Lemuel Shaw did as much work as any men in Massachusetts or Virginia; but if George Combe had come to this country, and said, " I want to see a specimen of the laboring class of the United States," I doubt whether any man would have sent him to Lemuel Shaw. I ask the critics of the Labor movement whether any man ever misunderstood this? Every man who reads of the Labor Question knows that it means the movement of the men that earn their living with their hands; that are employed, and paid in wages; are gathered under roofs of factories; sent out on farms; sent out on ships; gathered on the walls. In popular acceptation, the working class means the men that work with their hands, for wages, so many hours a day, employed by great capitalists; that work for everybody else.

Why do we move for this class? "Why," says Mr. Johnson, "don't

396

you move for all working-men? " Because, while Daniel Webster gets forty thousand dollars for arguing the Mexican claims, there is no need of anybody's moving for him. While Rufus Choate gets five thousand dollars for making one argument to a jury, there is no need of moving for him, or for the men that work with their brains, — that do highly disciplined and skilled labor, invent, and write books. The reason why the Labor movement confines itself to a single class is because that class of work does not get paid, does not get protection. Mental labor is adequately paid, and more than adequately protected. It can shift its channels; it can vary according to the supply and demand. If a man fails as a minister, why, he becomes a railway-conductor. If that doesn't suit him, he turns out, and becomes the agent of an insurance office. If that doesn't suit, he goes West, and becomes governor of a Territory. And if he finds himself incapable of either of these positions, he comes home, and gets to be a city editor. He varies his occupation as he pleases, and doesn't need protection. But the great mass, chained to a trade, doomed to be ground up in the mill of supply and demand, that work so many hours a day, and must run in the great ruts of business, — they are the men whose inadequate protection, whose unfair share of the general product claims a movement in their behalf.

Well, the third charge brought by Mr. Johnson against us is that we are cruel, — we combine; we prevent this man from laboring there, and we won't let that man learn our trade; we form trades-unions. To be sure we do. We say to the Chinese, " Stay at home. Don't come here by importation; come by immigration." We say to the crowding millions who try to swamp our trade, " Stand aloof; we won't teach you." We say to the mills of Lowell, who have turned us out of doors, " We'll starve you into submission." Well, " it's a narrow contest. It's an unjust, it's a cruel, it's an avaricious method." So it is. Where did we learn it? Learned it of capital, learned it of our enemies.

I know labor is narrow; I know she is aggressive; I know she arms herself with the best weapon that a corrupt civilization furnishes, — all true. Where do we get these ideas? Borrowed them from capital, every one of them; and when you advance to us on the level of peace, unarmed, we'll meet you on the same. While you combine and plot and defend, so will we.

But Mr. Johnson says, " Come into the world with the white banner of peace." Ay, we will, when you disarm. How foolish it would have been for Grant to send home his Sharp's rifles to Springfield, and garner all his cannon in New York, and put all his monitors in the harbor of Norfolk, and go down to Virginia with eighty thousand unarmed men, to look her in the face! Labor comes up, and says, " They have shotted their cannon to the lips; they have rough-ground their swords as in battle; they have adopted every new method; they have invented every dangerous machine, — and it is all planted like a great park of artillery against us. They have incorporated wealth; they have hidden behind banks; they have concealed themselves in taxation; they have passed rules to govern us, — and we will improve upon the lesson they have taught us. When they disarm, we will — not before."

Well, then, the fourth charge is found in the *Daily Advertiser*. We had a meeting at Framingham, and passed a set of resolutions; we adopted a platform; and the next day the *Daily Advertiser* granted us the condescension of an article, criticising our action, especially mine; and they described what we had adopted. They painted its horrible tendency. They said, " If you adopt that principle, it will lead you to that (and so on to that) till the final result will be — " I held my breath. I said to myself, " What will it probably be? Perhaps the stereotyped ghost of the French Revolution; that's what's coming." " The final result will be — " Horrible! I thought probably they would paint a millionaire hanging on every lamp-post. " The final result — " Perhaps it will be Mormonism; society dissolved into its original elements. Horrible! I began to feel a faint sensation; but I concluded to read on: " The final result will be an equalization of property." Horrible, horrible! Actually, men will be almost equal! An equalization of property! Any man that does that ought to be hanged. Well, we do mean it; we do mean just that. That's the meaning of the Labor movement, — an equalization of property. The *Advertiser* has found us out, actually discovered our plot. He's let the cat out of the bag. We didn't mean to have told you, but it is so. What we need is an equalization of property, — nothing else. My ideal of a civilization is a very high one; but the approach to it is a New England town of some two thousand inhabitants, with no rich man and no poor man in it, all mingling in the same society, every child at the same school, no poorhouse, no beggar, opportunities equal, nobody too proud to stand aloof, nobody too humble to be shut out. That's New England as it was fifty years ago, the horrible creature that the *Daily Advertiser* fears. That's what Framingham proposes to bring about. But why isn't Framingham contented? Because the civilization that lingers beautifully on the hillsides of New England, nestles sweetly in the valleys of Vermont, the moment it approaches a crowd like Boston, or a million of men gathered in one place like New York, — rots. It cannot force the crowd; it cannot stand the great centres of modern civilization.

Our civilization cannot stand the city. One reason is, it has got some hidden disease. Another reason is, the moment it flows out into the broad, deep activity of the nineteenth century, it betrays its weakness, and copies Europe. The moment this sweet-scented, dew-smelling Vermont flows down into the slums of New York, it becomes like London. The moment the North gathers its forces, and goes down the Mississippi Valley into New Orleans, social science stands aghast. Modern civilization shrinks back at the terrible evil which she can neither fathom nor cure, just as she does in Europe.

What is our cause? It is this: there are three hundred and fifty millions of human beings in what you call Christendom, and two hundred millions of them don't have enough to eat from January to December. I won't ask for culture, for opportunities for education, for travel, for society; but two hundred millions of men gathered under Christendom don't have even enough to eat. A hundred thousand men in the city of New York live in dwellings that a rich man wouldn't let his horse stay in a day.

But that isn't anything. You should go up to beautiful Berkshire with me, into the factories there. It shall be the day after a Presidential election. I will go with you into a counting-room, — four hundred employees. The partners are sitting down, the day after a Presidential election. They take the list of workmen, and sift them out; and every man that has not voted the ticket they wanted is thrown out to starve just as if he were cattle. That's Christian civilization! that's Massachusetts! I don't like that significant fact. I leap from that town into a large mill, with five hundred employees, and say to the master, " How about the dwellings of your operatives? How many hours do they have at home? " " Well, I hope they don't have any. The best-ventilated place they are ever in is my mill. They had better stay here sixteen hours out of the twenty-four; it keeps them out of mischief better than any other place. As long as they work, they are not doing worse. I cannot attend to their houses." I say to him, " It seems to me you do the same for your ox." That's another significant fact of our civilization. I go to Lowell, and I say to a young girl, wandering in the streets, " How is this? " " Well, I worked here seven years, and I thought I would leave that mill and go to another; and the corporation won't give me my ticket. I have sued them in the Supreme Court, and I cannot get it; and here I am, penniless, in Eastern Massachusetts." That's Christian civilization. I am picking up, not individual facts, but significant rules that were made for labor.

You say, "What does labor need in New England?" It needs justice. Mr. Stewart, in New York, has bought a whole town; and he is going to build model houses, and house there all the labor he can get to go into them. Yet the civilization which alone can look the New Testament in the face is a civilization where one man does not depend on the pity of another man's building him a model lodging-house; the civilization which alone can look the New Testament in the face is a civilization where one man could not build, and another man would not need, that sort of refuge.

[1871]

JOHN BROWN

[1800-1859]

HE WAS born in Torrington, Connecticut, of old New England stock. His father, a wandering jack-of-all-trades, removed the family to a village in Ohio, and there John grew up with little schooling and much freedom. Eventually he became a tanner, worked for his father, and then married and migrated to Pennsylvania, where he set up a tannery of his own. But he did not stay there long. Like his father, he moved frequently, going from one unsuccessful occupation and business venture to another. He was like his father in other respects as well: both were men of piety, both were abolitionists and agents of the underground railroad. It was not until he was well on in years, however, that he began to feel that he had a mission to free the slaves, dreaming of himself as the captain of a band which would swoop down upon slaveholders to release their blacks. In 1855 five of his sons went to Kansas to help win the territory for the free-soilers. Their father soon joined them, and in the guerrilla warfare of the time, " Old Ossawatomie," as he was called, was the terror of the pro-slavers. Several times he went east to Massachusetts to raise money and supplies. In the Concord-Cambridge circle of philosophers and poets he was regarded as a hero and saint. His forays into Missouri resulted in his being outlawed, but he succeeded in reaching Canada with a group of liberated Negroes. In 1859 he moved with his little band to the vicinity of Harper's Ferry. On the night of October 16 he raided the town in the hope of freeing what slaves were there; by morning he held the arsenal and bridges. The next night, however, a company of marines led by Robert E. Lee stormed his stronghold. He was captured after two of his sons had been mortally wounded. On December 2 he was hanged. It has been shown that there was insanity in his family and therefore it has been claimed that he too was insane. But such men as Thoreau, Theodore Parker, and Thomas Wentworth Higginson did not think him mad, and there have been many in our own day who have regarded him as a martyr. When he was hanged, the press of the country denounced him, but somehow the people remembered him and the Northern armies sang a song about his body and spirit as they marched to battle.

LAST SPEECH

I have, may it please the Court, a few words to say.

In the first place, I deny everything but what I have all along admitted — the design on my part to free the slaves. I intended certainly to have made a clear thing of that matter, as I did last winter, when I went into Missouri, and there took slaves without the snapping of a gun on either side, moved them through the country, and finally left them in Canada. I designed to have done the same thing again, on a larger scale. That was all I intended. I never did intend murder, or treason, or the destruction of property, or to excite or incite slaves to rebellion, or to make insurrection.

I have another objection: and that is, it is unjust that I should suffer such a penalty. Had I interfered in the manner which I admit, and which I admit has been fairly proved — (for I admire the truthfulness and candor of the greater portion of the witnesses who have testified in this case) — had I so interfered in behalf of the rich, the powerful, the intelligent, the so-called great, or in behalf of any of their friends, either father, mother, brother, sister, wife, or children, or any of that class, and suffered and sacrificed what I have in this interference, it would have been all right, and every man in this Court would have deemed it an act worthy of reward rather than punishment.

This Court acknowledges, as I suppose, the validity of the Law of God. I see a book kissed here which I suppose to be the Bible, or, at least, the New Testament. That teaches me that all things " whatsoever I would that men should do unto me, I should do even so to them." It teaches me, further, to " remember them that are in bonds as bound with them." I endeavored to act up to that instruction. I say, I am yet too young to understand that God is any respecter of persons. I believe that to have interfered as I have done, as I have always freely admitted I have done, in behalf of His despised poor, was not wrong, but right. Now, if it is deemed necessary that I should forfeit my life for the furtherance of the ends of justice, and mingle my blood further with the blood of my children, and with the blood of millions in this slave country whose rights are disregarded by wicked, cruel, and unjust enactments, I submit: so let it be done!

Let me say one word further.

I feel entirely satisfied with the treatment I have received on my trial. Considering all the circumstances, it has been more generous than I expected. But I feel no consciousness of guilt. I have stated from the first what was my intention and what was not. I never had any design against the life of any person, nor any disposition to commit treason, or excite slaves to rebel, or make any general insurrection. I never encouraged any man to do so, but always discouraged any idea of that kind.

Let me say, also, a word in regard to the statements made by some of those connected with me. I hear it has been stated by some of them that I have induced them to join me. But the contrary is true. I do not say this to injure them, but as regretting their weakness. There is not one of them but joined me of his own accord, and the greater part at their own expense. A number of them I never saw, and never had a word of conversation with, till the day they came to me, and that was for the purpose I have stated.

Now I have done.

[*1859*]

ABRAHAM LINCOLN

[1809–1865]

THE STORY of Abe Lincoln's life is too well known to need retelling here. Every schoolboy knows of his birth in a pioneer's log cabin in Kentucky; of his meager schooling and his arduous efforts to educate himself; of his failure as a store-keeper in New Salem, Illinois; and at least something of his career in politics, which was ended by a bullet fired by John Wilkes Booth six weeks after he began his second term as President of the United States.

He has become the purest and noblest symbol of American democracy, almost as much because of what he said as what he did. For in his later years Lincoln could speak and write magnificently, sometimes in homespun phrases, rich in the humor of the frontier, and sometimes in words profoundly dignified and serious, invested with an emotion that was almost mystical. A few of his speeches must rank with the world's masterpieces of oratory; others, straightforward and simple, express perfectly the ideas for which large numbers of Americans would prove willing to die.

It is impossible to reprint here every address or letter in which he said something notable and moving. The reader will not find, in the following pages, the pieces in which he remarked: " As I would not be a slave, so I would not be a master. This expresses my idea of democracy. Whatever differs from this, to the extent of the difference, is no democracy. . . ." " Why should there not be a patient confidence in the ultimate justice of the people? Is there any better or equal hope in the world? . . ." " In giving freedom to the slave we assure freedom to the free, — honorable alike in what we give and what we preserve. . . ." " This country, with its institutions, belongs to the people who inhabit it. Whenever they shall grow weary of the existing government, they can exercise their constitutional right of amending it, or their revolutionary right to dismember or overthrow it." (One of the finest ballads of our day was written around the last of these quotations.)

To read him is to understand why Lincoln has become a hero and a god to the American people. In the biographical essay which prefaces his volume of selections from Lincoln's writings, Philip Van Doren Stern wrote justly: " A popular hero is the living embodiment of his people, with all their characteristics, good and bad. He is one of them, lifted up and made great, yet never divorced from their earthiness, rooted deep in the soil from which he sprang. That the American people have chosen this man from among all others to be their representative in world mythology is evidence of their attachment to the principles of liberty, peace and justice for which he stood. And it is remarkable, too, that they have seen through the apparent disparities in his career to the essential underlying truths. They remember him as a man of peace and good will, although they know that he was a wartime leader. They cherish the words he spoke for freedom and democracy, although they realize that he was compelled by the emergency of war to suspend many of their most dearly defended civil rights. They know that he saw beyond the temporary measures of his day to ideals of eternal importance. They remember that he and the men of his time had to fight to preserve those ideals; they remember the part he played in this struggle; they know what he did and they will not forget what he said."

from

SPEECH AT PEORIA

We know the opening of new countries to slavery tends to the perpetuation of the institution, and so does keep men in slavery who would otherwise be free. This result we do not feel like favoring, and we are under no legal obligation to suppress our feelings in this respect.

Equal justice to the South, it is said, requires us to consent to the extension of slavery to new countries. That is to say, inasmuch as you do not object to my taking my hog to Nebraska, therefore I must not object to you taking your slave. Now, I admit that this is perfectly logical, if there is no difference between hogs and Negroes. But while you thus require me to deny the humanity of the Negro, I wish to ask whether you of the South, yourselves, have ever been willing to do as much? It is kindly provided that of all those who come into the world only a small percentage are natural tyrants. That percentage is no larger in the slave States than in the free. The great majority South, as well as North, have human sympathies, of which they can no more divest themselves than they can of their sensibility to physical pain. These sympathies in the bosoms of the Southern people manifest, in many ways, their sense of the wrong of slavery, and their consciousness that, after all, there is humanity in the Negro. If they deny this, let me address them a few plain questions. In 1820 you joined the North, almost unanimously, in declaring the African slave trade piracy, and in annexing to it the punishment of death. Why did you do this? If you did not feel that it was wrong, why did you join in providing that men should be hung for it? The practice was no more than bringing wild Negroes from Africa to such as would buy them. But you never thought of hanging men for catching and selling wild horses, wild buffaloes, or wild bears.

Again, you have among you a sneaking individual of the class of native tyrants known as the "Slave Dealer." He watches your necessities, and crawls up to buy your slave, at a speculating price. If you cannot help it, you sell to him; but if you can help it, you drive him from your door. You despise him utterly. You do not recognize him as a friend, or even as an honest man. Your children must not play with his; they may rollick freely with the little Negroes, but not with the slave dealer's children. If you are obliged to deal with him, you try to get through the job without so much as touching him. It is common with you to join hands with men you meet, but with the slave dealer you avoid the ceremony — instinctively shrinking from the snaky contact. If he grows rich and retires from business, you still remember him, and still keep up the ban of non-intercourse upon him and his family. Now why is this? You do not so treat the man who deals in corn, cotton, or tobacco.

And yet again. There are in the United States and Territories, including the District of Columbia, 433,643 free blacks. At five hundred dollars per head they are worth over two hundred millions of dollars. How comes this vast amount of property to be running about without owners? We do not see free horses or free cattle running at large. How is this? All these free blacks are the descendants of slaves, or have been slaves themselves; and they would be slaves now but for something which has operated on their white owners, inducing them at vast pecuniary sacrifice to liberate them. What is that something? Is there any mistaking it? In all these cases it is your sense of justice and human sympathy continually telling you that the poor Negro has some natural right to himself — that those who deny it and make mere merchandise of him deserve kickings, contempt, and death.

And now why will you ask us to deny the humanity of the slave, and estimate him as only the equal of the hog? Why ask us to do what you will not do yourselves? Why ask us to do for nothing what two hundred millions of dollars could not induce you to do?

But one great argument in support of the repeal of the Missouri Compromise is still to come. That argument is "the sacred right of self-government." It seems our distinguished Senator has found great difficulty in getting his antagonists, even in the Senate, to meet him fairly on this argument. Some poet has said:

Fools rush in where angels fear to tread.

At the hazard of being thought one of the fools of this quotation, I meet that argument — I rush in — I take that bull by the horns. I trust I understand and truly estimate the right of self-government. My faith in the proposition that each man should do precisely as he pleases with all which is exclusively his own lies at the foundation of the sense of justice there is in me. I extend the principle to communities of men as well as to individuals. I so extend it because it is politically wise, as well as naturally just: politically wise in saving us from broils about matters which do not concern us. Here, or at Washington, I would not trouble myself with the oyster laws of Virginia, or the cranberry laws of Indiana. The doctrine of self-government is right — absolutely and eternally right — but it has no just application as here attempted. Or perhaps I should rather say that whether it has such application depends upon whether a Negro is not or is a man. If he is not a man, in that case he who is a man may as a matter of self-government do just what he pleases with him.

But if the Negro is a man, is it not to that extent a total destruction of self-government to say that he too shall not govern himself? When the white man governs himself, that is self-government; but when he governs himself and also governs another man, that is more than self-government — that is despotism. If the Negro is a man, why then my ancient faith teaches me that " all men are created equal," and that there can be no moral right in connection with one man's making a slave of another.

Judge Douglas frequently, with bitter irony and sarcasm, paraphrases our argument by saying: "The white people of Nebraska are good enough to govern themselves, but they are not good enough to govern a few miserable Negroes! "

Well! I doubt not that the people of Nebraska are and will continue to be as good as the average of people elsewhere. I do not say the contrary. What I do say is that no man is good enough to govern another man without that other's consent. I say this is the leading principle, the sheet-anchor of American republicanism. Our Declaration of Independence says:

We hold these truths to be self-evident: That all men are created equal; that they are endowed by their Creator with certain inalienable rights; that among these are life, liberty and the pursuit of happiness. That to secure these rights, governments are instituted among men, DERIVING THEIR JUST POWERS FROM THE CONSENT OF THE GOVERNED.

I have quoted so much at this time merely to show that, according to our ancient faith, the just powers of governments are derived from the consent of the governed. Now the relation of master and slave is *pro tanto* a total violation of this principle. The master not only governs the slave without his consent, but he governs him by a set of rules altogether different from those which he prescribes for himself. Allow all the governed an equal voice in the government, and that, and that only, is self-government.

[1854]

from

A LETTER TO JOSHUA F. SPEED

Springfield, August 24, 1855

Dear Speed: You know what a poor correspondent I am. Ever since I received your very agreeable letter of the 22d of May I have been intending to write you an answer to it. You suggest that in political action, now, you and I would differ. I suppose we would; not quite as much, however, as you may think. You know I dislike slavery, and you fully admit the abstract wrong of it. So far there is no cause of difference. But you say that sooner than yield your legal right to the slave, especially at the bidding of those who are not themselves interested, you would see the Union dissolved. I am not aware that any one is bidding you yield that right; very certainly I am not. I leave that matter entirely to yourself. I also acknowledge your rights and my obligations under the Constitution in regard to your slaves. I confess I hate to see the poor creatures hunted down and caught and carried back to their stripes and unrequited toil; but I bite my lips and keep quiet.

In 1841 you and I had together a tedious low-water trip on a steamboat from Louisville to St. Louis. You may remember, as I well do, that from Louisville to the mouth of the Ohio there were on board ten or a dozen slaves shackled together with irons. That sight was a continued torment to me, and I see something like it every time I touch the Ohio or any other slave border. It is not fair for you to assume that I have no interest in a thing which has, and continually exercises, the power of making me miserable. You ought rather to appreciate how much the great body of the Northern people do crucify their feelings, in order to maintain their loyalty to the Constitution and the Union. I do oppose the extension of slavery because my judgment and feeling so prompt me, and I am under no obligations to the contrary. If for this you and I must differ, differ we must. . . .

You say that if Kansas fairly votes herself a free State, as a Christian you will rejoice at it. All decent slaveholders talk that way, and I do not doubt their candor. But they never vote that way. Although in a private letter or conversation you will express your preference that Kansas shall be free, you would vote for no man for Congress who would say the same thing publicly. No such man could be elected from any district in a slave State. You think Stringfellow and company ought to be hung; and yet at the next presidential election you will vote for the exact type and representative of Stringfellow. The slave breeders and slave traders are a small, odious, and detested class among you; and yet in politics they dictate the course of all of you, and are as completely your masters as you are the master of your own Negroes.

You inquire where I now stand. That is a disputed point. I think I am a Whig; but others say there are no Whigs, and that I am an Abolitionist. When I was at Washington, I voted for the Wilmot proviso as good as forty times; and I never heard of any one attempting to unwhig me for that. I now do no more than oppose the extension of slavery. I am not a Know-Nothing; that is certain. How could I be? How can any one who abhors the oppression of Negroes be in favor of degrading classes of white people? Our progress in degeneracy appears to me to be pretty rapid. As a nation we began by declaring that " all men are created equal." We now practically read it " all men are created equal, except Negroes." When the Know-Nothings get control, it will read " all men are created equal, except Negroes and foreigners and Catholics." When it comes to this, I shall prefer emigrating to some country where they make no pretense of loving liberty — to Russia, for instance, where despotism can be taken pure, and without the base alloy of hypocrisy.

Mary will probably pass a day or two in Louisville in October. My kindest regards to Mrs. Speed. On the leading subject of this letter, I have more of her sympathy than I have of yours; and yet let me say I am

Your friend forever,

A. *Lincoln*

[*1855*]

from

A SPEECH AT CHICAGO

We were often — more than once at least — in the course of Judge Douglas's speech last night reminded that this government was made for white men — that he believed it was made for white men. Well, that is putting it into a shape in which no one wants to deny it; but the judge then goes into his passion for drawing inferences that are not warranted. I protest, now and forever, against that counterfeit logic which presumes that because I do not want a Negro woman for a slave, I do necessarily want her for a wife. My understanding is that I need not have her for either; but, as God made us separate, we can leave one another alone, and do one another much good thereby. There are white men enough to marry all the white women, and enough black men to marry all the black women, and in God's name let them be so married. The judge regales us with the terrible enormities that take place by the mixture of races; that the inferior race bears the superior down. Why, Judge, if we do not let them get together in the Territories, they won't mix there. I should say at least that that is a self-evident truth.

Now, it happens that we meet together once every year, somewhere about the 4th of July, for some reason or other. These 4th of July gatherings I suppose have their uses. If you will indulge me, I will state what I suppose to be some of them.

We are now a mighty nation: we are thirty, or about thirty, millions of people, and we own and inhabit about one-fifteenth part of the dry land of the whole earth. We run our memory back over the pages of history for about eighty-two years, and we discover that we were then a very small people, in point of numbers vastly inferior to what we are now, with a vastly less extent of country, with vastly less of everything we deem desirable among men. We look upon the change as exceedingly advantageous to us and to our posterity, and we fix upon something that happened away back as in some way or other being connected with this rise of prosperity. We find a race of men living in that day whom we claim as our fathers and grandfathers; they were iron men; they fought for the principle that they were contending for; and we understood that by what they then did it has followed that the degree of prosperity which we now enjoy has come to us. We hold this annual celebration to remind ourselves of all the good done in this process of time, of how it was done and who did it, and how we are historically connected with it; and we go from these meetings in better humor with ourselves — we feel more attached the one to the other, and more firmly bound to the country we inhabit. In every way we are better men, in the age, and race, and country in which we live, for these celebrations. But after we have done all this, we have not yet reached the whole. There is something else connected with it. We have, besides these men — descended by blood from our ancestors — among us, perhaps half our people who are not descendants at all of these men; they are men who have come from Europe — German, Irish, French, and Scandinavian — men that have come from Europe themselves, or whose ancestors have come hither and settled here, finding themselves our equal in all things. If they look back through this history to trace their connection with those days by blood, they find they have none; they cannot carry themselves back into that glorious epoch and make themselves feel that they are part of us; but when they look through that old Declaration of Independence, they find that those old men say that "We hold these truths to be self-evident, that all men are created equal," and then they feel that the moral sentiment taught in that day evidences their relation to those men, that it is the father of all moral principle in them, and that they have a right to claim it as though they were blood of the blood, and flesh of the flesh, of the men who wrote that Declaration, and so they are. That is the electric cord in that Declaration that links the hearts of patriotic and liberty-loving men together, that will link those patriotic hearts as long as the love of freedom exists in the minds of men throughout the world.

Now, sirs, for the purpose of squaring things with this idea of "don't care if slavery is voted up or voted down," for sustaining the Dred

Scott decision, for holding that the Declaration of Independence did not mean anything at all, we have Judge Douglas giving his exposition of what the Declaration of Independence means, and we have him saying that the people of America are equal to the people of England. According to his construction, you Germans [1] are not connected with it. Now I ask you, in all soberness, if all these things, if indulged in, if ratified, if confirmed and indorsed, if taught to our children, and repeated to them, do not tend to rub out the sentiment of liberty in the country, and to transform this government into a government of some other form? Those arguments that are made, that the inferior race are to be treated with as much allowance as they are capable of enjoying; that as much is to be done for them as their condition will allow — what are these arguments? They are the arguments that kings have made for enslaving the people in all ages of the world. You will find that all the arguments in favor of kingcraft were of this class; they always bestrode the necks of the people — not that they wanted to do it, but because the people were better off for being ridden. That is their argument, and this argument of the judge is the same old serpent that says: "You work and I eat, you toil and I will enjoy the fruits of it." Turn in whatever way you will — whether it come from the mouth of a king, an excuse for enslaving the people of his country, or from the mouth of men of one race as a reason for enslaving the men of another race, it is all the same old serpent, and I hold if that course of argumentation that is made for the purpose of convincing the public mind that we should not care about this should be granted, it does not stop with the Negro. I should like to know — taking this old Declaration of Independence, which declares that all men are equal upon principle, and making exceptions to it — where will it stop? If one man says it does not mean a Negro, why not another say it does not mean some other man? If that Declaration is not the truth, let us get the statute-book in which we find it, and tear it out! Who is so bold as to do it? If it is not true, let us tear it out. [Cries of "No, no!"] Let us stick to it, then; let us stand firmly by it, then.

It may be argued that there are certain conditions that make necessities and impose them upon us, and to the extent that a necessity is imposed upon a man, he must submit to it. I think that was the condition in which we found ourselves when we established this government. We had slaves among us; we could not get our Constitution

---

[1] A German political club had just marched into the crowd.

unless we permitted them to remain in slavery; we could not secure the good we did secure if we grasped for more; but having by necessity submitted to that much, it does not destroy the principle that is the charter of our liberties. Let that charter stand as our standard.

My friend has said to me that I am a poor hand to quote Scripture. I will try it again, however. It is said in one of the admonitions of our Lord, "Be ye [therefore] perfect even as your Father which is in heaven is perfect." The Saviour, I suppose, did not expect that any human creature could be perfect as the Father in heaven; but he said, "As your Father in heaven is perfect, be ye also perfect." He set that up as a standard, and he who did most toward reaching that standard attained the highest degree of moral perfection. So I say in relation to the principle that all men are created equal, let it be as nearly reached as we can. If we cannot give freedom to every creature, let us do nothing that will impose slavery upon any other creature. Let us then turn this government back into the channel in which the framers of the Constitution originally placed it. Let us stand firmly by each other. If we do not do so, we are tending in the contrary direction that our friend Judge Douglas proposes — not intentionally — working in the traces that tend to make this one universal slave nation. He is one that runs in that direction, and as such I resist him.

My friends, I have detained you about as long as I desired to do, and I have only to say, let us discard all this quibbling about this man and the other man, this race and that race and the other race being inferior, and therefore they must be placed in an inferior position. Let us discard all these things, and unite as one people throughout this land, until we shall once more stand up declaring that all men are created equal.

My friends, I could not, without launching off upon some new topic, which would detain you too long, continue tonight. I thank you for this most extensive audience that you have furnished me tonight. I leave you, hoping that the lamp of liberty will burn in your bosoms until there shall no longer be a doubt that all men are created free and equal.

[1858]

from

A SPEECH AT EDWARDSVILLE, ILLINOIS

When . . . you have succeeded in dehumanizing the Negro; when you have put him down and made it impossible for him to be but as the beasts of the field; when you have extinguished his soul in this world and placed him where the ray of hope is blown out as in the darkness of the damned, are you quite sure that the demon you have roused will not turn and rend you? What constitutes the bulwark of our own liberty and independence? It is not our frowning battlements, our bristling sea coasts, our army and our navy. These are not our reliance against tyranny. All of those may be turned against us without making us weaker for the struggle. Our reliance is in the love of liberty which God has planted in us. Our defence is in the spirit which prized liberty as the heritage of all men, in all lands everywhere. Destroy this spirit and you have planted the seeds of despotism at your own doors. Familiarize yourselves with the chains of bondage and you prepare your own limbs to wear them. Accustomed to trample on the rights of others, you have lost the genius of your own independence and become the fit subjects of the first cunning tyrant who rises among you.

[1858]

from

THE MESSAGE TO CONGRESS
IN SPECIAL SESSION, 1861

It may be affirmed without extravagance that the free institutions we enjoy have developed the powers and improved the condition of our whole people beyond any example in the world. Of this we now have a striking and an impressive illustration. So large an army as the government has now on foot was never before known, without a soldier in it but who has taken his place there of his own free choice. But more than this, there are many single regiments whose members, one and another, possess full practical knowledge of all the arts, sciences, professions, and whatever else, whether useful or elegant, is known in the world; and there is scarcely one from which there could not be selected a President, a Cabinet, a Congress, and perhaps a court, abundantly competent to administer the government itself. Nor do I say this is not true also in the army of our late friends, now adversaries in this contest; but if it is, so much better the reason why the government which has conferred such benefits on both them and us should not be broken up. Whoever in any section proposes to abandon such a government would do well to consider in deference to what principle it is that he does it — what better he is likely to get in its stead — whether the substitute will give, or be intended to give, so much of good to the people? There are some foreshadowings on this subject. Our adversaries have adopted some declarations of independence in which, unlike the good old one, penned by Jefferson, they omit the words " all men are created equal." Why? They have adopted a temporary national constitution, in the preamble of which, unlike our good old one, signed by Washington, they omit " We, the People," and substitute, " We, the deputies of the sovereign and independent States." Why? Why this deliberate pressing out of view the rights of men and the authority of the people?

This is essentially a people's contest. On the side of the Union it is a struggle for maintaining in the world that form and substance of government whose leading object is to elevate the condition of men — to lift artificial weights from all shoulders; to clear the paths of laudable pursuit for all; to afford all an unfettered start, and a fair chance in the race of life. Yielding to partial and temporary departures, from necessity, this is the leading object of the government for whose existence we contend.

I am most happy to believe that the plain people understand and appreciate this. It is worthy of note that while in this, the government's hour of trial, large numbers of those in the army and navy who have been favored with the offices have resigned and proved false to the hand which had pampered them, not one common soldier or common sailor is known to have deserted his flag.

Great honor is due to those officers who remained true, despite the example of their treacherous associates; but the greatest honor, and most important fact of all, is the unanimous firmness of the common soldiers and common sailors. To the last man, so far as known, they have successfully resisted the traitorous efforts of those whose commands, but an hour before, they obeyed as absolute law. This is the patriotic instinct of the plain people. They understand, without an argument, that the destroying of the government which was made by Washington means no good to them.

Our popular government has often been called an experiment. Two points in it our people have already settled — the successful establishing and the successful administering of it. One still remains — its successful maintenance against a formidable internal attempt to overthrow it. It is now for them to demonstrate to the world that those who can fairly carry an election can also suppress a rebellion; that ballots are the rightful and peaceful successors of bullets; and that when ballots have fairly and constitutionally decided, there can be no successful appeal back to bullets; that there can be no successful appeal, except to ballots themselves, at succeeding elections. Such will be a great lesson of peace: teaching men that what they cannot take by an election, neither can they take it by a war; teaching all the folly of being the beginners of a war.

[*1861*]

from

THE ANNUAL MESSAGE TO CONGRESS, 1861

The insurrection is largely, if not exclusively, a war upon the first principle of popular government — the rights of the people. Conclusive evidence of this is found in the most grave and maturely considered public documents as well as in the general tone of the insurgents. In those documents we find the abridgment of the existing right of suffrage and the denial to the people of all right to participate in the selection of public officers except the legislative, boldly advocated, with labored arguments to prove that large control of the people in government is the source of all political evil. Monarchy itself is sometimes hinted at as a possible refuge from the power of the people.

In my present position I could scarcely be justified were I to omit raising a warning voice against this approach of returning despotism.

It is not needed nor fitting here that a general argument should be made in favor of popular institutions; but there is one point, with its connections, not so hackneyed as most others, to which I ask a brief attention. It is the effort to place capital on an equal footing with, if not above, labor, in the structure of government. It is assumed that labor is available only in connection with capital; that nobody labors unless somebody else, owning capital, somehow by the use of it induces him to labor. This assumed, it is next considered whether it is best that capital shall hire laborers, and thus induce them to work by their own consent, or buy them, and drive them to it without their consent. Having proceeded thus far, it is naturally concluded that all laborers are either hired laborers or what we call slaves. And, further, it is assumed that whoever is once a hired laborer is fixed in that condition for life.

Now, there is no such relation between capital and labor as assumed, nor is there any such thing as a free man being fixed for life in the condition of a hired laborer. Both these assumptions are false, and all inferences from them are groundless.

Labor is prior to, and independent of, capital. Capital is only the fruit of labor, and could never have existed if labor had not first existed. Labor is the superior of capital, and deserves much the higher consideration. Capital has its rights, which are as worthy of protection as any other rights. Nor is it denied that there is, and probably always will be, a relation between labor and capital producing mutual benefits. The error is in assuming that the whole labor of the community exists within that relation. A few men own capital, and that few avoid labor themselves, and with their capital hire or buy another few to labor for them. A large majority belong to neither class — neither work for others nor have others working for them. In most of the Southern States a majority of the whole people, of all colors, are neither slaves nor masters; while in the Northern a large majority are neither hirers nor hired. Men with their families — wives, sons, and daughters — work for themselves, on their farms, in their houses, and in their shops taking the whole product to themselves, and asking no favors of capital on the one hand, nor of hired laborers or slaves on the other. It is not forgotten that a considerable number of persons mingle their own labor with capital — that is, they labor with their own hands and also buy or hire others to labor for them; but this is only a mixed and not a distinct class. No principle stated is disturbed by the existence of this mixed class.

Again, as has already been said, there is not, of necessity, any such thing as the free hired laborer being fixed to that condition for life. Many independent men everywhere in these States, a few years back in their lives, were hired laborers. The prudent, penniless beginner in the world labors for wages awhile, saves a surplus with which to buy tools or land for himself, then labors on his own account another while, and at length hires another new beginner to help him. This is the just and generous and prosperous system which opens the way to all — gives hope to all, and consequent energy and progress and improvement of condition to all. No men living are more worthy to be trusted than those who toil up from poverty — none less inclined to take or touch aught which they have not honestly earned. Let them beware of surrendering a political power which they already possess, and which, if surrendered, will surely be used to close the door of advancement against such as they, and to fix new disabilities and burdens upon them, till all of liberty shall be lost.

[*1861*]

THE GETTYSBURG ADDRESS

Fourscore and seven years ago our fathers brought forth on this continent a new nation, conceived in liberty, and dedicated to the proposition that all men are created equal.

Now we are engaged in a great civil war, testing whether that nation, or any nation so conceived and so dedicated, can long endure. We are met on a great battlefield of that war. We have come to dedicate a portion of that field as a final resting-place for those who here gave their lives that that nation might live. It is altogether fitting and proper that we should do this.

But, in a larger sense, we cannot dedicate — we cannot consecrate — we cannot hallow — this ground. The brave men, living and dead, who struggled here, have consecrated it far above our poor power to add or detract. The world will little note nor long remember what we say here, but it can never forget what they did here. It is for us, the living, rather, to be dedicated here to the unfinished work which they

who fought here have thus far so nobly advanced. It is rather for us to be here dedicated to the great task remaining before us — that from these honored dead we take increased devotion to that cause for which they gave the last full measure of devotion; that we here highly resolve that these dead shall not have died in vain; that this nation, under God, shall have a new birth of freedom; and that government of the people, by the people, for the people, shall not perish from the earth.
[*1863*]

---

from

ADDRESS AT SANITARY FAIR IN BALTIMORE

The world has never had a good definition of the word liberty, and the American people, just now, are much in want of one. We all declare for liberty; but in using the same word we do not all mean the same thing. With some the word liberty may mean for each man to do as he pleases with himself, and the product of his labor; while with others the same word may mean for some men to do as they please with other men, and the product of other men's labor. Here are two, not only different, but incompatible things, called by the same name, liberty. And it follows that each of the things is, by the respective parties, called by two different and incompatible names — liberty and tyranny.

The shepherd drives the wolf from the sheep's throat, for which the sheep thanks the shepherd as his liberator, while the wolf denounces him for the same act, as the destroyer of liberty, especially as the sheep was a black one. Plainly, the sheep and the wolf are not agreed upon a definition of the word liberty; and precisely the same difference prevails today among us human creatures, even in the North, and all professing to love liberty. Hence we behold the process by which thousands are daily passing from under the yoke of bondage hailed by some as the advance of liberty, and bewailed by others as the destruction of all liberty.

[*1864*]

WALT WHITMAN

[1819–1892]

HE WAS born on Long Island, New York, and brought up in Brooklyn, where he attended a public grammar school. His father was a carpenter, and Walt himself learned the craft. But that was not his real trade; as a young boy he worked in printing shops until he became a skilled compositor — in which capacity he was employed by various newspapers and magazines. Soon he began to contribute to these periodicals, and by 1846 had gained sufficient reputation to be appointed editor of the *Brooklyn Daily Eagle*. He lost this job in 1848 because of his liberal politics. Then followed years of independent editorial work, free-lance writing, and carpentering. In 1855 he published the first edition of his *Leaves of Grass*. A few of the best minds in America, led by Emerson, immediately recognized its worth. In the years that followed, as Whitman brought out revised and fuller editions, it attracted an ever wider circle of admirers. It was viciously attacked for its unconventional poetic forms, its frank treatment of sex, and its radical sentiments, but its friends were eventually vindicated. It is now generally regarded as one of the few truly great volumes of poetry this country has produced.

During the Civil War Whitman went to Washington to work in the army hospitals. At the same time he wrote war correspondence, using much of his earnings, together with gifts solicited from others, to further his work among the wounded soldiers. In 1865 he was awarded a clerkship in the Indian Bureau, only to be discharged, six months later, for having written " an indecent book." The protests against this stupid action were prompt and vigorous. He was soon given a clerkship in the Attorney General's office and subsequently in the Treasury Department, where he remained on the payroll until 1874. From then until his death he lived on the rather modest proceeds of his writing, supplemented by funds donated by friends here and abroad.

There is no need today to argue either his rank or his significance. What Lincoln was in our public life, Whitman was in our literature: democracy's voice. No other American poet has so completely, profoundly, and consistently understood and appreciated the people — the plain people, the masses, the lowest in the social hierarchy. He sang for them, strove to express their passions and aspirations, defended them against snobs and tyrants, and pled their cause against tradition, prejudice, and skepticism. He stands close to Lincoln as an embodiment of the democratic spirit.

A SONG FOR OCCUPATIONS

1

A song for occupations!
In the labor of engines and trades and the labor of fields I find the
developments,
And find the eternal meanings.

Workmen and Workwomen!
Were all educations practical and ornamental well display'd out of me,
what would it amount to?
Were I as the head teacher, charitable proprietor, wise statesman, what
would it amount to?
Were I to you as the boss employing and paying you, would that
satisfy you?

The learn'd, virtuous, benevolent, and the usual terms,
A man like me and never the usual terms.

Neither a servant nor a master I,
I take no sooner a large price than a small price, I will have my own
whoever enjoys me,
I will be even with you and you shall be even with me.

If you stand at work in a shop I stand as nigh as the nighest in the
same shop,
If you bestow gifts on your brother or dearest friend I demand as good
as your brother or dearest friend,
If your lover, husband, wife, is welcome by day or night, I must be
personally as welcome,
If you become degraded, criminal, ill, then I become so for your sake,
If you remember your foolish and outlaw'd deeds, do you think I can-
not remember my own foolish and outlaw'd deeds?
If you carouse at the table I carouse at the opposite side of the table,
If you meet some stranger in the streets and love him or her, why I
often meet strangers in the street and love them.

Why what have you thought of yourself?
Is it you then that thought yourself less?

Is it you that thought the President greater than you?
Or the rich better off than you? or the educated wiser than you?

(Because you are greasy or pimpled, or were once drunk, or a thief,
Or that you are diseas'd, or rheumatic, or a prostitute,
Or from frivolity or impotence, or that you are no scholar and never saw
    your name in print,
Do you give in that you are any less immortal?)

2

Souls of men and women! it is not you I call unseen, unheard, un-
    touchable and untouching,
It is not you I go argue pro and con about, and to settle whether you
    are alive or no,
I own publicly who you are, if nobody else owns.

Grown, half-grown and babe, of this country and every country, in-
    doors and out-doors, one just as much as the other, I see,
And all else behind or through them.

The wife, and she is not one jot less than the husband,
The daughter, and she is just as good as the son,
The mother, and she is every bit as much as the father.

Offspring of ignorant and poor, boys apprenticed to trades,
Young fellows working on farms and old fellows working on farms,
Sailor-men, merchant-men, coasters, immigrants,
All these I see, but higher and farther the same I see,
None shall escape me and none shall wish to escape me.

I bring what you much need yet always have,
Not money, amours, dress, eating, erudition, but as good,
I send no agent or medium, offer no representative of value, but offer
    the value itself.

There is something that comes to one now and perpetually,
It is not what is printed, preach'd, discuss'd, it eludes discussion and
    print,
It is not to be put in a book, it is not in this book,

It is for you whoever you are, it is no farther from you than your hearing and sight are from you,
It is hinted by nearest, commonest, readiest, it is ever provoked by
them.

You may read in many languages, yet read nothing about it,
You may read the President's message and read nothing about it there,
Nothing in the reports from the State department or Treasury depart-
ment, or in the daily papers or weekly papers,
Or in the census or revenue returns, prices current, or any accounts
of stock.

3

The sun and stars that float in the open air,
The apple-shaped earth and we upon it, surely the drift of them is
something grand,
I do not know what it is except that it is grand, and that it is happiness,
And that the enclosing purport of us here is not a speculation or bon-
mot or reconnoissance,
And that it is not something which by luck may turn out well for us,
and without luck must be a failure for us,
And not something which may yet be retracted in a certain contingency.

The light and shade, the curious sense of body and identity, the greed
that with perfect complaisance devours all things,
The endless pride and outstretching of man, unspeakable joys and
sorrows,
The wonder every one sees in every one else he sees, and the wonders
that fill each minute of time forever,
What have you reckon'd them for, camerado?
Have you reckon'd them for your trade or farm-work? or for the profits
of your store?
Or to achieve yourself a position? or to fill a gentleman's leisure, or a
lady's leisure?

Have you reckon'd that the landscape took substance and form that
it might be painted in a picture?
Or men and women that they might be written of, and songs sung?
Or the attraction of gravity, and the great laws and harmonious com-

binations and the fluids of the air, as subjects for the savans?
Or the brown land and the blue sea for maps and charts?
Or the stars to be put in constellations and named fancy names?
Or that the growth of seeds is for agricultural tables, or agriculture
itself?

Old institutions, these arts, libraries, legends, collections, and the practice handed along in manufactures, will we rate them so high?
Will we rate our cash and business high? I have no objection,
I rate them as high as the highest — then a child born of a woman and
man I rate beyond all rate.

We thought our Union grand, and our Constitution grand,
I do not say they are not grand and good, for they are,
I am this day just as much in love with them as you,
Then I am in love with You, and with all my fellows upon the earth.

We consider bibles and religions divine — I do not say they are not
divine,
I say they have all grown out of you, and may grow out of you still,
It is not they who give the life, it is you who give the life,
Leaves are not more shed from the trees, or trees from the earth, than
they are shed out of you.

4

The sum of all known reverence I add up in you whoever you are,
The President is there in the White House for you, it is not you who
are here for him,
The Secretaries act in their bureaus for you, not you here for them,
The Congress convenes every Twelfth-month for you,
Laws, courts, the forming of States, the charters of cities, the going
and coming of commerce and mails, are all for you.

List close, my scholars dear,
Doctrines, politics and civilization exurge from you.
Sculpture and monuments and any thing inscribed anywhere are tallied
in you,
The gist of histories and statistics as far back as the records reach is
in you this hour, and myths and tales the same,

If you were not breathing and walking here, where would they all be?
The most renown'd poems would be ashes, orations and plays would
be vacuums.

All architecture is what you do to it when you look upon it,
(Did you think it was in the white or gray stone? or the lines of the
arches and cornices?)

All music is what awakes from you when you are reminded by the
instruments,
It is not the violins and the cornets, it is not the oboe nor the beating
drums, nor the score of the baritone singer singing his sweet ro-
manza, nor that of the men's chorus, nor that of the women's chorus,
It is nearer and farther than they.

5

Will the whole come back then?
Can each see signs of the best by a look in the looking-glass? is there
nothing greater or more?
Does all sit there with you, with the mystic unseen soul?

Strange and hard that paradox true I give,
Objects gross and the unseen soul are one.

House-building, measuring, sawing the boards,
Blacksmithing, glass-blowing, nail-making, coopering, tin-roofing,
shingle-dressing,
Ship-joining, dock-building, fish-curing, flagging of sidewalks by
flaggers,
The pump, the pile-driver, the great derrick, the coal-kiln and brick-
kiln,
Coal-mines and all that is down there, the lamps in the darkness, echoes,
songs, what meditations, what vast native thoughts looking through
smutch'd faces,
Iron-works, forge-fires in the mountains or by river-banks, men around
feeling the melt with huge crowbars, lumps of ore, the due combining of ore, limestone, coal,

The blast-furnace and the puddling-furnace, the loup-lump at the bottom of the melt at last, the rolling-mill, the stumpy bars of pig-
iron, the strong, clean-shaped T-rail for railroads,

Oil-works, silk-works, white-lead-works, the sugar-house, steam-saws,
the great mills and factories,

Stone-cutting, shapely trimming for façades or window or door-lintels,
the mallet, the tooth-chisel, the jib to protect the thumb,

The calking-iron, the kettle of boiling vault-cement, and the fire under
the kettle,

The cotton-bale, the stevedore's hook, the saw and buck of the sawyer,
the mould of the moulder, the working-knife of the butcher, the
ice-saw, and all the work with ice,

The work and tools of the rigger, grappler, sail-maker, block-maker,

Goods of gutta-percha, papier-maché, colors, brushes, brush-making,
glazier's implements,

The veneer and glue-pot, the confectioner's ornaments, the decanter
and glasses, the shears and flat-iron,

The awl and knee-strap, the pint measure and quart measure, the
counter and stool, the writing-pen of quill or metal, the making
of all sorts of edged tools,

The brewery, brewing, the malts, the vats, everything that is done by
brewers, wine-makers, vinegar-makers,

Leather-dressing, coach-making, boiler-making, rope-twisting, distilling, sign-painting, lime-burning, cotton-picking, electroplating,
electrotyping, stereotyping.

Stave-machines, planing-machines, reaping-machines, ploughing-
machines, thrashing-machines, steam wagons,

The cart of the carman, the omnibus, the ponderous dray,

Pyrotechny, letting off color'd fireworks at night, fancy figures and jets;

Beef on the butcher's stall, the slaughter-house of the butcher, the
butcher in his killing-clothes,

The pens of live pork, the killing-hammer, the hog-hook, the scalder's
tub, gutting, the cutter's cleaver, the packer's maul, and the plen-
teous winter-work of pork-packing,

Flour-works, grinding of wheat, rye, maize, rice, the barrels and the
half and quarter barrels, the loaded barges, the high piles on
wharves and levees,

The men and the work of the men on ferries, railroads, coasters, fish-
boats, canals;

426

The hourly routine of your own or any man's life, the shop, yard, store,
  or factory,
These shows all near you by day and night — workman! whoever you
  are, your daily life!
In that and them the heft of the heaviest — in that and them far more
  than you estimated, (and far less also,)
In them realities for you and me, in them poems for you and me,
In them, not yourself — you and your soul enclose all things, regard-
  less of estimation,
In them the development good — in them all themes, hints, possibilities.

I do not affirm that what you see beyond is futile, I do not advise you
  to stop,
I do not say leadings you thought great are not great,
But I say that none lead to greater than these lead to.

6

Will you seek afar off? you surely come back at last,
In things best known to you finding the best, or as good as the best,
In folks nearest to you finding the sweetest, strongest, lovingest,
Happiness, knowledge, not in another place but this place, nor for
  another hour but this hour,
Man in the first you see or touch, always in friend, brother, nighest
  neighbor — woman in mother, sister, wife,
The popular tastes and employments taking precedence in poems or
  anywhere,
You workwomen and workmen of these States having your own divine
  and strong life,
And all else giving place to men and women like you.

When the psalm sings instead of the singer,
When the script preaches instead of the preacher,
When the pulpit descends and goes instead of the carver that carved
  the supporting desk,
When I can touch the body of books by night or by day, and when
  they touch my body back again,
When a university course convinces like a slumbering woman and
  child convince,

When the minted gold in the vault smiles like the night-watchman's
daughter,
When warrantee deeds loafe in chairs opposite and are my friendly
companions,
I intend to reach them my hand, and make as much of them as I do
of men and women like you.

[*1855*]

SONG OF THE BROAD–AXE

1

Weapon shapely, naked, wan,
Head from the mother's bowels drawn,
Wooded flesh and metal bone, limb only one and lip only one,
Gray-blue leaf by red-heat grown, helve produced from a little seed
sown,
Resting the grass amid and upon,
To be lean'd and to lean on.

Strong shapes and attributes of strong shapes, masculine trades, sights
and sounds,
Long varied train of an emblem, dabs of music,
Fingers of the organist skipping staccato over the keys of the great
organ.

2

Welcome are all earth's lands, each for its kind,
Welcome are lands of pine and oak,
Welcome are lands of the lemon and fig,
Welcome are lands of gold,
Welcome are lands of wheat and maize, welcome those of the grape,
Welcome are lands of sugar and rice,
Welcome the cotton-lands, welcome those of the white potato and
sweet potato,
Welcome are mountains, flats, sands, forests, prairies,

Welcome the rich borders of rivers, table-lands, openings,
Welcome the measureless grazing-lands, welcome the teeming soil of
    orchards, flax, honey, hemp;
Welcome just as much the other more hard-faced lands,
Lands rich as lands of gold or wheat and fruit lands,
Lands of mines, lands of the manly and rugged ores,
Lands of coal, copper, lead, tin, zinc,
Lands of iron — lands of the make of the axe.

3

The log at the wood-pile, the axe supported by it,
The sylvan hut, the vine over the doorway, the space clear'd for a
    garden,
The irregular tapping of rain down on the leaves after the storm is
    lull'd,
The wailing and moaning at intervals, the thought of the sea,
The thought of ships struck in the storm and put on their beam ends,
    and the cutting away of masts,
The sentiment of the huge timbers of old-fashion'd houses and barns,
The remember'd print or narrative, the voyage at a venture of men,
    families, goods,
The disembarkation, the founding of a new city,
The voyage of those who sought a New England and found it, the
    outset anywhere,
The settlements of the Arkansas, Colorado, Ottawa, Willamette,
The slow progress, the scant fare, the axe, rifle, saddle-bags;
The beauty of all adventurous and daring persons,
The beauty of wood-boys and wood-men with their clear untrimm'd
    faces,
The beauty of independence, departure, actions that rely on themselves,
The American contempt for statutes and ceremonies, the boundless
    impatience of restraint,
The loose drift of character, the inkling through random types, the
    solidification;
The butcher in the slaughter-house, the hands aboard schooners and
    sloops, the raftsmen, the pioneer,
Lumbermen in their winter camp, daybreak in the woods, stripes of
    snow on the limbs of trees, the occasional snapping,

The glad clear sound of one's own voice, the merry song, the natural
 life of the woods, the strong day's work,
The blazing fire at night, the sweet taste of supper, the talk, the bed
 of hemlock-boughs and the bear-skin;
The house-builder at work in cities or anywhere,
The preparatory jointing, squaring, sawing, mortising,
The hoist-up of beams, the push of them in their places, laying them
 regular,
Setting the studs by their tenons in the mortises according as they were
 prepared,
The blows of mallets and hammers, the attitudes of the men, their
 curv'd limbs,
Bending, standing, astride the beams, driving in pins, holding on by
 posts and braces,
The hook'd arm over the plate, the other arm wielding the axe,
The floor-men forcing the planks close to be nail'd,
Their postures bringing their weapons downward on the bearers,
The echoes resounding through the vacant building;
The huge storehouse carried up in the city well under way,
The six framing-men, two in the middle and two at each end, care-
 fully bearing on their shoulders a heavy stick for a cross-beam,
The crowded line of masons with trowels in their right hands rap-
 idly laying the long side-wall, two hundred feet from front to
 rear,
The flexible rise and fall of backs, the continual click of the trowels
 striking the bricks,
The bricks one after another each laid so workmanlike in its place,
 and set with a knock of the trowel-handle,
The piles of materials, the mortar on the mortar-boards, and the steady
 replenishing by the hod-men;
Spar-makers in the spar-yard, the swarming row of well-grown ap-
 prentices,
The swing of their axes on the square-hew'd log shaping it toward the
 shape of a mast,
The brisk short crackle of the steel driven slantingly into the pine,
The butter-color'd chips flying off in great flakes and slivers,
The limber motion of brawny young arms and hips in easy costumes,
The constructor of wharves, bridges, piers, bulk-heads, floats, stays
 against the sea;

The city fireman, the fire that suddenly bursts forth in the close-pack'd
    square,
The arriving engines, the hoarse shouts, the nimble stepping and
    daring,
The strong command through the fire-trumpets, the falling in line, the
    rise and fall of the arms forcing the water,
The slender, spasmic, blue-white jets, the bringing to bear of the hooks
    and ladders and their execution,
The crash and cut away of connecting wood-work, or through floors
    if the fire smoulders under them,
The crowd with their lit faces watching, the glare and dense shadows;
The forger at his forge-furnace and the user of iron after him,
The maker of the axe large and small, and the welder and temperer,
The chooser breathing his breath on the cold steel and trying the edge
    with his thumb,
The one who clean-shapes the handle and sets it firmly in the socket;
The shadowy processions of the portraits of the past users also,
The primal patient mechanics, the architects and engineers,
The far-off Assyrian edifice and Mizra edifice,
The Roman lictors preceding the consuls,
The antique European warrior with his axe in combat,
The uplifted arm, the clatter of blows on the helmeted head,
The death-howl, the limpsy tumbling body, the rush of friend and foe
    thither,
The siege of revolted lieges determin'd for liberty,
The summons to surrender, the battering at castle gates, the truce and
    parley,
The sack of an old city in its time,
The bursting in of mercenaries and bigots tumultuously and disorderly,
Roar, flames, blood, drunkenness, madness,
Goods freely rifled from houses and temples, screams of women in the
    gripe of brigands,
Craft and thievery of camp-followers, men running, old persons
    despairing,
The hell of war, the cruelties of creeds,
The list of all executive deeds and words just or unjust,
The power of personality just or unjust.

431

4

Muscle and pluck forever!
What invigorates life invigorates death,
And the dead advance as much as the living advance,
And the future is no more uncertain than the present,
For the roughness of the earth and of man encloses as much as the
    delicatesse of the earth and of man,
And nothing endures but personal qualities.

What do you think endures?
Do you think a great city endures?
Or a teeming manufacturing state? or a prepared constitution? or the
    best built steamships?
Or hotels of granite and iron? or any chef-d'œuvres of engineering,
    forts, armaments?

Away! these are not to be cherish'd for themselves,
They fill their hour, the dancers dance, the musicians play for them,
The show passes, all does well enough of course,
All does very well till one flash of defiance.

A great city is that which has the greatest men and women,
If it be a few ragged huts it is still the greatest city in the whole world.

5

The place where a great city stands is not the place of stretch'd wharves,
    docks, manufactures, deposits of produce merely,
Nor the place of ceaseless salutes of new-comers or the anchor-lifters
    of the departing,
Nor the place of the tallest and costliest buildings or shops selling goods
    from the rest of the earth,
Nor the place of the best libraries and schools, nor the place where
    money is plentiest,
Nor the place of the most numerous population.

Where the city stands with the brawniest breed of orators and bards,
Where the city stands that is belov'd by these, and loves them in re-
    turn and understands them,

Where no monuments exist to heroes but in the common words and
   deeds,
Where thrift is in its place, and prudence is in its place,
Where the men and women think lightly of the laws,
Where the slave ceases, and the master of slaves ceases,
Where the populace rise at once against the never-ending audacity of
   elected persons,
Where fierce men and women pour forth as the sea to the whistle of
   death pours its sweeping and unript waves,
Where outside authority enters always after the precedence of inside
   authority,
Where the citizen is always the head and ideal, and President, Mayor,
   Governor and what not, are agents for pay,
Where children are taught to be laws to themselves, and to depend
   on themselves,
Where equanimity is illustrated in affairs,
Where speculations on the soul are encouraged,
Where women walk in public processions in the streets the same as
   the men,
Where they enter the public assembly and take places the same as
   the men;
Where the city of the faithfulest friends stands,
Where the city of the cleanliness of the sexes stands,
Where the city of the healthiest fathers stands,
Where the city of the best-bodied mothers stands,
There the great city stands.

6

How beggarly appear arguments before a defiant deed!
How the floridness of the materials of cities shrivels before a man's or
   woman's look!

All waits or goes by default till a strong being appears;
A strong being is the proof of the race and of the ability of the uni-
   verse,
When he or she appears materials are overaw'd,
The dispute on the soul stops,
The old customs and phrases are confronted, turn'd back, or laid away.

What is your money-making now? what can it do now?
What is your respectability now?
What are your theology, tuition, society, traditions, statute-books, now?
Where are your jibes of being now?
Where are your cavils about the soul now?

7

A sterile landscape covers the ore, there is as good as the best for all
    the forbidding appearance,
There is the mine, there are the miners,
The forge-furnace is there, the melt is accomplish'd, the hammers-men
    are at hand with their tongs and hammers,
What always served and always serves is at hand.

Than this nothing has better served, it has served all,
Served the fluent-tongued and subtle-sensed Greek, and long ere the
    Greek,
Served in building the buildings that last longer than any,
Served the Hebrew, the Persian, the most ancient Hindustanee,
Served the mound-raiser on the Mississippi, served those whose relics
    remain in Central America,
Served Albic temples in woods or on plains, with unhewn pillars and
    the druids,
Served the artificial clefts, vast, high, silent, on the snow-cover'd hills
    of Scandinavia,
Served those who time out of mind made on the granite walls rough
    sketches of the sun, moon, stars, ships, ocean waves,
Served the paths of the irruptions of the Goths, served the pastoral
    tribes and nomads,
Served the long distant Kelt, served the hardy pirates of the Baltic,
Served before any of those the venerable and harmless men of Ethiopia,
Served the making of helms for the galleys of pleasure and the making
    of those for war,
Served all great works on land and all great works on the sea,
For the mediæval ages and before the mediæval ages,
Served not the living only then as now, but served the dead.

434

8

I see the European headsman,
He stands mask'd, clothed in red, with huge legs and strong naked arms,
And leans on a ponderous axe.

(Whom have you slaughter'd lately, European headsman?
Whose is that blood upon you so wet and sticky?)

I see the clear sunsets of the martyrs,
I see from the scaffolds the descending ghosts,
Ghosts of dead lords, uncrown'd ladies, impeach'd ministers, rejected
    kings,
Rivals, traitors, poisoners, disgraced chieftains and the rest.

I see those who in any land have died for the good cause,
The seed is spare, nevertheless the crop shall never run out.
(Mind you, O foreign kings, O priests, the crop shall never run out.)

I see the blood wash'd entirely away from the axe,
Both blade and helve are clean,
They spirt no more the blood of European nobles, they clasp no more
    the necks of queens.

I see the headsman withdraw and become useless,
I see the scaffold untrodden and mouldy, I see no longer any axe
    upon it,
I see the mighty and friendly emblem of the power of my own race,
    the newest, largest race.

9

(America! I do not vaunt my love for you,
I have what I have.)

The axe leaps!
The solid forest gives fluid utterances,
They tumble forth, they rise and form,
Hut, tent, landing, survey,

Flail, plough, pick, crowbar, spade,
Shingle, rail, prop, wainscot, jamb, lath, panel, gable,
Citadel, ceiling, saloon, academy, organ, exhibition-house, library,
Cornice, trellis, pilaster, balcony, window, turret, porch,
Hoe, rake, pitchfork, pencil, wagon, staff, saw, jack-plane, mallet,
    wedge, rounce,
Chair, tub, hoop, table, wicket, vane, sash, floor,
Work-box, chest, string'd instrument, boat, frame, and what not,
Capitols of States, and capitol of the nation of States,
Long stately rows in avenues, hospitals for orphans or for the poor
    or sick,
Manhattan steamboats and clippers taking the measure of all seas.

The shapes arise!
Shapes of the using of axes anyhow, and the users and all that neigh-
    bors them,
Cutters down of wood and haulers of it to the Penobscot or Kennebec,
Dwellers in cabins among the Californian mountains or by the little
    lakes, or on the Columbia,
Dwellers south on the banks of the Gila or Rio Grande, friendly gath-
    erings, the characters and fun,
Dwellers along the St. Lawrence, or north in Kanada, or down by the
    Yellowstone, dwellers on coasts and off coasts,
Seal-fishers, whalers, arctic seamen breaking passages through the ice.

The shapes arise!
Shapes of factories, arsenals, foundries, markets,
Shapes of the two-threaded tracks of railroads,
Shapes of the sleepers of bridges, vast framework, girders, arches,
Shapes of the fleets of barges, tows, lake and canal craft, river craft,
Ship-yards and dry-docks along the Eastern and Western seas, and in
    many a bay and by-place,
The live-oak kelsons, the pine planks, the spars, the hackmatack-roots
    for knees,
The ships themselves on their ways, the tiers of scaffolds, the workmen
    busy outside and inside,
The tools lying around, the great auger and little auger, the adze, bolt,
    line, square, gouge, and bead-plane.

10

The shapes arise!
The shape measur'd, saw'd, jack'd, join'd, stain'd,
The coffin-shape for the dead to lie within in his shroud,
The shape got out in posts, in the bedstead posts, in the posts of the
bride's bed,
The shape of the little trough, the shape of the rockers beneath, the
shape of the babe's cradle,
The shape of the floor-planks, the floor-planks for dancers' feet,
The shape of the planks of the family home, the home of the friendly
parents and children,
The shape of the roof of the home of the happy young man and woman,
the roof over the well-married young man and woman,
The roof over the supper joyously cook'd by the chaste wife, and joyously eaten by the chaste husband, content after his day's work.

The shapes arise!
The shape of the prisoner's place in the court-room, and of him or her
seated in the place.
The shape of the liquor-bar lean'd against by the young rum-drinker
and the old rum-drinker,
The shape of the shamed and angry stairs trod by sneaking footsteps,
The shape of the sly settee, and the adulterous unwholesome couple,
The shape of the gambling-board with its devilish winnings and losings,
The shape of the step-ladder for the convicted and sentenced mur-
derer, the murderer with haggard face and pinion'd arms,
The sheriff at hand with his deputies, the silent and white-lipp'd crowd,
the dangling of the rope.

The shapes arise!
Shapes of doors giving many exits and entrances,
The door passing the dissever'd friend flush'd and in haste,
The door that admits good news and bad news,
The door whence the son left home confident and puff'd up,
The door he enter'd again from a long and scandalous absence, dis-
eas'd, broken down, without innocence, without means.

437

11

Her shape arises,
She less guarded than ever, yet more guarded than ever,
The gross and soil'd she moves among do not make her gross and
soil'd,
She knows the thoughts as she passes, nothing is conceal'd from her,
She is none the less considerate or friendly therefor,
She is the best belov'd, it is without exception, she has no reason to fear
and she does not fear,
Oaths, quarrels, hiccupp'd songs, smutty expressions are idle to her as
she passes,
She is silent, she is possess'd of herself, they do not offend her,
She receives them as the laws of Nature receive them, she is strong,
She too is a law of Nature — there is no law stronger than she is.

12

The main shapes arise!
Shapes of Democracy total, result of centuries,
Shapes ever projecting other shapes,
Shapes of turbulent manly cities,
Shapes of the friends and home-givers of the whole earth,
Shapes bracing the earth and braced with the whole earth.

[1856]

TO A FOIL'D EUROPEAN REVOLUTIONAIRE

Courage yet, my brother or my sister!
Keep on — Liberty is to be subserv'd whatever occurs;
That is nothing that is quell'd by one or two failures, or any number
of failures,
Or by the indifference or ingratitude of the people, or by any unfaith-
fulness,
Or the show of the tushes of power, soldiers, cannon, penal statutes.

What we believe in waits latent forever through all the continents,
Invites no one, promises nothing, sits in calmness and light, is positive
    and composed, knows no discouragement,
Waiting patiently, waiting its time.

(Not songs of loyalty alone are these,
But songs of insurrection also,
For I am the sworn poet of every dauntless rebel the world over,
And he going with me leaves peace and routine behind him,
And stakes his life to be lost at any moment.)

The battle rages with many a loud alarm and frequent advance and
    retreat,
The infidel triumphs, or supposes he triumphs,
The prison, scaffold, garrote, handcuffs, iron necklace and lead-balls do
    their work,
The named and unnamed heroes pass to other spheres,
The great speakers and writers are exiled, they lie sick in distant lands,
The cause is asleep, the strongest throats are choked with their own
    blood,
The young men droop their eyelashes toward the ground when they
    meet;
But for all this Liberty has not gone out of the place, nor the infidel
    enter'd into full possession.

When Liberty goes out of a place it is not the first to go, nor the sec-
    ond or third to go,
It waits for all the rest to go, it is the last.

When there are no more memories of heroes and martyrs,
And when all life and all the souls of men and women are discharged
    from any part of the earth,
Then only shall liberty or the idea of liberty be discharged from that
    part of the earth,
And the infidel come into full possession.

Then courage, European revolter, revoltress!
For till all ceases neither must you cease.

I do not know what you are for, (I do not know what I am for myself,
    nor what any thing is for,)
But I will search carefully for it even in being foil'd,
In defeat, poverty, misconception, imprisonment — for they too are
    great.

Did we think victory great?
So it is — but now it seems to me, when it cannot be help'd, that defeat
    is great,
And that death and dismay are great.

[1856]

EUROPE

The 72d and 73d Years of These States

Suddenly out of its stale and drowsy lair, the lair of slaves,
Like lightning it le'pt forth half startled at itself,
Its feet upon the ashes and the rags, its hands tight to the throats of
    kings.

O hope and faith!
O aching close of exiled patriots' lives!
O many a sicken'd heart!
Turn back unto this day and make yourselves afresh.

And you, paid to defile the People — you liars, mark!
Not for numberless agonies, murders, lusts,
For court thieving in its manifold mean forms, worming from his sim-
    plicity the poor man's wages,
For many a promise sworn by royal lips and broken and laugh'd at in
    the breaking,
Then in their power not for all these did the blows strike revenge, or
    the heads of the nobles fall;
The People scorn'd the ferocity of kings.

But the sweetness of mercy 'brew'd bitter destruction, and the fright-
en'd monarchs come back,
Each comes in state with his train, hangman, priest, tax-gatherer,
Soldier, lawyer, lord, jailer, and sycophant.

Yet behind all lowering stealing, lo, a shape,
Vague as the night, draped interminably, head, front and form, in
scarlet folds,
Whose face and eyes none may see,
Out of its robes only this, the red robes lifted by the arm,
One finger crook'd pointed high over the top, like the head of a snake
appears.

Meanwhile corpses lie in new-made graves, bloody corpses of young
men,
The rope of the gibbet hangs heavily, the bullets of princes are flying,
the creatures of power laugh aloud,
And all these things bear fruits, and they are good.

Those corpses of young men,
Those martyrs that hang from the gibbets, those hearts pierc'd by the
gray lead,
Cold and motionless as they seem live elsewhere with unslaughter'd
vitality.

They live in other young men, O kings!
They live in brothers again ready to defy you,
They were purified by death, they were taught and exalted.

Not a grave of the murder'd for freedom but grows seed for freedom,
in its turn to bear seed,
Which the winds carry afar and re-sow, and the rains and the snows
nourish.

Not a disembodied spirit can the weapons of tyrants let loose,
But it stalks invisibly over the earth, whispering, counseling, cau-
tioning.

441

Liberty, let others despair of you — I never despair of you.
Is the house shut? is the master away?
Nevertheless, be ready, be not weary of watching,
He will soon return, his messengers come anon.
[*1855*]

THE PRAIRIE–GRASS DIVIDING

The prairie-grass dividing, its special odor breathing,
I demand of it the spiritual corresponding,
Demand the most copious and close companionship of men,
Demand the blades to rise of words, acts, beings,
Those of the open atmosphere, coarse, sunlit, fresh, nutritious,
Those that go their own gait, erect, stepping with freedom and command, leading not following,
Those with a never-quell'd audacity, those with sweet and lusty flesh clear of taint,
Those that look carelessly in the faces of Presidents and governors, as to say *Who are you?*
Those of earth-born passion, simple, never constrain'd, never obedient,
Those of inland America.
[*1860*]

STARTING FROM PAUMANOK

1

Starting from fish-shaped Paumanok where I was born,
Well-begotten, and rais'd by a perfect mother,
After roaming many lands, lover of populous pavements,
Dweller in Mannahatta my city, or on southern savannas,
Or a soldier camp'd or carrying my knapsack and gun, or a miner in California,

Or rude in my home in Dakota's woods, my diet meat, my drink from
    the spring,
Or withdrawn to muse and meditate in some deep recess,
Far from the clank of crowds intervals passing rapt and happy,
Aware of the fresh free giver the flowing Missouri, aware of mighty
    Niagara,
Aware of the buffalo herds grazing the plains, the hirsute and strong-
    breasted bull,
Of earth, rock, Fifth-month flowers experienced, stars, rain, snow, my
    amaze,
Having studied the mocking-bird's tones and the flight of the mountain-
    hawk,
And heard at dawn the unrivall'd one, the hermit thrush from the
    swamp-cedars,
Solitary, singing in the West, I strike up for a New World.

2

Victory, union, faith, identity, time,
The indissoluble compacts, riches, mystery,
Eternal progress, the kosmos, and the modern reports.

This then is life,
Here is what has come to the surface after so many throes and con-
    vulsions.

How curious! how real!
Underfoot the divine soil, overhead the sun.

See revolving the globe,
The ancestor-continents away group'd together,
The present and future continents north and south, with the isthmus
    between.

See, vast trackless spaces,
As in a dream they change, they swiftly fill,
Countless masses debouch upon them,
They are now cover'd with the foremost people, arts, institutions,
    known.

443

See, projected through time,
For me an audience interminable.

With firm and regular step they wend, they never stop,
Successions of men, Americanos, a hundred millions,
One generation playing its part and passing on,
Another generation playing its part and passing on in its turn,
With faces turn'd sideways or backward towards me to listen,
With eyes retrospective towards me.

3

Americanos! conquerors! marches humanitarian!
Foremost! century marches! Libertad! masses!
For you a programme of chants.

Chants of the prairies,
Chants of the long-running Mississippi, and down to the Mexican sea,
Chants of Ohio, Indiana, Illinois, Iowa, Wisconsin and Minnesota,
Chants going forth from the centre from Kansas, and thence equi-
distant,
Shooting in pulses of fire ceaseless to vivify all.

4

Take my leaves America, take them South and take them North,
Make welcome for them everywhere, for they are your own offspring,
Surround them East and West, for they would surround you,
And you precedents, connect lovingly with them, for they connect
lovingly with you.

I conn'd old times,
I sat studying at the feet of the great masters,
Now if eligible O that the great masters might return and study me.

In the name of these States shall I scorn the antique?
Why these are the children of the antique to justify it.

5

Dead poets, philosophs, priests,
Martyrs, artists, inventors, governments long since,
Language-shapers on other shores,
Nations once powerful, now reduced, withdrawn, or desolate,
I dare not proceed till I respectfully credit what you have left wafted
  hither,
I have perused it, own it is admirable, (moving awhile among it,)
Think nothing can ever be greater, nothing can ever deserve more than
  it deserves,
Regarding it all intently a long while, then dismissing it,
I stand in my place with my own day here.

Here lands female and male,
Here the heir-ship and heiress-ship of the world, here the flame of
  materials,
Here spirituality the translatress, the openly-avow'd,
The ever-tending, the finale of visible forms,
The satisfier, after due long-waiting now advancing,
Yes here comes my mistress the soul.

6

The soul,
Forever and forever — longer than soil is brown and solid — longer
  than water ebbs and flows.
I will make the poems of materials, for I think they are to be the most
  spiritual poems,
And I will make the poems of my body and of mortality,
For I think I shall then supply myself with the poems of my soul and
  of immortality.

I will make a song for these States that no one State may under any
  circumstances be subjected to another State,
And I will make a song that there shall be comity by day and by night
  between all the States, and between any two of them,
And I will make a song for the ears of the President, full of weapons
  with menacing points,

And behind the weapons countless dissatisfied faces;
And a song make I of the One form'd out of all,
The fang'd and glittering One whose head is over all,
Resolute warlike One including and over all,
(However high the head of any else that head is over all.)

I will acknowledge contemporary lands,
I will trail the whole geography of the globe and salute courteously
    every city large and small,
And employments! I will put in my poems that with you is heroism
    upon land and sea,
And I will report all heroism from an American point of view.

I will sing the song of companionship,
I will show what alone must finally compact these,
I believe these are to found their own ideal of manly love, indicating
    it in me,
I will therefore let flame from me the burning fires that were threaten-
    ing to consume me,
I will lift what has too long kept down those smouldering fires,
I will give them complete abandonment,
I will write the evangel-poem of comrades and of love,
For who but I should understand love with all its sorrow and joy?
And who but I should be the poet of comrades?

7

I am the credulous man of qualities, ages, races,
I advance from the people in their own spirit,
Here is what sings unrestricted faith.

Omnes! omnes! let others ignore what they may,
I make the poem of evil also, I commemorate that part also,
I am myself just as much evil as good, and my nation is — and I say
    there is in fact no evil,
(Or if there is I say it is just as important to you, to the land or to me, as
    any thing else.)

I too, following many and follow'd by many, inaugurate a religion, I
    descend into the arena,

(It may be I am destin'd to utter the loudest cries there, the winner's
    pealing shouts,
Who knows? they may rise from me yet, and soar above every thing.)

Each is not for its own sake,
I say the whole earth and all the stars in the sky are for religion's sake.

I say no man has ever yet been half devout enough,
None has ever yet adored or worship'd half enough,
None has begun to think how divine he himself is, and how certain the
    future is.

I say that the real and permanent grandeur of these States must be their
    religion,
Otherwise there is no real and permanent grandeur;
(Nor character nor life worthy the name without religion,
Nor land nor man or woman without religion.)

8

What are you doing, young man?
Are you so earnest, so given up to literature, science, art, amours?
These ostensible realities, politics, points?
Your ambition or business whatever it may be?

It is well — against such I say not a word, I am their poet also,
But behold! such swiftly subside, burnt up for religion's sake,
For not all matter is fuel to heat, impalpable flame, the essential life of
    the earth,
Any more than such are to religion.

9

What do you seek so pensive and silent?
What do you need camerado?
Dear son do you think it is love?

Listen dear son — listen America, daughter or son,
It is a painful thing to love a man or woman to excess, and yet it satis-
    fies, it is great,

But there is something else very great, it makes the whole coincide,
It, magnificent, beyond materials, with continuous hands sweeps and
    provides for all.

10

Know you, solely to drop in the earth the germs of a greater religion,
The following chants each for its kind I sing.

My comrade!
For you to share with me two greatnesses, and a third one rising inclu-
    sive and more resplendent,
The greatness of Love and Democracy, and the greatness of Religion.

Melange mine own, the unseen and the seen,
Mysterious ocean where the streams empty,
Prophetic spirit of materials shifting and flickering around me.
Living beings, identities now doubtless near us in the air that we know
    not of,
Contact daily and hourly that will not release me,
These selecting, these in hints demanded of me.

Not he with a daily kiss onward from childhood kissing me,
Has winded and twisted around me that which holds me to him,
Any more than I am held to the heavens and all the spiritual world,
After what they have done to me, suggesting themes.

O such themes — equalities! O divine average!
Warblings under the sun, usher'd as now, or at noon, or setting,
Strains musical flowing through ages, now reaching hither,
I take to your reckless and composite chords, add to them, and cheer-
    fully pass them forward.

11

As I have walk'd in Alabama my morning walk,
I have seen where the she-bird the mocking-bird sat on her nest in the
    briers hatching her brood.

I have seen the he-bird also,
I have paus'd to hear him near at hand inflating his throat and joyfully
    singing.

And while I paus'd it came to me that what he really sang for was not
    there only,
Nor for his mate nor himself only, nor all sent back by the echoes,
But subtle, clandestine, away beyond,
A charge transmitted and gift occult for those being born.

12

Democracy! near at hand to you a throat is now inflating itself and joy-
    fully singing.

Ma femme! for the brood beyond us and of us,
For those who belong here and those to come,
I exultant to be ready for them will now shake out carols stronger and
    haughtier than have ever yet been heard upon earth.
I will make the songs of passion to give them their way,
And your songs outlaw'd offenders, for I scan you with kindred eyes,
    and carry you with me the same as any.
I will make the true poem of riches,
To earn for the body and the mind whatever adheres and goes forward
    and is not dropt by death;
I will effuse egotism and show it underlying all, and I will be the bard
    of personality,
And I will show of male and female that either is but the equal of the
    other,
And sexual organs and acts! do you concentrate in me, for I am deter-
    min'd to tell you with courageous clear voice to prove you illus-
    trious,
And I will show that there is no imperfection in the present, and can be
    none in the future,
And I will show that whatever happens to anybody it may be turn'd to
    beautiful results,
And I will show that nothing can happen more beautiful than death,
And I will thread a thread through my poems that time and events are
    compact,

449

And that all the things of the universe are perfect miracles, each as profound as any.

I will not make poems with reference to parts,
But I will make poems, songs, thoughts, with reference to ensemble,
And I will not sing with reference to a day, but with reference to all days,
And I will not make a poem nor the least part of a poem but has reference to the soul,
Because having look'd at the objects of the universe, I find there is no one nor any particle of one but has reference to the soul.

13

Was somebody asking to see the soul?
See, your own shape and countenance, persons, substances, beasts, the trees, the running rivers, the rocks and sands.

All hold spiritual joys and afterwards loosen them;
How can the real body ever die and be buried?

Of your real body and any man's or woman's real body,
Item for item it will elude the hands of the corpse-cleaners and pass to fitting spheres,
Carrying what has accrued to it from the moment of birth to the moment of death.

Not the types set up by the printer return their impression, the meaning, the main concern,
Any more than a man's substance and life or a woman's substance and life return in the body and the soul,
Indifferently before death and after death.

Behold, the body includes and is the meaning, the main concern, and includes and is the soul;
Whoever you are, how superb and how divine is your body, or any part of it!

14

Whoever you are, to you endless announcements!

Daughter of the lands did you wait for your poet?
Did you wait for one with a flowing mouth and indicative hand?
Toward the male of the States, and toward the female of the States,
Exulting words, words to Democracy's lands.

Interlink'd, food-yielding lands!
Land of coal and iron! land of gold! land of cotton, sugar, rice!
Land of wheat, beef, pork! land of wool and hemp! land of the apple
    and the grape!
Land of the pastoral plains, the grass-fields of the world! land of those
    sweet-air'd interminable plateaus!
Land of the herd, the garden, the healthy house of adobie!
Lands where the north-west Columbia winds, and where the south-
    west Colorado winds!
Land of the eastern Chesapeake! land of the Delaware!
Land of Ontario, Erie, Huron, Michigan!
Land of the Old Thirteen! Massachusetts land! land of Vermont and
    Connecticut!
Land of the ocean shores! land of sierras and peaks!
Land of boatmen and sailors! fishermen's land!
Inextricable lands! the clutch'd together! the passionate ones!
The side by side! the elder and younger brothers! the bony-limb'd!
The great women's land! the feminine! the experienced sisters and the
    inexperienced sisters!
Far breath'd land! Arctic braced! Mexican breez'd! the diverse! the
    compact!
The Pennsylvanian! the Virginian! the double Carolinian!
O all and each well-loved by me! my intrepid nations! O I at any rate
    include you all with perfect love!
I cannot be discharged from you! not from one any sooner than another!
O death! O for all that, I am yet of you unseen this hour with irrepres-
    sible love,
Walking New England, a friend, a traveler,
Splashing my bare feet in the edge of the summer ripples on Pau-
    manok's sands,

451

Crossing the prairies, dwelling again in Chicago, dwelling in every
    town,
Observing shows, births, improvements, structures, arts,
Listening to orators and oratresses in public halls,
Of and through the States as during life, each man and woman my
    neighbor,
The Louisianian, the Georgian, as near to me, and I as near to him and
    her,
The Mississippian and Arkansian yet with me, and I yet with any of
    them,
Yet upon the plains west of the spinal river, yet in my house of adobie,
Yet returning eastward, yet in the Seaside State or in Maryland,
Yet Kanadian cheerily braving the winter, the snow and ice welcome
    to me,
Yet a true son either of Maine or of the Granite State, or the Narragan-
    sett Bay State, or the Empire State,
Yet sailing to other shores to annex the same, yet welcoming every new
    brother,
Hereby applying these leaves to the new ones from the hour they unite
    with the old ones,
Coming among the new ones myself to be their companion and equal,
    coming personally to you now,
Enjoining you to acts, characters, spectacles, with me.

15

With me with firm holding, yet haste, haste on.

For your life adhere to me,
(I may have to be persuaded many times before I consent to give my-
    self really to you, but what of that?
Must not Nature be persuaded many times?)

No dainty dolce affettuoso I,
Bearded, sun-burnt, gray-neck'd, forbidding, I have arrived,
To be wrestled with as I pass for the solid prizes of the universe,
For such I afford whoever can persevere to win them.

16

On my way a moment I pause,
Here for you! and here for America!
Still the present I raise aloft, still the future of the States I harbinge
 glad and sublime,
And for the past I pronounce what the air holds of the red aborigines.

The red aborigines,
Leaving natural breaths, sounds of rain and winds, calls as of birds and
 animals in the woods, syllabled, to us for names,
Okonee, Koosa, Ottawa, Monongahela, Sauk, Natchez, Chattahoochee,
 Kaqueta, Oronoco,
Wabash, Miami, Saginaw, Chippewa, Oshkosh, Walla-Walla,
Leaving such to the States they melt, they depart, charging the water
 and the land with names.

17

Expanding and swift, henceforth,
Elements, breeds, adjustments, turbulent, quick and audacious,
A world primal again, vistas of glory incessant and branching,
A new race dominating previous ones and grander far, with new con-
 tests,
New politics, new literatures and religions, new inventions and arts.

These, my voice announcing — I will sleep no more but arise,
You oceans that have been calm within me! how I feel you, fathomless,
 stirring, preparing unprecedented waves and storms.

18

See, steamers steaming through my poems,
See, in my poems immigrants continually coming and landing,
See, in arriere, the wigwam, the trail, the hunter's hut, the flatboat, the
 maize-leaf, the claim, the rude fence, and the backwoods village,
See, on the one side the Western Sea and on the other the Eastern Sea,
 how they advance and retreat upon my poems as upon their own
 shores,

See, pastures and forests in my poems — see, animals wild and tame —
 see, beyond the Kaw, countless herds of buffalo feeding on short
 curly grass,
See, in my poems, cities, solid, vast, inland, with paved streets, with iron
 and stone edifices, ceaseless vehicles, and commerce,
See, the many-cylinder'd steam printing-press — see, the electric telegraph stretching across the continent,
See, through Atlantica's depths pulses American Europe reaching,
 pulses of Europe duly return'd,
See, the strong and quick locomotive as it departs, panting, blowing
 the steam-whistle,
See, ploughmen ploughing farms — see, miners digging mines — see, the
 numberless factories,
See, mechanics busy at their benches with tools — see from among
 them superior judges, philosophs, Presidents, emerge drest in working dresses,
See, lounging through the shops and fields of the States, me well-be-
 lov'd, close-held by day and night,
Hear the loud echoes of my songs there — read the hints come at last.

19

O camerado close! O you and me at last, and us two only.
O a word to clear one's path ahead endlessly!
O something ecstatic and undemonstrable! O music wild!
O now I triumph — and you shall also;
O hand in hand — O wholesome pleasure — O one more desirer and
 lover!
O to haste firm holding — to haste, haste on with me.
[*1860*]

FOR YOU O DEMOCRACY

Come, I will make the continent indissoluble,
I will make the most splendid race the sun ever shone upon,
I will make divine magnetic lands,

With the love of comrades,
　　With the life-long love of comrades.

I will paint companionship thick as trees along all the rivers of America,
　　and along the shores of the great lakes, and all over the prairies,
I will make inseparable cities with their arms about each other's necks,
　　By the love of comrades,
　　By the manly love of comrades.

For you these from me, O Democracy, to serve you ma femme!
For you, for you I am trilling these songs.
[*1860*]

from

DEMOCRATIC VISTAS

The People! Like our huge earth itself, which, to ordinary scansion, is
full of vulgar contradictions and offence, man, viewed in the lump,
displeases, and is a constant puzzle and affront to the merely educated
classes. The rare, cosmical, artist-mind, lit with the Infinite, alone confronts his manifold and oceanic qualities — but taste, intelligence and
culture (so-called) have been against the masses, and remain so.
There is plenty of glamour about the most damnable crimes and hog-
gish meannesses, special and general, of the feudal and dynastic world
over there, with its *personnel* of lords and queens and courts, so well-
dress'd and so handsome. But the People are ungrammatical, untidy,
and their sins gaunt and ill-bred.

Literature, strictly consider'd, has never recognized the People, and,
whatever may be said, does not to-day. Speaking generally, the tendencies of literature, as hitherto pursued, have been to make mostly
critical and querulous men. It seems as if, so far, there were some natural repugnance between a literary and professional life, and the rude
rank spirit of the democracies. There is, in later literature, a treatment
of benevolence, a charity business, rife enough it is true; but I know
nothing more rare, even in this country, than a fit scientific estimate and
reverent appreciation of the People — of their measureless wealth of

455

latent power and capacity, their vast, artistic contrasts of lights and shades — with, in America, their entire reliability in emergencies, and a certain breadth of historic grandeur, of peace or war, far surpassing all the vaunted samples of book-heroes, or any *haut ton* coteries, in all the records of the world.

The movements of the late secession war, and their results, to any sense that studies well and comprehends them, show that popular democracy, whatever its faults and dangers, practically justifies itself beyond the proudest claims and wildest hopes of its enthusiasts. Probably no future age can know, but I well know, how the gist of this fiercest and most resolute of the world's war-like contentions resided exclusively in the unnamed, unknown rank and file; and how the brunt of its labor of death was, to all essential purposes, volunteer'd. The People, of their own choice, fighting, dying for their own idea, insolently attack'd by the secession-slave-power, and its very existence imperil'd. Descending to detail, entering any of the armies, and mixing with the private soldiers, we see and have seen august spectacles. We have seen the alacrity with which the American-born populace, the peaceablest and most good-natured race in the world, and the most personally independent and intelligent, and the least fitted to submit to the irksomeness and exasperation of regimental discipline, sprang, at the first tap of the drum, to arms — not for gain, nor even glory, nor to repel invasion — but for an emblem, a mere abstraction — for the life, *the safety of the flag.* We have seen the unequal'd docility and obedience of these soldiers. We have seen them tried long and long by hopelessness, mismanagement, and by defeat; have seen the incredible slaughter toward or through which the armies (as at first Fredericksburg, and afterward at the Wilderness,) still unhesitatingly obey'd orders to advance. We have seen them in trench, or crouching behind breastwork, or tramping in deep mud, or amid pouring rain or thick-falling snow, or under forced marches in hottest summer (as on the road to get to Gettysburg) — vast suffocating swarms, divisions, corps, with every single man so grimed and black with sweat and dust, his own mother would not have known him — his clothes all dirty, stain'd and torn, with sour, accumulated sweat for perfume — many a comrade, perhaps a brother, sun-struck, staggering out, dying, by the roadside, of exhaustion — yet the great bulk bearing steadily on, cheery enough, hollow-bellied from hunger, but sinewy with unconquerable resolution.

We have seen this race proved by wholesale, by drearier, yet more fearful tests — the wound, the amputation, the shatter'd face or limb, the slow hot fever, long impatient anchorage in bed, and all the forms of maiming, operation and disease. Alas! America have we seen, though only in her early youth, already to hospital brought. There have we watch'd these soldiers, many of them only boys in years — mark'd their decorum, their religious nature and fortitude, and their sweet affection. Wholesale, truly. For at the front, and through the camps, in countless tents, stood the regimental, brigade and division hospitals; while everywhere amid the land, in or near cities, rose clusters of huge, white-wash'd, crowded, one-story wooden barracks; and there ruled agony with bitter scourge, yet seldom brought a cry; and there stalk'd death by day and night along the narrow aisles between the rows of cots, or by the blankets on the ground, and touch'd lightly many a poor sufferer, often with blessed, welcome touch.

I know not whether I shall be understood, but I realize that it is finally from what I learn'd personally mixing in such scenes that I am now penning these pages. One night in the gloomiest period of the war, in the Patent-office hospital in Washington city, as I stood by the bedside of a Pennsylvania soldier, who lay, conscious of quick approaching death, yet perfectly calm, and with noble, spiritual manner, the veteran surgeon, turning aside, said to me, that though he had witness'd many, many deaths of soldiers, and had been a worker at Bull Run, Antietam, Fredericksburg, etc., he had not seen yet the first case of man or boy that met the approach of dissolution with cowardly qualms or terror. My own observation fully bears out the remark.

What have we here, if not, towering above all talk and argument, the plentifully-supplied, last-needed proof of democracy, in its personalities? Curiously enough, too, the proof of this point comes, I should say, every bit as much from the south, as from the north. Although I have spoken only of the latter, yet I deliberately include all. Grand, common stock! to me the accomplish'd and convincing growth, prophetic of the future; proof undeniable to sharpest sense, of perfect beauty, tenderness and pluck, that never feudal lord, nor Greek, nor Roman breed, yet rival'd. Let no tongue ever speak in disparagement of the American races, north or south, to one who has been through the war in the great army hospitals.

Meantime, general humanity (for to that we return, as, for our purposes, what it really is, to bear in mind,) has always, in every department, been full of perverse maleficence, and is so yet. In downcast hours the soul thinks it always will be — but soon recovers from such sickly moods. I myself see clearly enough the crude, defective streaks in all the strata of the common people; the specimens and vast collections of the ignorant, the credulous, the unfit and uncouth, the incapable, and the very low and poor. The eminent person just mention'd sneeringly asks whether we expect to elevate and improve a nation's politics by absorbing such morbid collections and qualities therein. The point is a formidable one, and there will doubtless always be numbers of solid and reflective citizens who will never get over it. Our answer is general, and is involved in the scope and letter of this essay. We believe the ulterior object of political and all other government (having, of course, provided for the police, the safety of life, property, and for the basic statute and common law, and their administration, always first in order,) to be among the rest, not merely to rule, to repress disorder, etc., but to develop, to open up to cultivation, to encourage the possibilities of all beneficent and manly outcroppage, and of that aspiration for independence, and the pride and self-respect latent in all characters. (Or, if there be exceptions, we cannot, fixing our eyes on them alone, make theirs the rule for all.)

I say the mission of government, henceforth, in civilized lands, is not repression alone, and not authority alone, not even of law, nor by that favorite standard of the eminent writer, the rule of the best men, the born heroes and captains of the race, (as if such ever, or one time out of a hundred, get into the big places, elective or dynastic) — but higher than the highest arbitrary rule, to train communities through all their grades, beginning with individuals and ending there again, to rule themselves. What Christ appear'd for in the moral-spiritual field for human-kind, namely, that in respect to the absolute soul, there is in the possession of such by each single individual, something so transcendent, so incapable of gradations, (like life,) that, to that extent, it places all beings on a common level, utterly regardless of the distinctions of intellect, virtue, station, or any height or lowliness whatever — is tallied in like manner, in this other field, by democracy's rule that men, the nation, as a common aggregate of living identities, affording in each a separate and complete subject for freedom, worldly thrift and happiness, and for a fair chance for growth, and for protection in citizenship, etc., must, to the political extent of the suffrage or vote, if no further, be placed, in each and in the whole, on one broad, primary, universal, common platform.

The purpose is not altogether direct; perhaps it is more indirect. For it is not that democracy is of exhaustive account, in itself. Perhaps, indeed, it is (like Nature) of no account in itself. It is that, as we see, it is the best, perhaps only, fit and full means, formulater, general caller-forth, trainer, for the million, not for grand material personalities only, but for immortal souls. To be a voter with the rest is not so much; and this, like every institute, will have its imperfections. But to become an enfranchised man, and now, impediments removed, to stand and start without humiliation, and equal with the rest; to commence, or have the road clear'd to commence, the grand experiment of development, whose end (perhaps requiring several generations) may be the forming of a full-grown man or woman — that *is* something. . . .

When I pass to and fro, different latitudes, different seasons, beholding the crowds of the great cities, New York, Boston, Philadelphia, Cincinnati, Chicago, St. Louis, San Francisco, New Orleans, Baltimore — when I mix with these interminable swarms of alert, turbulent, good-natured, independent citizens, mechanics, clerks, young persons — at the idea of this mass of men, so fresh and free, so loving and so proud, a singular awe falls upon me. I feel, with dejection and amazement, that among our geniuses and talented writers or speakers, few or none have yet really spoken to this people, created a single image-making work for them, or absorb'd the central spirit and the idiosyncrasies which are theirs — and which, thus, in highest ranges, so far remain entirely uncelebrated, unexpress'd.

Dominion strong is the body's; dominion stronger is the mind's. What has fill'd, and fills to-day our intellect, our fancy, furnishing the standards therein, is yet foreign. The great poems, Shakspere included, are poisonous to the idea of the pride and dignity of the common people, the life-blood of democracy. The models of our literature, as we get it from other lands, ultra-marine, have had their birth in courts, and bask'd and grown in castle sunshine; all smells of princes' favors. Of workers of a certain sort, we have, indeed, plenty, contributing after their kind; many elegant, many learn'd, all complacent. But touch'd by the national test, or tried by the standards of democratic personality, they wither to ashes. I say I have not seen a single writer, artist, lecturer, or what-not, that has confronted the voiceless but ever erect and active, pervading, underlying will and typic aspiration of the land, in a spirit kindred to itself. Do you call those genteel little creatures American poets? Do you term that perpetual, pistareen, paste-pot work, American art, American drama, taste, verse? I think I hear, echoed as from some mountain-top afar in the west, the scornful laugh of the Genius of these States.

Democracry, in silence, biding its time, ponders its own ideals, not of literature and art only — not of men only, but of women. The idea of the women of America, (extricated from this daze, this fossil and un-healthy air which hangs about the word *lady,*) develop'd, raised to be-come the robust equals, workers, and, it may be, even practical and political deciders with the men — greater than man, we may admit, through their divine maternity, always their towering, emblematical attribute — but great, at any rate, as man, in all departments; or, rather, capable of being so, soon as they realize it, and can bring themselves to give up toys and fictions, and launch forth, as men do, amid real, in-dependent, stormy life.

Then, as towards our thought's finale, (and, in that, overarching the true scholar's lesson,) we have to say there can be no complete or epical presentation of democracy in the aggregate, or anything like it, at this day, because its doctrines will only be effectually incarnated in any one branch, when, in all, their spirit is at the root and centre. Far, far, indeed, stretch, in distance, our Vistas! How much is still to be disentangled, freed! How long it takes to make this American world see that it is, in itself, the final authority and reliance!

Did you, too, O friend, suppose democracy was only for elections, for politics, and for a party name? I say democracy is only of use there that it may pass on and come to its flower and fruits in manners, in the highest forms of interaction between men, and their beliefs — in re-ligion, literature, colleges, and schools — democracy in all public and private life, and in the army and navy.[1] I have intimated that, as a paramount scheme, it has yet few or no full realizers and believers. I do not see, either, that it owes any serious thanks to noted propagan-

---

[1] The whole present system of the officering and personnel of the army and navy of these States, and the spirit and letter of their trebly-aristocratic rules and regulations, is a monstrous exotic, a nuisance and revolt, and belong here just as much as orders of nobility, or the Pope's council of cardinals. I say if the present theory of our army and navy is sensible and true, then the rest of America is an unmitigated fraud.

dists or champions, or has been essentially help'd, though often harm'd, by them. It has been and is carried on by all the moral forces, and by trade, finance, machinery, intercommunications, and, in fact, by all the developments of history, and can no more be stopp'd than the tides, or the earth in its orbit. Doubtless, also, it resides, crude and latent, well down in the hearts of the fair average of the American-born people, mainly in the agricultural regions. But it is not yet, there or anywhere, the fully-receiv'd, the fervid, the absolute faith.

I submit, therefore, that the fruition of democracy, on aught like a grand scale, resides altogether in the future. As, under any profound and comprehensive view of the gorgeous-composite feudal world, we see in it, through the long ages and cycles of ages, the results of a deep, integral, human and divine principle, or fountain, from which issued laws, ecclesia, manners, institutes, costumes, personalities, poems, (hitherto unequall'd,) faithfully partaking of their source, and indeed only arising either to betoken it, or to furnish parts of that varied-flowing display, whose centre was one and absolute — so, long ages hence, shall the due historian or critic make at least an equal retrospect, an equal history for the democratic principle. It too must be adorn'd, credited with its results — then, when it, with imperial power, through amplest time, has dominated mankind — has been the source and test of all the moral, esthetic, social, political, and religious expressions and institutes of the civilized world — has begotten them in spirit and in form, and has carried them to its own unprecedented heights — has had (it is possible) monastics and ascetics, more numerous, more devout than the monks and priests of all previous creeds — has sway'd the ages with a breadth and rectitude tallying Nature's own — has fashion'd, systematized, and triumphantly finish'd and carried out, in its own interest, and with unparallel'd success, a new earth and a new man.

Thus we presume to write, as it were, upon things that exist not, and travel by maps yet unmade, and a blank. But the throes of birth are upon us; and we have something of this advantage in seasons of strong formations, doubts, suspense — for then the afflatus of such themes haply may fall upon us, more or less; and then, hot from surrounding war and revolution, our speech, though without polish'd coherence, and a failure by the standard called criticism, comes forth, real at least as the lightnings.

And may-be we, these days, have, too, our own reward — (for there are yet some, in all lands, worthy to be so encouraged). Though not for us the joy of entering at the last the conquer'd city — not ours the chance ever to see with our own eyes the peerless power and splendid *éclat* of the democratic principle, arriv'd at meridian, filling the world with effulgence and majesty far beyond those of past history's kings, or all dynastic sway — there is yet, to whoever is eligible among us, the prophetic vision, the joy of being toss'd in the brave turmoil of these times — the promulgation and the path, obedient, lowly reverent to the voice, the gesture of the god, or holy ghost, which others see not, hear not — with the proud consciousness that amid whatever clouds, seductions, or heart-wearying postponements, we have never deserted, never despair'd, never abandon'd the faith.

[*1871*]

DAVID R. LOCKE

[1833–1888]

UNDER the pseudonym of Petroleum V. Nasby, Locke was an exceedingly popular and influential satirist during and just after the Civil War. Locke's pieces were cast in the form of letters signed by Nasby, who was supposed to be a country preacher and politician of the Copperhead persuasion. That is to say, he was a Northern Democrat, sympathetic to the South, pro-slavery, and actively opposed to Lincoln's prosecution of the war. He is portrayed as a corrupt and cowardly man, a drunkard and a liar, and barely literate. His letters were written in atrocious style, with practically every word fantastically mis-spelled. This, by the way, was a favorite comic device in the journalistic humor of the time, having been practiced by Artemus Ward and other " primitive " humorists. Locke's pieces were extremely effective, in spite of their exaggerations. They reveal a shrewd mind and a knife-edged wit in their insight into the motives of cheap politicians and professional Negro-baiters. It was not for nothing that Lincoln admired and praised them.

Locke, who was born near Binghamton, New York, grew up in the newspaper business. At ten he was apprenticed to a local newspaper, became a printer and later an editor. At nineteen he founded a newspaper in a town in Ohio, and when he quit that enterprise he went to other towns in the same state. He published his Nasby papers from 1861 to 1887, at first in country papers and afterwards in the *Toledo Blade,* of which he was the editor and at last the chief owner.

from

THE STRUGGLES OF PETROLEUM V. NASBY

NEGRO EMIGRATION

Wingert's Corners, Ohio, April the 2d, 1862

There is now fifteen niggers, men, wimin, and childern, or ruther, mail, femail, and yung, in Wingert's Corners, and yisterday another arrove. I am bekomin alarmed, for, ef they inkreese at this rate, in suthin over sixty years they'll hev a majority in the town, and may, ef they git mean enuff, tyrannize over us, even ez we air tyrannizin over them. The danger is imminent! Alreddy our poor white inhabitants is out uv employment to make room for that nigger; even now our shops and factories is full uv that nigger, to the great detriment uv a white inhabitant who hez a family to support, and our poor-house and jail is full uv him.

I implore the peeple to wake up. Let us hold a mass meetin to take this subgik into considerashen, and, that biznis may be expeditid, I perpose the adopshen uv a series uv preamble and resolooshens, suthin like the follerin, to-wit:

WAREAS, We vew with alarm the ackshun uv the President uv the U. S., in recommendin the immejit emansipashun uv the slaves uv our misgidid Suthern brethrin, and his evident intenshun uv kolonizin on em in the North, and the heft on em in Wingert's Corners; and

WAREAS, In the event uv this imigrashun, our fellow-townsman, Abslum Kitt, and others, whose families depend upon their labor for support, wood be throde out of employment; and

WAREAS, When yoo giv a man a hoss, yoo air obleeged to also make him a present uv a silver-platid harnis and a $650 buggy, so ef we let the nigger live here, we are in dooty bound to marry him off-hand; and

WAREAS, When this stait uv affares arrives our kentry will be no fit place for men uv educashen and refinement; and

---

The great bugbear of the ignorant Democrats of the North, especially in the rural districts, was the fear of negro emigration, and consequently negro equality, and amalgamation. Antiquated females in Democratic processions carried banners bearing the touching appeal: " Fathers, save us from Nigger Equality! " " White husbands, or none!! " Amalgamation, negro equality, negro competition, were the dire array of calamities which were to befall the laboring men of the North, in case Republican measures and principles should prevail. With the predictions of the woes coming to Northern farmers and mechanics the campaign papers of the Democracy were filled.

WAREAS, Any man hevin the intellek uv a brass-mounted jackass kin easily see that the two races want never intendid to live together; and

WAREAS, Bein in the magority, we kin do as we please, and ez the nigger aint no vote he kant help hisself; therefore be it

Resolved, That the crude, undeodorizd Afrikin is a disgustin obgik.

Resolved, That this Convenshun, when it hez its feet washed, smells sweeter than the Afrikin in his normal condishun, and is therefore his sooperior.

Resolved, That the niggers be druv out uv Wingert's Corners, and that sich property ez they may hev accumulatid be confiscatid, and the proceeds applide to the follerin purposes, to-wit:

Payment uv the bills of the last Dimekratik Centrel Committee; payment uv the disintrestid patriots ez got up this meetin; the balance to remane in my hands.

Resolved, That the Ablishnists who oppose these resolushens all want to marry a nigger.

Resolved, That Dr. Petts, in rentin a part uv his bildin to niggers, hez struck a blow at the very foundashens uv sosiety.

Fellow-whites, arouse! The enemy is onto us! Our harths is in danger! When we hev a nigger for judge — niggers for teachers — niggers in pulpits — when niggers rool and controle society, then will yoo remember this warnin!

Arouse to wunst! Rally agin Conway! Rally agin Sweet. Rally agin Hegler! Rally agin Hegler's family! Rally agin the porter at the Reed House! Rally agin the cook at the Crook House! Rally agin the nigger widder in Vance's Addishun! Rally agin Missis Umstid! Rally agin Missis Umstid's childern by her first husband! Rally agin Missis Umstid's childern by her sekkund husband! Rally agin all the rest uv Missis Umstid's childern! Rally agin the nigger that cum yisterday! Rally agin the saddle-culurd girl that yoost to be hear! Ameriky for white men!

Petroleum V. Nasby

ORDAINS A MISSIONARY

Church uv the Noo Dispensashun ⎫
March the 17th, 1864 ⎭

Last Sunday we hed an improvin season. Robert Tooms Punt, who hez bin a studyin for the ministry with me for the past four weeks, wuz licenst and ordained. He is a youth uv much promise. He votid twict for Bookannon, and only 18 yeres old, swarin his votes in with a coolnis and ease that eggscitid the admirashen uv the patriarks at the biznis. I kin safely say that he hez whaled more Ablishnists, bustid more Methodist Brethrin, and other hetrodox Churches, than any Dimekrat uv his age in the Stait. He hez a brilliant future.

After the usual questions wuz put to him, and satisfactorily ansered, the congregashen wuz dismist, and, in the presence uv the elders and deacons alone, I delivered the follerin charge.

BROTHER: Hevin bin reglerly ordained, it only remains for me to give yoo a word uv council. Yoo are a goin into the apossel biznis at a rather unfavorable time. Man, wich is born uv woman, hez trouble for his inheritance. I've hed so much uv it that, ef I hed it to do over agin, I woodent be born at all.

The politikle heavins is orecast with portenshus clouds. The litenin uv wrath is leapin frum wun to another, whilst the thunder, wich wuz wunst at a distance, now roars angrily in our ears. The ole ship Dimokrasy is tossin madly onto the wild waves, with nary a sale set, her seams open, the water (a furrin element to her insides) a rushin in. The stiddiest part uv her crew hev seezed the boats and abandoned her, and the rest uv em are a fitin for the helm.

In the mean time the old ship is dashin past the haven uv Success, and is headin strate for the rocks uv Destrucshen. To yoo is intrusted a part uv the work uv savin her. Let me entreat yoo —

1. Avoid the soljers. With them yoo hev nothin in common. They will despitefully use yoo. Wunst a party uv em made me drink a pint uv water and take the oath uv allegianse, wich outrages wuz follered by conjestion uv the bowils and inflamashen uv the brain.

2. Alluz preech agin the nigger. It's soothin to a ginooine, constooshnel, suthern-rites Dimekrat to be constantly told that ther is a race uv men meaner than he is. Besides, it's safe — the nigger hez no vote. Ef he hed, we might vary.

3. Alluz hev a marter. The stait-rites Dimokrasy alluz sympathize with a man that's in basteels for sympathisin with the South, for nun uv em know how soon their turn may come.

4. Preech agin amalgamashen at leest four Sundays per month. A man uv straw that yoo set up yerself is the easiest knockt down, pertikelerly if yoo set him up with a view uv knockin uv him down.

5. Alluz diloot yoor wisky for new converts. It takes much to convert a Ablishnist, and ef yoo use the pure artikle, it wood kill a ordnary

constooshn afore he'd hev time to vote, wich wood be aggervatin.

6. Sarch the skripters faithfully for sich passages ez "Cussid be Kanan," "Servance, obey yoor masters," and sich.

7. Learn to read, or at least git the shape uv the letters so fixt in yoor mind that when yoo quote from a book or noosepaper, you will hold it rite side up. Eddicashen hez bin a grate help to me.

8. Learn to spell and pronounce Missenegenegenashun. It's a good word,

The great leadin ijees uv our sect, wich it is yoor dooty to inculcate, is these: The nigger's a ape, Linkin a goriller, Jeff Davis a chrischen gentleman, the rebellion a struggle for rites, the soljer a bluddy tool, Benbutler a beast, et settry. Yoo are never to bleeve in Fedral victorys, but must alluz credit Confedrit successes. I woodent advise yoo to let yoor faith in the Confedrisy go so fur as to take their skrip on yer salary, neither wood I burn greenbax. I hev dun. Go, my brother. Let yer polar star be Dimokrasy, yer rallyin cry, "The Yoonyun ez it wuz — the Constooshn ez it is," wich is latitoodinus; fite the good fite, and the day will cum wen yoo kin lay orf yer armor, and with "P. M." after yoor name, enjoy the repose that alluz follows well-directid and viggerus effort.

Brother Punt startid to-day for Suthern Illinoy, wher he hez a congregashen.

> *Petroleum V. Nasby*
> *Paster uv sed Church, in charge*

LAYS DOWN A PLATFORM

> Saint's Rest (*wich is in the Stait*
> *uv Noo Jersey*)
> *June the 23d, 1865*

These is the dark days uv the Dimokrasy. The misforchoons that befell our armies in front uv Richmond, the fall uv our capital, follered by the surrender uv our armies to Grant and Sherman, hez hurt us. Our leaders are either pinin in loathsome dunguns, incarseratid by the hevin-defyin, man-destroyin, tyrannical edix uv our late lamented President, or are baskin in the free air uv Italy and Canady. We hev

---

The Democracy of the North brought the negro more prominently forward than ever at the close of the war. The certainty that the ballot would very soon be given to that race, inflamed the lower strata of that party terribly, which feeling its leading men made good use of.

no way uv keepin our voters together. Opposin the war won't do no good, for before the next elecshun the heft uv our voters will hev diskiverd that the war is over. The fear uv drafts may do suthin in some parts uv Pennsylvany and Suthern Illinoy, for sum time yit, but that can't be depended on.

But we hev wun resource for a ishoo — ther will alluz be a Dimokrasy so long as ther's a nigger.

Ther is a uncompromisin dislike to the nigger in the mind uv a ginooine Dimekrat. The Spanish bull-fighter, when he wants to inflame the bull to extra cavortin, waves a red flag afore him. Wen yoo desire a Dimekrat to froth at the mouth, yoo will find a black face will anser the purpose. Therefore, the nigger is, to-day, our best and only holt. Let us use him.

For the guidance uv the faithful, I shel lay down a few plain rools to be observed, in order to make the most uv the capital we hev: —

1. Alluz assert that the nigger will never be able to take care uv hisself, but will alluz be a public burden. He may, possibly, give us the lie by goin to work. In sich a emergency, the dooty uv every Dimekrat is plane. He must not be allowed to work. Associashens must be organized, pledged to neither give him employment, to work with him, to work for any one who will give him work, or patronize any wun who duz. (I wood sejest that sich uv us ez hev bin forchoonit enuff to git credit, pay a trifle on account, so ez to make our patronage worth suthin.) This course, rigidly and persistently follerd, will drive the best uv em to stealin, und the balance to the poor-houses, provin wat we hev alluz claimed, that they are a idle and vishus race. Think, my brethren, wat a inspirin effeck our poor-houses and jails full uv niggers wood hev on the people! My sole expands ez I contemplate the deliteful vision.

2. Likewise assert that the nigger will come North, and take all the good places, throwin all our skilled mechanics out uv work by underbiddin uv em. This mite be open to two objecshuns, to-wit: It crosses slitely rool the 1, and white men mite say, ef there's jist enuff labor for wat's here, why not perhibit furriners frum comin? I anser: It's the biznis uv the voter to reconsile the contradicshun — he may beleeve either or both. Ez to the second objeckshun, wher is the Dimekrat who coodent be underbid, and stand it even to starvashen, ef the underbiddin wuz dun by a man uv the proud Caukashen race? and wher is the Dimekrat so lost to manhood ez not to drink blood, ef the same underbiddin is dun by a nigger? The starvin for work ain't the question

— it's the color uv the cause uv the starvashen that makes the difference.

Nigger equality may be worked agin to advantage. All men, without distincshun uv sex, are fond uv flatrin theirselves that somebody's lower down in the scale uv humanity than they is. Ef 'twan't for niggers, what wood the Dimokrasy do for sumbody to look down upon? It's also shoor to enlist wun style uv wimmen on our side. In times gone by, I've notist gushin virgins uv forty-five, full sixteen hands high and tough ez wire, holdin aloft banners onto wich wuz inscribd — " Save us from Nigger Equality." Yoo see it soothed em to hev a chanse uv advertisin, 1st, That they wuz frail, helplis critters; and, 2d, That, anshent and tough ez they wuz, some wun wuz still goin for em.

Ef ther ain't no niggers, central commities must furnish em. A half dozen will do for a ordinary county, ef they're hustled along with energy. Ef they won't steal, the central commities must do it their-selves. Show yer niggers in a township in the mornin, an the same nite rob the clothes-lines and hen-roosts. Ever willin to sacrifice myself for the cause, I volunteer to do this latter dooty in six populous counties.

These ijees, ef follered, will, no doubt, keep us together until our enemies split, when we will reap the reward uv our constancy and fidelity. May the Lord hasten the day.

Petroleum V. Nasby
Lait Paster uv the Church uv the Noo Dispensashun

NURSES THE LABOR MOVEMENT

Post Offis, Confedrit × *Roads*
(wich is in the Stait uv Kentucky)
May 28, 1869

The agitashen uv the question uv niggers labrin with white men in Washington reached the Corners four weeks ago, and perdoost, ez mite hev bin expectid, most profound feelin. Our white artisans assembled to-wunst and passed resolooshens in sympathy with their brethren in Washington, and urgin uv em to hold out to the bitter end rather than compermise their dignity by lowerin themselves to the level uv the greasy Afriken. The meetin wuznt a large one, for we hev only five mechanics uv the hawty Caucashen race at the Corners, but it wuz enthoosiastic. Three uv the five hed bin at Bascom's four days, hevin bin jist paid off by a new-comer, for a house they hed repaired for him, and they wuz in a frame uv mind for most anything that wuz eggs-citin.

469

I directed the attenshun uv these men to the fact that a nigger plasterer wuz even at that time employed in plasterin a house between the Corners and Garrettstown, and I askt em ef they wuz content to lay still and see an inferior race take the bread out uv their mouths in that way? I implored em, ez labrin men, to preserve the dignity uv labor. Shel niggers invade yoor okkepashens?

They wuznt none uv em plasterers, but they replied, "Never! Never!" and demanded, with the utmost promptitood, to be showd the wretch, that they mite go for him. But I restraned em till I hed organized em into a Free Labor Unyun, which perhibited anybody from workin at anythin which didn't jine it, and wich perhibited niggers from jinin it. This preliminary work accomplished, I remarkt, "Follow me!" They did it with alacrity.

On reachin the house we halted, and there our eyes rested onto a site wich blarsted em. There wuz a nigger, a full-blooded nigger, with a cap onto him, and overalls, plasterin away, whistlin and singin (sometimes one, sometimes another, and then agin both to-wunst) Methodist hymns. And ever and anon the unthinkin man of inferiority wood stop and execoot a break-down, and laff to hisself, so that he could be heard a mile. The disgustin wretch displayed his grovelin nacher by drinkin water out uv a bucket wich he hed handy by him.

We made short work uv it. We informed him that the laborers uv the Corners hed organized a Union, and that no one cood be permitted to work within its boundaries ceptin members thereof.

"Berry well!" remarkt the Afrikin cuss, calmly puttin on a dab uv mortar and smoothin it, "berry well! I'll jine the Yoonyun."

"But you can't. No nigger can be admitted."

"Den I specks I shel hev to go on and work widout bein a member. De ole woman and de babies must hab dar bread, yoo know."

Sich insolence cood not, uv course, be tolerated. We hed stated the case to him calmly and dispassionately. We hed informed him uv the laws we hed made, and this wretch deliberately defied us, by insistin that he shood go on with his work! Ther wuz but one course to take, and we took it. We snaked the platform out from under him; we tore up his mortar bed; we broke his trowel and other tools, and notified him offishelly that any attempt at resoomin work would result in lynchin uv him.

The next day we found that the nigger hed in trooth quit plasterin, but hed found employment ez a striker in a blacksmith shop. Uv course sich an outrage on the pure Caucashen employed in that shop, wich his name wuz O'Toole, cood not be permitted, and ez O'Toole refoosed to work with him, he wuz discharged. The next day I notist him on the streets, rather pale and haggard than otherwise, carryin home a shin bone uv beef wich he hed bought. The next day after I observed that he lookt better, and I diskivered that he hed found employment at last on a turnpike road wich is bein built east uv the town. Issaker Gavitt and me, the two champions uv labor for this seckshun (ez we don't work we hev time to attend to it), sejested to the noble Celts employed on the job the hidjusnis uv compellin em to work on an ekality with a nigger, and they struck agin it with the yoosual result. The nigger wuz discharged. He made but one or two more efforts. He undertook to git work at various places, but by this time it wuz well enuff knowd that the citizens uv the Corners wuz inflexibly opposed to the recognisin uv em in any capassity, and he yeelded. He got very thin, and pale, and haggard, and his large family likewise. It wuz evident that they wuznt feelin very well at home. Notis the nateral result of freedom! He ABSLOOTLY BEGGED! But uv course the Corners wood give nothin to a nigger. Then the instinktiv nateral cussidness uv the nigger — the infernal depravity wich is inherent into all uv em — began to display itself. He demoralized rapidly, and in a week became a most disgustin objick. He stole chickens uv Deekin Pogram, leastways Deekin Pogram's chickens wuz missin, and who should hev stole em but this nigger? He stole corn uv Elder Pennebacker, and wuz finally detected takin a ham from Bascom's smoke-house. There wuz no doubt ez to his guilt; he wuz taken in the act, with the fatal ham in his possession. He hed taken it home, and his wife wuz fryin large slices uv it.

There cood be but one endin to *sich* a succession uv crimes. The citizens were too much incensed to await the uncertain ackshen uv the law, and they hung him at site. The Corners will never tolerate a nigger theef in their midst, no how.

Uv course I improved the occasion. Ez his body wuz a swingin in the air, I askt our people to behold the fruits of Radicalism and Fanatycism. That nigger wuz wunst the happy slave uv a happy owner; there wuz atween em a nateral relashen. The nigger workt, and his owner eat, and thus wuz fulfilled the entire dooties uv life. He wuz not hung then, for he wuz worth too much money to hang. How hed it bin with him sense? He demanded to be made a free man; he wuz made a free man, and here he is. I told em that there wuz no need uv sayin more;

that body a danglin in the air, wich its sole wuz a marchin on, wuz the most elokent sermon wich cood be preacht.

The man whose house the nigger wuz a plasterin wuz in town yesterday, tryin to get Caucashin plasterers to finish the job; but ez ther ain't none uv em here, he isn't succeedin very well. He probably won't get into his new quarters this fall.

I am not certain wot become uv his family. There wuz a nigger woman's body pulled out uv the dam a day or two afterwards, wich somebody remarkt wuz the wife uv the deceast, and Captain McPelter remarkt that when he went to the cabin uv the deceest nigger to secoor his share of the furnitoor, that two leadin niggers from Garrettstown were notist makin off with the children. But there's no tellin whether there's any trooth in these rumors or not. I think I shel go to Washington, and put myself at the head uv the anti-nigger labor movement now bein inogurated there.

Petroleum V. Nasby, P. M.

(*wich is Postmaster*)

HARRIET BEECHER STOWE

[1811–1896]

DAUGHTER of Lyman Beecher, the famous Puritan minister of Litchfield, Connecticut, and sister of Henry Ward Beecher, who was to become the pastor of the Plymouth Church in Brooklyn, she was brought up in a rigorously Calvinist environment. Her education was mainly religious, but as she grew older she became increasingly skeptical of her father's austere theology and increasingly interested in secular problems. In 1832 the family moved to Cincinnati, where her father headed a seminary. This institution affected her in two ways: firstly, she met there, and married, Professor Calvin E. Stowe, teacher of Biblical literature; secondly, she was infected by the anti-slavery sentiment that was rampant in the school. She did not become an outspoken abolitionist, however, until she returned to New England in 1850, when the controversy over the Fugitive Slave Law was at its height. The immediate result of her great emotion was the novel which is permanently fixed in American history — *Uncle Tom's Cabin* (1852). Not so well known are her later books, the best of which are intimate portraits of New England life and people. Among them is the most charming thing she wrote: *Oldtown Folks*. The following selections are excellent sketches of the decline of theocracy and the rise of a democratic spirit in the Calvinist church.

---

from

OLDTOWN FOLKS

MY GRANDMOTHER'S BLUE BOOK

My grandmother was a character in her way, full of contradictions and inconsistencies, brave, generous, energetic, large-hearted, and impulsive. Theoretically she was an ardent disciple of the sharpest and severest Calvinism, and used to repeat Michael Wigglesworth's "Day of Doom" to us in the chimney-corner, of an evening, with a reverent acquiescence in all its hard sayings, while practically she was the most pitiful, easy-to-be-entreated old mortal on earth, and was ever falling

473

a prey to any lazy vagabond who chose to make an appeal to her abounding charity. She could not refuse a beggar that asked in a piteous tone; she could not send a child to bed that wanted to sit up; she could not eat a meal in peace when there were hungry eyes watching her; she could not, in cool, deliberate moments, even inflict transient and necessary pain for the greater good of a child, and resolutely shut her eyes to the necessity of such infliction. But there lay at the bottom of all this apparent inconsistency a deep cause that made it consistent, and that cause was the theologic stratum in which her mind, and the mind of all New England, was embedded.

Never, in the most intensely religious ages of the world, did the insoluble problem of the WHENCE, the WHY, and the WHITHER of mankind receive such earnest attention. New England was founded by a colony who turned their backs on the civilization of the Old World, on purpose that they might have nothing else to think of. Their object was to form a community that should think of nothing else.

Working on a hard soil, battling with a harsh, ungenial climate, everywhere being treated by Nature with the most rigorous severity, they asked no indulgence, they got none, and they gave none. They shut out from their religious worship every poetic drapery, every physical accessory that they feared would interfere with the abstract contemplation of hard, naked truth, and set themselves grimly and determinately to study the severest problems of the unknowable and the insoluble. Just as resolutely as they made their farms by blasting rocks and clearing land of ledges of stone, and founded thrifty cities and thriving money-getting communities in places which one would think might more properly have been left to the white bears, so resolutely they pursued their investigations amid the grim mysteries of human existence, determined to see and touch and handle everything for themselves, and to get at the absolute truth if absolute truth could be got at.

They never expected to find truth agreeable. Nothing in their experience of life had ever prepared them to think it would be so. Their investigations were made with the courage of the man who hopes little, but determines to know the worst of his affairs. They wanted no smoke of incense to blind them, and no soft opiates of pictures and music to lull them; for what they were after was *truth,* and not happiness, and they valued *duty* far higher than enjoyment.

The underlying foundation of life, therefore, in New England, was one of profound, unutterable, and therefore unuttered, melancholy, which regarded human existence itself as a ghastly risk, and, in the case of the vast majority of human beings, an inconceivable misfortune. . . .

As I have said, [my grandmother] was a great reader. On the round table that stood in her bedroom, next to the kitchen, there was an ample supply of books. Rollin's Ancient History, Hume's History of England, and President Edwards's Sermons, were among these.

She was not one of those systematic, skilful housewives who contrive with few steps and great method to do much in little time; she took everything the hardest end first, and attacked difficulties by sheer inconsiderate strength. For example, instead of putting on the great family pot, filling it with water, and afterwards putting therein the beef, pork, and vegetables of our daily meal, she would load up the receptacle at the sink in the back room, and then, with strong arm and cap-border erect, would fly across the kitchen with it and swing it over the fire by main strength. Thus inconsiderately she rushed at the daily battle of existence. But there was one point of system in which she never failed. There was, every day, a period, sacred and inviolable, which she gave to reading. The noon meal came exactly at twelve o'clock; and immediately after, when the dishes were washed and wiped, and the kitchen reduced to order, my grandmother changed her gown, and retired to the sanctuary of her bedroom to read. In this way she accomplished an amount which a modern housekeeper, with four servants, would pronounce to be wholly incredible. . . .

Her favorite books had different-colored covers, thriftily put on to preserve them from the wear of handling; and it was by these covers they were generally designated in the family. Hume's History of England was known as "the brown book"; Rollin's History was "the green book"; but there was one volume which she pondered oftener and with more intense earnestness than any other, which received the designation of "the blue book." This was a volume by the Rev. Dr. Bellamy of Connecticut, called "True Religion delineated, and distinguished from all Counterfeits." It was originally published by subscription, and sent out into New England with a letter of introduction and recommendation from the Rev. Jonathan Edwards, who earnestly set it forth as being a condensed summary, in popular language, of what it is vital and important for human beings to know for their spiritual progress. It was written in a strong, nervous, condensed, popular style, such as is fallen into by a practical man speaking to a practical people, by a man thoroughly in earnest to men as deeply in earnest, and lastly, by a man who believed without the shadow of a doubt, and without even the comprehension of the possibility of a doubt. . . .

My grandmother's blue book was published and recommended to the attention of New England, August 4, 1750, just twenty-six years before the Declaration of Independence. How popular it was, and how widely read in New England, appears from the list of subscribers which stands at the end of the old copy which my grandmother actually used. Almost every good old Massachusetts or Connecticut family name is there represented. We have the Emersons, the Adamses, the Brattles of Brattle Street, the Bromfields of Bromfield Street, the Brinsmaids of Connecticut, the Butlers, the Campbells, the Chapmans, the Cottons, the Daggetts, the Hawleys, the Hookers, with many more names of families yet continuing to hold influence in New England. How they regarded this book may be inferred from the fact that some subscribed for six books, some for twelve, some for thirty-six, and some for fifty. Its dissemination was deemed an act of religious ministry, and there is not the slightest doubt that it was heedfully and earnestly read in every good family of New England; and its propositions were discussed everywhere and by everybody. . . .

If any should ever be so curious as to read this old treatise, as well as most of the writings of Jonathan Edwards, they will perceive with singular plainness how inevitably monarchical and aristocratic institutions influence theology.

That " the king can do no wrong," — that the subject owes everything to the king, and the king nothing to the subject, — that it is the king's first duty to take care of himself, and keep up state, splendor, majesty, and royalty, and that it is the people's duty to give themselves up, body and soul, without a murmuring thought, to keep up this state, splendor, and royalty, — were ideas for ages so wrought into the human mind, and transmitted by ordinary generation, — they so reflected themselves in literature and poetry and art, and all the great customs of society, — that it was inevitable that systematic theology should be permeated by them.

The idea of God in which theologians delighted, and which the popular mind accepted, was not that of the Good Shepherd that giveth his life for the sheep, — of him that made himself of no reputation, and took unto himself the form of a servant, — of him who on his knees washed the feet of his disciples, and said that in the kingdom of heaven the greatest was he who served most humbly, — this aspect of a Divine Being had not yet been wrought into their systematic theology; because, while the Bible comes from God, theology is the outgrowth of the human mind, and therefore must spring from the movement of society.

When the Puritans arrived at a perception of the political rights of men in the state, and began to enunciate and act upon the doctrine that a king's right to reign was founded upon his power to promote the greatest happiness of his subjects, and when, in pursuance of this theory, they tried, condemned, and executed a king who had been false to the people, they took a long step forward in human progress. Why did not immediate anarchy follow, as when the French took such a step in regard to their king? It was because the Puritans transferred to God all those rights and immunities, all that unquestioning homage and worship and loyalty, which hitherto they had given to an earthly king. . . .

There is something most affecting in the submissive devotion of these old Puritans to their God. Nothing shows more completely the indestructible nature of the filial tie which binds man to God, of the filial yearning which throbs in the heart of a great child of so great a Father, than the manner in which these men loved and worshipped and trusted God as the ALL LOVELY, even in the face of monstrous assertions of theology ascribing to him deeds which no father could imitate without being cast out of human society, and no governor without being handed down to all ages as a monster.

These theologies were not formed by the Puritans; they were their legacy from past monarchical and mediæval ages; and the principles of true Christian democracy upon which they founded their new state began, from the time of the American Revolution, to act upon them with a constantly ameliorating power, so that whosoever should read my grandmother's blue book now would be astonished to find how completely New England theology has changed its base. . . .

It was inevitable that a people who had just carried through a national revolution and declared national independence on the principle that " governments owe their just power to the consent of the governed," and who recognized it as an axiom that the greatest good to the greatest number was the object to be held in view in all just governments, should very soon come into painful collision with forms of theological statement, in regard to God's government, which ap-

477

peared to contravene all these principles, and which could be supported only by referring to the old notion of the divine right and prerogative of the King Eternal.

President Edwards had constructed a marvellous piece of logic to show that, while true virtue in man consisted in supreme devotion to the general good of all, true virtue in God consisted in supreme regard for himself. This "Treatise on True Virtue" was one of the strongest attempts to back up by reasoning the old monarchical and aristocratic ideas of the supreme right of the king and upper classes. The whole of it falls to dust before the one simple declaration of Jesus Christ, that, in the eyes of Heaven, one lost sheep is more prized than all the ninety and nine that went not astray, and before the parable in which the father runs, forgetful of parental prerogative and dignity, to cast himself on the neck of the far-off prodigal. . . .

In the neighboring town of Adams there lived one of the most remarkable clergymen that New England has ever produced. His career influenced the thinking of Massachusetts, both in regard to those who adopted his opinions, and in the violent reaction from those opinions which was the result of his extreme manner of pushing them.

Dr. Moses Stern's figure is well remembered by me as I saw it in my boyhood. Everybody knew him, and when he appeared in the pulpit everybody trembled before him. He moved among men, but seemed not of men. An austere, inflexible, grand indifference to all things earthly seemed to give him the prestige and dignity of a supernatural being. His Calvinism was of so severe and ultra a type, and his statements were so little qualified either by pity of human infirmity, or fear of human censure, or desire of human approbation, that he reminded one of some ancient prophet, freighted with a mission of woe and wrath, which he must always speak, whether people would hear or whether they would forbear.

The Revolutionary war had introduced into the country a great deal of scepticism, of a type of which Paine's "Age of Reason" was an exponent; and, to meet this, the ministry of New England was not slow or unskilful.

Dr. Stern's mode of meeting this attitude of the popular mind was by an unflinching, authoritative, vehement reiteration of all the most unpopular and unpleasant points of Calvinism. Now as Nature is, in many of her obvious aspects, notoriously uncompromising, harsh, and severe, the Calvinist who begins to talk to common-sense people has this advantage on his side, — that the things which he represents the Author of Nature as doing and being ready to do, are not very different from what the common-sense man sees that the Author of Nature is already in the habit of doing.

The farmer who struggles with the hard soil, and with drouth and frost and caterpillars and fifty other insect plagues, — who finds his most persistent and well-calculated efforts constantly thwarted by laws whose workings he never can fully anticipate, and which never manifest either care for his good intentions or sympathy for his losses, is very apt to believe that the God who created nature may be a generally benevolent, but a severe and unsympathetic being, governing the world for some great, unknown purpose of his own, of which man's private improvement and happiness may or may not form a part.

Dr. Stern, with characteristic independence and fearlessness, on his own simple authority cut loose from and repudiated the whole traditional idea of the fall in Adam as having anything to do with the existence of human depravity; and made up his own theory of the universe, and began preaching it to the farmers of Adams. It was simply this: that the Divine Being is the efficient cause of all things, not only in matter but in mind, — that every good and every evil volition of any being in the universe is immediately caused by Him and tends equally well in its way to carry on his great designs. But, in order that this might not interfere with the doctrines of human responsibility, he taught that all was accomplished by Omniscient skill and knowledge in such a way as not in the slightest degree to interfere with human free agency; so that the whole responsibility of every human being's actions must rest upon himself.

Thus was this system calculated, like a skilful engine of torture, to produce all the mental anguish of the most perfect sense of helplessness with the most torturing sense of responsibility. Alternately he worked these two great levers with an almost supernatural power, — on one Sunday demonstrating with the most logical clearness, and by appeals to human consciousness, the perfect freedom of man, and, on the next, demonstrating with no less precision and logic the perfect power which an Omniscient Being possessed and exercised of controlling all his thoughts and volitions and actions.

Individually, Dr. Stern, like many other teachers of severe, uncompromising theories, was an artless, simple-hearted, gentle-mannered man. He was a close student, and wore two holes in the floor opposite his table in the spot where year after year his feet were placed in study. He refused to have the smallest thing to do with any temporal affair of this life. Like the other clergymen, he lived on a small salary, and the support of his family depended largely on the proceeds of a farm. But it is recorded of him, that once, when his whole summer's crop of hay was threatened with the bursting of a thunder-shower, and, farm-hands being short, he was importuned to lend a hand to save it, he resolutely declined, saying, that, if he once began to allow himself to be called on in any emergency for temporal affairs, he should become forgetful of his great mission.

The same inflexible, unbending perseverance he showed in preaching, on the basis of his own terrible theory, the most fearful doctrines of Calvinism. His sermons on Judas, on Jeroboam, and on Pharaoh, as practical examples of the doctrine of reprobation, were pieces of literature so startling and astounding, that, even in those days of interrupted travel, when there were neither railroads nor good roads of any kind, and almost none of our modern communicative system of magazines and newspapers, they were heard of all over New England. So great was the revulsion which his doctrines excited, that, when he exchanged with his brother ministers, his appearance in the pulpit was the signal for some of the most independent of the congregation to get up and leave the meeting-house. But, as it was one of his maxims that the minister who does not excite the opposition of the natural heart fails to do his work, he regarded such demonstrations as evident signs of a faithful ministry. . . .

In the town where he lived his preaching formed the strongest, most controlling of all forces. No human being could hear his sermons unmoved. He would not preach to an inattentive audience, and on one occasion, observing a large number of his congregation asleep, he abruptly descended from the pulpit and calmly walked off home, leaving the astonished congregation to their own reflections; nor would he resume public services until messages of contrition and assurances of better conduct had been sent him.

Dr. Stern was in his position irresistible, simply because he cared nothing at all for the things which men ordinarily care for, and which therefore could be used as motives to restrain the declarations and actions of a clergyman. He cared nothing about worldly prosperity; he was totally indifferent to money; he utterly despised fame and reputation and therefore from none of these sources could he be in the slightest degree influenced. Such a man is generally the king of his neighborhood, — the one whom all look up to, and all fear, and whose word in time becomes law.

Dr. Stern never sought to put himself forward otherwise than by the steady preaching of his system to the farming population of Adams. And yet, so great were his influence and his fame, that in time it became customary for young theological students to come and settle themselves down there as his students. This was done at first without his desire, and contrary to his remonstrance.

"I can't engage to teach you," he said; but still, when scholars came and continued to come, he found himself, without seeking it, actually at the head of a school of theology.

Let justice be done to all; it is due to truth to state that the theological scholars of Dr. Stern, wherever they went in the United States, were always marked men, — marked for an unflinching adherence to principle, and especially for a great power in supporting unpopular truths.

The Doctor himself lived to an extreme old age, always retaining and reiterating with unflinching constancy his opinions. He was the last of the New England ministers who preserved the old clerical dress of the theocracy. Long after the cocked hat and small-clothes, silk stockings and shoe-buckles, had ceased to appear in modern life, his venerable figure, thus apparelled, walked the ways of modern men, seeming like one of the primitive Puritans risen from the dead.

He was the last, also, of the New England ministers to claim for himself that peculiar position, as God's ambassador, which was such a reality in the minds of the whole early Puritan community. To extreme old age, his word was law in his parish, and he calmly and positively felt that it should be so. In time, his gray hairs, his fine, antique figure and quaint costume came to be regarded with the sort of appreciative veneration that every one gives to the monuments of the past. When he was near his ninetieth year, he was invited to New York to give the prestige of his venerable presence to the religious anniversaries which then were in the flush of newly organized enthusiasm, and which gladly laid hold of this striking accessory to the religious picturesque.

Dr. Stern was invited and fêted in the most select upper circles of New York, and treated with attentions which would have been flattering had he not been too entirely simple-minded and careless of such matters even to perceive what they meant.

481

But at this same time the Abolitionists, who were regarded as most improper people to be recognized in the religious circles of good society, came to New York, resolving to have their anniversary also; and, knowing that Dr. Stern had always professed to be an antislavery man, they invited him to sit on the stage with them; and Dr. Stern went. Shocking to relate, and dreadful to behold, this very cocked hat and these picturesque gray hairs, that had been brought to New York on purpose to ornament religious anniversaries which were all agreed in excluding and ignoring the Abolitionists, had gone right over into the camp of the enemy! and he was so entirely ignorant and uninstructible on the subject, and came back, after having committed this abomination, with a face of such innocent and serene gravity, that nobody dared to say a word to him on the subject.

He was at this time the accepted guest in a family whose very religion consisted in a gracious carefulness and tenderness lest they should wake up the feelings of their Southern brethren on the delicate subject of slavery. But then Dr. Stern was a man that it did no good to talk to, since it was well known that, wherever there was an unpopular truth to be defended, his cocked hat was sure to be in the front ranks.

Let us do one more justice to Dr. Stern, and say that his utter inflexibility toward human infirmity and human feeling spared himself as little as it spared any other. In his early life he records, in a most affecting autobiography, the stroke which deprived him, within a very short space, of a beloved wife and two charming children. In the struggle of that hour he says, with affecting simplicity, " I felt that I should die if I did not submit; and I did submit then, once for all." Thenceforward the beginning and middle and end of his whole preaching was *submission*, — utter, absolute, and unconditional.

In extreme old age, trembling on the verge of the grave, and looking back over sixty years of intense labor, he said, " After all, it is quite possible that I may not be saved"; but he considered himself as but one drop in the ocean, and his personal salvation as of but secondary account. His devotion to the King Eternal had no reference to a matter so slight. In all this, if there is something terrible and painful, there is something also which is grand, and in which we can take pride, as the fruit of our human nature. Peace to his ashes! he has learned better things ere now.

OUR MINISTER IN CLOUDLAND

The picture of our life in Cloudland [a village in which the writer of the narrative was attending school], and of the developing forces which were there brought to bear upon us, would be incomplete without the portrait of the minister.

Even during the course of my youth, the principles of democratic equality introduced and maintained in the American Revolution were greatly changing the social position and standing of the clergy. Ministers like Dr. Lothrop, noble men of the theocracy, men of the cocked hat, were beginning to pass away, or to appear among men only as venerable antiquities, and the present order of American citizen clergy was coming in.

Mr. Avery was a cheerful, busy, manly man, who posed himself among men as a companion and a fellow-citizen, whose word on any subject was to go only so far as its own weight and momentum should carry it. His preaching was a striking contrast to the elegant Addisonian essays of Parson Lothrop. It was a vehement address to our intelligent and reasoning powers, — an address made telling by a back force of burning enthusiasm. Mr. Avery preached a vigorous system of mental philosophy in theology, which made our Sundays, on the whole, about as intense an intellectual drill as any of our week-days. If I could describe its character by any one word, I should call it *manly* preaching.

Every person has a key-note to his mind which determines all its various harmonies. The key-note of Mr. Avery's mind was " the free agency of man." Free agency was with him the universal solvent, the philosopher's stone in theology; every line of his sermons said to every human being, " You are free, and you are able." And the great object was to intensify to its highest point, in every human being, the sense of individual, personal responsibility.

Of course, as a Calvinist, he found food for abundant discourse in reconciling this absolute freedom of man with those declarations in the standards of the Church which assert the absolute government of God over all his creatures and all their actions. But the cheerfulness and vigor with which he drove and interpreted and hammered in the most contradictory statements, when they came in the way of his favorite ideas, was really quite inspiring.

During the year we had a whole course of systematic theology, beginning with the history of the introduction of moral evil, the fall of the angels, and the consequent fall of man and the work of redemption resulting therefrom. In the treatment of all these subjects, the theology and imagery of Milton figured so largely that one might receive the impression that Paradise Lost was part of the sacred canon.

Mr. Avery not only preached these things in the pulpit, but talked them out in his daily life. His system of theology was to him the vital breath of his being. His mind was always running upon it, and all nature was, in his sight, giving daily tributary illustrations to it. In his farming, gardening, hunting, or fishing, he was constantly finding new and graphic forms of presenting his favorite truths. The most abstract subject ceased to be abstract in his treatment of it, but became clothed upon with the homely, every-day similes of common life. . . .

The Calvinism of Mr. Avery, though sharp and well defined, was not dull, as abstractions often are, nor gloomy and fateful like that of Dr. Stern. It was permeated through and through by cheerfulness and hope.

Mr. Avery was one of the kind of men who have a passion for saving souls. If there is such a thing as apostolic succession, this passion is what it ought to consist in. It is what ought to come with the laying on of hands, if the laying on of hands is what it is sometimes claimed to be.

Mr. Avery was a firm believer in hell, but he believed also that nobody need go there, and he was determined, so far as he was concerned, that nobody should go there if he could help it. Such a tragedy as the loss of any one soul in his parish he could not and would not contemplate for a moment; and he had such a firm belief in the truths he preached, that he verily expected with them to save anybody that would listen to him.

Goethe says, " Blessed is the man who believes that he has an idea by which he may help his fellow-creatures." Mr. Avery was exactly that man. He had such faith in what he preached that he would have gone with it to Satan himself, could he have secured a dispassionate and unemployed hour, with a hope of bringing him round.

Generous and ardent in his social sympathies, Mr. Avery never could be brought to believe that any particular human being had finally perished. At every funeral he attended he contrived to see a ground for hope that the departed had found mercy. Even the slightest hints of repentance were magnified in his warm and hopeful mode of presentation. He has been known to suggest to a distracted mother, whose thoughtless boy had been suddenly killed by a fall from a horse, the possibilities of the merciful old couplet, —

> " Between the saddle and the ground,
> Mercy was sought, and mercy found."

Like most of the New England ministers, Mr. Avery was a warm believer in the millennium. This millennium was the favorite recreation ground, solace, and pasture land, where the New England ministry fed their hopes and courage. Men of large hearts and warm benevolence, their theology would have filled them with gloom, were it not for this overplus of joy and peace to which human society on earth was in their view tending. Thousands of years, when the poor old earth should produce only a saintly race of perfected human beings, were to them some compensation for the darkness and losses of the great struggle.

Mr. Avery believed, not only that the millennium was coming, but that it was coming fast, and, in fact, was at the door. Every political and social change announced it. Our Revolution was a long step towards it, and the French Revolution, now in progress, was a part of that distress of nations which heralded it; and every month, when the Columbia Magazine brought in the news from Europe, Mr. Avery rushed over to Mr. Rossiter, and called him to come and hear how the thing was going.

Mr. Rossiter took upon himself that right which every free-born Yankee holds sacred, — the right of contravening his minister. Though, if he caught one of his boys swelling or ruffling with any opposing doctrine, he would scath and scorch the youngster with contemptuous irony, and teach him to comport himself modestly in talking of his betters, yet it was the employment of a great many of his leisure hours to run argumentative tilts against Mr. Avery. Sometimes, when we were sitting in our little garret window digging out the Greek lessons, such a war of voices and clangor of assertion and contradiction would come up from among the tassels of the corn, where the two were hoeing together in the garden, as would have alarmed people less accustomed to the vigorous manners of both the friends. . . .

It was this implied liberty of growth — the liberty to think and to judge freely upon all subjects — that formed the great distinctive educational force of New England life, particularly in this period of my youth. Monarchy, aristocracy, and theocracy, with their peculiar trains of ideas, were passing away, and we were coming within the sweep of pure republican influences, in which the *individual* is *everything*. Mr. Avery's enthusiastic preaching of free agency and personal responsibility was more than an *individual impulse*. It was the voice of a man whose ideas were the reflection of a period in American history. While New England theology was made by loyal monarchists, it reflected monarchical ideas. The rights and immunities of divine sovereignty were its favorite topics. When, as now, the government was becoming settled in the hands of the common people, the freedom of the individual, his absolute power of choice, and the consequent reasonableness of the duties he owed to the Great Sovereign Authority, began to be the favorite subjects of the pulpit.

Mr. Avery's preaching was immensely popular. There were in Cloudland only about half a dozen families of any prestige as to ancestral standing or previous wealth and cultivation. The old aristocratic idea was represented only in the one street that went over Cloudland Hill, where was a series of wide, cool, roomy, elm-shadowed houses, set back in deep door-yards, and flanked with stately, well-tended gardens. The doctor, the lawyer, the sheriff of the county, the schoolmaster, and the minister, formed here a sort of nucleus; but outlying in all the hills and valleys round were the mountain and valley farmers. Their houses sat on high hills or sunk in deep valleys, and their flaming windows at morning and evening looked through the encircling belts of forest solitudes as if to say, " We are here, and we are a power." These hard-working farmers formed the body of Mr. Avery's congregation. Sunday morning, when the little bell pealed out its note of invitation loud and long over the forest-feathered hills, it seemed to evoke a caravan of thrifty, well-filled farm-wagons, which, punctual as the village-clock itself, came streaming from the east and west, the north and south. Past the parsonage they streamed, with the bright cheeks and fluttering ribbons of the girls, and the cheery, rubicund faces of children, and with the inevitable yellow dog of the family faithfully pattering in the rear. The audience that filled the rude old meeting-house every Sunday would have astonished the men who only rode through the village of a week-day. For this set of shrewd, toil-hardened, vigorous, full-blooded republicans I can think of no preaching more admirably adapted than Mr. Avery's. It was preaching that was on the move, as their minds were, and which was slowly shaping out and elaborating those new forms of doctrinal statement that inevitably grow out of new forms of society. Living, as these men did, a lonely, thoughtful, secluded life, without any of the thousand stimulants which railroads and magazine and newspaper literature cast into our existence, their two Sunday sermons were the great intellectual stimulus which kept their minds bright, and they were listened to with an intense interest of which the scattered and diversified state of modern society gives few examples. They felt the compliment of being talked to as if they were capable of understanding the very highest of subjects, and they liked it. Each hard, heroic nature flashed like a flint at the grand thought of a free agency with which not even their Maker would interfere. Their God himself asked to reign over them, not by force, but by the free, voluntary choice of their own hearts. "*Choose* you this day whom ye will serve. If the Lord be God, serve him, and if Baal be God, serve him," was a grand appeal, fit for freemen.

The reasoning on moral government, on the history of man, — the theories of the universe past, present, and to come, — opened to these men a grand Miltonic poem, in which their own otherwise commonplace lives shone with a solemn splendor. Without churches or cathedrals or physical accessories to quicken their poetic nature, their lives were redeemed only by this poetry of ideas. . . .

Harry and I were often taken by Mr. Avery on his preaching tours to the distant farm parishes. There was a brown school-house in this valley, and a red school-house in that, and another on the hill, and so on for miles around, and Mr. Avery kept a constant stream of preaching going in one or other of these every evening. We liked these expeditions with him, because they were often excursions amid the wildest and most romantic of the mountain scenery, and we liked them furthermore because Mr. Avery was a man that made himself, for the time being, companionable to every creature of human shape that was with him.

With boys he was a boy, — a boy in the vigor of his animal life, his keen delight in riding, hunting, fishing. With farmers he was a farmer. Brought up on a farm, familiar during all his early days with its wholesome toils, he still had a farmer's eye and a farmer's estimates, and the working-people felt him bone of their bone, and flesh of their flesh. It used to be a saying among them, that, when Mr. Avery hoed more than usual in his potato-field, the Sunday sermon was sure to be better.

But the best sport of all was when some of Mr. Avery's preaching tours would lead up the course of a fine mountain trout-brook in the vicinity. Then sometimes Mr. Rossiter, Mr. Avery, Harry, and I would put our supper in our pockets, and start with the sun an hour or two high, designing to bring up at the red school-house, as the weekly notice phrased it, at " early candle-lighting."

A person who should accidentally meet Mr. Avery on one of these tours, never having seen him before, might imagine him to be a man who had never thought or dreamed of anything but catching trout all his days, he went into it with such *abandon.* Eye, voice, hand, thought, feeling, all were concentrated on trout. He seemed to have the quick perception, the rapid hand, and the noiseless foot of an Indian, and the fish came to his hook as if drawn there by magic. So perfectly absorbed was he that we would be obliged to jog his memory, and, in fact, often to drag him away by main force, when the hour for the evening lecture arrived. Then our spoils would be hid away among the bushes, and with wet feet he would hurry in; but, once in, he was as completely absorbed in his work of saving sinners as he had before been in his temporal fishery. He argued, illustrated, stated, guarded, answered objections, looking the while from one hard, keen, shrewd face to another, to see if he was being understood. The phase of Calvinism shown in my grandmother's blue book had naturally enough sowed through the minds of a thoughtful community hosts of doubts and queries. A great part of Mr. Avery's work was to remove these doubts by substituting more rational statements. It was essential that he should feel that he had made a hit somewhere, said something that answered a purpose in the minds of his hearers, and helped them at least a step or two on their way. . . .

[*1869*]

HENRY GEORGE

[1839–1897]

GEORGE was born in Philadelphia of a lower middle-class family. He had a good elementary schooling, but evidently had no scholastic ambitions, for he left high school in his first year and became, in turn, an errand-boy, clerk, sailor, and printer. In 1858 he arrived in San Francisco — voyaging as steward on a ship — drawn to the West by reports of high wages. The wages failed to materialize, so he tried store-keeping and gold-mining, and at last turned again to type-setting and printing. In 1861 he married. Years of poverty and struggle followed. Along with printing he eventually tried journalism, but even between the two he could barely make a living for some time. It was natural that he should begin to speculate on the causes of poverty, and this interest continued when he was a practicing newspaperman and editor. He began to publish articles and to lecture on the subject, gradually formulating a definite thesis. His study of the farmer's problems, of the way railroads became rich, of the rise of a city proletariat, led finally to the conclusion that the private ownership of land is the prime curse of modern society and that the cure is expropriatory taxation of rents. Since this was the only form of taxation George recommended, his doctrine was known as the Single Tax. Forcefully and clearly argued in his magnum opus, *Progress and Poverty,* his doctrine brought him international fame. He founded a movement which for some years had many adherents and which almost led to his election, in 1886, as mayor of New York City, where he had moved in 1880. Today his movement is obscure, almost forgotten except among economists. Yet his book lives — not because of its taxation theories, but because of its analysis of the spread of poverty coincidentally with technological progress and its strong plea for a just, equalitarian, and co-operative society.

from

PROGRESS AND POVERTY

THE LAW OF HUMAN PROGRESS

Compare society to a boat. Her progress through the water will not depend upon the exertion of her crew, but upon the exertion devoted to propelling her. This will be lessened by any expenditure of force required for bailing, or any expenditure of force in fighting among themselves, or in pulling in different directions.

Now, as in a separate state the whole powers of man are required to maintain existence, and mental power is set free for higher uses only by the association of men in communities, which permits the division of labor and all the economies which come with the co-operation of increased numbers, association is the first essential of progress. Improvement becomes possible as men come together in peaceful association, and the wider and closer the association, the greater the possibilities of improvement. And as the wasteful expenditure of mental power in conflict becomes greater or less as the moral law which accords to each an equality of rights is ignored or is recognized, equality (or justice) is the second essential of progress.

Thus association in equality is the law of progress. Association frees mental power for expenditure in improvement, and equality, or justice, or freedom — for the terms here signify the same thing, the recognition of the moral law — prevents the dissipation of this power in fruitless struggles.

Here is the law of progress, which will explain all diversities, all advances, all halts, and retrogressions. Men tend to progress just as they come closer together, and by co-operation with each other increase the mental power that may be devoted to improvement, but just as conflict is provoked, or association develops inequality of condition and power, this tendency to progression is lessened, checked, and finally reversed.

Given the same innate capacity, and it is evident that social development will go on faster or slower, will stop or turn back, according to the resistances it meets. In a general way these obstacles to improvement may, in relation to the society itself, be classed as external and internal — the first operating with greater force in the earlier stages of civilization, the latter becoming more important in the later stages.

Man is social in his nature. He does not require to be caught and tamed in order to induce him to live with his fellows. The utter helplessness with which he enters the world, and the long period required for the maturity of his powers, necessitate the family relation; which, as we may observe, is wider, and in its extensions stronger, among the ruder than among the more cultivated peoples. The first societies are families, expanding into tribes, still holding a mutual blood relationship, and even when they have become great nations claiming a common descent.

Given beings of this kind, placed on a globe of such diversified surface and climate as this, and it is evident that, even with equal capacity, and an equal start, social development must be very different. The first limit or resistance to association will come from the conditions of physical nature, and as these greatly vary with locality, corresponding differences in social progress must show themselves. The net rapidity of increase, and the closeness with which men, as they increase, can keep together, will, in the rude state of knowledge in which reliance for subsistence must be principally upon the spontaneous offerings of nature, very largely depend upon climate, soil, and physical conformation. Where much animal food and warm clothing are required; where the earth seems poor and niggard; where the exuberant life of tropical forests mocks barbarous man's puny efforts to control; where mountains, deserts, or arms of the sea separate and isolate men; association, and the power of improvement which it evolves, can at first go but a little way. But on the rich plains of warm climates, where human existence can be maintained with a smaller expenditure of force, and from a much smaller area, men can keep closer together, and the mental power which can at first be devoted to improvement is much greater. Hence civilization naturally first arises in the great valleys and table lands where we find its earliest monuments.

But these diversities in natural conditions, not merely thus directly produce diversities in social development, but, by producing diversities in social development, bring out in man himself an obstacle, or rather an active counterforce, to improvement. As families and tribes are separated from each other, the social feeling ceases to operate between them, and differences arise in language, custom, tradition, religion — in short, in the whole social web which each community, however small or large, constantly spins. With these differences, prejudices grow, animosities spring up, contact easily produces quarrels, aggres-

491

sion begets aggression, and wrong kindles revenge. And so between these separate social aggregates arises the feeling of Ishmael and the spirit of Cain, warfare becomes the chronic and seemingly natural relation of societies to each other, and the powers of men are expended in attack or defense, in mutual slaughter and mutual destruction of wealth, or in warlike preparations. How long this hostility persists, the protective tariffs and the standing armies of the civilized world to-day bear witness; how difficult it is to get over the idea that it is not theft to steal from a foreigner, the difficulty in procuring an international copyright act will show. Can we wonder at the perpetual hostilities of tribes and clans? Can we wonder that when each community was isolated from the others — when each, uninfluenced by the others, was spinning its separate web of social environment, which no individual can escape, that war should have been the rule and peace the exception? " They were even as we are."

Now, warfare is the negation of association. The separation of men into diverse tribes, by increasing warfare, thus checks improvement; while in the localities where a large increase in numbers is possible without much separation, civilization gains the advantage of exemption from tribal war, even when the community as a whole is carrying on warfare beyond its borders. Thus, where the resistance of nature to the close assocation of men is slightest, the counterforce of warfare is likely at first to be least felt; and in the rich plains where civilization first begins, it may rise to a great height while scattered tribes are yet barbarous. And thus, when small, separated communities exist in a state of chronic warfare which forbids advance, the first step to their civilization is the advent of some conquering tribe or nation that unites these smaller communities into a larger one, in which internal peace is preserved. Where this power of peaceable association is broken up, either by external assaults or internal dissensions, the advance ceases and retrogression begins.

But it is not conquest alone that has operated to promote association, and, by liberating mental power from the necessities of warfare, to promote civilization. If the diversities of climate, soil, and configuration of the earth's surface operate at first to separate mankind, they also operate to encourage exchange. And commerce, which is in itself a form of association or co-operation, operates to promote civilization, not only directly, but by building up interests which are opposed to warfare, and dispelling the ignorance which is the fertile mother of prejudices and animosities.

And so of religion. Though the forms it has assumed and the animosities it has aroused have often sundered men and produced warfare, yet it has at other times been the means of promoting association. A common worship has often, as among the Greeks, mitigated war and furnished the basis of union, while it is from the triumph of Christianity over the barbarians of Europe that modern civilization springs. Had not the Christian Church existed when the Roman Empire went to pieces, Europe, destitute of any bond of association, might have fallen to a condition not much above that of the North American Indians or only received civilization with an Asiatic impress from the conquering scimiters of the invading hordes which had been welded into a mighty power by a religion which, springing up in the deserts of Arabia, had united tribes separated from time immemorial, and, thence issuing, brought into the association of a common faith a great part of the human race.

Looking over what we know of the history of the world, we thus see civilization everywhere springing up where men are brought into association, and everywhere disappearing as this association is broken up. Thus the Roman civilization, spread over Europe by the conquests which insured internal peace, was overwhelmed by the incursions of the northern nations that broke society again into disconnected fragments; and the progress that now goes on in our modern civilization began as the feudal system again began to associate men in larger communities, and the spiritual supremacy of Rome to bring these communities into common relation, as her legions had done before. As the feudal bonds grew into national autonomies, and Christianity worked the amelioration of manners, brought forth the knowledge that during the dark days she had hidden, bound the threads of peaceful union in her all-pervading organization, and taught association in her religious orders, a greater progress became possible, which, as men have been brought into closer and closer association and co-operation, has gone on with greater and greater force.

But we shall never understand the course of civilization, and the varied phenomena which its history presents, without a consideration of what I may term the internal resistances, or counter forces, which arise in the heart of advancing society, and which can alone explain

493

how a civilization once fairly started should either come of itself to a halt or be destroyed by barbarians.

The mental power, which is the motor of social progress, is set free by association, which is, what, perhaps, it may be more properly called, an integration. Society in this process becomes more complex; its individuals more dependent upon each other. Occupations and functions are specialized. Instead of wandering, population becomes fixed. Instead of each man attempting to supply all of his wants, the various trades and industries are separated — one man acquires skill in one thing, and another in another thing. So, too, of knowledge, the body of which constantly tends to become vaster than one man can grasp, and is separated into different parts, which different individuals acquire and pursue. So, too, the performance of religious ceremonies tends to pass into the hands of a body of men specially devoted to that purpose, and the preservation of order, the administration of justice, the assignment of public duties and the distribution of awards, the conduct of war, etc., to be made the special functions of an organized government. In short, to use the language in which Herbert Spencer has defined evolution, the development of society is, in relation to its component individuals, the passing from an indefinite, incoherent homogeneity to a definite, coherent heterogeneity. The lower the stage of social development, the more society resembles one of those lowest of animal organisms which are without organs or limbs, and from which a part may be cut and yet live. The higher the stage of social development, the more society resembles those higher organisms in which functions and powers are specialized, and each member is vitally dependent on the others.

Now, this process of integration, of the specialization of functions and powers, as it goes on in society, is, by virtue of what is probably one of the deepest laws of human nature, accompanied by a constant liability to inequality. I do not mean that inequality is the necessary result of social growth, but that it is the constant tendency of social growth if unaccompanied by changes in social adjustments which, in the new conditions that growth produces, will secure equality. I mean, so to speak, that the garment of laws, customs, and political institutions, which each society weaves for itself, is constantly tending to become too tight as the society develops. I mean, so to speak, that man, as he advances, threads a labyrinth, in which, if he keeps straight ahead,

494

he will infallibly lose his way, and through which reason and justice can alone keep him continuously in an ascending path.

For, while the integration which accompanies growth tends in itself to set free mental power to work improvement, there is, both with increase of numbers and with increase in complexity of the social organization, a counter tendency set up to the production of a state of inequality, which wastes mental power, and, as it increases, brings improvement to a halt.

To trace to its highest expression the law which thus operates to evolve with progress the force which stops progress, would be, it seems to me, to go far to the solution of a problem deeper than that of the genesis of the material universe — the problem of the genesis of evil. Let me content myself with pointing out the manner in which, as society develops, there arise tendencies which check development.

There are two qualities of human nature which it will be well, however, to first call to mind. The one is the power of habit — the tendency to continue to do things in the same way; the other is the possibility of mental and moral deterioration. The effect of the first in social development is to continue habits, customs, laws, and methods, long after they have lost their original usefulness, and the effect of the other is to permit the growth of institutions and modes of thought from which the normal perceptions of men instinctively revolt.

Now the growth and development of society not merely tend to make each more and more dependent upon all, and to lessen the influence of individuals, even over their own conditions, as compared with the influence of society; but the effect of association or integration is to give rise to a collective power which is distinguishable from the sum of individual powers. Analogies, or, perhaps, rather illustrations of the same law, may be found in all directions. As animal organisms increase in complexity, there arise, above the life and power of the parts, a life and power of the integrated whole; above the capability of involuntary movements, the capability of voluntary movements. The actions and impulses of bodies of men are, as has often been observed, different from those which, under the same circumstances, would be called forth in individuals. The fighting qualities of a regiment may be very different from those of the individual soldiers. But there is no need of illustrations. In our inquiries into the nature and rise of rent, we traced the very thing to which I allude. Where population is sparse,

495

land has no value; just as men congregate together, the value of land appears and rises — a clearly distinguishable thing from the values produced by individual effort; a value which springs from association, which increases as association grows greater, and disappears as association is broken up. And the same thing is true of power in other forms than those generally expressed in terms of wealth.

Now, as society grows, the disposition to continue previous social adjustments tends to lodge this collective power, as it arises, in the hands of a portion of the community; and this unequal distribution of the wealth and power gained as society advances tends to produce greater inequality, since aggression grows by what it feeds on, and the idea of justice is blurred by the habitual toleration of injustice.

In this way the patriarchal organization of society can easily grow into hereditary monarchy, in which the king is as a god on earth, and the masses of the people mere slaves of his caprice. It is natural that the father should be the directing head of the family, and that at his death the eldest son, as the oldest and most experienced member of the little community, should succeed to the headship. But to continue this arrangement as the family expands, is to lodge power in a particular line, and the power thus lodged necessarily continues to increase, as the common stock becomes larger and larger, and the power of the community grows. The head of the family passes into the hereditary king, who comes to look upon himself and to be looked upon by others as a being of superior rights. With the growth of the collective power as compared with the power of the individual, his power to reward and to punish increases, and so increase the inducements to flatter and to fear him; until finally, if the process be not disturbed, a nation grovels at the foot of a throne, and a hundred thousand men toil for fifty years to prepare a tomb for one of their own mortal kind.

So the war-chief of a little band of savages is but one of their number, whom they follow as their bravest and most wary. But when large bodies come to act together, personal selection becomes more difficult, a blinder obedience becomes necessary and can be enforced, and from the very necessities of warfare when conducted on a large scale absolute power arises.

And so of the specialization of function. There is a manifest gain in productive power when social growth has gone so far that instead of every producer being summoned from his work for fighting purposes, a regular military force can be specialized; but this inevitably tends to the concentration of power in the hands of the military class or their chiefs. The preservation of internal order, the administration of justice, the construction and care of public works, and, notably, the observances of religion, all tend in similar manner to pass into the hands of special classes, whose disposition it is to magnify their function and extend their power.

But the great cause of inequality is in the natural monopoly which is given by the possession of land. The first perceptions of men seem always to be that land is common property; but the rude devices by which this is at first recognized — such as annual partitions or cultivation in common — are consistent with only a low stage of development. The idea of property, which naturally arises with reference to things of human production, is easily transferred to land, and an institution which when population is sparse merely secures to the improver and user the due reward of his labor, finally, as population becomes dense and rent arises, operates to strip the producer of his wages. Not merely this, but the appropriation of rent for public purposes, which is the only way in which, with anything like a high development, land can be readily retained as common property, becomes, when political and religious power passes into the hands of a class, the ownership of the land by that class, and the rest of the community become merely tenants. And wars and conquests, which tend to the concentration of political power and to the institution of slavery, naturally result, where social growth has given land a value, in the appropriation of the soil. A dominant class, who concentrate power in their hands, will likewise soon concentrate ownership of the land. To them will fall large partitions of conquered land, which the former inhabitants will till as tenants or serfs, and the public domain, or common lands, which in the natural course of social growth are left for a while in every country, and in which state the primitive system of village culture leaves pasture and woodland, are readily acquired, as we see by modern instances. And inequality once established, the ownership of land tends to concentrate as development goes on.

I am merely attempting to set forth the general fact that as a social development goes on, inequality tends to establish itself, and not to point out the particular sequence, which must necessarily vary with different conditions. But this main fact makes intelligible all the phenomena of petrifaction and retrogression. The unequal distribution of the power and wealth gained by the integration of men in society tends

497

to check, and finally to counterbalance, the force by which improvements are made and society advances. On the one side, the masses of the community are compelled to expend their mental powers in merely maintaining existence. On the other side, mental power is expended in keeping up and intensifying the system of inequality, in ostentation, luxury, and warfare. A community divided into a class that rules and a class that is ruled — into the very rich and the very poor, may "build like giants and finish like jewelers"; but it will be monuments of ruthless pride and barren vanity, or of a religion turned from its office of elevating man into an instrument for keeping him down. Invention may for a while to some degree go on; but it will be the invention of refinements in luxury, not the inventions that relieve toil and increase power. In the arcana of temples or in the chambers of court physicians knowledge may still be sought; but it will be hidden as a secret thing, or if it dares come out to elevate common thought or brighten common life, it will be trodden down as a dangerous innovator. For as it tends to lessen the mental power devoted to improvement, so does inequality tend to render men adverse to improvement. How strong is the disposition to adhere to old methods among the classes who are kept in ignorance by being compelled to toil for a mere existence, is too well known to require illustration; and on the other hand the conservatism of the classes to whom the existing social adjustment gives special advantages is equally apparent. This tendency to resist innovation, even though it be improvement, is observable in every special organization — in religion, in law, in medicine, in science, in trade guilds; and it becomes intense just as the organization is close. A close corporation has always an instinctive dislike of innovation and innovators, which is but the expression of an instinctive fear that change may tend to throw down the barriers which hedge it in from the common herd, and so rob it of importance and power; and it is always disposed to guard carefully its special knowledge or skill.

It is in this way that petrifaction succeeds progress. The advance of inequality necessarily brings improvement to a halt, and as it still persists or provokes unavailing reactions, draws even upon the mental power necessary for maintenance, and retrogression begins.

These principles make intelligible the history of civilization. . . .

The rise and growth of European civilization is too vast and complex a subject to be thrown into proper perspective and relation in a few

498

paragraphs; but in all its details, as in its main features, it illustrates the truth that progress goes on just as society tends towards closer association and greater equality. Civilization is co-operation. Union and liberty are its factors. The great extension of association — not alone in the growth of larger and denser communities, but in the increase of commerce and the manifold exchanges which knit each community together and link them with other though widely separated communities; the growth of international and municipal law; the advances in security of property and of person, in individual liberty, and towards democratic government — advances, in short, towards the recognition of the equal rights to life, liberty, and the pursuit of happiness — it is these that make our modern civilization so much greater, so much higher, than any that has gone before. It is these that have set free the mental power which has rolled back the veil of ignorance which hid all but a small portion of the globe from men's knowledge; which has measured the orbits of the circling spheres and bids us see moving, pulsing life in a drop of water; which has opened to us the antechamber of nature's mysteries and read the secrets of a long-buried past; which has harnessed in our service physical forces beside which man's efforts are puny; and increased productive power by a thousand great inventions. . . .

The law of human progress, what is it but the moral law? Just as social adjustments promote justice, just as they acknowledge the equality of right between man and man, just as they insure to each the perfect liberty which is bounded only by the equal liberty of every other, must civilization advance. Just as they fail in this, must advancing civilization come to a halt and recede. Political economy and social science cannot teach any lessons that are not embraced in the simple truths that were taught to poor fishermen and Jewish peasants by One who eighteen hundred years ago was crucified — the simple truths which, beneath the warpings of selfishness and the distortions of superstition, seem to underlie every religion that has ever striven to formulate the spiritual yearnings of man.

[*1879*]

HELEN HUNT JACKSON

[1830–1885]

SHE WAS born in Amherst, Massachusetts, the daughter of Nathan Fiske, teacher of Latin and philosophy at Amherst College. A neighbor and school-mate of Emily Dickinson, the two women were friends all their lives. Miss Fiske was educated at private schools in Ipswich and New York. In 1852 she married Edward B. Hunt, an army officer, and went with him wherever his duties took him. Eleven years after their marriage Major Hunt was ac-cidentally killed, and two years later her second son died (her first son had died in infancy). Until then her life had been that of any other genteel wife and mother, but now, in her loneliness, she turned to writing for the maga-zines. Poems, sketches, and book reviews flowed steadily into such mag-azines as the *Independent*, the *Nation*, *Hearth and Home*, and *Scribner's*. While traveling in Colorado in 1873–4 she met Williams S. Jackson, a banker, and they were married in 1875, settling down in Colorado Springs. Now she began to learn something about the Indians and their problems, was deeply moved, and undertook to call the public's attention to the situa-tion. After arduous research she produced a volume called *A Century of Dishonor* (1881), which she printed and sent to each member of Congress — at her own expense. It has remained one of the classic statements of the wrong done the Indian by the white men. In 1884 Mrs. Jackson published a novel, *Ramona*, on the same theme. It was enormously successful, but rather as a romance of California life than as a social criticism.

from

A CENTURY OF DISHONOR

There is not among these three hundred bands of Indians [in the United States] one which has not suffered cruelly at the hands either of the Government or of white settlers. The poorer, the more insignificant, the more helpless the band, the more certain the cruelty and outrage to which they have been subjected. This is especially true of the bands on the Pacific slope. These Indians found themselves of a sudden surrounded by and caught up in the great influx of gold-seeking settlers, as helpless creatures on a shore are caught up in a tidal wave. There was not time for the Government to make treaties; not even time for communities to make laws. The tale of the wrongs, the oppressions, the murders of the Pacific-slope Indians in the last thirty years would be a volume by itself, and is too monstrous to be believed.

It makes little difference, however, where one opens the record of the history of the Indians; every page and every year has its dark stain. The story of one tribe is the story of all, varied only by differences of time and place; but neither time nor place makes any difference in the main facts. Colorado is as greedy and unjust in 1880 as was Georgia in 1830, and Ohio in 1795; and the United States Government breaks promises now as deftly as then, and with added ingenuity from long practice.

One of its strongest supports in so doing is the wide-spread sentiment among the people of dislike to the Indian, of impatience with his presence as a " barrier to civilization," and distrust of it as a possible danger. The old tales of the frontier life, with its horrors of Indian warfare, have gradually, by two or three generations' telling, produced in the average mind something like an hereditary instinct of unquestioning and unreasoning aversion which it is almost impossible to dislodge or soften.

There are hundreds of pages of unimpeachable testimony on the side of the Indian; but it goes for nothing, is set down as sentimentalism or partisanship, tossed aside and forgotten.

President after president has appointed commission after commission to inquire into and report upon Indian affairs, and to make suggestions as to the best methods of managing them. The reports are filled with eloquent statements of wrongs done to the Indians, of perfidies on the part of the Government; they counsel, as earnestly as words can, a trial of the simple and unperplexing expedients of telling truth, keeping promises, making fair bargains, dealing justly in all ways and all things. These reports are bound up with the Government's Annual Reports, and that is the end of them. It would probably be no exaggeration to say that not one American citizen out of ten thousand ever sees them or knows that they exist, and yet any one of them, circulated throughout the country, read by the right-thinking, right-feeling men and women of this land, would be of itself a " campaign document " that would initiate a revolution which would not subside until the Indians' wrongs were, so far as is now left possible, righted.

In 1869 President Grant appointed a commission of nine men, representing the influence and philanthropy of six leading States, to visit the different Indian reservations, and to " examine all matters appertaining to Indian affairs."

In the report of this commission are such paragraphs as the following: " To assert that ' the Indian will not work ' is as true as it would be to say that the white man will not work.

" Why should the Indian be expected to plant corn, fence lands, build houses, or do anything but get food from day to day, when experience has taught him that the product of his labor will be seized by the white man to-morrow? The most industrious white man would become a drone under similar circumstances. Nevertheless, many of the Indians " (the commissioners might more forcibly have said 130,000 of the Indians) " are already at work, and furnish ample refutation of the assertion that ' the Indian will not work.' There is no escape from the inexorable logic of facts.

" The history of the Government connections with the Indians is a shameful record of broken treaties and unfulfilled promises. The history of the border white man's connection with the Indians is a sickening record of murder, outrage, robbery, and wrongs committed by the former, as the rule, and occasional savage outbreaks and unspeakably barbarous deeds of retaliation by the latter, as the exception.

" Taught by the Government that they had rights entitled to respect, when those rights have been assailed by the rapacity of the white man, the arm which should have been raised to protect them has ever been ready to sustain the aggressor.

" The testimony of some of the highest military officers of the United States is on record to the effect that, in our Indian wars, almost without exception, the first aggressions have been made by the white man; and the assertion is supported by every civilian of reputation who has studied the subject. In addition to the class of robbers and outlaws who find impunity in their nefarious pursuits on the frontiers, there is a large class of professedly reputable men who use every means in their power to bring on Indian wars for the sake of the profit to be realized from the presence of troops and the expenditures of Government funds in their midst. They proclaim death to the Indians at all times in words and publications, making no distinction between the innocent and the guilty. They irate the lowest class of men to the perpetration of the darkest deeds against their victims, and as judges and jurymen shield them from the justice due to their crimes. Every crime committed by a white man against an Indian is concealed or palliated. Every offence committed by an Indian against a white man is borne on the wings of the post or the telegraph to the remotest corner of the land, clothed with all the horrors which the reality or imagination can throw around it. Against such influences as these the people of the United States need to be warned."

To assume that it would be easy, or by any one sudden stroke of legislative policy possible, to undo the mischief and hurt of the long past, set the Indian policy of the country right for the future, and make the Indians at once safe and happy, is the blunder of a hasty and uninformed judgment. The notion which seems to be growing more prevalent, that simply to make all Indians at once citizens of the United States would be a sovereign and instantaneous panacea for all their ills and all the Government's perplexities, is a very inconsiderate one. To administer complete citizenship of a sudden, all round, to all Indians, barbarous and civilized alike, would be as grotesque a blunder as to dose them all round with any one medicine, irrespective of the symptoms and needs of their diseases. It would kill more than it would cure. Nevertheless, it is true, as was well stated by one of the superintendents of Indian Affairs in 1857, that, " so long as they are not citizens of the United States, their rights of property must remain insecure against invasion. The doors of the federal tribunals being barred against them while wards and dependents, they can only partially exercise the rights of free government, or give to those who make, execute, and construe the few laws they are allowed to enact, dignity sufficient to make them respectable. While they continue individually to gather the crumbs that fall from the table of the United States, idleness, improvidence, and indebtedness will be the rule, and industry, thrift, and freedom from debt the exception. The utter absence of individual title to particular lands deprives every one among them of the chief incentive to labor and exertion — the very mainspring on which the prosperity of a people depends."

All judicious plans and measures for their safety and salvation must embody provisions for their becoming citizens as fast as they are fit, and must protect them till then in every right and particular in which our laws protect other " persons " who are not citizens.

There is a disposition in a certain class of minds to be impatient with any protestation against wrong which is unaccompanied or unprepared with a quick and exact scheme of remedy. This is illogical. When pioneers in a new country find a tract of poisonous and swampy wilderness to be reclaimed, they do not withhold their hands from fire and axe till they see clearly which way roads should run, where good water will spring, and what crops will best grow on the redeemed land. They first clear the swamp. So with this poisonous and baffling part of the domain of our national affairs — let us first " clear the swamp."

However great perplexity and difficulty there may be in the details of any and every plan possible for doing at this late day anything like justice to the Indian, however hard it may be for good statesmen and good men to agree upon the things that ought to be done, there certainly is, or ought to be, no perplexity whatever, no difficulty whatever, in agreeing upon certain things that ought not to be done, and which must cease to be done before the first steps can be taken toward righting the wrongs, curing the ills, and wiping out the disgrace to us of the present condition of our Indians.

Cheating, robbing, breaking promises — these three are clearly things which must cease to be done. One more thing, also, and that is the refusal of the protection of the law to the Indian's rights of property, " of life, liberty, and the pursuit of happiness."

When these four things have ceased to be done, time, statesmanship, philanthropy, and Christianity can slowly and surely do the rest. Till these four things have ceased to be done, statesmanship and philanthropy alike must work in vain, and even Christianity can reap but small harvest.

[*1881*]

SAMUEL L. CLEMENS

[1835–1910]

AMONG the half-dozen great names in American literature is the pseudonym Mark Twain, used by this Missouri-born, poorly schooled, Mississippi riverboat pilot and unsuccessful miner. The death of his father when he was twelve years old forced young Clemens to leave school and become a printer's apprentice. The transition to newspaper work was easy. For a few years he was an itinerant journalist, then in 1857 apprenticed himself to a river pilot. In all he spent four years on the Mississippi, quitting it, as a licensed pilot, only when the Civil War put an end to the river traffic. He then went west — to try prospecting, but soon to become a reporter in Virginia City, Nevada. In 1864 he went on to California, and there, the following year, he published a story, " The Celebrated Jumping Frog of Calaveras County," which was a typical piece of frontier humor, but which had much more than a local success. A series of sketches from the Sandwich Islands gave him enough standing to justify a lecture tour, and this was followed by an excursion around the world, out of which grew the sketches that were later developed into his very popular book *The Innocents Abroad* (1869). Married in 1870 to Olivia Langdon — a conservative, middle-class woman to whom he was thoroughly devoted and who exercised a restraining influence upon his sometimes rough humor and unconventional views — he settled down to a literary career that made him a national hero. His output was large and uneven, but it included works that now seem imperishable: *The Adventures of Tom Sawyer* (1876), *Life on the Mississippi* (1883), *The Adventures of Huckleberry Finn* (1884), *A Connecticut Yankee at King Arthur's Court* (1889), *The Man That Corrupted Hadleyburg* (1900), and various shorter pieces.

Huckleberry Finn is, no doubt, his masterpiece. In the *Connecticut Yankee*, however, we find a particularly interesting expression of his feelings about society, class relations, and human progress. In a piece like " To a Person Sitting in Darkness " we find the " gentle " and " humorous " Mark Twain boiling with fury on the subject of imperialism. Those who know only his " boys' books " do not know Mark Twain. In numerous other works — such as *Hadleyburg*, *What is Man?* (1906), and *The Mysterious Stranger*, published posthumously in 1916 — he revealed a bitterness, a hatred for greed, selfishness, and hypocrisy, and a contempt for the shams of conventional society that are hardly matched in our literature. In his use of the

505

vernacular and of common materials he proved himself essentially a man of the people. By the views he expressed on a variety of social, moral, political, and religious problems he proved himself a passionate democrat.

from

A CONNECTICUT YANKEE IN
KING ARTHUR'S COURT

[*Hank Morgan of Hartford, a machinist at the Colt factory, is knocked unconscious. He dreams that he awakens in the year 513, when King Arthur reigned in England. His simple, mechanical tricks astound the court; he is regarded as a great magician; and thus he becomes the " King's right hand " and is known throughout England as The Boss. . . . In the first selection he is seeking knightly adventure, according to the custom of the times, in company with a fair young lady.*]

We came upon a group of ragged poor creatures who had assembled to mend the thing which was regarded as a road. They were as humble as animals to me; and when I proposed to breakfast with them, they were so flattered, so overwhelmed by this extraordinary condescension of mine that at first they were not able to believe that I was in earnest. My lady put up her scornful lip and withdrew to one side; she said in their hearing that she would as soon think of eating with the other cattle — a remark which embarrassed these poor devils merely because it referred to them, and not because it insulted or offended them, for it didn't. And yet they were not slaves, not chattels. By a sarcasm of law and phrase they were freemen. Seven-tenths of the free population of the country were of just their class and degree: small " independent " farmers, artisans, etc.; which is to say, they were the nation, the actual Nation; they were about all of it that was useful, or worth saving, or really respectworthy, and to subtract them would have been to subtract the Nation and leave behind some dregs, some refuse, in the shape of a king, nobility and gentry, idle, unproductive, acquainted mainly with the arts of wasting and destroying, and of no sort of use or value in any rationally constructed world. And yet, by ingenious contrivance, this gilded minority, instead of being in the tail of the procession where it belonged, was marching head up and banners flying, at the other end of it; had elected itself to be the Nation, and these innumerable clams had permitted it so long that they had come at last to accept it as a truth; and not only that, but to believe it right and as it should be. The priests had told their fathers and themselves that this ironical state of things was ordained of God; and so, not reflecting upon how unlike God it would be to amuse himself with sarcarsms, and especially such poor transparent ones as this, they had dropped the matter there and become respectfully quiet.

The talk of these meek people had a strange enough sound in a formerly American ear. They were freemen, but they could not leave the estates of their lord or their bishop without his permission; they could not prepare their own bread but must have their corn ground and their bread baked at his mill and his bakery, and pay roundly for the same; they could not sell a piece of their own property without paying him a handsome percentage of the proceeds, nor buy a piece of somebody else's without remembering him in cash for the privilege; they had to harvest his grain for him gratis, and be ready to come at a moment's notice, leaving their own crop to destruction by the threatened storm; they had to let him plant fruit trees in their fields, and then keep their indignation to themselves when his heedless fruit-gatherers trampled the grain around the trees; they had to smother their anger when his hunting-parties galloped through their fields laying waste the result of their patient toil; they were not allowed to keep doves themselves, and when the swarms from my lord's dovecote settled on their crops they must not lose their temper and kill a bird, for awful would the penalty be; when the harvest was at last gathered, then came the procession of robbers to levy their blackmail upon it; first the Church carted off its fat tenth, then the king's commissioner took his twentieth, then my lord's people made a mighty inroad upon the remainder; after which, the skinned freeman had liberty to bestow the remnant in his barn, in case it was worth the trouble; there were taxes, and taxes, and taxes, and more taxes, and taxes again, and yet other taxes — upon this free and independent pauper, but none upon his lord the baron or the bishop, none upon the wasteful nobility or the all-devouring Church; if the baron would sleep unvexed, the freeman must sit up all night after his day's work and whip the ponds to keep the frogs quiet; if the freeman's daughter — but no, that last infamy of monarchical government is unprintable; and finally, if the freeman, grown desperate with his tortures, found his life unendurable under such conditions, and sacrificed it and fled to death for mercy and refuge, the gentle Church condemned him to eternal fire, the gentle law buried him at midnight at the crossroads with a stake through his back, and his master the baron or the bishop confiscated all his property and turned his widow and his orphans out of doors.

And here were these freemen assembled in the early morning to work on their lord the bishop's road three days each — gratis; every head of a family, and every son of a family, three days each, gratis, and a day or so added for their servants. Why, it was like reading about France and the French, before the ever memorable and blessed Revolution, which swept a thousand years of such villainy away in one swift tidal wave of blood — one: a settlement of that hoary debt in the proportion of half a drop of blood for each hogshead of it that had been pressed by slow tortures out of that people in the weary stretch of ten centuries of wrong and shame and misery the like of which was not to be mated but in hell. There were two " Reigns of Terror," if we would but remember it and consider it; the one wrought murder in hot passion, the other in heartless cold blood; the one lasted mere months, the other had lasted a thousand years; the one inflicted death upon ten thousand persons, the other upon a hundred millions; but our shudders are all for the " horrors " of the minor Terror, the momentary Terror, so to speak; whereas, what is the horror of swift death by the ax compared with lifelong death from hunger, cold, insult, cruelty, and heartbreak? What is swift death by lightning compared with death by slow fire at the stake? A city cemetery could contain the coffins filled by that brief Terror which we have all been so diligently taught to shiver at and mourn over; but all France could hardly contain the coffins filled by that older and real Terror — that unspeakably bitter and awful Terror which none of us has been taught to see in its vastness or pity as it deserves.

These poor ostensible freemen who were sharing their breakfast and their talk with me, were as full of humble reverence for their king and Church and nobility as their worst enemy could desire. There was something pitifully ludicrous about it. I asked them if they supposed a nation of people ever existed, who, with a free vote in every man's hand, would elect that a single family and its descendants should reign over it forever, whether gifted or boobies, to the exclusion of all other families — including the voter's; and would also elect that a certain hundred families should be raised to dizzy summits of rank, and clothed on with offensive transmissible glories and privileges to the exclusion of the rest of the nation's families — *including his own.*

They all looked unhit, and said they didn't know; that they had never thought about it before, and it hadn't ever occurred to them that a nation could be so situated that every man *could* have a say in the government. I said I had seen one — and that it would last until it had an Established Church. Again they were all unhit — at first. But presently one man looked up and asked me to state that proposition again; and state it slowly, so it could soak into his understanding. I did it; and after a little he had the idea, and he brought his fist down and said *he* didn't believe a nation where every man had a vote would voluntarily get down in the mud and dirt in any such way; and that to steal from a nation its will and preference must be a crime and the first of all crimes. I said to myself:

" This one's a man. If I were backed by enough of his sort, I would make a strike for the welfare of this country, and try to prove myself its loyalest citizen by making a wholesome change in its system of government."

You see my kind of loyalty was loyalty to one's country, not to its institutions or its office-holders. The country is the real thing, the substantial thing, the eternal thing; it is the thing to watch over, and care for, and be loyal to; institutions are extraneous, they are its mere clothing, and clothing can wear out, become ragged, cease to be comfortable, cease to protect the body from winter, disease, and death. To be loyal to rags, to shout for rags, to worship rags, to die for rags — that is a loyalty of unreason, it is pure animal; it belongs to monarchy, was invented by monarchy; let monarchy keep it. I was from Connecticut, whose Constitution declares " that all political power is inherent in the people, and all free governments are founded on their authority and instituted for their benefit; and that they have *at all times* an undeniable and indefeasible right to *alter their form of government* in such a manner as they may think expedient."

Under that gospel, the citizen who thinks he sees that the commonwealth's political clothes are worn out, and yet holds his peace and does not agitate for a new suit, is disloyal; he is a traitor. That he may be the only one who thinks he sees this decay, does not excuse him; it is his duty to agitate anyway, and it is the duty of the others to vote him down if they do not see the matter as he does.

And now here I was, in a country where a right to say how the country should be governed was restricted to six persons in each thousand of its population. For the nine hundred and ninety-four to express dissatisfaction with the regnant system and propose to change it, would have made the whole six shudder as one man, it would have been so disloyal, so dishonorable, such putrid black treason. So to speak, I was become a stockholder in a corporation where nine hundred and ninety-four of the members furnished all the money and did all the work, and the other six elected themselves a permanent board of direction and took all the dividends. It seemed to me that what the nine hundred and ninety-four dupes needed was a new deal. The thing that would have best suited the circus side of my nature would have been to resign the Boss-ship and get up an insurrection and turn it into a revolution; but I knew that the Jack Cade or the Wat Tyler who tries such a thing without first educating his materials up to revolution grade is almost absolutely certain to get left. . . .

[*In the following two selections Morgan and King Arthur are wandering through England disguised as commoners. Arthur has some difficulty acting the part.*]

On the morning of the fourth day, when it was just sunrise, and we had been tramping an hour in the chill dawn, I came to a resolution: the king *must* be drilled; things could not go on so, he must be taken in hand and deliberately and conscientiously drilled, or we couldn't ever venture to enter a dwelling; the very cats would know this masquerader for a humbug and no peasant. So I called a halt and said:

"Sire, as between clothes and countenance, you are all right, there is no discrepancy; but as between your clothes and your bearing, you are all wrong, there is a most noticeable discrepancy. Your soldierly stride, your lordly port — these will not do. You stand too straight, your looks are too high, too confident. The cares of a kingdom do not stoop the shoulders, they do not droop the chin, they do not depress the high level of the eye-glance, they do not put doubt and fear in the heart and hang out the signs of them in slouching body and unsure step. It is the sordid cares of the lowly born that do these things. You must learn the trick; you must imitate the trade-marks of poverty, misery, oppression, insult, and the other several and common inhumanities that sap the manliness out of a man and make him a loyal and proper and approved subject and a satisfaction to his masters, or the very infants will know you for better than your disguise, and we shall go to pieces at the first hut we stop at. Pray try to walk like this."

The king took careful note, and then tried an imitation.

"Pretty fair — pretty fair. Chin a little lower, please — there, very good. Eyes too high; pray don't look at the horizon, look at the ground, ten steps in front of you. Ah — that is better, that is very good. Wait please; you betray too much vigor, too much decision; you want more of a shamble. Look at me, please — this is what I mean. . . . Now you are getting it; that is the idea — at least, it sort of approaches it. . . . Yes, that is pretty fair. *But!* There is a great big something wanting, I don't quite know what it is. Please walk thirty yards, so that I can get a perspective on the thing. . . . Now, then — your head's right, speed's right, shoulders right, eyes right, chin right, gait, carriage, general style right — everything's right! And yet the fact remains, the aggregate's wrong. The account don't balance. Do it again, please . . . *now* I think I begin to see what it is. Yes, I've struck it. You see, the genuine spiritlessness is wanting; that's what's the trouble. It's all *amateur* — mechanical details all right, almost to a hair; everything about the delusion perfect, except that it don't delude."

"What, then, must one do, to prevail?"

"Let me think. . . . I can't seem to quite get at it. In fact, there isn't anything that can right the matter but practice. This is a good place for it: roots and stony ground to break up your stately gait, a region not liable to interruption, only one field and one hut in sight, and they so far away that nobody could see us from there. It will be well to move a little off the road and put in the whole day drilling you, sire."

After the drill had gone on a little while, I said:

"Now, sire, imagine that we are at the door of the hut yonder, and the family are before us. Proceed, please — accost the head of the house."

The king unconsciously straightened up like a monument, and said, with frozen austerity:

"Varlet, bring a seat; and serve to me what cheer ye have."

"Ah, your grace, that is not well done."

"In what lacketh it?"

"These people do not call *each other* varlets."

"Nay, is that true?"

"Yes; only those above them call them so."

"Then must I try again. I will call him villein."

" No — no; for he may be a freeman."

" Ah — so. Then peradventure I should call him goodman."

" That would answer, your grace, but it would be still better if you said friend, or brother."

" Brother! — to dirt like that? "

" Ah, but *we* are pretending to be dirt like that, too."

" It is even true. I will say it. Brother, bring a seat, and thereto what cheer ye have, withal. *Now* 'tis right."

" Not quite, not wholly right. You have asked for one, not *us* — for one, not both; food for one, a seat for one."

The king looked puzzled — he wasn't a very heavy weight, intellectually. His head was an hour-glass; it could stow an idea, but it had to do it a grain at a time, not the whole idea at once.

" Would *you* have a seat also — and sit? "

" If I did not sit, the man would perceive that we were only pretending to be equals — and playing the deception pretty poorly, too."

" It is well and truly said! How wonderful is truth, come it in whatsoever unexpected form it may! Yes, he must bring out seats and food for both, and in serving us present not ewer and napkin with more show of respect to the one than to the other."

" And there is even yet a detail that needs correcting. He must bring nothing outside; we will go in — in among the dirt, and possibly other repulsive things — and take the food with the household, and after the fashion of the house, and all on equal terms, except the man be of the serf class; and finally, there will be no ewer and no napkin, whether he be serf or free. Please walk again, my liege. There — it is better — it is the best yet; but not perfect. The shoulders have known no ignobler burden than iron mail, and they will not stoop."

" Give me, then, the bag. I will learn the spirit that goeth with burdens that have not honor. It is the spirit that stoopeth the shoulders, I ween, and not the weight; for armor is heavy, yet it is a proud burden, and a man standeth straight in it. . . . Nay, but me no buts, offer me no objections. I will have the thing. Strap it upon my back."

He was complete now with that knapsack on, and looked as little like a king as any man I had ever seen. But it was an obstinate pair of shoulders; they could not seem to learn the trick of stooping with any sort of deceptive naturalness. The drill went on, I prompting and correcting:

" Now, make believe you are in debt, and eaten up by relentless creditors; you are out of work — which is horse-shoeing, let us say — and can get none; and your wife is sick, your children are crying because they are hungry — "

And so on, and so on, I drilled him as representing in turn all sorts of people out of luck and suffering dire privations and misfortunes. But lord, it was only just words, words — they meant nothing in the world to him. I might just as well have whistled. Words realize nothing, vivify nothing to you, unless you have suffered in your own person the thing which the words try to describe. There are wise people who talk ever so knowingly and complacently about "the working classes," and satisfy themselves that a day's hard intellectual work is very much harder than a day's hard manual toil, and is righteously entitled to much bigger pay. Why, they really think that, you know, because they know all about the one, but haven't tried the other. But I know all about both; and so far as I am concerned, there isn't money enough in the universe to hire me to swing a pickax thirty days, but I will do the hardest kind of intellectual work for just as near nothing as you can cipher it down — and I will be satisfied, too.

Intellectual "work" is misnamed; it is a pleasure, a dissipation, and is its own highest reward. The poorest paid architect, engineer, general, author, sculptor, painter, lecturer, advocate, legislator, actor, preacher, singer is constructively in heaven when he is at work; and as for the musician with the fiddle-bow in his hand who sits in the midst of a great orchestra with the ebbing and flowing tides of divine sound washing over him — why, certainly, he is at work, if you wish to call it that, but lord, it's a sarcasm just the same. The law of work does seem utterly unfair — but there it is, and nothing can change it: the higher the pay in enjoyment the worker gets out of it, the higher shall be his pay in cash, also. And it's also the very law of those transparent swindles, transmissible nobility and kingship. . . .

We stood there awhile, in the thick darkness and stillness, looking toward the red blur in the distance, and trying to make out the meaning of a far-away murmur that rose and fell fitfully on the night. Sometimes it swelled up and for a moment seemed less remote; but when we were hopefully expecting it to betray its cause and nature, it dulled and sank again, carrying its mystery with it. We started down the hill in its direction, and the winding road plunged us at once into almost solid darkness — darkness that was packed and crammed in between two

SAMUEL L. CLEMENS: *Connecticut Yankee*

tall forest walls. We groped along down for half a mile, perhaps, the murmur growing more and more distinct all the time, the coming storm threatening more and more, with now and then a little shiver of wind, a faint show of lightning, and dull grumblings of distant thunder. I was in the lead. I ran against something — a soft heavy something which gave, slightly, to the impulse of my weight; at the same moment the lightning glared out, and within a foot of my face was the writhing face of a man who was hanging from the limb of a tree! That is, it seemed to be writhing, but it was not. It was a gruesome sight. Straightway there was an ear-splitting explosion of thunder, and the bottom of heaven fell out; the rain poured down in a deluge. No matter, we must try to cut this man down, on the chance that there might be life in him yet, mustn't we? The lightning came quick and sharp now, and the place was alternately noonday and midnight. One moment the man would be hanging before me in an intense light and the next he was blotted out again in the darkness. I told the king we must cut him down. The king at once objected.

" If he hanged himself, he was willing to lose his property to his lord; so let him be. If others hanged him, belike they had the right — let him hang."

" But — "

" But me no buts, but even leave him as he is. And for yet another reason. When the lightning cometh again — there, look abroad."

Two others hanging, within fifty yards of us!

" It is not weather meet for doing useless courtesies unto dead folk. They are past thanking you. Come — it is unprofitable to tarry here."

There was reason in what he said, so we moved on. Within the next mile we counted six more hanging forms by the blaze of the lightning, and altogether it was a grisly excursion. That murmur was a murmur no longer, it was a roar; a roar of men's voices. A man came flying by now, dimly through the darkness, and other men chasing him. They disappeared. Presently another case of the kind occurred, and then another and another. Then a sudden turn of the road brought us in sight of that fire — it was a larger manor-house, and little or nothing was left of it — and everywhere men were flying and other men raging after them in pursuit.

I warned the king that this was not a safe place for strangers. We would better get away from the light, until matters should improve. We stepped back a little, and hid in the edge of the wood. From this hiding-place we saw both men and women hunted by the mob. The fearful work went on until nearly dawn. Then, the fire being out and the storm spent, the voices and flying footsteps presently ceased, and darkness and stillness reigned again.

We ventured out, and hurried cautiously away; and although we were worn out and sleepy, we kept on until we had put this place some miles behind us. Then we asked hospitality at the hut of a charcoal-burner, and got what was to be had. A woman was up and about, but the man was still asleep, on a straw shake-down, on the clay floor. The woman seemed uneasy until I explained that we were travelers and had lost our way and been wandering in the woods all night. She became talkative, then, and asked if we had heard of the terrible goings-on at the manor-house of Abblasoure. Yes, we had heard of them, but what we wanted now was rest and sleep. The king broke in:

" Sell us the house and take yourselves away, for we be perilous company, being late come from people that died at the Spotted Death."

It was good of him, but unnecessary. One of the commonest decorations of the nation was the waffle-iron face. I had noticed that the woman and her husband were both so decorated. She made us entirely welcome, and had no fears; and plainly she was immensely impressed by the king's proposition; for, of course, it was a good deal of an event in her life to run across a person of the king's humble appearance who was ready to buy a man's house for the sake of a night's lodging. It gave her a large respect for us, and she strained the lean possibilities of her hovel to the utmost to make us comfortable.

We slept till far into the afternoon, and then got up hungry enough to make cotter fare quite palatable to the king, the more particularly as it was scant in quantity. And also in variety; it consisted solely of onions, salt, and the national black bread — made out of horse-feed. The woman told us about the affair of the evening before. At ten or eleven at night, when everybody was in bed, the manor-house burst into flames. The countryside swarmed to the rescue, and the family were saved, with one exception, the master. He did not appear. Everybody was frantic over the loss, and two brave yeomen sacrificed their lives in ransacking the burning house seeking that valuable personage. But after a while he was found — what was left of him — which was his corpse. It was in a copse three hundred yards away, bound, gagged, stabbed in a dozen places.

Who had done this? Suspicion fell upon a humble family in the

515

neighborhood who had been lately treated with peculiar harshness by the baron; and from these people the suspicion easily extended itself to their relatives and familiars. A suspicion was enough; my lord's liveried retainers proclaimed an instant crusade against these people, and were promptly joined by the community in general. The woman's husband had been active with the mob, and had not returned home until nearly dawn. He was gone now to find out what the general result had been. While we were still talking he came back from his quest. His report was revolting enough. Eighteen persons hanged or butchered, and two yeomen and thirteen prisoners lost in the fire.

" And how many prisoners were there all together in the vaults? "

" Thirteen."

" Then every one of them was lost? "

" Yes, all."

. " But the people arrived in time to save the family; how is it they could save none of the prisoners? "

The man looked puzzled, and said:

"Would one unlock the vaults at such a time? Marry, some would have escaped."

" Then you mean that nobody *did* unlock them? "

" None went near them, either to lock or unlock. It standeth to reason that the bolts were fast; wherefore it was only needful to establish a watch, so that if any broke the bonds he might not escape, but be taken. None were taken."

" Natheless, three did escape," said the king, " and ye will do well to publish it and set justice upon their track, for these murthered the baron and fired the house."

I was just expecting he would come out with that. For a moment the man and his wife showed an eager interest in this news and an impatience to go out and spread it; then a sudden something else betrayed itself in their faces, and they began to ask questions. I answered the questions myself, and narrowly watched the effects produced. I was soon satisfied that the knowledge of who these three prisoners were had somehow changed the atmosphere; that our hosts' continued eagerness to go and spread the news was now only pretended and not real. The king did not notice the change, and I was glad of that. I worked the conversation around toward other details of the night's proceedings, and noted that these people were relieved to have it take that direction.

The painful thing observable about all this business was the alacrity with which this oppressed community had turned their cruel hands against their own class in the interest of the common oppressor. This man and woman seemed to feel that in a quarrel between a person of their own class and his lord, it was the natural and proper and rightful thing for that poor devil's whole caste to side with the master and fight his battle for him, without ever stopping to inquire into the rights or wrongs of the matter. This man had been out helping to hang his neighbors, and had done his work with zeal, and yet was aware that there was nothing against them but a mere suspicion, with nothing back of it describable as evidence, still neither he nor his wife seemed to see anything horrible about it.

This was depressing — to a man with the dream of a republic in his head. It reminded me of a time thirteen centuries away, when the "poor whites" of our South who were always despised and frequently insulted by the slavelords around them, and who owed their base condition simply to the presence of slavery in their midst, were yet pusillanimously ready to side with the slavelords in all political moves for the upholding and perpetuating of slavery, and did also finally shoulder their muskets and pour out their lives in an effort to prevent the destruction of that very institution which degraded them. And there was only one redeeming feature connected with that pitiful piece of history; and that was, that secretly the "poor white" did detest the slavelord, and did feel his own shame. That feeling was not brought to the surface, but the fact that it was there and could have been brought out, under favorable circumstances, was something — in fact, it was enough; for it showed that a man is at bottom a man, after all, even if it doesn't show on the outside.

Well, as it turned out, this charcoal-burner was just the twin of the Southern "poor white" of the far future. The king presently showed impatience, and said:

"An ye prattle here all the day, justice will miscarry. Think ye the criminals will abide in their father's house? They are fleeing, they are not waiting. You should look to it that a party of horse be set upon their track."

The woman paled slightly, but quite perceptibly, and the man looked flustered and irresolute. I said:

"Come, friend, I will walk a little way with you, and explain which direction I think they would try to take. If they were merely resisters of the gabelle or some kindred absurdity I would try to protect them

from capture; but when men murder a person of high degree and likewise burn his house, that is another matter."

The last remark was for the king — to quiet him. On the road the
man pulled his resolution together, and began the march with a steady
gait, but there was no eagerness in it. By and by I said:

"What relation were these men to you — cousins?"

He turned as white as his layer of charcoal would let him, and
stopped, trembling.

"Ah, my God, how know ye that?"

"I didn't know it; it was a chance guess."

"Poor lads, they are lost. And good lads they were, too."

"Were you actually going yonder to tell on them?"

He didn't quite know how to take this; but he said, hesitatingly:

"Ye-s."

"Then I think you are a damned scoundrel!"

It made him as glad as if I had called him an angel.

"Say the good words again, brother! for surely ye mean that ye would
not betray me an I failed of my duty."

"Duty? There is no duty in the matter, except the duty to keep still
and let those men get away. They've done a righteous deed."

He looked pleased; pleased, and touched with apprehension at the
same time. He looked up and down the road to see that no one was
coming, and then said in a cautious voice:

"From what land come you, brother, that you speak such perilous
words, and seem not to be afraid?"

"They are not perilous words when spoken to one of my own caste,
I take it. You would not tell anybody I said them?"

"I? I would be drawn asunder by wild horses first."

"Well, then, let me say my say. I have no fears of your repeating it.
I think devil's work has been done last night upon those innocent poor
people. That old baron got only what he deserved. If I had my way,
all his kind should have the same luck."

Fear and depression vanished from the man's manner, and grateful-
ness and a brave animation took their place:

"Even though you be a spy, and your words a trap for my undoing,
yet are they such refreshment that to hear them again and others like
to them, I would go to the gallows happy, as having had one good feast
at least in a starved life. And I will say my say now, and ye may report
it if ye be so minded. I helped to hang my neighbors for that it were

peril to my own life to show lack of zeal in the master's cause; the others helped for none other reason. All rejoice to-day that he is dead, but all do go about seemingly sorrowing, and shedding the hypocrite's tear, for in that lies safety. I have said the words, I have said the words! the only ones that have ever tasted good in my mouth, and the reward of that taste is sufficient. Lead on, an ye will, be it even to the scaffold, for I am ready."

There it was, you see. A man *is* a man, at bottom. Whole ages of abuse and oppression cannot crush the manhood clear out of him. Whoever thinks it a mistake is himself mistaken. Yes, there is plenty good enough material for a republic in the most degraded people that ever existed — even the Russians; plenty of manhood in them — even in the Germans — if one could but force it out of its timid and suspicious privacy, to overflow and trample in the mud any throne that ever was set up and any nobility that ever supported it. We should see certain things yet, let us hope and believe. First, a modified monarchy, till Arthur's days were done, then the destruction of the throne, nobility abolished, every member of it bound out to some useful trade, universal suffrage instituted, and the whole government placed in the hands of the men and women of the nation there to remain. Yes, there was no occasion to give up my dream. . . .

[*1889*]

---

from

TO THE PERSON SITTING IN DARKNESS

The following news from China appeared in the *Sun*, of New York, on Christmas Eve. The italics are mine:

The Rev. Mr. Ament, of the American Board of Foreign Missions, has returned from a trip which he made for the purpose of collecting indemnities for damages done by Boxers. *Everywhere he went he compelled the Chinese to pay.* He says that all his native Christians are now provided for. He had 700 of them under his charge, and 300 were killed. He has *collected 300 taels for each* of these murders, and has *compelled full payment for all the property belonging to Christians* that was destroyed. He also assessed *fines* amounting to THIRTEEN TIMES the amount of the indemnity. *This money will be used for the propagation of the Gospel.*

Mr. Ament declares that the compensation he has collected is *moderate* when compared with the amount secured by the Catholics, who demand, in addition to money, *head for head*. They collect 500 taels for each murder of a Catholic. In the Wenchiu country, 680 Catholics were killed, and for this the European Catholics here demand 750,000 strings of cash and 680 *heads*.

In the course of a conversation Mr. Ament referred to the attitude of the missionaries toward the Chinese. He said:

"I deny emphatically that the missionaries are *vindictive*, that they *generally* looted, or that they have done anything *since* the *siege* that *the circumstances did not demand*. I criticize the Americans. *The soft hand of the Americans is not as good as the mailed fist of the Germans.* If you deal with the Chinese with a soft hand they will take advantage of it.

"The statement that the French government will return the loot taken by the French soldiers is the source of the greatest amusement here. The French soldiers were more systematic looters than the Germans, and it is a fact that to-day *Catholic Christians*, carrying French flags and armed with modern guns, *are looting villages* in the Province of Chili."

By happy luck, we get these glad tidings on Christmas Eve — just in time to enable us to celebrate the day with proper gayety and enthusiasm. Our spirits soar, and we find we can even make jokes: Taels, I win, Heads you lose.

Our Reverend Ament is the right man in the right place. What we want of our missionaries out there is, not that they shall merely represent in their acts and persons the grace and gentleness and charity and loving-kindness of our religion, but that they shall also represent the American spirit. The oldest Americans are the Pawnees. . . .

Our Reverend Ament is justifiably jealous of those enterprising Catholics, who not only get big money for each lost convert, but get "head for head" besides. But he should soothe himself with the reflections that the entirety of their exactions are for their own pockets, whereas he, less selfishly, devotes only 300 taels per head to that service, and gives the whole vast thirteen repetitions of the property-indemnity to the service of propagating the Gospel. His magnanimity has won him the approval of his nation, and will get him a monument. Let him be content with these rewards. We all hold him dear for manfully defending his fellow missionaries from exaggerated charges which were beginning to distress us, but which his testimony has so considerably modified that we can now contemplate them without noticeable pain. For now we know that, even before the siege, the missionaries were not "generally" out looting, and that, "since the siege," they have acted quite handsomely, except when " circumstances " crowded them. I am arranging for the monument. Subscriptions for it can be sent to the American Board; designs for it can be sent to me. Designs must allegorically set forth the Thirteen Reduplications of the Indemnity, and the Object for which they were exacted; as Ornaments, the designs must exhibit 680 Heads, so disposed as to give a pleasing and pretty effect; for the Catholics have done nicely, and are entitled to notice in the monument. Mottoes may be suggested, if any shall be discovered that will satisfactorily cover the ground.

Mr. Ament's financial feat of squeezing a thirteen-fold indemnity out of the pauper peasants to square other people's offenses, thus condemning them and their women and innocent little children to inevitable starvation and lingering death, in order that the blood money so acquired might be *" used for the propagation of the Gospel,"* does not flutter my serenity; although the act and the words, taken together, concrete a blasphemy so hideous and so colossal that, without doubt, its mate is not findable in the history of this or of any other age. Yet, if a layman had done that thing and justified it with those words, I should have shuddered, I know. Or, if I had done the thing and said the words myself — However, the thought is unthinkable, irreverent as some imperfectly informed people think me. Sometimes an ordained minister sets out to be blasphemous. When this happens, the layman is out of the running; he stands no chance.

We have Mr. Ament's impassioned assurance that the missionaries are not " vindictive." Let us hope and pray that they will never become so, but will remain in the almost morbidly fair and just and gentle temper which is affording so much satisfaction to their brother and champion to-day.

The following is from the New York *Tribune* of Christmas Eve. It comes from that journal's Tokyo correspondent. It has a strange and impudent sound, but the Japanese are but partially civilized as yet. When they become wholly civilized they will not talk so:

The missionary question, of course, occupies a foremost place in the discussion. It is now felt as essential that the Western Powers take cognizance of the sentiment here, that religious invasions of Oriental countries by powerful Western organizations are tantamount to filibustering expeditions, and should not only be discountenanced, but that stern measures should be adopted for their suppression. The feeling here is that the missionary organizations constitute a constant menace to peaceful international relations.

Shall we? That is, shall we go on conferring our Civilization upon the peoples that sit in darkness, or shall we give those poor things a rest? Shall we bang right ahead in our old-time, loud, pious way, and commit the new century to the game; or shall we sober up and sit down and think it over first? Would it not be prudent to get our Civilization tools together, and see how much stock is left on hand in the way of Glass Beads and Theology, and Maxim Guns and Hymn Books, and Trade Gin and Torches of Progress and Enlightenment (patent adjustable ones, good to fire villages with, upon occasion), and balance the books, and arrive at the profit and loss, so that we may intelligently decide whether to continue the business or sell out the property and start a new Civilization Scheme on the proceeds?

Extending the Blessings of Civilization to our Brother who Sits in Darkness has been a good trade and has paid well, on the whole; and there is money in it yet, if carefully worked — but not enough, in my judgment, to make any considerable risk advisable. The People that Sit in Darkness are getting to be too scarce — too scarce and too shy. And such darkness as is now left is really of but an indifferent quality, and not dark enough for the game. The most of those People that Sit in Darkness have been furnished with more light than was good for them or profitable for us. We have been injudicious.

The Blessings-of-Civilization Trust, wisely and cautiously administered, is a Daisy. There is more money in it, more territory, more sovereignty, and other kinds of emolument, than there is in any other game that is played. But Christendom has been playing it badly of late years, and must certainly suffer by it, in my opinion. She has been so eager to get every stake that appeared on the green cloth, that the People who Sit in Darkness have noticed it — they have noticed it, and have begun to show alarm. They have become suspicious of the Blessings of Civilization. More — they have begun to examine them. This is not well. The Blessings of Civilization are all right, and a good commercial property; there could not be a better, in a dim light. . . .

It is a distress to look on and note the mismoves, they are so strange and so awkward. Mr. [Joseph] Chamberlain manufactures a war out of materials so inadequate and so fanciful that they make the boxes grieve and the gallery laugh, and he tries hard to persuade himself that it isn't purely a private raid for cash, but has a sort of dim, vague respectability about it somewhere, if he could only find the spot; and that, by and by, he can scour the flag clean again after he has finished dragging it through the mud, and make it shine and flash in the vault of heaven once more as it had shone and flashed there a thousand years in the world's respect until he laid his unfaithful hand upon it. It is bad play — bad. For it exposes the Actual Thing to Them that Sit in Darkness, and they say: "What! Christian against Christian? And only for money? Is *this* a case of magnanimity, forbearance, love, gentleness, mercy, protection of the weak — this strange and overshowy onslaught of an elephant upon a nest of field mice, on the pretext that the mice had squeaked an insolence at him — conduct which ' no self-respecting government could allow to pass unavenged '? as Mr. Chamberlain said. Was that a good pretext in a small case, when it had not been a good pretext in a large one? — for only recently Russia had affronted the elephant three times and survived alive and unsmitten. Is this Civilization and Progress? Is it something better than we already possess? These harryings and burnings and desert-makings in the Transvaal — is this an improvement on our darkness? Is it, perhaps, possible that there are two kinds of Civilization — one for home consumption and one for the heathen market? "

Then They that Sit in Darkness are troubled, and shake their heads; and they read this extract from a letter of a British private, recounting his exploits in one of Methuen's victories, some days before the affair of Magersfontein, and they are troubled again:

We tore up the hill and into the intrenchments, and the Boers saw we had them; so they dropped their guns and went down on their knees and put up their hands clasped, and begged for mercy. And we gave it them — *with the long spoon.*

The long spoon is the bayonet. See *Lloyd's Weekly,* London, of those days. The same number — and the same column — contained some quite unconscious satire in the form of shocked and bitter upbraidings of the Boers for their brutalities and inhumanities!

Next, to our heavy damage, the Kaiser went to playing the game without first mastering it. He lost a couple of missionaries in a riot in Shantung, and in his account he made an overcharge for them. China had to pay a hundred thousand dollars apiece for them, in money; twelve miles of territory, containing several millions of inhabitants and worth twenty million dollars; and to build a monument, and also a Christian church; whereas the people of China could have been depended upon to remember the missionaries without the help of these expensive memorials.

This was all bad play. Bad, because it would not, and could not, and will not now or ever, deceive the Person Sitting in Darkness. He knows that it was an overcharge. He knows that a missionary is like any other man: he is worth merely what you can supply his place for, and no more. He is useful, but so is a doctor, so is a sheriff, so is an editor; but a just Emperor does not charge war prices for such. A diligent, intelligent, but obscure missionary, and a diligent, intelligent country editor are worth much, and we know it; but they are not worth the earth. We esteem such an editor, and we are sorry to see him go; but, when he goes, we should consider twelve miles of territory, and a church, and a fortune, overcompensation for his loss. I mean, if he was a Chinese editor, and we had to settle for him. It is no proper figure for an editor or a missionary; one can get shop-worn kings for less. It was bad play on the Kaiser's part. It got this property, true; but it *produced the Chinese revolt*, the indignant uprising of China's traduced patriots, the Boxers. The results have been expensive to Germany, and to the other Disseminators of Progress and the Blessings of Civilization.

The Kaiser's claim was paid, yet it was bad play, for it could not fail to have an evil effect upon Persons Sitting in Darkness in China. They would muse upon the event, and be likely to say: " Civilization is gracious and beautiful, for such is its reputation; but can we afford it? There are rich Chinamen, perhaps they can afford it; but this tax is not laid upon them, it is laid upon the peasants of Shantung; it is they that must pay this mighty sum, and their wages are but four cents a day. Is this a better civilization than ours, and holier and higher and nobler? Is not this rapacity? Is not this extortion? . . ."

And next Russia must go and play the game injudiciously. She affronts England once or twice — with the Person Sitting in Darkness observing and noting; by moral assistance of France and Germany, she robs Japan of her hard-earned spoil, all swimming in Chinese blood — Port Arthur — with the Person again observing and noting; then she seizes Manchuria, raids its villages, and chokes its great river with the swollen corpses of countless massacred peasants — that astonished Person still observing and noting. And perhaps he is saying to himself: " It is yet *another* Civilized Power, with its banner of the Prince of Peace in one hand and its loot basket and its butcher knife in the other. Is there no salvation for us but to adopt Civilization and lift ourselves down to its level? "

And by and by comes America, and our Master of the Game [President McKinley] plays it badly — plays it as Mr. Chamberlain was playing it in South Africa. It was a mistake to do that; also, it was one which was quite unlooked for in a Master who was playing it so well in Cuba. In Cuba, he was playing the usual and regular *American* game, and it was winning, for there is no way to beat it. The Master, contemplating Cuba, said: " Here is an oppressed and friendless little nation which is willing to fight to be free, we go partners, and put up the strength of seventy million sympathizers and the resources of the United States: play! " Nothing but Europe combined could call that hand: and Europe cannot combine on anything. There, in Cuba, he was following our great traditions in a way which made us very proud of him, and proud of the deep dissatisfaction which his play was provoking in continental Europe. Moved by a high inspiration, he threw out those stirring words which proclaimed that forcible annexation would be " criminal aggression "; and in that utterance fired another " shot heard round the world." The memory of that fine saying will be outlived by the remembrance of no act of his but one — that he forgot it within the twelvemonth, and its honorable gospel along with it.

For, presently, came the Philippine temptation. It was strong; it was too strong, and he made that bad mistake: he played the European game, the Chamberlain game. It was a pity; it was a great pity, that error; that one grievous error, that irrevocable error. For it was the very place and time to play the American game again. And at no cost. Rich winnings to be gathered in, too; rich and permanent; indestructible; a fortune transmissible forever to the children of the flag. Not land, not money, not dominion — no, something worth many times more than that dross: our share, the spectacle of a nation of long harassed and persecuted slaves set free through our influence; our posterity's share, the golden memory of that fair deed. The game was in our hands. If it had been played according to the American rules, Dewey would have sailed away from Manila as soon as he had destroyed the Spanish fleet — after putting up a sign on shore guaranteeing foreign property and life against damage by the Filipinos, and warning the Powers that interference with the emancipated patriots would be regarded as an act unfriendly to the United States. The Powers cannot combine, in even a bad cause, and the sign would not have been molested.

Dewey could have gone about his affairs elsewhere, and left the competent Filipino army to starve out the little Spanish garrison and send it home, and the Filipino citizens to set up the form of government they

525

might prefer, and deal with the friars and their doubtful acquisitions according to Filipino ideas of fairness and justice — ideas which have since been tested and found to be of as high an order as any that prevail in Europe or America.

But we played the Chamberlain game, and lost the chance to add another Cuba and another honorable deed to our good record.

The more we examine the mistake, the more clearly we perceive that it is going to be bad for the Business. The Person Sitting in Darkness is almost sure to say: "There is something curious about this — curious and unaccountable. There must be two Americas: one that sets the captive free, and one that takes a once-captive's new freedom away from him, and picks a quarrel with him with nothing to found it on; then kills him to get his land."

The truth is, the Person Sitting in Darkness *is* saying things like that; and for the sake of the Business we must persuade him to look at the Philippine matter in another and healthier way. We must arrange his opinions for him. . . .

[*1901*]

EDWARD BELLAMY

[1850–1898]

THE MOST famous utopian romance of modern times was written by this son of a Baptist minister in Chicopee Falls, Massachusetts, where the author himself was born and lived most of his life. Even if this volume did not already contain evidence to the contrary, that fact alone should be sufficient reply to anyone who thinks that socialist sentiments are " foreign " ideas just recently imported. Bellamy was educated in the local schools, briefly at Union College, and privately in the law. He worked for a short time on newspapers in Springfield and New York, but was really interested in creative writing. He published some short stories and two "romances of immortality" before he began to work on his masterpiece, *Looking Backward*. He had long been interested in social questions, long been distressed by the poverty, economic waste, and oppression evident everywhere. In 1887 *Looking Backward* appeared. It was an international success, eventually selling well over a million copies. In it Bellamy described a socialist state — or at least a state of economic equality in which all significant property was nationally owned — which had been arrived at pacifically and by mutual consent, when men were persuaded that such a state was to their self-interest. Written with considerable charm, dramatically constructed, profoundly sincere in its appeal to his reader's humanity as well as his reason, it obviously satisfied the longings of great numbers of people who could no longer hope for a permanent frontier with theoretically unlimited opportunities.

from

LOOKING BACKWARD

[*Julian West awoke in the home of Dr. Leete from a trance which had lasted one hundred and thirteen years — from 1887 to 2000. At first he believed that he was the victim of a hoax, but one glance at his native city, Boston — beautifully and grandly rebuilt while he had been " sleeping " — convinced him that he was indeed in the first year of the twenty-first century. He began immediately to investigate his strange new world.*]

When in the course of the evening the ladies retired, leaving Dr. Leete and myself alone, he sounded me as to my disposition for sleep, saying that if I felt like it my bed was ready for me; but if I was inclined to wakefulness nothing would please him better than to bear me company. " I am a late bird, myself," he said, " and, without suspicion of flattery, I may say that a companion more interesting than yourself could scarcely be imagined. It is decidedly not often that one has a chance to converse with a man of the nineteenth century."

Now I had been looking forward all the evening with some dread to the time when I should be alone, on retiring for the night. Surrounded by these most friendly strangers, stimulated and supported by their sympathetic interest, I had been able to keep my mental balance. Even then, however, in pauses of the conversation I had had glimpses, vivid as lightning flashes, of the horror of strangeness that was waiting to be faced when I could no longer command diversion. I knew I could not sleep that night, and as for lying awake and thinking, it argues no cowardice, I am sure, to confess that I was afraid of it. When, in reply to my host's question, I frankly told him this, he replied that it would be strange if I did not feel just so, but that I need have no anxiety about sleeping; whenever I wanted to go to bed, he would give me a dose which would insure me a sound night's sleep without fail. Next morning, no doubt, I would awake with the feeling of an old citizen.

" Before I acquire that," I replied, " I must know a little more about the sort of Boston I have come back to. You told me when we were upon the house-top that though a century only had elapsed since I fell asleep, it had been marked by greater changes in the conditions of humanity than many a previous millennium. With the city before me I could well believe that, but I am very curious to know what some of the changes have been. To make a beginning somewhere, for the subject is doubtless a large one, what solution, if any, have you found for the labor question? It was the Sphinx's riddle of the nineteenth century, and when I dropped out the Sphinx was threatening to devour society, because the answer was not forthcoming. It is well worth sleeping a hundred years to learn what the right answer was, if, indeed, you have found it yet."

" As no such thing as the labor question is known nowadays," replied Dr. Leete, " and there is no way in which it could arise, I suppose we may claim to have solved it. Society would indeed have fully deserved being devoured if it had failed to answer a riddle so entirely simple. In fact, to speak by the book, it was not necessary for society to solve the riddle at all. It may be said to have solved itself. The solution came as the result of a process of industrial evolution which could not have terminated otherwise. All that society had to do was to recognize and co-operate with that evolution, when its tendency had become unmistakable."

"I can only say," I answered, "that at the time I fell asleep no such evolution had been recognized."

" It was in 1887 that you fell into this sleep, I think you said."

" Yes, May 30th, 1887."

My companion regarded me musingly for some moments. Then he observed, " And you tell me that even then there was no general recognition of the nature of the crisis which society was nearing? Of course, I fully credit your statement. The singular blindness of your contemporaries to the signs of the times is a phenomenon commented on by many of our historians, but few facts of history are more difficult for us to realize, so obvious and unmistakable as we look back seem the indications, which must also have come under your eyes, of the transformation about to come to pass. I should be interested, Mr. West, if you would give me a little more definite idea of the view which you and men of your grade of intellect took of the state and prospects of society in 1887. You must, at least, have realized that the widespread industrial and social troubles, and the underlying dissatisfaction of all classes with the inequalities of society, and the general misery of mankind, were portents of great changes of some sort."

" We did, indeed, fully realize that," I replied. " We felt that society was dragging anchor and in danger of going adrift. Whither it would drift nobody could say, but all feared the rocks."

" Nevertheless," said Dr. Leete, " the set of the current was perfectly perceptible if you had but taken pains to observe it, and it was not toward the rocks, but toward a deeper channel."

"We had a popular proverb," I replied, "that 'hindsight is better than foresight,' the force of which I shall now, no doubt, appreciate more fully than ever. All I can say is, that the prospect was such when I went into that long sleep that I should not have been surprised had I looked down from your house-top to-day on a heap of charred and moss-grown ruins instead of this glorious city."

Dr. Leete had listened to me with close attention and nodded thoughtfully as I finished speaking. "What you have said," he observed, "will be regarded as a most valuable vindication of Storiot, whose account of your era has been generally thought exaggerated in its picture of the gloom and confusion of men's minds. That a period of transition like that should be full of excitement and agitation was indeed to be looked for; but seeing how plain was the tendency of the forces in operation, it was natural to believe that hope rather than fear would have been the prevailing temper of the popular mind."

"You have not yet told me what was the answer to the riddle which you found," I said. "I am impatient to know by what contradiction of natural sequence the peace and prosperity which you now seem to enjoy could have been the outcome of an era like my own."

"Excuse me," replied my host, "but do you smoke?" It was not till our cigars were lighted and drawing well that he resumed. "Since you are in the humor to talk rather than to sleep, as I certainly am, perhaps I cannot do better than to try to give you enough idea of our modern industrial system to dissipate at least the impression that there is any mystery about the process of its evolution. The Bostonians of your day had the reputation of being great askers of questions, and I am going to show my descent by asking you one to begin with. What should you name as the most prominent feature of the labor troubles of your day?"

"Why, the strikes, of course," I replied.

"Exactly; but what made the strikes so formidable?"

"The great labor organizations."

"And what was the motive of these great organizations?"

"The workmen claimed they had to organize to get their rights from the big corporations," I replied.

"That is just it," said Dr. Leete; "the organization of labor and the strikes were an effect, merely, of the concentration of capital in greater masses than had ever been known before. Before this concentration began, while as yet commerce and industry were conducted by innumerable petty concerns with small capital, instead of a small number of great concerns with vast capital, the individual workman was relatively important and independent in his relations to the employer. Moreover, when a little capital or a new idea was enough to start a man in business for himself, workingmen were constantly becoming employers and there was no hard and fast line between the two classes. Labor unions were needless then, and general strikes out of the question. But when the era of small concerns with small capital was succeeded by that of the great aggregations of capital, all this was changed. The individual laborer, who had been relatively important to the small employer, was reduced to insignificance and powerlessness over against the great corporation, while at the same time the way upward to the grade of employer was closed to him. Self-defense drove him to union with his fellows.

"The records of the period show that the outcry against the concentration of capital was furious. Men believed that it threatened society with a form of tyranny more abhorrent than it had ever endured. They believed that the great corporations were preparing for them the yoke of a baser servitude than had ever been imposed on the race, servitude not to men but to soulless machines incapable of any motive but insatiable greed. Looking back, we cannot wonder at their desperation, for certainly humanity was never confronted with a fate more sordid and hideous than would have been the era of corporate tyranny which they anticipated. . . .

"To restore the former order of things, even if possible, would have involved returning to the day of stage-coaches. Oppressive and intolerable as was the régime of the great consolidations of capital, even its victims, while they cursed it, were forced to admit the prodigious increase of efficiency which had been imparted to the national industries, the vast economies effected by concentration of management and unity of organization, and to confess that since the new system had taken the place of the old the wealth of the world had increased at a rate before undreamed of. To be sure this vast increase had gone chiefly to make the rich richer, increasing the gap between them and the poor; but the fact remained that, as a means merely of producing wealth, capital had been proved efficient in proportion to its consolidation. The restoration of the old system with the subdivision of capital, if it were possible, might indeed bring back a greater equality of conditions, with more individual dignity and freedom, but it would be at the price of general poverty and the arrest of material progress.

"Was there, then, no way of commanding the services of the mighty wealth-producing principle of consolidated capital without bowing down to a plutocracy like that of Carthage? As soon as men began to ask themselves these questions, they found the answer ready for them. The movement toward the conduct of business by larger and larger aggregations of capital, the tendency toward monopolies, which had been so desperately and vainly resisted, was recognized at last, in its true significance, as a process which only needed to complete its logical evolution to open a golden future to humanity.

"Early in the last century the evolution was completed by the final consolidation of the entire capital of the nation. The industry and commerce of the country, ceasing to be conducted by a set of irresponsible corporations and syndicates of private persons at their caprice and for their profit, were intrusted to a single syndicate representing the people, to be conducted in the common interest for the common profit. . . ."

"Such a stupendous change as you describe," said I, "did not, of course, take place without great bloodshed and terrible convulsions."

"On the contrary," replied Dr. Leete, "there was absolutely no violence. The change had been long foreseen. Public opinion had become fully ripe for it, and the whole mass of the people was behind it. . . ."

Dr. Leete ceased speaking, and I remained silent, endeavoring to form some general conception of the changes in the arrangements of society implied in the tremendous revolution which he had described.

Finally I said, "The idea of such an extension of the functions of government is, to say the least, rather overwhelming."

"Extension! " he repeated, "where is the extension? "

"In my day," I replied, "it was considered that the proper functions of government, strictly speaking, were limited to keeping the peace and defending the people against the public enemy, that is, to the military and police powers."

"And, in heaven's name, who are the public enemies? " exclaimed Dr. Leete. "Are they France, England, Germany, or hunger, cold, and nakedness? In your day governments were accustomed, on the slightest international misunderstanding, to seize upon the bodies of citizens and deliver them over by hundreds of thousands to death and mutilation, wasting their treasures the while like water; and all this oftenest for no imaginable profit to the victims. We have no wars now, and our governments no war powers, but in order to protect every citizen against hunger, cold, and nakedness, and provide for all his physical and mental needs, the function is assumed of directing his industry for a term of years. No, Mr. West, I am sure on reflection you will perceive that it was in your age, not in ours, that the extension of the functions of governments was extraordinary. Not even for the best ends would men now allow their governments such powers as were then used for the most maleficent."

"Leaving comparisons aside," I said, "the demagoguery and corruption of our public men would have been considered, in my day, insuperable objections to any assumption by government of the charge of the national industries. We should have thought that no arrangement could be worse than to entrust the politicians with control of the wealth-producing machinery of the country. Its material interests were quite too much the football of parties as it was."

"No doubt you were right," rejoined Dr. Leete, "but all that is changed now. We have no parties or politicians, and as for demagoguery and corruption, they are words having only an historical significance."

"Human nature itself must have changed very much," I said.

"Not at all," was Dr. Leete's reply, "but the conditions of human life have changed, and with them the motives of human action. The organization of society with you was such that officials were under a constant temptation to misuse their power for the private profit of themselves or others. Under such circumstances it seems almost strange that you dared entrust them with any of your affairs. Nowadays, on the contrary, society is so constituted that there is absolutely no way in which an official, however ill-disposed, could possibly make any profit for himself or any one else by a misuse of his power. Let him be as bad an official as you please, he cannot be a corrupt one. There is no motive to be. The social system no longer offers a premium on dishonesty. But these are matters which you can only understand as you come, with time, to know us better."

"But you have not yet told me how you have settled the labor problem. It is the problem of capital which we have been discussing," I said. "After the nation had assumed conduct of the mills, machinery, railroads, farms, mines, and capital in general of the country, the labor question still remained. In assuming the responsibilities of capital the nation had assumed the difficulties of the capitalist's position."

"The moment the nation assumed the responsibilities of capital those difficulties vanished," replied Dr. Leete. "The national organization of labor under one direction was the complete solution of what was, in your day and under your system, justly regarded as the insoluble labor problem. When the nation became the sole employer, all the citizens, by virtue of their citizenship, became employees, to be distributed according to the needs of industry."

"That is," I suggested, "you have simply applied the principle of universal military service, as it was understood in our day, to the labor question."

"Yes," said Dr. Leete, "that was something which followed as a matter of course as soon as the nation had become the sole capitalist. The people were already accustomed to the idea that the obligation of every citizen, not physically disabled, to contribute his military services to the defense of the nation was equal and absolute. That it was equally the duty of every citizen to contribute his quota of industrial or intellectual services to the maintenance of the nation was equally evident, though it was not until the nation became the employer of labor that citizens were able to render this sort of service with any pretense either of universality or equity. No organization of labor was possible when the employing power was divided among hundreds or thousands of individuals and corporations, between which concert of any kind was neither desired, nor indeed feasible. It constantly happened then that vast numbers who desired to labor could find no opportunity, and on the other hand, those who desired to evade a part or all of their debt could easily do so."

"Service, now, I suppose, is compulsory upon all," I suggested.

"It is rather a matter of course than of compulsion," replied Dr. Leete. "It is regarded as so absolutely natural and reasonable that the idea of its being compulsory has ceased to be thought of. He would be thought to be an incredibly contemptible person who should need compulsion in such a case. Nevertheless, to speak of service being compulsory would be a weak way to state its absolute inevitableness. Our entire social order is so wholly based upon and deduced from it that if it were conceivable that a man could escape it, he would be left with no possible way to provide for his existence. He would have excluded himself from the world, cut himself off from his kind, in a word, committed suicide."

" I should not fail to mention," resumed the doctor, " that for those too deficient in mental or bodily strength to be fairly graded with the main body of workers, we have a separate grade, unconnected with the others, — a sort of invalid corps, the members of which are provided with a light class of tasks fitted to their strength. All our sick in mind and body, all our deaf and dumb, and lame and blind and crippled, and even our insane, belong to this invalid corps, and bear its insignia. The strongest often do nearly a man's work, the feeblest, of course, nothing; but none who can do anything are willing quite to give up. In their lucid intervals, even our insane are eager to do what they can."

" That is a pretty idea of the invalid corps," I said. " Even a barbarian from the nineteenth century can appreciate that. It is a very graceful way of disguising charity, and must be grateful to the feelings of its recipients."

" Charity! " repeated Dr. Leete. " Did you suppose that we consider the incapable class we are talking of objects of charity? "

" Why, naturally," I said, " inasmuch as they are incapable of self-support."

But here the doctor took me up quickly.

" Who is capable of self-support? " he demanded. " There is no such thing in a civilized society as self-support. In a state of society so barbarous as not even to know family co-operation, each individual may possibly support himself, though even then for a part of his life only; but from the moment that men begin to live together, and constitute even the rudest sort of society, self-support becomes impossible. As men grow more civilized, and the subdivision of occupations and services is carried out, a complex mutual dependence becomes the universal rule. Every man, however solitary may seem his occupation, is a member of a vast industrial partnership, as large as the nation, as large as humanity. The necessity of mutual dependence should imply the duty and guarantee of mutual support; and that it did not in your day constituted the essential cruelty and unreason of your system."

" That may all be so," I replied, " but it does not touch the case of those who are unable to contribute anything to the product of industry."

" Surely I told you this morning, at least I thought I did," replied Dr. Leete, " that the right of a man to maintenance at the nation's table depends on the fact that he is a man, and not on the amount of health and strength he may have, so long as he does his best."

"You said so," I answered, "but I supposed the rule applied only to the workers of different ability. Does it also hold of those who can do nothing at all?"

"Are they not also men?"

"I am to understand, then, that the lame, the blind, the sick, and the impotent, are as well off as the most efficient, and have the same income?"

"Certainly," was the reply.

"The idea of charity on such a scale," I answered, "would have made our most enthusiastic philanthropists gasp."

"If you had a sick brother at home," replied Dr. Leete, "unable to work, would you feed him on less dainty food, and lodge and clothe him more poorly, than yourself? More likely far, you would give him the preference; nor would you think of calling it charity. Would not the word, in that connection, fill you with indignation?"

"Of course," I replied; "but the cases are not parallel. There is a sense, no doubt, in which all men are brothers; but this general sort of brotherhood is not to be compared, except for rhetorical purposes, to the brotherhood of blood, either as to its sentiment or its obligations."

"There speaks the nineteenth century!" exclaimed Dr. Leete. "Ah, Mr. West, there is no doubt as to the length of time that you slept. If I were to give you, in one sentence, a key to what may seem the mysteries of our civilization as compared with that of your age, I should say that it is the fact that the solidarity of the race and the brotherhood of man, which to you were but fine phrases, are, to our thinking and feeling, ties as real and as vital as physical fraternity.

"But even setting that consideration aside, I do not see why it so surprises you that those who cannot work are conceded the full right to live on the produce of those who can. Even in your day, the duty of military service for the protection of the nation, to which our industrial service corresponds, while obligatory on those able to discharge it, did not operate to deprive of the privileges of citizenship those who were unable. They stayed at home, and were protected by those who fought, and nobody questioned their right to be, or thought less of them. So, now, the requirement of industrial service from those able to render it does not operate to deprive of the privileges of citizenship, which now implies the citizen's maintenance, him who cannot work.

The worker is not a citizen because he works, but works because he is a citizen. As you recognize the duty of the strong to fight for the weak, we, now that fighting is gone by, recognize his duty to work for him.

"A solution which leaves an unaccounted-for residuum is no solution at all; and our solution of the problem of human society would have been none at all had it left the lame, the sick, and the blind outside with the beasts, to fare as they might. Better far have left the strong and well unprovided for than these burdened ones, toward whom every heart must yearn, and for whom ease of mind and body should be provided, if for no others. Therefore it is, as I told you this morning, that the title of every man, woman, and child to the means of existence rests on no basis less plain, broad, and simple than the fact that they are fellows of one race — members of one human family. The only coin current is the image of God, and that is good for all we have.

"I think there is no feature of the civilization of your epoch so repugnant to modern ideas as the neglect with which you treated your dependent classes. Even if you had no pity, no feeling of brotherhood, how was it that you did not see that you were robbing the incapable class of their plain right in leaving them unprovided for?"

"I don't quite follow you there," I said. "I admit the claim of this class to our pity, but how could they who produced nothing claim a share of the product as a right?"

"How happened it," was Dr. Leete's reply, "that your workers were able to produce more than so many savages would have done? Was it not wholly on account of the heritage of the past knowledge and achievements of the race, the machinery of society, thousands of years in contriving, found by you ready-made to your hand? How did you come to be possessors of this knowledge and this machinery, which represent nine parts to one contributed by yourself in the value of your product? You inherited it, did you not? And were not these others, these unfortunate and crippled brothers whom you cast out, joint inheritors, co-heirs with you? What did you do with their share? Did you not rob them when you put them off with crusts, who were entitled to sit with the heirs, and did you not add insult to robbery when you called the crusts charity?

"Ah, Mr. West," Dr. Leete continued, as I did not respond, "what I do not understand is, setting aside all considerations either of justice or brotherly feeling toward the crippled and defective, how the workers of your day could have had any heart for their work, knowing that

537

their children, or grand-children, if unfortunate, would be deprived of the comforts and even necessities of life. It is a mystery how men with children could favor a system under which they were rewarded beyond those less endowed with bodily strength or mental power. For, by the same discrimination by which the father profited, the son, for whom he would give his life, being perchance weaker than others, might be reduced to crusts and beggary. How men dared leave children behind them, I have never been able to understand."

[1887]

GROVER CLEVELAND

[1837–1908]

THE SON of a Presbyterian clergyman, Grover Cleveland was born in Cald-well, New Jersey, but was brought up in the towns of western New York in which his father preached. The death of his father in 1853 forced young Cleveland to work for his living until he was taken into the family of a great-uncle who lived near Buffalo. He then studied law, was admitted to the bar in 1859, and in 1863 became assistant district attorney of Erie County. His known honesty and dependability led to political advancement. He be-came the county sheriff, then mayor of Buffalo, and in 1883 Governor of New York. The time was ripe for a Democrat who had a reputation as a reformer and as an enemy of Tammany and graft. Nominated for the presi-dency of the United States in 1884, he won the election against James G. Blaine, the slightly spotted candidate of the Republicans. Cleveland's ad-ministration was not successful. He lacked necessary tact and executive abil-ity. Moreover, the country was not at that moment in a mood for the low tariffs and governmental economies recommended by Cleveland. He lost the election in 1888 to Benjamin Harrison. But four years later, renominated, he defeated Harrison and began a second term that promised well but ended in distinct unpopularity. Bryanism was in the air after the panic of 1893 — and Cleveland was a "sound money" man. In 1894 he broke a railroad strike in Chicago by the use of troops against the wishes of the liberal Gov-ernor of Illinois, John P. Altgeld. In 1895 he came near bringing the country into a war with England over the question of Venezuela's boundaries. Nevertheless, it may fairly be stated that Cleveland's general policy repre-sented the liberal phase of capitalism in the nineteenth century. The message to Congress which follows is an excellent expression of the belief that there should be free and equal competition in business and that governments should be restricted in their activities. In it he anticipated many of the pro-gressive ideas of Theodore Roosevelt and some of Woodrow Wilson.

from

THE ANNUAL MESSAGE TO CONGRESS, 1888

The equal and exact justice of which we boast as the underlying principle of our institutions should not be confined to the relations of our citizens to each other. The Government itself is under bond to the American people that in the exercise of its functions and powers it will deal with the body of our citizens in a manner scrupulously honest and fair and absolutely just. It has agreed that American citizenship shall be the only credential necessary to justify the claim of equality before the law, and that no condition in life shall give rise to discrimination in the treatment of the people by their Government.

The citizen of our Republic in its early days rigidly insisted upon full compliance with the letter of this bond, and saw stretching out before him a clear field for individual endeavor. His tribute to the support of his Government was measured by the cost of its economical maintenance, and he was secure in the enjoyment of the remaining recompense of his steady and contented toil. In those days the frugality of the people was stamped upon their Government, and was enforced by the free, thoughtful, and intelligent suffrage of the citizen. Combinations, monopolies, and aggregations of capital were either avoided or sternly regulated and restrained. The pomp and glitter of governments less free offered no temptation and presented no delusion to the plain people who, side by side, in friendly competition, wrought for the ennoblement and dignity of man, for the solution of the problem of free government, and for the achievement of the grand destiny awaiting the land which God had given them.

A century has passed. Our cities are the abiding places of wealth and luxury; our manufactories yield fortunes never dreamed of by the fathers of the Republic; our business men are madly striving in the race for riches, and immense aggregations of capital outrun the imagination in the magnitude of their undertakings.

We view with pride and satisfaction this bright picture of our country's growth and prosperity, while only a closer scrutiny develops a somber shading. Upon more careful inspection we find the wealth and luxury of our cities mingled with poverty and wretchedness and unremunerative toil. A crowded and constantly increasing urban population suggests the impoverishment of rural sections and discontent with agricultural pursuits. The farmer's son, not satisfied with his father's simple and laborious life, joins the eager chase for easily acquired wealth.

We discover that the fortunes realized by our manufacturers are no longer solely the reward of sturdy industry and enlightened foresight, but that they result from the discriminating favor of the Government and are largely built upon undue exactions from the masses of our people. The gulf between employers and the employed is constantly widening, and classes are rapidly forming, one comprising the very rich and powerful, while in another are found the toiling poor.

As we view the achievements of aggregated capital, we discover the existence of trusts, combinations, and monopolies, while the citizen is struggling far in the rear or is trampled to death beneath an iron heel. Corporations, which should be the carefully restrained creatures of the law and the servants of the people, are fast becoming the people's masters.

Still congratulating ourselves upon the wealth and prosperity of our country and complacently contemplating every incident of change inseparable from these conditions, it is our duty as patriotic citizens to inquire at the present stage of our progress how the bond of the Government made with the people has been kept and performed.

Instead of limiting the tribute drawn from our citizens to the necessities of its economical administration, the Government persists in exacting from the substance of the people millions which, unapplied and useless, lie dormant in its Treasury. This flagrant injustice and this breach of faith and obligation add to extortion the danger attending the diversion of the currency of the country from the legitimate channels of business.

Under the same laws by which these results are produced the Government permits many millions more to be added to the cost of the living of our people and to be taken from our consumers, which unreasonably swell the profits of a small but powerful minority.

The people must still be taxed for the support of the Government under the operation of tariff laws. But to the extent that the mass of our citizens are inordinately burdened beyond any useful public purpose and for the benefit of a favored few, the Government, under pretext of an exercise of its taxing power, enters gratuitously into partnership with these favorites, to their advantage and to the injury of a vast majority of our people.

This is not equality before the law.

The existing situation is injurious to the health of our entire body politic. It stifles in those for whose benefit it is permitted all patriotic love of country, and substitutes in its place selfish greed and grasping avarice. Devotion to American citizenship for its own sake and for what it should accomplish as a motive to our nation's advancement and the happiness of all our people is displaced by the assumption that the Government, instead of being the embodiment of equality, is but an instrumentality through which especial and individual advantages are to be gained.

The arrogance of this assumption is unconcealed. It appears in the sordid disregard of all but personal interests, in the refusal to abate for the benefit of others one iota of selfish advantage, and in combinations to perpetuate such advantages through efforts to control legislation and improperly influence the suffrage of the people.

The grievances of those not included within the circle of these beneficiaries, when fully realized, will surely arouse irritation and discontent. Our farmers, long suffering and patient, struggling in the race of life with the hardest and most unremitting toil, will not fail to see, in spite of misrepresentations and misleading fallacies, that they are obliged to accept such prices for their products as are fixed in foreign markets where they compete with the farmers of the world; that their lands are declining in value while their debts increase, and that without compensating favor they are forced by the action of the Government to pay for the benefit of others such enhanced prices for the things they need that the scanty returns of their labor fail to furnish their support or leave no margin for accumulation.

Our workingmen, enfranchised from all delusions and no longer frightened by the cry that their wages are endangered by a just revision of our tariff laws, will reasonably demand through such revision steadier employment, cheaper means of living in their homes, freedom for themselves and their children from the doom of perpetual servitude, and an open door to their advancement beyond the limits of a laboring class. Others of our citizens, whose comforts and expenditures are measured by moderate salaries and fixed incomes, will insist upon the fairness and justice of cheapening the cost of necessaries for themselves and their families.

When to the selfishness of the beneficiaries of unjust discrimination under our laws there shall be added the discontent of those who suffer from such discrimination, we will realize the fact that the beneficent purposes of our Government, dependent upon the patriotism and contentment of our people, are endangered.

Communism is a hateful thing and a menace to peace and organized government; but the communism of combined wealth and capital, the outgrowth of overweening cupidity and selfishness, which insidiously undermines the justice and integrity of free institutions, is not less dangerous than the communism of oppressed poverty and toil, which, exasperated by injustice and discontent, attacks with wild disorder the citadel of rule.

He mocks the people who proposes that the Government shall protect the rich and that they in turn will care for the laboring poor. Any intermediary between the people and their Government or the least delegation of the care and protection the Government owes to the humblest citizen in the land makes the boast of free institutions a glittering delusion and the pretended boon of American citizenship a shameless imposition.

A just and sensible revision of our tariff laws should be made for the relief of those of our countrymen who suffer under present conditions. Such a revision should receive the support of all who love that justice and equality due to American citizenship; of all who realize that in this justice and equality our Government finds its strength and its power to protect the citizen and his property; of all who believe that the contented competence and comfort of many accord better with the spirit of our institutions than colossal fortunes unfairly gathered in the hands of a few; of all who appreciate that the forbearance and fraternity among our people, which recognize the value of every American interest, are the surest guaranty of our national progress, and of all who desire to see the products of American skill and ingenuity in every market of the world, with a resulting restoration of American commerce.

The necessity of the reduction of our revenues is so apparent as to be generally conceded, but the means by which this end shall be accomplished and the sum of direct benefit which shall result to our citizens present a controversy of the utmost importance. There should be no scheme accepted as satisfactory by which the burdens of the people are only apparently removed. Extravagant appropriations of public money, with all their demoralizing consequences, should not be tolerated, either as a means of relieving the Treasury of its present surplus or as furnishing pretext for resisting a proper reduction in tariff rates. Existing evils and injustice should be honestly recognized, boldly met, and effectively remedied. There should be no cessation of the struggle until a plan is perfected, fair and conservative toward existing industries, but which will reduce the cost to consumers of the necessaries of life, while it provides for our manufacturers the advantage of freer raw materials and permits no injury to the interests of American labor.

The cause for which the battle is waged is comprised within lines clearly and distinctly defined. It should never be compromised. It is the people's cause.

[1888]

WILLIAM DEAN HOWELLS

[1837–1920]

DURING the last few years of his life and for about ten years afterwards, it was fashionable to sneer at Howells and everything he stood for. This was part of the literary revolt against the genteel tradition, of which Howells was a leading exponent. But in the justifiable contempt for his gentility, other and more significant sides of his work were overlooked. Now that gentility has virtually disappeared from our literature, critics have begun to realize that he made certain valid and very desirable contributions to American letters. They have pointed out that he was an exceedingly good literary critic — one of the leaders of the realistic movement, one of the first to argue for the democratic spirit in modern fiction; that he was also a pioneer in the type of fiction for which he argued, his later novels being serious and conscientious studies of contemporary life; and, finally, that he was a courageous and generous man deeply concerned with the social problems of his day — and always from a humane point of view. All in all, he is now recognized as one of the great figures of the immediate past in our literature.

He was born in a hamlet in Ohio. His father, a poor anti-slavery journalist, could not afford to send him to school, and so at nine the boy became a typesetter in his father's shop. He read voraciously, learned several languages, began to write, at last joined the staff of the *Ohio State Journal* of Columbus. A campaign biography of Lincoln in 1860 led to his appointment to the consulate in Venice, where he remained until 1865. On his return he joined the staff of Godkin's *Nation,* but soon quit to accept a post at the *Atlantic Monthly,* of which he ultimately became editor-in-chief. Leaving in 1881, he began to write for the *Century* and *Harper's,* and to the latter he contributed a monthly critical article for many years. In the meantime he produced numerous novels, among them *A Modern Instance* (1882), *The Rise of Silas Lapham* (1885), *A Hazard of New Fortunes* (1890), and *The Quality of Mercy* (1892). His best work of criticism, based upon his *Harper's* pieces, was his *Criticism and Fiction* (1891). In his later years Howells was outspoken in defense of the underdog, interesting himself in strikes, denouncing imperialism, championing such humanitarian and radical novelists as Tolstoy and Zola. His utopian romance, *A Traveler from Altruria* (1894), is an example of his egalitarian sentiments. He outlived his time, yet he is honored in our own time.

from

A HAZARD OF NEW FORTUNES

[THE STRIKE]

The strike had made a good deal of talk in the office of *Every Other Week* — that is, it made Fulkerson talk a good deal. He congratulated himself that he was not personally incommoded by it, like some of the fellows who lived uptown, and had not everything under one roof, as it were. He enjoyed the excitement of it, and he kept the office-boy running out to buy the extras which the newsmen came crying through the street almost every hour with a lamentable, unintelligible noise. He read not only the latest intelligence of the strike, but the editorial comments on it, which praised the firm attitude of both parties, and the admirable measures taken by the police to preserve order. Fulkerson enjoyed the interviews with the police captains and the leaders of the strike; he equally enjoyed the attempts of the reporters to interview the road managers, which were so graphically detailed, and with such a fine feeling for the right use of scareheads as to have almost the value of direct expressions from them, though it seemed that they had resolutely refused to speak. He said, at second-hand from the papers, that if the men behaved themselves and respected the rights of property, they would have public sympathy with them every time; but just as soon as they began to interfere with the roads' right to manage their own affairs in their own way, they must be put down with an iron hand; the phrase " iron hand " did Fulkerson almost as much good as if it had never been used before. News began to come of fighting between the police and the strikers when the roads tried to move their cars with men imported from Philadelphia, and then Fulkerson rejoiced at the splendid courage of the police. At the same time he believed what the strikers said, and that the trouble was not made by them but by gangs of roughs acting without their approval. In this juncture he was relieved by the arrival of the State Board of Arbitration, which took up its quarters, with a great many scareheads, at one of the principal hotels, and invited the roads and the strikers to lay the matter in dispute before them; he said that now we should see the working of the greatest piece of social machinery in modern times. But it appeared to work only in the alacrity of the strikers to submit their grievance. The roads were as one road in declaring that there was nothing to arbitrate, and that they were merely asserting their right to manage their own affairs in their own way. One of the presidents was reported to have told a member of the Board, who personally summoned him, to get out and to go about his business. Then, to Fulkerson's extreme disappointment, the august tribunal, acting on behalf of the sovereign people in the interest of peace, declared itself powerless and got out, and would, no doubt, have gone about its business if it had had any. Fulkerson did not know what to say, perhaps because the extras did not; but March laughed at this result.

"It's a good deal like the military manœuvre of the King of France and his forty thousand men. I suppose somebody told him at the top of the hill that there was nothing to arbitrate, and to get out and go about his business, and that was the reason he marched down after he had marched up with all that ceremony. What amuses me is to find that in an affair of this kind the roads have rights and the strikers have rights, but the public has no rights at all. The roads and the strikers are allowed to fight out a private war in our midst — as thoroughly and precisely a private war as any we despise the Middle Ages for having tolerated — as any street war in Florence or Verona — and to fight it out at our pains and expense, and we stand by like sheep, and wait till we get tired. It's a funny attitude for a city of fifteen hundred thousand inhabitants."

"What would you do?" asked Fulkerson, a good deal daunted by this view of the case.

"Do? Nothing. Hasn't the State Board of Arbitration declared itself powerless? We have no hold upon the strikers; and we're so used to being snubbed and disobliged by common carriers that we have forgotten our hold on the roads, and always allow them to manage their own affairs in their own way, quite as if we had nothing to do with them, and they owed us no services in return for their privileges."

"That's a good deal so," said Fulkerson, disordering his hair. "Well, it's nuts for the colonel nowadays. He says if he was boss of this town he would seize the roads on behalf of the people, and man 'em with policemen, and run 'em till the managers had come to terms with the strikers; and he'd do that every time there was a strike."

"Doesn't that rather savour of the paternalism he condemned in Lindau?" asked March.

547

" I don't know. It savours of horse-sense."

" You are pretty far gone, Fulkerson. I thought you were the most engaged man I ever saw; but I guess you're more father-in-lawed. And before you're married too."

" Well, the colonel's a glorious old fellow, March. I wish he had the power to do that thing, just for the fun of looking on while he waltzed in. He's on the keen jump from morning till night, and he's up late and early to see the row. I'm afraid he'll get shot at some of the fights; he sees them all; *I* can't get any show at them: haven't seen a brickbat shied or a club swung yet. Have you? "

" No, I find I can philosophise the situation about as well from the papers, and that's what I really want to do, I suppose. Besides I'm solemnly pledged by Mrs. March not to go near any sort of crowd, under penalty of having her bring the children and go with me. Her theory is that we must all die together; the children haven't been at school since the strike began. There's no precaution that Mrs. March hasn't used. She watches me whenever I go out, and sees that I start straight for this office."

Fulkerson laughed and said: " Well, it's probably the only thing that's saved your life. Have you seen anything of Beaton lately? "

" No. You don't mean to say *he's* killed! "

" Not if he knows it. But I don't know — . What do you say, March? What's the reason you couldn't get us up a paper on the strike? "

" I knew it would fetch round to *Every Other Week*, somehow."

" No, but seriously. There'll be plenty of newspaper accounts. But you could treat it in the historical spirit — like something that happened several centuries ago; DeFoe's Plague of London style. Heigh? What made me think of it was Beaton. If I could get hold of him, you two could go round together and take down its æsthetic aspects. It's a big thing, March, this strike is. I tell you it's imposing to have a private war, as you say, fought out this way, in the heart of New York, and New York not minding it a bit. See? Might take that view of it. With your descriptions and Beaton's sketches — well, it would just be the greatest card! Come! What do you say? "

" Will you undertake to make it right with Mrs. March if I'm killed and she and the children are not killed with me? "

" Well, it would be difficult. I wonder how it would do to get Kendricks to do the literary part? "

548

" I've no doubt he'd jump at the chance. I've yet to see the form of literature that Kendricks wouldn't lay down his life for."

" Say! " March perceived that Fulkerson was about to vent another inspiration, and smiled patiently. " Look here! What's the reason we couldn't get one of the strikers to write it up for us? "

" Might have a symposium of strikers and presidents," March suggested.

" No; I'm in earnest. They say some of those fellows — especially the foreigners — are educated men. I know one fellow — a Bohemian — that used to edit a Bohemian newspaper here. He could write it out in his kind of Dutch, and we could get Lindau to translate it."

" I guess not," said March dryly.

" Why not? He'd do it for the cause, wouldn't he? Suppose you put it up on him, the next time you see him."

" I don't see Lindau any more," said March. He added, " I guess he's renounced me along with Mr. Dryfoos's money."

" Pshaw! You don't mean he hasn't been round since? "

" He came for a while, but he's left off coming now. I don't feel particularly gay about it," March said, with some resentment of Fulkerson's grin. " He's left me in debt to him for lessons to the children."

Fulkerson laughed out. " Well, he *is* the greatest old fool! Who'd 'a' thought he'd 'a' been in earnest with those ' brincibles ' of his? But I suppose there have to be just such cranks; it takes all kinds to make a world."

" There has to be *one* such crank, it seems," March partially assented. " One's enough for me."

" I reckon this thing is nuts for Lindau, too," said Fulkerson. " Why, it must act like a schooner of beer on him all the while, to see ' gabidal ' embarrassed like it is by this strike. It must make old Lindau feel like he was back behind those barricades at Berlin. Well, he's a splendid old fellow; pity he drinks, as I remarked once before."

When March left the office he did not go home so directly as he came, perhaps because Mrs. March's eye was not on him. He was very curious about some aspects of the strike, whose importance, as a great social convulsion, he felt people did not recognise; and with his temperance in everything, he found its negative expressions as significant as its more violent phases. He had promised his wife solemnly that he would keep away from these, and he had a natural inclination to keep his promise; he had no wish to be that peaceful spectator who always gets shot when there is any firing on a mob. He interested himself in the apparent indifference of the mighty city, which kept on about its business as tranquilly as if the private war being fought out in its midst were a vague rumour of Indian troubles on the frontier; and he realised how there might once have been a street feud of forty years in Florence without interfering materially with the industry and prosperity of the city. On Broadway there was a silence where a jangle and clatter of horse-car bells and hoofs had been, but it was not very noticeable; and on the avenues, roofed by the elevated roads, this silence of the surface tracks was not noticeable at all in the roar of the trains overhead. Some of the cross-town cars were beginning to run again; with a policeman on the rear of each; on the Third Avenue line, operated by non-union men, who had not struck, there were two policemen beside the driver of every car, and two beside the conductor, to protect them from the strikers. But there were no strikers in sight, and on Second Avenue they stood quietly about in groups on the corners. While March watched them at a safe distance, a car laden with policemen came down the track, but none of the strikers offered to molest it. In their simple Sunday best, March thought them very quiet, decent-looking people, and he could well believe that they had nothing to do with the riotous outbreaks in other parts of the city. He could hardly believe that there were any such outbreaks; he began more and more to think them mere newspaper exaggerations in the absence of any disturbance, or the disposition to it, that he could see. He walked on to the East River: Avenues A, B, and C presented the same quiet aspect as Second Avenue; groups of men stood on the corners, and now and then a police-laden car was brought unmolested down the tracks before them; they looked at it and talked together, and some laughed, but there was no trouble.

March got a cross-town car, and came back to the West side. A policeman, looking very sleepy and tired, lounged on the platform.

" I suppose you'll be glad when this cruel war is over," March suggested, as he got in.

The officer gave him a surly glance and made him no answer.

His behaviour, from a man born to the joking give and take of our life, impressed March. It gave him a fine sense of the ferocity which he had read of the French troops putting on toward the populace just before the *coup d'état;* he began to feel like populace; but he struggled with himself and regained his character of philosophical observer. In this character he remained in the car and let it carry him by the corner where he ought to have got out and gone home, and let it keep on with him to one of the furthermost tracks westward, where so much of the fighting was reported to have taken place. But everything on the way was as quiet as on the East side.

Suddenly the car stopped with so quick a turn of the brake that he was half thrown from his seat, and the policeman jumped down from the platform and ran forward. . . .

Dryfoos took the elevated road. The strike seemed a very far-off thing, though the paper he bought to look up the stock market was full of noisy typography about yesterday's troubles on the surface lines. Among the millions in Wall Street there was some joking and some swearing, but not much thinking about the six thousand men who had taken such chances in their attempt to better their condition. Dryfoos heard nothing of the strike in the lobby of the Stock Exchange, where he spent two or three hours watching a favourite stock of his go up and go down under the betting. By the time the Exchange closed it had risen eight points, and on this and some other investments he was five thousand dollars richer than he had been in the morning. But he had expected to be richer still, and he was by no means satisfied with his luck. All through the excitement of his winning and losing had played the dull, murderous rage he felt toward the child who had defied him and when the game was over and he started home, his rage mounted to a sort of frenzy. . . .

He suddenly decided to stop [at the office of *Every Other Week*] before he went home. . . .

There was nobody but Conrad in the counting-room, whither Dryfoos returned after glancing into Fulkerson's empty office. "Where's Fulkerson?" he asked, sitting down with his hat on.

"He went out a few moments ago," said Conrad, glancing at the clock. "I'm afraid he isn't coming back again to-day, if you wanted to see him."

Dryfoos twisted his head sideways and upward to indicate March's room. "That other fellow out, too?"

"He went just before Mr. Fulkerson," answered Conrad.

"Do you generally knock off here in the middle of the afternoon?" asked the old man.

" No," said Conrad, as patiently as if his father had not been there a score of times, and found the whole staff of *Every Other Week* at work between four and five. " Mr. March, you know, always takes a good deal of his work home with him, and I suppose Mr. Fulkerson went out so early because there isn't much doing to-day. Perhaps it's the strike that makes it dull."

" The strike — yes! It's a pretty piece of business to have everything thrown out because a parcel of lazy hounds want a chance to lay off and get drunk." Dryfoos seemed to think Conrad would make some answer to this, but the young man's mild face merely saddened, and he said nothing. " I've got a coupé out there now that I had to take because I couldn't get a car. If I had my way I'd have a lot of those vagabonds hung. They're waiting to get the city into a snarl, and then rob the houses — pack of dirty, worthless whelps. They ought to call out the militia, and fire into 'em. Clubbing is too good for them." Conrad was still silent, and his father sneered, " But I reckon *you* don't think so."

" I think the strike is useless," said Conrad.

" Oh, you *do,* do you? Comin' to your senses a little. Gettin' tired walkin' so much. I should like to know what your gentlemen over there on the East side think about the strike, anyway."

The young fellow dropped his eyes. " I am not authorized to speak for them."

" Oh, indeed! And perhaps you're not authorized to speak for yourself? "

" Father, you know we don't agree about these things. I'd rather not talk — "

" But I'm goin' to *make* you talk this time! " cried Dryfoos, striking the arm of the chair he sat in with the side of his fist. A maddening thought of Christine came over him. " As long as you eat my bread, you have got to do as I say. I won't have my children telling me what I shall do and sha'n't do, or take on airs of being holier than me. Now, you just speak up! Do you think those loafers are right, or don't you? Come! "

Conrad apparently judged it best to speak. " I think they were very foolish to strike — at this time, when the elevated roads can do the work."

" Oh, at this time, heigh! And I suppose they think over there on the East side that it'd been wise to strike before we got the elevated." Conrad again refused to answer, and his father roared, " What do you think? "

"I think a strike is always bad business. It's war; but sometimes there don't seem any other way for the working men to get justice. They say that sometimes strikes do raise the wages, after a while."

"Those lazy devils were paid enough already," shrieked the old man. "They got two dollars a day. How much do you think they ought to 'a' got? Twenty?"

Conrad hesitated, with a beseeching look at his father. But he decided to answer. "The men say that with partial work, and fines, and other things, they get sometimes a dollar, and sometimes ninety cents a day."

"They lie, and you *know* they lie," said his father, rising and coming toward him. "And what do you think the upshot of it all will be, after they've ruined business for another week, and made people hire hacks, and stolen the money of honest men? How is it going to end?"

"They will have to give in."

"Oh, give in, heigh! And what will you say *then*, I should like to know? How will you feel about it then? Speak!"

"I shall feel as I do now. I know you don't think that way, and I don't blame you — or anybody. But if I have got to say how I shall feel, why, I shall feel sorry they didn't succeed, for I believe they have a righteous cause, though they go the wrong way to help themselves."

His father came close to him, his eyes blazing, his teeth set. "Do you *dare* to say that to me?"

"Yes. I can't help it. I pity them; my whole heart is with those poor men."

"You impudent puppy!" shouted the old man. He lifted his hand and struck his son in the face. Conrad caught his hand with his own left, and while the blood began to trickle from a wound that Christine's intaglio ring had made in his temple, he looked at him with a kind of grieving wonder, and said, "Father!"

The old man wrenched his fist away, and ran out of the house. He remembered his address now, and he gave it as he plunged into the coupé. He trembled with his evil passion, and glared out of the windows at the passers as he drove home; he only saw Conrad's mild grieving, wondering eyes, and the blood slowly trickling from the wound in his temple.

Conrad went to the neat set-bowl in Fulkerson's comfortable room, and washed the blood away, and kept bathing the wound with the cold water till it stopped bleeding. The cut was not deep, and he

553

thought he would not put anything on it. After a while he locked up the office, and started out, he hardly knew where. But he walked on, in the direction he had taken, till he found himself in Union Square, on the pavement in front of Brentano's. It seemed to him that he heard some one calling gently to him, " Mr. Dryfoos! "

Conrad looked confusedly around, and the same voice said again, " Mr. Dryfoos! " and he saw that it was a lady speaking to him from a coupé beside the curbing, and then he saw that it was Miss Vance.

She smiled when he gave signs of having discovered her, and came up to the door of her carriage. "I am so glad to meet you. I have been longing to talk to somebody; nobody seems to feel about it as I do. Oh, isn't it horrible? *Must* they fail? I saw cars running on all the lines as I came across; it made me sick at heart. *Must* those brave fellows give in? And everybody seems to hate them so — I can't bear it." Her face was estranged with excitement, and there were traces of tears on it. "You must think me almost crazy to stop you in the street this way; but when I caught sight of you I had to speak. I knew you would sympathise — I knew you would feel as I do. Oh, how can anybody help honouring those poor men for standing by one another as they do? They are risking all they have in the world for the sake of justice! Oh, they are true heroes! They are staking the bread of their wives and children on the dreadful chance they've taken! But no one seems to understand it. No one seems to see that they are willing to suffer more now that other poor men may suffer less hereafter. And those wretched creatures that are coming in to take their places — those traitors — "

" We can't blame them for wanting to earn a living, Miss Vance," said Conrad.

" No, no! I don't blame them. Who am I, to do such a thing? It's *we* — people like me, of my class — who make the poor betray one another. But this dreadful fighting — this hideous paper is full of it! " She held up an extra, crumpled with her nervous reading. " Can't something be done to stop it? Don't you think that if some one went among them, and tried to make them see how perfectly hopeless it was to resist the companies, and drive off the new men, he might do some good? I have wanted to go and try; but I am a woman, and I mustn't! I shouldn't be afraid of the strikers, but I'm afraid of what people would say! " Conrad kept pressing his handkerchief to the

554

cut in his temple, which he thought might be bleeding, and now she noticed this. "Are you hurt, Mr. Dryfoos? You look so pale."

"No, it's nothing — a little scratch I've got."

"Indeed you look pale. Have you a carriage? How will you get home? Will you get in here with me, and let me drive you?"

"No, no," said Conrad, smiling at her excitement. "I'm perfectly well — "

"And you don't think I'm foolish and wicked for stopping you here, and talking in this way? But I know you feel as I do!"

"Yes, I feel as you do. You are right — right in every way — I mustn't keep you — Good-bye." He stepped back to bow, but she put her beautiful hand out of the window, and when he took it she wrung his hand hard.

"Thank you, thank you! You are good and you are just! But no one can do anything. It's useless!"

The type of irreproachable coachman on the box whose respectability had suffered through the strange behaviour of his mistress in this interview, drove quickly off at her signal, and Conrad stood a moment looking after the carriage. His heart was full of joy; it leaped; he thought it would burst. As he turned to walk away it seemed to him as if he mounted upon the air. The trust she had shown him, the praise she had given him; that crush of the hand: he hoped nothing, he formed no idea from it, but it all filled him with love that cast out the pain and shame he had been suffering. He believed that he could never be unhappy any more; the hardness that was in his mind toward his father went out of it; he saw how sorely he had tried him; he grieved that he had done it, but the means, the difference of his feeling about the cause of their quarrel, he was solemnly glad of that since she shared it. He was only sorry for his father. "Poor father!" he said under his breath as he went along. He explained to her about his father in his reverie, and she pitied his father too.

He was walking over toward the West side, aimlessly at first, and then at times with the longing to do something to save those mistaken men from themselves forming itself into a purpose. Was not that what she meant, when she bewailed her woman's helplessness? She must have wished him to try, if he, being a man, could not do something; or if she did not, still he would try, and if she heard of it, she would recall what she had said, and would be glad he understood her so.

555

Thinking of her pleasure in what he was going to do, he forgot almost what it was; but when he came to a street-car track he remembered it, and looked up and down to see if there were any turbulent gathering of men, whom he might mingle with and help to keep from violence. He saw none anywhere; and then suddenly, as if at the same moment, for in his exalted mood all events had a dream-like simultaneity, he stood at the corner of an avenue, and in the middle of it, a little way off, was a street-car, and around the car a tumult of shouting, cursing, struggling men. The driver was lashing his horses forward, and a policeman was at their heads, with the conductor, pulling them; stones, clubs, brick-bats hailed upon the car, the horses, the men trying to move them. The mob closed upon them in a body, and then a patrol-wagon whirled up from the other side, and a squad of policemen leaped out, and began to club the rioters. Conrad could see how they struck them under the rims of their hats; the blows on their skulls sounded as if they had fallen on stone; the rioters ran in all directions.

One of the officers rushed up toward the corner where Conrad stood, and then he saw at his side a tall old man with a long white beard. He was calling out at the policeman: "Ah yes! Glup the strikerss — gif it to them! Why don't you co and glup the bresidents that insoalt your lawss, and gick your Boart of Arpidration out-of-toors? Glup the strikerss — they cot no friendts! They cot no money to pribe you, to dreat you!"

The officer lifted his club, and the old man threw his left arm up to shield his head. Conrad recognised Lindau, and now he saw the empty sleeve dangle in the air, over the stump of his wrist. He heard a shot in that turmoil beside the car, and something seemed to strike him in the breast. He was going to say to the policeman, "Don't strike him! He's an old soldier! You see he has no hand!" but he could not speak, he could not move his tongue. The policeman stood there; he saw his face: it was not bad, not cruel; it was like the face of a statue, fixed, perdurable; a mere image of irresponsible and involuntary authority. Then Conrad fell forward, pierced through the heart by that shot fired from the car.

March heard the shot as he scrambled out of his car, and at the same moment he saw Lindau drop under the club of the policeman, who left him where he fell, and joined the rest of the squad in pursuing the rioters. The fighting round the car in the avenue ceased; the driver whipped his horses into a gallop, and the place was left empty.

March would have liked to run; he thought how his wife had implored him to keep away from the rioting; but he could not have left Lindau lying there if he would. Something stronger than his will drew him to the spot, and there he saw Conrad dead beside the old man.

[*1890*]

from

CRITICISM AND FICTION

" How few materials," said Emerson, " are yet used by our arts! The mass of creatures and of qualities are still hid and expectant," and to break new ground is still one of the uncommonest and most heroic of the virtues. The artists are not alone to blame for the timidity that keeps them in the old furrows of the worn-out fields; most of those whom they live to please, or live by pleasing, prefer to have them remain there; it wants rare virtue to appreciate what is new, as well as to invent it; and the " easy things to understand" are the conventional things. This is why the ordinary English novel, with its hackneyed plot, scenes, and figures, is more comfortable to the ordinary American than an American novel, which deals, at its worst, with comparatively new interests and motives. To adjust one's self to the enjoyment of these costs an intellectual effort, and an intellectual effort is what no ordinary person likes to make. It is only the extraordinary person who can say, with Emerson: " I ask not for the great, the remote, the romantic. . . . I embrace the common; I sit at the feet of the familiar and the low. . . . Man is surprised to find that things near are not less beautiful and wondrous than things remote. . . . The perception of the worth of the vulgar is fruitful in discoveries. . . . The foolish man wonders at the unusual, but the wise man at the usual. . . . To-day always looks mean to the thoughtless; but to-day is a king in disguise. . . . Banks and tariffs, the newspaper and caucus, Methodism and Unitarianism, are flat and dull to dull people, but rest on the same foundations of wonder as the town of Troy and the temple of Delphos."

Perhaps we ought not to deny their town of Troy and their temple

557

of Delphos to the dull people; but if we ought, and if we did, they would still insist upon having them. An English novel, full of titles and rank, is apparently essential to the happiness of such people; their weak and childish imagination is at home in its familiar environment; they know what they are reading; the fact that it is hash many times warmed over reassures them; whereas a story of our own life, honestly studied and faithfully represented, troubles them with varied misgiving. They are not sure that it is literature; they do not feel that it is good society; its characters, so like their own, strike them as commonplace; they say they do not wish to know such people.

Everything in England is appreciable to the literary sense, while the sense of the literary worth of things in America is still faint and weak with most people, with the vast majority who " ask for the great, the remote, the romantic," who cannot " embrace the common," cannot " sit at the feet of the familiar and the low," in the good company of Emerson. We are all, or nearly all, struggling to be distinguished from the mass, and to be set apart in select circles and upper classes like the fine people we have read about. We are really a mixture of the plebeian ingredients of the whole world; but that is not bad; our vulgarity consists in trying to ignore " the worth of the vulgar," in believing that the superfine is better.

But, the humanitarian impulse . . . I think . . . has never so generally characterized all fiction. One may refuse to recognize this impulse; one may deny that it is in any greater degree shaping life than ever before, but no one who has the current of literature under his eye can fail to note it there. People are thinking and feeling generously, if not living justly, in our time; it is a day of anxiety to be saved from the curse that is on selfishness, of eager question how others shall be helped, of bold denial that the conditions in which we would fain have rested are sacred or immutable. Especially in America, where the race has gained a height never reached before, the eminence enables more men than ever before to see how even here vast masses of men are sunk in misery that must grow every day more hopeless, or embroiled in a struggle for mere life that must end in enslaving and imbruting them.

Art, indeed, is beginning to find out that if it does not make friends with Need it must perish. It perceives that to take itself from the many and leave them no joy in their work, and to give itself to the few whom it can bring no joy in their idleness, is an error that kills. This has long been the burden of Ruskin's message: and if we can believe William Morris, the common people have heard him gladly, and have felt the truth of what he says. " They see the prophet in him rather than the fantastic rhetorician, as more superfine audiences do "; and the men and women who do the hard work of the world have learned from him and from Morris that they have a right to pleasure in their toil, and that when justice is done them they will have it. In all ages poetry has affirmed something of this sort, but it remained for ours to perceive it and express it somehow in every form of literature. But this is only one phase of the devotion of the best literature of our time to the service of humanity. No book written with a low or cynical motive could succeed now, no matter how brilliantly written; and the work done in the past to the glorification of mere passion and power, to the deification of self, appears monstrous and hideous. The romantic spirit worshipped genius, worshipped heroism, but at its best, in such a man as Victor Hugo, this spirit recognized the supreme claim of the lowest humanity. Its error was to idealize the victims of society, to paint them impossibly virtuous and beautiful; but truth, which has succeeded to the highest mission of romance, paints these victims as they are, and bids the world consider them not because they are beautiful and virtuous, but because they are ugly and vicious, cruel, filthy, and only not altogether loathsome because the divine can never wholly die out of the human. The truth does not find these victims among the poor alone, among the hungry, the houseless, the ragged; but it also finds them among the rich, cursed with the aimlessness, the satiety, the despair of wealth, wasting their lives in a fool's paradise of shows and semblances, with nothing real but the misery that comes of insincerity and selfishness.

It is needless for me to say, either to the many whom my opinions on this point incense or to the few who accept them, that I do not think the fiction of our own time even always equal to this work, or perhaps more than seldom so. But as I have before expressed, to the still-reverberating discontent of two continents, fiction is now a finer art than it has ever been hitherto, and more nearly meets the requirements of the infallible standard. I have hopes of real usefulness in it, because it is at last building on the only sure foundation; but I am by no means certain that it will be the ultimate literary form, or will remain as important as we believe it is destined to become. On the

559

contrary, it is quite imaginable that when the great mass of readers, now sunk in the foolish joys of mere fable, shall be lifted to an interest in the meaning of things through the faithful portrayal of life in fiction, then fiction the most faithful may be superseded by a still more faithful form of contemporaneous history. I willingly leave the precise character of this form to the more robust imagination of readers whose minds have been nurtured upon romantic novels, and who really have an imagination worth speaking of, and confine myself, as usual, to the hither side of the regions of conjecture.

The art which in the mean time disdains the office of teacher is one of the last refuges of the aristocratic spirit which is disappearing from politics and society, and is now seeking to shelter itself in æsthetics. The pride of caste is becoming the pride of taste; but as before, it is averse to the mass of men; it consents to know them only in some conventionalized and artificial guise. It seeks to withdraw itself, to stand aloof; to be distinguished, and not to be identified. Democracy in literature is the reverse of all this. It wishes to know and tell the truth, confident that consolation and delight are there; it does not care to paint the marvellous and impossible for the vulgar many, or to sentimentalize and falsify the actual for the vulgar few. Men are more like than unlike one another: let us make them know one another better, that they may be all humbled and strengthened with a sense of their fraternity. Neither arts, nor letters, nor sciences, except as they somehow, clearly or obscurely, tend to make the race better and kinder, are to be regarded as serious interests; they are all lower than the rudest crafts that feed and house and clothe, for except they do this office they are idle; and they cannot do this except from and through the truth.

[*1892*]

CHARLES ELIOT NORTON

[1827–1908]

EULOGIES of Norton as a " gentleman scholar," as a humanist, as an inspiring teacher, as a student of medieval architecture and ancient art, have been frequent. Some of us, however, have preferred to remember him as a distinguished example of that remarkable breed (now, alas, becoming rare) — the New England aristocrat with a sense of civic duty and devotion to the commonweal, and with the courage to stand up for his convictions despite vituperation and calumny. Norton was born in Cambridge, Massachusetts. His father was a Biblical scholar at Harvard and his mother came from the wealthy Eliot family of Boston. He was educated at Harvard, spent a few years in business, and then traveled leisurely in Asia and Europe. The rest of his life was devoted to study, writing, travel, teaching, and correspondence with the literary notables of England — a pleasant way of life, but one which did not make him indifferent to the things that were happening around him. While in business, just after leaving Harvard, he spent his evenings establishing night schools for men in Cambridge. During the 1850's he made his anti-slavery views unmistakably clear; he admired John Brown. Subsequently he promoted Negro education. With his friend George William Curtis, he worked for civil-service reforms. He was forthright in expressing his views as a free-thinker. Finally, and most courageous of all, were his open attacks upon imperialism, which reached their logical climax in his denunciation of the Spanish-American War. His famous speech on this issue (delivered on June 7, 1898, to a church group in Cambridge), together with two letters on its consequences, are here reprinted. His stand brought threats of grave personal injury, but he never wavered or recanted.

TRUE PATRIOTISM

There are moments in every man's life, in the life of every nation, when, under the excitement of passion, the simple truths which in common times are the foundation upon which the right order and conduct of life depend are apt to be forgotten and disregarded. I shall venture to-night to recall to you some of these commonplace truths,

561

which in these days of war need more than ever to be kept in mind.

There never was a land that better deserved the love of her people than America, for there never was a mother-country kinder to her children. She has given to them all that she could give. Her boundless resources have lain open to them, to use at their will. And the consequence has been that never in the history of man has there been so splendid a spectacle of widely diffused and steadily increasing material welfare as America has displayed during the last hundred years. Millions upon millions of men have lived here with more comfort, with less fear, than any such numbers elsewhere in any age have lived. Countless multitudes, whose forefathers from the beginning of human life on earth have spent weary lives in unrewarded toil, in anxiety, in helplessness, in ignorance, have risen here, in the course of even a single generation, to the full and secure enjoyment of the fruits of their labour, to confident hope, to intelligent possession of their own faculties. Is not the land to be dearly loved in which this has been possible, in which this has been achieved?

But there is a deeper source of love of country than the material advantages and benefits it may afford. It is in the character of its people, in their moral life, in the type of civilization which they exhibit. The elements of human nature are indeed so fixed that favourable or unfavourable circumstances have little effect upon its essential constitution, but prosperity or the reverse brings different traits into prominence. The conditions which have prevailed in America have, if broadly considered, tended steadily and strongly to certain good results in the national character; not, indeed, to unmixed good, but to a preponderance of good. The institutions established for self-government have been founded with intent to secure justice and independence for all. The social relations among the whole body of the people, are humane and simple. The general spirit of the people is liberal, is kindly, is considerate. The ideas for the realization of which in private and public conduct there is more or less steady and consistent effort, are as high and as worthy as any which men have pursued. Every genuine American holds to the ideal of justice for all men, of independence, including free speech and free action within the limits of law, of obedience to law, of universal education, of material well-being for all the well-behaving and industrious, or peace and good-will among men. These, however far short the nation may fall in expressing them in its actual life, are, no one will deny it, the ideals of our American democracy. And it is because America represents these ideals that the deepest love for his country glows in the heart of the American, and inspires him with that patriotism which counts no cost, which esteems no sacrifice too great to maintain and to increase the influence of these principles which embody themselves in the fair shape of his native land, and have their expressive symbol in her flag. The spirit of his patriotism is not an intermittent impulse; it is an abiding principle; it is the strongest motive of his life; it is his religion.

And because it is so, and just in proportion to his love of the ideals for which his country stands, is his hatred of whatever is opposed to them in private conduct or public policy. Against injustice, against dishonesty, against lawlessness, against whatever may make for war instead of peace, the good citizen is always in arms.

No thoughtful American can have watched the course of affairs among us during the last thirty years without grave anxiety from the apparent decline in power to control the direction of public and private conduct, of the principles upon regard for which the permanent and progressive welfare of America depends; and especially the course of events during the last few months and the actual condition of the country to-day, should bring home to every man the question whether or not the nation is true to one of the chief of the ideals to which it has professed allegiance. A generation has grown up that has known nothing of war. The blessings of peace have been poured out upon us. We have congratulated ourselves that we were free from the misery and the burdens that war and standing armies have brought upon the nations of the Old World. " Their fires " — I cite a fine phrase of Sir Philip Sidney in a letter to Queen Elizabeth — " Their fires have given us light to see our own quietness." And now of a sudden, without cool deliberation, without prudent preparation, the nation is hurried into war, and America, she who more than any other land was pledged to peace and good-will on earth, unsheathes her sword, compels a weak and unwilling nation to a fight, rejecting without due consideration her earnest and repeated offers to meet every legitimate demand of the United States. It is a bitter disappointment to the lover of his country; it is a turning-back from the path of civilization to that of barbarism.

" There never was a good war," said Franklin. There have indeed been many wars in which a good man must take part, and take part with grave gladness to defend the cause of justice, to die for it if need

563

be, a willing sacrifice, thankful to give life for what is dearer than life, and happy that even by death in war he is serving the cause of peace. But if a war be undertaken for the most righteous end, before the resources of peace have been tried and proved vain to secure it, that war has no defence; it is a national crime. And however right, however unavoidable a way may be, and those of us who are old enough to remember the war for the Union know that war may be right and unavoidable, yet, I repeat the words of Franklin, " There never was a good war." It is evil in itself, it is evil in its never-ending train of consequences. No man has known the nature of war better than General Sherman, and in his immortal phrase he has condensed its description — " War is hell." " From the earliest dawnings of policy to this day," said Edmund Burke, more than a hundred years ago, " the invention of men has been sharpening and improving the mystery of murder, from the first rude essays of clubs and stones to the present perfection of gunnery, cannoneering, bombarding, mining, and all these species of artificial, learned and refined cruelty in which we are now so expert, and which make a principal part of what politicians have taught us to believe is our principal glory." And it is now, at the end of this century, the century in which beyond any other in history knowledge has increased and the arts of peace have advanced, that America has been brought by politicians and writers for the press, faithless to her noble ideals, against the will of every right-minded citizen, to resort to these cruel arts, these arts of violence, these arts which rouse the passions of the beast in man, before the resources of peace had been fairly tested and proved insufficient to secure the professed ends, which, however humane and desirable, afford no sufficient justification for resorting to the dread arbitrament of arms.

There are, indeed, many among us who find justification of the present war in the plea that its motive is to give independence to the people of Cuba, long burdened by the oppressive and corrupt rule of Spain, and especially to relieve the suffering of multitudes deprived of their homes and of means of subsistence by the cruel policy of the general who exercised for a time a practical dictatorship over the island. The plea so far as it is genuine deserves the respect due to every humane sentiment. But independence secured for Cuba by forcible overthrow of the Spanish rule means either practical anarchy or the substitution of the authority of the United States for that of Spain. Either alternative might well give us pause. And as for the relief of suffering, surely it is a strange procedure to begin by inflicting worse suffering still. It is fighting the devil with his own arms. That the end justifies the means is a dangerous doctrine, and no wise man will advise doing evil for the sake of an uncertain good. But the plea that the better government of Cuba and the relief of the reconcentrados could only be secured by war is the plea either of ignorance or of hypocrisy.

But the war is declared; and on all hands we hear the cry that he is no patriot who fails to shout for it, and to urge the youth of the country to enlist, and to rejoice that they are called to the service of their native land. The sober counsels that were appropriate before the war was entered upon must give way to blind enthusiasm, and the voice of condemnation must be silenced by the thunders of the guns and the hurrahs of the crowd. Stop! A declaration of war does not change the moral law. " The ten commandments will not budge " at a joint resolve of Congress. Was James Russell Lowell aught but a good patriot when during the Mexican war he sent the stinging shafts of his matchless satire at the heart of the monstrous iniquity, or when, years afterward, he declared, that he thought at the time and that he still thought the Mexican war was a national crime? Did John Bright ever render greater service to his country than when, during the Crimean war, he denounced the Administration which had plunged England into it, and employed his magnificent power of earnest and incisive speech in the endeavour to repress the evil spirit which it evoked in the heart of the nation? No! the voice of protest, of warning, of appeal is never more needed than when the clamour of fife and drum, echoed by the press and too often by the pulpit, is bidding all men fall in and keep step and obey in silence the tyrannous word of command. Then, more than ever, it is the duty of the good citizen not to be silent, and spite of obloquy, misrepresentation and abuse, to insist on being heard, and with sober counsel to maintain the everlasting validity of the principles of the moral law.

So confused are men by false teaching in regard to national honour and the duty of the citizen that it is easy to fall into the error of holding a declaration of war, however brought about, as a sacred decision of the national will, and to fancy that a call to arms from the Administration has the force of a call from the lips of the country, of the America to whom all her sons are ready to pay the full measure of devotion. This is indeed a natural and for many a youth not a discreditable error. But if the nominal, though authorized, representatives of the country have brought us into a war that might and should have been avoided, and which consequently is an unrighteous war, then, so long as the safety of the State is not at risk, the duty of the good citizen is plain. He is to help to provide the Administration responsible for the conduct of the war with every means that may serve to bring it to the speediest end. He is to do this alike that the immediate evils of the war may be as brief and as few as possible, and also that its miserable train of after evils may be diminished and the vicious passions excited by it be the sooner allayed. Men, money, must be abundantly supplied. But must he himself enlist or quicken the ardent youth to enter service in such a cause? The need is not yet. The country is in no peril. There is always in a vast population like ours an immense, a sufficient supply of material of a fighting order, often of a heroic courage, ready and eager for the excitement of battle, filled with the old notion that patriotism is best expressed in readiness to fight for our country, be she right or wrong. Better the paying of bounties to such men to fill the ranks than that they should be filled by those whose higher duty is to fit themselves for the service of their country in the patriotic labours of peace. We mourn the deaths of our noble youth fallen in the cause of their country when she stands for the right; but we may mourn with a deeper sadness for those who have fallen in a cause which their generous hearts mistook for one worthy of the last sacrifice.

My friends, America has been compelled against the will of all her wisest and best to enter into a path of darkness and peril. Against their will she has been forced to turn back from the way of civilization to the way of barbarism, to renounce for the time her own ideals. With grief, with anxiety must the lover of his country regard the present aspect and the future prospect of the nation's life. With serious purpose, with utter self-devotion he should prepare himself for the untried and difficult service to which it is plain he is to be called in the quick-coming years.

Two months ago America stood at the parting of the ways. Her first step is irretrievable. It depends on the virtue, on the enlightened patriotism of her children whether her future steps shall be upward to the light or downward to the darkness.

" Nil desperandum de republica."

[*1898*]

566

LETTERS ON THE SPANISH WAR

TO LESLIE STEPHEN

I have been silent too long, — partly because this iniquitous and perilous war has made me averse to letter-writing. The days are grave and disheartening, and the prospect is dark. We have been living in a Fool's Paradise, hoping that in the long run the better elements in our national life would get the upper hand, and that we should stumble along, with many a slip indeed, but on the whole in the right direction. But the war has suddenly roused us from this dream. America has rejected her old ideals, turned her back on her past, and chosen the path of barbarism. All the evil spirits of the Old World which we trusted were exorcised in the New, have taken possession of her, and under their influence she has gone mad. A mere accident, — the report of some words which, at the moment of the declaration of war, I spoke to my class on the nature of true patriotism, brought me into transient prominence and made me the subject of a good deal of newspaper obloquy. I stated my opinions more fully in a speech to a young men's club, and unexpectedly found myself in the position of representative of the rights of independent individual judgment and expression. The attacks made upon me would have been simply humorous, had they not been indicative of the blindness and despotism of popular passion. One of our Irish patriots, a man prominent in politics, in a speech in my own native Cambridge, intimated that a coat of tar and feathers would be a proper suit for me, and the suggestion was repeated in a Chicago newspaper! My mail was loaded down with letters and post-cards full of abuse, mostly anonymous, some of them going so far as to bid me look out for a stray bullet! But the storm is ceasing and will soon die wholly away. . . .

[*1898*]

TO EDWARD LEE-CHILDE

My dear Childe, — Your letter of six weeks ago gave me much pleasure, and I should have thanked you for it before now, but for the fact that owing to the position I have taken in regard to this wretched, needless and, consequently, iniquitious war, I have been burdened with letters which demanded immediate attention, from a great number of known and unknown correspondents, more of them denouncing my course than expressing sympathy with it. . . .

The old America, the America of our hopes and our dreams has come to an end, and a new America is entering on the false course which has been tried so often and which has often led to calamity. This war will in the long run result in far more evil to the United States than to Spain. We shall nominally win, but at the cost of what infinite loss!

The world is uglier physically, and in part morally, than when we were born, — but I believe that in the portion of it which we call civilized there is less misery. At any rate, I comfort myself with what may, after all, be a delusion. . . .

[*1898*]

WILLIAM JENNINGS BRYAN

[1860–1925]

BRYAN WAS born of farmer stock in Salem, Illinois, and educated at a small local college. He studied law in Chicago and practiced in an Illinois town from 1883 to 1887, moving in the latter year to Lincoln, Nebraska. There he practiced his profession for only a few years, deserting it to enter politics. In 1890 he was elected to Congress as a Democrat, and in 1892 he was re-elected. He failed in his candidacy for the Senate in 1894, but continued his political activities through writing and lecturing. Gradually he came to the forefront as a champion of Populism — the vigorous agrarian movement of that period. In the Democratic Convention at Chicago in 1896 he made his greatest speech. It was not merely a plea for currency reform; if his advocacy of the free coinage of silver were all that that speech contained it would have been forgotten long ago. It was a great speech — it is remembered — because it was a plea for economic justice for the working farmers of this country and an impassioned denunciation of the privileged classes. Bryan was nominated for the presidency, but lost to McKinley. He ran again in 1900 and once again in 1908. After these unsuccessful attempts he gave up all hope of entering the White House. He remained a potent figure in the Democratic Party, however. He helped to nominate Woodrow Wilson and was Secretary of State in Wilson's first cabinet, resigning when he realized that Wilson was leading the country to war. In later years Bryan was conspicuous as a prohibitionist and religious fundamentalist. His last public appearance was at the Scopes trial in Dayton, Tennessee, where he helped the state prosecute Scopes for teaching Darwinism. It is sometimes said that Clarence Darrow's knife-edged cross-examination of Bryan caused the latter's death. He died five days after the trial ended. For twenty years a symbol of Middle Western democracy, at the end he was a symbol of intellectual backwardness.

from
SPEECH AT CHICAGO, 1896

I would be presumptuous, indeed, to present myself against the distinguished gentlemen to whom you have listened if this were a mere measuring of abilities; but this is not a contest between persons. The humblest citizen in all the land, when clad in the armor of a righteous cause, is stronger than all the hosts of error. I come to speak to you in defense of a cause as holy as the cause of liberty — the cause of humanity.

When this debate is conluded, a motion will be made to lay upon the table the resolution offered in commendation of the administration, and also the resolution offered in condemnation of the administration. We object to bringing this question down to the level of persons. The individual is but an atom; he is born, he acts, he dies; but principles are eternal; and this has been a contest over a principle.

Never before in the history of this country has there been witnessed such a contest as that through which we have just passed. Never before in the history of American politics has a great issue been fought out as this issue has been, by the voters of a great party. On the fourth of March, 1895, a few Democrats, most of them members of Congress, issued an address to the Democrats of the nation, asserting that the money question was the paramount issue of the hour; declaring that a majority of the Democratic party had the right to control the action of the party on this paramount issue; and concluding with the request that the believers in the free coinage of silver in the Democratic party should organize, take charge of, and control the policy of the Democratic party. Three months later, at Memphis, an organization was perfected, and the silver Democrats went forth openly and courageously proclaiming their belief, and declaring that, if successful, they would crystallize into a platform the declaration which they had made. Then began the conflict. With a zeal approaching the zeal which inspired the crusaders who followed Peter the Hermit, our silver Democrats went forth from victory unto victory until they are now assembled, not to discuss, not to debate, but to enter up the judgment already rendered by the plain people of this country. In this contest brother has been arrayed against brother, father against son. The warmest ties of love, acquaintance and association have been disregarded; old leaders have been cast aside when they have refused to give expression to the sentiments of those whom they would lead, and new leaders have sprung up to give direction to this cause of truth. Thus has the contest been waged, and we have assembled here under as binding and solemn instructions as were ever imposed upon representatives of the people.

We do not come as individuals. As individuals we might have been glad to compliment the gentleman from New York [Senator Hill], but we know that the people for whom we speak would never be willing to put him in a position where he could thwart the will of the Democratic party. I say it was not a question of persons; it was a question of principle, and it is not with gladness, my friends, that we find ourselves brought into conflict with those who are now arrayed on the other side.

The gentleman who preceded me [ex-Governor Russell] spoke of the State of Massachusetts; let me assure him that not one present in all this convention entertains the least hostility to the people of the State of Massachusetts, but we stand here representing people who are the equals, before the law, of the greatest citizens in the State of Massachusetts. When you [turning to the gold delegates] come before us and tell us that we are about to disturb your business interests, we reply that you have disturbed our business interests by your course.

We say to you that you have made the definition of a business man too limited in its application. The man who is employed for wages is as much a business man as his employer, the attorney in a country town is as much a business man as the corporation counsel in a great metropolis; the merchant at the cross-roads store is as much a business man as the merchant of New York; the farmer who goes forth in the morning and toils all day—who begins in the spring and toils all summer — and who by the application of brain and muscle to the natural resources of the country creates wealth, is as much a business man as the man who goes upon the board of trade and bets upon the price of grain; the miners who go down a thousand feet into the earth, or climb two thousand feet upon the cliffs, and bring forth from their hiding places the precious metals to be poured into the channels of trade are as much business men as the few financial magnates who, in a back room, corner the money of the world. We come to speak for this broader class of business men.

Ah, my friends, we say not one word against those who live upon the Atlantic coast, but the hardy pioneers who have braved all the dangers of the wilderness, who have made the desert to blossom as the rose — the poineers away out there [pointing to the West], who rear their children near to Nature's heart, where they can mingle their voices with the voices of the birds — out there where they have erected schoolhouses for the education of their young, churches where they praise their Creator, and cemeteries where rest the ashes of their dead — these people, we say, are as deserving of the consideration of our party as any people in this country. It is for these that we speak. We do not come as aggressors. Our war is not a war of conquest; we are fighting in the defense of our homes, our families, and posterity. We have petitioned, and our petitions have been scorned; we have entreated, and our entreaties have been disregarded; we have begged, and they have mocked when our calamity came. We beg no longer; we entreat no more; we petition no more. We defy them.

The gentleman from Wisconsin has said that he fears a Robespierre. My friends, in this land of the free you need not fear that a tyrant will spring up from among the people. What we need is an Andrew Jackson to stand, as Jackson stood, against the encroachments of organized wealth.

They tell us that this platform was made to catch votes. We reply to them that changing conditions make new issues; that the principles upon which Democracy rests are as everlasting as the hills, but that they must be applied to new conditions as they arise. Conditions have arisen, and we are here to meet these conditions. They tell us that the income tax ought not to be brought in here; that it is a new idea. They criticize us for our criticism of the Supreme Court of the United States. My friends, we have not criticized; we have simply called attention to what you already know. If you want criticisms, read the dissenting opinions of the court. There you will find criticisms. They say that we passed an unconstitutional law; we deny it. The income tax law was not unconstitutional when it was passed; it was not unconstitutional when it went before the Supreme Court for the first time; it did not become unconstitutional until one of the judges changed his mind, and we cannot be expected to know when a judge will change his mind. The income tax is just. It simply intends to put the burdens of government justly upon the backs of the people. I am in favor of an income tax. When I find a man who is not willing to bear his share of the burdens of the government which protects him,

I find a man who is unworthy to enjoy the blessings of a government like ours.

They say that we are opposing national bank currency; it is true. If you will read what Thomas Benton said, you will find he said that, in searching history, he could find but one parallel to Andrew Jackson; that was Cicero, who destroyed the conspiracy of Catiline and saved Rome. Benton said that Cicero only did for Rome what Jackson did for us when he destroyed the bank conspiracy and saved America. We say in our platform that we believe that the right to coin and issue money is a function of government. We believe it. We believe that it is a part of sovereignty, and can no more with safety be delegated to private individuals than we could afford to delegate to private individuals the power to make penal statutes or levy taxes. Mr. Jefferson, who was once regarded as good Democratic authority, seems to have differed in opinion from the gentleman who has addressed us on the part of the minority. Those who are opposed to this proposition tell us that the issue of paper money is a function of the bank, and that the Government ought to go out of the banking business. I stand with Jefferson rather than with them, and tell them as he did, that the issue of money is a function of government, and that the banks ought to go out of the governing business.

They complain about the plank which declares against life tenure in office. They have tried to strain it to mean that which it does not mean. What we oppose by that plank is the life tenure which is being built up in Washington, and which excludes from participation in official benefits the humbler members of society. . . .

And now, my friends, let me come to the paramount issue. If they ask us why it is that we say more on the money question than we say upon the tariff question, I reply that, if protection has slain its thousands, the gold standard has slain its tens of thousands. If they ask us why we do not embody in our platform all the things that we believe in, we reply that when we have restored the money of the Constitution all other necessary reforms will be possible; but that until this is done there is no other reform that can be accomplished.

Why is it that within three months such a change has come over the country? Three months ago, when it was confidently asserted that those who believe in the gold standard would frame our platform and nominate our candidates, even the advocates of the gold standard did not think that we could elect a President. And they had good reason for their doubt, because there is scarcely a State here to-day asking for the gold standard which is not in the absolute control of the Republican party. But note the change. Mr. McKinley was nominated at St. Louis upon a platform which declared for the maintenance of the gold standard until it can be changed into bimetallism by international agreement. Mr. McKinley was the most popular man among the Republicans, and three months ago everybody in the Republican party prophesied his election. How is it to-day? Why, the man who was once pleased to think that he looked like Napoleon — that man shudders to-day when he remembers that he was nominated on the anniversary of the battle of Waterloo. Not only that, but as he listens he can hear with ever-increasing distinctness the sound of the waves as they beat upon the lonely shores of St. Helena.

Why this change? Ah, my friends, is not the reason for the change evident to any one who will look at the matter? No private character, however pure, no personal popularity, however great, can protect from the avenging wrath of an indignant people a man who will declare that he is in favor of fastening the gold standard upon this country, or who is willing to surrender the right of self-government and place the legislative control of our affairs in the hands of foreign potentates and powers.

We go forth confident that we shall win. Why? Because upon the paramount issue of this campaign there is not a spot of ground upon which the enemy will dare to challenge battle. If they tell us that the gold standard is a good thing, we shall point to their platform and tell them that their platform pledges the party to get rid of the gold standard and substitute bimetallism. If the gold standard is a good thing, why try to get rid of it? I call your attention to the fact that some of the very people who are in this convention to-day and who tell us that we ought to declare in favor of international bimetallism — thereby declaring that the gold standard is wrong and that the principle of bimetallism is better — these very people four months ago were open and avowed advocates of the gold standard, and were then telling us that we could not legislate two metals together, even with the aid of all the world. If the gold standard is a good thing, we ought to declare in favor of its retention and not in favor of abandoning it; and if the gold standard is a bad thing why should we wait until other nations are willing to help us to let go? Here is the line of battle, and we care not upon which issue they force the fight; we

574

are prepared to meet them on either issue or on both. If they tell us that the gold standard is the standard of civilization, we reply to them that this, the most enlightened of all the nations of the earth, has never declared for a gold standard and that both the great parties this year are declaring against it. If the gold standard is the standard of civilization, why, my friends, should we not have it? If they come to meet us on that issue we can present the history of our nation. More than that; we can tell them that they will search the pages of history in vain to find a single instance where the common people of any land have ever declared themselves in favor of the gold standard. They can find where the holders of fixed investments have declared for a gold standard, but not where the masses have.

Mr. Carlisle said in 1878 that this was a struggle between " the idle holders of idle capital " and " the struggling masses, who produce the wealth and pay the taxes of the country "; and, my friends, the question we are to decide is: Upon which side will the Democratic party fight; upon the side of " the idle holders of idle capital " or upon the side of " the struggling masses "? That is the question which the party must answer first, and then it must be answered by each individual hereafter. The sympathies of the Democratic party, as shown by the platform, are on the side of the struggling masses who have ever been the foundation of the Democratic party. There are two ideas of government. There are those who believe that, if you will only legislate to make the well-to-do prosperous, their prosperity will leak through on those below. The Democratic idea, however, has been that if you legislate to make the masses prosperous, their prosperity will find its way up through every class which rests upon them.

You come to us and tell us that the great cities are in favor of the gold standard; we reply that the great cities rest upon our broad and fertile prairies. Burn down your cities and leave our farms, and your cities will spring up again as if by magic; but destroy our farms and the grass will grow in the streets of every city in the country.

My friends, we declare that this nation is able to legislate for its own people on every question, without waiting for the aid or consent of any other nation on earth; and upon that issue we expect to carry every State in the Union. I shall not slander the inhabitants of the fair State of Massachusetts nor the inhabitants of the State of New York by saying that, when they are confronted with the proposition, they will declare that this nation is not able to attend to its own business.

It is the issue of 1776 over again. Our ancestors, when but three millions in number, had the courage to declare their political independence of every other nation; shall we, their descendants, when we have grown to seventy millions, declare that we are less independent than our forefathers? No, my friends, that will never be the verdict of our people. Therefore, we care not upon what lines the battle is fought. If they say bimetallism is good, but that we cannot have it until other nations help us, we reply that, instead of having a gold standard because England has, we will restore bimetallism, and then let England have bimetallism because the United States has it. If they dare to come out in the open field and defend the gold standard as a good thing, we will fight them to the uttermost. Having behind us the producing masses of this nation and the world, supported by the commercial interests, the laboring interests, and the toilers everywhere, we will answer their demand for a gold standard by saying to them: You shall not press down upon the brow of labor this crown of thorns, you shall not crucify mankind upon a cross of gold.

[*1896*]

EDWIN MARKHAM

[1852–1940]

HE WAS born of a family of pioneers, in Oregon City, Oregon. His father was the captain of one of the covered-wagon trains and in the new settlement became a farmer and hunter; his mother kept a store. When he was five years old he was taken to California, where he grew up, was educated, and was trained to be a school-teacher at the State Normal School in San Jose. He was teaching in a hamlet in the Sierras when he began to write his one great and deservedly famous poem, " The Man with the Hoe." When it was published it immediately attracted attention, was widely reprinted, was made the subject of countless editorials and sermons. No American poem had ever so sharply and bitterly accused society of injustice and exploitation — and the time was ripe for it. For this was a time of rising social protest, of acute labor struggles, of increasing humanitarian sentiment among educated people, for it was a time when no one could fail to see the ugly results of boom capitalism after the Civil War in the spread of slums, breadlines, and violence. Churchmen, in particular, were becoming alarmed and indignant, and " Christian Socialism " was attracting idealistic ministers. Markham's poem was a wonderful text for the rebel in the pulpit. Markham published many volumes during the course of his long life, but nothing he ever wrote equaled, in either power or popularity, " The Man with the Hoe." He died still believing in the ideals of social democracy which he had professed in his youth.

THE MAN WITH THE HOE

Written after Seeing Millet's World-Famous Painting

God made man in His own image, in the image of God made He him.
                                                    — GENESIS.

> Bowed by the weight of centuries he leans
> Upon his hoe and gazes on the ground,
> The emptiness of ages in his face,

And on his back the burden of the world.
Who made him dead to rapture and despair,
A thing that grieves not and that never hopes,
Stolid and stunned, a brother to the ox?
Who loosened and let down this brutal jaw?
Whose was the hand that slanted back this brow?
Whose breath blew out the light within this brain?

Is this the Thing the Lord God made and gave
To have dominion over sea and land;
To trace the stars and search the heavens for power;
To feel the passion of Eternity?
Is this the Dream He dreamed who shaped the suns
And marked their ways upon the ancient deep?
Down all the stretch of Hell to its last gulf
There is no shape more terrible than this —
More tongued with censure of the world's blind greed —
More filled with signs and portents for the soul —
More fraught with danger to the universe.

What gulfs between him and the seraphim!
Slave of the wheel of labor, what to him
Are Plato and the swing of Pleiades?
What the long reaches of the peaks of song,
The rift of dawn, the reddening of the rose?
Through this dread shape the suffering ages look;
Time's tragedy is in that aching stoop;
Through this dread shape humanity betrayed,
Plundered, profaned and disinherited,
Cries protest to the Judges of the World,
A protest that is also prophecy.

O masters, lords and rulers in all lands,
Is this the handiwork you give to God,
This monstrous thing distorted and soul-quenched?
How will you ever straighten up this shape;
Touch it again with immortality;
Give back the upward looking and the light;

Rebuild in it the music and the dream;
Make right the immemorial infamies,
Perfidious wrongs, immedicable woes?

O masters, lords and rulers in all lands,
How will the Future reckon with this Man?
How answer his brute question in that hour
When whirlwinds of rebellion shake the world?
How will it be with kingdoms and with kings —
With those who shaped him to the thing he is —
When this dumb Terror shall reply to God,
After the silence of the centuries?

[*1899*]

FINLEY PETER DUNNE

[1867–1936]

THE CASUAL newspaper humorist who uses his humor to attack social and political evils has had a long tradition in America. Among the greatest in that line was Dunne, creator of " Mr. Dooley," an Irish saloon-keeper in Chicago who commented bitingly on the affairs of the day. Dunne invented him in 1893, when he was working on the Chicago *Evening Post*. The " Mr. Dooley " articles — short dialogues in Irish dialect — were at first intended only to blast corrupt politicians in Chicago, but soon Dunne widened their scope. The Spanish War inspired several particularly savage articles which, significantly, won him wide popularity. Labor problems, national policy, education, snobbishness, anti-Semitism, high finance — everything was grist to " Mr. Dooley's " mill. The articles were later collected into books — *Mr. Dooley in Peace and in War* (1898), *Mr. Dooley in the Hearts of His Countrymen* (1898), *Mr. Dooley's Philosophy* (1900), *Mr. Dooley Says* (1910), and others — which were very successful. Those who read them as mere humor misunderstood them. As Franklin P. Adams once wrote, " When the Dunnes and the Lardners die, the papers print editorials saying that there was no malice in their writing and no bitterness in their humor. Few popular writers ever wrote more maliciously and bitterly than Lardner and Dunne. They resented injustice, they loathed sham, and they hated the selfish stupidity that went with them." Dunne was born in Chicago and educated in its public schools. At seventeen he became a newspaperman. He worked in his native city until 1900, when he came to New York. After several years of magazine and newspaper editing, he retired to concentrate upon his own writing. He became inactive after the World War. (The footnotes in the following selections are by Professor Elmer Ellis, who edited *Mr. Dooley at His Best.*)

MR. DOOLEY ON EXPANSION [1]

"Whin we plant what Hogan calls th' starry banner iv Freedom in th' Ph'lippeens," said Mr. Dooley, "an' give th' sacred blessin' iv liberty to the poor, downtrodden people iv thim unfortunate isles — damn thim! — we'll larn thim a lesson."

"Sure," said Mr. Hennessy, sadly, "we have a thing or two to larn oursilves."

"But it isn't f'r thim to larn us," said Mr. Dooley. "'Tis not f'r thim wretched an' degraded crathers, without a mind or a shirt iv their own, f'r to give lessons in politeness an' liberty to a nation that mannyfacthers more dhressed beef than anny other imperyal nation in th' wurruld. We say to thim: 'Naygurs,' we say, 'poor, dissolute, uncovered wretches,' says we, 'whin th' crool hand iv Spain forged man'cles f'r ye'er limbs, as Hogan says, who was it crossed th' say an' sthruck off th' comealongs? We did — by dad, we did. An' now, ye mis'rable, childish-minded apes, we propose f'r to larn ye th' uses iv liberty. In ivry city in this unfair land we will erect schoolhouses an' packin' houses an' houses iv correction; an' we'll larn ye our language, because 'tis aisier to larn ye ours than to larn oursilves yours. An' we'll give ye clothes, if ye pay f'r thim; an', if ye don't ye can go without. An', whin ye're hungry, ye can go to th' morgue — we mane th' resth'rant — an' ate a good square meal iv ar-rmy beef. An' we'll sind th' gr-reat Gin'ral Eagan over f'r to larn ye etiquette, an' Andhrew Carnegie to larn ye pathritism with blow-holes into it, an' Gin'ral Alger to larn ye to hould onto a job; an', whin ye've become edycated an' have all th' blessin's iv civilization that we don't want, that'll count ye one. We can't give ye anny votes, because we haven't more thin enough to go round now; but we'll threat ye th' way a father shud threat his childher if we have to break ivry bone in ye'er bodies. So come to our ar-rms,' says we.

"But, glory be, 'tis more like a rasslin' match than a father's embrace. Up gets this little monkey iv an Aggynaldoo, an' says he, 'Not for us,' he says. 'We thank ye kindly; but we believe,' he says, 'in

---

[1] The Filipinos under Aguinaldo's leadership did not take kindly to American rule. . . . Andrew Carnegie's steel company had been accused of supplying armor plate to the navy that had blow-holes in it. Nevertheless, the steel-maker had come out of the war a vigorous anti-imperialist. Commissary-General C. P. Eagan had gained notoriety by appearing before a board of inquiry and reading a paper filled with filthy abuse of General Miles.

pathronizin' home industhries,' he says. ' An',' he says, ' I have on hand,' he says, ' an' f'r sale,' he says, ' a very superyor brand iv home-made liberty, like ye'er mother used to make,' he says. ' 'Tis a long way fr'm ye'er plant to here,' he says, ' an' be th' time a cargo iv liberty,' he says, ' got out here an' was handled be th' middlemen,' he says, ' it might spoil,' he says. ' We don't want anny col' storage or embalmed liberty,' he says. ' What we want an' what th' ol' reliable house iv Aggynaldoo,' he says, ' supplies to th' thrade,' he says, ' is fr-resh liberty r-right off th' far-rm,' he says. ' I can't do annything with ye'er proposition,' he says. ' I can't give up,' he says, ' th' rights f'r which f'r five years I've fought an' bled ivry wan I cud reach,' he says. ' Onless,' he says, ' ye'd feel like buyin' out th' whole business,' he says. ' I'm a pathrite,' he says; ' but I'm no bigot,' he says.

"An' there it stands, Hinnissy, with th' indulgent parent kneelin' on th' stomach iv his adopted child, while a dillygation fr'm Boston bastes him with an umbrella. There it stands, an' how will it come out I dinnaw. I'm not much iv an expansionist mesilf. F'r th' las' tin years I've been thryin' to decide whether 'twud be good policy an' thrue to me thraditions to make this here bar two or three feet longer, an' manny's th' night I've laid awake tryin' to puzzle it out. But I don't know what to do with th' Ph'lippeens anny more thin I did las' summer, befure I heerd tell iv thim. We can't giv thim to anny wan without makin' th' wan that gets thim feel th' way Doherty felt to Clancy whin Clancy med a frindly call an' give Doherty's childher th' measles. We can't sell thim, we can't ate thim, an' we can't throw thim into th' alley whin no wan is lookin'. An' 'twud be a disgrace f'r to lave befure we've pounded these frindless an' ongrateful people into insinsibility. So I suppose, Hinnissy, we'll have to stay an' do th' best we can, an' lave Andhrew Carnegie secede fr'm th' Union. They'se wan consolation; an' that is, if th' American people can govern thimsilves, they can govern annything that walks."

" 'Twill cost a power iv money," said Mr. Hennessy, the prudent.

" Expand, ixpind," said Mr. Dooley. " That's a joke, an' I med it."

[*1899*]

MR. DOOLEY ON MR. CARNEGIE'S GIFT [1]

" Tin millyon dollars to make th' Scotch a larned people," said Mr. Dooley.

" Who done that? " asked Mr. Hennessy.

" Andhrew Carnaygie," says Mr. Dooley. " He reaches down into his pocket where he keeps th' change an' pulls up tin millyon bawbies, an' says he: ' Boys, take ye'er fill iv larnin,' an' charge it to me,' he says. ' Divvle hang th' expinse,' he says. ' Th' more th' merryer," he says. ' A short life an' a happy wan,' he says. ' Larn annything ye like,' he says. ' Name ye'er priference,' he says, ' an' put it all down to Carnaygie,' he says. . . .

" Th' day whin we millyonaires bought yachts an' brownstone houses with mansard roofs onto thim an' were proud iv havin' thim has gone by, Hinnissy. 'Twill not be long befure none will be so poor as not to own a private yacht, an' th' nex' time a Coxey army starts f'r Wash'n'ton, it'll ride in a specyal vestibule thrain. What was luxuries a few years ago is mere necessities now. Pierpont Morgan calls in wan iv his office boys, th' prisidint iv a naytional bank, an' says he, ' James,' he says, ' take some change out iv th' damper an' r-run out an' buy Europe f'r me,' he says. ' I intind to re-organize it an' put it on a paying basis,' he says. ' Call up th' Czar an' th' Pope an' th' Sultan an' th' Impror Willum, an' tell thim we won't need their sarvices afther nex' week,' he says. ' Give thim a year's salary in advance. An', James,' he says, ' ye bether put that r-red-headed book-keeper near th' dure in charge iv th' continent. He doesn't seem to be doin' much,' he says. Ye see, Hinnissy, th' game has got so much bigger since we first made our money that if Jay Gould was to come back to earth with some iv th' plays we used to wondher about, he'd feel like an old-clothes man. So, 'tis nawthin' strange whin Jawn D., or Andhrew, or mesilf, buys a string iv universities an' puts in tin millyons to teach th' young idee how to loot. Befure long we'll be

---

[1] The Carnegie Trust for Scottish Universities was created in 1901 with a ten-million-dollar endowment. Carnegie had turned over active control of his steel company the same year to the United States Steel Corporation, which J. P. Morgan had created as the most powerful corporation in the United States, with the possible exception of the Standard Oil Company. John D. Rockefeller, of the latter corporation, was contributing heavily to the support of the University of Chicago. Homestead, Pennsylvania, was the location of one of the Carnegie steel mills, well known to newspaper readers because of the sanguinary labor troubles there in 1892.

racin' thim. I don't know but what 'tis th' finest kind iv spoort th' wurruld has iver heerd about.

"Father Kelly don't think as much iv it as I do. He was in here las' night, an' says he: 'Ye can't buy idjacation f'r people,' he says. 'If ye cud, th' on'y man in th' wurruld that knew annything wud be Jawn D. Rockefeller,' he says. 'Idjacation,' he says, 'is something that a man has to fight f'r an' pull out iv its hole be th' hair iv its head,' he says. 'That's th' reason it's so precious,' he says. 'They'se so little iv it, an' it's so hard to get,' he says. 'They'se anny quantity iv gab that looks like it, but it ain't th' rale thing,' he says. 'Th' wurruld is full iv people wearin' false joolry iv that kind,' he says, 'but afther they've had it f'r a long time, it tur-rns green an' blue, an' some day whin they thry to get something on it, th' pawnbroker throws thim out. No, sir, idjacation means throuble an' wurruk an' worry, an' Andhrew Carnaygie himsilf is th' on'y wan I know that's been able to pick it up in th' brief inthervals between wan dollar an' another,' he says. 'Th' smartest man in my day at th' Colledge iv th' Sacred Heart was a la-ad who used to come to school with a half a dozen biled potatoes in an ol' newspaper, an' sawed wood all evenin' to pay f'r his larnin'. Annything that boy larned, he larned, ye bet. Ivry line iv Latin he knew riprisinted a stick iv wood, an' belonged to him. 'Twasn't borrowed at th' back dure iv a millyonaire. He knew more thin anny man I iver see, an' he's now at th' head iv wan iv th' best little wan-room schools in Du Page County,' he says. 'Andhrew Carnaygie's tin millyons won't make anny Robert Burns,' he says. 'It may make more Andhrew Carnaygies,' says I. 'They'se enough to go round now,' says he.

"I don't know that he' right. I don't know f'r sure that Father Kelly is r-right, Hinnissy. I don't think it makes anny difference wan way or th' other how free ye make idjacation. Men that wants it 'll have it be hook an' be crook, an' thim that don't ra-aly want it niver will get it. Ye can lade a man up to th' university, but ye can't make him think. But if I had as much money as I said I had a minyit ago, I'd endow a bar'l iv oatmeal f'r ivry boy in Scotland that wanted an idjacation, an' lave it go at that. Idjacation can always be had, but they'se niver enough oatmeal in Scotland."

"Or Homestead," said Mr. Hennessy.

"Or Homestead," said Mr. Dooley.

[*1901*]

WILLIAM VAUGHN MOODY

[1869–1910]

HE WAS born in Spencer, Indiana, and educated locally and at Harvard, completing the four-year college course in three years despite the fact that he had to support himself by tutoring and typing. After taking his master's degree in 1894, he served a year as an assistant in the English department, then went to the University of Chicago as an instructor. In 1907, when he retired from academic work, he held the title of assistant professor. During the last three years of his short life he devoted all his time to writing. His most famous work is his play *The Great Divide,* produced in New York in 1906 with Henry Miller and Margaret Anglin in the leading roles. It was an immediate and outstanding success and has often been revived. To students Moody is perhaps best known for the textbook he wrote with Robert Morss Lovett, *A First View of English Literature* (1905). But literary critics remember him chiefly for his poems, a volume of which was published in 1901. And above all they remember him for the two poems which follow — surely two of the most eloquent poetic expressions of the democratic spirit that that period produced. The first is a plea for social justice, the second an outcry against the rise of imperialism after the Spanish War.

GLOUCESTER MOORS

A mile behind is Gloucester town
Where the fishing fleets put in,
A mile ahead the land dips down
And the woods and farms begin.
Here, where the moors stretch free
In the high blue afternoon,
Are the marching sun and talking sea,
And the racing winds that wheel and flee
On the flying heels of June.

Jill-o'er-the-ground is purple blue,
Blue is the quaker-maid.
The wild geranium holds its dew
Long in the boulder's shade.
Wax-red hangs the cup
From the huckleberry boughs,
In barberry bells the grey moths sup
Or where the choke-cherry lifts high up
Sweet bowls for their carouse.

Over the shelf of the sandy cove
Beach-peas blossom late.
By copse and cliff the swallows rove
Each calling to his mate.
Seaward the sea-gulls go,
And the land-birds all are here;
That green-gold flash was a vireo,
And yonder flame where the marsh-flags grow
Was a scarlet tanager.

This earth is not the steadfast place
We landsmen build upon;
From deep to deep she varies pace,
And while she comes is gone.
Beneath my feet I feel
Her smooth bulk heave and dip;
With velvet plunge and soft upreel
She swings and steadies to her keel
Like a gallant, gallant ship.

These summer clouds she sets for sail,
The sun is her masthead light,
She tows the moon like a pinnace frail
Where her phosphor wake churns bright.
Now hid, now looming clear,
On the face of the dangerous blue
The star fleets tack and wheel and veer,
But on, but on does the old earth steer
As if her port she knew.

God, dear God! Does she know her port,
Though she goes so far about?
Or blind astray, does she make her sport
To brazen and chance it out?
I watched when her captains passed:
She were better captainless.
Men in the cabin, before the mast,
But some were reckless and some aghast,
And some sat gorged at mess.

By her battened hatch I leaned and caught
Sounds from the noisome hold, —
Cursing and sighing of souls distraught
And cries too sad to be told.
Then I strove to go down and see;
But they said, " Thou art not of us! "
I turned to those on the deck with me
And cried, " Give help! " But they said, " Let be:
Our ship sails faster thus."

Jill-o'er-the-ground is purple blue,
Blue is the quaker-maid,
The alder-clump where the brook comes through
Breeds cresses in its shade.
To be out of the moiling street
With its swelter and its sin!
Who has given to me this sweet,
And given my brother dust to eat?
And when will his wage come in?

Scattering wide or blown in ranks,
Yellow and white and brown,
Boats and boats from the fishing banks
Come home to Gloucester town.
There is cash to purse and spend,
There are wives to be embraced,
Hearts to borrow and hearts to lend,
And hearts to take and keep to the end, —
O little sails, make haste!

But thou, vast outbound ship of souls,
What harbor town for thee?
What shapes, when thy arriving tolls,
Shall crowd the banks to see?
Shall all the happy shipmates then
Stand singing brotherly?
Or shall a haggard ruthless few
Warp her over and bring her to,
While the many broken souls of men
Fester down in the slaver's pen,
And nothing to say or do?

[*1901*]

from

AN ODE IN TIME OF HESITATION

[*The time referred to is the time when America waged war against the Filipinos.*]

Was it for this our fathers kept the law?
This crown shall crown their struggle and their ruth?
Are we the eagle nation Milton saw
Mewing its mighty youth,
Soon to possess the mountain winds of truth,
And be a swift familiar of the sun
Where aye before God's face his trumpets run?
Or have we but the talons and the maw,
And for the abject likeness of our heart
Shall some less lordly bird be set apart? —
Some gross-billed wader where the swamps are fat?
Some gorger in the sun? Some prowler with the bat?

Ah, no!
We have not fallen so.
We are our fathers' sons: let those who lead us know!

'Twas only yesterday sick Cuba's cry
Came up the tropic wind, " Now help us, for we die! "
Then Alabama heard,
And rising, pale, to Maine and Idaho
Shouted a burning word.
Proud state with proud impassioned state conferred,
And at the lifting of a hand sprang forth,
East, west, and south, and north,
Beautiful armies. Oh, by the sweet blood and young
Shed on the awful hill slope at San Juan,
By the unforgotten names of eager boys
Who might have twisted girls' love and been stung
With the old mystic joys
And starry griefs, now the spring nights come on,
But that the heart of youth is generous, —
We charge you, ye who lead us,
Breathe on their chivalry no hint of stain!
Turn not their new-world victories to gain!
One least leaf plucked for chaffer from the bays
Of their dear praise,
One jot of their pure conquest put to hire,
The implacable republic will require;
With clamor, in the glare and gaze of noon,
Or subtly, coming as a thief at night,
But surely, very surely, slow or soon,
That insult deep we deeply will requite.
Tempt not our weakness, our cupidity!
For save we let the island men go free,
Those baffled and dislaureled ghosts
Will curse us from the lamentable coasts
Where walk the frustrate dead.
The cup of trembling shall be drainèd quite,
Eaten the sour bread of astonishment,
With ashes of the hearth shall be made white
Our hair, and wailing shall be in the tent;
Then on your guiltier head
Shall our intolerable self-disdain
Wreak suddenly its anger and its pain;

For manifest in that disastrous light
We shall discern the right
And do it, tardily. — O ye who lead,
Take heed!
Blindness we may forgive, but baseness we will smite.
[*1901*]

W. E. BURGHARDT DU BOIS

[1868–   ]

FOR more than thirty years Du Bois has been one of the intellectual leaders of the Negro people in America. He was born in Great Barrington, Massachusetts, and was educated at Fisk University, the University of Berlin, and Harvard, where he earned his Ph.D. with a thesis on the slave trade. He taught at Wilberforce University in Ohio and then, as head of the department of economics, at Atlanta University, where he remained for thirteen years. In 1903 he published his partly autobiographical volume, *The Souls of Black Folk*. It was a bitter condemnation of race discrimination and prejudice and a demand for full political and economic rights. Included was a vigorous attack upon the philosophy of Booker T. Washington, who had inferentially accepted an inferior social position for the Negro and had sought to direct Negro education into channels designed to keep black men a permanent working class under white domination. Du Bois spoke for the tiny but ambitious class of Negro intellectuals and middle-class professionals. Since then Washington has been praised by whites more often than blacks. Du Bois's book pictured the common life of the rural Negro vividly and poignantly, and it is the latter aspect of the work that is represented here. In 1910 Du Bois left Atlanta to become director of the National Association for the Advancement of Colored People and founder of its magazine, *The Crisis*. He is still head of the N.A.A.C.P. He has published many other works on Negro problems, as well as two novels.

---

from

THE SOULS OF BLACK FOLK

OF THE MEANING OF PROGRESS

Once upon a time I taught school in the hills of Tennessee, where the broad dark vale of the Mississippi begins to roll and crumple to greet the Alleghanies. I was a Fisk student then, and all Fisk men thought that Tennessee — beyond the Veil — was theirs alone, and in vacation time they sallied forth in lusty bands to meet the county school-commissioners. Young and happy, I too went, and I shall not soon forget that summer, seventeen years ago. . . .

Sprinkled over hill and dale lay cabins and farmhouses, shut out from the world by the forests and the rolling hills toward the east. There I found at last a little school. Josie told me of it; she was a thin, homely girl of twenty, with a dark-brown face and thick, hard hair. I had crossed the stream at Watertown, and rested under the great willows; then I had gone to the little cabin in the lot where Josie was resting on her way to town. The gaunt farmer made me welcome, and Josie, hearing my errand, told me anxiously that they wanted a school over the hill; that but once since the war had a teacher been there; that she herself longed to learn, — and thus she ran on, talking fast and loud, with much earnestness and energy.

Next morning I crossed the tall round hill, lingered to look at the blue and yellow mountains stretching toward the Carolinas, then plunged into the wood, and came out at Josie's home. It was a dull frame cottage with four rooms, perched just below the brow of the hill, amid peach-trees. The father was a quiet, simple soul, calmly ignorant, with no touch of vulgarity. The mother was different, — strong, bustling, and energetic, with a quick, restless tongue, and an ambition to live " like folks." There was a crowd of children. Two boys had gone away. There remained two growing girls; a shy midget of eight; John, tall, awkward, and eighteen; Jim, younger, quicker, and better looking; and two babies of indefinite age. Then there was Josie herself. She seemed to be the centre of the family; always busy at service, or at home, or berry-picking; a little nervous and inclined to scold, like her mother, yet faithful, too, like her father. She had about her a certain fineness, the shadow of an unconscious moral heroism that would willingly give all of life to make life broader, deeper, and fuller for her and hers. I saw much of this family afterwards, and grew to love them for their honest efforts to be decent and comfortable, and for their knowledge of their own ignorance. There was with them no affectation. The mother would scold the father for being so " easy "; Josie would roundly berate the boys for carelessness; and all knew that it was a hard thing to dig a living out of a rocky side-hill.

I secured the school. I remember the day I rode horseback out to the commissioner's house with a pleasant young white fellow who wanted the white school. The road ran down the bed of a stream; the sun laughed and the water jingled, and we rode on. " Come in," said the commissioner, — " come in. Have a seat. Yes, that certificate will do. Stay to dinner. What do you want a month? " " Oh," thought I, " this is lucky "; but even then fell the awful shadow of the Veil, for they ate first, then I — alone.

The schoolhouse was a log hut, where Colonel Wheeler used to shelter his corn. It sat in a lot behind a rail fence and thorn bushes, near the sweetest of springs. There was an entrance where a door once was, and within, a massive rickety fireplace; great chinks between the logs served as windows. Furniture was scarce. A pale blackboard crouched in the corner. My desk was made of three boards, reinforced at critical points, and my chair, borrowed from the landlady, had to be returned every night. Seats for the children — these puzzled me much. I was haunted by a New England vision of neat little desks and chairs, but, alas! the reality was rough plank benches without backs, and at times without legs. They had the one virtue of making naps dangerous — possibly fatal, for the floor was not to be trusted.

It was a hot morning late in July when the school opened. I trembled when I heard the patter of little feet down the dusty road, and saw the growing row of dark solemn faces and bright eager eyes facing me. First came Josie and her brothers and sisters. The longing to know, to be a student in the great school at Nashville, hovered like a star above this child-woman amid her work and worry, and she studied doggedly. There were the Dowells from their farm over toward Alexandria, — Fanny, with her smooth black face and wondering eyes; Martha, brown and dull; the pretty girl-wife of a brother, and the younger brood.

There were the Burkes, — two brown and yellow lads, and a tiny haughty-eyed girl. Fat Reuben's little chubby girl came, with golden face and old-gold hair, faithful and solemn. 'Thenie was on hand early, — a jolly, ugly, good-natured girl, who slyly dipped snuff and looked after her little bow-legged brother. When her mother could spare her, 'Tildy came, — a midnight beauty, with starry eyes and tapering limbs; and her brother, correspondingly homely. And then the big boys, — the hulking Lawrences; the lazy Neills, unfathered sons of mother and daughter; Hickman, with a stoop in his shoulders; and the rest.

There they sat, nearly thirty of them, on the rough benches, their faces shading from a pale cream to a deep brown, the little feet bare and swinging, the eyes full of expectation, with here and there a twinkle of mischief, and the hands grasping Webster's blue-back spelling-book. I loved my school, and the fine faith the children had in the wisdom of their teacher was truly marvellous. We read and spelled together, wrote a little, picked flowers, sang, and listened to stories of the world beyond the hill. At times the school would dwindle away, and I would start out. I would visit Mun Eddings, who lived in two very dirty rooms, and ask why little Lugene, whose flaming face seemed ever ablaze with the dark-red hair uncombed, was absent all last week, or why I missed so often the inimitable rags of Mack and Ed. Then the father, who worked Colonel Wheeler's farm on shares, would tell me how the crops needed the boys; and the thin, slovenly mother, whose face was pretty when washed, assured me that Lugene must mind the baby. "But we'll start them again next week." When the Lawrences stopped, I knew that the doubts of the old folks about book-learning had conquered again, and so, toiling up the hill, and getting as far into the cabin as possible, I put Cicero " pro Archia Poeta " into the simplest English with local applications, and usually convinced them — for a week or so.

On Friday nights I often went home with some of the children, — sometimes to Doc Burke's farm. He was a great, loud, thin Black, ever working, and trying to buy the seventy-five acres of hill and dale where he lived; but people said that he would surely fail, and the " white folks would get it all." His wife was a magnificent Amazon, with saffron face and shining hair, uncorseted and barefooted, and the children were strong and beautiful. They lived in a one-and-a-half-room cabin in the hollow of the farm, near the spring. The front room was full of great fat white beds, scrupulously neat; and there were bad chromos on the walls, and a tired centre-table. In the tiny back kitchen I was often invited to " take out and help " myself to fried chicken and wheat biscuit, " meat " and corn pone, string-beans and berries. At first I used to be a little alarmed at the approach of bedtime in the one lone bedroom, but embarrassment was very deftly avoided. First, all the children nodded and slept; and were stowed away in one great pile of goose feathers; next, the mother and the father discreetly slipped away to the kitchen while I went to bed; then, blowing out the dim light, they retired in the dark. In the morning all were up and away before I thought of awaking. Across the road, where fat Reuben lived, they all went outdoors while the teacher retired, because they did not boast the luxury of a kitchen.

I liked to stay with the Dowells, for they had four rooms and plenty of good country fare. Uncle Bird had a small, rough farm, all woods and hills, miles from the big road; but he was full of tales, — he preached now and then, — and with his children, berries, horses, and wheat he was happy and prosperous. Often, to keep the peace, I must go where life was less lovely; for instance, 'Tildy's mother was incorrigibly dirty, Reuben's larder was limited seriously, and herds of untamed insects wandered over the Eddingses' beds. Best of all I loved to go to Josie's, and sit on the porch, eating peaches, while the mother bustled and talked: how Josie had bought the sewing-machine; how Josie worked at service in winter, but that four dollars a month was "mighty little" wages; how Josie longed to go away to school, but that it "looked like" they never could get far enough ahead to let her; how the crops failed and the well was yet unfinished; and, finally, how "mean" some of the white folks were.

For two summers I lived in this little world; it was dull and humdrum. The girls looked at the hill in wistful longing, and the boys fretted and haunted Alexandria. Alexandria was "town," — a straggling, lazy village of houses, churches, and shops, and an aristocracy of Toms, Dicks, and Captains. Cuddled on the hill to the north was the village of the colored folks, who lived in three- or four-room unpainted cottages, some neat and homelike, and some dirty. The dwellings were scattered rather aimlessly, but they centred about the twin temples of the hamlet, the Methodist, and the Hard-Shell Baptist churches. These, in turn, leaned gingerly on a sad-colored schoolhouse. Hither my little world wended its crooked way on Sunday to meet other worlds, and gossip, and wonder, and make the weekly sacrifice with frenzied priest at the altar of the "old-time religion." Then the soft melody and mighty cadences of Negro song fluttered and thundered.

I have called my tiny community a world, and so its isolation made it; and yet there was among us but a half-awakened common consciousness, sprung from common joy and grief, at burial, birth, or wedding; from a common hardship in poverty, poor land, and low wages; and, above all, from the sight of the Veil that hung between us and Opportunity. All this caused us to think some thoughts together; but these, when ripe for speech, were spoken in various languages. Those whose eyes twenty-five and more years before had seen "the glory of the coming of the Lord," saw in every present hindrance or help a dark fatalism bound to bring all things right in His own good time. The mass of those to whom slavery was a dim recollection of childhood found the world a puzzling thing: it asked little of them, and they answered with little, and yet it ridiculed their offering. Such a paradox they could not understand, and therefore sank into listless indifference, or shiftlessness, or reckless bravado. There were, however, some, — such as Josie, Jim, and Ben — to whom War, Hell, and Slavery were but childhood tales, whose young appetites had been whetted to an edge by school and story and half-awakened thought. Ill could they be content, born without and beyond the World. And their weak wings beat against their barriers, — barriers of caste, of youth, of life; at last, in dangerous moments, against everything that opposed even a whim.

The ten years that follow youth, the years when first the realization comes that life is leading somewhere, — these were the years that passed after I left my little school. When they were past, I came by chance once more to the walls of Fisk University, to the halls of the chapel of melody. As I lingered there in the joy and pain of meeting old school-friends, there swept over me a sudden longing to pass again beyond the blue hill, and to see the homes and the school of other days, and to learn how life had gone with my school-children; and I went.

Josie was dead, and the gray-haired mother said simply, "We've had a heap of trouble since you've been away." I had feared for Jim. With a cultured parentage and a social caste to uphold him, he might have made a venturesome merchant or a West Point cadet. But here he was, angry with life and reckless; and when Farmer Durham charged him with stealing wheat, the old man had to ride fast to escape the stones which the furious fool hurled after him. They told Jim to run away; but he would not run, and the constable came that afternoon. It grieved Josie, and great awkward John walked nine miles every day to see his little brother through the bars of Lebanon jail. At last the two came back together in the dark night. The mother cooked supper, and Josie emptied her purse, and the boys stole away. Josie grew thin and silent, yet worked the more. The hill became steep for the quiet old father, and with the boys away there was little to do in the valley. Josie helped them to sell the old farm, and they moved nearer town. Brother Dennis, the carpenter, built a new house with six rooms; Josie toiled a year in Nashville, and brought back ninety dollars to furnish the house and change it to a home.

When the spring came, and the birds twittered, and the stream ran proud and full, little sister Lizzie, bold and thoughtless, flushed with the passion of youth, bestowed herself on the tempter, and brought home a nameless child. Josie shivered and worked on, with the vision of schooldays all fled, with a face wan and tired, — worked until, on a summer's day, some one married another; then Josie crept to her mother like a hurt child, and slept — and sleeps.

I paused to scent the breeze as I entered the valley. The Lawrences have gone, — father and son forever, — and the other son lazily digs in the earth to live. A new young widow rents out their cabin to fat Reuben. Reuben is a Baptist preacher now, but I fear as lazy as ever, though his cabin has three rooms; and little Ella has grown into a bouncing woman, and is ploughing corn on the hot hillside. There are babies a-plenty, and one half-witted girl. Across the valley is a house I did not know before, and there I found, rocking one baby and expecting another, one of my schoolgirls, a daughter of Uncle Bird Dowell. She looked somewhat worried with her new duties, but soon bristled into pride over her neat cabin and the tale of her thrifty husband, the horse and cow, and the farm they were planning to buy.

My log schoolhouse was gone. In its place stood Progress; and Progress, I understand, is necessarily ugly. The crazy foundation stones still marked the former site of my poor little cabin, and not far away, on six weary boulders, perched a jaunty board house, perhaps twenty by thirty feet, with three windows and a door that locked. Some of the window-glass was broken, and part of an old iron stove lay mournfully under the house. I peeped through the window half reverently, and found things that were more familiar. The blackboard had grown by about two feet, and the seats were still without backs. The county owns the lot now, I hear, and every year there is a session of school. As I sat by the spring and looked on the Old and the New I felt glad, very glad, and yet —

After two long drinks I started on. There was the great double log-house on the corner. I remembered the broken, blighted family that used to live there. The strong, hard face of the mother, with its wilderness of hair, rose before me. She had driven her husband away, and while I taught school a strange man lived there, big and jovial, and people talked. I felt sure that Ben and 'Tildy would come to naught from such a home. But this is an odd world; for Ben is a busy farmer in Smith County, "doing well, too," they say, and he had cared for little 'Tildy until last spring, when a lover married her. A hard life the lad had led, toiling for meat, and laughed at because he was homely and crooked. There was Sam Carlon, an impudent old skinflint, who had definite notions about "niggers," and hired Ben a summer and would not pay him. Then the hungry boy gathered his sacks together, and in broad daylight went into Carlon's corn; and when the hard-fisted farmer set upon him the angry boy flew at him like a beast. Doc Burke saved a murder and a lynching that day.

The story reminded me again of the Burkes, and an impatience seized me to know who won in the battle, Doc or the seventy-five acres. For it is a hard thing to make a farm out of nothing, even in fifteen years. So I hurried on, thinking of the Burkes. They used to have a certain magnificent barbarism about them that I liked. They were never vulgar, never immoral, but rather rough and primitive, with an unconventionality that spent itself in loud guffaws, slaps on the back, and naps in the corner. I hurried by the cottage of the misborn Neill boys. It was empty, and they were grown into fat, lazy farm-hands. I saw the home of the Hickmans, but Albert, with his stooping shoulders, had passed from the world. Then I came to the Burkes' gate and peered through; the inclosure looked rough and untrimmed, and yet there were the same fences around the old farm save to the left, where lay twenty-five other acres. And lo! the cabin in the hollow had climbed the hill and swollen to a half-finished six-room cottage.

The Burkes held a hundred acres, but they were still in debt. Indeed, the gaunt father who toiled night and day would scarcely be happy out of debt, being so used to it. Some day he must stop, for his massive frame is showing decline. The mother wore shoes, but the lion-like physique of other days was broken. The children had grown up. Rob, the image of his father, was loud and rough with laughter. Birdie, my school baby of six, had grown to a picture of maiden beauty, tall and tawny. "Edgar is gone," said the mother, with head half bowed, — "gone to work in Nashville; he and his father couldn't agree."

Little Doc, the boy born since the time of my school, took me horse-back down the creek next morning toward Farmer Dowell's. The road and the stream were battling for mastery, and the stream had the better of it. We splashed and waded, and the merry boy, perched behind me, chattered and laughed. He showed me where Simon Thompson had bought a bit of ground and a home; but his daughter Lana, a plump, brown, slow girl,was not there. She had married a man and a farm twenty miles away. We wound on down the stream till we came to a gate that I did not recognize, but the boy insisted that it was " Uncle

Bird's." The farm was fat with the growing crop. In that little valley was a strange stillness as I rode up; for death and marriage had stolen youth and left age and childhood there. We sat and talked that night after the chores were done. Uncle Bird was grayer, and his eyes did not see so well, but he was still jovial. We talked of the acres bought, — one hundred and twenty-five, — of the new guest-chamber added, of Martha's marrying. Then we talked of death: Fanny and Fred were gone; a shadow hung over the other daughter, and when it lifted she was to go to Nashville to school. At last we spoke of the neighbors, and as night fell, Uncle Bird told me how, on a night like that, 'Thenie came wandering back to her home over yonder, to escape the blows of her husband. And next morning she died in the home that her little bow-legged brother, working and saving, had bought for their widowed mother.

My journey was done, and behind me lay hill and dale, and Life and Death. How shall man measure Progress there where the dark-faced Josie lies? How many heartfuls of sorrow shall balance a bushel of wheat? How hard a thing is life to the lowly, and yet how human and real! And all this life and love and strife and failure, — is it the twilight of nightfall or the flush of some faint-dawning day?

Thus sadly musing, I rode to Nashville in the Jim Crow car.

[*1903*]

HAMLIN GARLAND

[1860–1940]

HE WAS a man of the people — a fact worth emphasizing because there were
so few in our literature at the time he began to write. His father had been a
clerk before migrating to the frontier to take up farming. Born in Wisconsin
and raised in Iowa, Hamlin Garland was educated at Cedar Valley Seminary
in Osage, Iowa, working on the family farm half of every school year. For
a while he taught school in Illinois, then farmed in North Dakota, finally, in
1884, went to Boston to become a writer. He lived on a few dollars a week,
studied, taught, began to write. In 1887 he went back to the Middle West;
and the bleak villages, the mean farms, and the broken and wasted lives, now
observed with fresh and mature eyes, gave him his subject matter for his
finest books. In 1891 came *Main-Travelled Roads*, short stories depicting his
native region and its people. The volume won him critical acclaim, chief
among his sponsors being William Dean Howells. In 1894 came *Crumbling
Idols*, literary essays in defense of realism and asserting the claims of a literature which would truthfully portray the common people in their struggles
for existence. There are some critics who regard this as his most interesting
work, but his best known is certainly his autobiographical narrative *A Son
of the Middle Border* (1917), which contains unforgettable descriptions of
his background. In him the agrarian protest against the pressures of industrial capitalism found its first significant voice in literature.

from

A SON OF THE MIDDLE BORDER

A VISIT TO THE WEST

At twenty-seven years of age, and after having been six years absent
from Osage, the little town in which I went to school, I found myself
able to re-visit it. . . .

Once out of the city, I absorbed " atmosphere " like a sponge. It was
with me no longer (as in New England) a question of warmed-over

themes and appropriated characters. Whittier, Hawthorne, Holmes, had no connection with the rude life of these prairies. Each weedy field, each wire fence, the flat stretches of grass, the leaning Lombardy trees, — everything was significant rather than beautiful, familiar rather than picturesque.

Something deep and resonant vibrated within my brain as I looked out upon this monotonous commonplace landscape. I realized for the first time that the east had surfeited me with picturesqueness. It appeared that I had been living for six years amidst painted, neatly arranged pasteboard scenery. Now suddenly I dropped to the level of nature unadorned, down to the ugly unkempt lanes I knew so well, back to the pungent realities of the streamless plain.

Furthermore I acknowledged a certain responsibility for the conditions of the settlers. I felt related to them, an intolerant part of them. Once fairly out among the fields of northern Illinois everything became so homely, uttered itself so piercingly to me that nothing less than song could express my sense of joy, of power. This was my country — these my people.

It was the third of July, a beautiful day with a radiant sky, darkened now and again with sudden showers. Great clouds, trailing veils of rain, enveloped the engine as it roared straight into the west, — for an instant all was dark, then forth we burst into the brilliant sunshine careening over the green ridges as if drawn by run-away dragons with breath of flame.

It was sundown when I crossed the Mississippi river (at Dubuque) and the scene which I looked out upon will forever remain a splendid page in my memory. The coaches lay under the western bluffs, but away to the south the valley ran, walled with royal purple, and directly across the flood, a beach of sand flamed under the sunset light as if it were a bed of pure untarnished gold. Behind this an island rose, covered with noble trees which suggested all the romance of the immemorial river. The redman's canoe, the explorer's batteau, the hunter's lodge, the emigrant's cabin, all stood related to that inspiring vista. For the first time in my life I longed to put this noble stream into verse.

All that day I had studied the land, musing upon its distinctive qualities, and while I acknowledged the natural beauty of it, I revolted from the gracelessness of its human habitations. The lonely box-like farmhouses on the ridges suddenly appeared to me like the dens of wild animals. The lack of color, of charm in the lives of the people anguished me. I wondered why I had never before perceived the futility of woman's life on a farm.

I asked myself, " Why have these stern facts never been put into our literature as they have been used in Russia and in England? Why has this land no story-tellers like those who have made Massachusetts and New Hampshire illustrious? "

These and many other speculations buzzed in my brain. Each moment was a revelation of new uglinesses as well as of remembered beauties. . . .

[As] the train . . . rattled away to the north and I drew closer to the scenes of my boyhood, my memory quickened. The Cedar rippling over its limestone ledges, the gray old mill and the pond where I used to swim, the farm-houses with their weedy lawns, all seemed not only familiar but friendly, and when at last I reached the station (the same grimy little den from which I had started forth six years before), I rose from my seat with the air of a world-traveller and descended upon the warped and splintered platform, among my one time friends and neighbors, with quickened pulse and seeking eye.

It was the fourth of July and a crowd was at the station, but though I recognized half the faces, not one of them lightened at sight of me. The 'bus driver, the ragged old dray-man (scandalously profane), the common loafers shuffling about, chewing and spitting, seemed absolutely unchanged. One or two elderly citizens eyed me closely as I slung my little Boston valise with a long strap over my shoulder and started up the billowing board sidewalk toward the center of the town, but I gave out no word of recognition. Indeed I took a boyish pride in the disguising effect of my beard.

How small and flat and leisurely the village seemed! The buildings which had once been so imposing in my eyes were now of very moderate elevation indeed, and the opera house was almost indistinguishable from the two-story structures which flanked it; but the trees had increased in dignity, and some of the lawns were lovely.

With eyes singling out each familiar object I loitered along the walk. There stood the grimy wagon shop from which a hammer was ringing cheerily, like the chirp of a cricket, – just as aforetime. Orrin Blakey stood at the door of his lumber yard surveying me with curious eyes but I passed him in silence. I wished to spend an hour or two in going about in guise of a stranger. There was something instructive as well as deliciously exciting in thus seeing old acquaintances as from behind a mask. They were at once familiar and mysterious — mysterious with my new question, " Is this life worth living? "

The Merchants' Hotel which once appeared so luxurious (within the reach only of great lecturers like Joseph Cook and Wendell Phillips) had declined to a shabby frame tavern, but entering the dining room I selected a seat near an open window, from which I could look out upon the streets and survey the throng of thickening sightseers as they moved up and down before me like the figures in a vitascope.

I was waited upon by a slatternly girl and the breakfast she brought to me was so bad (after Mary's cooking) that I could only make a pretense of eating it, but I kept my seat, absorbed by the forms coming and going, almost within the reach of my hand. Among the first to pace slowly by was Lawyer Ricker, stately, solemn and bibulous as ever, his red beard flowing over a vest unbuttoned in the manner of the old-fashioned southern gentleman, his spotless linen and neat tie showing that his careful, faithful wife was still on guard.

Him I remembered for his astounding ability to recite poetry by the hour and also because of a florid speech which I once heard him make in the court room. For six mortal hours he spoke on a case involving the stealing of a horse-blanket worth about four dollars and a half. In the course of his argument he ranged with leisurely self-absorption, from ancient Egypt and the sacred Crocodile down through the dark ages, touching at Athens and Mount Olympus, reviewing Rome and the court of Charlemagne, winding up at four P.M. with an impassioned appeal to the jury to remember the power of environment upon his client. I could not remember how the suit came out, but I did recall the look of stupefaction which rested on the face of the accused as he found himself likened to Gurth the swine-herd and a peasant of Carcassonne.

Ricker seemed quite unchanged save for the few gray hairs which had come into his beard and, as he stood in conversation with one of the merchants of the town, his nasal voice, his formal speech and the grandiloquent gesture of his right hand brought back to me all the stories I had heard of his drinking and of his wife's heroic rescuing expeditions to neighboring saloons. A strange, unsatisfactory end to a man of great natural ability.

Following him came a young girl leading a child of ten. I knew them at once. Ella McKee had been of the size of the little one, her sister, when I went away, and nothing gave me a keener realization of the

603

years which had passed than the flowering of the child I had known into this charming maiden of eighteen. Her resemblance to her sister Flora was too marked to be mistaken, and the little one by her side had the same flashing eyes and radiant smile with which both of her grown-up sisters were endowed. Their beauty fairly glorified the dingy street as they walked past my window.

Then an old farmer, bent and worn of frame, halted before me to talk with a merchant. This was David Babcock, Burton's father, one of our old-time neighbors, a little more bent, a little thinner, a little grayer — that was all, and as I listened to his words I asked, "What purpose does a man serve by toiling like that for sixty years with no increase of leisure, with no growth in mental grace?"

There was a wistful note in his voice which went straight to my heart. He said: "No, our wheat crop ain't a-going to amount to much this year. Of course we don't try to raise much grain — it's mostly stock, but I thought I'd try wheat again. I wisht we could get back to the good old days of wheat raising — it w'ant so confining as stock-raisin'." His good days were also in the past!

As I walked the street I met several neighbors from Dry Run as well as acquaintances from the Grove. Nearly all, even the young men, looked worn and weatherbeaten and some appeared both silent and sad. Laughter was curiously infrequent and I wondered whether in my days on the farm they had all been as rude of dress, as misshapen of form and as wistful of voice as they now seemed to me to be. "Have times changed? Has a spirit of unrest and complaining developed in the American farmer?"

I perceived the town from the triple viewpoint of a former resident, a man from the city, and a reformer, and every minutest detail of dress, tone and gesture revealed new meaning to me. Fancher and Gammons were feebler certainly, and a little more querulous with age, and their faded beards and rough hands gave pathetic evidence of the hard wear of wind and toil. At the moment nothing glozed the essential tragic futility of their existence.

Then down the street came "The Ragamuffins," the little Fourth of July procession, which in the old days had seemed so funny, so exciting to me. I laughed no more. It filled me with bitterness to think that such a makeshift spectacle could amuse anyone. "How dull and eventless life must be to enable such a pitiful travesty to attract and hold the attention of girls like Ella and Flora," I thought as I saw them standing with their little sister to watch " the parade."

From the window of a law office, Emma and Matilda Leete were leaning and I decided to make myself known to them. Emma, who had been one of my high admirations, had developed into a handsome and interesting woman with very little of the village in her dress or expression, and when I stepped up to her and asked, " Do you know me? " her calm gray eyes and smiling lips denoted humor. " Of course I know you — in spite of the beard. Come in and sit with us and tell us all about yourself."

As we talked, I found that they, at least, had kept in touch with the thought of the east, and Ella understood in some degree the dark mood which I voiced. She, too, occasionally doubted whether the life they were all living was worth while. " We make the best of it," she said, " but none of us are living up to our dreams."

Her musical voice, thoughtful eyes and quick intelligence, re-asserted their charm, and I spent an hour or more in her company talking of old friends. It was not necessary to talk down to her. She was essentially urban in tone while other of the girls who had once impressed me with their beauty had taken on the airs of village matrons and did not interest me. If they retained aspirations they concealed the fact. Their husbands and children entirely occupied their minds.

Returning to the street, I introduced myself to Uncle Billy Fraser and Osmund Button and other Sun Prairie neighbors and when it became known that " Dick Garland's boy " was in town, many friends gathered about to shake my hand and inquire concerning " Belle " and " Dick."

The hard, crooked fingers which they laid in my palm completed the sorrowful impression which their faces had made upon me. A twinge of pain went through my heart as I looked into their dim eyes and studied their heavy knuckles. I thought of the hand of Edwin Booth, of the flower-like palm of Helena Modjeska, of the subtle touch of Inness, and I said, " Is it not time that the human hand ceased to be primarily a bludgeon for hammering a bare living out of the earth? Nature all bountiful, undiscriminating, would, under justice, make such toil unnecessary." My heart burned with indignation. With William Morris and Henry George I exclaimed, " Nature is not to blame. Man's laws are to blame," — but of this I said nothing at the time — at least not to men like Babcock and Fraser.

Next day I rode forth among the farms of Dry Run, retracing familiar lanes, standing under the spreading branches of the maple trees I had planted fifteen years before. I entered the low stone cabin wherein Neighbor Button had lived for twenty years (always intending some-time to build a house and make a granary of this), and at the table with the family and the hired men, I ate again of Ann's "riz" biscuit and sweet melon pickles. It was not a pleasant meal, on the contrary it was depressing to me. The days of the border were over, and yet Arvilla his wife was ill and aging, still living in pioneer discomfort, toil-ing like a slave.

At neighbor Gardner's home, I watched his bent complaining old wife housekeeping from dawn to dark, literally dying on her feet. William Knapp's home was somewhat improved but the men still came to the table in their shirt sleeves smelling of sweat and stinking of the stable, just as they used to do, and Mrs. Knapp grown more gouty, more unwieldly than ever (she spent twelve or fourteen hours each day on her swollen and aching feet), moved with a waddling motion because, as she explained, "I can't limp — I'm just as lame in one laig as I am in t'other. But 'tain't no use to complain, I've just so much work to do and I might as well go ahead and do it."

I slept that night in her "best room," yes, at last, after thirty years of pioneer life, she had a guest chamber and a new "bed-room soot." With open pride and joy she led Belle Garland's boy in to view this precious acquisition, pointing out the soap and towels, and carefully removing the counterpane! I understood her pride, for my mother had not yet acquired anything so luxurious as this. She was still on the border!

Next day, I called upon Andrew Ainsley and while the women cooked in a red-hot kitchen, Andy stubbed about the barnyard in his bare feet, showing me his hogs and horses. Notwithstanding his town-visitor and the fact that it was Sunday, he came to dinner in a dirty, sweaty, collarless shirt, and I, sitting at his oil-cloth covered table, slipped back, deeper, ever deeper among the stern realities of the life from which I had emerged. I recalled that while my father had never allowed his sons or the hired men to come to the table unwashed or uncombed, we usually ate while clothed in our sweaty garments, glad to get food into our mouths in any decent fashion, while the smell of the horse and the cow mingled with the savor of the soup. There is no escape even on a modern "model farm" from the odor of the barn.

Every house I visited had its individual message of sordid struggle and half-hidden despair. Agnes had married and moved away to Dakota, and Bess had taken upon her girlish shoulders the burdens of wifehood and motherhood almost before her girlhood had reached its first period of bloom. In addition to the work of being cook and scrub-woman, she was now a mother and nurse. As I looked around upon her worn chairs, faded rag carpets, and sagging sofas, — the bare walls of her pitiful little house seemed a prison. I thought of her as she was in the days of her radiant girlhood and my throat filled with rebellious pain.

All the gilding of farm life melted away. The hard and bitter realities came back upon me in a flood. Nature was as beautiful as ever. The soaring sky was filled with shining clouds, the tinkle of the bobolink's fairy bells rose from the meadow, a mystical sheen was on the odorous grass and waving grain, but no splendor of cloud, no grace of sunset could conceal the poverty of these people, on the contrary they brought out, with a more intolerable poignancy, the gracelessness of these homes, and the sordid quality of the mechanical daily routine of these lives.

I perceived beautiful youth becoming bowed and bent. I saw lovely girlhood wasting away into thin and hopeless age. Some of the women I had known had withered into querulous and complaining spinster-hood, and I heard ambitious youth cursing the bondage of the farm. "Of such pain and futility are the lives of the average man and woman of both city and country composed," I acknowledged to myself with savage candor. "Why lie about it?"

Some of my playmates opened their acrid hearts to me. My presence stimulated their discontent. I was one of them, one who having escaped had returned as from some far-off glorious land of achievement. My improved dress, my changed manner of speech, everything I said, roused in them a kind of rebellious rage and gave them unwonted power of expression. Their mood was no doubt transitory, but it was as real as my own.

Men who were growing bent in digging into the soil spoke to me of their desire to see something of the great eastern world before they died. Women whose eyes were faded and dim with tears, listened to me with almost breathless interest whilst I told them of the great cities I had seen, of wonderful buildings, of theaters, of the music of the sea. Young girls expressed to me their longing for a life which was better worth while, and lads, eager for adventure and excitement, confided to me their secret intention to leave the farm at the earliest moment. "I don't intend to wear out my life drudging on this old place," said Wesley Fancher with a bitter oath.

In those few days, I perceived life without its glamor. I no longer looked upon these toiling women with the thoughtless eyes of youth. I saw no humor in the bent forms and graying hair of the men. I began to understand that my own mother had trod a similar slavish round with never a full day of leisure, with scarcely an hour of escape from the tugging hands of children, and the need of mending and washing clothes. I recalled her as she passed from the churn to the stove, from the stove to the bedchamber, and from the bedchamber back to the kitchen, day after day, year after year, rising at daylight or before, and going to her bed only after the evening dishes were washed and the stockings and clothing mended for the night.

The essential tragedy and hopelessness of most human life under the conditions into which our society was swiftly hardening embittered me, called for expression, but even then I did not know that I had found my theme. I had no intention at the moment of putting it into fiction.

The reader may interrupt at this point to declare that all life, even the life of the city is futile, if you look at it in that way, and I reply by saying that I still have moments when I look at it that way. What is it all about, anyhow, this life of ours? Certainly to be forever weary and worried, to be endlessly soiled with thankless labor and to grow old before one's time soured and disappointed, is not the whole destiny of man!

Some of these things I said to Emma and Matilda but their optimism was too ingrained to yield to my gray mood. "We can't afford to grant too much," said Emma. "We are in it, you see."

Leaving the village of Osage, with my mind still in a tumult of revolt, I took the train for the Northwest, eager to see my mother and my little sister, yet beginning to dread the changes which I must surely find in them. Not only were my senses exceedingly alert and impressionable, my eyes saw nothing but the loneliness and the lack of beauty in the landscape, and the farther west I went, the lonelier became the box-like habitations of the plain. Here were the lands over which we had hurried in 1881, lured by the "Government Land" of the farther west. Here, now, a kind of pioneering behind the lines was going on. The

free lands were gone and so, at last, the price demanded by these speculators must be paid.

This wasteful method of pioneering, this desolate business of lonely
settlement took on a new and tragic significance as I studied it. Instructed by my new philosophy I now perceived that these plowmen,
these wives and daughters had been pushed out into these lonely ugly
shacks by the force of landlordism behind. These plodding Swedes
and Danes, these thrifty Germans, these hairy Russians had all fled
from the feudalism of their native lands and were here because they
had no share in the soil from which they sprung, and because in the
settled communities of the eastern states, the speculative demand for
land had hindered them from acquiring even a leasing right to the
surface of the earth.

I clearly perceived that our Song of Emigration had been, in effect,
the hymn of fugitives!

And yet all this did not prevent me from acknowledging the beauty
of the earth. On the contrary, social injustice intensified nature's prod-
igality. I said, "Yes, the landscape is beautiful, but how much of its
beauty penetrates to the heart of the men who are in the midst of it
and battling with it? How much of consolation does the worn and
weary renter find in the beauty of cloud and tree or in the splendor of
the sunset? — Grace of flower does not feed or clothe the body, and
when the toiler is both badly clothed and badly fed, bird-song and leaf-
shine cannot bring content." Like Millet, I asked, "Why should all of
a man's waking hours be spent in an effort to feed and clothe his family?
Is there not something wrong in our social scheme when the unremitting
toiler remains poor?"

With such thoughts filling my mind, I passed through this belt of
recent settlement and came at last into the valley of the James. One by
one the familiar flimsy little wooden towns were left behind (strung
like beads upon a string), and at last the elevator at Ordway appeared
on the edge of the horizon, a minute, wavering projection against the
skyline, and half an hour later we entered the village, a sparse collection
of weatherbeaten wooden houses, without shade of trees or grass of
lawns, a desolate, drab little town. . . .

[1917]

JACK LONDON

[1876–1916]

ONE of the fabulously successful writers of our century, he was also one of its most radical. His origins help to explain that paradox. He was born in San Francisco of an extremely poor family and brought up on the Oakland waterfront. He was a leader of a boys' gang which hung around the saloons and dives. After school hours he sold newspapers, worked on an ice wagon, in a bowling alley, in a cannery. At fifteen, having completed grammar school, he bought a sloop and became an oyster pirate. Later a sailor, mill-hand, stoker, tramp, and janitor, he got to know all there was to know about the life of the underdog. At nineteen he suddenly decided to acquire an education. He studied for a year at the Oakland High School, crammed sufficiently to take college entrance examinations, and spent a semester at the University of California. Then followed work in a laundry, a voyage to the Yukon, and finally the decision to try writing. A few short stories, a minor novel, and a socialist tract were followed by *The Call of the Wild* (1903). It was a sensational best-seller. From then on he earned incredible sums of money with such books as *The Sea Wolf* (1904), *Before Adam* (1907), *Martin Eden* (1909), and *The Abysmal Brute* (1913). He lived extravagantly and romantically — which is the way he wrote, too. Yet he remained a revolutionary socialist, and with such books as *The Iron Heel* (1908) and *War of the Classes* (1905) he made himself a hero of socialist workers throughout the world. The sketch which follows has been widely reprinted. It is an excellent self-portrait.

WHAT LIFE MEANS TO ME

I was born in the working-class. Early I discovered enthusiasm, ambition, and ideals; and to satisfy these became the problem of my child-life. My environment was crude and rough and raw. I had no outlook, but an uplook rather. My place in society was at the bottom. Here life offered nothing but sordidness and wretchedness, both of the flesh and the spirit; for here flesh and spirit were alike starved and tormented.

Above me towered the colossal edifice of society, and to my mind the only way out was up. Into this edifice I early resolved to climb. Up above, men wore black clothes and boiled shirts, and women dressed in beautiful gowns. Also, there were good things to eat, and there was plenty to eat. This much for the flesh. Then there were the things of the spirit. Up above me, I knew, were unselfishnesses of the spirit, clean and noble thinking, keen intellectual living. I knew all this because I read "Seaside Library" novels, in which, with the exception of the villains and adventuresses, all men and women thought beautiful thoughts, spoke a beautiful tongue, and performed glorious deeds. In short, as I accepted the rising of the sun, I accepted that up above me was all that was fine and noble and gracious, all that gave decency and dignity to life, all that made life worth living and that remunerated one for his travail and misery.

But it is not particularly easy for one to climb up out of the working-class — especially if he is handicapped by the possession of ideals and illusions. I lived on a ranch in California, and I was hard put to find the ladder whereby to climb. I early inquired the rate of interest on invested money, and worried my child's brain into an understanding of the virtues and excellencies of that remarkable invention of man, compound interest. Further, I ascertained the current rates of wages for workers of all ages, and the cost of living. From all this data I concluded that if I began immediately and worked and saved until I was fifty years of age, I could then stop working and enter into participation in a fair portion of the delights and goodnesses that would then be open to me higher up in society. Of course, I resolutely determined not to marry, while I quite forgot to consider at all that great rock of disaster in the working-class world — sickness.

But the life that was in me demanded more than a meagre existence of scraping and scrimping. Also, at ten years of age, I became a newsboy on the streets of a city, and found myself with a changed uplook. All about me were still the same sordidness and wretchedness, and up above me was still the same paradise waiting to be gained; but the ladder whereby to climb was a different one. It was now the ladder of business. Why save my earnings and invest in government bonds, when, by buying two newspapers for five cents, with a turn of the wrist I could sell them for ten cents and double my capital? The business ladder was the ladder for me, and I had a vision of myself becoming a baldheaded and successful merchant prince.

Alas for visions! When I was sixteen I had already earned the title of " prince." But this title was given me by a gang of cut-throats and thieves, by whom I was called " The Prince of the Oyster Pirates." And at that time I had climbed the first rung of the business ladder. I was a capitalist. I owned a boat and a complete oyster-pirating outfit. I had begun to exploit my fellow-creatures. I had a crew of one man. As captain and owner I took two-thirds of the spoils, and gave the crew one-third, though the crew worked just as hard as I did and risked just as much his life and liberty.

This one rung was the height I climbed up the business ladder. One night I went on a raid amongst the Chinese fishermen. Ropes and nets were worth dollars and cents. It was robbery, I grant, but it was precisely the spirit of capitalism. The capitalist takes away the possessions of his fellow-creatures by means of a rebate, or of a betrayal of trust, or by the purchase of senators and supreme-court judges. I was merely crude. That was the only difference. I used a gun.

But my crew that night was one of those inefficients against whom the capitalist is wont to fulminate, because, forsooth, such inefficients increase expenses and reduce dividends. My crew did both. What of his carelessness he set fire to the big mainsail and totally destroyed it. There weren't any dividends that night, and the Chinese fishermen were richer by the nets and ropes we did not get. I was bankrupt, unable just then to pay sixty-five dollars for a new mainsail. I left my boat at anchor and went off on a bay-pirate boat on a raid up the Sacramento River. While away on this trip, another gang of bay pirates raided my boat. They stole everything, even the anchors; and later on, when I recovered the drifting hulk, I sold it for twenty dollars. I had slipped back the one rung I had climbed, and never again did I attempt the business ladder.

From then on I was mercilessly exploited by other capitalists. I had the muscle, and they made money out of it while I made but a very indifferent living out of it. I was a sailor before the mast, a longshoreman, a roustabout; I worked in canneries, and factories, and laundries; I mowed lawns, and cleaned carpets, and washed windows. And I never got the full product of my toil. I looked at the daughter of the cannery owner, in her carriage, and knew that it was my muscle, in part, that helped drag along that carriage on its rubber tires. I looked at the son of the factory owner, going to college, and knew that it was my muscle that helped, in part, to pay for the wine and good fellowship he enjoyed.

But I did not resent this. It was all in the game. They were the strong. Very well, I was strong. I would carve my way to a place amongst them and make money out of the muscles of other men. I was not afraid of work. I loved hard work. I would pitch in and work harder than ever and eventually become a pillar of society.

And just then, as luck would have it, I found an employer that was of the same mind. I was willing to work, and he was more than willing that I should work. I thought I was learning a trade. In reality, I had displaced two men. I thought he was making an electrician out of me; as a matter of fact, he was making fifty dollars per month out of me. The two men I had displaced had received forty dollars each per month; I was doing the work of both for thirty dollars per month.

This employer worked me nearly to death. A man may love oysters, but too many oysters will disincline him toward that particular diet. And so with me. Too much work sickened me. I did not wish ever to see work again. I fled from work. I became a tramp, begging my way from door to door, wandering over the United States and sweating bloody sweats in slums and prisons.

I had been born in the working-class, and I was now, at the age of eighteen, beneath the point at which I had started. I was down in the cellar of society, down in the subterranean depths of misery about which it is neither nice nor proper to speak. I was in the pit, the abyss, the human cesspool, the shambles and charnel-house of our civilization. This is the part of the edifice of society that society chooses to ignore. Lack of space compels me here to ignore it, and I shall say only that the things I there saw gave me a terrible scare.

I was scared into thinking. I saw the naked simplicities of the complicated civilization in which I lived. Life was a matter of food and shelter. In order to get food and shelter men sold things. The merchant sold shoes, the politician sold his manhood, and the representative of the people, with exceptions, of course, sold his trust; while nearly all sold their honor. Women, too, whether on the street or in the holy bond of wedlock, were prone to sell their flesh. All things were commodities, all people bought and sold. The one commodity that labor had to sell was muscle. The honor of labor had no price in the market-place. Labor had muscle, and muscle alone, to sell.

But there was a difference, a vital difference. Shoes and trust and honor had a way of renewing themselves. They were imperishable stocks. Muscle, on the other hand, did not renew. As the shoe merchant sold shoes, he continued to replenish his stock. But there was no way of replenishing the laborer's stock of muscle. The more he sold of his muscle, the less of it remained to him. It was his one commodity, and each day his stock of it diminished. In the end, if he did not die before, he sold out and put up his shutters. He was a muscle bankrupt, and nothing remained to him but to go down into the cellar of society and perish miserably.

I learned, further, that brain was likewise a commodity. It, too, was different from muscle. A brain seller was only at his prime when he was fifty or sixty years old, and his wares were fetching higher prices than ever. But a laborer was worked out or broken down at forty-five or fifty. I had been in the cellar of society, and I did not like the place as a habitation. The pipes and drains were unsanitary, and the air was bad to breathe. If I could not live on the parlor floor of society, I could, at any rate, have a try at the attic. It was true, the diet there was slim, but the air at least was pure. So I resolved to sell no more muscle, and to become a vender of brains.

Then began a frantic pursuit of knowledge. I returned to California and opened the books. While thus equipping myself to become a brain merchant, it was inevitable that I should delve into sociology. There I found, in a certain class of books, scientifically formulated, the simple sociological concepts I had already worked out for myself. Other and greater minds, before I was born, had worked out all that I had thought and a vast deal more. I discovered that I was a socialist.

The socialists were revolutionists, inasmuch as they struggled to overthrow the society of the present, and out of the material to build the society of the future. I, too, was a socialist and a revolutionist. I joined the groups of working-class and intellectual revolutionists, and for the first time came into intellectual living. Here I found keen-flashing intellects and brilliant wits; for here I met strong and alert-brained, withal horny-handed, members of the working-class; unfrocked preachers too wide in their Christianity for any congregation of Mammon-worshippers; professors broken on the wheel of university subservience to the ruling class and flung out because they were quick with knowledge which they strove to apply to the affairs of mankind.

Here I found, also, warm faith in the human, glowing idealism, sweetnesses of unselfishness, renunciation, and martyrdom — all the splendid, stinging things of the spirit. Here life was clean, noble, and alive. Here life rehabilitated itself, became wonderful and glorious; and I was glad to be alive. I was in touch with great souls who exalted flesh and spirit over dollars and cents, and to whom the thin wail of the starved slum child meant more than all the pomp and circumstance of commercial expansion and world empire. All about me were nobleness of purpose and heroism of effort, and my days and nights were sunshine and starshine, all fire and dew, with before my eyes, ever burning and blazing, the Holy Grail, Christ's own Grail, the warm human, long-suffering and maltreated, but to be rescued and saved at the last.

And I, poor foolish I, deemed all this to be a mere foretaste of the delights of living I should find higher above me in society. I had lost many illusions since the day I read " Seaside Library " novels on the California ranch. I was destined to lose many of the illusions I still retained.

As a brain merchant I was a success. Society opened its portals to me. I entered right in on the parlor floor, and my disillusionment proceeded rapidly. I sat down to dinner with the masters of society, and with the wives and daughters of the masters of society. The women were gowned beautifully, I admit; but to my naïve surprise I discovered that they were of the same clay as all the rest of the women I had known down below in the cellar. " The colonel's lady and Judy O'Grady were sisters under their skins " — and gowns.

It was not this, however, so much as their materialism, that shocked me. It is true, these beautifully gowned, beautiful women prattled sweet little ideals and dear little moralities; but in spite of their prattle the dominant key of the life they lived was materialistic. And they were so sentimentally selfish! They assisted in all kinds of sweet little charities, and informed one of the fact, while all the time the food they ate and the beautiful clothes they wore were bought out of dividends stained with the blood of child labor, and sweated labor, and of prostitution itself. When I mentioned such facts, expecting in my innocence that these sisters of Judy O'Grady would at once strip off their blood-dyed silks and jewels, they became excited and angry, and read me preachments about the lack of thrift, the drink, and the innate depravity that caused all the misery in society's cellar. When I mentioned that I couldn't quite see that it was the lack of thrift, the intemperance, and the depravity of a half-starved child of six that made it work twelve hours every night in a Southern cotton mill, these sisters of Judy O'Grady attacked my private life and called me an " agitator " — as though that, forsooth, settled the argument.

Nor did I fare better with the masters themselves. I had expected to find men who were clean, noble, and alive, whose ideals were clean, noble, and alive. I went about amongst the men who sat in the high places — the preachers, the politicians, the business men, the professors, and the editors. I ate meat with them, drank wine with them, automobiled with them, and studied them. It is true, I found many that were clean and noble; but with rare exceptions, they were not *alive*. I do verily believe I could count the exceptions on the fingers of my two hands. Where they were not alive with rottenness, quick with unclean life, they were merely the unburied dead — clean and noble, like well-preserved mummies, but not alive. In this connection I may especially mention the professors I met, the men who live up to that decadent university ideal, " the passionless pursuit of passionless intelligence."

I met men who invoked the name of the Prince of Peace in their diatribes against war, and who put rifles in the hands of Pinkertons with which to shoot down strikers in their own factories. I met men incoherent with indignation at the brutality of prize-fighting, and who, at the same time, were parties to the adulteration of food that killed each year more babies than even red-handed Herod had killed.

I talked in hotels and clubs and homes and Pullmans and steamer-chairs with captains of industry, and marvelled at how little travelled they were in the realm of intellect. On the other hand, I discovered that their intellect, in the business sense, was abnormally developed. Also, I discovered that their morality, where business was concerned, was nil.

This delicate, aristocratic-featured gentleman was a dummy director and a tool of corporations that secretly robbed widows and orphans. This gentleman, who collected fine editions and was an especial patron of literature, paid blackmail to a heavy-jowled, black-browed boss of a municipal machine. This editor, who published patent medicine advertisements and did not dare print the truth in his paper about said patent medicines for fear of losing the advertising, called me a scoundrelly demagogue because I told him that his political economy was antiquated and that his biology was contemporaneous with Pliny.

This senator was the tool and the slave, the little puppet of a gross, uneducated machine boss; so was this governor and this supreme court judge; and all three rode on railroad passes. This man, talking soberly and earnestly about the beauties of idealism and the goodness of God, had just betrayed his comrades in a business deal. This man, a pillar of the church and heavy contributor to foreign missions, worked his shop girls ten hours a day on a starvation wage and thereby directly encouraged prostitution. This man, who endowed chairs in universities, perjured himself in courts of law over a matter of dollars and cents. And this railroad magnate broke his word as a gentleman and a Christian when he granted a secret rebate to one of two captains of industry locked together in a struggle to the death.

It was the same everywhere, crime and betrayal, betrayal and crime — men who were alive, but who were neither clean nor noble, men who were clean and noble but who were not alive. Then there was a great, hopeless mass, neither noble nor alive, but merely clean. It did not sin positively nor deliberately; but it did sin passively and ignorantly by acquiescing in the current immorality and profiting by it. Had it been noble and alive it would not have been ignorant, and it would have refused to share in the profits of betrayal and crime.

I discovered that I did not like to live on the parlor floor of society. Intellectually I was bored. Morally and spiritually I was sickened. I remembered my intellectuals and idealists, my unfrocked preachers, broken professors, and clean-minded, class-conscious workingmen. I remembered my days and nights of sunshine and starshine, where life was all a wild sweet wonder, a spiritual paradise of unselfish adventure and ethical romance. And I saw before me, ever blazing and burning, the Holy Grail.

So I went back to the working-class, in which I had been born and where I belonged. I care no longer to climb. The imposing edifice of society above my head holds no delights for me. It is the foundation of the edifice that interests me. There I am content to labor, crowbar in hand, shoulder to shoulder with intellectuals, idealists, and class-conscious workingmen, getting a solid pry now and again and setting the whole edifice rocking. Some day, when we get a few more hands and crowbars to work, we'll topple it over, along with all its rotten life and unburied dead, its monstrous selfishness and sodden materialism. Then we'll cleanse the cellar and build a new habitation for mankind, in which there will be no parlor floor, in which all the rooms will be bright and airy, and where the air that is breathed will be clean, noble, and alive.

Such is my outlook. I look forward to a time when man shall progress upon something worthier and higher than his stomach, when there will be a finer incentive to impel men to action than the incentive of to-day, which is the incentive of the stomach. I retain my belief in the nobility and excellence of the human. I believe that spiritual sweetness and unselfishness will conquer the gross gluttony of to-day. And last of all, my faith is in the working-class. As some Frenchman has said, " The stairway of time is ever echoing with the wooden shoe going up, the polished boot descending."

[*1906*]

HERBERT CROLY

[1869-1930]

CROLY was born in New York City and was educated at the College of the City of New York and Harvard. From 1900 to 1906 he was the editor of the *Architectural Record*. In 1914, on funds supplied by Mr. and Mrs. Willard Straight, he founded the *New Republic,* and for sixteen years thereafter he was its chief editor. Under his guidance, and through the efforts of such co-workers as Walter Lippmann, Francis Hackett, Walter Weyl, George Soule, and Bruce Bliven, it became one of the foremost journals of liberal opinion in America, exercising an extraordinary influence in academic, journalistic, and political circles. Croly's ideas were admirably formulated in a volume entitled *The Promise of American Life* (1909), and from its concept of a liberal democracy he never deviated. It was a perfect expression of the sentiments behind the progressive movement which found its political leaders in Theodore Roosevelt and Woodrow Wilson. There is, indeed, evidence that Croly influenced both men. As for the direct effect of his book, we have the word of Robert Morss Lovett that when it " came into the hands of progressive teachers it lifted the study of political science in American colleges to a higher plane," and of Mr. Justice Frankfurter that it was " seminal in American political thinking." Croly's chief subsequent work was his volume *Progressive Democracy* (1914).

---

from

THE PROMISE OF AMERICAN LIFE

The moral and social aspiration proper to American life is, of course, the aspiration vaguely described by the word democratic; and the actual achievement of the American nation points towards an adequate and fruitful definition of the democratic ideal. Americans are usually satisfied by a most inadequate verbal description of democracy, but their national achievement implies one which is much more comprehensive and formative. In order to be true to their past, the increasing comfort and economic independence of an ever increasing proportion of the population must be secured, and it must be secured by a combination of individual effort and proper political organization. Above all, however, this economic and political system must be made to secure results of moral and social value. It is the seeking of such results which converts democracy from a political system into a constructive social ideal; and the more the ideal significance of the American national Promise is asserted and emphasized, the greater will become the importance of securing these moral and social benefits.

The fault in the vision of our national future possessed by the ordinary American does not consist in the expectation of some continuity of achievement. It consists rather in the expectation that the familiar benefits will continue to accumulate automatically. In his mind the ideal Promise is identified with the processes and conditions which hitherto have very much simplified its fulfillment, and he fails sufficiently to realize that the conditions are themselves changing, in such wise that hereafter the ideal Promise, instead of being automatically fulfilled, may well be automatically stifled. For two generations and more the American people were, from the economic point of view, most happily situated. They were able, in a sense, to slide down hill into the valley of fulfillment. Economic conditions were such that, given a fair start, they could scarcely avoid reaching a desirable goal. But such is no longer the case. Economic conditions have been profoundly modified, and American political and social problems have been modified with them. The Promise of American life must depend less than it did upon the virgin wilderness and the Atlantic Ocean, for the virgin wilderness has disappeared, and the Atlantic Ocean has become merely a big channel. The same results can no longer be achieved by the same easy methods. Ugly obstacles are peculiarly dangerous to a person who is sliding down hill. The man who is clambering up hill is in a much better position to evade or overcome them. Americans will possess a safer as well as a worthier vision of their national Promise as soon as they give it a house on a hill-top rather than in a valley.

The very genuine experience upon which American optimistic fatalism rests, is equivalent, because of its limitations, to a dangerous inexperience, and of late years an increasing number of Americans have been drawing this inference. They have been coming to see themselves more as others see them; and as an introduction to a consideration of this more critical frame of mind, I am going to quote [a] foreigner's view of American life, — the foreigner in this case being an Englishman and writing in 1893.

"The American note," says Mr. James Muirhead in his "Land of Contrasts," "includes a sense of illimitable expansion and possibility, an almost childlike confidence in human ability and fearlessness of both the present and the future, a wider realization of human brotherhood than has yet existed, a greater theoretical indifference to authority and a positive predilection for innovation, a marked alertness of mind, and a manifold variety of interest — above all, an inextinguishable hopefulness and courage. It is easy to lay one's finger in America upon almost every one of the great defects of civilization — even those defects which are specially characteristic of the civilization of the Old World. The United States cannot claim to be exempt from manifestations of economic slavery, of grinding the faces of the poor, of exploitation of the weak, of unfair distribution of wealth, of unjust monopoly, of unequal laws, of industrial and commercial chicanery, of disgraceful ignorance, of economic fallacies, of public corruption, of interested legislation, of want of public spirit, of vulgar boasting and chauvinism, of snobbery, of class prejudice, of respect of persons, and of a preference of the material over the spiritual. In a word, America has not attained, or nearly attained, perfection. But below and behind, and beyond all its weakness and evils, there is the grand fact of a noble national theory founded on reason and conscience." The reader will remark in the foregoing quotation that Mr. Muirhead is equally emphatic in his approval and in his disapproval. He generously recognizes almost as much that is good about Americans and their ways as our most vivacious patriotic orators would claim, while at the same time he has marshaled an army of abuses and sins which sound like an echo of the pages of the *London Saturday Review*. In the end he applies a friendly dash of whitewash by congratulating us on the "grand fact of our noble national theory," but to a discerning mind the consolation is not very consoling. The trouble is that the sins with which America is charged by Mr. Muirhead are flagrant violations of our noble national theory. So far as his charges are true, they are a denial that the American political and economic organization is accomplishing the results which its traditional claims require. If, as Mr. Muirhead charges, Americans permit the existence of economic slavery, if they grind the face of the poor, if they exploit the weak and distribute wealth unjustly, if they allow monopolies to prevail and laws to be unequal, if they are disgracefully ignorant, politically corrupt, commercially unscrupulous, socially snobbish, vulgarly boastful, and morally coarse, — if the substance of the foregoing indictment is really true, why, the less that is said about a noble national theory, the better. A man who is a sturdy sinner all the week hardly improves his moral standing by attending church on Sunday and professing a noble Christian theory of life. There must surely be some better way of excusing our sins than by raising aloft a noble theory of which these sins are a glaring violation.

I have quoted from Mr. Muirhead, not because his antithetic characterization of American life is very illuminating, but because of the precise terms of his charges against America. His indictment is practically equivalent to the assertion that the American system is not, or at least is no longer, achieving as much as has been claimed on its behalf. A democratic system may permit undefiled the existence of many sins and abuses, but it cannot permit the exploitation of the ordinary man by means of unjust laws and institutions. Neither can this indictment be dismissed without argument. When Mr. Muirhead's book was written sixteen years ago, the majority of good Americans would assuredly have read the charge with an incredulous smile; but in the year 1909 they might behave differently. The sins of which Mr. Muirhead accused Americans sixteen years ago are substantially the sins of which to-day they are accusing themselves — or rather one another. A numerous and powerful group of reformers has been collecting whose whole political policy and action is based on the conviction that the " common people " have not been getting the Square Deal to which they are entitled under the American system; and these reformers are carrying with them a constantly increasing body of public opinion. A considerable proportion of the American people is beginning to exhibit economic and political, as well as personal, discontent. A generation ago the implication was that if a man remained poor and needy, his poverty was his own fault, because the American system was giving all its citizens a fair chance. Now, however, the discontented poor are beginning to charge their poverty to an unjust political and economic organization, and reforming agitators do not hesitate to support them in this contention. Manifestly a threatened obstacle has been raised against the anticipated realization of our national Promise. Unless the great majority of Americans not only have, but believe they have, a fair chance, the better American future will be dangerously compromised.

The conscious recognition of grave national abuses casts a deep shadow across the traditional American patriotic vision. The sincere and candid reformer can no longer consider the national Promise as destined to automatic fulfillment. The reformers themselves are, no doubt, far from believing that whatever peril there is cannot be successfully averted. They make a point of being as patriotically prophetic as the most "old-fashioned Democrat." They proclaim even more loudly their conviction of an indubitable and a beneficent national future. But they do not and cannot believe that this future will take care of itself. As reformers they are bound to assert that the national body requires for the time being a good deal of medical attendance, and many of them anticipate that even after the doctors have discontinued their daily visits the patient will still need the supervision of a sanitary specialist. He must be persuaded to behave so that he will not easily fall ill again, and so that his health will be permanently improved. Consequently, just in so far as reformers are reformers they are obliged to abandon the traditional American patriotic fatalism. The national Promise has been transformed into a closer equivalent of a national purpose, the fulfillment of which is a matter of conscious work.

The transformation of the old sense of a glorious national destiny into the sense of a serious national purpose will inevitably tend to make the popular realization of the Promise of American life both more explicit and more serious. As long as Americans believed they were able to fulfill a noble national Promise merely by virtue of maintaining intact a set of political institutions and by the vigorous individual pursuit of private ends, their allegiance to their national fulfillment remained more a matter of words than of deeds; but now that they are being aroused from their patriotic slumber, the effect is inevitably to disentangle the national idea and to give it more dignity. The redemption of the national Promise has become a cause for which the good American must fight, and the cause for which a man fights is a cause which he more than ever values. The American idea is no longer to be propagated merely by multiplying the children of the West and by granting ignorant aliens permission to vote. Like all sacred causes, it must be propagated by the Word and by that right arm of the Word, which is the Sword.

The more enlightened reformers are conscious of the additional dignity and value which the popularity of reform has bestowed upon the American idea, but they still fail to realize the deeper implications of their own programme. In abandoning the older conception of an automatic fulfillment of our national destiny, they have abandoned more of the traditional American point of view than they are aware. The traditional American optimistic fatalism was not of accidental origin, and it cannot be abandoned without involving in its fall some other important ingredients in the accepted American tradition. Not only was it dependent on economic conditions which prevailed until comparatively recent times, but it has been associated with certain erroneous but highly cherished political theories. It has been wrought into the fabric of our popular economic and political ideas to such an extent that its overthrow necessitates a partial revision of some of the most important articles in the traditional American creed.

The extent and the character of this revision may be inferred from a brief consideration of the effect upon the substance of our national Promise of an alteration in its proposed method of fulfillment. The substance of our national Promise has consisted, as we have seen, of an improving popular economic condition, guaranteed by democratic political institutions, and resulting in moral and social amelioration. These manifold benefits were to be obtained merely by liberating the enlightened self-interest of the American people. The beneficent result followed inevitably from the action of wholly selfish motives — provided, of course, the democratic political system of equal rights was maintained in its integrity. The fulfillment of the American Promise was considered inevitable because it was based upon a combination of self-interest and the natural goodness of human nature. On the other hand, if the fulfillment of our national Promise can no longer be considered inevitable, if it must be considered as equivalent to a conscious national purpose instead of an inexorable national destiny, the implication necessarily is that the trust reposed in individual self-interest has been in some measure betrayed. No pre-established harmony can then exist between the free and abundant satisfaction of private needs and the accomplishment of a morally and socially desirable result. The Promise of American life is to be fulfilled — not merely by a maximum amount of economic freedom, but by a certain measure of discipline; not merely by the abundant satisfaction of individual desires, but by a large measure of individual subordination

624

and self-denial. And this necessity of subordinating the satisfaction of individual desires to the fulfillment of a national purpose is attached particularly to the absorbing occupation of the American people, — the occupation, viz.: of accumulating wealth. The automatic fulfillment of the American national Promise is to be abandoned, if at all, precisely because the traditional American confidence in individual freedom has resulted in a morally and socially undesirable distribution of wealth.

In making the concluding statement of the last paragraph I am venturing, of course, upon very debatable ground. Neither can I attempt in this immediate connection to offer any justification for the statement which might or should be sufficient to satisfy a stubborn skeptic. I must be content for the present with the bare assertion that the prevailing abuses and sins, which have made reform necessary, are all of them associated with the prodigious concentration of wealth, and of the power exercised by wealth, in the hands of a few men. I am far from believing that this concentration of economic power is wholly an undesirable thing, and I am also far from believing that the men in whose hands this power is concentrated deserve, on the whole, any exceptional moral reprobation for the manner in which it has been used. In certain respects they have served their country well, and in almost every respect their moral or immoral standards are those of the great majority of their fellow-countrymen. But it is none the less true that the political corruption, the unwise economic organization, and the legal support afforded to certain economic privileges are all under existing conditions due to the malevolent social influence of individual and incorporated American wealth; and it is equally true that these abuses, and the excessive " money power " with which they are associated, have originated in the peculiar freedom which the American tradition and organization have granted to the individual. Up to a certain point that freedom has been and still is beneficial. Beyond that point it is not merely harmful; it is by way of being fatal. Efficient regulation there must be; and it must be regulation which will strike, not at the symptoms of the evil, but at its roots. The existing concentration of wealth and financial power in the hands of a few irresponsible men is the inevitable outcome of the chaotic individualism of our political and economic organization, while at the same time it is inimical to democracy, because it tends to erect political abuses and social inequalities into a system. The inference which follows may be disagreeable, but it is not to be escaped. In becoming responsible for the subordination of the individual to the demand of a dominant and constructive national purpose, the American state will in effect be making itself responsible for a morally and socially desirable distribution of wealth.

The consequences, then, of converting our American national destiny into a national purpose are beginning to be revolutionary. When the Promise of American life is conceived as a national ideal, whose fulfillment is a matter of artful and laborious work, the effect thereof is substantially to identify the national purpose with the social problem. What the American people of the present and the future have really been promised by our patriotic prophecies is an attempt to solve that problem. They have been promised on American soil comfort, prosperity, and the opportunity for self-improvement; and the lesson of the existing crisis is that such a Promise can never be redeemed by an indiscriminate individual scramble for wealth. The individual competition, even when it starts under fair conditions and rules, results, not only, as it should, in the triumph of the strongest, but in the attempt to perpetuate the victory; and it is this attempt which must be recognized and forestalled in the interest of the American national purpose. The way to realize a purpose is, not to leave it to chance, but to keep it loyally in mind, and adopt means proper to the importance and the difficulty of the task. No voluntary association of individuals, resourceful and disinterested though they be, is competent to assume the responsibility. The problem belongs to the American national democracy, and its solution must be attempted chiefly by means of official national action.

Neither can its attempted solution be escaped. . . . In so far as the social problem is a real problem and the economic grievance a real grievance, they are bound under the American political system to come eventually to the surface and to demand express and intelligent consideration. A democratic ideal makes the social problem inevitable and its attempted solution indispensable.

[*1909*]

626

THEODORE ROOSEVELT

[1858–1919]

THIS son of a wealthy New York family was carefully sheltered during his childhood and schooled by private tutors, yet he ended his life as a symbol of America's aggressive virility and "practical idealism." On his graduation from Harvard in 1880 he turned to the study and writing of history, but two years later was persuaded to run for the New York State legislature. He was elected and served until 1884, distinguishing himself by his interest in political reform and civil service standards. In 1889 he was appointed United States Civil Service Commissioner, in 1895 New York Police Commissioner. At the outbreak of the Spanish-American War he helped to organize and headed a cavalry regiment — the Rough Riders — which saw action in Cuba. The resulting publicity, which he enjoyed thoroughly, enabled him to be elected governor of his native state in 1898. His political career was now assured. In 1900 he was put on the Republican national ticket as candidate for the vice-presidency, and McKinley carried him into office. The next year McKinley was assassinated and the aristocratic reformer became our twenty-sixth President. From then until 1908, the end of his second term, he was a belligerent exponent of American power and prestige and at the same time a foe of monopoly and a crusader for honest politics. Thus he reflected the "muckraking" trend and anticipated some of the liberalism of Wilson and Franklin D. Roosevelt. By 1910 the Republican Party was split between progressive and conservative forces, with President Taft torn between them. Roosevelt re-entered the political arena, assuming leadership of the liberals. At Ossawatomie, Kansas, while on a tour of the country to argue his principles, he made the famous speech of which the following is an excerpt. In 1912 he formed a third party and ran for the presidency against Taft, but succeeded only in winning the election for Wilson.

---

from

THE NEW NATIONALISM

We come here to-day to commemorate one of the epoch-making events of the long struggle for the rights of man — the long struggle for the uplift of humanity. Our country — this great republic — means

627

nothing unless it means the triumph of a real democracy, the triumph of popular government, and, in the long run, of an economic system under which each man shall be guaranteed the opportunity to show the best that there is in him. That is why the history of America is now the central feature of the history of the world; for the world has set its face hopefully toward our democracy; and, O my fellow citizens, each one of you carries on your shoulders not only the burden of doing well for the sake of your own country, but the burden of doing well and of seeing that this nation does well for the sake of mankind.

There have been two great crises in our country's history: first, when it was formed, and then, again, when it was perpetuated; and, in the second of these great crises — in the time of stress and strain which culminated in the Civil War, on the outcome of which depended the justification of what had been done earlier, you men of the Grand Army, you men who fought through the Civil War, not only did you justify your generation, not only did you render life worth living for our generation, but you justified the wisdom of Washington and Washington's colleagues. If this republic had been founded by them only to be split asunder into fragments when the strain came, then the judgment of the world would have been that Washington's work was not worth doing. . . .

It was a heroic struggle; and, as is inevitable with all such struggles, it had also a dark and terrible side. Very much was done of good, and much also of evil; and, as was inevitable in such a period of revolution, often the same man did both good and evil. For our great good fortune as a nation, we, the people of the United States as a whole, can now afford to forget the evil, or, at least, to remember it without bitterness, and to fix our eyes with pride only on the good that was accomplished. Even in ordinary times there are very few of us who do not see the problems of life as through a glass, darkly; and when the glass is clouded by the murk of furious popular passion, the vision of the best and the bravest is dimmed. Looking back, we are all of us now able to do justice to the valor and the disinterestedness and the love of the right, as to each it was given to see the right, shown both by the men of the North and the men of the South in that contest which was finally decided by the attitude of the West. We can admire the heroic valor, the sincerity, the self-devotion shown alike by the men who wore the blue and the men who wore the gray; and our sadness that such men should have had to fight one another is tempered by the glad knowledge that ever hereafter their descendants shall be found fighting side by side, struggling in peace as well as in war for the uplift of their common country, all alike resolute to raise to the highest pitch of honor and usefulness the nation to which they all belong. . . .

In every wise struggle for human betterment one of the main objects, and often the only object, has been to achieve in large measure equality of opportunity. In the struggle for this great end, nations rise from barbarism to civilization, and through its people press forward from one stage of enlightenment to the next. One of the chief factors in progress is the destruction of special privilege. The essence of any struggle for healthy liberty has always been, and must always be, to take from some one man or class of men, the right to enjoy power, or wealth, or position, or immunity, which has not been earned by service to his or their fellows. That is what you fought for in the Civil War, and that is what we strive for now.

At many stages in the advance of humanity, this conflict between the men who possess more than they have earned and the men who have earned more than they possess is the central condition of progress. In our day it appears as the struggle of free men to gain and hold the right of self-government as against the special interests, who twist the methods of free government into machinery for defeating the popular will. At every stage, and under all circumstances, the essence of the struggle is to equalize opportunity, destroy privilege, and give to the life and citizenship of every individual the highest possible value both to himself and to the commonwealth. . . .

I stand for the square deal. But when I say that I am for the square deal, I mean not merely that I stand for fair play under the present rules of the game, but that I stand for having those rules changed so as to work for a more substantial equality of opportunity and of reward for equally good service. One word of warning, which, I think, is hardly necessary in Kansas. When I say I want a square deal for the poor man, I do not mean that I want a square deal for the man who remains poor because he has not got the energy to work for himself. If a man who has had a chance will not make good, then he has got to quit. And you men of the Grand Army, you want justice for the brave man who fought, and punishment for the coward who shirked his work. Is not that so?

Now, this means that our government, national and state, must be freed from the sinister influence or control of special interests. Exactly as the special interests of cotton and slavery threatened our political integrity before the Civil War, so now the great special business interests too often control and corrupt the men and methods of government for their own profit. We must drive the special interests out of politics. That is one of our tasks to-day. Every special interest is entitled to justice — full, fair, and complete, — and, now, mind you, if there were any attempt by mob violence to plunder and work harm to the special interest, whatever it may be, that I most dislike, and the wealthy man, whomsoever he may be, for whom I have the greatest contempt, I would fight for him, and you would if you were worth your salt. He should have justice. For every special interest is entitled to justice, but not one is entitled to a vote in Congress, to a voice on the bench, or to representation in any public office. The Constitution guarantees protection to property, and we must make that promise good. But it does not give the right of suffrage to any corporation.

The true friend of property, the true conservative, is he who insists that property shall be the servant and not the master of the commonwealth; who insists that the creature of man's making shall be the servant and not the master of the man who made it. The citizens of the United States must effectively control the mighty commercial forces which they have themselves called into being. . . .

We grudge no man a fortune which represents his own power and sagacity, when exercised with entire regard to the welfare of his fellows. Again, comrades over there, take the lesson from your own experience. Not only did you not grudge, but you gloried in the promotion of the great generals who gained their promotion by leading the army to victory. So it is with us. We grudge no man a fortune in civil life if it is honorably obtained and well used. It is not even enough that it should have been gained without doing damage to the community. We should permit it to be gained only so long as the gaining represents benefit to the community. This, I know, implies a policy of a far more active governmental interference with social and economic conditions in this country than we have yet had, but I think we have got to face the fact that such an increase in governmental control is now necessary. . . .

But I think we may go still further. The right to regulate the use of wealth in the public interest is universally admitted. Let us admit also the right to regulate the terms and conditions of labor, which is the chief element of wealth, directly in the interest of the common good.

The fundamental thing to do for every man is to give him a chance to reach a place in which he will make the greatest possible contribution to the public welfare. Understand what I say there. Give him a chance, not push him up if he will not be pushed. Help any man who stumbles; if he lies down, it is a poor job to try to carry him; but if he is a worthy man, try your best to see that he gets a chance to show the worth that is in him. No man can be a good citizen unless he has a wage more than sufficient to cover the bare cost of living, and hours of labor short enough so that after his day's work is done he will have time and energy to bear his share in the management of the community, to help in carrying the general load. We keep countless men from being good citizens by the conditions of life with which we surround them. We need comprehensive workmen's compensation acts, both state and national laws to regulate child labor and work for women, and, especially, we need in our common schools not merely education in book learning, but also practical training for daily life and work. We need to enforce better sanitary conditions for our workers in industry and commerce, both within and between the states. Also, friends, in the interest of the workingman himself we need to set our faces like flint against mob violence just as against corporate greed; against violence and injustice and lawlessness by wage workers just as much as against lawless cunning and greed and selfish arrogance of employers. If I could ask but one thing of my fellow countrymen, my request would be that, whenever they go in for reform, they remember the two sides, and that they always exact justice from one side as much as from the other. . . .

I do not ask for overcentralization; but I do ask that we work in a spirit of broad and far-reaching nationalism when we work for what concerns our people as a whole. We are all Americans. Our common interests are as broad as the continent. I speak to you here in Kansas exactly as I would speak in New York or Georgia, for the most vital problems are those which affect us all alike. The national government belongs to the whole American people, and where the whole American people are interested, that interest can be guarded effectively only by the national government. The betterment which we seek must be accomplished, I believe, mainly through the national government.

[*1910*]

WOODROW WILSON

[1856-1924]

THE TWENTY-EIGHTH President of the United States was born in Staunton, Virginia. He was the son of a Presbyterian minister and teacher in a theological seminary, and was thus brought up in a pious and bookish atmosphere. Educated at Davidson College, Princeton, and the University of Virginia, he practiced law for one year, then entered Johns Hopkins as a graduate student of history and politics. In 1885 he went to Bryn Mawr to teach, in 1888 to Wesleyan, and in 1890 to Princeton. In 1902 he became president of Princeton. His progressive educational policies attracted sufficient attention to lead to his nomination for the governorship of New Jersey. Elected in 1910, he immediately became a hero of the reform movement of the time. In 1912 he won the nomination of the Democratic Party for the presidency and was elected because of a split in the Republican Party. His campaign was based upon an appeal to liberal and reform groups, and his election was a triumph of the "little man" against the big industrialist. His campaign speeches were collected by William Bayard Hale into a volume called *The New Freedom* (1913), which became a bible of pre-war liberalism. Wilson's first administration witnessed many governmental reforms, but it was his peace plea that won him a second administration. A year after his re-election he brought the United States into the World War with a humanitarian program for the future. It is a matter of record that the program was not adopted and that Wilson became an embittered and broken man. A military era is hardly congenial to liberal ideals, and it was inevitable that the end of Wilson's reign should have been marked by reaction.

---

from

THE NEW FREEDOM

LIFE COMES FROM THE SOIL

When I look back on the processes of history, when I survey the genesis of America, I see this written over every page: that the nations are renewed from the bottom, not from the top; that the genius which springs up from the ranks of unknown men is the genius which renews the youth and energy of the people. Everything I know about history, every bit of experience and observation that has contributed to my thought, has confirmed me in the conviction that the real wisdom of human life is compounded out of the experiences of ordinary men. The utility, the vitality, the fruitage of life does not come from the top to the bottom; it comes, like the natural growth of a great tree, from the soil, up through the trunk into the branches to the foliage and the fruit. The great struggling unknown masses of the men who are at the base of everything are the dynamic force that is lifting the levels of society. A nation is as great, and only as great, as her rank and file.

So the first and chief need of this nation of ours to-day is to include in the partnership of government all those great bodies of unnamed men who are going to produce our future leaders and renew the future energies of America. And as I confess that, as I confess my belief in the common man, I know what I am saying. The man who is swimming against the stream knows the strength of it. The man who is the mêlée knows what blows are being struck and what blood is being drawn. The man who is on the make is the judge of what is happening in America, not the man who has made good; not the man who has emerged from the flood; not the man who is standing on the bank looking on, but the man who is struggling for his life and for the lives of those who are dearer to him than himself. That is the man whose judgment will tell you what is going on in America; that is the man by whose judgment I, for one, wish to be guided.

We have had the wrong jury; we have had the wrong group, — no, I will not say the wrong group, but too small a group, — in control of the policies of the United States. The average man has not been consulted, and his heart had begun to sink for fear he never would be consulted again. Therefore, we have got to organize a government whose sympathies will be open to the whole body of the people of the United States, a government which will consult as large a proportion of the people of the United States as possible before it acts. Because the great problem of government is to know what the average man is experiencing and is thinking about. Most of us are average men; very few of us rise, except by fortunate accident, above the general level of the community about us; and therefore the man who thinks common thoughts, the man who has had common experiences, is almost always the man who interprets America aright. Isn't that the reason that we are proud of such stories as the story of Abraham Lincoln, — a man who rose out of the ranks and interpreted America better than any man had interpreted it who had risen out of the privileged classes or the educated classes of America?

The hope of the United States in the present and in the future is the same that it has always been: it is the hope and confidence that out of unknown homes will come men who will constitute themselves the masters of industry and of politics. The average hopefulness, the average welfare, the average enterprise, the average initiative, of the United States are the only things that make it rich. We are not rich because a few gentlemen direct our industry; we are rich because of our own intelligence and our own industry. America does not consist of men who get their names into the newspapers; America does not consist politically of the men who set themselves up to be political leaders; she does not consist of the men who do most of her talking, — they are important only so far as they speak for that great voiceless multitude of men who constitute the great body and the saving force of the nation. Nobody who cannot speak the common thought, who does not move by the common impulse, is the man to speak for America, or for any of her future purposes. Only he is fit to speak who knows the thoughts of the great body of citizens, the men who go about their business every day, the men who toil from morning till night, the men who go home tired in the evenings, the men who are carrying on the things we are so proud of.

You know how it thrills our blood sometimes to think how all the nations of the earth wait to see what America is going to do with her power, her physical power, her enormous resources, her enormous wealth. The nations hold their breath to see what this young country will do with her young unspoiled strength; we cannot help but be proud that we are strong. But what has made us strong? The toil of millions of men, the toil of men who do not boast, who are inconspicuous, but who live their lives humbly from day to day; it is the great body of toilers that constitutes the might of America. It is one of the glories of our land that nobody is able to predict from what family, from what region, from what race, even, the leaders of the country are going to come. The great leaders of this country have not come very often from the established, " successful " families.

I remember speaking at a school not long ago where I understood that almost all the young men were the sons of very rich people, and I told them I looked upon them with a great deal of pity, because, I said: " Most of you fellows are doomed to obscurity. You will not do anything. You will never try to do anything, and with all the great tasks of the country waiting to be done, probably you are the very men who will decline to do them. Some man who has been ' up against it,' some man who has come out of the crowd, somebody who has had the whip of necessity laid on his back, will emerge out of the crowd, will show that he understands the crowd, understands the interests of the nation, united and not separated, and will stand up and lead us."

If I may speak of my own experience, I have found audiences made up of the " common people " quicker to take a point, quicker to understand an argument, quicker to discern a tendency and to comprehend a principle, than many a college class that I have lectured to, — not because the college class lacked the intelligence, but because college boys are not in contact with the realities of life, while " common " citizens are in contact with the actual life of day by day; you do not have to explain to them what touches them to the quick.

There is one illustration of the value of the constant renewal of society from the bottom that has always interested me profoundly. The only reason why government did not suffer dry rot in the Middle Ages under the aristocratic system which then prevailed was that so many of the men who were efficient instruments of government were drawn from the church, — from that great religious body which was then the only church, that body which we now distinguish from other religious bodies as the Roman Catholic Church. The Roman Catholic Church was then, as it is now, a great democracy. There was no peasant so humble that he might not become a priest, and no priest so obscure that he might not become Pope of Christendom; and every chancellery in Europe, every court in Europe, was ruled by these learned, trained and accomplished men, — the priesthood of that great and dominant body. What kept government alive in the Middle Ages was this constant rise of the sap from the bottom, from the rank and file of the great body of the people through the open channels of the priesthood. That, it seems to me, is one of the most interesting and convincing illustrations that could possibly be adduced of the thing that I am talking about.

The only way that government is kept pure is by keeping these channels open, so that nobody may deem himself so humble as not to constitute a part of the body politic, so that there will constantly be coming new blood into the veins of the body politic; so that no man is so obscure that he may not break the crust of any class he may belong to, may not spring up to higher levels and be counted among the leaders of the state. Anything that depresses, anything that makes the organization greater than the man, anything that blocks, discourages, dismays the humble man, is against all the principles of progress. When I see alliances formed, as they are now being formed, by successful men of business with successful organizers of politics, I know that something has been done that checks the vitality and progress of society. Such an alliance, made at the top, is an alliance made to depress the levels, to hold them where they are, if not to sink them; and, therefore, it is the constant business of good politics to break up such partnerships, to re-establish and reopen the connections between the great body of the people and the offices of government.

To-day, when our government has so far passed into the hands of special interests; to-day, when the doctrine is implicitly avowed that only select classes have the equipment necessary for carrying on government; to-day, when so many conscientious citizens, smitten with the scene of social wrong and suffering, have fallen victims to the fallacy that benevolent government can be meted out to the people by kind-hearted trustees of prosperity and guardians of the welfare of dutiful employees, — to-day, supremely, does it behoove this nation to remember that a people shall be saved by the power that sleeps in its own deep bosom, or by none; shall be renewed in hope, in conscience, in strength, by waters welling up from its own sweet, perennial springs. Not from above; not by patronage of its aristocrats. The flower does not bear the root, but the root the flower. Everything that blooms in beauty in the air of heaven draws its fairness, its vigor, from its roots. Nothing living can blossom into fruitage unless through nourishing stalks deep-planted in the common soil. The rose is merely the evidence of the vitality of the root; and the real source of its beauty, the very blush that it wears upon its tender cheek, comes from those silent sources of life that lie hidden in the chemistry of the soil. Up from that soil, up from the silent bosom of the earth, rise the currents of life and energy. Up from the common soil, up from the quiet heart of the people, rise joyously to-day streams of hope and determination bound to renew the face of the earth in glory.

I tell you, the so-called radicalism of our times is simply the effort of nature to release the generous energies of our people. This great American people is at bottom just, virtuous, and hopeful; the roots of its being are in the soil of what is lovely, pure, and of good report, and the need of the hour is just that radicalism that will clear a way for the realization of the aspirations of a sturdy race.

[*1912–13*]

from

WAR MESSAGE TO CONGRESS

With a profound sense of the solemn and even tragical character of the step I am taking and of the grave responsibilities which it involves, but in unhesitating obedience to what I deem my constitutional duty, I advise that the Congress declare the recent course of the Imperial German Government to be in fact nothing less than war against the Government and people of the United States; that it formally accept the status of belligerent which has thus been thrust upon it; and that it take immediate steps not only to put the country in a more thorough state of defense but also to exert all its power and employ all its resources to bring the Government of the German Empire to terms and end the war. . . .

While we do these things, these deeply momentous things, let us be very clear, and make very clear to all the world what our motives and our objects are. My own thought has not been driven from its habitual and normal course by the unhappy events of the last two months, and I do not believe that the thought of the nation has been altered or clouded by them. I have exactly the same things in mind now that I had in mind when I addressed the Senate on the twenty-second of January last; the same that I had in mind when I addressed the Congress on the third of February and on the twenty-sixth of February. Our object now, as then, is to vindicate the principles of peace and justice in the life of the world as against selfish and autocratic power and to set up amongst the really free and self-governed peoples of the world such a concert of purpose and of action as will henceforth ensure the observance of those principles. Neutrality is no longer feasible or desirable where the peace of the world is involved and the freedom of its peoples, and the menace to that peace and freedom lies in the existence of autocratic governments backed by organized force which is controlled wholly by their will, not by the will of their people. We have seen the last of neutrality in such circumstances. We are at the beginning of an age in which it will be insisted that the same standards of conduct and of responsibility for wrong done shall be observed among nations and their governments that are observed among the individual citizens of civilized states.

We have no quarrel with the German people. We have no feeling towards them but one of sympathy and friendship. It was not upon their impulse that their Government acted in entering this war. It was not with their previous knowledge or approval. It was a war determined upon as wars used to be determined upon in the old, unhappy days when peoples were nowhere consulted by their rulers and wars were provoked and waged in the interests of dynasties or of little groups of ambitious men who were accustomed to use their fellow men as pawns and tools. Self-governed nations do not fill their neighbor states with spies or set the course of intrigue to bring about some critical posture of affairs which will give them an opportunity to strike and make conquest. Such designs can be successfully worked out only under cover and where no one has the right to ask questions. Cunningly contrived plans of deception or aggression, carried, it may be, from generation to generation, can be worked out and kept from the light only within the privacy of courts or behind the carefully guarded confidences of a narrow and privileged class. They are happily impossible where public opinion commands and insists upon full information concerning all the nation's affairs.

A steadfast concert for peace can never be maintained except by a partnership of democratic nations. No autocratic government could be trusted to keep faith within it or observe its covenants. It must be a league of honor, a partnership of opinion. Intrigue would eat its vitals away; the plottings of inner circles who could plan what they would and render account to no one would be a corruption seated at its very heart. Only free peoples can hold their purpose and their honor steady to a common end and prefer the interests of mankind to any narrow interest of their own.

Does not every American feel that assurance has been added to our hope for the future peace of the world by the wonderful and heartening things that have been happening within the last few weeks in Russia? Russia was known by those who knew it best to have been always in fact democratic at heart, in all the vital habits of her thought, in all the intimate relationships of her people that spoke their natural instinct, their habitual attitude towards life. The autocracy that crowned the summit of her political structure, long as it had stood and terrible as was the reality of its power, was not in fact Russian in origin, character, or purpose; and now it has been shaken off and the great, generous Russian people have been added in all their naïve majesty and might to the forces that are fighting for freedom in the world, for justice, and for peace. Here is a fit partner for a League of Honor.

One of the things that has served to convince us that the Prussian autocracy was not and could never be our friend is that from the very outset of the present war it has filled our unsuspecting communities and even our offices of government with spies and set criminal intrigues everywhere afoot against our national unity of counsel, our peace within and without, our industries and our commerce. Indeed it is now evident that its spies were here even before the war began; and it is unhappily not a matter of conjecture but a fact proved in our courts of justice that the intrigues which have more than once come perilously near to disturbing the peace and dislocating the industries of the country have been carried on at the instigation, with the support, and even under the personal direction of official agents of the Imperial Government accredited to the Government of the United States. Even in checking these things and trying to extirpate them we have sought to put the most generous interpretation possible upon them because we knew that their source lay, not in any hostile feeling or purpose of the German people towards us (who were, no doubt, as ignorant of them as we ourselves were), but only in the selfish designs of a Government that did what it pleased and told its people nothing. But they have played their part in serving to convince us at last that that Government entertains no real friendship for us and means to act against our peace and security at its convenience. That it means to stir up enemies against us at our very doors the intercepted note to the German Minister at Mexico City is eloquent evidence.

We are accepting this challenge of hostile purpose because we know that in such a Government, following such methods, we can never have a friend; and that in the presence of its organized power, always lying in wait to accomplish we know not what purpose, there can be no assured security for the democratic governments of the world. We are now about to accept gauge of battle with this natural foe to liberty and shall, if necessary, spend the whole force of the nation to check and nullify its pretensions and its power. We are glad, now that we see the facts with no veil of false pretense about them, to fight thus for the ultimate peace of the world and for the liberation of its peoples, the German peoples included: for the rights of nations great and small and the privilege of men everywhere to choose their way of life and of obedience. The world must be made safe for democracy. Its peace must be planted upon the tested foundations of political liberty. We must have no selfish ends to serve. We desire no conquest, no dominion. We seek no indemnities for ourselves, no material compensation for the sacrifices we shall freely make. We are but one of the champions of the rights of mankind. We shall be satisfied when those rights have been made as secure as the faith and the freedom of nations can make them.

Just because we fight without rancor and without selfish object, seeking nothing for ourselves but what we shall wish to share with all free peoples, we shall, I feel confident, conduct our operations as belligerents without passion and ourselves observe with proud punctilio the principles of right and of fair play we profess to be fighting for.

I have said nothing of the governments allied with the Imperial Government of Germany because they have not made war upon us or challenged us to defend our right and our honor. The Austro-Hungarian Government has, indeed, avowed its unqualified endorsement and acceptance of the reckless and lawless submarine warfare adopted now without disguise by the Imperial German Government, and it has therefore not been possible for this Government to receive Count Tarnowski, the Ambassador recently accredited to this Government by the Imperial and Royal Government of Austria-Hungary; but that Government has not actually engaged in warfare against citizens of the United States on the seas, and I take the liberty, for the present at least, of postponing a discussion of our relations with the authorities at Vienna. We enter this war only where we are clearly forced into it because there are no other means of defending our rights.

It will be all the easier for us to conduct ourselves as belligerents in a high spirit of right and fairness because we act without animus, not in enmity towards a people or with the desire to bring an injury or disadvantage upon them, but only in armed opposition to an irresponsible government which has thrown aside all considerations of humanity and of right and is running amuck. We are, let me say again, the sincere friends of the German people, and shall desire nothing so much as the early re-establishment of intimate relations of mutual advantage between us — however hard it may be for them, for the time being, to believe that this is spoken from our hearts. We have borne with their present government through all these bitter months because of that friendship — exercising a patience and forbearance which would otherwise have been impossible. We shall, happily, still have an opportunity to prove that friendship in our daily attitude and actions towards the millions of men and women of German birth and native sympathy who live amongst us and share our life, and we shall be proud to prove it towards all who are in fact loyal to their neighbors and to the Government in the hour of test. They are, most of them, as true and loyal Americans as if they had never known any other fealty or allegiance. They will be prompt to stand with us in rebuking and restraining the few who may be of a different mind and purpose. If there should be disloyalty, it will be dealt with with a firm hand of stern repression; but, if it lifts its head at all, it will lift it only here and there and without countenance except from a lawless and malignant few.

It is a distressing and oppressive duty, Gentlemen of the Congress, which I have performed in thus addressing you. There are, it may be, many months of fiery trial and sacrifice ahead of us. It is a fearful thing to lead this great peaceful people into war, into the most terrible and disastrous of all wars, civilization itself seeming to be in the balance. But the right is more precious than peace, and we shall fight for the things which we have always carried nearest our hearts — for democracy, for the right of those who submit to authority to have a voice in their own governments, for the rights and liberties of small nations, for a universal dominion of right by such a concert of free peoples as shall bring peace and safety to all nations and make the world itself at last free. To such a task we can dedicate our lives and our fortunes, everything that we are and everything that we have, with the pride of those who know that the day has come when America is privileged to spend her blood and her might for the principles that gave her birth and happiness and the peace which she has treasured. God helping her, she can do no other.

[*1917*]

VAN WYCK BROOKS

[1886–   ]

His two recent works — *The Flowering of New England* (1936) and *New England: Indian Summer* (1940) — have been best-sellers, which is a gratifying fact, for seldom do such humane and liberal narratives of our literary and cultural history reach a wide public. But it is not through such rather non-critical works that he achieved his eminence in American letters. He has been one of the most influential critics of our time because of such books as *America's Coming-of-Age* (1915) and *Letters and Leadership* (1918), in which he analyzed brilliantly the effects upon our literature of economic materialism on the one hand and idealism divorced from social action on the other. Brooks was born in Plainfield, New Jersey, of Yankee stock, and was educated in local schools and at Harvard, receiving his degree in 1907. Editorial jobs in publishing houses, with an interval of teaching at Stanford University, occupied him until 1917. Then he became associate editor of the *Seven Arts* magazine, afterwards of the *Freeman*. Since 1924 he has devoted all his time to writing.

---

from

AMERICA'S COMING–OF–AGE

Twenty, even ten years, ago, it would have been universally assumed that the only hope for American society lay in somehow lifting the "Lowbrow" elements to the level of the "Highbrow" elements. But the realism of contemporary thought makes it plain that the mere idealism of university ethics, the loftiness of what is called culture, the purity of so-called Good Government, left to themselves, produce a glassy inflexible priggishness on the upper levels that paralyzes life. It is equally plain that the lower levels have a certain humanity, flexibility, tangibility which are indispensable in any programme: that Tammany has quite as much to teach Good Government as Good Government has to teach Tammany, that slang has quite as much in store for culture as culture has for slang — that the universities, while emphatically not becoming more "practical," must base their disinterestedness on human, moral, social, artistic and personal needs, impulses and experience.

But society cannot become humane of itself; and it is for this reason that the movements of Reform are so external and so superficial. The will-to-reform springs from a conviction *ex post facto*. It suggests the frame of mind of business men who retire at sixty and collect pictures. Nothing so exemplifies it as the spectacle of Andrew Carnegie spending three-quarters of his life in providing steel for battleships and the last quarter of it in trying to abolish war. He himself surely was not conscious of any inward revolution; plainly with him as with others the will to create disorder, or what amounts to this, and the will to reform it sprang from the same inner condition of mind. The impetus of reform is evidently derived from the hope that a sufficient number of reformers can be trained and brought into the field to match the forces of business — the one group cancelling the other group. The ideal of reform, in short, is the attainment of zero.

Nothing is more absurd than to attack business as such. But the motives and circumstances of business vary from age to age, and there is a world of difference between industry conceived as a social process and trade conceived as a private end. A familiar distinction between the nineteenth and the twentieth centuries is that the problem of civilization is no longer the problem of want but the problem of surplus. Roughly speaking the hereditary American class — the prevailing class, I mean — is faced with the problem not of making money but of spending it; the prevailing American class is in a position of relative, but relatively great, economic freedom, and under these conditions it is plain that in them economic self-assertion ("enterprise") has become to a large extent a vicious anachronism. But force of habit, the sheer impetus and ground-swell of an antiquated pioneering spirit finds them with no means of personal outlet except, on the one hand, a continued economic self-assertion and on the other a reckless overflow of surplus wealth that takes the form of doing what everybody else does, and doing it as much more so as possible.

Because it was for so long the law of the tribe, economic self-assertion still remains to most Americans a sort of moral obligation, while self-fulfillment still looks like a pretty word for selfishness. Yet self-fulfillment through science, or literature, or mechanics, or industry itself — the working out of one's own personality, one's own inventiveness through forms of activity that are directly social, as all these activities *are* directly social, gives a man, through his very sociality, through the feeling he has that, as a good workman, he is cooperating with all other good workmen, a life-interest apart from his rewards. And as this principle is diffused and understood, the incentive is withdrawn from economic self-assertion, a relative competence being notoriously satisfying to the man whose prime end is the fulfilling of his own creative instincts; and the wealth of the world is already socialized.

One cannot have personality, one cannot have the expressions of personality so long as the end of society is an impersonal end like the accumulation of money. For the individual whose personal end varies too greatly from the end of the mass of men about him suffers acutely and becomes abnormal; indeed, he actually cannot accomplish anything healthily fine at all. The best and most disinterested individual can only express the better intuitions and desires of his age and place; — there must be some sympathetic touch between him and some visible or invisible host about him, since the mind is a flower that has an organic connection with the soil from which it springs.

The only serious approach to society is the personal approach, and the quickening realism of contemporary social thought is at bottom simply a restatement for the mass of commercialized men, and in relation to issues that directly concern men as a whole, of those personal instincts that have been the essence of art, religion, literature — the essence of personality itself — since the beginning of things. It will remain of the least importance to patch up politics, to become infected with social consciousness, or to do any of the other easy popular contemporary things unless, in some way, personality can be made to release itself on a middle plane between vaporous idealism and self-interested practicality; unless, in short, self-fulfillment as an ideal can be substituted for self-assertion as an ideal. On the economic plane, this implies socialism; on every other plane it implies something which a majority of Americans in our day certainly do not possess — an object in living. . . .

Something, in American literature, has always been wanting — every one, I think, feels that. Aside from the question of talent, there is not, excepting Walt Whitman, one American writer who comes home to a modern American with that deep, moving, shaking impact of personality for which one turns to the abiding poets and writers of the world. A certain density, weight and richness, a certain poignancy, a "something far more deeply interfused," simply is not there.

Above all, the Americanism of our old writers appears to have had no faculty of development and adaptation. With the death of Emerson, Lowell, Holmes and their group, something in the American mind really came to an end. The generation that has passed since then is a generation which has produced no indisputable leader of thought and letters, which has destroyed the coherence of the old American circle of ideas, and left us at the height of the second immigration among the chaotic raw materials of a perhaps altogether new attitude of mind.

It is, in fact, the plain, fresh, homely, impertinent, essentially innocent old America that has passed, and in its passing the allegory of Rip Van Winkle has been filled with a new meaning. Hendrik Hudson and his men, we see, have begun another game of bowls, and the reverberations are heard in many a summer thunderstorm; but they have been miraculously changed into Jews, Lithuanians, Magyars and German socialists. Rip is that old innocent America which has fallen asleep and which hears and sees in a dream the movement of peoples, the thunder of alien wants. And when after twenty years he awakens again, stretches his cold rheumatic limbs, and discovers the long white beard, he will once more set out for home. But when he arrives will he be recognized?

What emotions pass through an hereditary American when he calls to mind the worthies who figured in that ubiquitous group of "Our Poets" which occupied once so prominent a place in so many domestic interiors? Our Poets were commonly six in number, kindly, grey-bearded, or otherwise grizzled old men. One recalls a prevailing six, with variations. Sometimes a venerable historian was included, a novelist or so, and even Bayard Taylor.

Nothing could make one feel so like a prodigal son as to look at that picture. So much for the first glance, the first quick impression after one has come home to it from the far wanderings of an ordinary profane existence. But more complicated emotions supervene. What a world within a world that picture summons up! Frankly, we feel in ourselves, we are no longer so fortunate as in those days. It could really have been said of us then, as it cannot now be said at all, that as a folk we had won a certain coherence, a certain sort of ripeness in the better part of ourselves, which was reflected in the coherence of our men of letters.

645

Whittier, for example, was a common basis, and a very sweet and elevating basis, for a national programme of emotions the like of which no poet since his time has been able to compass. One recalls that fact, so full of meaning; and then, deep down, a forgotten world sweeps back over one, a world of memory, sentiment and association, a world of influences the most benign — like a mournful autumn wind stirring in forsaken places. But sooner or later the ordinary profane existence reasserts itself; and we have to put it to ourselves with equal frankness — has any one of these men, or any one of these influences, the power at bottom to make it less profane? The most benign sentiment in the world will not do so unless it has in it that which grips in some way at the root of personality.

It is no use to go off into a corner with American literature, as most of the historians have done, — in a sulky, private sort of way, taking it for granted that if we give up world values we are entitled to our own little domestic rights and wrongs, criticism being out of place by the fireside. "But oh, wherever else I am accounted dull," wrote Cowper in one of his letters, "let me pass for a genuis at Olney." This is the method of the old-fashioned camp in American criticism, just as the method of the contemporary camp is the method of depreciative comparison with better folk than our own.

The only fruitful approach is the personal approach, and to me, at least Thoreau, Emerson, Poe and Hawthorne are possessions forever. This does not alter the fact that if my soul were set on the accumulation of dollars not one of them would have the power to move me from it. And this I take to be a suggestive fact. Not one of them, not all of them, have had the power to move the soul of America from the accumulation of dollars; and when one has said this, one has arrived at some sort of basis for literary criticism.

Plainly enough, during what has been called the classical period of American literature, the soul of America did not wish to be moved from the accumulation of dollars; plainly enough, the pioneering instinct of economic self-assertion was the law of the tribe. And if the New England writers were homogeneous with the American people as no other group, scarcely any other individual, has been since, it is equally plain that they themselves and all their works must have accorded with the law of the tribe. The immense, vague cloud-canopy of idealism which hung over the American people during the nineteenth century was never permitted, in fact, to interfere with the practical conduct of life.

Never permitted, I say, although it is a more accurate explanation that, being essentially impersonal itself, the essence of this idealism lay in the very fact that it had and could have no connection with the practical conduct of life. The most successful and famous writers, Bryant and Longfellow, for example, promoted this idealism, being, so far as one can see, generally satisfied with the ordinary practices of society; they tacitly accepted the peculiar dualism that lies at the root of our national point of view. Emerson's really equivocal individualism on the one hand asserted the freedom and self-reliance of the spirit and on the other appeared to justify the unlimited private expediency of the business man. And as a suggestive corollary of this, the two principal artists in American literature, Poe and Hawthorne, were out of touch with society as few other artists in the world had been before: to their contemporaries they seemed spectral and aloof, scarcely human, and equally marked was the reaction upon their work of a world to them essentially unreal.

Granting these facts, and granting the still more significant fact of the absence from our literature of that deep, moving, shaking impact of personality which would have brought it into more permanent touch with American life, I do not see how we can escape the general axiom: that a society whose end is impersonal and antisocial cannot produce an ideal reflex in literature which is personal and social, and conversely, that the ideal reflex in literature produced by such a society will be unable to educate its own personal and social instincts. In effect, an examination of American literature will show, I think, that those of our writers who have possessed a vivid personal genius have been paralyzed by the want of a social background, while those who have possessed a vivid social genius have been equally unable to develop their personalities.

[1915]

VACHEL LINDSAY

[1879–1931]

LINDSAY was born in Springfield, Illinois, and was educated in the local public schools and at Hiram College. This was the period of Populism — the political movement of the Mid-Western small farmers revolting against the policies and controls of Eastern capitalists. It was a democratic movement that grew out of the conditions described in Hamlin Garland's works, and Lindsay was infected by its spirit and became one of its great voices. But first he tried to become an artist — in Chicago and New York, where he studied under Robert Henri. He failed to sell his drawings, came near starving, and at last resolved to become a tramp and beggar. At the same time he began seriously to write poetry. For several years he wandered through the country, distributing a leaflet called *Rhymes to be Traded for Bread* and giving recitations of his verses. A deeply religious man, influenced by mystical Swedenborgianism, he became a lecturer for the Y.M.C.A. and for the Anti-Saloon League. In 1913 he published his first volume, *General William Booth Enters into Heaven,* and in 1914 *The Congo and Other Poems.* These volumes established him, and from then on he wrote copiously and gave readings of his works in schools and colleges. His poetry employed the vernacular, was compounded of the rhythms of contemporary life, and was designed to be read aloud, to be chanted and sung. His poems were often noisy, usually sentimental. They expressed an identity with and sympathy for the common people. Lincoln was Lindsay's god, William Jennings Bryan one of his prophets.

FACTORY WINDOWS ARE ALWAYS BROKEN

Factory windows are always broken.
Somebody's always throwing bricks,
Somebody's always heaving cinders,
Playing ugly Yahoo tricks.

Factory windows are always broken.
Other windows are let alone.
No one throws through the chapel-window
The bitter, snarling, derisive stone.

Factory windows are always broken.
Something or other is going wrong.
Something is rotten — I think, in Denmark.
End of the factory-window song.
[*1914*]

TOLSTOI IS PLOWING YET

Tolstoi is plowing yet. When the smoke-clouds break,
High in the sky shines a field as wide as the world.
There he toils for the Kingdom of Heaven's sake.

Ah, he is taller than clouds of the little earth.
Only the congress of planets is over him,
And the arching path where new sweet stars have birth.

Wearing his peasant dress, his head bent low,
Tolstoi, that angel of Peace, is plowing yet;
Forward across the field, his horses go.
[*1915*]

BRYAN, BRYAN, BRYAN, BRYAN

*The Campaign of Eighteen Ninety-Six, As Viewed at
the Time by a Sixteen-Year-Old, etc.*

I

In a nation of one hundred fine, mob-hearted, lynching, relenting, re-
penting millions,
There are plenty of sweeping, swinging, stinging, gorgeous things to
shout about,
And knock your old blue devils out.

649

I brag and chant of Bryan, Bryan, Bryan,
Candidate for president who sketched a silver Zion,
The one American Poet who could sing outdoors,
He brought in tides of wonder, of unprecedented splendor,
Wild roses from the plains, that made hearts tender,
All the funny circus silks
Of politics unfurled,
Bartlett pears of romance that were honey at the cores,
And torchlights down the street, to the end of the world.

There were truths eternal in the gab and tittle-tattle.
There were real heads broken in the fustian and the rattle.
There were real lines drawn:
Not the silver and the gold,
But Nebraska's cry went eastward against the dour and old,
The mean and cold.

It was eighteen ninety-six, and I was just sixteen
And Altgeld ruled in Springfield, Illinois,
When there came from the sunset Nebraska's shout of joy:
In a coat like a deacon, in a black Stetson hat
He scourged the elephant plutocrats
With barbed wire from the Platte.
The scales dropped from their mighty eyes.
They saw that summer's noon
A tribe of wonders coming
To a marching tune.

Oh, the longhorns from Texas,
The jay hawks from Kansas,
The plop-eyed bungaroo and giant giassicus,
The varmint, chipmunk, bugaboo,
The horned-toad, prairie-dog and ballyhoo,
From all the newborn states arow,
Bidding the eagles of the west fly on,
Bidding the eagles of the west fly on.
The fawn, prodactyl and thing-a-ma-jig,
The rakaboor, the hellangone,
The whangdoodle, batfowl and pig,

The coyote, wild-cat and grizzly in a glow,
In a miracle of health and speed, the whole breed abreast,
They leaped the Mississippi, blue border of the West,
From the Gulf to Canada, two thousand miles long: —
Against the towns of Tubal Cain,
Ah, — sharp was their song.
Against the ways of Tubal Cain, too cunning for the young,
The longhorn calf, the buffalo and wampus gave tongue.

These creatures were defending things Mark Hanna never dreamed:
The moods of airy childhood that in desert dews gleamed,
The gossamers and whimsies,
The monkeyshines and didoes
Rank and strange
Of the canyons and the range,
The ultimate fantastics
Of the far western slope,
And of prairie schooner children
Born beneath the stars,
Beneath falling snows,
Of the babies born at midnight
In the sod huts of lost hope,
With no physician there,
Except a Kansas prayer,
With the Indian raid a howling through the air.

And all these in their helpless days
By the dour East oppressed,
Mean paternalism
Making their mistakes for them,
Crucifying half the West,
Till the whole Atlantic coast
Seemed a giant spiders' nest.

And these children and their sons
At last rode through the cactus,
A cliff of mighty cowboys
On the lope,
With gun and rope.

And all the way to frightened Maine the old East heard them call,
And saw our Bryan by a mile lead the wall
Of men and whirling flowers and beasts,
The bard and the prophet of them all.
Prairie avenger, mountain lion,
Bryan, Bryan, Bryan, Bryan,
Gigantic troubadour, speaking like a siege gun,
Smashing Plymouth Rock with his boulders from the West,
And just a hundred miles behind, tornadoes piled across the sky,
Blotting out sun and moon,
A sign on high.

Headlong, dazed and blinking in the weird green light,
The scalawags made moan,
Afraid to fight.

II

When Bryan came to Springfield, and Altgeld gave him greeting,
Rochester was deserted, Divernon was deserted,
Mechanicsburg, Riverton, Chickenbristle, Cotton Hill,
Empty: for all Sangamon drove to the meeting —
In silver-decked racing cart,
Buggy, buckboard, carryall,
Carriage, phaeton, whatever would haul,
And silver-decked farm-wagons gritted, banged and rolled,
With the new tale of Bryan by the iron tires told.

The State House loomed afar,
A speck, a hive, a football,
A captive balloon!
And the town was all one spreading wing of bunting, plumes, and sun-
     shine,
Every rag and flag, and Bryan picture sold,
When the rigs in many a dusty line
Jammed our streets at noon,
And joined the wild parade against the power of gold.

We roamed, we boys from High School,
With mankind,
While Springfield gleamed,

Silk-lined.
Oh, Tom Dines, and Art Fitzgerald,
And the gangs that they could get!
I can hear them yelling yet.
Helping the incantation,
Defying aristocracy,
With every bridle gone,
Ridding the world of the low down mean,
Bidding the eagles of the West fly on,
Bidding the eagles of the West fly on,
We were bully, wild and woolly,
Never yet curried below the knees.
We saw flowers in the air,
Fair as the Pleiades, bright as Orion,
— Hopes of all mankind,
Made rare, resistless, thrice refined.
Oh, we bucks from every Springfield ward!
Colts of democracy —
Yet time-winds out of Chaos from the star-fields of the Lord.

The long parade rolled on. I stood by my best girl.
She was a cool young citizen, with wise and laughing eyes.
With my necktie by my ear, I was stepping on my dear,
But she kept like a pattern, without a shaken curl.

She wore in her hair a brave prairie rose.
Her gold chums cut her, for that was not the pose.
No Gibson Girl would wear it in that fresh way.
But we were fairy Democrats, and this was our day.

The earth rocked like the ocean, the sidewalk was a deck.
The houses for the moment were lost in the wide wreck.
And the bands played strange and stranger music as they trailed along.
Against the ways of Tubal Cain,
Ah, sharp was their song!
The demons in the bricks, the demons in the grass,
The demons in the bank-vaults peered out to see us pass,
And the angels in the trees, the angels in the grass,
The angels in the flags, peered out to see us pass.

And the sidewalk was our chariot, and the flowers bloomed higher,
And the street turned to silver and the grass turned to fire,
And then it was but grass, and the town was there again,
A place for women and men.

III

Then we stood where we could see
Every band,
And the speaker's stand.
And Bryan took the platform.
And he was introduced.
And he lifted his hand
And cast a new spell.
Progressive silence fell
In Springfield,
In Illinois,
Around the world.
Then we heard these glacial boulders across the prairie rolled:
" *The people have a right to make their own mistakes.* . . .
You shall not crucify mankind
Upon a cross of gold."

And everybody heard him —
In the streets and State House yard.
And everybody heard him
In Springfield,
In Illinois,
Around and around and around the world,
That danced upon its axis
And like a darling broncho whirled.

IV

July, August, suspense.
Wall Street lost to sense.
August, September, October,
More suspense,
And the whole East down like a wind-smashed fence.

Then Hanna to the rescue,
Hanna of Ohio,
Rallying the roller-tops,
Rallying the bucket-shops.
Threatening drouth and death,
Promising manna,
Rallying the trusts against the bawling flannelmouth;
Invading misers' cellars,
Tin-cans, socks,
Melting down the rocks,
Pouring out the long green to a million workers,
Spondulix by the mountain-load, to stop each new tornado,
And beat the cheapskate, blatherskite,
Populistic, anarchistic,
Deacon — desperado.

V

Election night at midnight:
Boy Bryan's defeat.
Defeat of western silver.
Defeat of the wheat.
Victory of letterfiles
And plutocrats in miles
With dollar signs upon their coats,
Diamond watchchains on their vests
And spats on their feet.
Victory of custodians,
Plymouth Rock,
And all that inbred landlord stock.
Victory of the neat.
Defeat of the aspen groves of Colorado valleys,
The blue bells of the Rockies,
And blue bonnets of old Texas,
By the Pittsburg alleys.
Defeat of alfalfa and the Mariposa lily.
Defeat of the Pacific and the long Mississippi.
Defeat of the young by the old and silly.
Defeat of tornadoes by the poison vats supreme.
Defeat of my boyhood, defeat of my dream.

VI

Where is McKinley, that respectable McKinley,
The man without an angle or a tangle,
Who soothed down the city man and soothed down the farmer,
The German, the Irish, the Southerner, the Northerner,
Who climbed every greasy pole, and slipped through every crack;
Who soothed down the gambling hall, the bar-room, the church,
The devil vote, the angel vote, the neutral vote,
The desperately wicked, and their victims on the rack,
The gold vote, the silver vote, the brass vote, the lead vote,
Every vote? . . .

Where is McKinley, Mark Hanna's McKinley,
His slave, his echo, his suit of clothes?
Gone to join the shadows, with the pomps of that time,
And the flame of that summer's prairie rose.

Where is Cleveland whom the Democratic platform
Read from the party in a glorious hour,
Gone to join the shadows with pitchfork Tillman,
And sledge-hammer Altgeld who wrecked his power.

Where is Hanna, bulldog Hanna.
Low-browed Hanna, who said: " Stand pat "?
Gone to his place with old Pierpont Morgan.
Gone somewhere . . . with lean rat Platt.

Where is Roosevelt, the young dude cowboy,
Who hated Bryan, then aped his way?
Gone to join the shadows with mighty Cromwell
And tall King Saul, till the Judgment Day.

Where is Altgeld, brave as the truth,
Whose name the few still say with tears?
Gone to join the ironies with Old John Brown,
Whose fame rings loud for a thousand years.

656

Where is that boy, that Heaven-born Bryan,
That Homer Bryan, who sang from the West?
Gone to join the shadows with Altgeld the Eagle,
Where the kings and the slaves and the troubadours rest.

[*1919*]

A NET TO SNARE THE MOONLIGHT

(*What the Man of Faith Said*)

The dew, the rain and moonlight
All prove our Father's mind.
The dew, the rain and moonlight
Descend to bless mankind.

Come, let us see that all men
Have land to catch the rain,
Have grass to snare the spheres of dew,
And fields spread for the grain.

Yea, we would give to each poor man
Ripe wheat and poppies red, —
A peaceful place at evening
With the stars just overhead:

A net to snare the moonlight,
A sod spread to the sun,
A place of toil by daytime,
Of dreams when toil is done.

[*1920*]

657

JOHN DEWEY

[1859–   ]

HE WAS born in Burlington, Vermont, and educated in the local schools and at the University of Vermont, receiving his bachelor's degree in 1879. Five years later he took his Ph.D. at Johns Hopkins. He taught at the universities of Minnesota, Michigan, Chicago, and, after 1904, at Columbia, with which he is still associated. He has lectured in cities all over the world. In Chicago Dewey was one of the first members of the board of trustees at Hull House and ever since he has taken an active interest in social-welfare and political-reform movements. He made headlines a few years ago when he rendered a report, as the head of a voluntary committee of inquiry, exonerating Leon Trotsky of the Soviet government's charges against him. It is not in politics, however, but in the fields of education and philosophy that his real influence has been exerted — and especially in education. Such works as *The School and Society* (1889) and *Democracy and Education* (1916), in addition to numerous articles in periodicals, have helped greatly to liberalize the American school systems. Among his best known philosophical works are *Experience and Nature* (1925), *The Quest for Certainty* (1929), and *Art as Experience* (1934).

---

from

DEMOCRACY AND EDUCATION

The devotion of democracy to education is a familiar fact. The superficial explanation is that a government resting upon popular suffrage cannot be successful unless those who elect and who obey their governers are educated. Since a democratic society repudiates the principle of external authority, it must find a substitute in voluntary disposition and interest; these can be created only by education. But there is a deeper explanation. A democracy is more than a form of government; it is primarily a mode of associated living, of conjoint communicated experience. The extension in space of the number of individuals who participate in an interest so that each has to refer his own action to that of others, and to consider the action of others to give point and direction to his own, is equivalent to the breaking down of those barriers of class, race, and national territory which kept men from perceiving the full import of their activity. These more numerous and more varied points of contact denote a greater diversity of stimuli to which an individual has to respond; they consequently put a premium on variation in his action. They secure a liberation of powers which remain suppressed as long as the incitations to action are partial, as they must be in a group which in its exclusiveness shuts out many interests.

The widening of the area of shared concerns, and the liberation of a greater diversity of personal capacities which characterize a democracy, are not of course the product of deliberation and conscious effort. On the contrary, they were caused by the development of modes of manufacture and commerce, travel, migration, and intercommunication which flowed from the command of science over natural energy. But after greater individualization on one hand, and a broader community of interest on the other have come into existence, it is a matter of deliberate effort to sustain and extend them. Obviously a society to which stratification into separate classes would be fatal, must see to it that intellectual opportunities are accessible to all on equable and easy terms. A society marked off into classes need be specially attentive only to the education of its ruling elements. A society which is mobile, which is full of channels for the distribution of a change occurring anywhere, must see to it that its members are educated to personal initiative and adaptability. Otherwise, they will be overwhelmed by the changes in which they are caught and whose significance or connections they do not perceive. The result will be a confusion in which a few will appropriate to themselves the results of the blind and externally directed activities of others.

Probably the most deep-seated antithesis which has shown itself in educational history is that between education in preparation for useful labor and education for a life of leisure. The bare terms " useful labor " and " leisure " confirm the statement already made that the segregation and conflict of values are not self-inclosed, but reflect a division within social life. Were the two functions of gaining a livelihood by work and enjoying in a cultivated way the opportunities of leisure, distributed equally among the different members of a community, it would not occur to any one that there was any conflict of educational agencies and aims involved. It would be self-evident that the question was how education could contribute most effectively to both. And while it might be found that some materials of instruction chiefly accomplished one result and other subject matter the other, it would be evident that care must be taken to secure as much overlapping as conditions permit; that is, the education which had leisure more directly in view should indirectly reinforce as much as possible the efficiency and the enjoyment of work, while that aiming at the latter should produce habits of emotion and intellect which would procure a worthy cultivation of leisure.

These general considerations are amply borne out by the historical development of educational philosophy. The separation of liberal education from professional and industrial education goes back to the time of the Greeks, and was formulated expressly on the basis of a division of classes into those who had to labor for a living and those who were relieved from this necessity. The conception that liberal education, adapted to men in the latter class, is intrinsically higher than the servile training given to the former class reflected the fact that one class was free and the other servile in its social status. The latter class labored not only for its own subsistence, but also for the means which enabled the superior class to live without personally engaging in occupations taking almost all the time and not of a nature to engage or reward intelligence.

That a certain amount of labor must be engaged in goes without saying. Human beings have to live and it requires work to supply the resources of life. Even if we insist that the interests connected with getting a living are only material and hence intrinsically lower than those connected with enjoyment of time released from labor, and even if it were admitted that there is something engrossing and insubordinate in material interests which leads them to strive to usurp the place belonging to the higher ideal interests, this would not — barring the fact of socially divided classes — lead to neglect of the kind of education which trains men for the useful pursuits. It would rather lead to scrupulous care for them, so that men were trained to be efficient in them and yet to keep them in their place; education would see to it that we avoided the evil results which flow from their being allowed to flourish in obscure purlieus of neglect. Only when a division of these interests coincides with the division of an inferior and a superior social class will preparation for useful work be looked upon with contempt as an unworthy thing: a fact which prepares one for the conclusion that the rigid identification of work with material interests, and leisure with ideal interests is itself a social product.

The educational formulations of the social situation made over two thousand years ago have been so influential and give such a clear and logical recognition of the implications of the division into laboring and leisure classes, that they deserve especial note. According to them, man occupies the highest place in the scheme of animate existence. In part, he shares the constitution and functions of plants and animals — nutritive, reproductive, motor or practical. The *distinctively* human function is reason existing for the sake of beholding the spectacle of the universe. Hence the truly human end is the fullest possible of this distinctive human prerogative. The life of observation, meditation, cogitation, and speculation pursued as an end in itself is the proper life of man. From reason moreover proceeds the proper control of the lower elements of human nature — the appetites and the active, motor, impulses. In themselves greedy, insubordinate, lovers of excess, aiming only at their own satiety, they observe moderation — the law of the mean — and serve desirable ends as they are subjected to the rule of reason.

Such is the situation as an affair of theoretical psychology and as most adequately stated by Aristotle. But this state of things is reflected in the constitution of classes of men and hence in the organization of society. Only in a comparatively small number is the function of reason capable of operating as a law of life. In the mass of people, vegetative and animal functions dominate. Their energy of intelligence is so feeble and inconstant that it is constantly overpowered by bodily appetite and passion. Such persons are not truly ends in themselves, for only reason constitutes a final end. Like plants, animals and physical tools, they are means, appliances, for the attaining of ends beyond them, selves, although unlike them they have enough intelligence to exercise a certain discretion in the execution of the tasks committed to them. Thus by nature, and not merely by social convention, there are those who are slaves — that is, means for the ends of others. The great body of artisans are in one important respect worse off than even slaves. Like the latter they are given up to the service of ends external to themselves; but since they do not enjoy the intimate association with the free superior class experienced by domestic slaves they remain on a lower plane of excellence. Moreover, women are classed with slaves and craftsmen as factors among the animate instrumentalities of production and reproduction of the means for a free or rational life.

Individually and collectively there is a gulf between merely living and living worthily. In order that one may live worthily he must first live, and so with collective society. The time and energy spent upon mere life, upon the gaining of subsistence, detracts from that available for activities that have an inherent rational meaning; they also unfit for the latter. Means are menial, the serviceable is servile. The true life is possible only in the degree in which the physical necessities are had without effort and without attention. Hence slaves, artisans, and women are employed in furnishing the means of subsistence in order that others, those adequately equipped with intelligence, may live the life of leisurely concern with things intrinsically worth while.

To these two modes of occupation, with their distinction of servile and free activities (or " arts ") correspond two types of education: the base or mechanical and the liberal or intellectual. Some persons are trained by suitable practical exercises for capacity in *doing* things, for ability to use the mechanical tools involved in turning out physical commodities and rendering personal service. This training is a mere matter of habituation and technical skill; it operates through repetition and assiduity in application, not through awakening and nurturing thought. Liberal education aims to train intelligence for its proper office: to know. The less this knowledge has to do with practical affairs, with making or producing, the more adequately it engages intelligence. . . .

We are in a position honestly to criticize the division of life into separate functions and of society into separate classes only so far as we are free from responsibility for perpetuating the educational practices which train the many for pursuits involving mere skill in production, and the few for a knowledge that is an ornament and a cultural embellishment. In short, ability to transcend the Greek philosophy of life and education is not secured by a mere shifting about of the theoretical symbols meaning free, rational, and worthy. It is not secured by a change of sentiment regarding the dignity of labor, and the superiority of a life of service to that of an aloof self-sufficing independence. Important as these theoretical and emotional changes are, their importance consists in their being turned to account in the development of a truly democratic society, a society in which all share in useful

662

service and all enjoy a worthy leisure. It is not a mere change in the concepts of culture — or a liberal mind — and social service which requires an educational reorganization; but the educational transformation is needed to give full and explicit effect to the changes implied in social life. The increased political and economic emancipation of the " masses " has shown itself in education; it has effected the development of a common school system of education, public and free. It has destroyed the idea that learning is properly a monopoly of the few who are predestined by nature to govern social affairs. But the revolution is still incomplete. The idea still prevails that a truly cultural or liberal education cannot have anything in common, directly at least, with industrial affairs, and that the education which is fit for the masses must be a useful or practical education in a sense which opposes useful and practical to nurture of appreciation and liberation of thought. . . .

There is . . . an opportunity for an education which, keeping in mind the larger features of work, will reconcile liberal nurture with training in social serviceableness, with ability to share efficiently and happily in occupations which are productive. And such an education will of itself tend to do away with the evils of the existing economic situation. In the degree in which men have an active concern in the ends that control their activity, their activity becomes free or voluntary and loses its externally enforced and servile quality, even though the physical aspect of behavior remain the same. In what is termed politics, democratic social organization makes provision for this direct participation in control; in the economic region, control remains external and autocratic. Hence the split between inner mental action and outer physical action of which the traditional distinction between the liberal and the utilitarian is the reflex. An education which should unify the disposition of the members of society would do much to unify society itself.

[*1916*]

RANDOLPH BOURNE

[1886–1918]

BOURNE was born in Bloomfield, New Jersey, and educated in the local
schools. At seventeen he went to work — and he continued to work even
when he entered Columbia in 1909. He was a brilliant student, received his
degree in 1912, and was awarded a fellowship which enabled him to travel
abroad for a year. On his return he began to contribute reviews and essays
to the magazines and quickly earned a reputation as a liberal thinker. He
joined the editorial staff of the *New Republic,* but when America entered
the World War he resigned. For Bourne was an uncompromising pacifist,
and the *New Republic* was martial. He then wrote such essays as " The War
and the Intellectuals " and " Twilight of Idols," which have never been forgotten because of their insight into the relation of war to social progress and
culture, and because they were written with great force and beautiful clar-
ity. They were published in the *Seven Arts* magazine — and they led the
magazine's backers to withdraw their support. He was hounded by the
secret service, arrested, cartooned and lampooned, lived miserably, at last
died of pneumonia. Since then — to a lamentably small circle of people —
Bourne has become one of the heroes of American intellectual life.

from

THE WAR AND THE INTELLECTUALS

To those of us who still retain an irreconcilable animus against war,
it has been a bitter experience to see the unanimity with which the
American intellectuals have thrown their support to the use of war-
technique in the crisis in which America found herself. Socialists, college professors, publicists, new-republicans, practitioners of literature,
have vied with each other in confirming with their intellectual faith the
collapse of neutrality and the riveting of the war-mind on a hundred
million more of the world's people. And the intellectuals are not content with confirming our belligerent gesture. They are now complacently asserting that it was they who effectively willed it, against the

hesitation and dim perceptions of the American democratic masses. A war made deliberately by the intellectuals! A calm moral verdict, arrived at after a penetrating study of inexorable facts! Sluggish masses, too remote from the world-conflict to be stirred, too lacking in intellect to perceive their danger! An alert intellectual class, saving the people in spite of themselves, biding their time with Fabian strategy until the nation could be moved into war without serious resistance! An intellectual class, gently guiding a nation through sheer force of ideas into what the other nations entered only through predatory craft or popular hysteria or militarist madness! A war free from any taint of self-seeking, a war that will secure the triumph of democracy and internationalize the world! This is the picture which the more self-conscious intellectuals have formed of themselves, and which they are slowly impressing upon a population which is being led no man knows whither by an indubitably intellectualized President. And they are right, in that the war certainly did not spring from either the ideals or the prejudices, from the national ambitions or hysteria, of the American people, however acquiescent the masses prove to be, and however clearly the intellectuals prove their putative intuition.

Those intellectuals who have felt themselves totally out of sympathy with this drag toward war seek some explanation for this joyful leadership. They will want to understand this willingness of the American intellect to open the sluices and flood us with the sewage of the war spirit. We cannot forget the virtuous horror and stupefaction which filled our college professors when they read the famous manifesto of their ninety-three German colleagues in defense of their war. To the American academic mind of 1914 defense of war was inconceivable. From Bernhardi it recoiled as from a blasphemy, little dreaming that two years later would find it creating its own cleanly reasons for imposing military service on the country and for talking of the rough rude currents of health and regeneration that war would send through the American body politic. They would have thought any one mad who talked of shipping American men by the hundreds of thousands — conscripts — to die on the fields of France. Such a spiritual change seems catastrophic when we shoot our minds back to those days when neutrality was a proud thing. But the intellectual progress has been so gradual that the country retains little sense of the irony. The war sentiment, begun so gradually but so perseveringly by the preparedness advocates who came from the ranks of big business, caught hold of one after another of the intellectual groups. With the aid of Roosevelt, the murmurs became a monotonous chant, and finally a chorus so mighty that to be out of it was at first to be disreputable and finally almost obscene. And slowly a strident rant was worked up against Germany which compared very creditably with the German fulminations against the greedy power of England. The nerve of the war-feeling centered, of course, in the richer and older classes of the Atlantic seaboard, and was keenest where there were French or English business and particularly social connections. The sentiment then spread over the country as a class-phenomenon, touching everywhere those upper-class elements in each section who identified themselves with this Eastern ruling group. It must never be forgotten that in every community it was the least liberal and least democratic elements among whom the preparedness and later the war sentiment was found. The farmers were apathetic, the small business men and workingmen are still apathetic towards the war. The election was a vote of confidence of these latter classes in a President who would keep the faith of neutrality. The intellectuals, in other words, have identified themselves with the least democratic forces in American life. They have assumed the leadership for war of those very classes whom the American democracy has been immemorially fighting. Only in a world where irony was dead could an intellectual class enter war at the head of such illiberal cohorts in the avowed cause of world-liberalism and world-democracy. No one is left to point out the undemocratic nature of this war-liberalism. In a time of faith, skepticism is the most intolerable of all insults. . . .

The results of war on the intellectual class are already apparent. Their thought becomes little more than a description and justification of what is going on. They turn upon any rash one who continues idly to speculate. Once the war is on, the conviction spreads that individual thought is helpless, that the only way one can count is as a cog in the great wheel. There is no good holding back. We are told to dry our unnoticed and ineffective tears and plunge into the great work. Not only is every one forced into line, but the new certitude becomes idealized. It is a noble realism which opposes itself to futile obstruction and the cowardly refusal to face facts. This realistic boast is so loud and sonorous that one wonders whether realism is always a stern and intelligent grappling with realities. May it not be sometimes a mere surrender to the actual, an abdication of the ideal through a sheer

666

fatigue from intellectual suspense? The pacifist is roundly scolded for refusing to face the facts, and for retiring into his own world of senti-mental desire. But is the realist, who refuses to challenge or criticize facts, entitled to any more credit than that which comes from follow-ing the line of least resistance? The realist thinks he at least can control events by linking himself to the forces that are moving. Perhaps he can. But if it is a question of controlling war, it is difficult to see how the child on the back of a mad elephant is to be any more effective in stopping the beast than is the child who tries to stop him from the ground. The ex-humanitarian, turned realist, sneers at the snobbish neutrality, colossal conceit, crooked thinking, dazed sensibilities, of those who are still unable to find any balm of consolation for this war. We manufacture consolations here in America while there are probably not a dozen men fighting in Europe who did not long ago give up every reason for their being there except that nobody knew how to get them away.

But the intellectuals whom the crisis has crystallized into an accept-ance of war have put themselves into a terrifyingly strategic position. It is only on the craft, in the stream, they say, that one has any chance of controlling the current forces for liberal purposes. If we obstruct, we surrender all power for influence. If we responsibly approve, we then retain our power for guiding. We will be listened to as responsible thinkers, while those who obstructed the coming of war have com-mitted intellectual suicide and shall be cast into outer darkness. Criti-cism by the ruling powers will only be accepted from those intellectuals who are in sympathy with the general tendency of the war. Well, it is true that they may guide, but if their stream leads to disaster and the frustration of national life, is their guiding any more than a preference whether they shall go over the right-hand or the left-hand side of the precipice? Meanwhile, however, there is comfort on board. Be with us, they call, or be negligible, irrelevant. Dissenters are already ex-communicated. Irreconcilable radicals, wringing their hands among the débris, become the most despicable and impotent of men. There seems no choice for the intellectual but to join the mass of accept-ance. But again the terrible dilemma arises, — either support what is going on, in which case you count for nothing because you are swallowed in the mass and great incalculable forces bear you on; or remain aloof, passively resistant, in which case you count for nothing because you are outside the machinery of reality.

667

Is there no place left, then, for the intellectual who cannot yet crystallize, who does not dread suspense, and is not yet drugged with fatigue? The American intellectuals, in their preoccupation with reality, seem to have forgotten that the real enemy is War rather than imperial Germany. There is work to be done to prevent this war of ours from passing into popular mythology as a holy crusade. What shall we do with leaders who tell us that we go to war in moral spotlessness, or who make "democracy" synonymous with a republican form of government? There is work to be done in still shouting that all the revolutionary by-products will not justify the war, or make war anything else than the most noxious complex of all the evils that afflict men. There must be some to find no consolation whatever, and some to sneer at those who buy the cheap emotion of sacrifice. There must be some irreconcilables left who will not even accept the war with walrus tears. There must be some to call unceasingly for peace, and some to insist that the terms of settlement shall be not only liberal but democratic. There must be some intellectuals who are not willing to use the old discredited counters again and to support a peace which would leave all the old inflammable materials of armament lying about the world. There must still be opposition to any contemplated "liberal" world-order founded on military coalitions. The "irreconcilable" need not be disloyal. He need not even be "impossibilist." His apathy towards war would take the form of a heightened energy and enthusiasm for the education, the art, the interpretation that make for life in the midst of the world of death. The intellectual who retains his animus against war will push out more boldly than ever to make his case solid against it. The old ideals crumble; new ideals must be forged. . . .

[*1917*]

from

UNFINISHED FRAGMENT ON THE STATE

Government is synonymous with neither State nor Nation. It is the machinery by which the nation, organized as a State, carries out its State functions. Government is a framework of the administration of laws, and the carrying out of the public force. Government is the idea of the

State put into practical operation in the hands of definite, concrete, fallible men. It is the visible sign of the invisible grace. It is the word made flesh. And it has necessarily the limitations inherent in all practicality. Government is the only form in which we can envisage the State, but it is by no means identical with it. That the State is a mystical conception is something that must never be forgotten. Its glamor and its significance linger behind the framework of Government and direct its activities.

Wartime brings the ideal of the State out into very clear relief, and reveals attitudes and tendencies that were hidden. In times of peace the sense of the State flags in a republic that is not militarized. For war is essentially the health of the State. The ideal of the State is that within its territory its power and influence should be universal. As the Church is the medium for the spiritual salvation of men, so the State is thought of as the medium for his political salvation. Its idealism is a rich blood flowing to all the members of the body politic. And it is precisely in war that the urgency for union seems greatest, and the necessity for universality seems most unquestioned. The State is the organization of the herd to act offensively or defensively against another herd similarly organized. The more terrifying the occasion for defense, the closer will become the organization and the more coercive the influence upon each member of the herd. War sends the current of purpose and activity flowing down to the lowest level of the herd, and to its most remote branches. All the activities of society are linked together as fast as possible to this central purpose of making a military offensive or a military defense, and the State becomes what in peace times it has vainly struggled to become — the inexorable arbiter and determinant of men's businesses and attitudes and opinions. The slack is taken up, the cross-currents fade out, and the nation moves lumberingly and slowly, but with ever accelerated speed and integration, towards the great end, towards that "peacefulness of being at war," of which L. P. Jacks has so unforgettably spoken.

The classes which are able to play an active and not merely a passive role in the organization for war get a tremendous liberation of activity and energy. Individuals are jolted out of their old routine, many of them are given new positions or responsibility, new techniques must be learnt. Wearing home ties are broken and women who would have remained attached with infantile bonds are liberated for service overseas. A vast sense of rejuvenescence pervades the significant classes, a

669

sense of new importance in the world. Old national ideals are taken out, re-adapted to the purpose and used as universal touchstones, or molds into which all thought is poured. Every individual citizen who in peacetimes had no function to perform by which he could imagine himself an expression or living fragment of the State becomes an active amateur agent of the Government in reporting spies and disloyalists, in raising Government funds, or in propagating such measures as are considered necessary by officialdom. Minority opinion, which in times of peace was only irritating and could not be dealt with by law unless it was conjoined with actual crime, becomes, with the outbreak of war, a case for outlawry. Criticism of the State, objections to war, lukewarm opinions concerning the necessity or the beauty of conscription, are made subject to ferocious penalties, far exceeding in severity those affixed to actual pragmatic crimes. Public opinion, as expressed in the newspapers, and the pulpits and the schools, becomes one solid block. "Loyalty," or rather war orthodoxy, becomes the sole test for all professions, techniques, occupations. Particularly is this true in the sphere of the intellectual life. There the smallest taint is held to spread over the whole soul, so that a professor of physics is *ipso facto* disqualified to teach physics or to hold honorable place in a university — the republic of learning — if he is at all unsound on the war. Even mere association with persons thus tainted is considered to disqualify a teacher. Anything pertaining to the enemy becomes taboo. His books are suppressed wherever possible, his language is forbidden. His artistic products are considered to convey in the subtlest spiritual way taints of vast poison to the soul that permits itself to enjoy them. So enemy music is suppressed, and energetic measures of opprobrium taken against those whose artistic consciences are not ready to perform such an act of self-sacrifice. The rage for loyal conformity works impartially, and often in diametric opposition to other orthodoxies and traditional conformities, or even ideals. The triumphant orthodoxy of the State is shown at its apex perhaps when Christian preachers lose their pulpits for taking on more or less literal terms the Sermon on the Mount, and Christian zealots are sent to prison for twenty years for distributing tracts which argue that war is unscriptural.

War is the health of the State. It automatically sets in motion throughout society those irresistible forces for uniformity, for passionate cooperation with the Government in coercing into obedience the minority groups and individuals which lack the larger herd sense. The machinery of government sets and enforces the drastic penalties, the minorities are either intimidated into silence, or brought slowly around by a subtle process of persuasion which may seem to them really to be converting them. Of course the ideal of perfect loyalty, perfect uniformity is never really attained. The classes upon whom the amateur work of coercion falls are unwearied in their zeal, but often their agitation instead of converting, merely serves to stiffen their resistance. Minorities are rendered sullen, and some intellectual opinion bitter and satirical. But in general, the nation in war-time attains a uniformity of feeling, a hierarchy of values culminating at the undisputed apex of the State ideal, which could not possibly be produced through any other agency than war. Other values such as artistic creation, knowledge, reason, beauty, the enhancement of life, are instantly and almost unanimously sacrificed, and the significant classes who have constituted themselves the amateur agents of the State, are engaged not only in sacrificing these values for themselves but in coercing all other persons into sacrificing them. . . .

In other quieter moments, the Nation or Country forms the basic idea of society. We think vaguely of a loose population spreading over a certain geographical portion of the earth's surface, speaking a common language, and living in a homogeneous civilization. Our idea of Country concerns itself with the non-political aspects of a people, its ways of living, its personal traits, its literature and art, its characteristic attitudes towards life. We are Americans because we live in a certain bounded territory, because our ancestors have carried on a great enterprise of pioneering and colonization, because we live in certain kinds of communities which have a certain look and express their aspirations in certain ways. We can see that our civilization is different from contiguous civilizations like the Indian and Mexican. The institutions of our country form a certain network which affects us vitally and intrigues our thoughts in a way that these other civilizations do not. We are a part of country, for better or for worse. We have arrived in it through the operation of physiological laws, and not in any way through our own choice. By the time we have reached what are called years of discretion, its influences have molded our habits, our values, our ways of thinking, so that however aware we may become, we never

671

really lose the stamp of our civilization, or could be mistaken for the child of any other country. Our feeling for our fellow-countrymen is one of similarity or of mere acquaintance. We may be intensely proud of and congenial to our particular network of civilization, or we may detest most of its qualities and rage at its defects. This does not alter the fact that we are inextricably bound up in it. The Country, as an inescapable group into which we are born, and which makes us its particular kind of a citizen of the world, seems to be a fundamental fact of our consciousness, an irreducible minimum of social feeling.

Now this feeling for country is essentially non-competitive; we think of our own people merely as living on the earth's surface along with other groups, pleasant or objectionable as they may be, but fundamentally as sharing the earth with them. In our simple conception of country there is no more feeling of rivalry with other peoples than there is in our feeling for our family. Our interest turns within rather than without, is intensive and not belligerent. We grow up and our imaginations gradually stake out the world we live in, they need no greater conscious satisfaction for the gregarious impulses than this sense of a great mass of people to whom we are more or less attuned, and in whose institutions we are functioning. The feeling for country would be an uninflatable maximum were it not for the ideas of State and Government which are associated with it. Country is a concept of peace, of tolerance, of living and letting live. But State is essentially a concept of power, of competition; it signifies a group in its aggressive aspects. And we have the misfortune of being born not only into a country but into a State, and as we grow up we learn to mingle the two feelings into a hopeless confusion.

The State is the country acting as a political unit, it is the group acting as a repository of force, determiner of law, arbiter of justice. International politics is a "power politics" because it is a relation of States and that is what States infallibly and calamitously are, huge aggregations of human and industrial force that may be hurled against each other in war. When a country acts as a whole in relation to another country, or in imposing laws on its own inhabitants, or in coercing or punishing individuals or minorities, it is acting as a State. The history of America as a country is quite different from that of America as a State. In one case it is the drama of the pioneering conquest of the land, of the growth of wealth and the ways in which it was used, of the enterprise of education, and the carrying out of spiritual ideals, of the struggle of economic classes. But as a State, its history is that of playing a part in the world, making war, obstructing international trade, preventing itself from being split to pieces, punishing those citizens whom society agrees are offensive, and collecting money to pay for all. . . .

[*1919*]

673

EDGAR LEE MASTERS

[1869–   ]

BORN in a village in Kansas of an old American family, he was taken to Illinois, where his father became a successful lawyer and politician. He was brought up in Petersburg and Lewistown (the latter being five miles from the Spoon River) and was educated in the local schools. He learned the printer's trade, studied law with his father, and at the same time contributed poems to Chicago newspapers. In 1891 he was admitted to the bar. A year later he went to Chicago to pursue his profession, remaining in practice until 1920. From 1898 to 1914 he published several volumes of verse and political essays. William Marion Reedy, enterprising and courageous editor of *Reedy's Mirror*, in St. Louis, is said to have introduced Masters to the *Greek Anthology*. At any rate, that work gave Masters the idea for his *Spoon River Anthology*, which Reedy published serially in 1914, and which came out in book form a year later. Its scheme was simple: the men and women buried in the cemetery at Spoon River spoke from their graves to explain themselves — to reveal the truth about their lives and thoughts. It created a furore. Here was realism and a clean break with the genteel tradition; here was a powerful expression of the barren and mean life of a small town in the Middle West; here was a cry against moral and social hypocrisy, against greed and injustice. By virtue of its immense success, it became one of the beacons in the literary revolt against convention and smug materialism. In 1920 he published *Domesday Book*, a narrative in verse in which various people testify at an inquest on the death of a young woman. These volumes, together with his *New Spoon River* (1924), are the basis of his continuing reputation.

---

from

SPOON RIVER ANTHOLOGY

ENGLISH THORNTON

Here! You sons of the men
Who fought with Washington at Valley Forge,
And whipped Black Hawk at Starved Rock,

Arise! Do battle with the descendants of those
Who bought land in the loop when it was waste sand,
And sold blankets and guns to the army of Grant,
And sat in legislatures in the early days,
Taking bribes from the railroads!
Arise! Do battle with the fops and bluffs,
The pretenders and figurantes of the society column
And the yokel souls whose daughters marry counts;
And the parasites on great ideas,
And the noisy riders of great causes,
And the heirs of ancient thefts.
Arise! And make the city yours,
And the State yours —
You who are sons of the hardy yeomanry of the forties!
By God! If you do not destroy these vermin
My avenging ghost will wipe out
Your city and your state.

HARRY WILMANS

I was just turned twenty-one,
And Henry Phipps, the Sunday-school superintendent,
Made a speech in Bindle's Opera House.
"The honor of the flag must be upheld," he said,
"Whether it be assailed by a barbarous tribe of Tagalogs
Or the greatest power in Europe."
And we cheered and cheered the speech and the flag he waved
As he spoke.
And I went to the war in spite of my father,
And followed the flag till I saw it raised
By our camp in a rice field near Manila,
And all of us cheered and cheered it.
But there were flies and poisonous things;
And there was the deadly water,
And the cruel heat,
And the sickening, putrid food;
And the smell of the trench just back of the tents
Where the soldiers went to empty themselves;
And there were the whores who followed us, full of syphilis;

And beastly acts between ourselves or alone,
With bullying, hatred, degradation among us,
And days of loathing and nights of fear
To the hour of the charge through the steaming swamp,
Following the flag,
Till I fell with a scream, shot through the guts.
Now there's a flag over me in Spoon River!
A flag! A flag!

JOHN WASSON

Oh! the dew-wet grass of the meadow in North Carolina
Through which Rebecca followed me wailing, wailing,
One child in her arms, and three that ran along wailing,
Lengthening out the farewell to me off to the war with the British,
And then the long, hard years down to the day of Yorktown.
And then my search for Rebecca,
Finding her at last in Virginia,
Two children dead in the meanwhile.
We went by oxen to Tennessee,
Thence after years to Illinois,
At last to Spoon River.
We cut the buffalo grass,
We felled the forests,
We built the school houses, built the bridges,
Leveled the roads and tilled the fields
Alone with poverty, scourges, death —
If Harry Wilmans who fought the Filipinos
Is to have a flag on his grave
Take it from mine!

[1914–15]

676

OLIVER WENDELL HOLMES

[1841-1935]

In Justice Holmes the great liberal tradition of New England once again found an eloquent voice. During the 30 years in which he served as an associate justice of the Supreme Court of the United States, he was almost always on the liberal side of the court's decisions; and, as might be expected, his side was frequently the dissenting side. He was the son and namesake of the Boston physician who became the most popular poet and essayist of the genteel tradition. On being graduated from Harvard in 1861 he joined a regiment of Massachusetts volunteers and during the course of the Civil War fought in some of the bloodiest battles, was thrice wounded, and rose from a lieutenant to a lieutenant colonel. At the end of the war he entered Harvard Law School and on receiving his law degree began to practice in Boston. A distinguished career at the bar and as a teacher of law at Harvard ended with his appointment to the bench of the Supreme Court of Massachusetts, and finally in 1902 he was appointed to the Supreme Court of the United States.

THE ABRAMS CASE

This case involved a conviction under the Espionage Act of 1917. Abrams and his associates were charged with four counts: conspiring to print and publish " disloyal . . . and abusive language about the form of government of the United States," using " language intended to bring the form of government of the United States into contempt . . . disrepute," intending " to incite, provoke, and encourage resistance to the United States in said war [against Germany]," " to urge, incite, and advocate curtailment of production of things and products, to wit, ordnance and ammunition, necessary and essential to the prosecution of the war." The conviction of Abrams was affirmed in a majority opinion written by Justice Clarke. Holmes and Brandeis dissented. Holmes's opinion follows:

677

This indictment is founded wholly upon the publication of two leaflets which I shall describe in a moment. . . . The first of these leaflets says that the President's cowardly silence about the intervention in Russia reveals the hypocrisy of the plutocratic gang in Washington. It intimates that "German militarism combined with allied capitalism to crush the Russian Revolution"; goes on that the tyrants of the world fight each other until they see a common enemy, — working class enlightenment, when they combine to crush it; and that now militarism and capitalism combined, though not openly, to crush the Russian Revolution. It says that there is only one enemy of the workers of the world and that is capitalism; that it is a crime for workers of America, etc., to fight the workers' republic of Russia, and ends, "Awake! Awake, you workers of the world! Revolutionists." A note adds: "It is absurd to call us pro-German. We hate and despise German militarism more than do you hypocritical tyrants. We have more reason for denouncing German militarism than has the coward of the White House."

The other leaflet, headed "Workers — Wake Up," with abusive language says that America, together with the Allies, will march for Russia to help the Czecho-Slovaks in their struggle against the Bolsheviki, and that this time the hypocrites shall not fool the Russian emigrants and friends of Russia in America. It tells the Russian emigrants that they now must spit in the face of the false military propaganda by which their sympathy and help to the prosecution of the war have been called forth, and says that with the money they have lent or are going to lend "they will make bullets not only for the Germans, but also for the worker soviets of Russia," and further, "Workers in the ammunition factories, you are producing bullets, bayonets, cannon to murder not only the Germans, but also your dearest, best, who are in Russia fighting for freedom." It then appeals to the same Russian emigrants at some length not to consent to the "inquisitionary expedition in Russia," and says that the destruction of the Russia Revolution is "the politics of the march on Russia." The leaflet winds up by saying: "Workers, our reply to this barbaric intervention has to be a general strike!" And after a few words on the spirit of revolution, exhortations not to be afraid, and some usual tall talk, ends, "Woe unto those who will be in the way of progress. Let solidarity live! The Rebels."

No argument seems to me necessary to show that these pronunciamentos in no way attack the form of government of the United States,

or that they do not support either of the first two counts. What little
I have to say about the third count may be postponed until I have
considered the fourth. With regard to that it seems too plain to be
denied that the suggestion to workers in the ammunition factories that
they are producing bullets to murder their dearest, and the further
advocacy of a general strike, both in the second leaflet, do urge curtailment of production of things necessary to the prosecution of the
war within the meaning of the Act of May 16, 1918. But to make the
conduct criminal, that statute requires that it should be " with intent
by such curtailment to cripple or hinder the United States in the
prosecution of the war." It seems to me that no such intent is proved.

I am aware, of course, that the word " intent " as vaguely used in ordinary legal discussion means no more than knowledge at the time
of the act that the consequences said to be intended will ensue. Even
less than that will satisfy the general principle of civil and criminal
liability. A man may have to pay damages, may be sent to prison, at
common law might be hanged, if at the time of his act he knew facts
from which common experience showed that the consequences would
follow, whether he individually could foresee them or not. But, when
words are used exactly, a deed is not done with intent to produce a
consequence unless that consequence is the aim of the deed. It may be
obvious, and obvious to the actor, that the consequence will follow, and
he may be liable for it even if he regrets it, but he does not do the act
with intent to produce it unless the aim to produce it is the proximate
motive of the specific act, although there may be some deeper motive
behind.

It seems to me that this statute must be taken to use its words in
a strict and accurate sense. They would be absurd in any other. A
patriot might think that we were wasting money on aeroplanes, or
making more cannon of a certain kind than we needed, and might
advocate curtailment with success; yet, even if it turned out that the
curtailment hindered and was thought by other minds to have been
obviously likely to hinder the United States in the prosecution of the
war, no one would hold such conduct a crime. I admit that my illustration does not answer all that might be said, but it is enough to show
what I think and to let me pass to a more important aspect of the case.
I refer to the 1st Amendment to the Constitution that Congress shall
make no law abridging the freedom of speech.

I never have seen any reason to doubt that the questions of law that alone were before this court in the cases of Schenck, Frohwerk, and Debs, 249 U. S. 47, 204, 211, ante, 470, 561, 566, were rightly decided. I do not doubt for a moment that by the same reasoning that would justify punishing persuasion to murder, the United States constitutionally may punish speech that produces or is intended to produce a clear and imminent danger that it will bring about forthwith certain substantive evils that the United States constitutionally may seek to prevent. The power undoubtedly is greater in time of war than in time of peace because war opens dangers that do not exist at other times.

But, as against dangers peculiar to war, as against others, the principle of the right to free speech is always the same. It is only the present danger of immediate evil or an intent to bring it about that warrants Congress in setting a limit to the expression of opinion where private rights are not concerned. Congress certainly cannot forbid all effort to change the mind of the country. Now nobody can suppose that the surreptitious publishing of a silly leaflet by an unknown man, without more, would present any immediate danger that its opinions would hinder the success of the government arms or have any appreciable tendency to do so. Publishing those opinions for the very purpose of obstructing, however, might indicate a greater danger, and at any rate would have the quality of an attempt. So I assume that the second leaflet, if published for the purposes alleged in the fourth count, might be punishable. But it seems pretty clear to me that nothing less than that would bring these papers within the scope of this law. An actual intent in the sense that I have explained is necessary to constitute an attempt, where a further act of the same individual is required to complete the substantive crime, for reasons given in Swift & Co. v. United States, 196 U. S. 375, 396. It is necessary where the success of the attempt depends upon others, because if that intent is not present, the actor's aim may be accomplished without bringing about the evils sought to be checked. An intent to prevent interference with the revolution in Russia might have been satisfied without any hindrance to carrying on the war in which we were engaged.

I do not see how anyone can find the intent required by the statute in any of the defendants' words. The second leaflet is the only one that affords even a foundation for the charge, and there, without invoking the hatred of German militarism expressed in the former one, it is evident from the beginning to the end that the only object of the paper is to help Russia and stop American intervention there against the popular government, — not to impede the United States in the war that it was carrying on. To say that two phrases, taken literally, might import a suggestion of conduct that would have interference with the war as an indirect and probably undesired effect, seems to me by no means enough to show an attempt to produce that effect.

I return for a moment to the third count. That charges an intent to provoke resistance to the United States in its war with Germany. Taking the clause in the statute that deals with that in connection with the other elaborate provisions of the act, I think that resistance to the United States means some forcible act of opposition to some proceeding of the United States in pursuance of the war. I think the intent must be the specific intent that I have described, and for the reasons that I have given I think that no such intent was proved or existed in fact. I also think that there is no hint at resistance to the United States, as I construe the phrase.

In this case sentences of twenty years' imprisonment have been imposed for the publishing of two leaflets that I believe the defendants had as much right to publish as the government has to publish the Constitution of the United States now vainly invoked by them. Even if I am technically wrong, and enough can be squeezed from these poor and puny anonymities to turn the color of legal litmus paper, — I will add, even if what I think the necessary intent were shown, — the most nominal punishment seems to me all that possibly could be inflicted, unless the defendants are to be made to suffer not for what the indictment alleges, but for the creed that they avow, — a creed that I believe to be the creed of ignorance and immaturity when honestly held, as I see no reason to doubt that it was held here, but which, although made the subject of examination at the trial, no one has a right even to consider in dealing with the charges before the court.

Persecution for the expression of opinions seems to me perfectly logical. If you have no doubt of your premises or power and want a certain result with all your heart you naturally express your wishes in law and sweep away all opposition. To allow opposition by speech seems to indicate that you think the speech impotent, as when a man says that he has squared the circle, or that you do not care wholeheartedly for the result, or that you doubt either your power or your premises. But when men have realized that time has upset many fighting faiths, they may come to believe even more than they believe the very foundations of their own conduct that the ultimate good desired is better reached by free trade in ideas, — that the best test of truth is the power of the thought to get itself accepted in the competition of the market; and that truth is the only ground upon which their wishes safely can be carried out. That, at any rate, is the theory of our Constitution. It is an experiment as all life is an experiment. Every year, if not every day, we have to wager our salvation upon some prophecy based upon imperfect knowledge. While that experiment is part of our system I think that we should be eternally vigilant against attempts to check the expression of opinions that we loathe and believe to be fraught with death, unless they so imminently threaten immediate interference with the lawful and pressing purposes of the law that an immediate check is required to save the country. I wholly disagree with the argument of the government that the 1st Amendment left the common law as to seditious libel in force. History seems to me against the notion. I had conceived that the United States through many years had shown its repentance for the Sedition Act of July 14, 1798, by repaying fines that it imposed. Only the emergency that makes it immediately dangerous to leave the correction of evil counsels to time warrants making any exception to the sweeping command, " Congress shall make no law . . . abridging the freedom of speech." Of course I am speaking only of expressions of opinion and exhortations, which were all that were uttered here; but I regret that I cannot put into more impressive words my belief that in their conviction upon this indictment the defendants were deprived of their rights under the Constitution of the United States.

[*1919*]

THE ROSIKA SCHWIMMER CASE

When Miss Schwimmer, well known as a militant pacifist, applied for United States citizenship, she was asked, " If necessary, are you willing to take up arms in defense of this country? " She replied that she would not do so personally. The courts refused to grant her citizenship, on the ground that the Naturalization Act of 1906 requires that the applicant agree to "support and defend the Constitution and laws of the United States against all enemies." Miss Schwimmer stated that she was prepared to fulfill all the obligations of citizenship except take up arms, and that she would defend the United States against its enemies by other means than arms. The Supreme Court ruled against her, Justice Butler writing the majority opinion. Holmes, Brandeis, and Sanford dissented. Holmes's opinion follows:

The applicant seems to be a woman of superior character and intelligence, obviously more than ordinarily desirable as a citizen of the United States. It is agreed that she is qualified for citizenship except so far as the views set forth in a statement of facts "may show that the applicant is not attached to the principles of the Constitution of the United States and well disposed to the good order and happiness of the same, and except in so far as the same may show that she cannot take the oath of allegiance without a mental reservation." The views referred to are an extreme opinion in favor of pacifism and a statement that she would not bear arms to defend the Constitution. So far as the adequacy of her oath is concerned, I hardly can see how that is affected by the statement, inasmuch as she is a woman over fifty years of age, and would not be allowed to bear arms if she wanted to. And as to the opinion the whole examination of the applicant shows that she holds none of the now-dreaded creeds, but thoroughly believes in organized government and prefers that of the United States to any other in the world. Surely it cannot show lack of attachment to any principles of the Constitution that she thinks that it can be improved. I suppose that most intelligent people think that it might be. Her particular improvement looking to the abolition of war seems to me not materially different in its bearing on this case from a wish to establish cabinet government as in England, or a single house, or one term of seven years for the President. To touch a more burning question, only a judge mad with partisanship would exclude because the applicant thought that the 18th Amendment should be repealed.

Of course, the fear is that if a war came the applicant would exert activities such as were dealt with in Schenck v. U. S., 249 U. S. 47. . . . But that seems to me unfounded. Her position and motives are wholly different from those of Schenck. She is an optimist and states in strong and, I do not doubt, sincere words her belief that war will disappear and that the impending destiny of mankind is to unite in peaceful leagues. I do not share that optimism nor do I think that a philosophic view of the world would regard war as absurd. But most people who have known it regard it with horror, as a last resort, and, even if not yet ready for cosmopolitan efforts, would welcome any practicable combinations that would increase the power on the side of peace. The notion that the applicant's optimistic anticipations would make her a worse citizen is sufficiently answered by her examination, which seems to me a better argument for her admission than any I can offer. Some of her answers might excite popular prejudice, but if there is any principle of the Constitution that more imperatively calls for attachment than any other it is the principle of free thought — not free thought for those who agree with us but freedom for the thought that we hate. I think that we should adhere to that principle with regard to admission into, as well as to life within, this country. And, recurring to the opinion that bars this applicant's way, I would suggest that the Quakers have done their share to make the country what it is, that many citizens agree with the applicant's belief, and that I had not supposed hitherto that we regretted our inability to expel them because they believe more than some of us do in the teachings of the Sermon on the Mount.

[*1929*]

LOUIS D. BRANDEIS

[1856–1941]

FOR 15 of the 23 years in which he served as an associate justice of the Supreme Court of the United States, his name was constantly linked with that of Justice Holmes. For during that period his views almost invariably coincided with Holmes's, which is to say that he was on the liberal side of the court's decisions, and thus more frequently than not on the dissenting side. Case after case involving civil liberties or democratic rights, decided conservatively by the majority of the court, produced a brilliant dissenting decision written by either Holmes or Brandeis with the other concurring in the dissent. There was a difference between them, however: Holmes was more interested in and consistent about civil liberties, Brandeis more concerned with economic and industrial democracy. Brandeis's interests were self-evident before his appointment to the court: he figured prominently in a number of investigations and court tests concerned with precisely such questions, and he figured in them as a protagonist of the little people against monopolists. Born in Louisville, Kentucky, and educated in the schools of his native city and in Dresden, Germany, he took his law degree at Harvard and practiced in Boston for more than 35 years. His appointment to the Supreme Court by President Wilson aroused a storm of controversy instigated chiefly by big business men and their newspapers. Wilson forced the issue successfully, and there are some who think that it was one of his greatest contributions to American liberalism.

[ON INDUSTRIAL RELATIONS]

My observation leads me to believe that while there are many contributing causes to unrest, that there is one cause which is fundamental. That is the necessary conflict — the contrast between our political liberty and our industrial absolutism. We are as free politically, perhaps, as free as it is possible for us to be. Every male has his voice and vote; and the law has endeavored to enable, and has succeeded practically, in enabling him to exercise his political franchise without fear. He therefore has his part; and certainly can secure an adequate part in the government of the country in all of its political relations; that is, in all relations which are determined directly by legislation or governmental administration.

On the other hand, in dealing with industrial problems the position of the ordinary worker is exactly the reverse. The individual employee has no effective voice or vote. And the main objection, as I see it, to the very large corporation is, that it makes possible — and in many cases makes inevitable — the exercise of industrial absolutism. It is not merely the case of the individual worker against the employer which, even if he is a reasonably sized employer, presents a serious situation calling for the interposition of a union to protect the individual. But we have the situation of an employer so potent, so well organized, with such concentrated forces and with such extraordinary powers of reserve and the ability to endure against strikes and other efforts of a union, that the relatively loosely organized masses of even strong unions are unable to cope with the situation. We are dealing here with a question, not of motive, but of condition. Now, the large corporation and the managers of the powerful corporation are probably in large part actuated by motives just the same as an employer of a tenth of their size. Neither of them, as a rule, wishes to have his liberty abridged; but the smaller concern usually comes to the conclusion that it is necessary that it should be, where an important union must be dealt with. But when a great financial power has developed — when there exists these powerful organizations, which can successfully summon forces from all parts of the country, which can afford to use tremendous amounts of money in any conflict to carry out what they deem to be their business principle, and can also afford to suffer large losses — you have necessarily a condition of inequality between the two contending forces. Such contests, though undertaken with the best motives and with strong conviction on the part of the corporate managers that they are seeking what is for the best interests not only of the company but of the community, lead to absolutism. The result, in the cases of these large corporations, may be to develop a benevolent absolutism, but it is an absolutism all the same; and it is that which makes the great corporation so dangerous. There develops within the State a state so powerful that the ordinary social and industrial forces existing are insufficient to cope with it.

Unrest, to my mind, never can be removed — and fortunately never can be removed — by mere improvement of the physical and material condition of the workingman. If it were possible we should run great risk of improving their material condition and reducing their manhood. We must bear in mind all the time, that however much we may desire material improvement and must desire it for the comfort of the individual, that the United States is a democracy, and that we must have, above all things, men. It is the development of manhood to which any industrial and social system should be directed. We Americans are committed not only to social justice in the sense of avoiding things which bring suffering and harm, like unjust distribution of wealth; but we are committed primarily to democracy. The social justice for which we are striving is an incident of democracy — perhaps its finest expression — but it rests upon democracy, which implies the rule by the people. And therefore the end for which we must strive is the attainment of rule by the people, and that involves industrial democracy as well as political democracy. That means that the problems of a trade should be no longer the problems of the employer alone. The problems of his business, and it is not the employer's business alone, are the problems of all in it. The union cannot shift upon the employer the responsibility for conditions, nor can the employer insist upon determining, according to his will, the conditions which shall exist. The problems which exist are the problems of the trade; they are the problems of employer and employee. Profit sharing, however liberal, cannot meet the situation. That would mean merely dividing the profits of business. Such a division may do harm or it might do good, dependent on how it is applied.

There must be a division not only of profits, but a division also of responsibilities. The employees must have the opportunity of participating in the decisions as to what shall be their condition and how the business shall be run. They must learn also in sharing that responsibility that they, too, must bear the suffering arising from grave mistakes, just as the employer must. But the right to assist in making the decisions, the right of making their own mistakes, if mistakes there must be, is a privilege which should not be denied to labor. We must insist upon labor sharing the responsibilities for the result of the business.

Now, to a certain extent we are gradually getting it — in smaller businesses. The grave objection to the large business is that, almost inevitably, the form of organization, the absentee stock holdings, and its remote directorship prevent participation, ordinarily, of the employees in such management. The executive officials become stewards in charge of the details of the operation of the business, they alone coming into direct relation with labor. Thus we lose that necessary co-operation which naturally flows from contact between employers and employees — and which the American aspirations for democracy demand. It is in the resultant absolutism that you will find the fundamental cause of prevailing unrest; no matter what is done with the superstructure, no matter how it may be improved in one way or the other, unless we eradicate that fundamental difficulty, unrest will not only continue, but, in my opinion, will grow worse. . . .

It is almost inconceivable to my mind that a corporation with powers so concentrated as the Steel Corporation could get to a point where it would be willing to treat with the employees on equal terms. And unless they treat on equal terms then there is no such thing as democratization. The treatment on equal terms with them involves not merely the making of a contract; it must develop into a continuing relation. The making of a contract with a union is a long step. It is collective bargaining — a great advance. But it is only the first step. In order that collective bargaining should result in industrial democracy it must go further and create practically an industrial government — a relation between employer and employee where the problems as they arise from day to day, or from month to month, or from year to year, may come up for consideration and solution as they come up in our political government. . . .

I think all of our human experience shows that no one with absolute power can be trusted to give it up even in part. That has been the experience with political absolutism; it must prove the same with industrial absolutism. Industrial democracy will not come by gift. It has got to be won by those who desire it. And if the situation is such that a voluntary organization like a labor union is powerless to bring about the democratization of a business, I think we have in this fact some proof that the employing organization is larger than is consistent with the public interest. I mean by larger, is more powerful, has a financial influence too great to be useful to the State; and the State must in some way come to the aid of the workingmen if democratization is to be secured. . . .

[*1915*]

THE CASE OF DUPLEX VS. DEERING

This case grew out of an attempt by the International Association of Machinists to unionize the Michigan factory of the Duplex Company, manufacturers of printing presses. The union sought to persuade the New York customers of Duplex to refrain from purchasing Duplex presses; and the union asked the workers in these New York plants not to handle Duplex presses. In short, a general boycott of Duplex products was undertaken. The company sought an injunction against the New York local of the union, was refused it by the lower courts, but granted it by the Supreme Court. Justices Brandeis, Holmes, and Clarke dissented from the majority opinion. Brandeis's opinion follows:

The Duplex Company, a manufacturer of newspaper printing presses, seeks to enjoin officials of the machinists' and affiliated unions from interfering with its business by inducing their members not to work for plaintiff or its customers in connection with the setting up of presses made by it. . . . There is here no charge that defendants are inducing employees to break their contracts. Nor is it now urged that defendants threaten acts of violence. But plaintiff insists that the acts complained of violate both the common law of New York and the Sherman Act, and that, accordingly, it is entitled to relief by injunction under the State law and under § 16 of the Clayton Act, October 15, 1914, c. 323, 38 Stat. 730, 737.

The defendants admit interference with plaintiff's business but justify on the following ground: There are in the United States only four manufacturers of such presses; and they are in active competition. Between 1909 and 1913 the machinists' union induced three of them to recognize and deal with the union, to grant the eight-hour day, to establish a minimum wage scale, and to comply with other union requirements. The fourth, the Duplex Company, refused to recognize the union; insisted upon conducting its factory on the open shop principle; refused to introduce the eight-hour day and operated, for the most part, ten hours a day; refused to establish a minimum wage scale; and disregarded other union standards. Thereupon two of the three manufacturers who had assented to union conditions notified the union that they should be obliged to terminate their agreements with it unless their competitor, the Duplex Company, also entered into the agreement with the union, which, in giving more favorable terms to labor, imposed correspondingly greater burdens upon the employer. Because the Duplex Company refused to enter into such an agreement, and in order to induce it to do so, the machnists' union declared a strike at its factory, and in aid of that strike instructed its members and the members of affiliated unions not to work on the installation of presses which plaintiff had delivered in New York. Defendants insisted that by the common law of New York, where the acts complained of were done, and where this suit was brought, and also by § 20 of the Clayton Act, 38 Stat. 730, 738, the facts constitute a justification for this interference with plaintiff's business.

First. As to the rights at common law: Defendants' justification is that of self-interest. They have supported the strike at the employer's factory by a strike elsewhere against its product. They have injured the plaintiff, not maliciously, but in self-defense. They contend that the Duplex Company's refusal to deal with the machinists' union and to observe its standards threatened the interest, not only of such union members as were its factory employees, but even more of all members of the several affiliated unions employed by plaintiff's competitors and by others whose more advanced standards the plaintiff was, in reality, attacking; and that none of the defendants and no person whom they are endeavoring to induce to refrain from working in connection with the setting up of presses made by plaintiff is an outsider, an interloper. In other words, that the contest between the company and the machinists' union involves vitally the interest of every person whose cooperation is sought. May not all with a common interest join in refusing to expend their labor upon articles whose very production constitutes an attack upon their standard of living and the institution which they are convinced supports it? Applying common-law principles the answer should, in my opinion, be: Yes, if as a matter of fact those who so cooperate have a common interest.

The change in the law by which strikes once illegal and even criminal are now recognized as lawful was effected in America largely without the intervention of legislation. This reversal of a common-law rule was not due to the rejection by the courts of one principle and the adoption in its stead of another, but to a better realization of the facts of industrial life. It is conceded that, although the strike of the workmen in

690

plaintiff's factory injured its business, the strike was not an actionable wrong; because the obvious self-interest of the strikers constituted a justification. . . . Even after strikes to raise wages or reduce hours were held to be legal because of the self-interest, some courts held that there was not sufficient causal relationship between a strike to unionize a shop and the self-interest of the strikers to justify injuries inflicted. . . . But other courts, repeating the same legal formula, found that there was justification, because they viewed the facts differently. . . .

When centralization in the control of business brought its corresponding centralization in the organization of workingmen, new facts had to be appraised. A single employer might, as in this case, threaten the standing of the whole organization and the standards of all its members; and when he did so the union, in order to protect itself, would naturally refuse to work on his materials wherever found. When such a situation was first presented to the courts, judges concluded that the intervention of the purchaser of the materials established an insulation through which the direct relationship of the employer and the workingmen did not penetrate; and the strike against the material was considered a strike against the purchaser by unaffected third parties. . . . But other courts, with better appreciation of the facts of industry, recognized the unity of interest throughout the union, and that, in refusing to work on materials which threatened it, the union was only refusing to aid in destroying itself. . . .

So, in the case at bar, deciding a question of fact upon the evidence introduced and matters of common knowledge, I should say, as the two lower courts have said, that the defendants and those from whom they sought cooperation have a common interest which the plaintiff threatened. This view is in harmony with the views of the Court of Appeals of New York. For in New York, although boycotts like that in *Loewe v. Lawlor*, 208 U. S. 274, are illegal because they are conducted, not against a product, but against those who deal in it, and are carried out by a combination of persons, not united by common interest, but only by sympathy ; . . , it is lawful for all members of a union by whomever employed to refuse to handle materials whose production weakens the union. . . .

In my opinion, therefore, plaintiff had no cause of action by the common law of New York.

Second. As to the anti-trust laws of the United States: § 20 of the Clayton Act declares:

" Nor shall any of the acts specified in this paragraph be considered or held to be violations of any law of the United States."

The acts which are thus referred to are, whether performed singly or in concert:

" Terminating any relation of employment, or . . . ceasing to perform any work or labor, or . . . recommending, advising or persuading others by peaceful means so to do; or . . . attending at any place where such person or persons may lawfully be, for the purpose of obtaining or communicating information, or . . . peacefully persuading any person to work or abstain from working; or . . . ceasing to patronize or employ any party to such dispute, or . . . recommending, advising, or persuading others by peaceful and lawful means so to do; or . . . paying or giving to, or withholding from, any person engaged in such dispute, any strike benefits or other moneys or things of value; or peacefully assembling in a lawful manner and for lawful purposes; or . . . doing any act or thing which might lawfully be done in the absence of such dispute by any party thereto."

This statute was the fruit of unceasing agitation, which extended over more than twenty years and was designed to equalize before the law the position of workingmen and employer as industrial combatants. Aside from the use of the injunction, the chief source of dissatisfaction with the existing law lay in the doctrine of malicious combination, and, in many parts of the country, in the judicial declarations of the illegality at common law of picketing and persuading others to leave work. The grounds for objection to the latter are obvious. The objection to the doctrine of malicious combinations requires some explanation. By virtue of that doctrine, damage resulting from conduct such as striking or withholding patronage or persuading others to do either, which without more might be *damnum absque injuria* because the result of trade competition, became actionable when done for a purpose which a judge considered socially or economically harmful and therefore branded as malicious and unlawful. It was objected that, due largely to environment, the social and economic ideas of judges, which thus became translated into law, were prejudicial to a position of equality between workingmen and employer; that due to this dependence upon the individual opinion of the judges great confusion existed as to what purposes were lawful and what unlawful; and that in any event Congress, not the judges, was the body which should declare what public policy in regard to the industrial struggle demands.

By 1914 the ideas of the advocates of legislation had fairly crystallized upon the manner in which the inequality and uncertainty of the law should be removed. It was to be done by expressly legalizing certain acts regardless of the effects produced by them upon other persons. As to them Congress was to extract the element of *injuria* from the damages thereby inflicted, instead of leaving judges to determine according to their own economic and social views whether the damage inflicted on an employer in an industrial struggle was *damnum absque injuria,* because an incident of trade competition, or a legal injury, because in their opinion, economically and socially objectionable. This idea was presented to the committees which reported the Clayton Act. The resulting law set out certain acts which had previously been held unlawful, whenever courts had disapproved of the ends for which they were performed; it then declared that, when these acts were committed in the course of an industrial dispute, they should not be held to violate any law of the United States. In other words the Clayton Act substituted the opinion of Congress as to the propriety of the purpose for that of differing judges; and thereby it declared that the relations between employers of labor and workingmen were competitive relations, that organized competition was not harmful and that it justified injuries necessarily inflicted in its course. Both the majority and the minority reports of the House Committee indicate that such was its purpose. If, therefore, the Act applies to the case at bar, the acts here complained of cannot " be considered or held to be violations of any law of the United States," and hence do not violate the Sherman Act. . . .

Because I have come to the conclusion that both the common law of a State and a statute of the United States declare the right of industrial combatants to push their struggle to the limits of the justification of self-interest, I do not wish to be understood as attaching any constitutional or moral sanction to that right. All rights are derived from the purposes of the society in which they exist; above all rights rises duty to the community. The conditions developed in industry may be such that those engaged in it cannot continue their struggle without danger to the community. But it is not for judges to determine whether such conditions exist, nor is it their function to set the limits of permissible contest and to declare the duties which the new situation demands. This is the function of the Legislature which, while limiting individual and group rights of aggression and defense, may substitute processes of justice for the more primitive method of trial by combat.

[*1921*]

VERNON LOUIS PARRINGTON

[1871–1929]

HE WAS born in Aurora, Illinois, but was brought up in Kansas, where his father practiced law. He studied at the College of Emporia for several years, then went to Harvard, where he was admitted as a junior to the class of 1893. After being graduated he returned to Emporia to teach. Five years later he became a professor of English at the University of Oklahoma; in 1908 he went to the University of Washington, and there he taught until his death. There, too, he created the series of lectures on the history of American thought and literature from which grew his great work, *Main Currents in American Thought*. He was a popular and admired teacher, but he was hardly known outside his own campus, for he published very little — and that little was of no real importance — until at last he produced his *Main Currents*. The first two volumes of this work appeared in 1927; the third and concluding volume, uncompleted because of his sudden death, appeared in 1931. Immediately upon its publication, it was recognized as a masterpiece in its field. Its brilliant and eloquent style, its passionate defense of democratic ideals, its sympathy for those who strove to express the struggles of the common people against snobbery, exploitation, and a static social structure, informed and illuminated its interpretation of our literary and intellectual development. Its influence in both academic and journalistic circles has been profound.

---

from

MAIN CURRENTS IN AMERICAN THOUGHT

ANDREW JACKSON: AGRARIAN LIBERAL

Clay's pleasant dream of a paternalistic prosperity for America got its first rude awakening from General Jackson and his motley following of western equalitarians and eastern proletarians. Gentlemen were suddenly reminded that the plain people had been overlooked in the distribution of benefits. The waters of prosperity, it would seem, had been trickling somewhat too scantily to them from the great reservoirs

694

where they were impounded; and as they saw the wealth pouring into private ponds through governmental pipe lines, a natural human envy took possession of them. In theory the pipe lines belonged to them, and the impounded waters were to be used for common irrigation; but in practice the mains seemed to conduct only to Lowell industrialists and Philadelphia and New York capitalists, and the waters turned out to be privately owned. As the recognition of this fact came home to the producing mass it provided a rallying point for an anti-monopolist movement and determined the great objective of the Jacksonian attack, the assault on the Bank.

The driving force of the new Democracy was the same class-feeling that had done service a generation before, the will to destroy the aristocratic principle in government. This conscious class-feeling had been strengthened by the spread of the dogma of equalitarianism through the frontier, and this in turn had brought about an extension of manhood suffrage which enfranchised a numerous body of voters who turned against an aristocracy that had long resisted their demands for the vote. The spirit of 1798 was rising afresh, and the re-alignment assumed the form of a democratic-aristocratic struggle, which for the moment obscured the more significant fact of an emerging middle class. The battle seemed to lie between homespun and broadcloth for control of government, and this serves to explain the odium that quickly attached to Jacksonian Democracy in polite circles. In drawing together mechanics and frontiersmen, the new party inevitably became a lower-class instrument, offensive to gentlemen of the old school of politics. The records of the times carry abundant evidence, often amusing, of this aristocratic contempt. In the early forties a girl of seventeen living on a Mississippi plantation, describing Jefferson Davis — whose wife she afterwards became — was surprised at the contrast between his politics and his manners. " Would you believe it," she wrote, " he is refined and cultivated, and yet he is a Democrat! " (*Jefferson Davis, A Memoir by his Wife*, Vol. I, p. 192.)

There were quite evident reasons for his aristocratic contempt. The new Democracy was heavily weighted with what gentlemen were pleased to call the rabble. Fresh Democratic recruits had been gathering since Jefferson molded the first party of protest. Industrialism was creating a city proletariat, and the frontier was producing the coonskin voter; neither as yet possessed any adequate political philosophy, but they needed no philosophy to enlist against the traditional privileges and perquisites of broadcloth. They had had their fill of such rule. The stake-in-society theory was worn threadbare, and other philosophies were preparing. Meanwhile in the person of Old Hickory they saw the visible embodiment of their vague aspirations, and they turned to him with an unquestioning loyalty that nothing could weaken. He was our first great popular leader, our first man of the people. If he aroused a wild enthusiasm in breasts covered by linsey-woolsey, it was because he believed that linsey-woolsey had its stake-in-society equally with broadcloth. He was one of our few Presidents whose heart and sympathy were with the plain people, and who clung to the simple faith that government must deal as justly with the poor as with the rich. Believing so, he could not be turned aside from his course by paid clamor, but with a courage rare in the White House he dared make a frontal attack on the citadel of exploitation in the face of an army of mercenaries.

The dramatic career of Andrew Jackson, so unlike that of Jefferson, which was determined by a speculative temperament and founded on a critical examination of diverse systems of society and politics, was shaped in large measure by prejudice and circumstance. A man of iron will and inflexible purpose, he was almost wholly lacking in political and social philosophy. His conclusions were the reactions of a simple nature of complete integrity, in contact with plain fact. Fundamentally realistic, he cherished few romanticisms. There was no subtlety in his mental processes and this lack kept him free from the temptation to follow devious paths beloved of politicians. He must take the shortest way to his objective, crashing through such obstacles as lay in his path. He was never a bookish man. He was surprisingly ill read, and his grammar and spelling were those of the plain people. He loved horse racing and was a master of profanity; yet in spite of characteristics that link him with Davy Crockett, he possessed an innate dignity and chivalry that set him far above the wag of the canebrakes. He was a born leader whose headlong onslaughts and rash mistakes might imperil the cause but could not shake the confidence of his followers. All who knew a man when they saw one respected Andrew Jackson. Imperious and dictatorial, he knew how to command but not to obey; he took orders from no one, not even his superiors, unless such orders fell in with his own plans. In short General Jackson represented the best which the new West could breed in the way of capable and self-reliant individualism, and the backwoodsmen loved him for the enemies he made, and backed him loudly in his fight against the aristocratic East.

When Jackson settled in Nashville in 1788, at the age of twenty-one, the Cumberland valley had somewhat under five thousand inhabitants scattered a distance of eighty-five miles along the river. The first settlements had been made only nine years before, and Nashville was a frontier post with frontier manners. Into this rough society the young Scotch-Irishman fitted easily. His smattering of the law sufficed to gain him clients and he soon became a local political leader. When he was only twenty-nine he was sent to Philadelphia as the first Congressman from the state of Tennessee, where he came in contact with the " aristocratic Neebobs " of the government and heartily disliked them. The next year he was sent to the Senate, but a single session satisfied him and he resigned to accept a judgeship in the state Supreme Court, which post he held for six years. During these early years he was unconsciously following the path that conducted straight to a middle-class philosophy. He threw himself into speculation, bought and sold land in great blocks, traded in horses and slaves, set up a general store, and was well on the road to wealth when the panic of 1795 caught him unprepared. He lost most of his extensive holdings, including his homestead and many of his slaves, and removed to a six hundred and forty acre tract eight miles from Nashville — the Hermitage — which was to become one of the famous places of America. With this removal his middle-class ambitions fell away and he became a planter with a simple agrarian point of view; and this old-fashioned agrarianism became in later years the determining force in all his political thinking.

He was fifty-eight when he emerged as a potential candidate for the Presidency in 1822, and for years his sole interests, other than those of his plantation, had been military. He was singularly wanting in any formulated political philosophy, and his reelection to the Senate two years later did little to supply the lack. He had picked up some shreds of the protectionist theory and in a letter written in 1824 he went so far as to declare for a " judicious " protective tariff, basing his view on the grounds of the country's economic unpreparedness at the time of the War of 1812, on the lack of markets for the produce of western farms, and on the desirability of drawing labor from the farm to the factory. But he added a significant passage that reveals the agrarian bias of his mind. To the end of his life he insisted that he was an old Republican of 1798, and this comment of 1824 suffices to connect his later attack on the Bank with Jefferson's attack on Hamilton's fiscal policy.

Beyond this, I look at the Tariff with an eye to the proper distribution of labor and revenue; and with a view to discharge our national debt. I am one of those who do not believe that a national debt is a national blessing, but rather a curse to a republic; inasmuch as it is calculated to raise around the administration a moneyed aristocracy dangerous to the liberties of the country. (Quoted in Bassett, *Life of Andrew Jackson,* Vol. I, p. 346.)

The tariff was the only question on which he was receptive to Whiggish arguments, and although he never openly repudiated a protectionist policy he soon grew lukewarm in its support. Such other fragments of Whiggery as found accidental lodgment in his mind were swept away in the fierce struggles that marked his years in the White House. During those eight years Jackson found himself, and the man who emerged from the struggle was an agrarian of the old Virginian school. As he came to understand the significance of the principle of exploitation he learned to interpret social classes in terms of economics. He instinctively hated all aristocrats, extending his dislike to the circle that pretended to social preeminence in Tennessee, speaking of them contemptuously as the "aristocrats of Nashville." But in these later years a change in his vocabulary appeared; his favorite phrases became " the monied capitalists " and the " hydra of corruption." He had come to associate aristocracy with the control of the economics of society. He was learning how aristocracies are built up through the instrumentality of the state; and as that lesson sank into his mind his opposition to such class favoritism hardened into adamant. He would put a stop to such practices, cost what it might. His attack on the Bank was perhaps the most courageous act in our political history; he knew how fiercely it would be defended; yet he was amazed at the number of hornets that issued from the shaken nest. " Such has been the scenes of corruption in our last congress," he wrote in 1833, " that I loath the corruption of human nature and long for retirement, and repose on the Hermitage. But until I can strangle this hydra of corruption, the Bank, I will not shrink from my duty." And a little later, " I want relaxation from business and rest, but where can I get rest; I fear not on this earth " (Bassett, *Life of Andrew Jackson,* Vol. II, pp. 635, 637).

As his policy unfolded it became clear that Jackson had not changed with the changing times. He remained to the last the product of an earlier domestic economy, with an old-fashioned horror of debt. He was too generous to be frugal, too kind-hearted to be thrifty, too honest to live above his means. He desired a simple independence for himself and for his country. He believed that the government should pay its debt, reduce its revenues, and live simply. In his austere personal rectitude he exhibited a Puritan conviction of the sacredness of stewardship; he must return to the common poeple, who had put their trust in him, an honest reckoning of that trust. It was not in his nature to betray their faith. He would have nothing to do with the new theory that government is an agency to help business. To take profits from an instrument erected supposedly for the common good was abhorrent to his old-fashioned views; it was impossible for him to lend the sanction of his office to particular or special interests; and when circumstances made the Bank the central vexing problem of his administration, his position was predetermined by every conviction of his mind. While he was President he would not allow the government to be used for business ends; he would not permit its funds or credit to be turned to private profits; he would not tolerate a money monopoly, no matter how conventionally correct its operations might be proved to be, that challenged the sovereignty of the national government. The twin powers of the purse and sword — to recall Clay's famous phrase that every Whig orator used on the stump — were in Jackson's opinion the ultimate tests of sovereignty; and to turn over the money of the government to private hands for private use, he believed, was as grave an abrogation of sovereign rights as would be the use of the army and navy by private interests for private ends.

In the judgment of many critics Jackson, in his ignorance of the intricacies of capitalistic finance, wantonly destroyed a necessary credit system, thereby bringing a devastating panic on the country. Whether or not that judgment is true is of little importance today. More interesting historically is the fact that in his attitude towards the Bank, as in his attitude towards internal improvements, Jackson returned to the agrarian position of Jefferson and John Taylor, nullifying for a time the victories gained by the middle class during the boom period of nationalism. The more he learned about the methods of capitalistic finance, the more he distrusted it. His prejudices were his strength. He disliked speculation and he could see nothing permanently wise or sound in a speculative economy that put American industry at the mercy of bankers to expand or contract credit. With an old-fashioned love of a stable currency he gave his warm support to the project to return the country to a specie basis. " The great desideratum, in modern times," he said in his message to the twenty-fourth Congress, " is an efficient check upon the power of banks, preventing that excessive issue of paper whence arise those fluctuations in the standard of value which render uncertain the rewards of labor." The establishment of additional mints to provide an adequate coinage of gold or silver became therefore a natural corollary of his attack upon bank currency. It was John Taylor's economics written into the law of the land.

In his attitude towards the state Jackson followed the nationalistic tendencies of the West. He was as patriotic as Clay, and in spite of strong states-rights sympathies he contemptuously rejected Calhoun's theory of nullification. But he had no love for an omnicompetent state. More and more he drifted back to the Jeffersonian position in his conception of the powers and duties of the federal government. Replying to the vote of censure of 1834, he stated his ideal of government in words that would have become Jefferson's first inaugural speech. He had been charged with being ambitious, to which he replied:

The ambition which leads me on, is an anxious desire and a fixed determination, to return to the people, unimpaired, the sacred trust they have confided to my charge — to heal the wounds of the constitution and preserve it from further violation; to persuade my countrymen, so far as I may, that it is not in a splendid government, supported by powerful monopolies and aristocratical establishments, that they will find happiness, or their liberties protected, but in a plain system, void of pomp — protecting all, and granting favors to none — dispensing its blessings like the dews of heaven, unseen and unfelt, save in the freshness and beauty they contribute to produce. It is such a government that the genius of our people requires — such a one only under which our States may remain for ages to come, united, prosperous, and free. (Benton, *Thirty Years' View*, Vol. I, p. 427.)

The evils entailed on America by the Jacksonian revolution were many, but they cannot properly be charged against Andrew Jackson. They came in spite of him, and they came as a result of the great object lesson in the manipulation of the majority will that his popularity had laid bare. His instincts and the main outline of his policy were Jeffersonian; but neither he nor any other man was strong enough to stop the current of middle-class individualism then running. The American people were wanting in an adequate democratic program suited to the changing times, as they were wanting in desire for a social democracy. And when his capable hands fell from the machine he had created, it was seized by the politicians and used for narrow partisan ends. Yet one far-reaching result survived the movement, the popularization of the name of democracy and the naive acceptance of the belief that the genius of America was democratic. In choosing a party name the Jacksonians were shrewder politicians and better prophets than the Whigs. For better or worse the American masses, and in particular the nationalistic West, had espoused the principle of democracy, and interpreted it in terms of political equalitarianism — a principle that had inspired a fanatical hatred in the breasts of old Federalists. To gentlemen of that earlier school democracy had meant the right of the propertyless majority to plunder the minority in the name of the law. The later Whigs did not make so blundering a mistake. Instead of proclaiming democracy the mother of all mischiefs, they welcomed it as an effective aid in vote-getting. Learning their lesson from Jackson, the Whig politicians outdid him in democratic professions. They had discovered that business has little to fear from a skillfully guided electorate; that quite the safest way, indeed, to reach into the public purse is to do it in the sacred name of the majority will. Perhaps the rarest bit of irony in American history is the later custodianship of democracy by the middle class, who while perfecting their tariffs and subsidies, legislating from the bench, exploiting the state and outlawing all political theories but their own, denounce all class consciousness as unpatriotic and all agrarian or proletarian programs as undemocratic. But it was no fault of Andrew Jackson if the final outcome of the great movement of Jacksonian democracy was so untoward; it was rather the fault of the times that were not ripe for democracy.

[*1927*]

NICOLA SACCO

[1891-1927]

and

BARTOLOMEO VANZETTI

[1888-1927]

ONE need only mention the Sacco-Vanzetti case to adult Americans to evoke a flood of uncomfortable memories. It was the *cause célèbre* of the 1920's.

They were Italian immigrants. Both arrived here in 1908. Sacco became a shoe-worker around Boston; Vanzetti became a restaurant-worker and heavy laborer in New York, Springfield, and elsewhere, at last settling in Plymouth, Massachusetts, where eventually he worked as a fish-peddler. Both went to Mexico during the war in order to avoid the draft. Both were radical idealists and were active in labor struggles, earning reputations as agitators. Both became pacifists and anarchists. They were friends.

They were on a street car in Brockton, Massachusetts, when they were arrested on May 5, 1920 — charged with having perpetrated a hold-up and two murders in South Braintree. Soon great numbers of private citizens — writers, artists, lawyers, workers, teachers — came to their defense in the belief that these men were being " framed " because of their radicalism. It was a period of reaction. The agitation in their favor spread throughout the world. For seven years there were trials, appeals, petitions, mass meetings, examinations. On August 22, 1927, they were executed. Today practically no one who has studied their case believes in their guilt.

When Sacco and Vanzetti were imprisoned they knew virtually no English. They studied in prison — and wrote letters. The letters they wrote toward the end are remarkable documents. The three which follow speak for themselves.

LETTERS OF SACCO AND VANZETTI

SACCO TO HIS DAUGHTER INES

I would like that you should understand what I am going to say to you, and I wish I could write you so plain, for I long so much to have you hear all the heart-beat eagerness of your father, for I love you so much as you are the dearest little beloved one. . . .

It was the greatest treasure and sweetness in my struggling life that I could have lived with you and your brother Dante and your mother in a neat little farm, and learn all your sincere words and tender affection. Then in the summertime to be sitting with you in the home nest under the oak tree shade — beginning to teach you of life and how to read and write, to see you running, laughing, crying and singing through the verdent fields picking the wild flowers here and there from one tree to another, and from the clear, vivid stream to your mother's embrace.

The same I have wished to see for other poor girls, and their brothers, happy with their mother and father as I dreamed for us — but it was not so and the nightmare of the lower classes saddened very badly your father's soul.

For the things of beauty and of good in this life, mother nature gave to us all, for the conquest and the joy of liberty. The men of this dying old society, they brutally have pulled me away from the embrace of your brother and your poor mother. But, in spite of all, the free spirit of your father's faith still survives, and I have lived for it and for the dream that some day I would have come back to life, to the embrace of your dear mother, among our friends and comrades again, but woe is me!

I know that you are good and surely you love your mother, Dante and all the beloved ones — and I am sure that you love me also a little, for I love you much and then so much. You do not know Ines, how often I think of you every day. You are in my heart, in my vision, in every angle of this sad walled cell, in the sky and everywhere my gaze rests.

Meantime, give my best paternal greetings to all the friends and comrades, and doubly so to our beloved ones. Love and kisses to your brother and mother.

With the most affectionate kiss and ineffable caress from him who loves you so much that he constantly thinks of you. Best warm greetings from Bartolo to you all.

[*1927*]

SACCO TO HIS "SON AND COMPANION," DANTE

Since the day I saw you last I had always the idea to write you this letter, but the length of my hunger strike and the thought I might not be able to explain myself, made me put it off all this time.

The other day, I ended my hunger strike and just as soon as I did that I thought of you to write to you, but I find that I did not have enough strength and I cannot finish it at one time. However, I want to get it down in any way before they take us again to the death-house, because it is my conviction that just as soon as the court refuses a new trial to us they will take us there. And between Friday and Monday, if nothing happens, they will electrocute us right after midnight, on August 22nd. Therefore, here I am, right with you with love and with open heart as ever I was yesterday. . . .

Well, my dear boy, after your mother had talked to me so much and I had dreamed of you day and night, how joyful it was to see you at last. To have talked with you like we used to in the days — in those days. Much I told you on that visit and more I wanted to say, but I saw that you will remain the same affectionate boy, faithful to your mother who loves you so much, and I did not want to hurt your sensibilities any longer, because I am sure that you will continue to be the same boy and remember what I have told you. I knew that and what here I am going to tell you will touch your sensibilities, but don't cry Dante, because many tears have been wasted, as your mother's have been wasted for seven years, and never did any good. So, Son, instead of crying, be strong, so as to be able to comfort your mother, and when you want to distract your mother from the discouraging soulness, I will tell you what I used to do. To take her for a long walk in the quiet country, gathering wild flowers here and there, resting under the shade of trees, between the harmony of the vivid stream and the gentle tranquility of the mothernature, and I am sure that she will enjoy this very much, as you surely would be happy for it. But remember always, Dante, in the play of happiness, don't you use all for yourself only, but down yourself just one step, at your side and help the weak ones that cry for help, help the prosecuted and the victim, because that are your better friends; they are the comrades that fight and fall as your father and Bartolo fought and fell yesterday for the conquest of the joy of freedom for all and the poor workers. In this struggle of life you will find more love and you will be loved.

I am sure that from what your mother told me about what you said during these last terrible days when I was lying in the iniquitous death-house — that description gave me happiness because it showed you will be the beloved boy I had always dreamed.

Therefore whatever should happen tomorrow, nobody knows, but if they should kill us, you must not forget to look at your friends and comrades with the smiling gaze of gratitude as you look at your beloved ones, because they love you as they love every one of the fallen perse-cuted comrades. I tell you, your father that is all the life to you, your father that loved you and saw them, and knows their noble faith (that is mine) their supreme sacrifice that they are still doing for our freedom, for I have fought with them, and they are the ones that still hold the last of our hope that today they can still save us from electrocution, it is the struggle and fight between the rich and the poor for safety and freedom. Son, which you will understand in the future of your years to come, of this unrest and struggle of life's death.

Much I thought of you when I was lying in the death house — the singing, the kind tender voices of the children from the playground, where there was all the life and the joy of liberty — just one step from the wall which contains the buried agony of three buried souls. It would remind me so often of you and your sister Ines, and I wish I could see you every moment. But I feel better that you did not come to the death-house so that you could not see the horrible picture of three lying in agony waiting to be electrocuted, because I do not know what effect it would have on your young age. But then, in another way if you were not so sensitive it would be very useful to you tomorrow when you could use this horrible memory to hold up to the world the shame of the coun-try in this cruel persecution and unjust death. Yes, Dante, they can crucify our bodies today as they are doing, but they cannot destroy our ideas, that will remain for the youth of the future to come.

Dante, when I said three human lives buried, I meant to say that with us there is another young man by the name of Celestino Maderios that is to be electrocuted at the same time with us. He has been twice before in that horrible death-house, that should be destroyed with the hammers of real progress — that horrible house that will shame forever the future of the citizens of Massachusetts. They should destroy that house and put up a factory or school, to teach many of the hundreds of the poor orphan boys of the world.

Dante, I say once more to love and be nearest to your mother and the beloved ones in these sad days, and I am sure that with your brave heart and kind goodness they will feel less discomfort. And you will also not forget to love me a little for I do — O, Sonny! thinking so much and so often of you.

Best fraternal greetings to all the beloved ones, love and kisses to your little Ines and mother. Most hearty affectionate embrace.

[*1927*]

VANZETTI TO DANTE SACCO

I still hope, and we will fight until the last moment, to revindicate our right to live and to be free, but all the forces of the State and of the money and reaction are deadly against us because we are libertarians or anarchists.

I write little of this because you are now and yet too young to understand these things and other things of which I would like to reason with you.

But, if you do well, you will grow and understand your father's and my case and your father's and my principles, for which we will soon be put to death.

I tell you now that all that I know of your father, he is not a criminal, but one of the bravest men I ever knew. Some day you will understand what I am about to tell you. That your father has sacrificed everything dear and sacred to the human heart and soul for his fate in liberty and justice for all. That day you will be proud of your father, and if you come brave enough, you will take his place in the struggle between tyranny and liberty and you will vindicate his (our) names and our blood.

If we have to die now, you shall know, when you will be able to understand this tragedy in its fullest, how good and brave your father has been with you, your father and I, during these eight years of struggle, sorrow, passion, anguish and agony.

Even from now you shall be good, brave with your mother, with Ines, and with Susie — brave, good Susie [1] — and do all you can to console and help them.

I would like you to also remember me as a comrade and friend to your father, your mother and Ines, Susie and you, and I assure you that neither have I been a criminal, that I have committed no robbery and no murder, but only fought modestly to abolish crimes from among mankind and for the liberty of all.

Remember Dante, each one who will say otherwise of your father and I, is a liar, insulting innocent dead men who have been brave in their life. Remember and know also, Dante, that if your father and I would have been cowards and hypocrits and rinnegetors of our faith, we would not have been put to death. They would not even have convicted a lebbrous dog; not even executed a deadly poisoned scorpion on such evidence as that they framed against us. They would have given a new trial to a matricide and abitual felon on the evidence we presented for a new trial.

Remember, Dante, remember always these things; we are not criminals; they convicted us on a frame-up; they denied us a new trial; and if we will be executed after seven years, four months and seventeen days of unspeakable tortures and wrong, it is for what I have already told you; because we were for the poor and against the exploitation and oppression of the man by the man.

The documents of our case, which you and other ones will collect and preserve, will prove to you that your father, your mother, Ines, my family and I have sacrificed by and to a State Reason of the American Plutocratic reaction.

The day will come when you will understand the atrocious cause of the above written words, in all its fullness. Then you will honor us.

Now, Dante, be brave and good always. I embrace you.

---

[1] Faithful friend of Mrs. Sacco, with whom she and her children lived during the last years of the case.

P.S. I left the copy of *An American Bible* to your mother now, for she will like to read it, and she will give it to you when you will be bigger and able to understand it. Keep it for remembrance. It will also testify to you how good and generous Mrs. Gertrude Winslow has been with us all. Good-bye Dante.

[*1927*]

HEYWOOD BROUN

[1888–1939]

MORE than any other newspaperman of our time, he seemed like the personification of whatever is still romantic and courageous in his profession. Born in Brooklyn, New York, he was educated at the Horace Mann School and at Harvard. In 1912 he went to work on the *New York Tribune,* first as a rewrite man, next as a baseball reporter, and then as dramatic critic. In 1917 he was a correspondent with the A.E.F. in Europe. He came back a pacifist. After the war he worked for the *New York World* as dramatic and literary critic and at last as a daily columnist. His column, entitled "It Seems to Me," made him famous, for he succeeded in making a work of art out of this traditional journalistic form. Sometimes his pieces were light and charming, sometimes angry and bitter; occasionally they were highly personal, more often they dealt with important public events. Rarely were they anything but admirably written. What really distinguished them, however, was their viewpoint — the viewpoint of an impassioned democrat. His piece on the Sacco-Vanzetti case, in 1927, led to his being suppressed by the publisher of the *World.* He promptly resigned. In 1928 he returned to the *World,* but a magazine article he wrote in which he denied that the *World* was truly a liberal paper led to his being discharged. When the *World* was taken over by the Scripps-Howard *Telegram,* his column reappeared, and for ten years thereafter — right to the day of his death — it continued to appear. During this period he became one of America's great champions of the underdog. Consistently, unequivocally, he spoke for the underprivileged and the dispossessed. The climax of his career was his work as a founder and president of the American Newspaper Guild.

from

IT SEEMS TO ME

THE MIRACLE OF DEBS

Eugene V. Debs is dead and everybody says that he was a good man. He was no better and no worse when he served a sentence at Atlanta. I imagine that now it would be difficult to find many to defend the jailing of Debs. But at the time of the trial he received little support outside the radical ranks.

The problem involved was not simple. I hated the thing they did to Debs even at the time, and I was not then a pacifist. Yet I realize that almost nobody means precisely what he says when he makes the declaration, " I'm in favor of free speech." I think I mean it, but it is not difficult for me to imagine situations in which I would be gravely tempted to enforce silence on anyone who seemed to be dangerous to the cause I favored.

Free speech is about as good a cause as the world has ever known. But, like the poor, it is always with us and gets shoved aside in favor of things which seem at some given moment more vital. They never are more vital. Not when you look back at them from a distance. When the necessity of free speech is most important we shut it off. Everybody favors free speech in the slack moments when no axes are being ground.

It would have been better for America to have lost the war than to lose free speech. I think so, but I imagine it is a minority opinion. However, a majority right now can be drummed up to support the contention that it was wrong to put Debs in prison. That won't keep the country from sending some other Debs to jail in some other day when panic psychology prevails.

You see, there was another aspect to the Debs case, a point of view which really begs the question. It was foolish to send him to jail. His opposition to the war was not effective. A wise dictator, someone like Shaw's Julius Cæsar, for instance, would have given Debs better treatment than he got from our democracy.

Eugene Debs was a beloved figure and a tragic one. All his life he led lost causes. He captured the intense loyalty of a small section of our people, but I think that he affected the general thought of his time to a slight degree. Very few recognized him for what he was. It became the habit to speak of him a man molded after the manner of Lenin or Trotzky. And that was a grotesque misconception. People were constantly overlooking the fact that Debs was a Hoosier, a native product in every strand of him. He was a sort of Whitcomb Riley turned politically minded.

It does not seem to me that he was a great man. At least he was not a great intellect. But Woodward has argued persuasively that neither was George Washington. In summing up the Father of His Country, this most recent biographer says in effect that all Washington had was character. By any test such as that Debs was great. Certainly he had character. There was more of goodness in him than bubbled up in any other American of his day. He had some humor, or otherwise a religion might have been built up about him, for he was thoroughly Messianic. And it was a strange quirk which set this gentle, sentimental Middle-Westerner in the leadership of a party often fierce and militant.

Though not a Christian by any precise standard, Debs was the Christian-Socialist type. That, I'm afraid, is outmoded. He did feel that wrongs could be righted by touching the compassion of the world. Perhaps they can. It has not happened yet. Of cold, logical Marxianism, Debs possessed very little. He was never the brains of his party. I never met him, but I read many of his speeches, and most of them seemed to be second-rate utterances. But when his great moment came a miracle occurred. Debs made a speech to the judge and jury at Columbus after his conviction, and to me it seems one of the most beautiful and moving passages in the English language. He was for that one afternoon touched with inspiration. If anybody told me that tongues of fire danced upon his shoulders as he spoke, I would believe it.

Whenever I write anything about churches, ministers write in and say: " But of course you have no faith in miracles and the supernatural." And that is a long way off the target. For better or worse I can't stand out for a minute against mysticism. I think there are very few ministers ready to believe in as many miracles as I accept, because I cannot help myself. The speech which Debs made is to me a thing miraculous, because in it he displayed a gift for singing prose which was never with him on any other day of his life. And if you ask me, I'll also have to admit that I don't see how Lincoln came to the Gettysburg Address by any pathway which can be charted. There was in that nothing to suggest the utterance of a man who had been a small time politician and who might reasonably be expected to have formed his habits of speech in the rough and tumble school of give and take political debate in which his formative years were spent.

Something was in Debs, seemingly, that did not come out unless you saw him. I'm told that even those speeches of his which seemed to any reader indifferent stuff, took on vitality from his presence. A hard-bitten Socialist told me once, " Gene Debs is the only one who can get away with the sentimental flummery that's been tied onto Socialism in this country. Pretty nearly always it gives me a swift pain to go around to meetings and have people call me ' comrade.' That's a lot of bunk. But the funny part of it is that when Debs says 'comrade' it's all right. He means it. That old man with the burning eyes actually believes that there can be such a thing as the brotherhood of man. And that's not the funniest part of it. As long as he's around I believe it myself."

With the death of Debs, American Socialism is almost sure to grow more scientific, more bitter, possibly more effective. The party is not likely to forget that in Russia it was force which won the day, and not persuasion.

I've said that it did not seem to me that Debs was a great man in life, but he will come to greatness by and by. There are in him the seeds of symbolism. He was a sentimental Socialist, and that line has dwindled all over the world. Radicals talk now in terms of men and guns and power, and unless you get in at the beginning of the meeting and orient yourself, this could just as well be Security Leaguers or any other junkers in session.

The Debs idea will not die. To be sure, it was not his first at all. He carried on an older tradition. It will come to pass. There can be a brotherhood of man.

[*1926*]

SACCO AND VANZETTI

When at last Judge Thayer in a tiny voice passed sentence upon Sacco and Vanzetti, a woman in the court room said with terror: "It is death condemning life!"

The men in Charlestown Prison are shining spirits, and Vanzetti has spoken with an eloquence not known elsewhere within our time. They are too bright, we shield our eyes and kill them. We are the dead, and in us there is not feeling nor imagination nor the terrible torment of lust for justice. And in the city where we sleep smug gardeners walk to keep the grass above our little houses sleek and cut whatever blade thrusts up a head above its fellows.

"The decision is unbelievably brutal," said the chairman of the Defense Committee, and he was wrong. The thing is worthy to be believed. It has happened. It will happen again, and the shame is wider than that which must rest upon Massachusetts. I have never believed that the trial of Sacco and Vanzetti was one set apart from many by reason of the passion and prejudice which encrusted all the benches. Scratch through the varnish of any judgment seat and what will you strike but hate thick-clotted from centuries of angry verdicts? Did any man ever find power within his hand except to use it as a whip?

Governor Alvan T. Fuller never had any intention in all his investigation but to put a new and higher polish upon the proceedings. The justice of the business was not his concern. He hoped to make it respectable. He called old men from high places to stand behind his chair so that he might seem to speak with all the authority of a high priest or a Pilate.

What more can these immigrants from Italy expect? It is not every prisoner who has a president of Harvard University throw on the switch for him. And Robert Grant is not only a former judge but one of the most popular dinner guests in Boston. If this is a lynching, at least the fish peddler and his friend the factory hand may take unction to their souls that they will die at the hands of men in dinner coats or academic gowns, according to the conventionalities required by the hour of execution.

Already too much has been made of the personality of Webster Thayer. To sympathizers of Sacco and Vanzetti he has seemed a man with a cloven hoof. But in no usual sense of the term is this man a villain. Although probably not a great jurist, he is without doubt as capable and conscientious as the average Massachusetts judge, and if that's enough to warm him in wet weather by all means let him stick the compliment against his ribs.

Webster Thayer has a thousand friends. He has courage, sincerity and convictions. Judge Thayer is a good man, and when he says that he made every effort to give a fair trial to the anarchists brought before him, undoubtedly he thinks it and he means it. Quite often I've heard the remark: " I wonder how that man sleeps at night? " On this point I have no first hand information, but I venture to guess that he is no more beset with uneasy dreams than most of us. He saw his duty and he thinks he did it.

And Governor Fuller, also, is not in any accepted sense of the word a miscreant. Before becoming Governor he manufactured bicycles. Nobody was cheated by his company. He loves his family and pays his debts. Very much he desires to be Governor again, and there is an excellent chance that this ambition will be gratified. Other governors of Massachusetts have gone far, and it is not fantastic to assume that some day he might be President. His is not a master mind, but he is a solid and substantial American, chiming in heartily with all our national ideals and aspirations.

To me the tragedy of the conviction of Sacco and Vanzetti lies in the fact that this was not a deed done by crooks and knaves. In that case we would have a campaign with the slogan " Turn the rascals out," and set up for a year or two a reform administration. Nor have I had much patience with any who would like to punish Thayer by impeachment or any other process. Unfrock him and his judicial robes would fall upon a pair of shoulders not different by the thickness of a fingernail. Men like Holmes and Brandeis do not grow on bushes. Popular government, as far as the eye can see, is always going to be administered by the Thayers and Fullers.

It has been said that the question at issue was not the guilt or inno-cence of Sacco and Vanzetti but whether or not they received a fair trial. I will admit that this commands my interest to some extent, but still I think it is a minor phase in the whole matter. From a Utopian point of view the trial was far from fair, but it was not more biased than a thousand which take place in this country every year. It has been pointed out that the public prosecutor neglected to call certain witnesses because their testimony would not have been favorable to his case. Are there five district attorneys, is there one, in the whole country who would do otherwise?

Again Professor Frankfurter has most clearly shown that the prose-cution asked a trick question in regard to the pistol and made the expert seem to testify far more concretely than he was willing to commit him-self. That was very wrong, but not unique. Our judicial processes are so arranged that it is to the interest of district attorneys to secure con-victions rather than to ascertain justice, and if it would profit his case, there is not one who would not stoop to confuse the issue in the minds of the jurymen.

Eleven of the twelve who convicted Sacco and Vanzetti are still alive, and Governor Fuller talked to them. He reports somewhat naively that they all told him that they considered the trial fair. Did he expect them to report, " Why, no, Governor, we brought in a verdict of guilty just out of general depravity "?

By now there has been a long and careful sifting of the evidence in

714

the case. It is ridiculous to say that Sacco and Vanzetti are being rail-roaded to the chair. The situation is much worse than that. This is a thing done cold-bloodedly and with deliberation. But care and delib-eration do not guarantee justice. Even if every venerable college presi-dent in the country tottered forward to say "guilty" they could not alter facts. The tragedy of it all lies in the fact that though a Southern moun-tain man may move more quickly to a dirty deed of violence, his feet are set no more firmly in the path of prejudice than a Lowell ambling se-dately to a hanging.

I said of Calvin Coolidge that I admired his use of "I do not choose," but he was dealing with a problem wholly personal, and had every right to withhold his reasons. For Governor Fuller I can't say the same. These are the lives of others with which he is dealing. In his fairly long statement he answers not a single point which has been made against the justice of the conviction. The deliberations of himself and his associates were secret, and seemingly it is his intention that they shall remain secret. A gentleman does not investigate and tell.

I've said these men have slept, but from now on it is our business to make them toss and turn a little, for a cry should go up from many mil-lion voices before the day set for Sacco and Vanzetti to die. We have a right to beat against tight minds with our fists and shout a word into the ears of the old men. We want to know, we will know — "Why?"
[*1927*]

TWO-GUN CROWLEY

One hundred and fifty heavily armed policemen fought for two hours with gas and revolvers and ax and captured Two-Gun Crowley. With him they took his girl and his confederate.

It was good police work, sharp pursuit by the detectives and a diffi-cult task carried out efficiently. In spite of the number of attackers the work was dangerous, for desperate armed men in hiding can easily pick off many who seek to dislodge them.

And credit should go to Commissioner Mulrooney. They say that he prides himself on being a good cop. That compliment he deserves, although some may withhold complete approval of his abilities as an executive.

But if the police came out of the Crowley man hunt with credit you and I did not. It is wasteful and an unimaginative way of life to spend so much effort and risk of life upon the capture of a criminal when such indifference and carelessness have been shown in the matter of his genesis. We should catch our gunmen younger and long before they have taken their posts behind a barricade prepared to shoot it out.

The existence of a Two-Gun Crowley is not accidental. In all probability he will be executed and the community will sit back with the feeling that the case is ended and a problem has been solved. Then we will wait until some other gangster very like him provides a similar city melodrama and a first page story.

Even more important than catching a Crowley, convicting and punishing him is the task of finding out what he is all about. You must dig for the whys. This is more vital than even the finest detective work in tracking down the outlaws. We need another sort of detective. It is up to us to create a class of men capable of solving the intricate and subtle trail which comes before the crime.

Here he is: Francis Crowley, 20 years old, 5 feet 3 inches tall, a little more than 100 pounds in weight. He was born in a New York slum. Before he was a year old his mother turned him over to a woman who ran a baby farm. His first job was with a gang of laborers, and he quit this after a little while to steal parcels off the rear ends of trucks. And a little later he became an automobile thief.

By now we have our subject well on the way to the final crimes for which he was arrested. And the law will concern itself with those episodes and leave the earlier trail alone.

It has been charged that many of the more modern students of crime tend to sentimentalize the criminal. It seems to me that the approach which they suggest is far more realistic than the notion that an electric chair can be a complete solvent for a social problem.

Take the background of Crowley: Slum-bred, under-nourished, undereducated, underpaid. Not every man who goes through this mill becomes a vicious criminal. But I rather feel that may be the way to bet. At any rate, no one will pretend this furnishes a reasonable school for citizenship.

It would take money to tear down all the hovels in which the Crowleys are born. But it also takes a lot of money to catch the adult

Crowleys. We might very likely need something as radical as free medicine and milk to raise up the slum children physically stunted by lack of nourishment and sun.

There is, I believe, a very possible connection between the meagerness of this man and his passion to play the desperado. He couldn't have been much good at heavy labor — this skinny 5-foot waif. To him a gun provided ego satisfaction.

I am not consumed with pity for Crowley the individual. But it would be dull not to realize that he, like his sort, is governed by precise rules of cause and effect. And that is where the guilt of you and me creeps in. We can get excited about a killer. Ten thousand stand to cheer the police in their dangerous work of digging him out of a top floor apartment. Very probably many of the citizens gathered around would have been glad to volunteer their assistance in the man hunt. The police cut holes through the roof to get at the desperadoes.

All right! But how about more radical digging and deeper cutting? Can't somebody lift for us the roof of the house in which Crowley was born? Let us have slits through the tenement walls of the place in which he lived. If he went to a city school we might inquire and try to ascertain in just what respects the system failed him.

It is true that as things stand he is an enemy of society. But inevitably there is some point along the journey where we failed him. I am not pretending that the task is easy or that psychiatry, to mention one phase of the study, has advanced to the point of ultimate wisdom. But we should try.

If the city had never produced more than a single Crowley it would be enough to track him down, try him and convict him. But we know of gangsters who have been and of those who will come after.

And so I suggest that there ought to be some court intent upon facts far more fundamental. The detectives of the force did skillful work in solving the problem, "Where is Crowley?" It still remains for us to meet that even more important query, "Why is Crowley?"

[*1931*]

MICHAEL GOLD

[1896–   ]

THE SON of working-class immigrant parents, he was born on the East Side of New York, one of the city's slum areas and at that time a red-light district. At twelve he went to work in a factory making incandescent gas mantles, and later he worked for the Adams Express Company as a driver's helper and night watchman. When he was nineteen he went to Boston, began to work for radical papers, and became a labor organizer. When he returned to New York, he got a job with the socialist newspaper, the *Call*. After that he wandered across the country, sometimes working as a laborer, sometimes as a newspaperman. For two years he lived in Mexico. When he again returned to New York, he got a job on the *Liberator,* then edited by Max Eastman. Subsequently he was co-editor with Claude McKay — until the magazine failed. He was one of the founders of the *New Masses* and has long written a column for the *Daily Worker*. In short, he is an outspoken Communist and his writings usually express his politics. It happens, however, that his magnum opus is an autobiographical volume, *Jews Without Money* (1930), which has been read and admired by thousands of anti-Communist readers. For it is not a " party " document but simply a vivid and touching picture of Jewish proletarian life, protesting against the conditions suffered by the poor immigrants of our large cities.

---

from

JEWS WITHOUT MONEY

MUSHROOMS IN BRONX PARK

1

The summer. It was painful to draw one's breath. The sun blazed with sheer murder all day. At night, steam rose from the ghetto stones like a Russian vapor bath. There was never any relief from the weight pressing on our necks and skulls. People were sick, doctors were busy.

The Jewish babies whimpered and died. The flies thrived. Every one was nervous; there were quarrels down the airshaft. I would wake in the dead of night and hear the tenement groaning and twisting in bedrooms. People went exploring for sleep as for a treasure. Hollow-eyed ghosts tramped the streets all night. Families slept on the docks, in the parks, on the roofs. But the world was hot.

2

Some nights my mother laid bedding on the sidewalk before our tenement. While she and my father fanned themselves on the stoop and gossiped with the neighbors, my sister and I slept in the street.

The street cars, the wagons, the talk, the sudden shrieks, the million shoes of passers-by grinding like an emery wheel on the pavements did not disturb our sleep. But one night something did happen that left a permanent mark on my mind.

It was the evening before the Fourth of July. There was the usual debauch of patriotism. Kids were shooting off toy cannons, firecrackers and their fingers in every street. The night was lit with a city's bombardment. Grinning Italians shot their revolvers at the sky. Roman candles popped red, blue and yellow balls at the sky. Pinwheels whirled, Catherine wheels fizzed and turned, torpedoes crackled, and rockets flew like long golden winged snakes above the tenements. It was fun. But I tired at last and fell asleep on the bedding spread by my mother in front of the tenement.

I had slept an hour, when some careless person threw a lighted cannon cracker out of a window. It exploded on the pillow beside my face. I leaped up with a scream of fright, and ran to my mother. I trembled and sobbed, and saw my blood stream. A big slice of flesh had been torn from my left shoulder; I still bear the scar.

This shattered meat healed quickly; the blood was soon forgotten. What remained was the nightmare. For weeks after that Fourth of July I woke every night, with a scream. I was re-living the explosion. My parents did not know what to do. The fat and cheerful Dr. Axelrod gave me pink pills to take. They did not help. The thin and gloomy young Dr. Solow mumbled something about sending me to the country. But was that possible? my parents asked. So he gave me greenish medicine to take. It did not help.

I was losing weight. My mother took the advice of a neighbor and called in a Speaker-woman, Baba Sima the witch-doctor. It was she who cured me.

3

There were many such old women on the East Side. They were held in great respect. The East Side worshiped doctors, but in nervous cases, or in mishaps of the personal life, it sometimes reverted to medievalism.

Lovers sought philters of the old Babas, to win a victory over a rival in love. Deserted wives paid these women money to model little wax figures of their wandering husbands and torture them until the false one returned.

Baba Sima called one summer night, as I lay pale and exhausted by the dark mental shadows. She was a humpbacked old crone in a kerchief and apron, with red rheumy eyes, and protruding belly. Her flabby mouth was devoid of teeth. It was sunk so deeply that her nose and chin almost met. She was dressed as poorly as any old synagogue beggar. She sniffled and panted after the climb upstairs, and my mother gave her tea. She talked a bit, took a pinch of snuff, then waddled into the bedroom to look at me.

" *Nu, nu,*" she said, cheerfully, wiping her nose and sweaty face with a rag out of her mysterious satchel, " if it was only a firecracker, I can cure him. The boy has been frightened, but I will pass the fright away. He will be sound in a few weeks, with God's help."

She turned me on my stomach, and with a blunt knife traced magic designs on my bare back, mumbling over and over in singsong:

> " *Tanti beovati,*
> *Tanti sabatanu.*
> *Tanti Keeliati,*
> *Tanti lamachtanu.*"

" To him, and to her, and to us, and to it! The serpent and the fire, the ocean and the sun! God is Jehovah, and Jehovah is God! Rushyat! Cushyat! Cum! Tum! Sum! "

She rubbed my back lightly with a pungent oil, and wiped her hands. The first treatment was over. My mother paid her a dollar and invited her to more tea. The old lady grew amazingly greedy; she drank four glasses of tea heaped high with my mother's best rose-leaf jam. She gobbled at least a dozen butter cookies. Then she sniffled off to her next call.

I was left irritable and skeptical. This foreign hocus-pocus did not appeal to me, an American boy. I was ashamed of it. I feared the boys in my gang would hear of it, and would tease me. My mother stroked my hair.

"My dear," said my mother, "no one will tease you. Don't you want to be cured of your fright? It isn't good to be frightened in this world, one can't go through life with a fright. One is not a man. This is a famous Speaker; your poppa knew her in Roumania. She knows more than many Doctors. She learned her wisdom from a famous Zaddik. She is sure to make you well."

The next visit Baba Sima went through the same ritual and drank another gallon of tea with dozens of cookies. The third visit she left a prescription. My mother was to walk through the pushcart market on Orchard Street, and buy a glass at the first pushcart selling household things. She was forbidden to bargain, but to pay the first price the peddler demanded. The same night, I was to take this glass to the East River. If there was a moon, I was to drink a glass of river water; no moon, two glasses. Then I was to throw the glass into the river, and repeat the words: Cum, tum, sum.

I did this. On the fourth visit the Magic-Maker prescribed a paste of horse-droppings gathered in the street; mixed with a spider's web, honey, grits, thyme, my own urine, and pepper. This was smeared on my forehead for a week.

On the fourth visit the Magic-Maker brought many things in her bag. She set them out in the kitchen; a little tin pail, a ladle, and some lead. She melted the lead over our kitchen stove, muttering weird rhymes. Then she poured the lead from the melting ladle into the pail. The lead hissed and steamed as it dropped into the water. As it cooled, it took on jagged outlines. The Magic-Maker regarded the lead long and painfully. Her toothless jaws worked; her eyes watered as if she were crying. She took many pinches of snuff.

"It is a horse!" she announced triumphantly at last. Our family group, watching her fearfully in the gaslight, was startled. "Give me another glass of tea; my cure is done, it is a horse!"

We stared at the chunk of jagged lead. Yes, we assured each other in amazement, it had taken on the shape of a horse. And the next night, exactly at midnight, my father led me into the livery stable, and I whispered into the ear of one of the coach horses:

"My fright in your body; God is Jehovah," I said, giving the horse an apple which he munched sleepily. "Cum! Tum! Sum!"

Thus I was cured. The nightmare did not return. I woke no longer screaming in the night. Yet I was skeptical, and could not believe in the magic. I asked Vassa the stable-hand whether the horse now woke at night, screaming. He said the horse didn't. But I was cured. That greedy, dirty, foolish old woman knew some deep secrets, evidently. She had cured me. I never told my friends, I was too ashamed. But I marveled that summer, and not even my parents could explain it all. They had not heard of the greater magic: Suggestion.

4

After I was cured, our family life went back to its normal summer routine. My father left us mornings for his work, my mother cooked and baked, my sister Esther played jacks and skipped the rope with her girls. I played with my own gang, I fought, stole apples, read Buffalo Bill stories, went swimming, watched the prostitutes. At night my father told fairy-tales to his admiring friends, and we drank beer. Then we searched for sleep on the roof, or on the sidewalks. The world was hot.

Every Sunday morning in summer my father itched to be off somewhere. He did not want to stay in town on his one free day. But my mother hated trips. When he rode to Coney Island to swim in the ocean my mother never went along. She hated the pushing and excitement of a million frantic people.

"It's a madhouse," she grumbled. "Why must I fight a lot of hooligans because it is Sunday? I can rest better sitting here on my own stoop."

She made my father angry. He loved swimming; he could swim way out beyond the lifelines. And he loved, too, as much as I did, the razzle-dazzle, the mechanical blare, the gaudy savage joys of Coney Island.

"But the fare is cheap, only a nickel," he said. "Where else can one go for a nickel?"

"I don't care," said my mother, "it's a madhouse. Coney Island is a place for monkeys."

" Bah! " my father sneered. " You are an old Baba grandmother. You would like to sit by the stove all your life! "

" No," said my mother, calmly, " in Hungary I went to places. I used to walk there in the fields and the woods. But Coney Island is different. It has no fields."

" *Nu*," said my father, irritably, " let us go to the fields then. I will take you to Bronx Park next Sunday."

" Has it a forest there? " asked my mother.

" Yes, it has a forest," said my father.

" *Nu*, we will see then," said my mother, casually, " maybe I will go." She was not enthusiastic. My mother had the peasant's aversion to travel. In her Hungarian village no one ever traveled far, except to America. The East Side was her village now, and she saw no reason for leaving it even on Sunday. She still lives on the East Side, on the same street, in the same tenement, an unhurried peasant. She has never been out of New York City. There are millions of such peasants in New York.

5

Sunday came. My mother had evidently decided to make the trip to Bronx Park. She rose at six to get things ready. She ironed a dress for Esther, a waist for me; she darned our stockings, and packed a lunch of salami sandwiches, pickles, cake, oranges and hard-boiled eggs. Then she swept the house, cooked breakfast, and woke us.

" Stand up! " she said, yanking off our bedclothes.

" Why so early? " my father groaned sleepily.

" We are going to Bronx Park," said my mother. " Have you forgotten? "

At breakfast my sister and I were crazy with excitement over the trip. My mother had to slap us. She was flustered and grumbly; the thought of travel confused her.

In the elevated train her face flushed purple with heat and bewilderment. No wonder; the train was worse than a cattle car. It was crowded with people to the point of nausea. Excited screaming mothers, fathers sagging under enormous lunch baskets, children yelling, puking and running under every one's legs, an old graybeard fighting with the conductor, a gang of tough Irish kids in baseball suits who persisted in swinging from the straps — sweating bodies and exasperated nerves —

grinding lurching train, sudden stops when a hundred bodies battered into each other, bedlam of legs and arms, sneezing, spitting, cursing, sighing — a super-tenement on wheels.

Northward to the Bronx! And at every station new mobs of frenzied sweating families loaded with lunch baskets and babies burst through the doors. There was no room for them, but they made it for themselves by standing on our feet.

My father cursed each time a fat wet matron flopped in his lap or trod on his corns.

This was New York on Sunday. All the trains and street cars were crowded like this. Seven million people rushing to find a breath of fresh air! " *Pfui!* " said my father.

" In Roumania it is a little walk to the country," he said. " Here it is a fight for one's life. What a crazy land! "

But my mother became happier as the train rolled on. She leaned out of the window and smiled. In the streets below, the solid palisades of tenement had disappeared. There were small houses, each set among green weedy lots, and there were trees.

" It's a pleasure to see green things again," she said. " Look, another tree! I am glad we came, Herman! When we come to Bronx Park I will take off my shoes and walk in the grass. I haven't done it for fifteen years."

" They will arrest you," snarled my father, as he glared at the fat Jewish woman standing next to him, who persisted in grabbing him around the neck each time the train lurched.

" I want to pick daisies! " cried my little sister.

" Yes, yes, my darling," said my mother, fondly, " daisies and mushrooms, too. I will show you how to find mushrooms. It is more fun than picking daisies."

6

At last the Bronx Park! My father bought us popcorn to eat, and red balloons. Then we walked through some green fields. My mother sighed as she sniffed the fragrant air.

" Ach," said my happy mother, " it's like Hungary! There is much room, and the sky is so big and blue! One can breathe here! "

So we walked until we came to a menagerie. Here we saw a gang of crazy monkeys in a cage. They were playing tag. We fed them peanuts and watched them crack open the shells. Then we saw a lion, two tigers, a white bear, some snakes, birds, and an elephant. All of them we gave peanuts.

Then we walked far into a big lonesome country. It had a big field with no one in it. It had a forest at one end. We looked for signs: KEEP OFF THE GRASS. There were no signs. So we walked into the middle of the field, and found a wonderful tree. This tree we made our own.

We spread newspapers under the tree, and my mother laid out the lunch. We were hungry after our long ride and walk. So we ate the salami sandwiches and other good things.

My father drank two bottles of beer. Then he stretched on his back, smoked his pipe, and looked at the sky. He sang Roumanian shepherd songs. Then he fell asleep, and snored.

My mother cleaned away the newspapers. Then she looked to see if no policeman was near. There was no policeman. So she took off her shoes and stockings and walked around on the grass.

My sister and I left her and went hunting for daisies. We found some and brought them to her. She wove for us two daisy crowns out of them, the sort children wear in Hungary.

Then my mother took our hands. "Come," she said, in a whisper, "while poppa sleeps we will go into the forest and hunt mushrooms."

My father heard the whisper. His snores abruptly ended.

"Don't get lost," he mumbled, not opening his sleepy eyes.

"Pooh," said my mother, "lost in a forest? Me?"

"All right," said my father, turning on his side and snoring again.

7

In the forest everything suddenly became cool and green. It was like going into a mysterious house. The trees were like walls, their leaves made a ceiling. Clear, sweet voices sang through the house. These were the birds. The birds lived in the house. Little ants and beetles ran about under our feet. They lived on the floor of the house.

I smelled queer, garlicky smells. I saw a large gold coin lying in a bed of green. I looked closer, and knew I was fooled. It was sunlight. The sun made other golden lines and circles. I heard running water.

My mother walked in front of us. Her face looked younger. She stopped mysteriously every few minutes, and sniffed the air.

"I am smelling out the mushrooms," she explained. "I know how to do that. I learned it in Hungary. Each mushroom has its own smell. The best ones grow under oak trees."

" I want to pick some," said Esther.

" No! " said my mother, sharply, " you must never do that. You are an American child, and don't know about these things. Some mushrooms are poison! They will kill you! Never pick them! "

" Do they come on strings? " I asked.

" Those are the grocery store mushrooms," explained my mother. " Ach, America, the thief, where children only see dry, dead mushrooms in grocery stores! Wait, I will show you! "

There was a flush of excitement on her black, gypsy face. We were surprised at our mother. She was always so slow-moving and careful. Now she jumped over big rocks and puddles and laughed like a girl.

" Stop! I think there are mushrooms under those leaves! " she said. " Let me scratch a little and find out. Yes, yes! do you see? My nose is still sharp after all these years! What a pretty silver cap it has! It is a birch mushroom. Its parents are those birch trees. When mushrooms grow near pine trees they are green, and taste of pine. But the oak mushroom is the finest of all. It is a beautiful brown."

She broke off pieces of the mushroom for us to nibble. " It is better with salt," she said. " But how good it is! It is not like the rubbish they grow here in cellars! No, the American mushrooms have no worth. They taste and look like paper. A real mushroom should taste of its own earth or tree. In Hungary we know that! "

We followed her, as she poked around under the trees and bushes for her beloved mushrooms. She found many, and lifted her skirt to make a bag for them. Each new mushroom reminded her of Hungary and of things she had never told us. She talked in a low, caressing voice. She stooped to the mushrooms, and her eyes shone like a child's.

" Ach, how people love the mushrooms in Hungary! In the season every one is in the forest with a big basket to hunt. We had our own favorite spots where we went year after year. We never plucked mushrooms, but cut them close to the roots, like this. It means they will grow again next year. Two other Jewish girls and I always went hunting together."

" Momma, can mushrooms talk to each other? "

" Some people say so. Some people say that at night mushrooms not only talk, but dance with each other. They turn into jolly old men with beards. In the morning they become mushrooms again.

"Birds talk to each other, too, people say. I used to know the names of all the birds, and their songs. I knew good snakes and bad, and killed the bad ones with a stick. I knew where to find blueberries and huckleberries. I could walk twenty miles in a forest and find my way back. Once, two girls and I were lost in a forest for days and found our way back. Ach, what fun there was in Hungary!"

Suddenly my mother flung her arms around each of us, and kissed Esther and me.

"Ach, Gott!" she said, "I'm so happy in a forest! You American children don't know what it means! I am happy!"

[1930]

EDNA ST. VINCENT MILLAY

[1892–   ]

MISS MILLAY has had a long and distinguished career and is now the most widely read of our serious poets. She was born in Rockland, Maine, and was educated in local schools and at Vassar, from which she was graduated in 1917. While at college she won an intercollegiate poetry prize. When she went down to New York she soon became prominent in the bohemian literary life of the city, which then flourished in Greenwich Village. She was active in the Provincetown Theatre and in the Theatre Guild. She wrote the libretto for an opera called *The King's Henchman* — music by Deems Taylor — which the Metropolitan Opera House produced in 1927. In 1923 her *The Harpweaver and Other Poems* was awarded the Pulitzer Prize. Other successful volumes have been *The Buck in the Snow* (1928), *Wine from These Grapes* (1934), *Conversation at Midnight* (1937), and *Huntsman, What Quarry?* (1939). Miss Millay has often been interested in liberal causes — notably the Sacco-Vanzetti case — and in libertarian ideals, and these interests have found expression in her poetry. Her most recent poems have been tributes to Britain.

JUSTICE DENIED IN MASSACHUSETTS

Let us abandon then our gardens and go home
And sit in the sitting-room.
Shall the larkspur blossom or the corn grow under this cloud?
Sour to the fruitful seed
Is the cold earth under this cloud,
Fostering quack and weed, we have marched upon but cannot conquer;
We have bent the blades of our hoes against the stalks of them.

Let us go home, and sit in the sitting-room.
Not in our day
Shall the cloud go over and the sun rise as before,

728

Beneficent upon us
Out of the glittering bay,
And the warm winds be blown inward from the sea
Moving the blades of corn
With a peaceful sound.
Forlorn, forlorn,
Stands the blue hay-rack by the empty mow.
And the petals drop to the ground,
Leaving the tree unfruited.
The sun that warmed our stooping backs and withered the weed up
    rooted —
We shall not feel it again.
We shall die in darkness, and be buried in the rain.

What from the splendid dead
We have inherited —
Furrows sweet to the grain, and the weed subdued —
See now the slug and the mildew plunder.
Evil does overwhelm
The larkspur and the corn;
We have seen them go under.

Let us sit here, sit still,
Here in the sitting-room until we die;
At the step of Death on the walk, rise and go;
Leaving to our children's children this beautiful doorway,
And this elm,
And a blighted earth to till
With a broken hoe.
[*1928*]

CZECHO–SLOVAKIA

If there were balm in Gilead, I would go
To Gilead for your wounds, unhappy land,
Gather you balsam there, and with this hand,

Made deft by pity, cleanse and bind and sew
And drench with healing, that your strength might grow,
(Though love be outlawed, kindness contraband)
And you, O proud and felled, again might stand;
But where to look for balm, I do not know.
The oils and herbs of mercy are so few;
Honour's for sale; allegiance has its price;
The barking of a fox has bought us all;
We save our skins a craven hour or two. —
While Peter warms him in the servants' hall
The thorns are platted and the cock crows twice.

[*1938*]

SAY THAT WE SAW SPAIN DIE

Say that we saw Spain die. O splendid bull, how well you fought!
Lost from the first.
         . . . the tossed, the replaced, the watchful *torero* with
    gesture elegant and spry,
Before the dark, the tiring but the unglazed eye deploying the bright
    cape,
Which hid for once not air, but the enemy indeed, the authentic shape,
A thousand of him, interminably into the ring released . . . the turning
    beast at length between converging colours caught.

Save for the weapons of its skull, a bull
Unarmed, considering, weighing, charging
Almost a world, itself without ally.

Say that we saw the shoulders more than the mind confused, so pro-
    fusely
Bleeding from so many more than the accustomed barbs, the game gone
    vulgar, the rules abused.

Say that we saw Spain die from loss of blood, a rustic reason in a rein-
    forced
And proud punctilious land, no *espada* —

730

A hundred men unhorsed,
A hundred horses gored, and the afternoon aging, and the crowd growing restless (all, all so much later than planned),
And the big head heavy, sliding forward in the sand, and the tongue dry
   with sand, — no *espada*
Toward that hot neck, for the delicate and final thrust, having dared
   thrust forth his hand.

[*1938*]

LINCOLN STEFFENS

[1866–1936]

HE WAS born in San Francisco and educated at the University of California, receiving his bachelor's degree in 1889. Then for three years he was abroad studying philosophy in the universities of Berlin, Heidelberg, Leipzig, and Paris. On his return he went into newspaper work, joining the staff of the New York *Evening Post*. After six years there, he worked for four years as city editor of the *Commercial Advertiser*. From 1902 to 1906 he was managing editor of *McClure's Magazine*, from 1906 to 1911 associate editor of the *American Magazine* and *Everybody's*. From almost the beginning of his career he was known as a first-rate observer of the political scene, and soon he became more than an observer — he became an active reformer. He was perhaps the most famous of the "muckrakers" — the clan of journalists who devoted themselves to exposing corruption in government and finance. His books *The Shame of the Cities* (1904) and *The Struggle for Self-Government* (1906) were widely read. During the war he was a free-lance writer, advised men in high places, participated in the Bullitt Mission to Russia. In 1931 he published his great *Autobiography* — an engaging and acute record of a lifetime of adventuring in journalism and politics.

---

from

AUTOBIOGRAPHY OF LINCOLN STEFFENS

THE PEACEMAKER

Armistice Day — and night — was a spectacle of joy in Paris. The French government let the people have their way, and their way was singing and dancing, madly, gladly, sadly. There were regrets and doubts, but the rejoicing prevailed. And the next days — after joy — came hope, the hope for peace, a real peace. Was it possible? No more wars? The sophisticated sneered, the newspapers mocked, but there was a chance. President Wilson was coming; and the people, the French, the Germans, the English — all the common peoples were putting their hope in the American president whose advent was Messianic.

Wilson came on a ship, with a cargo of commissioners, secretaries, secret service men, and correspondents, all in the ordinary, but *Le Temps*, the leading government organ, described his approach as the French people saw it. The great American prophet of peace was sailing on a cloud through the air to save the Old World, and the cynical editor predicted that the savior would come down to earth for his landing. But there were some fears even in that quarter that he might not fall so hard, that he might indeed make the peace without conquest that he had promised. The Germans had so understood his words; the French folk did; you could hear that in what they were saying all about you. And the Italians — the simple masses, who wanted peace, believed that he had said and meant peace. Our American propaganda, the masterly work of George Creel and the president, had lifted to the pitch of faith the simple, blinding hope of a continent. No European leader, whether reactionary or radical, could have won such trust; the old peoples have had experience of their own leaders; but " Meester Wilson " was a new kind of leader, and his kind of people, the American soldiers, had kept their word. The Europeans believed in us, in our president, but they feared for him. And they prayed for him. Literally. When Wilson traveled by train from his port of landing to Paris, by night, we heard that peasant families had been seen here and there all along the way kneeling beside the track in the dark to pray for him and his mission. And in Paris, when he arrived and had rested, the streets were packed mile on mile to watch him pass in parade, quiet crowds who wanted to look into his face to see, as they said, whether he meant and had the strength to do what he promised.

It was said that he understood this and that he wished to make those hops of his to London and to Rome to gather up the confidence and the strength of the people. I went along with him on those trips; the press was invited in mass, and we could see and hear and feel that the American president was making himself the world leader of all the democracies, the hope of the race. He succeeded in that. When he returned to Paris to go to work with the premiers and peace delegates, Woodrow Wilson was the spokesman of public opinion and the potential ruler of Europe. Whether he realized it or no, we newspaper men knew it, and we knew, too, that the statesmen of Europe knew it and feared it. They had to yield to his first demands: for open sessions of the peace conference, for open covenants openly arrived at. If he had gone on to his other terms! But open sessions was enough; even that was impossible, they said, in Europe, as impossible as open sessions of a Legislature or a political convention in America! How could burglars plan burglary, how could conquerors divide the loot of empire, in public? The imperialists had to agree to open sessions, but Mr. Wilson had to agree to private meetings of the " big four " to prepare for the formal, public meetings. The correspondents fought for press tickets, and they reported solemnly the staged shows which the world watched till we learned what they were. After that the correspondents hung around the lobbies, traded gossip, cultivated leaks, and so watched as best they could the private, very secret sessions of the four or five peacemakers in fact; even the little allies' representatives were excluded from these sessions and depended in part at least upon the press for information. The commanding victors alone made that treaty of peace. They were dividing the earth, and their problem was to manipulate and, if possible, break the American president, break his plan, break his personal strength, which they called his obstinacy, break his power and popularity. And the French led in this process of attrition. Clemenceau was the man who broke Wilson. Wilson was pitied, Clemenceau was execrated or adored, for this; but the conflict of these two men goes deeper, I think. It was a struggle of American idealism and good will against French realism, of the American reformer, the Anglo-Saxon liberal, against the intelligent French radical; and when the good American president fell before the wicked French premier, it was our moral American culture that went down under the clear, logical, conscious intelligence of French culture.

On the afternoon of the third day of the private meetings of the premiers two French newspaper men came in to the American press room at the Hotel Crillon. There were only a few American correspondents there. It was teatime, as the Frenchmen remarked in some surprise, and no tea; they did not know that tea is an English, not an American, institution. We were working when they marched in like a couple of gendarmes, but I rose to meet them, and others came up to make them welcome. They were polite for a few moments; then they said that they had come to verify a bit of news. Had we heard of a little scene at the meeting of the president and the premiers? We looked at one another, we Americans, and I said, " No, nothing. Why? What had they heard? " They exchanged glances, and one of them spoke for them both.

"We heard — but only from French sources, and we can't use it unless we get American confirmation of it — we heard that M. Clemenceau challenged M. Wilson to make a permanent peace. Have you heard anything about the scene?"

"No," I said for myself, and the other Americans present nodded no. "Tell us about it," I urged. "Describe the scene."

Then one of them told how, when the president and the premiers sat down at the table that morning and were about to proceed to business, M. Clemenceau, who was fiddling with his gray silk gloves, said, "One moment, gentlemen. I desire before we go any further to be made clear on one very essential point." The French reporter was entering into his story; he mimicked Clemenceau, drawing tight and smooth his little silk gloves, and bowing sweetly and smiling sardonically. And the reporter acted the parts he quoted.

The president and the premiers halted and looked up expectantly at M. Clemenceau, who said: "I have heard something about a permanent peace. There has been a great deal of talk about a peace to end war forever, and I am interested in that. All Frenchmen would like to make permanent peace. But I would like to know — all the French would like to know — whether you mean it, the permanent peace."

He looked at his colleagues and they nodded.

"So," Clemenceau said, "you really mean it! Well, it is possible. We can do it; we can make the permanent peace. And we French need, we very much need, the permanent peace. Every time you, our neighbors, get into a fight, France is the battlefield, and our population, our armies, do not increase. If there is not an end of wars we French may be all wiped out some day. So, you see, it is we French more than you remote Americans, Mr. President, more than you safe islanders, Mr. Lloyd George, who require the security of the real peace. But we French cannot quite believe that you, our friends, neighbors, allies — that you really mean what you say. Do you, Mr. President?"

Mr. Wilson did.

"And you, Mr. Premier?"

Mr. Lloyd George did.

And the Italians did, of a certainty, yes.

"Very important," M. Clemenceau muttered, as if convinced, as if the whole prospect were changing, and his whole policy. "Very important. We can make this permanent peace; we can remove all the causes of war and set up no new causes of war. It is very, very important what you say, what you have been so long saying, Mr. President. We here now have the opportunity to make a peace that shall last forever, and the French people, diminishing, will be safe. And you are sure you propose to seize this opportunity?"

They did, they emphatically did.

Clemenceau clucked in his throat; he pressed tight down the fingers of his gloves. "And — you have counted the cost of such a peace?" he asked.

There was some hesitation at that. "What costs?"

"Well," said the French intelligence, "if we give up all future wars — if we are to prevent war, we must give up our empires and all hope of empire. You, Mr. Lloyd George, you English will have to come out of India, for example; we French shall have to come out of North Africa; and you Americans, Mr. President, you must get out of the Philippines and Porto Rico and leave Cuba alone and — Mexico. Oh, we can all go to these and other countries, but as tourists, traders, travelers; we cannot any more govern them or exploit or have the inside track in them. We cannot possess the keys to trade routes and spheres of influence. And, yes, we shall have to tear down our tariff walls and open the whole world to free trade and traffic. Those are some of the costs of permanent peace; there are other sacrifices we, the dominant powers, would have to make. It is very expensive, peace. We French are willing, but are you willing, to pay the price, all those costs of no more war in the world?"

The French correspondents became personal; they smiled. They said that the president and the premiers protested that they did not mean all that, that that was not necessary, not all at once. "No, no, they did not mean that, exactly."

"Then," said Clemenceau, sitting up straight and fisting the table sharply once, "then you don't mean peace. You mean war. And the time for us French to make war is now, when we have got one of our neighbors down; we shall finish him and get ready for — the next war."

The French correspondents rested a moment, smiling; they asked again if we had heard this. When we repeated that it was news to us, they were sorry. "We can't print it — from French sources only. It would be discourteous." They bowed and went out. We Americans separated, without comment, and I assumed that the story would be investigated and reported. I wasn't attached to any news service myself, but if I had been I would have reported the incident just as we got it. For those French correspondents were certainly "inspired" to sound us with that story. I thought that some one very near Clemenceau had sent them to us, but whether it was authentic or not, their gossip was significant. French correspondents, coming as a couple, one to talk, the other to bear witness, were acting on orders from some editor, statesman, or party leader. Some French mind as French, as intelligent, and as representative as Clemenceau's had made that story, if not the Tiger himself. In a word, it was the French view of the peace and of American and English ideals. It is in this sense a true story; it has served me as the key to all the French maneuvers then and since; it flashed out the difference between Wilson and Clemenceau, and it explained Wilson's typical failure.

Wilson did not mean peace, not literally; nor do we Americans, nor do the British, mean peace. We do not want war; nobody in the world wants war; but some of us do want the things we can't have without war. That's what the French see. And they see that we wish, like them, for peace; we will work and we will pray for it, but we have not noted and we will not give up the things that cause wars. Clemenceau and the French would, I think, if we would. But Clemenceau, like so many of the leading French politicians, had seen things as a radical once. As a young man he learned that there are causes of war and that the way to end war is to prevent war: by dealing with the causes thereof. No treaties, no scraps of paper, no partial and no complete disarmament, can hold off very long a war that we have planted in our maladjustment of conflicting economic interests. That was, that *is*, the French view, and so obvious is it to those clear minds that they think we are hypocrites; we must see it, too, they think. And we don't.

[*1931*]

JOHN DOS PASSOS

[1896–   ]

HE WAS born in Chicago of a well-to-do family and was educated at the Choate School and Harvard, from which he was graduated in 1916. Soon afterwards he enlisted in an ambulance corps of the French army, later joined the Red Cross in Italy, and finally entered the medical corps of the American army. In 1921 he published a novel called *Three Soldiers* which attempted to present a realistic picture of the war and its effects upon three contrasting characters. It was a cynical and bitter work, reflecting the postwar disillusionment. It was a critical but hardly a popular success. The latter he achieved in 1925 with *Manhattan Transfer,* a novel of New York life. He has since published plays, essays, and travel sketches, but his great reputation now rests principally on *U. S. A.,* a trilogy consisting of *The 42nd Parallel* (1930), *1919* (1932), and *The Big Money* (1936). In this huge novel he has succeeded in picturing the conflicting social forces in America in our times — ending with the coming of the depression. The work is built up out of sections of objective narrative, newspaper headlines, impressionistic autobiographical sketches, and a series of remarkable biographies of representative contemporary figures (both actual and symbolic). The latter are truly memorable, and three of them appear here. While visiting Spain during the civil war he was sympathetic to the anarchists and antagonistic to the communists — a point of view which found expression in his last novel, *Adventures of a Young Man* (1939).

---

from

U. S. A.

FIGHTING BOB

La Follette was born in the town limits of Primrose; he worked on a farm in Dane County, Wisconsin, until he was nineteen.

At the university of Wisconsin he worked his way through. He wanted to be an actor, studied elocution and Robert Ingersoll and Shakespeare and Burke;

(who will ever explain the influence of Shakespeare in the last century, Marc Antony over Cæsar's bier, Othello to the Venetian Senate and Polonius, everywhere Polonius?)

riding home in a buggy after commencement he was Booth and Wilkes writing the Junius papers and Daniel Webster and Ingersoll defying God and the togaed great grave and incorruptible as statues magnificently spouting through the capitoline centuries;

he was the star debater in his class,

and won an interstate debate with an oration on the character of Iago.

He went to work in a law office and ran for district attorney. His schoolfriends canvassed the county riding round evenings. He bucked the machine and won the election.

It was the revolt of the young man against the state republican machine

and Boss Keyes the postmaster in Madison who ran the county was so surprised he about fell out of his chair.

That gave La Follette a salary to marry on. He was twentyfive years old.

Four years later he ran for congress; the university was with him again; he was the youngsters' candidate. When he was elected he was the youngest representative in the house

He was introduced round Washington by Philetus Sawyer the Wisconsin lumber king who was used to stacking and selling politicians the way he stacked and sold cordwood.

He was a Republican and he'd bucked the machine. Now they thought they had him. No man could stay honest in Washington.

Booth played Shakespeare in Baltimore that winter. Booth never would go to Washington on account of the bitter memory of his brother. Bob La Follette and his wife went to every performance.

In the parlor of the Plankinton Hotel in Milwaukee during the state fair, Boss Sawyer the lumber king tried to bribe him to influence his brother-in-law who was presiding judge over the prosecution of the Republican state treasurer;

Bob La Follette walked out of the hotel in a white rage. From that time it was war without quarter with the Republican machine in Wisconsin until he was elected governor and wrecked the Republican machine;

this was the tenyears war that left Wisconsin the model state where the voters, orderloving Germans and Finns, Scandinavians fond of their own opinion, learned to use the new leverage, direct primaries, referendum and recall.

La Follette taxed the railroads.

John C. Payne said to a group of politicians in the lobby of the Ebbitt House in Washington "La Follette's a damn fool if he thinks he can buck a railroad with five thousand miles of continuous track, he'll find he's mistaken . . . We'll take care of him when the time comes."

But when the time came the farmers of Wisconsin and the young lawyers and doctors and businessmen just out of school

took care of him

and elected him governor three times

and then to the United States Senate,

where he worked all his life making long speeches full of statistics, struggling to save democratic government, to make a farmers' and small businessmen's commonwealth, lonely with his back to the wall, fighting corruption and big business and high finance and trusts and combinations of combinations and the miasmic lethargy of Washington.

He was one of " the little group of wilful men expressing no opinion but their own "

who stood out against Woodrow Wilson's armed ship bill that made war with Germany certain; they called it a filibuster but it was six men with nerve straining to hold back a crazy steamroller with their bare hands;

the press pumped hatred into its readers against La Follette,

the traitor,

they burned him in effigy in Illinois;

in Wheeling they refused to let him speak.

In nineteen twentyfour La Follette ran for president and without money or political machine rolled up four and a half million votes

but he was a sick man, incessant work and the breathed out air of
committee rooms and legislative chambers choked him

and the dirty smell of politicians,

and he died,

an orator haranguing from the capitol of a lost republic;

but we will remember

how he sat firm in March nineteen seventeen while Woodrow Wilson
was being inaugurated for the second time, and for three days held the
vast machine at deadlock. They wouldn't let him speak; the galleries
glared hatred at him; the senate was a lynching party,

a stumpy man with a lined face, one leg stuck out in the aisle and his
arms folded and a chewed cigar in the corner of his mouth

and an undelivered speech on his desk,

a wilful man expressing no opinion but his own.

THE HOUSE OF MORGAN

I commit my soul into the hands of my savior, wrote John Pierpont
Morgan in his will, *in full confidence that having redeemed it and
washed it in His most precious blood, He will present it faultless before
my heavenly father, and I intreat my children to maintain and defend
at all hazard and at any cost of personal sacrifice the blessed doctrine of
complete atonement for sin through the blood of Jesus Christ once
offered and through that alone,*

and into the hands of the House of Morgan represented by his son,

he committed,

when he died in Rome in 1913,

the control of the Morgan interests in New York, Paris and London,
four national banks, three trust companies, three life insurance companies, ten railroad systems, three street railway companies, an express
company, the International Mercantile Marine,

power,

on the cantilever principle, through interlocking directorates

over eighteen other railroads, U. S. Steel, General Electric, American
Tel and Tel, five major industries;

741

the interwoven cables of the Morgan Stillman Baker combination held credit up like a suspension bridge, thirteen percent of the banking resources of the world.

The first Morgan to make a pool was Joseph Morgan, a hotelkeeper in Hartford Connecticut who organized stagecoach lines and bought up Ætna Life Insurance stock in a time of panic caused by one of the big New York fires in the 1830's;

his son Junius followed in his footsteps, first in the drygoods business, and then as partner to George Peabody, a Massachusetts banker who built up an enormous underwriting and mercantile business in London and became a friend of Queen Victoria;

Junius married the daughter of John Pierpont, a Boston preacher, poet, eccentric, and abolitionist; and their eldest son,

John Pierpont Morgan

arrived in New York to make his fortune

after being trained in England, going to school at Vevey, proving himself a crack mathematician at the University of Göttingen,

a lanky morose young man of twenty,

just in time for the panic of '57.

(war and panics on the stock exchange, bankruptcies, warloans, good growing weather for the House of Morgan.)

When the guns started booming at Fort Sumter, young Morgan turned some money over reselling condemned muskets to the U. S. army and began to make himself felt in the gold room in downtown New York; there was more in trading in gold than in trading in muskets; so much for the Civil War.

During the Franco-Prussian war Junius Morgan floated a huge bond issue for the French government at Tours.

At the same time young Morgan was fighting Jay Cooke and the German-Jew bankers in Frankfort over the funding of the American war debt (he never did like the Germans or the Jews).

The panic of '75 ruined Jay Cooke and made J. Pierpont Morgan the boss croupier of Wall Street; he united with the Philadelphia Drexels and built the Drexel building where for thirty years he sat in his glassedin office, redfaced and insolent, writing at his desk, smoking great black cigars, or, if important issues were involved, playing soli-

742

taire in his inner office; he was famous for his few words, Yes or No, and for his way of suddenly blowing up in a visitor's face and for that special gesture of the arm that meant, *What do I get out of it?*

In '77 Junius Morgan retired; J. Pierpont got himself made a member of the board of directors of the New York Central railroad and launched the first *Corsair*. He liked yachting and to have pretty actresses call him Commodore.

He founded the Lying-In Hospital on Stuyvesant Square, and was fond of going into St. George's church and singing a hymn all alone in the afternoon quiet.

In the panic of '93

at no inconsiderable profit to himself

Morgan saved the U. S. Treasury; gold was draining out, the country was ruined, the farmers were howling for a silver standard, Grover Cleveland and his cabinet were walking up and down in the blue room at the White House without being able to come to a decision, in Congress they were making speeches while the gold reserves melted in the Subtreasuries; poor people were starving; Coxey's army was marching to Washington; for a long time Grover Cleveland couldn't bring himself to call in the representative of the Wall Street moneymasters; Morgan sat in his suite at the Arlington smoking cigars and quietly playing solitaire until at last the president sent for him;

he had a plan all ready for stopping the gold hemorrhage.

After that what Morgan said went; when Carnegie sold out he built the Steel Trust.

J. Pierpont Morgan was a bullnecked irascible man with small black magpie's eyes and a growth on his nose; he let his partners work themselves to death over the detailed routine of banking, and sat in his back office smoking black cigars; when there was something to be decided he said Yes or No or just turned his back and went back to his solitaire.

Every Christmas his librarian read him Dickens' *A Christmas Carol* from the original manuscript.

He was fond of canarybirds and pekinese dogs and liked to take pretty actresses yachting. Each *Corsair* was a finer vessel than the last.

When he dined with King Edward he sat at His Majesty's right; he

743

ate with the Kaiser tête-à-tête; he liked talking to cardinals or the pope, and never missed a conference of Episcopal bishops;

Rome was his favorite city.

He liked choice cookery and old wines and pretty women and yachting, and going over his collections, now and then picking up a jewelled snuffbox and staring at it with his magpie's eyes.

He made a collection of the autographs of the rulers of France, owned glass cases full of Babylonian tablets, seals, signets, statuettes, busts,

Gallo-Roman bronzes,

Merovingian jewels, miniatures, watches, tapestries, porcelains, cuneiform inscriptions, paintings by all the old masters, Dutch, Italian, Flemish, Spanish,

manuscripts of the gospels and the Apocalypse,

a collection of the works of Jean-Jacques Rousseau,

and the letters of Pliny the Younger.

His collectors bought anything that was expensive or rare or had the glint of empire on it, and he had it brought to him and stared hard at it with his magpie's eyes. Then it was put in a glass case.

The last year of his life he went up the Nile on a dahabiyeh and spent a long time staring at the great columns of the Temple of Karnak.

The panic of 1907 and the death of Harriman, his great opponent in railroad financing, in 1909, had left him the undisputed ruler of Wall Street, most powerful private citizen in the world;

an old man tired of the purple, suffering from gout, he had deigned to go to Washington to answer the questions of the Pujo Committee during the Money Trust Investigation: Yes, I did what seemed to me to be for the best interests of the country.

So admirably was his empire built that his death in 1913 hardly caused a ripple in the exchanges of the world: the purple descended to his son, J. P. Morgan,

who had been trained at Groton and Harvard and by associating with the British ruling class

to be a more constitutional monarch: *J. P. Morgan suggests. . . .*

By 1917 the Allies had borrowed one billion, nine-hundred million dollars through the House of Morgan: we went overseas for democracy and the flag;

and by the end of the Peace Conference the phrase *J. P. Morgan suggests* had compulsion over a power of seventyfour billion dollars.

J. P. Morgan is a silent man, not given to public utterances, but during the great steel strike, he wrote Gary: *Heartfelt congratulations on your stand for the open shop, with which I am, as you know, absolutely in accord. I believe American principles of liberty are deeply involved, and must win if we stand firm.*

(Wars and panics on the stock exchange,
machinegunfire and arson,
bankruptcies, warloans,
starvation, lice, cholera and typhus:
good growing weather for the House of Morgan.)

THE BODY OF AN AMERICAN

Whereasthe Congressoftheunitedstates byaconcurrentresolutionadopted on the4thdayofmarch lastauthorizedthe Secretaryofwar to cause to be brought to theunitedstatesthe body of an Americanwhowasamemberoftheamerican expeditionaryforcesineurope wholosthislifeduringtheworldwarandwhoseidentityhasnotbeenestablished for burial inthememorialamphitheatreofthenational cemeteryatarlingtonvirginia

In the tarpaper morgue at Chalons-sur-Marne in the reek of chloride of lime and the dead, they picked out the pine box that held all that was left of

enie menie minie moe plenty other pine boxes stacked up there containing what they'd scraped up of Richard Roe

and other person or persons unknown. Only one can go. How did they pick John Doe?

Make sure he aint a dinge, boys,

make sure he aint a guinea or a kike,

how can you tell a guy's a hundredpercent when all you've got's a gunnysack full of bones, bronze buttons stamped with the screaming eagle and a pair of roll puttees?

. . . and the gagging chloride and the puky dirtstench of the year-old dead . . .

745

The day withal was too meaningful and tragic for applause. Silence, tears, songs and prayer, muffled drums and soft music were the instrumentalities today of national approbation.

John Doe was born (thudding din of blood in love into the shuddering soar of a man and woman alone indeed together lurching into
and ninemonths sick drowse waking into scared agony and the pain and blood and mess of birth). John Doe was born
and raised in Brooklyn, in Memphis, near the lake-front in Cleveland, Ohio, in the stench of the stockyards in Chi, on Beacon Hill, in an old brick house in Alexandria Virginia, on Telegraph Hill, in a halftimbered Tudor cottage in Portland the city of roses,
in the Lying-In Hospital old Morgan endowed on Stuyvesant Square,
across the railroad tracks, out near the country club, in a shack cabin tenement apartmenthouse exclusive residential suburb;
scion of one of the best families in the social register, won first prize in the baby parade at Coronado Beach, was marbles champion of the Little Rock grammarschools, crack basketballplayer at the Booneville High, quarterback at the State Reformatory, having saved the sheriff's kid from drowning in the Little Missouri River was invited to Washington to be photographed shaking hands with the President on the White House steps; —

though this was a time of mourning, such an assemblage necessarily has about it a touch of color. In the boxes are seen the court uniforms of foreign diplomats, the gold braid of our own and foreign fleets and armies, the black of the conventional morning dress of American statesmen, the varicolored furs and outdoor wrapping garments of mothers and sisters come to mourn, the drab and blue of soldiers and sailors, the glitter of musical instruments and the white and black of a vested choir

— busboy harveststiff hogcaller boyscout champeen cornshucker of Western Kansas bellhop at the United States Hotel at Saratoga Springs office boy callboy fruiter telephone lineman longshoreman lumberjack plumber's helper,
worked for an exterminating company in Union City, filled pipes in an opium joint in Trenton, N. J.
Y.M.C.A. secretary, express agent, truckdriver, fordmechanic, sold books in Denver Colorado: Madam would you be willing to help a young man work his way through college?
President Harding, with a reverence seemingly more significant because of his high temporal station, concluded his speech:

746

We are met today to pay the impersonal tribute;
the name of him whose body lies before us took flight with his imperish-
able soul . . .
as a typical soldier of this representative democracy he fought and died
believing in the indisputable justice of his country's cause . . .

by raising his right hand and asking the thousands within the sound
of his voice to join in the prayer:

Our Father which art in heaven hallowed be thy name . . .

Naked he went into the army;
they weighed you, measured you, looked for flat feet, squeezed your
penis to see if you had clap, looked up your anus to see if you had
piles, counted your teeth, made you cough, listened to your heart and
lungs, made you read the letters on the card, charted your urine and
your intelligence,
gave you a service record for a future (imperishable soul)
and an identification tag stamped with your serial number to hang
around your neck, issued O D regulation equipment, a condiment can
and a copy of the articles of war.
Atten'SHUN suck in your gut you c——r wipe that smile off your
face eyes right wattja tink dis is a choirch-social? For-war-D'ARCH.

John Doe
and Richard Roe and other person or persons unknown
drilled hiked, manual of arms, ate slum, learned to salute, to soldier,
to loaf in the latrines, forbidden to smoke on deck, overseas guard
duty, forty men and eight horses, shortarm inspection and the ping of
shrapnel and the shrill bullets combing the air and the sorehead wood-
peckers the machineguns mud cooties gasmasks and the itch.
Say feller tell me how I can get back to my outfit.

John Doe had a head
for twentyodd years intensely the nerves of the eyes the ears the
palate the tongue the fingers the toes the armpits, the nerves warm-
feeling under the skin charged the coiled brain with hurt sweet warm
cold mine must dont sayings print headlines:
Thou shalt not the multiplication table long division, Now is the time
for all good men knocks but once at a young man's door, It's a great life
if Ish gebibbel, The first five years'll be the Safety First, Suppose a hun

747

tried to rape your my country right or wrong, Catch 'em young, What he dont know wont treat 'em rough, Tell 'em nothin, He got what was coming to him he got his, This is a white man's country, Kick the bucket, Gone west, If you dont like it you can croaked him

Say buddy cant you tell me how I can get back to my outfit?

Cant help jumpin when them things go off, give me the trots them things do. I lost my identification tag swimmin in the Marne, roughhousin with a guy while we was waiting to be deloused, in bed with a girl named Jeanne (Love moving picture wet French postcard dream began with saltpeter in the coffee and ended at the propho station); —

Say soldier for chrissake cant you tell me how I can get back to my outfit?

John Doe's
heart pumped blood:
alive thudding silence of blood in your ears
down in the clearing in the Oregon forest where the punkins were punkincolor pouring into the blood through the eyes and the fallcolored trees and the bronze hoopers were hopping through the dry grass, where tiny striped snails hung on the underside of the blades and the flies hummed, wasps droned, bumblebees buzzed, and the woods smelt of wine and mushrooms and apples, homey smell of fall pouring into the blood,
and I dropped the tin hat and the sweaty pack and lay flat with the dogday sun licking my throat and adamsapple and the tight skin over the breastbone.

The shell had his number on it.

The blood ran into the ground.

The service record dropped out of the filing cabinet when the quartermaster sergeant got blotto that time they had to pack up and leave the billets in a hurry.
The identification tag was in the bottom of the Marne.

The blood ran into the ground, the brains oozed out of the cracked skull and were licked up by the trenchrats, the belly swelled and raised a generation of bluebottle flies,

and the incorruptible skeleton,
and the scraps of dried viscera and skin bundled in khaki

they took to Chalons-sur-Marne
and laid it out neat in a pine coffin
and took it home to God's Country on a battleship
and buried it in a sarcophagus in the Memorial Amphitheatre in the
Arlington National Cemetery
and draped the Old Glory over it
and the bugler played taps
and Mr. Harding prayed to God and the diplomats and the generals
and the admirals and the brasshats and the politicians and the handsomely dressed ladies out of the society column of the *Washington Post*
stood up solemn
and thought how beautiful sad Old Glory God's Country it was to
have the bugler play taps and the three volleys made their ears ring.

Where his chest ought to have been they pinned
the Congressional Medal, the D.S.C., the Medaille Militaire, the
Belgian Croix de Guerre, the Italian gold medal, the Vitutea Militara
sent by Queen Marie of Rumania, the Czechoslovak war cross, the
Virtuti Militari of the Poles, a wreath sent by Hamilton Fish, Jr., of
New York, and a little wampum presented by a deputation of Arizona
redskins in warpaint and feathers. All the Washingtonians brought
flowers.

Woodrow Wilson brought a bouquet of poppies.
[*1930–36*]

749

THEODORE DREISER

[1871–   ]

DREISER was born in Terre Haute, Indiana, of a poor Catholic family. He attended parochial and public schools in several Indiana cities and towns and at sixteen went to Chicago to work at various meagerly paid jobs. At eighteen he entered the University of Indiana, spent a year there, and returned to Chicago to look for a newspaper job — which he got, in 1892, on the *Chicago Daily Globe*. Years of newspaper reporting and magazine editing in St. Louis, Pittsburgh, and New York followed. Not until 1910 did he leave journalism for good — resigning, that year, from the editorship of the Butterick publications. Ten years before, he had published a novel, *Sister Carrie*. It was a milestone in American literature — perhaps the greatest of the early realistic novels. In 1911 came his second masterpiece, *Jennie Gerhardt*. Then followed lesser novels, *The Financier* (1912), *The Titan* (1914), and *The Genius* (1915). In 1925 he published his monumental *An American Tragedy*. These novels, at their best, were significant because they revealed a humane man groping for an understanding of the social forces which determine the fate of individual human lives. Dreiser has also published plays, stories, verse, essays, and two exceptionally interesting autobiographical volumes, *A Book about Myself* (1922) and *Dawn* (1931). In recent years he has been a vigorous exponent of radical political movements.

---

from

A BOOK ABOUT MYSELF

[PITTSBURGH]

I came to Pittsburgh through the brown-blue mountains of Western Pennsylvania, and all day long we had been winding at the base of one or another of them, following the bed of a stream or turning out into a broad smooth valley, crossing directly at the center of it, or climbing some low ridge with a puff-puff-puff and then clattering almost recklessly down the other slope. I had never before seen any mountains.

The sight of sooty-faced miners at certain places, their little oil and tow tin lamps fastened to their hats, their tin dinnerpails on their arms, impressed me as something new and faintly reminiscent of the one or two small coal mines about Sullivan, Indiana, where I had lived when I was a boy of seven. Along the way I saw a heavy-faced and heavy-bodied type of peasant woman, with a black or brown or blue or green skirt and a waist of a contrasting color, a headcloth or neckerchief of still another, trailed by a few children of equally solid proportions, hanging up clothes or doing something else about their miserable places. These were the much-maligned hunkies just then being imported by the large manufacturing and mining and steel-making industries of the country to take the place of the restless and less docile American working man and woman. I marveled at their appearance and number, and assumed, American-fashion, that in their far-off and unhappy lands they had heard of the wonderful American Constitution, its guaranty of life, liberty and the pursuit of happiness, as well as of the bounteous opportunities afforded by this great land, and that they had forsaken their miseries to come all this distance to enjoy these greater blessings.

I did not then know of the manufacturers' foreign labor agent with his lying propaganda among ignorant and often fairly contented peasants, painting America as a country rolling in wealth and opportunity, and then bringing them here to take the places of more restless and greatly underpaid foreigners who, having been brought over by the same gay pictures, were becoming irritated and demanded more pay. I did not then know of the padrone, the labor spy, the company store, five cents an hour for breaker children, the company stockade, all in full operation at this time. All I knew was that there had been a great steel strike in Pittsburgh recently, that Andrew Carnegie, as well as other steel manufacturers (the Olivers, for one), had built fences and strung them with electrified barbed wire in order to protect themselves against the " lawless " attacks of " lawless " workingmen. . . .

Our mid-Western papers, up to the day of Cleveland's election in 1892 and for some time after, had been full of the merits of this labor dispute, with long and didactic editorials, intended in the main to prove that the workingman was not so greatly underpaid, considering the type of labor he performed and the intelligence he brought to his task; that the public was not in the main vastly interested in labor disputes, both parties to the dispute being unduly selfish; that it would be a severe blow to the prosperity of the country if labor disputes were too long continued; that unless labor was reasonable in its demands capital would become disheartened and leave the country. I had not made up my mind that the argument was all on one side, although I knew that the average man in America, despite its great and boundless opportunities, was about as much put upon and kicked about and underpaid as any other. This growing labor problem or the general American dissatisfaction with poor returns upon efforts made crystallized three years later in the Free Silver campaign and the " gold parades." The " full dinner-pail " was then invented as a slogan to counteract the vast economic unrest, and the threat to close down and so bring misery to the entire country unless William McKinley was elected was also freely posted. Henry George, Father McGlynn, Herr Most, Emma Goldman, and a score of others were abroad voicing the woes of hundreds of thousands who were supposed to have no woes.

At that time, as I see it now, America was just entering upon the most lurid phase of that vast, splendid, most lawless and most savage period in which the great financiers were plotting and conniving at the enslavement of the people and belaboring each other. Those crude parvenu dynasties which now sit enthroned in our democracy, threatening its very life with their pretensions and assumptions, were then in their very beginning. John D. Rockefeller was still in Cleveland; Flagler, William Rockefeller, H. H. Rogers, were still comparatively young and secret agents; Carnegie was still in Pittsburgh, an iron master, and of all his brood of powerful children only Frick had appeared; William H. Vanderbilt and Jay Gould had only recently died; Cleveland was President, and Mark Hanna was an unknown business man in Cleveland. The great struggles of the railroads, the coal companies, the gas companies, to overawe and tax the people were still in abeyance, or just being born. The multi-millionaire had arrived, it is true, but not the billionaire. On every hand were giants plotting, fighting, dreaming; and yet in Pittsburgh there was still something of a singing spirit.

When I arrived here and came out of the railway station, which was directly across the Monongahela River from the business center, I was impressed by the huge walls of hills that arose on every hand, a great black sheer ridge rising to a height of five or six hundred feet to my right and enclosing this river, on the bosom of which lay steamboats of good size. From the station a pleasingly designed bridge of fair size led to the city beyond, and across it trundled in unbroken lines street-cars and wagons and buggies of all sizes and descriptions. The city itself was already smartly outlined by lights, a galaxy climbing the hills in every direction, and below me as I walked out upon this bridge was an agate stream reflecting the lights from either shore. Below this was another bridge, and upstream another. The whole river for a mile or more was suddenly lit to a rosy glow, a glow which, as I saw upon turning, came from the tops of some forty or fifty stacks belching a deep orange-red flame. At the same time an enormous pounding and crackling came from somewhere, as though titans were at work upon subterranean anvils. I stared and admired. I felt that I was truly adventuring into a new and strange world. . . .

Something about the city drew me intensely. I wished I might remain for a time. The next morning I was up bright and early to look up the morning papers and find out the names of the afternoon papers. I found that there were four: the *Dispatch* and *Times,* morning papers, and the *Gazette-Telegraph* and *Leader,* afternoon. I thought them most interesting and different from those of other cities in which I had worked.

" Andy Pastor had his right hand lacerated while at work in the 23-inch mill yesterday."

" John Kristoff had his right wrist sprained while at work in the 140-inch mill yesterday."

" Joseph Novic is suffering from contused wounds of the left wrist received while at work in the 23-inch mill yesterday."

" A train of hot metal, being hauled from a mixing-house to open hearth No. 2, was side-swiped by a yard engine near the 48-inch mill. The impact tilted the ladles of some of the cars and the hot metal spilled in a pool of water along the track. Antony Brosak, Constantine Czernik and Kafros Maskar were seriously wounded by the exploding metal."

Such items arrested my attention at once; and then such names as Squirrel Hill, Sawmill Run, Moon Run, Hazelwood, Wind Gap Road, Braddock, McKeesport, Homestead, Swisvale, somehow made me wish to know more of this region.

The *Dispatch* was Republican, the *Times* Democratic. Both were evidently edited with much conservatism as to local news. I made haste to visit the afternoon newspaper offices, only to discover that they were fully equipped with writers. I then proceeded in search of a room and finally found one in Wylie Avenue, a curious street that climbed a hill to its top and then stopped. Here, almost at the top of this hill,

753

in an old yellow stonefront house the rear rooms of which commanded a long and deep canyon or "run," I took a room for a week. The family of this house rented rooms to several others, clerks who looked and proved to be a genial sort, holding a kind of court on the front steps of an evening.

I now turned to the morning papers, going first to the *Times,* which had its offices in a handsome building, one of the two or three high office buildings in the city. The city editor received me graciously but could promise nothing. At the *Dispatch,* which was published in a three-story building at Smithfield and Diamond streets, I found a man who expressed much more interest. He was a slender, soft-spoken, one-handed man. On very short acquaintance I found him to be shrewd and canny, gracious always, exceedingly reticent and uncommunicative and an excellent judge of news, and plainly holding his job not so much by reason of what he put into his paper as by what he kept out of it. He wanted to know where I had worked before I came to Pittsburgh, whether I had been connected with any paper here, whether I had ever done feature stuff. I described my experiences as nearly as I could, and finally he said that there was nothing now but he was expecting a vacancy to occur soon. If I could come around in the course of a week or ten days (I drooped sadly) — well, then, in three or four days, he thought he might do something for me. The salary would not be more than eighteen the week. My spirits fell at that, but his manner was so agreeable and his hope for me so keen that I felt greatly encouraged and told him I would wait a few days anyhow. . . .

I . . . took a car which followed the Monongahela upstream to Homestead, and here for the first time had a view of that enormous steel plant which only recently (June to December, 1892) had played such a great part in the industrial drama of America. The details of the quarrel were fairly fresh in my mind: how the Carnegie Steel Company had planned, with the technicalities of a wage-scale readjustment as an excuse, to break the power of the Amalgamated Steel Workers, who were becoming too forceful and who were best organized in their plant, and how the Amalgamated, resenting the introduction of three hundred Pinkerton guards to "protect" the plant, had attacked them, killing several and injuring others, and so permitting the introduction of the State militia, which speedily and permanently broke the power of the strikers. They could only wait then and starve, and so they had waited and starved for six months, when they finally returned to work, such of them as would be received. When I reached there in April, 1894, the battle was already fifteen months past, but the feeling was still alive. I did not then know what it was about this town of Homestead that was so depressing, but in the six months of my stay here I found that it was a compound of a sense of defeat and sullen despair. The men had not forgotten. Even then the company was busy, and had been for months, importing Poles, Hungarians, Lithuanians, to take the places of the ousted strikers. Whole colonies were already here, housed under the most unsatisfactory conditions, and more were coming. Hence the despair of those who had been defeated.

Along the river sprawled for a quarter of a mile or more the huge low length of the furnaces, great black bottle-like affairs with rows of stacks and long low sheds or buildings paralleling them, sheds from which came a continuous hammering and sputtering and the glow of red fire. The whole was shrouded by a pall of gray smoke, even in the bright sunshine. Above the plant, on a slope which rose steeply behind it, were a few moderately attractive dwellings grouped about two small parks, the trees of which were languishing for want of air. Behind and to the sides of these were the spires of several churches, those soporifics against failure and despair. Turning up side streets one found, invariably, uniform frame houses, closely built and dulled by smoke and grime, and below, on the flats behind the mill, were cluttered alleys so unsightly and unsanitary as to shock me into the belief that I was once more witnessing the lowest phases of Chicago slum-life, the worst I had ever seen. The streets were mere mud-tracks. Where there were trees (and there were few) they were dwarfed and their foliage withered by a metallic fume which was over all. Though the sun was bright at the top of the hill, down here it was gray, almost cloudy, at best a filtered dull gold haze.

The place held me until night. I browsed about its saloons, of which there was a large number, most of them idle during the drift of the afternoon. The open gates of the mill held my interest also for through them I could see furnaces, huge cranes, switching engines, cars of molten iron being hauled to and fro, and mountains of powdered iron ore and scrap iron piled here and there awaiting the hour of new birth in the smelting vats. When the sun had gone down, and I had watched a shift of men coming out with their buckets and coats over their arms, and

755

other hundreds entering in a rush, I returned to the city with a sense of the weight and breadth and depth of huge effort. Here bridges and rail and plate steel were made for all the world. But of all these units that dwelt and labored here scarce a fraction seemed even to sense a portion of the meaning of all they did. I knew that Carnegie had become a multi-millionaire, as had Phipps and others, and that he was beginning to give libraries, that Phipps had already given several floral conservatories, and that their "lobbies" in Congress were even then bartering for the patronage of the government on their terms; but the poor units in these hovels at Homestead — what did they know?

On another day I explored the east end of Pittsburgh, which was the exclusive residence section of the city and a contrast to such hovels and deprivation as I had witnessed at Homestead and among the shacks across the Monongahela and below Mt. Washington. Never in my life, neither before nor since, in New York, Chicago or elsewhere, was the vast gap which divides the rich from the poor in America so vividly and forcefully brought home to me. I had seen on my map a park called Schenley, and thinking that it might be interesting I made my way out a main thoroughfare called (quite appropriately, I think) Fifth Avenue, lined with some of the finest residences of the city. Never did the mere possession of wealth impress me so keenly. Here were homes of the most imposing character, huge, verandaed, tree-shaded, with immense lawns, great stone or iron or hedge fences and formal gardens and walks of a most ornate character. It was a region of well-curbed, well-drained and well-paved thoroughfares. Even the street-lamps were of a better design than elsewhere, so eager was a young and democratic municipality to see that superior living conditions were provided for the rich. There were avenues lined with well-cropped trees, and at every turn one encountered expensive carriages, their horses jingling silver or gold-gilt harness, their front seats occupied by one or two footmen in livery, while reclining was Madam or Sir, or both, gazing condescendingly upon the all too comfortable world about them.

In Schenley Park was a huge and interesting arboretum or botanical garden under glass, a most oriental affair given by Phipps of the Carnegie Company. A large graceful library of white limestone, perhaps four or five times the size of the one in Allegheny, given by Andrew Carnegie, was in process of construction. And he was another of the chief beneficiaries of Homestead, the possessor of a great house in this region, another in New York and still another in Scotland, a man for whom the unwitting "Pinkertons" and contending strikers had been killed. Like huge ribbons of fire these and other names of powerful steel men — the Olivers, Thaws, Fricks, Thompsons — seemed to rise and band the sky. It seemed astonishing to me that some men could thus rise and soar about the heavens like eagles, while others, drab sparrows all, could only pick among the offal of the hot ways below. What were these things called democracy and equality about which men prated? Had they any basis in fact? There was constant palaver about the equality of opportunity which gave such men as these their chance, but I could not help speculating as to the lack of equality of opportunity these men created for others once their equality at the top had made them. If equality of opportunity had been so excellent for them why not for others, especially those in their immediate care? True, all men had not the brains to seize upon and make use of that which was put before them, but again, not all men of brains had the blessing of opportunity as had these few men. Strength, as I felt, should not be too arrogant or too forgetful of the accident or chance by which it had arrived. It might do something for the poor — pay them decent living wages, for instance. Were these giants planning to subject their sons and daughters to the same "equality of opportunity" which had confronted them at the start and which they were so eager to recommend to the attention of others? Not at all. In this very neighborhood I passed an exclusive private school for girls, with great grounds and a beautiful wall — another sample of equality of opportunity.

On the fourth day of my stay here I called again at the *Dispatch* office and was given a position. . . .

In a very little while I came to be on friendly terms with the men of this and some other papers, men who, because of their intimate contact with local political and social conditions, were well fitted to enlighten me as to the exact economic and political conditions here. Two in particular, the political and labor men of this paper were most helpful. The former, a large, genial, commercial-drummer type, who might also have made an excellent theatrical manager or promoter, provided me with a clear insight into the general cleavage of local and State politics and personalities. I liked him very much. The other, the labor man, was a slow, silent, dark, square-shouldered and almost square-headed youth, who drifted in and out of the office irregularly. He it was who attended, when permitted by the working people themselves, all labor meetings in the city or elsewhere, as far east at times as the hard coal regions about Wilkes-Barre and Scranton. As he himself told me, he was the paper's sole authority for such comments or assertions as it dared to make in connection with the mining of coal and the manufacture of steel. He was an intense sympathizer with labor, but not so much with organized as with unorganized workers. He believed that labor here had two years before lost a most important battle, one which would show in its contests with money in the future: which was true. He pretended to know that there was a vast movement on foot among the moneyed elements in America to cripple if not utterly destroy organized labor, and to that end he assured me once that all the great steel and coal and oil magnates were in a conspiracy to flood the country with cheap foreign labor, which they had lured or were luring here by all sorts of dishonest devices; once here, these immigrants were to be used to break the demand of better-paid and more intelligent labor. He pretended to know that in the coal and steel regions thousands had already been introduced and more were on their way, and that all such devices as showy churches and schools for defectives, etc., were used to keep ignorant and tame those already here.

"But you can't say anything about it in Pittsburgh," he said to me. "If I should talk I'd have to get out of here. The papers here won't use a thing unfavorable to the magnates in any of these fields. I write all sorts of things, but they never get in. . . ."

My friend Martyn . . . grew melodramatic as he told me where these men lived and how they lived, and finally took me in order that I might see for myself. Afterward, in the course of my reportorial work, I came upon some of these neighborhoods and individuals, and since they are all a part of the great fortune-building era, and illustrate how democracy works in America, and how some great fortunes were built, I propose to put down here a few pictures of things that I saw. . . .

I recall visiting a two-room tenement in a court, the character of which first opened my eyes to the type of home these workers endured. This court consisted of four sides with an open space in the center. Three of these sides were smoke-grimed wooden houses three stories in height; the fourth was an ancient and odorous wooden stable, where the horses of a contractor were kept. In the center of this court stood a circular wooden building or lavatory with ten triangular compartments, each opening into one vault or cesspool. Near this was one hydrant, the only water-supply for all these homes or rooms. These two conveniences served twenty families, Polish, Hungarian, Slavonic, Jewish, Negro, of from three to five people each, living in the sixty-three rooms which made up the three grimy sides above mentioned. There were twenty-seven children in these rooms, for whom this court was their only playground. For twenty housewives this was the only place where they could string their wash-lines. For twenty tired, sweaty, unwashed husbands this was, aside from the saloon, the only near and neighborly recreation and companionship center. Here of a sweltering summer night, after playing cards and drinking beer, they would frequently stretch themselves to sleep. . . .

It was to Martyn and his interest that I owed still other views. He took me one day to a boardinghouse in which lived twenty-four people, all in two rooms, and yet, to my astonishment and confusion, it was not so bad as that other court, so great apparently is the value of intimate human contact. Few of the very poor day laborers, as Martyn explained to me, who were young and unmarried, cared how they lived so long as they lived cheaply and could save a little. This particular boardinghouse in Homestead was in a court such as I have described, and consisted of two rooms, one above the other, each measuring perhaps 12 x 20. In the kitchen at the time was the wife of the boarding boss cooking dinner. Along one side of the room was an oilcloth-covered table with a plank bench on each side; above it was a rack holding a long row of white cups, and a shelf with tin knives and forks. Near the up-to-date range, the only real piece of furniture in the room, hung the buckets in which all mill men carried their noon or midnight meals. A crowd of men were lounging cheerfully about, talking, smoking and enjoying life, one of them playing a concertina. They were making the most of a brief spell before their meal and departure for work. In the room above, as the landlord cheerfully showed us, were double iron bedsteads set close together and on them comfortables neatly laid.

In these two rooms lived, besides the boarding boss and his wife, both stalwart Bulgarians, and their two babies, twenty men. They were those who handled steel billets and bars, unloaded and loaded trains, worked in cinder pits, filled steel buckets with stock, and what not. They all worked twelve hours a day, and their reward was this and what they could save over and above it out of nine-sixty per week. Martyn said a good thing about them at the time: " I don't know how it is. I know these people are exploited and misused. The mill-owners pay them the lowest wages, the landlords exploit these boardinghouse keepers as well as their boarders, and the community which they make by their work don't give a damn for them, and yet they are happy, and I'll be hanged if they don't make me happy. It must be that just work is happiness," and I agreed with him. Plenty of work, something to do, the ability to avoid the ennui of idleness and useless, pensive, futile thought! . . .

In the meantime I was going about my general work, and an easy task it proved. My city editor, cool, speculative, diplomatic soul, soon instructed me as to the value of news and its limitations here. "We don't touch on labor conditions except through our labor man," he told me, "and he knows what to say. There's nothing to be said about the rich or religious in a derogatory sense: they're all right in so far as we know. We don't touch on scandals in high life. The big steel men here just about own the place, so we can't. Some papers out West and down in New York go in for sensationalism, but we don't. I'd rather have some simple little feature any time, a story about some old fellow with eccentric habits, than any of these scandals or trage- dies. Of course we do cover them when we have to, but we have to be mighty careful what we say."

So much for a free press in Pittsburgh, A.D. 1893!

[*1922*]

CHARLES A. BEARD

[1874–   ]

HE WAS born in Knightstown, Indiana, of a long line of farmers and artisans, but his own father was a man of means, president of the local bank, and owner of a fine library, which he taught the boy to use. He was educated at De Pauw University, Oxford, Cornell, and Columbia, the last of these awarding him his Ph.D. in 1904. He remained at Columbia as a teacher of politics until 1917, when he resigned from a professorship in protest against violations of academic freedom. Nevertheless, his influence among students of political science and history continued to increase. He became known as one of the foremost liberal scholars in his field, and in later years — through his periodical writing and his books for the layman — he became an important and distinguished public figure. Best known among his many works are *An Economic Interpretation of the Constitution* (1913), *Economic Origins of Jeffersonian Democracy* (1915), *The Rise of American Civilization* (with Mary R. Beard — 1927), and *America in Midpassage* (1939). The essay which follows is characteristic of his vigorous and caustic style and his liberal viewpoint.

---

from

THE MYTH OF RUGGED AMERICAN
INDIVIDUALISM

"The House of Bishops would be as much at sea in Minneapolis as at Atlantic City." This bit of delicious humor, all too rare in America's solemn assemblies, sparkled at a tense moment in the late conference of the Episcopalian magnates at Denver when the respective merits of the two cities as future meeting places were under debate. But the real cause of the caustic comment seems to have been a heated discussion, led by the Honorable George W. Wickersham, over a dangerous proposal to modify . . . the sacred creed of rugged American individualism.

That contest had been precipitated by the report of a special com﹒ mission in which occurred these highly inflammatory words: " It is becoming increasingly evident that the conception of society as made up of autonomous, independent individuals is as faulty from the point of view of economic realism as it is from the standpoint of Christian idealism. Our fundamental philosophy of rugged individualism must be modified to meet the needs of a co-operative age." This frightful conclusion flowed from a fact statement which the commission summarized in the following language: " Side by side with such misery and idleness, there are warehouses bursting with goods which cannot be bought; elevators full of wheat while bread lines haunt our cities; carefully protected machinery lying idle, while jobless men throng our streets; money in the banks available at low rates."

These shocking passages Mr. Wickersham read to the assembled delegates with considerable indignation, and denied their truth. Then he added an illuminating exposition all his own: " I think this is an expression of a social philosophy that is expressed by the Soviet Government of Russia. It is a negation of the whole concept of American civilization. I think it would be a sad day when the American people abandon the principles on which they have grown to greatness." Coming to specifications, he particularly attacked a point in the report, that " compulsory unemployment insurance is feasible." Realizing that Mr. Wickersham was a specialist in individualism, since he was the chief author of a collective report from which each individual signer apparently dissented, the congregated deputies at Denver voted down the proposal that the commission's statement should be taken as " representing the mind of the Church," and substituted a mere pious recommendation that it should be given " careful consideration " by members of the Church. Such, at least, is the story reported in the press.

This in only one of many straws in the wind indicating a movement to exalt rugged individualism into a national taboo beyond the reach of inquiring minds. From day to day it becomes increasingly evident that some of our economic leaders (by no means all of them) are using the phrase as an excuse for avoiding responsibility, for laying the present depression on " government interference," and for seeking to escape from certain forms of taxation and regulation which they do not find to their interest. If a smoke screen big enough can be laid on the land, our commercial prestidigitators may work wonders — for themselves. . . .

Hence it is important to ask, calmly and without reference to election heats, just what all this means. In what way is the Government "in business" and how did it get there? Here we climb down out of the muggy atmosphere of controversy and face a few stubborn facts. They are entered in the indubitable records of the Government of the United States and are as evident as the hills to them that have eyes to see. Let us catalogue a few of them *seriatim* for the first time in the history of this adventure in logomachy.

1. Government Regulations of Railways, from 1887 to the last Act of Congress. How did the Government get into this business? The general cause was the conduct of railway corporations under the rule of rugged individualism — rebates, pools, stock watering, bankruptcy-juggling, all the traffic will bear, savage rate slashing, merciless competition, and the rest of it. If anyone wants to know the facts, let him read the history of railroading in the sixties, seventies, and early eighties, or, if time is limited, the charming illustrations presented in Charles Francis Adams' "A Chapter of Erie." And what was the immediate cause of the Government's intervention? The insistence of business men, that is, shippers, who were harassed and sometimes ruined by railway tactics, and of farmers, the most rugged of all the rugged individualists the broad land of America has produced. And the result? Let the gentle reader compare the disastrous railway bankruptcies that flowed from the panic of 1873, including bloodshed and arson, with the plight of railways now, bad as it is. Government regulation is not a utopian success, but it is doubtful whether any of our great business men would like to get the Government entirely out of this business and return to the magnificent anarchy of Jay Gould's age. President Hoover has not even suggested it.

2. Waterways. Since its foundation the Government has poured hundreds of millions into rivers, harbors, canals, and other internal improvements. It is still pouring in millions. Some of our best economists have denounced it as wasteful and have demonstrated that most of it does not pay in any sense of the word. But President Hoover, instead of leaving this work to private enterprise, insists on projecting and executing the most elaborate undertakings, in spite of the fact that some of them are unfair if not ruinous to railways. Who is back of all this? Business men and farmers who want lower freight rates. There is not a chamber of commerce on any Buck Creek in America that will not cheer until tonsils are cracked any proposal to make the said creek navi-

gable. Dredging companies want the good work to go on, and so do the concerns that make dredging machinery. Farmers are for it also and they are, as already said, the ruggedest of rugged individuals — so rugged in fact that the vigorous efforts of the Farm Board to instill co-operative reason into them have been almost as water on a duck's back.

3. The United States Barge Corporation. Who got the Government into the job of running barges on some of its improved waterways? Certainly not the socialists, but good Republicans and Democrats speaking for the gentlemen listed under 2 above.

4. The Shipping Business. The World War was the occasion, but not the cause of this departure. For more than half a century the politicians of America fought ship subsidies against business men engaged in the shipbuilding and allied industries. At last, under the cover of war necessities, the Government went into the shipping business, with cheers from business. Who is back of the huge expenditures for the merchant marine? Business men. Who supports huge subsidies under the guise of " lucrative mail contracts," making a deficit in postal finances to be used as proof that the Government cannot run any business? Business men clamor for three mail subsidies and receive them. Who put the Government into the business of providing cheap money for ship building? Business men did it. . . .

5. Aviation. The Government is " in " this business. It provides costly airway services free of charge and subsidizes air mail. Who is behind this form of Government enterprise? Gentlemen engaged in aviation and the manufacture of planes and dirigibles. Then the government helps by buying planes for national defense. Who is opposed to air mail subsidies? A few despised " politicians."

6. Canals. Who zealously supported the construction of the Panama Canal? Shippers on the Pacific Coast who did not like the railway rates. Also certain important shipping interests on both coasts — all controlled by business men. Who insisted that the Government should buy the Cape Cod Canal? The business men who put their money into the enterprise and found that it did not pay. Then they rejoiced to see the burden placed on the broad back of our dear Uncle Sam.

7. Highway Building. Who has supported Federal highway aid — the expenditures of hundreds of millions on roads involving the taxation of railways to pay for ruinous competition? Everybody apparently, but specifically business men engaged in the manufacture and sale of

automobiles and trucks. Who proposes to cut off every cent of that outlay? Echoes do not answer.

8. The Department of Commerce, its magnificent mansion near the Treasury Department, and its army of hustlers scouting for business at the uttermost ends of the earth. Who is responsible for loading on the Government the job of big drummer at large for business? Why shouldn't these rugged individualists do their own drumming instead of asking the taxpayers to do it for them? Business men have been behind this enormous expansion, and Mr. Hoover, as Secretary of Commerce, outdid every predecessor in the range of his activities and the expenditure of public money. Who proposes to take the Government out of the business of hunting business for men who ought to know their own business?

9. The Big Pork Barrel — appropriations for public buildings, navy yards, and army posts. An interesting enterprise for the United States Chamber of Commerce would be to discover a single piece of pork in a hundred years that has not been approved by local business men as beneficiaries. When Bill Tillman shouted in the Senate that he intended to steal a hog every time a Yankee got a ham, he knew for whom the speaking was done.

10 The Bureau of Standards. Besides its general services, it renders valuable aid to business undertakings. Why shouldn't they do their own investigating at their own expense, instead of turning to the Government?

11. The Federal Trade Commission. Who runs there for rulings on " fair practices "? Weary consumers? Not often. Principally, business men who do not like to be outwitted or cheated by their competitors. If we are rugged individualists, why not let every individualist do as he pleases, without invoking government intervention at public expense?

·12. The Anti-Trust Acts. Business men are complaining against these laws on the ground that they cannot do any large-scale planning without incurring the risk of prosecution. The contention is sound, but who put these laws on the books and on what theory were they based? They were the product of a clamor on the part of farmers and business men against the practices of great corporations. Farmers wanted lower prices. Business men of the smaller variety objected to being undersold, beaten by clever tricks, or crushed to the wall by competitors with immense capital. And what was the philosophy behind the Sherman Act and the Clayton Act? Individualism, pure and undefiled, " The

New Freedom " as President Wilson phrased it in literary language. " Break up the trusts and let each tub stand on its own bottom." That was the cry among little business men. As lawyers put it in their somber way, " the natural person's liberty should not be destroyed by artificial persons known as corporations created under the auspices of the State." Whether any particular business man is for or against the anti-trust laws depends upon his particular business and the state of its earnings.

13. The Tariff. On this tender subject it is scarcely possible to speak soberly. It seems safe to say, however, that if all the business men who demand this kind of " interference " — with the right of capital to find its most lucrative course, industry and intelligence their natural re-ward, commodities their fair price, and idleness and folly their natural punishment — were to withdraw their support for protection, cease their insistence on it, then the politicians would probably reduce the levy or go over to free trade; with what effect on business no one can cor-rectly predict. At all events there are thousands of business men who want to keep the Government in the business of protecting their business against foreign competition. If competition is good, why not stand up and take it?

14. The Federal Farm Board. This collectivist institution is the prod-uct of agrarian agitation, on the part of our most stalwart individualists, the free and independent farmers; but President Hoover sponsored it and signed the bill that created it. Now what is its avowed purpose as demonstrated by the language of the statute, the publications of the Farm Board, and the activities carried out under its auspices? It is primarily and fundamentally intended to stabilize prices and production through co-operative methods. And what has the Board done? It has encouraged the development of co-operation as distinguished from individualism among farmers; it has financed co-operative associations; it has denounced individualistic farmers who insist on growing as much as they please, and has tried to get them to increase their earnings by a common limitation of production. If the Agricultural Marketing Act means anything, if the procedure of the Farm Board is not a delusion, then co-operation is to be substituted for individualism in agricultural production and marketing. If there is ever to be a rational adjustment of supply to demand in this field, the spirit and letter of President Hoover's measure must be realized through organized action by millions of farmers under federal auspices. The other alternative is simon-pure

766

individualism: let each farmer produce what he likes, as much of it as he likes, and sell it at any price he can get. But under the happy title " Grow Less — Get More," the Farm Board has given instructions to farmers: " One thing the successful manufacturers learned long ago was that they could not make money when they produced more than they could sell at a profit." The obvious moral is for farmers to get together under Government leadership or hang separately.

15. The Moratorium and Frozen Assets. The latest form of government interference with " the natural course " of economy is the suspension of payments due the United States from foreign powers on account of lawful debts and the proposal to give public support to "frozen assets." What was the source of inspiration here? American investment bankers having got themselves into a jam in their efforts to make easy money now demand government assistance. In 1927 one of the most distinguished German economists told the writer of this article that the great game in his country, as in other parts of Europe, was to borrow billions from private bankers in the United States, so that it would ultimately be impossible to pay reparations, the debts due the Federal Government, *and* then the debts owed to private parties. The expected result? American bankers would then force their Government to forego its claims for the benefit of private operators who wanted to make bankers' commissions and eight or ten per cent on their money. Well, the game worked. American taxpayers are to be soaked and American bankers are to collect — perhaps. . . .

In this survey of a few leading economic activities of the Federal Government the emphasis is not critical; so far as the present argument is concerned, any or all of these functions may be justified with respect to national interest. Indeed it is difficult to find any undertaking of the Government which is not supported by some business men on the ground of national defense. In the early days of our history even those statesmen who generally espoused free trade or low tariffs were willing to concede the importance of making the nation independent in the manufacture of munitions of war. And in the latest hour, subsidies to the merchant marine, to aviation, and to waterways development are stoutly defended in the name of preparedness. Transforming a creek into a river navigable by outboard motor boats can be supported by military engineers on the theory that it gives them practice in their art. No; the emphasis here is not critical. The point is that the Federal

Government does not operate in a vacuum, but under impulsion from without; and all of the measures which put the Government into business have been supported by rugged individualists — business men or farmers or both. The current tendency to describe the Government as a meddling busybody, prying around and regulating for the mere pleasure of taking the joy out of somebody's life, betrays an ignorance of the facts in the case. The Government of the United States operates continually in the midst of the most powerful assembly of lobbyists the world has ever seen — the representatives of every business interest that has risen above the level of a corner grocery; and there is not a single form of government interference with business that does not have the approval of one or more of these interests — except perhaps the taxation of incomes for the purpose, among other things, of paying the expenses of subsidizing and regulating business.

For forty years or more there has not been a President, Republican or Democrat, who has not talked against government interference and then supported measures adding more interference to the huge collection already accumulated. Take, for instance, President Wilson. He made his campaign in 1912 on the classical doctrine of individualism; he blew mighty blasts in the name of his new freedom against the control of the Government by corporate wealth and promised to separate business and government, thus setting little fellows free to make money out of little business. The heir of the Jeffersonian tradition, he decried paternalism of every kind. Yet look at the statutes enacted under his benign administration: the trainmen's law virtually fixing wages on interstate railways for certain classes of employees; the shipping board law; the farm loan act; federal aid for highway construction; the Alaskan railway; the federal reserve act; the water power act; and the rest of the bills passed during his regime. Only the Clayton anti-trust law can be called individualistic. No wonder Mr. E. L. Doheny exclaimed to Mr. C. W. Barron that President Wilson was a college professor gone Bolshevist! And why did Democrats who had been saying "the less government the better" operate on the theory that the more government the better? Simply because their mouths were worked by ancient memories and their actions were shaped by inexorable realities.

Then the Republicans came along in 1921 and informed the country that they were going back to normalcy, were determined to take the Government out of business. Well, did they repeal a single one of the important measures enacted during the eight years of President Wilson's rule? It would be entertaining to see the sanhedrin of the United States Chamber of Commerce trying to make out a list of laws repealed in the name of normalcy and still more entertaining to watch that august body compiling a list of additional laws interfering with "the natural course of business" enacted since 1921. Heirs of the Hamiltonian tradition, the Republicans were not entitled to talk about separating the Government from business. Their great spiritual teacher, Daniel Webster, a pupil of Hamilton, had spoken truly when he said that one of the great reasons for framing the Constitution was the creation of a government that could regulate commerce. They came honestly by subsidies, bounties, internal improvements, tariffs, and other aids to business. What was the trouble with them in the age of normalcy? Nothing; they just wanted their kind of government intervention in the "natural course of industry." Evidently, then, there is some confusion on this subject of individualism, and it ought to be examined dispassionately in the light of its history with a view to discovering its significance and its limitations; for there is moral danger in saying one thing and doing another — at all events too long.

Historically speaking, there are two schools of individualism: one American, associated with the name of Jefferson, and the other English, associated with the name of Cobden. The former was agrarian in interest, the latter capitalist. Jefferson wanted America to be a land of free, upstanding farmers with just enough government to keep order among them; his creed was an agrarian creed nicely fitted to a civilization of sailing ships, ox carts, stagecoaches, wooden plows, tallow dips, and home-made bacon and sausages; and since most of the people in the United States, during the first century of their independence, were engaged in agriculture, they thought highly of Jefferson's praise of agriculture and his doctrine of anarchy plus the police constable. Cobden's individualism was adapted to capitalist England at the middle of the nineteenth century — early industrial England. At that moment his country was the workshop of the world, was mistress of the world market in manufactured commodities, and feared no competition from any foreign country. English capitalists thus needed no protective tariffs and subsidies and, therefore, wanted none. Hence they exalted free trade to the level of a Mosaic law, fixed and eternal. They wanted to employ labor on their own terms and turn working people out to starve when no profitable business was at hand; so they quite naturally believed that any government interference with their right to do as they pleased was "bad." Their literary apologist, Macaulay, clothed their articles of faith in such magnificent rhetoric that even the tiredest business man could keep awake reading it at night.

Closely examined, what is this creed of individualism? Macaulay defines it beautifully. . . . Let the Government maintain peace, defend property, reduce the cost of litigation, and observe economy in expenditure — that is all. Do American business men want peace all the time, in Nicaragua, for instance, when their undertakings are disturbed? Or in Haiti or Santo Domingo? Property must be defended, of course. But whose property? And what about the cost of litigation and economy in expenditures? If they would tell their hired men in law offices to cut the cost of law, something might happen. As for expenditures, do they really mean to abolish subsidies, bounties, and appropriations-in-aid from which they benefit? Speaking brutally, they do not. That is not the kind of economy in expenditures which they demand; they prefer to cut off a few dollars from the Children's Bureau.

Then comes Macaulay's system of private economy: let capital find its most lucrative course alone, unaided: no government tariffs, subsidies, bounties, and special privileges. That is the first item. Do American business men who shout for individualism believe in that? Certainly not. So that much is blown out of the water. Macaulay's next item is: let commodities find their fair price. Do the gentlemen who consolidate, merge, and make price understandings want to allow prices to take their "natural course"? By no means; they are trying to effect combinations that will hold prices up to the point of the largest possible profit. Macaulay's third item is: let industry and intelligence receive their natural reward. Whose industry and intelligence and what industry and intelligence? When these questions are asked all that was clear and simple dissolves in mist.

Then there is Macaulay's last item: let idleness and folly reap their natural punishment. That was a fundamental specification in the bill of Manchesterism. Malthus made it a law for the economists: the poor are poor because they have so many babies and are improvident; nothing can be done about it, at least by any government, even though it enforces drastic measures against the spread of information on birth control. Darwin made a natural science of it: biology sanctified the tooth and claw struggle of business by proclaiming the eternal tooth and claw struggle of the jungle. If the government will do nothing whatever, all people will rise or sink to the level which their industry or idleness, their intelligence or folly commands. No distinction was made between those who were idle because they could find no work and those who just loved idleness for its own sake — either in slums or mansions. Those who hit bottom and starved simply deserved it. That is the good, sound, logical creed of simon-pure individualism which Herbert Spencer embedded in fifty pounds of printed matter. To him and all his devotees, even public schools and public libraries were anathema: let the poor educate themselves at their own expense; to educate them at public expense is robbery of the taxpayer — that industrious, intelligent, provident person who is entitled to keep his " natural reward."

Do any stalwart individualists believe that simple creed now? Not in England, where Liberals, professing to carry on the Cobden-Bright tradition, vote doles for unemployed working people. Why not let idleness and folly get their natural punishment? Why not, indeed? There must be a reason. Either the individualists betray their own faith, or, as some wag has suggested, they are afraid that they might find themselves hanging to a lantern if they let the idle and the foolish starve, that is, reap the natural punishment prescribed by Macaulay. Nor do American individualists propose to let nature take her course in this country. There is no danger of revolution here; as Mr. Coolidge has said, " we have had our revolution "; yet business men agree with the politicians on feeding the hungry. It is true that they seem to be trying to obscure the issues and the facts by talking about the beneficence of private charity while getting most of the dole from public treasuries; but that is a detail. Although our rugged individualists advertise Macaulay's creed, their faith in it appears to be shaky or their courage is not equal to their hopes. Then why should they try to delude themselves and the public?

There is another side to this stalwart individualism that also deserves consideration. Great things have been done in its name, no doubt, and it will always have its place in any reasoned scheme of thinking. Individual initiative and energy are absolutely indispensable to the successful conduct of any enterprise, and there is ample ground for fearing the tyranny and ineptitude of governments. In the days of pioneering industry in England, in our pioneering days when forests were to be cut and mountain fastnesses explored, individualism was the great dynamic which drove enterprise forward. But on other pages of the doom book other entries must be made. In the minds of most people who shout for

771

individualism vociferously, the creed, stripped of all flashy rhetoric, means getting money, simply that and nothing more. And to this creed may be laid most of the shame that has cursed our cities and most of the scandals that have smirched our Federal Government. . . .

The cold truth is that the individualist creed of everybody for himself and the devil take the hindmost is principally responsible for the distress in which Western civilization finds itself — with investment racketeering at one end and labor racketeering at the other. Whatever merits the creed may have had in days of primitive agriculture and industry, it is not applicable in an age of technology, science, and rationalized economy. Once useful, it has become a danger to society. . . .

[1931]

ERSKINE CALDWELL

[1903–   ]

THE SON of a Presbyterian minister, Caldwell was born in a village in Georgia and brought up in various parts of the South. He spent three years at the University of Virginia, but his real education for his career as a writer came from his contacts with the poor whites of the Georgia hill country and with the workers of the various cities in which he was employed as a laborer, hack-man, cook, and waiter. He published two unsuccessful novels before his now famous *Tobacco Road* (1932), and that was followed by another success, *God's Little Acre* (1933) These works are now generally accepted as the truest pictures we have ever had of the tragic degeneracy of Southern backwoods people — a race ground down by poverty, disease, and ignorance. The grim humor of these novels serves merely to emphasize the tragedy of the scenes and characters depicted. Caldwell's best short stories, included in such volumes as *Kneel to the Rising Sun* (1935) and *Southways* (1938), have usually dealt with similar subjects — poor whites, Negro share-croppers, small-town workers. Many of them are ranked among contemporary master-pieces in this field.

DAUGHTER

At sunrise a Negro on his way to the big house to feed the mules had taken the word to Colonel Henry Maxwell, and Colonel Henry 'phoned the sheriff. The sheriff had hustled Jim into town and locked him up in the jail, and then he went home and ate breakfast.

Jim walked around the empty cellroom while he was buttoning his shirt, and after that he sat down on the bunk and tied his shoelaces. Everything that morning had taken place so quickly that he had not even had time to get a drink of water. He got up and went to the water bucket near the door, but the sheriff had forgotten to put water in it.

By that time there were several men standing in the jailyard. Jim

773

went to the window and looked out when he heard them talking. Just then another automobile drove up, and six or seven men got out. Other men were coming towards the jail from both directions of the street.

"What was the trouble out at your place this morning, Jim?" somebody said.

Jim stuck his chin between the bars and looked at the faces in the crowd. He knew everyone there.

While he was trying to figure out how everybody in town had heard about his being there, somebody else spoke to him.

"It must have been an accident, wasn't it, Jim?"

A colored boy hauling a load of cotton to the gin drove up the street. When the wagon got in front of the jail, the boy whipped up the mules with the ends of the reins and made them trot.

"I hate to see the State have a grudge against you, Jim," somebody said.

The sheriff came down the street swinging a tin dinner-pail in his hand. He pushed through the crowd, unlocked the door, and set the pail inside.

Several men came up behind the sheriff and looked over his shoulder into the jail.

"Here's your breakfast my wife fixed up for you, Jim. You'd better eat a little, Jim boy."

Jim looked at the pail, at the sheriff, at the open jail door, and he shook his head.

"I don't feel hungry," he said. "Daughter's been hungry, though.— awful hungry."

The sheriff backed out the door, his hand going to the handle of his pistol. He backed out so quickly that he stepped on the toes of the men behind him.

"Now, don't you get careless, Jim boy," he said. "Just sit and calm yourself."

He shut the door and locked it. After he had gone a few steps towards the street, he stopped and looked into the chamber of his pistol to make sure it had been loaded.

The crowd outside the window pressed in closer. Some of the men rapped on the bars until Jim came and looked out. When he saw them, he stuck his chin between the iron and gripped his hands around it.

"How come it to happen, Jim?" somebody asked. "It must have been an accident, wasn't it?"

Jim's long thin face looked as if it would come through the bars. The sheriff came up to the window to see if everything was all right.

"Now, just take it easy, Jim boy," he said.

The man who had asked Jim to tell what had happened, elbowed the sheriff out of the way. The other men crowded closer.

"How come, Jim?" the man said. "Was it an accident?"

"No," Jim said, his fingers twisting about the bars. "I picked up my shotgun and done it."

The sheriff pushed towards the window again.

"Go on, Jim, and tell us what it's all about."

Jim's face squeezed between the bars until it looked as though only his ears kept his head from coming through.

"Daughter said she was hungry, and I just couldn't stand it no longer. I just couldn't stand to hear her say it."

"Don't get all excited now, Jim boy," the sheriff said, pushing forward one moment and being elbowed away the next.

"She waked up in the middle of the night again and said she was hungry. I just couldn't stand to hear her say it."

Somebody pushed all the way through the crowd until he got to the window.

"Why, Jim, you could have come and asked me for something for her to eat, and you know I'd have given you all I got in the world."

The sheriff pushed forward once more.

"That wasn't the right thing to do," Jim said. "I've been working all year and I made enough for all of us to eat."

He stopped and looked down into the faces on the other side of the bars.

"I made enough working on shares, but they came and took it all away from me. I couldn't go around begging after I'd made enough to keep us. They just came and took it all off. Then Daughter woke up again this morning saying she was hungry, and I just couldn't stand it no longer."

"You'd better go and get on the bunk now, Jim boy," the sheriff said.

"It don't seem right that the little girl ought to be shot like that," somebody said.

"Daughter said she was hungry," Jim said. "She'd been saying that for all of the past month. Daughter'd wake up in the middle of the night and say it. I just couldn't stand it no longer."

"You ought to have sent her over to my house, Jim. Me and my wife could have fed her something, somehow. It don't look right to kill a little girl like her."

"I made enough for all of us," Jim said. "I just couldn't stand it no longer. Daughter'd been hungry all the past month."

"Take it easy, Jim boy," the sheriff said, trying to push forward.

The crowd swayed from side to side.

"And so you just picked up the gun this morning and shot her?" somebody asked.

"When she woke up this morning saying she was hungry, I just couldn't stand it."

The crowd pushed closer. Men were coming towards the jail from all directions, and those who were then arriving pushed forward to hear what Jim had to say.

"The State has got a grudge against you now, Jim," somebody said, "but somehow it don't seem right."

"I can't help it," Jim said. "Daughter woke up again this morning that way."

The jailyard, the street, and the vacant lot on the other side were filled with men and boys. All of them were pushing forward to hear Jim. Word had spread all over town by that time that Jim Carlisle had shot and killed his eight-year-old daughter, Clara.

"Who does Jim share-crop for?" somebody asked.

"Colonel Henry Maxwell," a man in the crowd said. "Colonel Henry has had Jim out there about nine or ten years."

"Henry Maxwell didn't have no business coming and taking all the shares. He's got plenty of his own. It ain't right for Henry Maxwell to come and take Jim's, too."

The sheriff was pushing forward once more.

"The State's got a grudge against Jim now," somebody said. "Somehow it doesn't seem right, though."

The sheriff pushed his shoulder into the crowd of men and worked his way in closer.

A man shoved the sheriff away.

"Why did Henry Maxwell come and take your share of the crop, Jim?"

"He said I owed it to him because one of his mules died about a month ago."

The sheriff got in front of the barred window.

"You ought to go to the bunk now and rest some, Jim boy," he said. "Take off your shoes and stretch out, Jim boy."

He was elbowed out of the way.

"You didn't kill the mule, did you, Jim?"

"The mule dropped dead in the barn," Jim said. "I wasn't nowhere around. It just dropped dead."

The crowd was pushing harder. The men in front were jammed against the jail, and the men behind were trying to get within earshot. Those in the middle were squeezed against each other so tightly they could not move in any direction. Everyone was talking louder.

Jim's face pressed between the bars and his fingers gripped the iron until the knuckles were white.

The milling crowd was moving across the street to the vacant lot. Somebody was shouting. He climbed up on an automobile and began swearing at the top of his lungs.

A man in the middle of the crowd pushed his way out and went to his automobile. He got in and drove off alone.

Jim stood holding to the bars and looking through the window. The sheriff had his back to the crowd, and he was saying something to Jim. Jim did not hear what he said.

A man on his way to the gin with a load of cotton stopped to find out what the trouble was. He looked at the crowd in the vacant lot for a moment, and then he turned around and looked at Jim behind the bars. The shouting across the street was growing louder.

"What's the trouble, Jim?"

Somebody on the other side of the street came to the wagon. He put his foot on a spoke in the wagon wheel and looked up at the man on the cotton while he talked.

"Daughter woke up this morning again saying she was hungry," Jim said.

The sheriff was the only person who heard him.

The man on the load of cotton jumped to the ground, tied the reins to the wagon wheel, and pushed through the crowd to the car where all the shouting and swearing was being done. After listening for a while, he came back to the street, called a Negro who was standing with several other Negroes on the corner, and handed him the reins. The Negro drove off with the cotton towards the gin, and the man went back into the crowd.

Just then the man who had driven off alone in his car came back. He sat for a moment behind the steering wheel, and then he opened the door and jumped to the ground. He opened the rear door and took out a crowbar that was as long as he was tall.

"Pry that jail door open and let Jim out," somebody said. "It ain't right for him to be in there."

The crowd in the vacant lot was moving again. The man who had been standing on top of the automobile jumped to the ground, and the men moved towards the street in the direction of the jail.

The first man to reach it jerked the six-foot crowbar out of the soft earth where it had been jabbed.

The sheriff backed off.

"Now, take it easy, Jim boy," he said.

He turned and started walking rapidly up the street towards his house.

[*1935*]

STEPHEN VINCENT BENÉT

[1898–1943]

BENÉT was born in Bethlehem, Pennsylvania, and brought up in California and Georgia, where his father, an army man, was stationed at government arsenals. He was educated at Summerville Academy and Yale, from which he was graduated in 1919. He took his master's degree the following year and then studied briefly at the Sorbonne in Paris. From 1921 until his death he supported himself by writing. Short stories, novels, poems, and essays poured from his pen, but while he wrote many good tales, it is in the field of poetry that he won his major honors. In 1926 he was awarded a Guggenheim fellowship which enabled him to spend two years writing an epic poem on the Civil War. It was published as *John Brown's Body* in 1928, was extremely successful, and was awarded the Pulitzer Prize in Poetry for that year. His collected *Ballads and Poems* was published in 1931, and a notable new volume, *Burning City*, in 1936. The selections which follow are from the last of these.

ODE TO THE AUSTRIAN SOCIALISTS

(*February 12–February 15, 1934*)

They shot the Socialists at half-past five
In the name of victorious Austria.
         The sky
Was blue with February those four cold days
And the little snow lay lightly on the hard ground.
(Vienna's the laughing city of tunes and wine,
Of *Schlagobers* and starved children . . . and a great ghost. . . .)
They had called the general strike but the plans went wrong
Though the lights failed, that first night.
         It is odd to turn

779

The switch by your bed and have no lamp go on
And then look out of the windows at the black street
Empty, except for a man with a pistol, running.
We have built our cities for lights and the harsh glare
And, when the siren screams at the winter stars,
It is only a fire, an ambulance, nothing wrong,
Just part of the day. You can walk to the corner store
And never duck at a bullet. The lights are there
And, if you see a man with a pistol, running,
You phone the police or wait for tomorrow's papers.
It is different, with the lights out and the shots beginning. . . .

These were ordinary people.
The kind that go to the movies and watch parades,
Have children, take them to parks, ride the trolley cars,
The workmen at the next bench, the old, skilful foreman;
You have seen the backs of their necks a million times
In any crowd and forgotten — seen their faces,
Anonymous, tired, good-humored, faces of skill.
(The quick hands moving deftly among machines,
Hands of the baker and the baker's wife,
Hands gloved with rubber, mending the spitting wire,
Hands on controls and levers, big, square-palmed hands
With the dint of the tool upon them,
Dull, clumsy fingers laboring a dull task
And others, writing and thoughtful, or sensitive
As a setter's mouth.) You have seen their hats and their shoes
Everywhere, in every city. They wear no costumes.
Their pockets have lint in them, and tobacco-dust.
Their faces are the faces of any crowd.

It was Monday when this began.
                                They were slow to start it
But they had been pushed to the wall. They believed in peace,
Good houses, meetings, elections and resolutions,
Not the sudden killing in corners, the armored cars
Sweeping the square, the bombs and the bloody heads,
But they'd seen what happened next door, in another country,
To people who believed in peace and elections

And the same tide was rising here. They could hear the storm.
They took to their guns at last, in the workmen's quarters,
Where they'd built the houses for peace and the sure future.

The houses were tall and fine,
Great blocks of manstone, built by people for people,
Not to make one man rich. When you do not build
To make one man rich, you can give people light and air,
You can have room to turn round — room after the day —
You can have books and clean water and healthy sleep,
A place for children to grow in.
All over the world men knew about those houses.

Let us remember Karl Marx Hof, Goethe Hof,
The one called Matteoti and all the rest.
They were little cities built by people for people.
They were shelled by six-inch guns.
                              It is strange to go
Up the known stairs to the familiar room
And point the lean machine-gun out of the window,
Strange to see the black of that powder upon your hands. . . .

They had hidden arms against need but they could not find them
In many cases, being ordinary people.
The other side was much readier — Fey and Dollfuss
And all the shirts were quite ready.
                              When you believe
In parks and elections and meetings and not in death,
Not in Cæsar,
It is hard to realize that the day may come
When you send your wife and children down to the cellar
To be out of the way of shells, and mount the known
Countable stairs to the familiar room,
The unfamiliar pistol cold in your fist
And your mouth dry with despair.
                              It is hard to think
In spite of all oppression, all enmity,
That that is going to happen.
And so, when it does happen, your plans go wrong.

781

(White flags on the Karl Marx Hof and the Goethe Hof
And the executions, later.)
                                        A correspondent
Of the British press remarked, when the thing was done
And they let him in to see it, that on the whole
The buildings were less damaged than you'd expect
From four days' bullets. True, he had seen, before,
A truckload of undertakers and cheap, pine coffins
Go to the disputed district.
But the buildings stood, on the whole. They had built them well.

These were ordinary people and they are dead.
Dead where they lived, by violence, in their own homes,
Between the desk and the door and the kitchen chair,
Dead in the courtyards where the children played
(The child's jaw smashed by a bullet, the bloody crib,
The woman sprawled like a rag on the clean stairs)
Uncæsarlike, unwarlike, merely dead.

Dead, or in exile many, or afraid
(And those who live there still and wake in the night,
Remembering the free city)
Silent or hunted and their leaders slimed.
The communists said they would not fight but they fought
Four days of bitter February,
Ill-led, outnumbered, the radio blaring lies
And the six-inch guns against them and all hope gone,
Four days in the Karl Marx Hof and the Goethe Hof
And nobody knows yet how many dead
And sensible men give in and accept the flag,
The badge, the arm-band, the gag, the slave-tyranny,
The shining, tin peace of Cæsar.
                                        They were not sensible,
Four days of February, two years ago.

Bring no flowers here,
Neither of mountain nor valley,
Nor even the common flowers of the waste field
That still are free to the poor;

No wreaths upon these graves, these houseless graves;
But bring alone the powder-blackened brass
Of the shell-case, the slag of bullets, the ripped steel
And the bone-spattering lead,
Infertile, smelling acridly of death,
And heap them here, till the rusting of guns, for remembrance.
[*1936*]

from

ODE TO WALT WHITMAN

(*May 31, 1819–March 26, 1892*)

It is Fourth Month now and spring in another century,
Let us go to the hillside and ask; he will like to hear us;
" Is it good, the sleep? "

      " It is good, the sleep and the waking.
I have picked out a bit of hill where the south sun warms me.
I like to be near the trees."

Nay, let him ask, rather.
" Is it well with you, comrades?
The cities great, portentous, humming with action?
The bridges mightily spanning wide-breasted rivers?
The great plains growing the wheat, the old lilac hardy, well-budded?
Is it well with these States? "

" The cities are great, portentous, a world-marvel,
The bridges arched like the necks of beautiful horses.
We had made the dry land bloom and the dead land blossom."

" Is it well with these States? "

" The old wound of your war is healed and we are one nation.
We have linked the whole land with the steel and the hard highways.

783

We have fought new wars and won them. In the French field
There are bones of Texarkana and Little Falls,
Aliens, our own; in the low-lying Belgian ground;
In the cold sea of the English; in dark-faced islands.
Men speak of them well or ill; they themselves are silent."

" Is it well with these States? "

" We have made many, fine new toys.
We —
There is a rust on the land.
A rust and a creeping blight and a scaled evil,
For six years eating, yet deeper than those six years,
Men labor to master it but it is not mastered.
There is the soft, grey, foul tent of the hatching worm
Shrouding the elm, the chestnut, the Southern cypress.
There is shadow in the bright sun, there is shadow upon the streets.
They burn the grain in the furnace while men go hungry.
They pile the cloth of the looms while men go ragged.
We walk naked in our plenty."

" My tan-faced children? "

" These are your tan-faced children.
These skilled men, idle, with the holes in their shoes.
These drifters from State to State, these wolvish, bewildered boys
Who ride the blinds and the box-cars from jail to jail,
Burnt in their youth like cinders of hot smokestacks,
Learning the thief's crouch and the cadger's whine,
Dishonored, abandoned, disinherited.
These, dying in the bright sunlight they cannot eat,
Or the strong men, sitting at home, their hands clasping nothing,
Looking at their lost hands.
These are your tan-faced children, the parched young,
The old man rooting in waste-heaps, the family rotting
In the flat, before eviction,
With the toys of plenty about them,
The shiny toys making ice and music and light,
But no price for the shiny toys and the last can empty.

784

The sleepers in blind corners of the night.
The women with dry breasts and phantom eyes.
The walkers upon nothing, the four million.
These are your tan-faced children."

"But the land?"

" Over the great plains of the buffalo-land
The dust-storm blows, the choking, sifting, small dust.
The skin of that land is ploughed by the dry, fierce wind
And blown away, like a torrent;
It drifts foot-high above the young sprouts of grain
And the water fouls, the horses stumble and sicken,
The wash-board cattle stagger and die of drought.
We tore the buffalo's pasture with the steel blade.
We made the waste land blossom and it has blossomed.
That was our fate; now that land takes its own revenge,
And the giant dust-flower blooms above five States."

" But the gains of the years, who got them? "

"Many, great gains.
Many, yet few; they robbed us in the broad daylight,
Saying, ' Give us this and that; we are kings and titans;
We know the ropes; we are solid; we are hard-headed;
We will build you cities and railroads ' — as if *they* built them!
They, the preying men, the men whose hearts were like engines,
Gouging the hills for gold, laying waste the timber,
The men like band-saws, moving over the land.
And, after them, the others,
Soft-bodied, lacking even the pirate's candor,
Men of paper, robbing by paper, with paper faces,
Rustling like frightened paper when the storm broke.
The men with the jaws of moth and aphis and beetle,
Boring the dusty, secret hole in the corn,
Fixed, sucking the land, with neither wish nor pride
But the wish to suck and continue.
They have been sprayed, a little.
But they say they will have the land back again, these men."

" There were many such in my time.
I have seen the rich arrogant and the poor oppressed.
I have seen democracy, also. I have seen
The good man slain, the knave and the fool in power,
The democratic vista botched by the people,
Yet not despaired, loving the giant land,
Though I prophesied to these States."

" Now they say we must have one tyranny or another
And a dark bell rings in our hearts."

" Was the blood spilt for nothing, then? "
[*1936*]

786

LEANE ZUGSMITH

[1903–   ]

MISS ZUGSMITH was born in Louisville, Kentucky, but spent most of her childhood in Philadelphia and Atlantic City. She attended Goucher College, the University of Pennsylvania, and Columbia. She held editorial jobs on pulp magazines, lived in Europe for a year, and then worked for many years in book-publishing houses. She has produced six novels, among them *A Time to Remember* (1936) and *The Summer Soldier* (1938), and one volume of short stories, *Home Is Where You Hang Your Childhood* (1937). Her novels have revealed a consistent advance not only in skill and sensitiveness, but also in understanding of the political forces which are her chief preoccupation. Especially fine, however, are the stories in which she deals with the domestic effects of social tragedy. Her stories have appeared in such magazines as the *New Yorker*, the *Atlantic Monthly*, the *New Masses, Collier's,* and *Story Magazine*. Until recently she has been a special-feature writer on the staff of the New York newspaper *PM*.

ROOM IN THE WORLD

When she heard Ab's footsteps approaching the door, she knew, without having to see or to hear him, that it had been the same as yesterday and all the days before, since he had been fired from the job he had held as watchman for the office building. He couldn't do anything but talk about it all night long, and every day he went back trying to get to some one higher up who would tell the new superintendent: "Ab's been with us nine years, there ain't no reason to let him go." If she was him, Pauline thought, she'd give it up and if, like he said, there wasn't no job for him no place, she'd go on Relief. With a five-months-old baby and a three-year-old boy growing so fast that the Lord only knew how she was going to make this suit of his any bigger, and a girl of eight, already in the second grade, she'd give it up. But Ab was bullheaded, always had been, and maybe he'd get back, like he said.

As Ab came in, she hastened to close the door leading off the kitchen into the room where Jappy was taking his nap. Even when Ab raised his voice, it wouldn't wake the baby in the market basket near the stove. She was a dandy sleeper, better than Jappy, much better than Frances ever had been.

She thrust the needle into the material, waiting to see if Ab was going to speak first. If he kept on staring at her, it was up to her and it meant he was good and sore. After a while, she knew it was up to her.

"Either the clock's fast," she said in the casual, conversational tone she had lately learned to use, "or Frances must of been kept in."

Gloomily he stared at her.

"She done her homework, I know." Pauline turned Jappy's drawers inside out and studied the problem of enlarging them.

"I tried every God-damned one of them," he said between his teeth. "I seen all their chippy secretaries. They're all too God-damned busy to see me. I'm only working there *nine* years. Maybe that ain't long enough."

"No one can say you ain't tried," she said.

"Tried? I done everything but crawl along the corridors on my belly. It's 'see the super. It's up to the super.' Nuts!"

"Them real-estate people are over the super," she said sympathetically and she thought: He won't give it up yet. No use telling him about the gas or how they wouldn't give her credit at the other grocery store she tried out.

"They won't even see me. You seen what they written me."

"It was a sin the old super had to die," she said.

"The new one will take me back," he said ominously. "I ain't saying how but I'm gonta get back on the job."

Hooding her anxious eyes as she watched him to read what was in his mind, she heard Frances at the door. She hurried to open it, her mind still on her husband's words. The kid was all excited about something, the way she got sometimes, dancing around the room. She sure was high-strung; good thing the baby didn't seem to take after her. Pauline was afraid she'd begin to bother her pa, but he didn't seem to take notice, banging his hand down on the kitchen table, crying out:

"I ain't going back crawling to them, neither, to get it!"

She cast a swift look at the baby to see if she had been disturbed by the noise. " Maybe — " Pauline began.

" Maybe, nothing! I'll be back on the job, wait and see."

Frances kept tugging at her arm. " *Ma,* I been telling you."

Ab glared at his daughter.

" We're talking now, Pa and me," Pauline said quickly.

" Only, Ma, let me tell about the new little girl, she came today. She's got curls just like Shirley Temple." Frances's voice went up high.

" Shut up! " said Ab.

" The new little girl, she looks just like Shirley Temple."

" Play in the other room." Her mother pinched her cheek. " Jappy's asleep in yours and his."

" No I don't wanta. I wanta tell you about the new little girl, Ma, she's got red paint on her fingernails. Can't I have — "

Her mother interrupted her. " You're getting your Pa worked up, not minding." She reached for a tin pail. " Go on down and get me five cents' worth of milk, hear me. Tell him your Ma said she'd stop in and pay up tomorrow."

Ab breathed heavily after the little girl had left the room. Without looking up from her sewing, his wife said calmly: " She's only eight." And she thought: In a while, when we can't get no credit no place, there won't be that much spirit in any of them.

" I'm trying to think out what to do, and she comes in babbling till she gets me all mixed up."

" Try to think what you was thinking before."

" What do you think I'm trying to do? "

The tick of the clock sounded loud now. The baby's occasional soft snores could be heard. Pauline kept her head bent over her sewing until Ab spoke up.

" You know how they do when a lot of them go out on strike," he said.

" Well? "

" Like I read once in a newspaper, see, a fellow and his whole family, they go out with signs, asking for his job back."

Her face became thoughtful. " Like them pickets is what you mean? "

" You got me."

She ceased to sew. " I couldn't leave Frances take care of the baby."

" No. She'd let it smother or something." He looked down at his hands for a while. Presently he said: " I could take the two kids, see, all of us wearing signs asking for my job back."

"I could make the signs O. K., if we had some kind of stiff paper," she said. "You wouldn't walk Jappy too long, would you, Ab? He don't stand much walking."

Ab stood up, his face lighted. "That would get them, all right, you bet! Maybe them newspaper guys will come around and take our pictures." He pulled a pencil from his vest pocket and smoothed the wrinkles from a brown paper bag.

"Maybe down at the corner, they'd give you some stiff paper," said Pauline.

He wet the pencil, leaning over the kitchen table, too elated to sit down. "Now, we'll say —" He wet the pencil once more. "What'll we say?"

"If the sign's for the kids it had oughta say something about 'my Pa' and so on."

"You got brains, Pauline," he said. "'Please get my Pa back his job.' How's that?"

"O. K."

"We'll make Jappy's and Frances's alike. Now mine." He wet the pencil. "What would you say?"

"'Get me back my job at the Stark Building,' how about that?"

"No," he said. He started to print letters. "How's this? 'Fired for no reason after nine years being watchman at the Stark Building.'"

"That's O. K.," she said.

"O. K.? It's the nuts!" he cried out gleefully. "Wait till I see the faces of them birds who thinks they ain't gonta take me back!"

It was getting past the baby's feeding time; Pauline thanked her stars that she was so good she wouldn't start bawling right off. She couldn't pick her up with Jappy goose-stepping around, already dressed to go out, the sign flapping as he thrust each leg straight out before him, Frances trying to see how the sign looked on her before the little mirror over the dresser, and Ab yelling: "Let's go to town. Come on, you kids."

Jappy couldn't be held down. He kept singing: "I'm a picket, I'm a picket, I'm a picket," until they couldn't help laughing.

"Them signs are going to blow all around on them," Pauline said.

"Don't worry about them signs," Ab cried out. "Come on, you kids."

"I'm a picket," shouted Jappy. In a fit of wildness, he dug his forefinger into the top of his cap and began whirling around.

"You'll get dizzy. Stop it!" his mother called out.

Frances ran in. "I can't see what I look like, Ma," she complained.

Jappy started going round too fast and fell down.

"You bent the sign," his father said crossly, picking him up.

Jappy smiled when he saw that he didn't have to cry.

"It'll only take a minute." Pauline threaded a needle and began to sew the bottom corners of the sign on to Jappy's little coat. "I'll sew on yours, too," she told Frances.

"Lift me up, Pa, in by the looking-glass, so's I can see," Frances begged.

As Ab took her into the other room, Pauline said to her son with exasperation: "Keep still, will you!"

"I'm gonta be a picket," he screamed joyfully. "I'm gonta go up to them dopes —"

"Where did you learn that?" She bit off the thread.

"I'm gonta be a dope, I'm gonta be a picket."

Frances came back, saying sulkily: "I can't read what it says in the looking-glass."

"You know what it says. I told her." Ab followed her.

"What's mine say?" cried Jappy.

"It says 'Give my Pa back his job,'" said Frances, holding still while her mother sewed the bottom corners of her sign on to her jacket.

"Give my Pa back his job," Jappy chanted, starting once more to goose-step.

Ab grabbed his hand. "Come on. I ain't gonna wait another minute."

Picking up the baby, Pauline followed them to the door. As soon as she had closed it, she heard sounds of bawling outside. It was Jappy, all right. She opened the door. Ab called angrily to her from the stairs. "He wantsta take his Popeye doll along with him. He ain't gonta."

Jappy's cries were louder now that he knew his mother was listening. "Let him," she said. "It won't do no harm." Might do good, she thought, them seeing a little kid with a doll. "I'll get it."

"Make it snappy," Ab called back.

She found the wooden figure from which all the paint had streaked. Jappy was back at the door with Frances just behind. The little boy smirked. "Popeye the Sailor's gonta be a picket," he said.

"Hurry up!" Ab called out.

"Popeye wants a sign." Jappy held the doll up to his mother. "Make him a sign." His chin was beginning to tremble.

She snatched a fragment of paper from the table, scribbled on it and attached it precariously to the doll. "Hurry." She gave both children little pushes and then stood with her ear to the crack of the door where she could hear them talking as they went toward the stairs.

"Popeye's sign says 'Give my Pa back his job,'" said Jappy.

"It don't say nothing," said Frances. "It's only scribble."

"It do, too," he said.

Then their voices became fainter. She wished she could see the street from their windows to watch them walking away. Hope Ab don't forget he shouldn't keep them out too long. The baby began to whimper, and she patted its back as she unbuttoned her blouse. It don't do no good for me to skimp on eating, she thought, or I'll only take it away from the baby.

When they came back, Ab couldn't talk of anything but the expression on the new super's face and how people had stopped them and they almost had their pictures taken. As Pauline ripped the stitches off Jappy's sign, she noticed that he was almost asleep on his feet. When she started to rip the stitches off Frances's sign, she saw that her skinny legs were trembling. She looked up into the little girl's miserable face. "Why, what's the matter, honey?"

Before Frances could get out a word, she began to bawl. She bawled just like she did when she was a baby.

"What happened to her?" Pauline turned to Ab.

"I don't know." He was beginning to be gloomy again.

Pauline put her arms around Frances. "Tell Ma," she said.

Her breath catching, the tears streaming down the monkey face she was making, Frances said: "The new little girl seen me."

"A lot of people seen you," said Pauline. "That don't make no difference." She was trying to keep her voice steady.

Frances struggled out of her mother's reach.

"The new little girl seen me," she got out between sobs and ran from the room.

"I try to get back my job," said Ab heavily, "and that's the thanks I get."

Before she spoke, she looked around for Jappy and, finding him asleep on the floor, she said, trying to pick her words:

"She got a crush on some little girl at school she says looks like Shirley Temple."

"That ain't gonta get my job back." Ab bent his head over the table where his sign and Jappy's lay.

Both of them could hear, through the closed door, Frances's frenzy of weeping.

Pauline swallowed. "Other people seeing her don't make no difference, on account of she's at the age, see what I mean?"

"No," he said, but his lowered voice had in it a curious strain.

"She's highstrung, Ab. To some other kid it mightn't mean nothing, only with her it might set her back, you know how kids are."

She waited for him to reply, watching him make marks on the back of his sign with his pencil. It was the truth, he might as well admit it. Other people didn't have to take out their kids with signs on them begging for their Pa's job. The weeping in the next room had subsided into long sighs and occasional hiccups.

Presently, without looking up, he said: "I shouldn't oughta take her tomorrow."

"Jappy likes it." Pauline said hopefully.

He made more marks on the back of the sign. Still without looking up, he said: "We could change the words tomorrow." He pushed the lettering toward her, keeping his eyes averted. The crooked printing read:

"Ain't there room in the world for us?"

Now it's gonta bust out, she thought. Only you can't let it go, not with the kid bawling in the other room and him so down in the mouth. She swallowed the thing in her throat. And, searching for it, she found the tone she had lately learned to use.

"It don't seem like 'ain't' is the right word there," she said in a casual, conversational voice.

[*1936*]

JAMES WELDON JOHNSON

[1871–1938]

A LEADER of the Negro people in their political and social activities, he was also a poet of some distinction. He was born in Jacksonville, Florida, where he received his elementary education. In 1894 he was graduated from Atlanta University. He became principal of the colored high school in Jacksonville, studied law, was admitted to the Florida bar in 1897, and practiced until 1901, when he moved to New York to write light opera with his brother J. Rosamond Johnson. In 1906 he was appointed to a U. S. consulate in Venezuela, in 1909 transferred to Nicaragua. From 1916 to 1930 he was secretary of the National Association for the Advancement of Colored People, in which position he fought against lynching and Jim Crowism. His investigation of American military rule in Haiti led to the restoration of a native Haitian government. In 1930 he became a professor of literature at Fisk University. He was a trustee of Atlanta University and of the Garland Fund. Johnson published a novel, *The Autobiography of an Ex-Colored Man* (1912), and a history of the Negro in New York, *Black Manhattan* (1930), as well as verse. The two short poems which follow indicate the rise of emotions new in Negro poetry — protest instead of supplication, bitterness instead of self-pity.

TO AMERICA

How would you have us, as we are?
Or sinking 'neath the load we bear?
Our eyes fixed forward on a star?
Or gazing empty at despair?

Rising or falling? Men or things?
With dragging pace or footsteps fleet?
Strong, willing sinews in your wings?
Or tightening chains about your feet?
[*1917*]

THE BLACK MAMMY

O whitened head entwined in turban gay,
O kind black face, O crude, but tender hand,
O foster-mother in whose arms there lay
The race whose sons are masters of the land!
It was thine arms that sheltered in their fold,
It was thine eyes that followed through the length
Of infant days these sons. In times of old
It was thy breast that nourished them to strength.

So often hast thou to thy bosom pressed
The golden head, the face and brow of snow;
So often has it 'gainst thy broad, dark breast
Lain, set off like a quickened cameo.
Thou simple soul, as cuddling down that babe
With thy sweet croon, so plaintive and so wild,
Came ne'er the thought to thee, swift like a stab,
That it some day might crush thine own black child?

[1917]

COUNTEE CULLEN

[1903–   ]

HE IS perhaps the most skillful Negro poet of our day. Writing usually in traditional forms, his lyrics have won him a rather larger audience than that enjoyed by any other contemporary colored poet. He has thus satisfied his own standard, for he has said that the fact of race should not be a criterion of literary judgment. Nevertheless, the fact of race is a considerable factor in his writing. It is not for his lyrics on conventional themes that he is best known, but for such poems as those that follow. In them we see some traces of an earlier tradition in Negro verse — a touch of sentimentality, of pathos, of a certain modesty in expressing tragedy. Cullen was born in New York in 1903 and " reared in the conservative atmosphere of a Methodist parsonage." He was educated in the public schools of the city, at New York University, and at Harvard. Among his books are *Color* (1925) and *Copper Sun* (1927). He is on the staff of *Opportunity: A Journal of Negro Life*.

INCIDENT

Once riding in old Baltimore,
    Heart-filled, head-filled with glee,
I saw a Baltimorean
    Keep looking straight at me.

Now I was eight and very small,
    And he was no whit bigger,
And so I smiled, but he poked out
    His tongue and called me, " Nigger."

I saw the whole of Baltimore
    From May until December:
Of all the things that happened there
    That's all that I remember

[1925]

YET DO I MARVEL

I doubt not God is good, well-meaning, kind,
And did he stoop to quibble could tell why
The little buried mole continues blind,
Why flesh that mirrors him must some day die,
Make plain the reason tortured Tantalus
Is baited with the fickle fruit, declare
If merely brute caprice dooms Sisyphus
To struggle up a never-ending stair.

Inscrutable His ways are and immune
To catechism by a mind too strewn
With petty cares to slightly understand
What awful brain compels His awful hand;
Yet do I marvel at this curious thing:
To make a poet black, and bid him sing!

[1925]

LANGSTON HUGHES

[1902–   ]

BORN in Joplin, Missouri, he was brought up in Lawrence, Kansas, and Cleveland, Ohio — and in the last city he attended high school and began writing poems for the school magazine. When he was graduated, he spent a year in Mexico, where his father owned a ranch, then returned to the United States. For one year he attended classes at Columbia, after which he went to sea and for three years wandered around Europe and Africa. In Paris he worked in night-clubs; in Italy he was " on the beach." He arrived in New York in 1924, voyaging as an ordinary seaman on a freighter. Soon afterwards he got a job as a busboy in the Wardman Park Hotel, Washington, D.C. He was now again writing poetry. One day Vachel Lindsay was dining at the hotel and Hughes gave him three poems to read. That evening Lindsay read them to his audience in the hotel auditorium — and Hughes was acclaimed. In 1925 he won a poetry prize given by the Negro magazine *Opportunity*. In 1926 he went back to college, this time to Lincoln University, for another brief excursion into academic work. Since then he has supported himself by writing. Among his works are two volumes of poetry, *The Weary Blues* (1926) and *Fine Clothes to the Jew* (1927), a novel, *Not without Laughter* (1930), a volume of short stories, *The Ways of White Folks* (1934), and an autobiography, *The Big Sea* (1940). Even the most careless reader of the poems which follow will realize that the colored race has in Hughes not merely a gifted writer, but one who speaks forthrightly for his people — one who neither begs nor weeps, but *demands* justice, and one who, at the same time, rises above race to speak for all the lowly.

CROSS

My old man's a white old man
And my old mother's black.
If ever I cursed my white old man
I take my curses back.

If ever I cursed my black old mother
And wished she were in hell,
I'm sorry for that evil wish
And now I wish her well.

My old man died in a fine big house.
My ma died in a shack.
I wonder where I'm gonna die,
Being neither white nor black?
[*1926*]

I, TOO, SING AMERICA

I, too, sing America.

I am the darker brother.
They send me to eat in the kitchen
When company comes,
But I laugh,
And eat well,
And grow strong.

Tomorrow,
I'll sit at the table
When company comes.
Nobody'll dare
Say to me,
" Eat in the kitchen,"
Then.

Besides,
They'll see how beautiful I am
And be ashamed, —

I, too, am America.
[*1926*]

799

LET AMERICA BE AMERICA AGAIN

Let America be America again.
Let it be the dream it used to be.
Let it be the pioneer on the plain
Seeking a home where he himself is free.

(America never was America to me.)

Let America be the dream the dreamers dreamed —
Let it be that great strong land of love
Where never kings connive nor tyrants scheme
That any man be crushed by one above.

(It never was America to me.)

O, let my land be a land where Liberty
Is crowned with no false patriotic wreath,
But opportunity is real, and life is free,
Equality is in the air we breathe.

(There's never been equality for me,
Nor freedom in this " homeland of the free.")

Say who are you that mumbles in the dark?
And who are you that draws your veil across the stars?

I am the poor white, fooled and pushed apart,
I am the Negro bearing slavery's scars.
I am the red man driven from the land,
I am the immigrant clutching the hope I seek —
And finding only the same old stupid plan.
Of dog eat dog, of mighty crush the weak.

I am the young man, full of strength and hope,
Tangled in that ancient endless chain
Of profit, power, gain, of grab the land!
Of grab the gold! Of grab the ways of satisfying need!

Of work the men! Of take the pay!
Of owning everything for one's own greed!

I am the farmer, bondsman to the soil.
I am the worker sold to the machine.
I am the Negro, servant to you all.
I am the people, humble, hungry, mean —
Hungry yet today despite the dream.
Beaten yet today — O, Pioneers!
I am the man who never got ahead,
The poorest worker bartered through the years.

Yet I'm the one who dreamt our basic dream
In that Old World while still a serf of kings,
Who dreamt a dream so strong, so brave, so true,
That even yet its mighty daring sings
In every brick and stone, in every furrow turned
That's made America the land it has become.
O, I'm the man who sailed those early seas
In search of what I meant to be my home —
For I'm the one who left dark Ireland's shore,
And Poland's plain, and England's grassy lea,
And torn from Black Africa's strand I came
To build a " homeland of the free."

The free?

Who said the free? Not me?
Surely not me? The millions on relief today?
The millions shot down when we strike?
The millions who have nothing for our pay?
For all the dreams we've dreamed
And all the songs we've sung
And all the hopes we've held
And all the flags we've hung,
The millions who have nothing for our pay —
Except the dream that's almost dead today.

O, let America be America again —
The land that never has been yet —

And yet must be — the land where *every* man is free.
The land that's mine — the poor man's, Indian's, Negro's, ME —
Who made America,
Whose sweat and blood, whose faith and pain,
Whose hand at the foundry, whose plow in the rain,
Must bring back our mighty dream again.

Sure, call me any ugly name you choose —
The steel of freedom does not stain.
From those who live like leeches on the people's lives,
We must take back our land again,
America!

O, yes,
I say it plain,
America never was America to me,
And yet I swear this oath —
America will be!

Out of the rack and ruin of our gangster death,
The rape and rot of graft, and stealth, and lies,
We, the people, must redeem
The land, the mines, the plants, the rivers,
The mountains and the endless plain —
All, all the stretch of these great green states —
And make America again!

[*1938*]

RICHARD WRIGHT

[1908–   ]

HE WAS born on a plantation twenty-five miles from Natchez, Mississippi, but spent most of his boyhood in Memphis, Tennessee. Like most other Negroes, he saw much of poverty and little of school. His father disappeared, his mother took in washing, and the boy grew up on the streets. At fifteen he left home and went to work. Two years later he went to Chicago, where he was a ditch-digger, dishwasher, street-cleaner, porter, and post-office clerk. But somehow he had learned to enjoy reading, and, as often happens among untutored and undisciplined readers, he read everything that fell into his hands. He says that "accidentally, I came across H. L. Mencken's *Book of Prefaces,* which served as a literary Bible for me for some years." He decided to become a writer. After experimenting with poetry, he turned to fiction. A series of short stories, collected into a volume entitled *Uncle Tom's Children* (1938), was the result. It marked the arrival of a new talent. In 1940 came his novel *Native Son* — a grim and terrifying picture of Negro life, bristling with condemnation of the white world. It was spectacularly successful — a Book-of-the-Month Club selection and a best-seller. In the spring of 1941 it was dramatized by Wright and Paul Green and produced successfully on Broadway by Orson Welles.

from

NATIVE SON

He went down the steps into the vestibule and stood looking out into the street through the plate glass of the front door. Now and then a street car rattled past over steel tracks. He was sick of his life at home. . . . But what could he do? Each time he asked himself that question his mind hit a blank wall and he stopped thinking. . . . Yes, he could take the job at Dalton's and be miserable, or he could refuse it and starve. It maddened him to think that he did not have a wider choice of action. Well, he could not stand here all day like this. What was he to do with himself? He tried to decide if he wanted to buy a ten-cent magazine, or go to a movie, or go to the poolroom and talk with the gang, or just loaf around. . . .

He opened the door and met the morning air. He went along the side-walk with his head down, fingering the quarter in his pocket. He stopped and searched all of his pockets; in his vest pocket he found a lone copper cent. That made a total of twenty-six cents, fourteen cents of which would have to be saved for carfare to Mr. Dalton's; that is, if he decided to take the job. In order to buy a magazine and go to the movies he would have to have at least twenty cents more. " Goddammit, I'm always broke! " he mumbled.

He stood on the corner in the sunshine, watching cars and people pass. He needed more money; if he did not get more than he had now he would not know what to do with himself for the rest of the day. He wanted to see a movie; his senses hungered for it. In a movie he could dream without effort; all he had to do was lean back in a seat and keep his eyes open.

He thought of Gus and G. H. and Jack. Should he go to the poolroom and talk with them? But there was no use in his going unless they were ready to do what they had been long planning to do. If they could, it would mean some sure and quick money. From three o'clock to four o'clock in the afternoon there was no policeman on duty in the block where Blum's Delicatessen was and it would be safe. One of them could hold a gun on Blum and keep him from yelling; one could watch the front door; one could watch the back; and one could get the money from the box under the counter. Then all four of them could lock Blum in the store and run out through the back and duck down the alley and meet an hour later, either at Doc's poolroom or at the South Side Boys' Club, and split the money.

Holding up Blum ought not to take more than two minutes, at the most. And it would be their last job. But it would be the toughest one that they had ever pulled. All the other times they had raided news-stands, fruit stands, and apartments. And, too, they had never held up a white man before. They had always robbed Negroes. They felt that it was much easier and safer to rob their own people, for they knew that white policemen never really searched diligently for Negroes who committed crimes against other Negroes. For months they had talked of robbing Blum's, but had not been able to bring themselves to do it. They had the feeling that the robbing of Blum's would be a violation of ultimate taboo; it would be a trespassing into territory where the full wrath of an alien white world would be turned loose upon them; in short, it would be a symbolic challenge of the white world's rule over them; a challenge which they yearned to make, but were afraid to. Yes; if they could rob Blum's, it would be a real hold-up, in more senses than one. In comparison, all of their other jobs had been play. . . .

He walked toward the poolroom. When he got to the door he saw Gus half a block away, coming toward him. He stopped and waited. It was Gus who had first thought of robbing Blum's.

"Hi, Bigger!"

"What you saying, Gus?"

"Nothing. Seen G. H. or Jack yet?"

"Naw. You?"

"Naw. Say, got a cigarette?"

"Yeah."

Bigger took out his pack and gave Gus a cigarette; he lit his and held the match for Gus. They leaned their backs against the red-brick wall of a building, smoking, their cigarettes slanting white across their black chins. To the east Bigger saw the sun burning a dazzling yellow. In the sky above him a few big white clouds drifted. He puffed silently, relaxed, his mind pleasantly vacant of purpose. Every slight movement in the street evoked a casual curiosity in him. Automatically, his eyes followed each car as it whirred over the smooth black asphalt. A woman came by and he watched the gentle sway of her body until she disappeared into a doorway. He sighed, scratched his chin and mumbled,

"Kinda warm today."

"Yeah," Gus said.

"You get more heat from this sun than from them old radiators at home."

"Yeah; them old white landlords sure don't give much heat."

"And they always knocking at your door for money."

"I'll be glad when summer comes."

"Me too," Bigger said.

He stretched his arms above his head and yawned; his eyes moistened. The sharp precision of the world of steel and stone dissolved into blurred waves. He blinked and the world grew hard again, mechanical, distinct. A weaving motion in the sky made him turn his eyes upward; he saw a slender streak of billowing white blooming against the deep blue. A plane was writing high up in the air.

"Look!" Bigger said.

"What?"

"That plane writing up there," Bigger said, pointing.

"Oh!"

They squinted at a tiny ribbon of unfolding vapor that spelled out the word: USE. . . . The plane was so far away that at times the strong glare of the sun blanked it from sight.

"You can hardly see it," Gus said.

"Looks like a little bird," Bigger breathed with childlike wonder.

"Them white boys sure can fly," Gus said.

"Yeah," Bigger said, wistfully. "They get a chance to do everything."

Noiselessly, the tiny plane looped and veered, vanishing and appearing, leaving behind it a long trail of white plumage, like coils of fluffy paste being squeezed from a tube; a plume-coil that grew and swelled and slowly began to fade into the air at the edges. The plane wrote another word: SPEED. . . .

"How high you reckon he is?" Bigger asked.

"I don't know. Maybe a hundred miles; maybe a thousand."

"I could fly one of them things if I had a chance," Bigger mumbled reflectively, as though talking to himself.

Gus pulled down the corners of his lips, stepped out from the wall, squared his shoulders, doffed his cap, bowed low and spoke with mock deference:

"Yessuh."

"You go to hell," Bigger said, smiling.

"Yessuh," Gus said again.

"I *could* fly a plane if I had a chance," Bigger said.

"If you wasn't black and if you had some money and if they'd let you go to that aviation school, you *could* fly a plane," Gus said.

For a moment Bigger contemplated all the "ifs" that Gus had mentioned. Then both boys broke into hard laughter, looking at each other through squinted eyes. When their laughter subsided, Bigger said in a voice that was half-question and half-statement:

"It's funny how the white folks treat us, ain't it?"

"It better be funny," Gus said.

"Maybe they right in not wanting us to fly," Bigger said. "'Cause if I took a plane up I'd take a couple of bombs along and drop 'em as sure as hell. . . ."

They laughed again, still looking upward. The plane sailed and dipped and spread another word against the sky: GASOLINE. . . .

" Use Speed Gasoline," Bigger mused, rolling the words slowly from his lips. " God, I'd like to fly up there in that sky."

" God'll let you fly when He gives you your wings up in heaven," Gus said.

They laughed again, reclining against the wall, smoking, the lids of their eyes drooped softly against the sun. Cars whizzed past on rubber tires. Bigger's face was metallically black in the strong sunlight. There was in his eyes a pensive, brooding amusement, as of a man who had been long confronted and tantalized by a riddle whose answer seemed always just on the verge of escaping him, but prodding him irresistibly on to seek its solution. The silence irked Bigger; he was anxious to do something to evade looking so squarely at this problem.

" Let's play ' white,' " Bigger said, referring to a game of play-acting in which he and his friends imitated the ways and manners of white folks.

" I don't feel like it," Gus said.

" General! " Bigger pronounced in a sonorous tone, looking at Gus expectantly.

" Aw, hell! I don't want to play," Gus whined.

" You'll be court-martialed," Bigger said, snapping out his words with military precision.

" Nigger, you nuts! " Gus laughed.

" General! " Bigger tried again, determinedly.

Gus looked wearily at Bigger, then straightened, saluted and answered:

" Yessuh."

" Send your men over the river at dawn and attack the enemy's left flank," Bigger ordered.

" Yessuh."

" Send the Fifth, Sixth, and Seventh Regiments," Bigger said, frowning. " And attack with tanks, gas, planes, and infantry."

" Yessuh! " Gus said again, saluting and clicking his heels.

For a moment they were silent, facing each other, their shoulders thrown back, their lips compressed to hold down the mounting impulse to laugh. Then they guffawed, partly at themselves and partly at the vast white world that sprawled and towered in the sun before them.

" Say, what's a ' left flank '? " Gus asked.

" I don't know," Bigger said. " I heard it in the movies."

They laughed again. After a bit they relaxed and leaned against the wall, smoking. Bigger saw Gus cup his left hand to his ear, as though holding a telephone receiver; and cup his right hand to his mouth, as though talking into a transmitter.

" Hello," Gus said.

" Hello," Bigger said. " Who's this? "

" This is Mr. J. P. Morgan speaking," Gus said.

" Yessuh, Mr. Morgan," Bigger said; his eyes filled with mock adulation and respect.

" I want you to sell twenty thousand shares of U. S. Steel in the market this morning," Gus said.

" At what price, suh? " Bigger asked.

" Aw, just dump 'em at any price," Gus said with casual irritation. " We're holding too much."

" Yessuh," Bigger said.

" And call me at my club at two this afternoon and tell me if the President telephoned," Gus said.

" Yessuh, Mr. Morgan," Bigger said.

Both of them made gestures signifying that they were hanging up telephone receivers; then they bent double, laughing.

" I bet that's *just* the way they talk," Gus said.

" I wouldn't be surprised," Bigger said.

They were silent again. Presently, Bigger cupped his hand to his mouth and spoke through an imaginary telephone transmitter.

" Hello."

" Hello," Gus answered. " Who's this? "

" This is the President of the United States speaking," Bigger said.

" Oh, yessuh, Mr. President," Gus said.

" I'm calling a cabinet meeting this afternoon at four o'clock and you, as Secretary of State, *must* be there."

" Well now, Mr. President," Gus said, " I'm pretty busy. They raising sand over there in Germany and I got to send 'em a note. . . ."

" But this is important," Bigger said.

" What you going to take up at this cabinet meeting? " Gus asked.

" Well, you see, the niggers is raising sand all over the country," Bigger said, struggling to keep back his laughter. " We've got to do something with these black folks. . . ."

" Oh, if it's about the niggers, I'll be right there, Mr. President," Gus said.

They hung up imaginary receivers and leaned against the wall and laughed. A street car rattled by. Bigger sighed and swore.

"Goddammit!"

"What's the matter?"

"They don't let us do *nothing*."

"Who?"

"The *white* folks."

"You talk like you just now finding that out," Gus said.

"Naw. But I just can't get used to it," Bigger said. "I swear to God I can't. I know I oughtn't think about it, but I can't help it. Every time I think about it I feel like somebody's poking a red-hot iron down my throat. Goddammit, look! We live here and they live there. We black and they white. They got things and we ain't. They do things and we can't. It's just like living in jail. Half the time I feel like I'm on the outside of the world peeping in through a knot-hole in the fence. . . ."

"Aw, ain't no use feeling that way about it. It don't help none," Gus said.

"You know one thing?" Bigger said.

"What?"

"Sometimes I feel like something awful's going to happen to me," Bigger spoke with a tinge of bitter pride in his voice.

"What you mean?" Gus asked, looking at him quickly. There was fear in Gus's eyes.

"I don't know. I just feel that way. Every time I get to thinking about me being black and they being white, me being here and they being there, I feel like something awful's going to happen to me. . . ."

"Aw, for Chrissakes! There ain't nothing you can do about it. How come you want to worry yourself? You black and they make the laws. . . ."

"Why they make us live in one corner of the city? Why don't they let us fly planes and run ships? . . ."

Gus hunched Bigger with his elbow and mumbled good-naturedly, "Aw, nigger, quit thinking about it. You'll go nuts."

The plane was gone from the sky and the white plumes of floating smoke were thinly spread, vanishing. Because he was restless and had time on his hands, Bigger yawned again and hoisted his arms high above his head.

"Nothing ever happens," he complained.

"What you want to happen?"

"Anything," Bigger said with a wide sweep of his dingy palm, a sweep that included all the possible activities of the world.

Then their eyes were riveted; a slate-colored pigeon swooped down to the middle of the steel car tracks and began strutting to and fro with ruffled feathers, its fat neck bobbing with regal pride. A street car rumbled forward and the pigeon rose swiftly through the air on wings stretched so taut and sheer that Bigger could see the gold of the sun through their translucent tips. He tilted his head and watched the slate-colored bird flap and wheel out of sight over the edge of a high roof.

"Now, if I could only do that," Bigger said.

Gus laughed.

"Nigger, you nuts."

"I reckon we the only things in this city that can't go where we want to go and do what we want to do."

"Don't think about it," Gus said.

"I can't help it."

"That's why you feeling like something awful's going to happen to you," Gus said. "You think too much."

"What in hell can a man do?" Bigger asked, turning to Gus.

"Get drunk and sleep it off."

"I can't. I'm broke."

Bigger crushed his cigarette and took out another one and offered the package to Gus. They continued smoking. A huge truck swept past, lifting scraps of white paper into the sunshine; the bits settled down slowly.

"Gus?"

"Hunh?"

"You know where the white folks live?"

"Yeah," Gus said, pointing eastward. "Over across the 'line'; over there on Cottage Grove Avenue."

"Naw; they don't," Bigger said.

"What you mean?" Gus asked, puzzled. "Then, where do they live?"

Bigger doubled his fist and struck his solar plexus.

"Right down here in my stomach," he said.

Gus looked at Bigger searchingly, then away, as though ashamed.

"Yeah; I know what you mean," he whispered.

"Every time I think of 'em, I *feel* 'em," Bigger said.

"Yeah; and in your chest and throat, too," Gus said.

"It's like fire."

"And sometimes you can't hardly breathe. . . ."

Bigger's eyes were wide and placid, gazing into space.

"That's when I feel like something awful's going to happen to me.
. . ." Bigger paused, narrowed his eyes. "Naw; it ain't like something
going to happen to me. It's . . . It's like I was going to do something
I can't help. . . ."

"Yeah!" Gus said with uneasy eagerness. His eyes were full of a
look compounded of fear and admiration for Bigger. "Yeah; I know
what you mean. It's like you going to fall and don't know where you
going to land. . . ."

Gus's voice trailed off. The sun slid behind a big white cloud and the
street was plunged in cool shadow; quickly the sun edged forth again
and it was bright and warm once more. A long sleek black car, its
fenders glinting like glass in the sun, shot past them at high speed and
turned a corner a few blocks away. Bigger pursed his lips and sang:

"Zoooooooooom!"

"They got everything," Gus said.

"They own the world," Bigger said.

"Aw, what the hell," Gus said. "Let's go in the poolroom."

"O. K."

They walked toward the door of the poolroom. . . .

[*1940*]

GENEVIEVE TAGGARD

[1894–   ]

MISS TAGGARD was born in Waitsburg, Washington. When she was two years old her family moved to Hawaii to establish a school and a mission, and there she was brought up and educated. In 1914 she left Hawaii to enter the University of California, from which she was graduated in 1919. The following year she went to New York. She helped found and edit a poetry magazine, the *Measure,* and became a contributor to the *Masses.* Her first book of verse, *For Eager Lovers,* was published in 1922. Since 1929 she has taught English at women's colleges — Mount Holyoke, Bennington, and at present Sarah Lawrence. In 1931 she was awarded a Guggenheim fellowship which enabled her to spend a year in Mallorca writing poetry. Her *Collected Poems* was published in 1938. She is also the author of a biography, *The Life and Mind of Emily Dickinson* (1930). From the beginning of her career Miss Taggard's work has been informed by a militantly humanitarian spirit.

SILENCE IN MALLORCA

I

Our stony island, Spain's laconic child
Quiet. Nada. Cover the glowing spark.
Hush all the hótas and hush hush the wild

Arabian cries. Now in Europe's dark
Whisper weep secretly plot but never sing.
On cliffs against the sky moves the new mark

Shape of the plane, the loathed imperial thing
The hawk from Italy, the spy of black.
Ground where we labor darkens with its wing.

A few shot first. Then nothing. Then the attack.
Terror of the invader. Puff of shells,
And Juan our best man ambushed in the back.

Hide hide in the caves; listen in the dry wells. . . .
Clang — the obedient treachery of church bells.

II

They shot the mayor of Inca. They jailed
The poor the free the poor the free the brave.
Out of the puerto when the felucca sailed

Planes roared and swooped and shot them on the wave.
Our people serve the invader and his gun.
Our people, Spain. Slow tempo of the slave.

We are cut off. Africa's blazing sun
Knew these same hawks that now around us prey.
And Barcelona suffers. Is there no one

To save us but ourselves? From far away
After victorious battle. . . . Cry, we cry
Brothers, Comrades help us. Where are they?

Our island lying open to the sky.
Mallorca, the first to fall, the last to die.

III

O wild west wind. . . . Liberty's open roar,
Blow on this island, blow the ocean clean,
Drown our tormentors, blow equinox, blow war

Away from the world. Drive to us the unseen
Battalions, clouds of planes by workers flown,
Give us our land again, quiet and green,

Our children singing and our land, our own
Ways, our wives, our delegates. Blow here.
The indifferent sea washes the beach of stone,

813

And Mediterranean silence, primitive fear
Steps in the foot of Tomàs, the new slave.
Moves in the hovering hawk, spiraling near.

We bend, we work, — this island inferno and grave.
Come with the wind of your wings. And save.

[*1938*]

LONG VIEW

Never heard happier laughter.
        Where did you hear it?
Somewhere in the future.
        Very far in the future?
Oh no. It was natural. It sounded
Just like our own, American, sweet and easy.
People were talking together. They sat on the ground. It was summer.
And the old told stories of struggle.
The young listened. I overheard
Our own story, retold. They looked up at the stars
Hearing the serious words. Someone sang.
They loved us who had passed away.
They forgot all our errors. Our names were mixed. The story was long.
The young people danced. They brought down
New boughs for the flame. They said, Go on with the story now.
What happened next?
        For us there was silence
Something like pain or tears. But they took us with them.
Their laughter was peace. I never heard happier.
Their children large and beautiful. Like us, but new-born.
This was in the mountains of the west.
They were resting. They knew each other well.
The trees and rivers are on the map, but the time
Is not yet. I listened again. Their talk was ours
With many favorite words. I heard us all speaking.

But they spoke of better things, soberly. They were wise
And learned. They sang not only of us.
They remembered thousands, and many countries, far away.
One poet who sat there with them began to talk of the future.
Then they were silent again. And they looked at the sky.
And then in the light of the stars they banked their fire as we do
Scuffing the ground, and said goodnight.
                This poem I bring back to you
Knowing that you wonder often, that you want
Word of these people.

[*1940*]

DOROTHY PARKER

[1893–   ]

MISS PARKER was born in West End, New Jersey, and educated at a private school and in a convent. Her first important literary job was that of dramatic critic of *Vanity Fair* in the years 1917–20. She began, at the same time, to contribute light verse to F. P. A.'s column, which then appeared in the *New York Daily Mail*. After leaving *Vanity Fair* she became an unusually successful free-lance writer, publishing satirical sketches and stories, as well as verse, in a variety of magazines. She was one of the original editors of the *New Yorker* and for many years was its literary critic. Her volumes of verse, *Enough Rope* (1926), *Sunset Gun* (1928), and *Not So Deep as a Well* (1936), and her collections of stories, *Laments for the Living* (1930), *After Such Pleasures* (1933), and *Here Lies* (1939), have been phenomenally popular. Miss Parker was neatly classified as a " sophisticate," a writer of " smart " things, and as a wit in the literary world of Manhattan, when the crisis of the 1930's deepened and the civil war broke out in Spain. In this fateful period she began to publish things which indicated a new point of view — a serious, deeply felt social consciousness. She visited Spain at this time and was there moved to write some memorable pieces, one of which, a poignant story which first appeared in the *New Yorker*, follows. She has since been active in behalf of many liberal causes.

SOLDIERS OF THE REPUBLIC

That Sunday afternoon we sat with the Swedish girl in the big café in Valencia. We had vermouth in thick goblets, each with a cube of honeycombed gray ice in it. The waiter was so proud of that ice he could hardly bear to leave the glasses on the table, and thus part from it forever. He went to his duty — all over the room they were clapping their hands and hissing to draw his attention — but he looked back over his shoulder.

It was dark outside, the quick, new dark that leaps down without dusk on the day; but, because there were no lights in the streets, it seemed as set and as old as midnight. So you wondered that all the babies were still up. There were babies everywhere in the café, babies serious without solemnity and interested in a tolerant way in their surroundings.

At the table next ours, there was a notably small one; maybe six months old. Its father, a little man in a big uniform that dragged his shoulders down, held it carefully on his knee. It was doing nothing whatever, yet he and his thin young wife, whose belly was already big again under her sleazy dress, sat watching it in a sort of ecstasy of admiration, while their coffee cooled in front of them. The baby was in Sunday white; its dress was patched so delicately that you would have thought the fabric whole had not the patches varied in their shades of whiteness. In its hair was a bow of new blue ribbon, tied with absolute balance of loops and ends. The ribbon was of no use; there was not enough hair to require restraint. The bow was sheerly an adornment, a calculated bit of dash.

"Oh, for God's sake, stop that!" I said to myself. "All right, so it's got a piece of blue ribbon on its hair. All right, so its mother went without eating so it could look pretty when its father came home on leave. All right, so it's her business, and none of yours. All right, so what have you got to cry about?"

The big, dim room was crowded and lively. That morning there had been a bombing from the air, the more horrible for broad daylight. But nobody in the café sat tense and strained, nobody desperately forced forgetfulness. They drank coffee or bottled lemonade, in the pleasant, earned ease of Sunday afternoon, chatting of small, gay matters, all talking at once, all hearing and answering.

There were many soldiers in the room, in what appeared to be the uniforms of twenty different armies until you saw that the variety lay in the differing ways the cloth had worn or faded. Only a few of them had been wounded; here and there you saw one stepping gingerly, leaning on a crutch or two canes, but so far on toward recovery that his face had color. There were many men, too, in civilian clothes — some of them soldiers home on leave, some of them governmental workers, some of them anybody's guess. There were plump, comfortable wives, active with paper fans, and old women as quiet as their grandchildren. There were many pretty girls and some beauties, of whom you did not remark, "There's a charming Spanish type," but said, "What a beautiful girl!" The women's clothes were not new, and their material was too humble ever to have warranted skillful cutting.

"It's funny," I said to the Swedish girl, "how when nobody in a place is best-dressed, you don't notice that everybody isn't."

"Please?" the Swedish girl said.

No one, save an occasional soldier, wore a hat. When we had first come to Valencia, I lived in a state of puzzled pain as to why everybody on the streets laughed at me. It was not because "West End Avenue" was writ across my face as if left there by a customs officer's chalked scrawl. They like Americans in Valencia, where they have seen good ones — the doctors who left their practices and came to help, the calm young nurses, the men of the International Brigade. But when I walked forth, men and women courteously laid their hands across their splitting faces and little children, too innocent for dissembling, doubled with glee and pointed and cried, "*Olé!*" Then, pretty late, I made my discovery, and left my hat off; and there was laughter no longer. It was not one of those comic hats, either; it was just a hat.

The café filled to overflow, and I left our table to speak to a friend across the room. When I came back to the table, six soldiers were sitting there. They were crowded in, and I scraped past them to my chair. They looked tired and dusty and little, the way that the newly dead look little, and the first things you saw about them were the tendons in their necks. I felt like a prize sow.

They were all in conversation with the Swedish girl. She has Spanish, French, German, anything in Scandinavian, Italian, and English. When she has a moment for regret, she sighs that her Dutch is so rusty she can no longer speak it, only read it, and the same is true of her Rumanian.

They had told her, she told us, that they were at the end of forty-eight hours' leave from the trenches, and, for their holiday, they had all pooled their money for cigarettes, and something had gone wrong, and the cigarettes had never come through to them. I had a pack of American cigarettes — in Spain rubies are as nothing to them — and I brought it out, and by nods and smiles and a sort of breast stroke, made it understood that I was offering it to those six men yearning for tobacco. When they saw what I meant, each one of them rose and shook my hand. Darling of me to share my cigarettes with the men on their way back to the trenches. Little Lady Bountiful. The prize sow.

Each one lit his cigarette with a contrivance of yellow rope that stank when afire and was also used, the Swedish girl translated, for igniting grenades. Each one received what he had ordered, a glass of coffee, and each one murmured appreciatively over the tiny cornucopia of coarse sugar that accompanied it. Then they talked.

They talked through the Swedish girl, but they did to us that thing we all do when we speak our own language to one who has no knowledge of it. They looked us square in the face, and spoke slowly, and pronounced their words with elaborate movements of their lips. Then, as their stories came, they poured them at us so vehemently, so emphatically that they were sure we must understand. They were so convinced we would understand that we were ashamed for not understanding.

But the Swedish girl told us. They were all farmers and farmers' sons, from a district so poor that you try not to remember there is that kind of poverty. Their village was next that one where the old men and the sick men and women and children had gone, on a holiday, to the bull-ring; and the planes had come over and dropped bombs on the bull-ring, and the old men and the sick men and the women and the children were more than two hundred.

They had all, the six of them, been in the war for over a year, and most of that time they had been in the trenches. Four of them were married. One had one child, two had three children, one had five. They had not had word from their families since they had left for the front. There had been no communication; two of them had learned to write from men fighting next them in the trench, but they had not dared to write home. They belonged to a union, and union men, of course, are put to death if taken. The village where their families lived had been captured, and if your wife gets a letter from a union man, who knows but they'll shoot her for the connection?

They told about how they had not heard from their families for more than a year. They did not tell it gallantly or whimsically or stoically. They told it as if — Well, look. You have been in the trenches, fighting, for a year. You have heard nothing of your wife and your children. They do not know if you are dead or alive or blinded. You do not know where they are, or if they are. You must talk to somebody. That is the way they told about it.

One of them, some six months before, had heard of his wife and his three children — they had such beautiful eyes, he said — from a brother-in-law in France. They were all alive then, he was told, and had a bowl of beans a day. But his wife had not complained of the food, he heard. What had troubled her was that she had no thread to mend the children's ragged clothes. So that troubled him, too.

"She has no thread," he kept telling us. "My wife has no thread to mend with. No thread."

We sat there, and listened to what the Swedish girl told us they were saying. Suddenly one of them looked at the clock, and then there was excitement. They jumped up, as a man, and there were calls for the waiter and rapid talk with him, and each of them shook the hand of each of us. We went through more swimming motions to explain to them that they were to take the rest of the cigarettes — fourteen cigarettes for six soldiers to take to war — and then they shook our hands again. Then all of us said "*Salud!*" as many times as could be for six of them and three of us, and then they filed out of the café, the six of them, tired and dusty and little, as men of the mighty horde are little.

Only the Swedish girl talked, after they had gone. The Swedish girl has been in Spain since the start of the war. She has nursed splintered men, and she has carried stretchers into the trenches and, heavier laden, back to the hospital. She has seen and heard too much to be knocked into silence.

Presently it was time to go, and the Swedish girl raised her hands above her head and clapped them twice together to summon the waiter. He came, but he only shook his head and his hand, and moved away.

The soldiers had paid for our drinks.

[*1938*]

JONATHAN DANIELS

[1902–   ]

THE SON of Josephus Daniels, who was Secretary of the Navy in Woodrow Wilson's cabinet and has been Ambassador to Mexico during Franklin D. Roosevelt's administration, Jonathan Daniels was born in Raleigh, North Carolina. He was educated at the University of North Carolina, receiving the degree of M.A. in 1922, and attended the Columbia Law School in 1922–3. He then went to work on his father's newspaper, the *Raleigh News and Observer*, and since 1933 he has been its editor. In 1938 he published a significant book, *A Southerner Discovers the South,* recording his impressions of an extended automobile trip up and down and across his native region. It is significant because it represents a genuinely progressive and democratic attitude toward Southern life and problems. It is not unique in that respect, but it is a particularly attractive example of recent Southern liberalism.

---

from

A SOUTHERNER DISCOVERS THE SOUTH

A traveler comes to destinations. Or hopes to.

I remember when I was young and Admiral Robert E. Peary and Dr. Frederick Cook were quarreling (I was a great and small partisan of Dr. Cook) that I conceived of the North Pole as such a trimmed tree trunk as the Southern Bell Telephone Company or the Carolina Power & Light Company sometimes imbedded in the sidewalk before our house. I would not have been surprised, of course, had the North Pole been a little more ornate, and a trifle more impervious to heat and cold and bug and polar bear. But it provided a definite destination for explorers. And I think that the moment when loss of faith in Dr. Cook began to set in was when he failed to show a lantern slide of it in his illustrated lecture at the Academy of Music.

Certainly now at the end of my travels in discovery of the South I wish I had a definite destination to report — or a plan. Certainly a plan. For the South, the Philosophers at Chapel Hill tell me, will not escape without a plan or at least a planning. I agree.

All people are planners.

"I aim to plant lespedeza in that field if I ever get around to it. But it just seems natural somehow to put it in cotton."

All people are regionalists.

I discovered that when I was twelve. And I still believe that Dr. Howard W. Odum missed one of the best indices of the Southern region when he failed to determine a line on one side of which all nice children say, "No, ma'am," and "Yes, ma'am," to the teacher and on the other side of which they get laughed at for saying it by all including teacher. Such a line, I understand, no longer exists. At any rate, when I asked my daughter about it she said, "Hunh?"

But certainly all people are planners and regionalists. The plan may not extend beyond dinner time and the region may not reach beyond the creek. Indeed, in one section of North Carolina plan and region are combined.

"Well, I guess we'll do like the folks across the river do."

"How's that?"

"Do without."

In more ways than one that has been the regional plan of the American South, and I for one Southerner, speaking also without fear of contradiction for 25,000,000 others, am ready to find another.

This program was adopted shortly after the surrender at Appomattox and has been in force almost without interruption since. That was a grand war for the poets and the politicians, but I am beginning to wonder quite seriously whether the Civil War itself ever made any really profound difference in the life and history of the South. The war itself seems a detail almost insignificant between what went before and what came after. Mine, I suppose, was the last Southern generation reared in a combination of indignation and despair. Now, fortunately, save in a few groups devoted to a form of rebel yelling which is also a form of ancestor whooping, the Civil War as such plays little or no part in the life and thinking of the South. That means, I hope, escape from the old Do-Without Economy of the Southern States, for the chief injury inflicted upon us late confederates by the war was the excuse which it gave us for giving up and sitting in the sun. The

South was poor; the war caused it. The South was ignorant; the war made us too poor to educate. The South was slow; well, after what the damyankees did it wasn't any use to stir. The war provided a satisfying, acceptable and even mildly exhilarating excuse for everything from Captain Seabrook's wooden leg to the quality of education dispensed at the Centennial School.

Unfortunately, like a great many simple explanations this one did not explain. The tariff did at least as much damage in Dixie as Sherman and Grant together in making the South poor and keeping it poor. Indeed, while Grant and Sherman have gone to whatever they had coming to them, the tariff remains. The process of selling the fertility of the land along with the cotton began a long time before the Civil War and had reduced Virginia gentlemen to the unpleasant business of breeding slaves for the Deep South markets. Even now men tremble over the possible loss of cotton markets; it is a trembling like that of the old slave fearful of losing his chains. The contempt for labor which everywhere and in all times has been an inevitable item of slavery was full grown before 1860. The hookworm was in the South but not discovered. Yellow fever, typhoid and malaria were there but not understood. Pellagra was seen as clay eating and was considered a perverse habit of the perverted po' whites. Most of the white people were desperately poor. Most of the Negroes had instinctively developed an apparently racial shiftlessness as a shrewd labor defense under slavery long before ladies and gentlemen on the Charleston housetops applauded the firing on Fort Sumter. And Reconstruction: Mississippi had defaulted on its bonds sometime in the 40's. The Rothschilds were involved, and if Mississippi paid her debts, the Governor said, he was fearful that they might use the money to gain control of the sepulcher of Our Blessed Saviour. That would never do, so Mississippi defaulted, and there was not a Negro in the Legislature that did it.

The Civil War killed men and broke hearts and caused a tremendous amount of private suffering. But war is too spectacular. All of the major faults and flaws in Southern economy were on the way to full growth before the war began. But it served as an alibi — a magnificent alibi — for them all, and for those that came after, too. In a false present, the South had begun the adoration of a fictitious past. It luxuriated in its tragedy. The South, like some ladies in it, enjoyed ill-health. Delicacy of constitution became a positive social virtue. And generally the fact was overlooked that as early after Appomattox as 1870 the South produced more cotton than it did in 1860 and got more for it, the most, indeed, that it had ever received.

The South's faults were many, but the South's faults were not alone. The war and Reconstruction were important as memory of them served as a screen of emotionalism behind which moved, ever praising Lee, those unemotional gentlemen from the North who knew what they wanted and how much they would have to pay for it, which was not much. This second wave of carpetbaggers was received with honors and banquets and bands. They were the agents of the new and ever greater absentee ownership of the South. They came from the North with excellent financial connections to buy up broken down Southern railroads and other properties and they picked up some pretty bargains and some pretty Southerners. The town was properly impressed when Colonel Cadwallader entertained Mr. Prentiss, the Boston banker. (It continues impressed when his name is Manaccus and he is in the garment business.) The banks of those same gentlemen who bought up Southern railroads were also deeply interested in Northern railroads. It has even been suggested that while they were ever willing to make money they were also careful not to build up Southern traffic and industry at the expense of those older developed areas of the North and East through which their older lines ran. Freight rates certainly have not been shaped to aid the industrial development of the South; instead they still sit providing inland the protection which tariffs provide on coast and frontier. Some trade tacticians feel that freight rate and tariff together made a prettier pincher than that which Grant and Sherman applied on the Confederacy.

Of course, all ownership in this modern corporate civilization assumes the pattern of absentee ownership. Stockholders, South as North, are increasingly irresponsible and uncreative as individual capitalists. But the control of capital is in the North and East and it may be significant that the only industrial development which has taken place in the South since the industrial North overcame the country culture of the South has been in the widely dispersed manufacture of textiles and in the new big industry of the cigarette. Otherwise the South, devoted to the culture of cotton and tobacco, the prices of which are fixed in world markets, still buys from the protected factories of the North. Its new overseers, faithful to the absentee owners, beg and plead and promise for more absentee investment and control while simultaneously they cry to hysteria in condemnation of foreign agitators among nice native labor.

There is reason for both fear and elation. The new pincher movement upon the South has not been applied in recent years with the precision which Grant and Sherman exercised, or perhaps the body seized is a good deal less easily grasped than was the old half-dead Confederacy between Richmond and Atlanta. At any rate those capitalists, local and absentee, who are concerned for low wages in the South, and those who are concerned for sales in the South do not seem to be acting in perfect unity. The most profoundly disturbing foreign agitators in the region are the salesmen of Chevrolets and radios, gaudy machine-stitched dresses and other shining gadgets and gewgaws. Even the power companies, incited by TVA, are filling the tow-heads and the burr-heads with glittering dreams. Not only the spindle has come South, so also has the automobile. The worker and the mill have both become mobile. As whole mills may move from Massachusetts to Mississippi so may whole philosophies.

It is not the Communists who are coming but the advertisers. The cabins of the South are wall papered with the pages of newspapers and magazines and so much advertising has practically permanent appeal. There may not come to the cabin in a year enough money to meet for a month the requirements of the persuasive suggestion that it is easy to own a Packard. But if all of those who see the walls cannot read them, all of them can desire. If they lack the money, they can wish for it. They can be dissatisfied with the old Do-Without Plan of the Southern regions of the United States. They are. And those new absentees who are coming South in a movement which New England Governors call "a threat from the South" should come warned: the South has much to offer, place and people and resources and power, but it does not honestly have docility to offer. Such as it possessed is disappearing before the building of desire. And the first problem of the South today is people. It is by no means limited to the South. Indeed, it is the newly exciting question of the possibility of democracy. In contemplation of it too many people have been looking at Italy and Spain and Russia and Germany, as well as at the old democracies of England and France. It is less disturbing to consider it over water, perhaps, but the seeing is clearer in the South. Contemplate the questions:

Are the Southern people capable of serving, governing and saving themselves?

Or must they depend for guidance in government and to decency and adequacy in living upon an oligarchy of so-called aristocrats, a committee of experts, a ring of politicians? Upon plutocrat, demagogue or professor?

Is democracy possible in the South? (Is it possible anywhere?)

Surely, those questions are properly raised with regard to the folk of a region in which the sharp-eyed regional planners have found natural resources in superabundance, population in abundance, but a deficiency in science, skills, technology and organization, waste in its general economy and a richness, combined with immaturity and multiple handicaps, in its culture. The trends they discovered show hesitancy and relative regression in many aspects of culture. They found the lowest incomes and the poorest fed people in America in a region which should be a garden.

Beyond those findings, I pretend to no simple, certain answers to the questions. In the first place, of course, the Southern people will not show their capability or the lack of it in a vacuum. They must work in a realm not only patterned by their past and their prejudices, but also one definitely shaped by tariffs and freight rates fixed largely at the North for the benefit of the North. It is a region governed in important degree by absentee owners and one which has been stirred deeply more frequently by reflex response to exterior criticism than by agitators, native or foreign, at work within. It is a sensitive region, more romantic than idealistic, and one which is expiating for more sins than its own, though there are enough of them.

The answers like the questions go deep into the past. Important aspects of democracy grew in the South. Much of its philosophy was shaped at Monticello by Thomas Jefferson. But Jefferson in Virginia and John Adams in Massachusetts died on the same afternoon in 1826. And sometime thereafter, perhaps at the very time it began to become solidly Democratic, the South discarded democracy. Or perhaps more fairly stated, its democracy was destroyed. From the beginning there were Southerners, big and rich, who held to the faith that wisdom reposed only in the big and the rich and that therefore the franchise should be restricted to them. More and more democracy asserted itself against them. Requirements for voting and office were slowly but steadily scaled down. And then after a long and passionate war, in the South the electorate was enlarged, by force from without, by thousands of Negroes and decreased by thousands of white men who had formerly borne arms as Southerners and so as Confederates and so as Rebels. The result was a condition which seemed intolerable to the most faithful Democrats. Perhaps at that time no entry of any sort by the Negroes into the rights of citizenship would have been tolerable to the South. Certainly, however, the Negroes were given no chance to be absorbed. They were hurried from slavery into a power which, in general, other men misused. Any unemotional reader of history must recognize the similarity between the Ku Klux of the South and the Brown Shirts of Germany and the Black Shirts of Italy and the similarity of the conditions which created them. They provided a rank and file violence. But in the South they brought the Bourbons to power. And the native Bourbon has steadily served the large prop-ertied classes, absentee or local, in the exploitation of the South. Al-most without exception the rout of the carpetbaggers, the Negroes and the scallywags carried the old planter class and a new promoter class to power also over the vast white mass of little farmers and storekeepers, mechanics and laborers. For them as for the Negroes to too great an extent democracy was in the years afterwards effectually denied. But little men stir: and men to lead them. There was, for instance, Benjamin Ryan Tillman in South Carolina. And " Pitchfork Ben " was by no means the only name applied to him. Low Country aristocrats still snort to speak of him. After him there were others like him — and not like him. There will be more. They are Southern demagogues, some better and some worse, but all indicative of a Southern unwillingness to leave government entirely to the political gentlemen of the gentlemen of business — gentlemen who know exactly what they want and how much they will pay for it. It is only an alternative, when as in the case of such a man as Huey Long, he leaves as a political estate a power to plunder. Neither he nor his inheritors discovered that power. It always exists when the people are incapable of government or careless of government. And Southerners might be plundered by the very peo-ple who made them also for a time incapable of government. They were. And those who plundered them also saw sign of inferiority in the poverty that was left.

There are Southerners still who would more quickly deny the ability of the people of the South to manage the South than any people outside of it. They are the persisting and ineradicable Bourbons and Brigadiers

who are devoted to a class before a region. That made them readier
to serve as the agents of the new mastery. They still serve it and serving
also themselves believe they serve the South. Their minds are still
patterned in that master-slave concept which in the sense of superiority
applied not only to slaves but to white men lacking slaves. They apply
it now to the cotton mill as well as to the plantation. Many aristocrats in the South — and that is the name for both the Coca-Cola
bottler and the member of the Society of the Cincinnati — do not believe and never have believed that the people should — if they could
— govern the South. Such a faith or faithlessness leads to the unin-
corporated mill village and the company union. Included under it are
both the kindliest paternalism and the most vicious and careless exploitation.

This lack of faith by the new great in the many small seems to me
sad, but the saddest thing in the South is the fact that those at the top
who do not believe in the intelligence of those at the bottom have
not shown themselves capable of a leadership satisfactory to the people
they assume to lead — nor, so far as I could discover, to anybody else.
The market for stuffed shirts is glutted.

Finally, the people are not as disturbing as the patricians. The most
encouraging thing is that the ordinary Southern whites, given fair
chance and training, are showing themselves capable of performing
the best types of work. This is so in the South. TVA discovered it
and was surprised. Others are discovering it. And in the black and
white migration to the North this generation of Southern immigrants
has been able to compete with the workers already on the ground. The
depression saw them shivering and jobless in every Northern city: by
the thousands it sent them scurrying home again. Now they and more
beside them move again. They are, of course, inadequately trained,
inadequately skilled. Sometimes they are underfed. Sometimes they
are sick. Sometimes they are criminal, feeble-minded, perverted, insane. But they move and they will move. They march to eat. They
will not be stopped. They need not be feared unless they are resisted.
But fear in the South has slandered both of them:

The Southern Negro is not an incurably ignorant ape.

The Southern white masses are not biologically degenerate.

Both are peoples capable of vastly more training than they possess.
Both are peoples who may hang heavy on the national advance, or help
to speed and sustain it. Both are peoples who could consume and

produce more wealth. And they are capable of happy, productive, peaceful life, side by side. White men and black men have shared the South's too little for a long time and, though there is more than a casual connection between hunger and lynchings, they have shared it in relative quiet, decency and peace. They would be able to build a South in terms of the South's potentiality, if together they had a chance to make and share plenty. . . .

A plan for a new, free, fed, housed, happy South must include not merely program at home for improvement but also program in the nation for the relinquishment of advantages elsewhere over the South. Perhaps those advantages are so deeply fixed as in freight rate and tariff that to change them to give the South a chance might do vast harm elsewhere, might cause much suffering in the areas which have grown rich on advantage, like that which wrings the hearts of Northerners when they see it in the South. Perhaps the South, as New England seems now fearing, may be able to escape its single-slavery to cotton and advance to a diverse industrial and agricultural development despite the imperial advantages which New England took as its loot after the Civil War. There was some sort of bargain then, now dimly seen. The Negroes were sold down the river again after emancipation, and the price paid was a fixed economic differentiation which left the whole South in slavery to New England instead of some of the South in slavery to other Southerners. But I mean to start no new war: the South is at last escaping from the more destructive Reconstruction which economically continued the South as captive. And New England is afraid: the terrible danger is that it is about to lose at last the slavery from which it profited long after Lincoln in a manner of speaking set the Negroes free. Of course everybody was free in the South, free to fight among themselves for the too little that was left when tribute was paid.

Cato the Elder was no more implacable than the Brahmans of Boston who came after the Abolitionists with considerably cooler heads. The South was not plowed up and planted with salt as Carthage was. If no more generous, Bostonians (citizens of a region and an attitude and not a town) were less wasteful. They recognized that the South kept in its place (a place in the nation geographically similar to that of the Negro in the South) might be useful and profitable. It was. And as Southerner at the end of discovery I ask now only that they recognize the poverty of the South as a part of the same civilization as Harvard and in a measure as the creation of the same people. Cato did not ride through Carthage on the train and blame its condition on the Carthaginians. That much only I ask of the Yankees.

A good deal more is necessary for the Southerners. Item one is escape from pretentiousness. The Southerner has deluded only himself. The boy who was brought in to Savannah from Bryan County with malaria, pellagra, hookworm and a pelvis pierced by his thigh bone as a result of malnutrition nevertheless insisted in the hospital that he was the best alligator catcher on the coast of Georgia. Perhaps he was. Maybe still one Reb can beat ten Yankees. It is irrelevant. But planning in the South must begin at the bottom where so many of its people are. There is no handle on its top by which it can be lifted. . . .

[*1938*]

ARCHIBALD MACLEISH

[1892–   ]

HE WAS born in Glencoe, Illinois, and was educated at the Hotchkiss School and Yale. While at college he was prominent in both athletic and literary activities. On being graduated in 1915, he entered the Harvard Law School. In 1917 he joined a hospital unit and went to France, in 1918 he transferred to the field artillery. He was a captain when the war ended. He returned to the Harvard Law School, taught for a year, then practiced law in Boston for three years. He quit his profession to write poetry. Several volumes appeared which attracted the attention of discriminating critics. In 1932 came his *Conquistador,* which won him the Pulitzer Prize in Poetry. *Frescoes for Mr. Rockefeller's City* came in 1933, *Public Speech* in 1936. In the meantime he became one of the editors of *Fortune.* In 1938–9 he was custodian of the Nieman Collection of Journalism at Harvard, in 1939 he was appointed Librarian of Congress. Mr. MacLeish is the author of several plays in verse, two of which, *The Fall of the City* (1937) and *Air Raid* (1938), were designed for radio broadcasting. During the mid-1930's much of his poetry was inspired by a deep concern with the grave social and political crises of the period, and the inspiration manifested itself in a vigorous libertarian and democratic spirit. Previously some critics had suspected a strain of snobbishness in his writing. Since the outbreak of the Second World War, Mr. MacLeish has been interested chiefly in polemics against isolationism and defeatism and for democratic war aims.

POLE STAR FOR THIS YEAR

Where the wheel of light is turned:
Where the axle of the night is
Turned: is motionless: where holds
And has held ancient sureness always:

Where of faring men the eyes
At oar bench at the rising bow

831

Have seen — torn shrouds between — the Wain
And that star's changelessness: not changing:

There upon that intent star:
Trust of wandering men: of truth
The most reminding witness: we
Fix our eyes also: waylost: the wanderers:

We too turn now to that star:
We too in whose trustless hearts
All truth alters and the lights
Of earth are out now turn to that star:

Liberty of man and mind
That once was mind's necessity
And made the West blaze up has burned
To bloody embers and the lamp's out:

Hope that was a noble flame
Has fanned to violence and feeds
On cities and the flesh of men
And chokes where unclean smoke defiles it:

Even the small spark of pride
That taught the tyrant once is dark
Where gunfire rules the starving street
And justice cheats the dead of honor:

Liberty and pride and hope
And every guide-mark of the mind
That led our blindness once has vanished.
This star will not. Love's star will not.

Love that has beheld the face
A man has with a man's eyes in it
Bloody from the slugger's blows
Or heard the cold child cry for hunger —

Love that listens where the good:
The virtuous: the men of faith:

Proclaim the paradise on earth
And murder, starve and burn to make it —

Love that cannot either sleep
Or keep rich music in the ear
Or lose itself for the wild beat
The anger in the blood makes raging —

Love that hardens into hate —
Love like hatred and as bright —
Love is that one waking light
That leads now when all others darken.

[*1936*]

SPEECH TO A CROWD

Tell me my patient friends — awaiters of messages —
From what other shore: from what stranger:
Whence was the word to come? Who was to lesson you?

Listeners under a child's crib in a manger —
Listeners once by the oracles: now by the transoms —
Whom are you waiting for? Who do you think will explain?

Listeners thousands of years and still no answer —
Writers at night to Miss Lonely-Hearts: awkward spellers —
Open your eyes! There is only earth and the man!

There is only you: there is no one else on the telephone:
No one else is on the air to whisper:
No one else but you will push the bell.

No one knows if you don't: neither ships
Nor landing-fields decode the dark between:
You have your eyes and what your eyes see *is*.

833

The earth you see is really the earth you are seeing:
The sun is truly excellent: truly warm:
Women are beautiful as you have seen them —

Their breasts (believe it) like cooing of doves in a portico:
They bear at their breasts tenderness softly. Look at them!
Look at yourselves. You are strong. You are well formed.

Look at the world — the world you never took!
It is really true you may live in the world heedlessly:
Why do you wait to read it in a book then?

Write it yourselves! Write to yourselves if you need to!
Tell yourselves there is sun and the sun will rise:
Tell yourselves the earth has food to feed you: —

Let the dead men say that men must die!
Who better than you can know what death is?
How can a bone or a broken body surmise it?

Let the dead shriek with their whispering breath:
Laugh at them! Say the murdered gods may wake
But we who work have end of work together:

Tell yourselves the earth is yours to take!

Waiting for messages out of the dark you were poor.
The world was always yours: you would not take it.
[*1936*]

THOMAS WOLFE

[1900–1938]

HE WAS the son of a stone-cutter in Asheville, North Carolina. A sensitive, introspective boy, he had an unhappy childhood — a fact obvious to readers of his novels. He studied from 1916 to 1920 at the University of North Carolina, edited the college paper, and wrote plays. From North Carolina he went to Harvard, where he attended the famous playwriting class of Professor George P. Baker. In 1922 Harvard gave him a master's degree. After a period of travel abroad, he became an instructor in English at Washington Square College, New York University. He taught there from 1924 to 1930, resigning to devote himself to writing. In 1929 his first novel, *Look Homeward, Angel,* had been published, and there were critics who said then that it was the best first novel they had seen in a decade. Three huge novels followed, *Of Time and the River* (1935), *The Web and the Rock* (1939), and *You Can't Go Home Again* (1940), the last two published posthumously. The subtitle of *Of Time and the River* is " A Legend of Man's Hunger in His Youth "; the publishers' description of his last work is " A Novel about a Lost Modern Who Found Himself." In those phrases are summed up the motifs of all his novels. He symbolized in himself, as well as in his work, the " homeless " generation of the 1930's which sought an understanding of the forces that were transforming American life — a generation in search of a faith and a " home." That Wolfe found what he wanted is suggested by the " credo " which concludes his last novel.

---

from

OF TIME AND THE RIVER

[*Eugene, a young writer whose whole life has been one of struggle, arrives at the home of his friend Joel Pierce for a brief visit. He finds a typical estate of the Hudson River Valley — a great mansion set in the midst of beautiful lawns and wide fields. In the following scene he meets, and is examined by, his friend's mother.*]

Mrs. Pierce stood at the foot of the stairs surveying this young stranger from the outside world with a tolerant but glacially detached smile of impersonal curiosity:

" . . . Joel tells me that you like to stay up all night and prowl around. What do you do on these prowling expeditions? "

He wanted to answer her with simple eloquence and grace and warmth, he wanted to paint a picture of his midnight wanderings that would hold her there in fascinated interest, but the glacial impersonality of the woman's smile, the proud and haughty magnificence of her person, froze all the ardors of enthusiasm and conviction with which, he felt, he might have spoken, it even seemed to numb and thicken the muscles of his tongue, and he stood there gaping at her awkwardly, cutting a sorry figure, and flushing crimson with anger and vexation at his lame, stupid, halting tongue, and stammered out, replying:

" I — I walk," he mumbled. " I — I take walks."

" You — *what?* " she said kindly enough, but sharply, with a kind of peremptory authority that told him that she must already be growing weary and impatient of his stammering, incoherent speech, his mumbling awkwardness:

" Oh — *walk!* " she cried, with an air of swift enlightenment, as if her puzzled mind had just succeeded in translating his jargon. " Oh," she said quietly, and looked at him for a moment steadily with her fixed and glacial smile, " you do."

It seemed to him that those brief words were already pregnant with a cold indifferent dismissal: in them he seemed to feel the impregnable indifference of her cold detachment — the yawning gulf that separated her life from his. Already it seemed to him that she had turned away from him, dismissing him as not worthy even of such amused attention as she had given him. But after a moment, as she continued to look at him with her brilliant, glacial, detached, yet not unkindly smile, she continued:

" And what do you do on these walks? Where do you go? "

— Where? Where? Where indeed? His mind groped desperately over the whole nocturnal pattern of the city — over the lean, gaunt webbing of Manhattan with the barren angularity of its streets, the splintered, glacial soar of its terrific buildings, and the silent, frozen harshness of its streets of old brown houses, grimy brick and rusty, age-encrusted stone.

Oh, he thought that he could tell her all that could be told, that youth could know, that any man had ever known about night and time and darkness, and about the city's dark and secret heart, and what lay buried in the dark and secret heart of all America. He thought that

836

he could tell her all that any man could ever know about the huge, attentive secrecy of night, and of man's silent heart of buried, waiting, and intolerable desire, about the thing that waits there in the night-time in America, that lies buried at the city's secret heart of night, the mute and single tongue of man's intolerable desire, the silence of his single heart in all its overwhelming eloquence, the great tide flowing in the hearts of men, as dark and as mysterious as the great, unceasing river, the thing that waits and does not speak and is forever silent and that knows forever, and that has no words to say, no tongue to speak, and that unites six million celled and lonely sleepers at the heart of night and silence, in the great dark tide of the unceasing river, and of all our buried songs of hopes and joy and wild desire that live for-ever in the heart of night and of America.

Yes, he thought that he could tell her all of this, but when he spoke, with thickened tongue, a numb and desperate constraint, all that he could mutter thickly was: " I — I walk."

" But *where?* " she said, a trifle more sharply, still looking at him with her glacial, curious smile. " That's what I'd like to know. Where do you go? What do you see that's so interesting? What do you find that's worth staying up all night for? Where do you go when you make these expeditions? " she again demanded. " Up to Broadway? "

" Yes," he mumbled thickly, " — sometimes — and — and — sometimes — I go down town."

" Down town? " the cool incisive inflection of the voice, the glacial gray-green of the eye bored through him like a steel-blue drill. " Down town *where?* To the Battery? "

" Y-y-yes — sometimes. . . . And — and along the East Side, too," he mumbled.

" *Where?* " she cried sharply, smiling, but manifestly impatient with his mumbled, tongue-tied answers. " *Oh* — the East Side! " she cried again, with the air of glacial enlightenment. " — In the tenement section! "

" Yes — yes," he stumbled on desperately, " — and along Fourteenth Street and Second Avenue — and Grand Street — and — and Delancey — and — and the Bowery — and all the docks and piers and all," he blurted out, conscious of Joel's eager, radiant smile of hopeful kindness, and the miserable clown he was making of himself.

" But I should think you would find all that dreadfully boring." Mrs. Pierce's voice was now tinged with cool and mild surprise. " And awfully ugly, isn't it? . . . I mean, if you've got to prowl around at night, you might hunt for something a little more attractive than the East Side, couldn't you? . . . After all, we still have Riverside Drive — I suppose even that has changed a great deal, but in my childhood it was quite a lovely place. Or the Park? " she said, a little more kindly and persuasively. "If you want to take a walk before going to bed, why wouldn't it be better to take it in the Park — where you could see an occasional tree or a little grass. . . . Or even Fifth Avenue and around Washington Square — that used to be quite pleasant! But the East *Side!* Heavens! My dear boy, what on earth do you ever find in a place like that to interest you? "

He was absolutely speechless, congealed, actually terrified by the haughty magnificence, the glacial and almost inhuman detachment, of her person. His mouth gaped, he gulped, his lips quivered and made soundless efforts for a moment, and then he stammered:

"You — you find — you find — p-p-p-people there," he said.

"*People?*" Again, her thin eyebrows arched in fine surprise. "But of course you find people there! You find people everywhere you go. . . . Only," she added, "I shouldn't think you'd find many people anywhere at two o'clock in the morning. I should think most of them would be in bed — even on the East Side."

"They — they stay up late over there."

"But why? " she now cried with a good-natured but frank impatience. "That's just what I'm trying to find out! . . . What's it all about? What's all the *shooting* for? " she said humorously, repeating a phrase which was in current use at that time. " — What's the big attraction? What do they find to do that's so interesting that it can keep them out of bed half through the night? . . . Really," she cried, "if it's so amusing as all that, I think I'll go and have a look myself. What do they *do?* " she again insisted. "That's what I want to know."

"They — they sit around and talk."

"But *where? Where?* " she now cried with frank despair. "My dear boy, that's what I want you to tell me."

" Oh, in — in lunch-rooms — and restaurants — and speakeasies — and — and places like that."

"Yes," she nodded, with an air of satisfaction. "Good. At least, we have *that* settled. And you go to these places, too — and sit around — and watch — and listen to them. Is that it? "

"Yes," he said helplessly, nodding, her words suddenly making all this restless and unceasing explanation of the night seem reasonless, foolish, pitifully absurd, " sometimes."

" And what kind of people do you find in those places? " she said curiously. " I've often wondered what kind of people go there."

Kind? He stared at her foolishly with gaping jaw, and gaped and muttered wordlessly, and could not find a word to say to her. Kind? Great God, what word could ever shape them, what phrase could ever utter the huge swarm and impact of just one moment, out of all those million swarming memories of kaleidoscopic night! Kind? Great God, the kind of all the earth, the kind of the whole world, the unnumbered, nameless, swarming, and illimitable kind that make all living! Kind? The mongrel compost of a hundred races — the Jews, the Irish, the Italians, and the niggers, the Swedes, the Germans, the Lithuanians and the Poles, the Russians, Czechs, and Greeks, the Syrians, Turks, and Armenians, the nameless hodge-podge of the Balkans, as well as Chinese, Japs, and dapper little Filipinos — a hundred tongues, a thousand tribes, unnumbered colonies of life, all poured in through the lean gateways of the sea, all poured in upon that rock of life, to join the countless freightage of that ship of living stone, all nurtured and sustained upon the city's strong breast — a thousand kinds, a single substance, all fused and joined there at the heart of night, all moving with that central, secret and dynamic energy, all wrought and woven in, with all their swarming variousness, into the great web of America — with all its clamor, naked struggle, blind and brutal strife, with all its violence, ignorance, and cruelty, and with its terror, joy, and mystery, its undying hope, its everlasting life.

All he could do was gape and mumble foolishly again, and stammer finally: " There — there are all kinds, I guess," and plunge on desperately, " and then — and then — there are the wharves and piers and docks — the Battery and the City Hall — and — then — and then," he stumbled on, " — the Bridge — the Bridge is good."

" The Bridge? " Again the pencilled brows of arched surprise, the glacial curiosity. " What bridge? "

What bridge? Great God, the only bridge, the bridge of power, life and joy, the bridge that was a span, a cry, an ecstasy — that was America. What bridge? The bridge whose wing-like sweep that was like space and joy and ecstasy was mixed like music in his blood, would beat like flight and joy and triumph through the conduits of his life forever. What bridge? The bridge whereon at night he had walked and stood and watched a thousand times, until every fabric of its soaring web was inwrought in his memory, and every stone of its twin terrific arches was in his heart, and every living sinew of its million cabled nerves had throbbed and pulsed in his own spirit like his soul's anatomy.

"The — the Brooklyn Bridge," he mumbled. "The — the Bridge is good."

"Good? How do you mean — good?" The glacial and amused inquiry pierced his consciousness again with confusion, numb paralysis of speech, and incoherence. And at this moment Joel, seeing his agonizing embarrassment, came to his rescue with the exquisite, radiant kindliness that was the constant evidence of his fine character.

"Um. Yes," he could hear Joel whispering in a thoughtful and convinced way. "He's dead right about it, Mums. I've gone with him once or twice — and the Bridge *is* good! . . . and the East Side has good things in it, too," he whispered generously. "I saw some good bits there — street corners, a store front, alleys — there's good color — I'd like to go back sometime and paint it."

For the first time Mrs. Pierce broke into a robust, free and hearty laugh.

"Joel!" she cried. "You can get the most insane notions in your head of any boy I ever knew! If I didn't watch you, I believe you'd be painting ash-cans! . . . My dear boy," she said laughing, "you'd better stick to what you're doing. I don't think you've had much experience with low-life — if that's what you want I'll find plenty of it for you right here in Rhinekill or on the farm. . . . If you want low-life," here she paused and laughed heartily again, "go down to Granny's tomorrow and paint the expression of those nine maids of hers when she tells them she's decided to bob their hair because it fits in so nicely with the new decoration — Hah! Hah! Hah! Hah! Hah!" — Mrs. Pierce cast back her hand and laughed again, a full free hearty laugh of robust humor, in which Joel joined enthusiastically, almost suddenly, with a face radiant with glee — "I'd just like to be there when she tells them, that'll be low-life enough," she said.

"*Simply* incredible!" Joel whispered, his face still radiant with its gleeful merriment.

"But no," his mother went on more casually, and with humorous tolerance. " — You finish up what you're doing first — finish those screens you're doing for Madge Telfair — then we'll talk about low-life. . . . But I hardly think your talent lies in that direction," she said good-humoredly but with an ironically knowing smile. "I haven't been your mother all these years without finding out something about your abilities — and I hardly think they lie in that direction. So you just stick to what you're doing for the present — and if there's any low-life to be done, just let me do the choosing. . . . Well, then, good-night," she said quietly, kindly, and good-naturedly to the young man, as she turned to go upstairs. "Joel has told me so much about your nocturnal habits that I was curious to meet you and find out what you did. I'm glad to get the mystery cleared up. . . . I suppose," she said, with an idle and detached curiosity, "that when one is all alone and knows no one in the city, he is driven to do almost anything for amusement. . . . Where are you from?" she said curiously.

"From — from the South," he answered.

"Oh," she stared at him a moment longer with her cold, fixed smile. "Yes," she said, "I can see you are. I thought so. . . . Well, children," she said with an air of finality, "you can burn the candle at both ends if that's what you want to do — go out and bay the moon, if you like — but not too near the house," she said good-naturedly. "Your *mother's* going to bed. . . . Joel," she said quietly, "you'll be in to see me, of course, before you turn in."

"Yes, Mums," he whispered, eager, radiant, his tall, thin figure bent forward reverentially as he looked up at her, his eyebrows arching with their characteristic expression of fine surprise. — "But of course!" he said.

"Very well," she said quietly. "And now good-night to all of you."

Turning, she went swiftly up the stairs, a tall, magnificently haughty figure of a woman, holding rustling and luxurious skirts.

"And now," Joel whispered, when his mother had departed, "I'll show you your room — and how to find the kitchen — and tell you anything you want to know — and after *that*," he whispered, laughing and stroking his head, "you can do as you please, stay up as long as you like — but *I'm* going to bed."

With these words he took his guest's valise and started up the stairs. The young man followed him: he had been given a room on the second floor on the river side of the house. It was a magnificent spacious room so richly, softly carpeted that the foot sank down with velvet firmness to a noiseless tread. The quality of the room was the quality of the whole house — a kind of chateau-like grandeur and solidity, combined with the warmth, comfort and simplicity of a country house. Joel pressed buttons, flooding the great room with light. The wide and snowy covers of the great bed had been drawn back for the night. It was a bed fit for a king, and long and spacious enough for a man of seven feet: it waited there with a kind of still embrace, a silent and yet animate invitation that was eloquent with the promise of a strange and sweet repose.

Joel opened the door of the bathroom — it was a miracle of shining tile and creamy porcelain and gleaming silver and heavy, robe-like towels. Then Joel raised the shades, drew the curtains apart and opened the window: the fragrance of the night came in slowly, sustaining gauzy curtains on its breath of coolness like a cloud of gossamer. And through the opened window was revealed anew the haunting loneliness of that enchanted landscape: the vast sweep of velvet-rounded lawn that slept in moonlight, and the sleeping and moon-haunted woods below and to each side, and down below them in the distance the great wink and scallop-dance and dark unceasing mystery of the lovely and immortal river — a landscape such as one might see in dreams, in dreams forever haunted by the thought of home.

The feeling of happiness that filled the youth was so grand, so wonderful and so overpowering that he could not speak. It seemed that all his life he had dreamed of one day finding such a life as this, and now that he had found it, it seemed to him that all he had dreamed was but a poor and shabby counterfeit of this reality — all he had imaged as a boy in his unceasing visions of the shining city, and of the glamorous men and women, the fortunate, good, and happy life that he would find there, seemed nothing but a shadowy and dim prefigurement of the radiant miracle of this actuality.

It was not merely the wealth, the luxury and the comfort of the scene that filled his heart with a sense of joy and victory. Far more than this, it was the feeling that this life of wealth and luxury and comfort was so beautiful and right and good. At the moment it seemed to him to be the life for which all men on the earth are seeking, about which all men living dream, toward which all the myriads of the earth aspire; and the thing, above all, which made this life seem so beautiful and good was the conviction that filled him at that moment of its essential incorruptible righteousness. It seemed to him to be the most wonderful and beautiful life on earth, not only because it existed for the comfort and the soul-enrichment of its choice few, but because it stood there as a beacon and a legend in the hearts of all men living — a symbol of what all life on earth should be, a promise of what every man on earth should have.

In that blind surge of youth and joy, the magic of that unbelievable discovery, he could not estimate the strange and bitter chance of destiny, nor ravel out that grievous web, that dense perplexity. He could not see how men had groped and toiled and mined, and grown blind and bent and gray, deep in the dark bowels of the earth, to wreak this moonlight loveliness upon a hill; nor know how men had sweat and women worked, how youth had struck its fire and grown old, how hope and faith and even love had died, how many nameless lives had labored, grieved, and come to naught in order that this fragile image of compacted night, this priceless distillation of its rare and chosen loveliness, should blossom to a flower of moonlight beauty on a hill. . . .

[*1935*]

from

YOU CAN'T GO HOME AGAIN

CREDO

I believe that we are lost here in America, but I believe we shall be found. And this belief, which mounts now to the catharsis of knowledge and conviction, is for me — and I think for all of us — not only our own hope, but America's everlasting, living dream. I think the life which we have fashioned in America, and which has fashioned us — the forms we made, the cells that grew, the honeycomb that was created — was self-destructive in its nature, and must be destroyed. I think these forms are dying, and must die, just as I know that America and the people in it are deathless, undiscovered, and immortal, and must live.

I think the true discovery of America is before us. I think the true fulfillment of our spirit, of our people, of our mighty and immortal land, is yet to come. I think the true discovery of our own democracy is still before us. And I think that all these things are certain as the morning, as inevitable as noon. I think I speak for most men living when I say that our America is Here, is Now, and beckons on before us, and that this glorious assurance is not only our living hope, but our dream to be accomplished.

I think the enemy is here before us, too. But I think we know the forms and faces of the enemy, and in the knowledge that we know him, and shall meet him, and eventually must conquer him is also our living hope. I think the enemy is here before us with a thousand faces, but I think we know that all his faces wear one mask. I think the enemy is single selfishness and compulsive greed. I think the enemy is blind, but has the brutal power of his blind grab. I do not think the enemy was born yesterday, or that he grew to manhood forty years ago, or that he suffered sickness and collapse in 1929, or that we began without the enemy, and that our vision faltered, that we lost the way, and suddenly were in his camp. I think the enemy is old as Time, and evil as Hell, and that he has been here with us from the beginning. I think he stole our earth from us, destroyed our wealth, and ravaged and despoiled our land. I think he took our people and enslaved them, that he polluted the fountains of our life, took unto himself the rarest treasures of our own possession, took our bread and left us with a crust, and, not content, for the nature of the enemy is insatiate — tried finally to take from us the crust.

I think the enemy comes to us with the face of innocence and says to us:

"I am your friend."

I think the enemy deceives us with false words and lying phrases, saying:

"See, I am one of you — I am one of your children, your son, your brother, and your friend. Behold how sleek and fat I have become — and all because I am just one of you, and your friend. Behold how rich and powerful I am — and all because I am one of you — shaped in your way of life, of thinking, of accomplishment. What I am, I am because I am one of you, your humble brother and your friend. Behold," cries Enemy, "the man I am, the man I have become, the thing I have accomplished — and reflect. Will you destroy this thing? I assure you that it is the most precious thing you have. It is yourselves, the projection of each of you, the triumph of your individual lives, the thing that is rooted in your blood, and native to your stock, and inherent in the traditions of America. It is the thing that all of you may hope to be," says Enemy, "for —" humbly — "am I not just one of you? Am I not just your brother and your son? Am I not the living image of what each of you may hope to be, would wish to be, would desire for his own son? Would you destroy this glorious incarnation of your own heroic self? If you do, then," says Enemy, " you destroy yourselves — you kill the thing that is most gloriously American, and in so killing, kill yourselves."

He lies! And now we know he lies! He is not gloriously, or in any other way, ourselves. He is not our friend, our son, our brother. And he is not American! For, although he has a thousand familiar and convenient faces, his own true face is old as Hell.

Look about you and see what he has done.

[*1940*]

SINCLAIR LEWIS

[1885–   ]

THE SON of a country doctor, he was born in a prairie village — Sauk Center, Minnesota. He was a thin, nervous youth, something less than proficient in his studies, but very fond of reading. He entered Yale in 1903. Paying little attention to conventional campus activities, he cultivated his interest in literature and became editor of the *Yale Literary Magazine*. In 1906, tired of college, he went off to join a socialist colony run by Upton Sinclair, worked there for a while as janitor, then tried free-lancing, and finally returned to Yale, from which he was graduated in 1908. After a period of newspaper work and free-lancing, he joined the staff of a book-publishing house, and in this field he worked from 1910 to 1916, after which he devoted himself to writing. Popular magazine stories of no literary merit were followed by two enormously successful novels, *Main Street* (1920) and *Babbitt* (1922). In the first he depicted small-town life in America, in the second he caricatured the manners and mind of the " booster " type of business man. They are the classic criticisms of contemporary American civilization. From them he went on to *Arrowsmith* (1925) and *Elmer Gantry* (1927), which also dealt caustically with aspects of American life. Subsequently, in *It Can't Happen Here* (1935), he wrote a savage story of a possible fascist triumph based on native characteristics and tendencies. Unfortunately, in such other novels as *Mantrap* (1926), *Ann Vickers* (1933), and *The Prodigal Parents* (1938), Lewis has proved himself still capable of trivial stuff. In 1930 he was awarded the Nobel Prize in Literature — the first American to be so honored.

---

from

IT CAN'T HAPPEN HERE

As he . . . drove up Pleasant Hill to Tasbrough's, Doremus Jessup . . . let himself be absorbed in the hills, as it had been his habit for the fifty-three years, out of his sixty years of life, that he had spent in Fort Beulah, Vermont.

Legally a city, Fort Beulah was a comfortable village of old red brick, old granite workshops, and houses of white clapboards or gray shingles, with a few smug little modern bungalows, yellow or seal brown. There was but little manufacturing: a small woolen mill, a sash-and-door factory, a pump works. The granite which was its chief produce came from quarries four miles away; in Fort Beulah itself were only the offices . . . all the money . . . the meager shacks of most of the quarry workers. It was a town of perhaps ten thousand souls, inhabiting about twenty thousand bodies — the proportion of soul-possession may be too high.

There was but one (comparative) skyscraper in town: the six-story Tasbrough Building, with the offices of the Tasbrough & Scarlett Granite Quarries; the offices of Doremus's son-in-law, Fowler Greenhill, M.D., and his partner, old Dr. Olmsted, of Lawyer Mungo Kitterick, of Harry Kindermann, agent for maple syrup and dairying supplies, and of thirty or forty other village samurai.

It was a downy town, a drowsy town, a town of security and tradition, which still believed in Thanksgiving, Fourth of July, Memorial Day, and to which May Day was not an occasion for labor parades but for distributing small baskets of flowers.

It was a May night — late in May of 1936 — with a three-quarter moon. Doremus's house was a mile from the business-center of Fort Beulah, on Pleasant Hill, which was a spur thrust like a reaching hand out from the dark rearing mass of Mount Terror. Upland meadows, moon-glistening, he could see, among the wildernesses of spruce and maple and poplar on the ridges far above him; and below, as his car climbed, was Ethan Creek flowing through the meadows. Deep woods — rearing mountain bulwarks — the air like spring-water — serene clap-boarded houses that remembered the War of 1812 and the boyhoods of those errant Vermonters, Stephen A. Douglas, the "Little Giant," and Hiram Powers and Thaddeus Stevens and Brigham Young and President Chester Alan Arthur.

"No — Powers and Arthur — they were weak sisters," pondered Doremus. "But Douglas and Thad Stevens and Brigham, the old stallion — I wonder if we're breeding up any paladins like those stout, grouchy old devils? — if we're producing 'em anywhere in New England? — anywhere in America? — anywhere in the world? They had guts. Independence. Did what they wanted to and thought what they liked, and everybody could go to hell. The youngsters today — Oh, the aviators have plenty of nerve. The physicists, these twenty-five-year-old Ph.D.'s that violate the inviolable atom, they're pioneers. But most of the wish-washy young people today — Going seventy miles an hour but not going anywhere — not enough imagination to *want* to go anywhere! Getting their music by turning a dial. Getting their phrases from the comic strips instead of from Shakespeare and the Bible and Veblen and Old Bill Sumner. Pap-fed flabs! Like this smug pup Malcolm Tasbrough. . . ."

Mr. Francis Tasbrough was the president, general manager, and chief owner of the Tasbrough & Scarlett Granite Quarries, at West Beulah, four miles from "the Fort." He was rich, persuasive, and he had constant labor troubles. He lived in a new Georgian brick house on Pleasant Hill, a little beyond Doremus Jessup's, and in that house he maintained a private barroom luxurious as that of a motor company's advertising manager at Grosse Point. It was no more the traditional New England than was the Catholic part of Boston; and Frank himself boasted that, though his family had for six generations lived in New England, he was no tight Yankee but in his Efficiency, his Salesmanship, the complete Pan-American Business Executive.

He was a tall man, Tasbrough, with a yellow mustache and a monotonously emphatic voice. He was fifty-four, six years younger than Doremus Jessup, and when he had been four, Doremus had protected him from the results of his singularly unpopular habit of hitting the other small boys over the head with things — all kinds of things — sticks and toy wagons and lunch boxes and dry cow flops.

Assembled in his private barroom tonight, after the Rotarian Dinner, were Frank himself, Doremus Jessup, Medary Cole, the miller, Superintendent of Schools Emil Staubmeyer, R. C. Crowley — Roscoe Conkling Crowley, the weightiest banker in Fort Beulah — and, rather surprisingly, Tasbrough's pastor, the Episcopal minister, the Rev. Mr. Falck, his old hands as delicate as porcelain, his wilderness of hair silk-soft and white, his unfleshly face betokening the Good Life. Mr. Falck came from a solid Knickerbocker family, and he had studied in Edinburgh and Oxford along with the General Theological Seminary of New York; and in all of the Beulah Valley there was, aside from Doremus, no one who more contentedly hid away in the shelter of the hills.

The barroom had been professionally interior-decorated by a young New York gentleman with the habit of standing with the back of his right hand against his hip. It had a stainless-steel bar, framed illustrations from *La Vie Parisienne*, silvered metal tables, and chromium-plated aluminum chairs with scarlet leather cushions.

All of them except Tasbrough, Medary Cole (a social climber to whom the favors of Frank Tasbrough were as honey and fresh ripened figs), and "Professor" Emil Staubmeyer were uncomfortable in this parrot-cage elegance, but none of them, including Mr. Falck, seemed to dislike Frank's soda and excellent Scotch or the sardine sandwiches.

"And I wonder if Thad Stevens would of liked this, either?" considered Doremus. "He'd of snarled. Old cornered catamount. But probably not at the whisky!"

"Doremus," demanded Tasbrough, "why don't you take a tumble to yourself? All these years you've had a lot of fun criticizing — always being agin the government — kidding everybody — posing as such a Liberal that you'll stand for all these subversive elements. Time for you to quit playing tag with crazy ideas and come in and join the family. These are serious times — maybe twenty-eight million on relief, and beginning to get ugly — thinking they've got a vested right now to be supported.

"And the Jew Communists and Jew financiers plotting together to control the country. I can understand how, as a younger fellow, you could pump up a little sympathy for the unions and even for the Jews — though, as you know, I'll never get over being sore at you for taking the side of the strikers when those thugs were trying to ruin my whole business — burn down my polishing and cutting shops — why, you were even friendly with that alien murderer Karl Pascal, who started the whole strike — maybe I didn't enjoy firing *him* when it was all over!

"But anyway, these labor racketeers are getting together now, with Communist leaders, and determined to run the country — to tell men like *me* how to run our business! — and just like General Edgeways said, they'll refuse to serve their country if we should happen to get dragged into some war. Yessir, a mighty serious hour, and it's time for you to cut the cackle and join the really responsible citizens."

Said Doremus, "Hm. Yes, I agree it's a serious time. With all the discontent there is in the country to wash him into office, Senator Windrip has got an excellent chance to be elected President, next November, and if he is, probably his gang of buzzards will get us into some war, just to grease their insane vanity and show the world that we're the huskiest nation going. And then I, the Liberal, and you, the Plutocrat, the bogus Tory, will be led out and shot at 3 A.M. Serious? Huh! "

" Rats! You're exaggerating! " said R. C. Crowley.

Doremus went on: " If Bishop Prang, our Savonarola in a Cadillac 16, swings his radio audience and his League of Forgotten Men to Buzz Windrip, Buzz will win. People will think they're electing him to create more economic security. Then watch the Terror! God knows there's been enough indication that we *can* have tyranny in America — the fix of the Southern share-croppers, the working conditions of the miners and garment-makers, and our keeping Mooney in prison so many years. But wait till Windrip shows us how to say it with machine guns! Democracy — here and in Britain and France, it hasn't been so universal a sniveling slavery as Naziism in Germany, such an imagination-hating, pharisaic materialism as Russia — even if it has produced industrialists like you, Frank, and bankers like you, R. C., and given you altogether too much power and money. On the whole, with scandalous exceptions, Democracy's given the ordinary worker more dignity than he ever had. That may be menaced now by Windrip — all the Windrips. All right! Maybe we'll have to fight paternal dictatorship with a little sound patricide — fight machine guns with machine guns. Wait till Buzz takes charge of us. A real Fascist dictatorship! "

" Nonsense! Nonsense! " snorted Tasbrough. " That couldn't happen here in America, not possibly! We're a country of freemen."

" The answer to that," suggested Doremus Jessup, " if Mr. Falck will forgive me, is ' the hell it can't! ' Why, there's no country in the world that can get more hysterical — yes, or more obsequious! — than America. Look how Huey Long became absolute monarch over Louisiana, and how the Right Honorable Mr. Senator Berzelius Windrip owns *his* State. Listen to Bishop Prang and Father Coughlin on the radio — divine oracles, to millions. Remember how casually most Americans have accepted Tammany grafting and Chicago gangs and the crookedness of so many of President Harding's appointees? Could Hitler's bunch, or Windrip's, be worse? Remember the Ku Klux Klan? Remember our war hysteria, when we called sauerkraut ' Liberty cabbage ' and somebody actually proposed calling German measles ' Liberty measles '? And wartime censorship of honest papers? Bad as Russia! Remember our kissing the — well, the feet of Billy Sunday, the million-dollar evangelist, and of Aimee McPherson, who swam from the Pacific Ocean clear into the Arizona desert and got away with it? Remember Voliva and Mother Eddy? . . . Remember our Red scares and our Catholic scares, when all well-informed people knew that the O.G.P.U. were hiding out in Oskaloosa, and the Republicans campaigning against Al Smith told the Carolina mountaineers that if Al won the Pope would illegitimatize their children? Remember Tom Heflin and Tom Dixon? Remember when the hick legislators in certain states, in obedience to William Jennings Bryan, who learned his biology from his pious old grandma, set up shop as scientific experts and made the whole world laugh itself sick by forbidding the teaching of evolution? . . . Remember the Kentucky night-riders? Remember how trainloads of people have gone to enjoy lynchings? Not happen here? Prohibition — shooting down people just because they *might* be transporting liquor — no, that couldn't happen in *America!* Why, where in all history has there ever been a people so ripe for a dictatorship as ours! We're ready to start on a Children's Crusade — only of adults — right now, and the Right Reverend Abbots Windrip and Prang are all ready to lead it! "

"Well, what if they are? " protested R. C. Crowley. "It might not be so bad. I don't like all these irresponsible attacks on us bankers all the time. Of course, Senator Windrip has to pretend publicly to bawl the banks out, but once he gets into power he'll give the banks their proper influence in the administration and take our expert financial advice. Yes. Why are you so afraid of the word ' Fascism,' Doremus? Just a word — just a word! And might not be so bad, with all the lazy bums we got panhandling relief nowadays, and living on my income tax and yours — not so worse to have a real Strong Man, like Hitler or Mussolini — like Napoleon or Bismarck in the good old days — and have 'em really *run* the country and make it efficient and prosperous again. 'Nother words, have a doctor who won't take any back-chat, but really boss the patient and make him get well whether he likes it or not! "

"Yes! " said Emil Staubmeyer. "Didn't Hitler save Germany from the Red Plague of Marxism? I got cousins there. I *know!* "

"Hm," said Doremus, as often Doremus did say it. " Cure the evils of Democracy by the evils of Fascism! Funny therapeutics. I've heard of their curing syphilis by giving the patient malaria, but I've never heard of their curing malaria by giving the patient syphilis! "

"Think that's nice language to use in the presence of the Reverend Falck? " raged Tasbrough.

Mr. Falck piped up, " I think it's quite nice language, and an interesting suggestion, Brother Jessup! "

" Besides," said Tasbrough, " this chewing the rag is all nonsense, anyway. As Crowley says, might be a good thing to have a strong man in the saddle, but — it just can't happen here in America."

And it seemed to Doremus that the softly moving lips of the Reverend Mr. Falck were framing, " The hell it can't! . . ."

[*1935*]

JOHN STEINBECK

[1902–   ]

IN ANY list of contemporary American novelists likely to endure, Steinbeck's would be one of the leading names. His is certainly the highest achievement of the 1930's. He was born in Salinas, California, educated in local schools and at Stanford University. While attending school and for some years afterwards he worked at jobs that gave him an insight into the life of the common people. In 1929 he published his first novel, *Cup of Gold* — a failure. Two other undistinguished novels followed. In 1935 he published *Tortilla Flat,* which attracted attention as a sympathetic picture of Mexican workers in southern California. *In Dubious Battle* (1936), the story of a strike, was evidence of his ripening talents, for it was tightly written and well constructed and showed that he was attempting to comprehend major social forces. His next work, *Of Mice and Men* (1937), a novelette about migratory workers, was a brilliant success. Finally, *The Grapes of Wrath* appeared in 1939, and there could no longer be any doubt about his powers. It has been called the *Uncle Tom's Cabin* of our generation — an unforgettable picture of an oppressed and exploited minority, so compellingly presented that it awakens the conscience of the nation — the minority in this case being the dispossessed farmers of the " dust bowl " who join the horde of migratory workers in California. The fact that this novel has been one of the best-sellers of the past decade is proof that the democratic spirit of America flourishes.

---

from

THE GRAPES OF WRATH

The owners of the land came onto the land, or more often a spokesman for the owners came. They came in closed cars, and they felt the dry earth with their fingers, and sometimes they drove big earth augers into the ground for soil tests. The tenants, from their sunbeaten dooryards, watched uneasily when the closed cars drove along the fields. And at last the owner men drove into the dooryards and sat in their cars to talk out of the windows. The tenant men stood beside the cars for a while, and then squatted on their hams and found sticks with which to mark the dust.

In the open doors the women stood looking out, and behind them the children — corn-headed children, with wide eyes, one bare foot on top of the other bare foot, and the toes working. The women and the children watched their men talking to the owner men. They were silent.

Some of the owner men were kind because they hated what they had to do, and some of them were angry because they hated to be cruel, and some of them were cold because they had long ago found that one could not be an owner unless one were cold. And all of them were caught in something larger than themselves. Some of them hated the mathematics that drove them, and some were afraid, and some worshiped the mathematics because it provided a refuge from thought and from feeling. If a bank or a finance company owned the land, the owner man said, The Bank — or the Company — needs — wants — insists — must have — as though the Bank or the Company were a monster, with thought and feeling, which had ensnared them. These last would take no responsibility for the banks or the companies because they were men and slaves, while the banks were machines and masters all at the same time. Some of the owner men were a little proud to be slaves to such cold and powerful masters. The owner men sat in the cars and explained. You know the land is poor. You've scrabbled at it long enough, God knows.

The squatting tenant men nodded and wondered and drew figures in the dust, and yes, they knew, God knows. If the dust only wouldn't fly. If the top would only stay on the soil, it might not be so bad.

The owner men went on leading to their point: You know the land's getting poorer. You know what cotton does to the land; robs it, sucks all the blood out of it.

The squatters nodded — they knew, God knew. If they could only rotate the crops they might pump blood back into the land.

Well, it's too late. And the owner men explained the workings and the thinkings of the monster that was stronger than they were. A man can hold land if he can just eat and pay taxes; he can do that.

Yes, he can do that until his crops fail one day and he has to borrow money from the bank.

But — you see, a bank or a company can't do that, because those creatures don't breathe air, don't eat side-meat. They breathe profits; they eat the interest on money. If they don't get it, they die the way you die without air; without side-meat. It is a sad thing, but it is so. It is just so.

The squatting men raised their eyes to understand. Can't we just hang on? Maybe the next year will be a good year. God knows how much cotton next year. And with all the wars — God knows what price cotton will bring. Don't they make explosives out of cotton? And uniforms? Get enough wars and cotton'll hit the ceiling. Next year, maybe. They looked up questioningly.

We can't depend on it. The bank — the monster has to have profits all the time. It can't wait. It'll die. No, taxes go on. When the monster stops growing, it dies. It can't stay one size.

Soft fingers began to tap the sill of the car window, and hard fingers tightened on the restless drawing sticks. In the doorways of the sun-beaten tenant houses, women sighed and then shifted feet so that the one that had been down was now on top, and the toes working. Dogs came sniffing near the owner cars and wetted on all four tires one after another. And chickens lay in the sunny dust and fluffed their feathers to get the cleansing dust down to the skin. In the little sties the pigs grunted inquiringly over the muddy remnants of the slops.

The squatting men looked down again. What do you want us to do? We can't take less share of the crop — we're half starved now. The kids are hungry all the time. We got no clothes, torn an' ragged. If all the neighbors weren't the same, we'd be ashamed to go to meeting.

And at last the owner men came to the point. The tenant system won't work any more. One man on a tractor can take the place of twelve or fourteen families. Pay him a wage and take all the crop. We have to do it. We don't like to do it. But the monster's sick. Something's happened to the monster.

But you'll kill the land with cotton.

We know. We've got to take cotton quick before the land dies. Then we'll sell the land. Lots of families in the East would like to own a piece of land.

The tenant men looked up alarmed. But what'll happen to us? How'll we eat?

You'll have to get off the land. The plows'll go through the dooryard.

And now the squatting men stood up angrily. Grampa took up the land, and he had to kill the Indians and drive them away. And Pa was born here, and he killed weeds and snakes. Then a bad year came and he had to borrow a little money. An' we was born here. There in the door — our children born here. And Pa had to borrow money. The bank owned the land then, but we stayed and we got a little bit of what we raised.

We know that — all that. It's not us, it's the bank. A bank isn't like a man. Or an owner with fifty thousand acres, he isn't like a man either. That's the monster.

Sure, cried the tenant men, but it's our land. We measured it and broke it up. We were born on it, and we got killed on it, died on it. Even if it's no good, it's still ours. That's what makes it ours — being born on it, working it, dying on it. That makes ownership, not a paper with numbers on it.

We're sorry. It's not us. It's the monster. The bank isn't like a man.

Yes, but the bank is only made of men.

No, you're wrong there — quite wrong there. The bank is something else than men. It happens that every man in a bank hates what the bank does, and yet the bank does it. The bank is something more than men, I tell you. It's the monster. Men made it, but they can't control it.

The tenants cried, Grampa killed Indians, Pa killed snakes for the land. Maybe we can kill banks — they're worse than Indians and snakes. Maybe we got to fight to keep our land, like Pa and Grampa did.

And now the owner men grew angry. You'll have to go.

But it's ours, the tenant men cried. We —

No. The bank, the monster owns it. You'll have to go.

We'll get our guns, like Grampa when the Indians came. What then?

Well — first the sheriff, and then the troops. You'll be stealing if you try to stay, you'll be murderers if you kill to stay. The monster isn't men, but it can make men do what it wants.

But if we go, where'll we go? How'll we go? We got no money.

We're sorry, said the owner men. The bank, the fifty-thousand-acre owner can't be responsible. You're on land that isn't yours. Once over the line maybe you can pick cotton in the fall. Maybe you can go on relief. Why don't you go west to California? There's work there, and it never gets cold. Why, you can reach out anywhere and pick an orange. Why, there's always some kind of crop to work in. Why don't you go there? And the owner men started their cars and rolled away.

The tenant men squatted down on their hams again to mark the dust with a stick, to figure, to wonder. Their sunburned faces were dark, and their sun-whipped eyes were light. The women moved cautiously out of the doorways toward their men, and the children crept behind the women, cautiously, ready to run. The bigger boys squatted beside their fathers, because that made them men. After a time the women asked, What did he want?

And the men looked up for a second, and the smolder of pain was in their eyes. We got to get off. A tractor and a superintendent. Like factories.

Where'll we go? the women asked.

We don't know. We don't know.

And the women went quickly, quietly back into the houses and herded the children ahead of them. They knew that a man so hurt and so perplexed may turn in anger, even on people he loves. They left the men alone to figure and to wonder in the dust.

After a time perhaps the tenant man looked about — at the pump put in ten years ago, with a goose-neck handle and iron flowers on the spout, at the chopping block where a thousand chickens had been killed, at the hand plow lying in the shed, and the patent crib hanging in the rafters over it.

The children crowded about the women in the houses. What we going to do, Ma? Where we going to go?

The women said, We don't know, yet. Go out and play. But don't go near your father. He might whale you if you go near him. And the women went on with the work, but all the time they watched the men squatting in the dust — perplexed and figuring.

The tractors came over the roads and into the fields, great crawlers moving like insects, having the incredible strength of insects. They crawled over the ground, laying the track and rolling on it and picking it up. Diesel tractors, puttering while they stood idle; they thundered when they moved, and then settled down to a droning roar. Snub-nosed monsters, raising the dust and sticking their snouts into it, straight down the country, across the country, through fences, through dooryards, in and out of gullies in straight lines. They did not run on the ground, but on their own roadbeds. They ignored hills and gulches, water courses, fences, houses.

The man sitting in the iron seat did not look like a man; gloved, goggled, rubber dust mask over nose and mouth, he was a part of the monster, a robot in the seat. The thunder of the cylinders sounded through the country, became one with the air and the earth, so that earth and air muttered in sympathetic vibration. The driver could not control it — straight across country it went, cutting through a dozen farms and straight back. A twitch at the controls could swerve the cat', but the driver's hands could not twitch because the monster that built the tractor, the monster that sent the tractor out, had somehow got into the driver's hands, into his brain and muscle, had goggled him and muzzled him — goggled his mind, muzzled his speech, goggled his perception, muzzled his protest. He could not see the land as it was, he could not smell the land as it smelled; his feet did not stamp the clods or feel the warmth and power of the earth. He sat in an iron seat and stepped on iron pedals. He could not cheer or beat or curse or encourage the extension of his power, and because of this he could not cheer or whip or curse or encourage himself. He did not know or own or trust or beseech the land. If a seed dropped did not germinate, it was nothing. If the young thrusting plant withered in drought or drowned in a flood of rain, it was no more to the driver than to the tractor.

He loved the land no more than the bank loved the land. He could admire the tractor — its machined surfaces, its surge of power, the roar of its detonating cylinders; but it was not his tractor. Behind the tractor rolled the shining disks, cutting the earth with blades — not plowing but surgery, pushing the cut earth to the right where the second row of disks cut it and pushed it to the left; slicing blades shining, polished by the cut earth. And pulled behind the disks, the harrows combing with iron teeth so that the little clods broke up and the earth lay smooth. Behind the harrows, the long seeders — twelve curved iron penes erected in the foundry, orgasms set by gears, raping methodically, raping without passion. The driver sat in his iron seat and he was proud of the straight lines he did not will, proud of the tractor he did not own or love, proud of the power he could not control. And when that crop grew, and was harvested, no man had crumbled a hot clod in his fingers and let the earth sift past his fingertips. No man had touched the seed, or lusted for the growth. Men ate what they had not raised, had no connection with the bread. The land bore under iron, and under iron gradually died; for it was not loved or hated, it had no prayers or curses.

858

At noon the tractor driver stopped sometimes near a tenant house and opened his lunch: sandwiches wrapped in waxed paper, white bread, pickle, cheese, Spam, a piece of pie branded like an engine part. He ate without relish. And tenants not yet moved away came out to see him, looked curiously while the goggles were taken off, and the rubber dust mask, leaving white circles around the eyes and a large white circle around nose and mouth. The exhaust of the tractor puttered on, for fuel is so cheap it is more efficient to leave the engine running than to heat the Diesel nose for a new start. Curious children crowded close, ragged children who ate their fried dough as they watched. They watched hungrily the unwrapping of the sandwiches, and their hunger-sharpened noses smelled the pickle, cheese, and Spam. They didn't speak to the driver. They watched his hand as it carried food to his mouth. They did not watch him chewing; their eyes followed the hand that held the sandwich. After a while the tenant who could not leave the place came out and squatted in the shade beside the tractor.

"Why, you're Joe Davis's boy!"

"Sure," the driver said.

"Well, what you doing this kind of work for — against your own people?"

"Three dollars a day. I got damn sick of creeping for my dinner — and not getting it. I got a wife and kids. We got to eat. Three dollars a day, and it comes every day."

"That's right," the tenant said. "But for your three dollars a day fifteen or twenty families can't eat at all. Nearly a hundred people have to go out and wander on the roads for your three dollars a day. Is that right?"

And the driver said, "Can't think of that. Got to think of my own kids. Three dollars a day, and it comes every day. Times are changing, mister, don't you know? Can't make a living on the land unless you've got two, five, ten thousand acres and a tractor. Crop land isn't for little guys like us any more. You don't kick up a howl because you can't make Fords, or because you're not the telephone company. Well, crops are like that now. Nothing to do about it. You try to get three dollars a day someplace. That's the only way."

The tenant pondered. "Funny thing how it is. If a man owns a little property, that property is him, it's part of him, and it's like him. If he owns property only so he can walk on it and handle it and be sad when it isn't doing well, and feel fine when the rain falls on it, that property is him, and some way he's bigger because he owns it. Even if he isn't successful he's big with his property. That is so."

And the tenant pondered more. "But let a man get property he doesn't see, or can't take time to get his fingers in, or can't be there to walk on it — why, then the property is the man. He can't do what he wants, he can't think what he wants. The property is the man, stronger than he is. And he is small, not big. Only his possessions are big — and he's the servant of his property. That is so, too."

The driver munched the branded pie and threw the crust away. "Times are changed, don't you know? Thinking about stuff like that don't feed the kids. Get your three dollars a day, feed your kids. You got no call to worry about anybody's kids but your own. You get a reputation for talking like that, and you'll never get three dollars a day. Big shots won't give you three dollars a day if you worry about anything but your three dollars a day."

"Nearly a hundred people on the road for your three dollars. Where will we go?"

"And that reminds me," the driver said, "you better get out soon. I'm going through the dooryard after dinner."

"You filled in the well this morning."

"I know. Had to keep the line straight. But I'm going through the dooryard after dinner. Got to keep the lines straight. And — well, you know Joe Davis, my old man, so I'll tell you this. I got orders wherever there's a family not moved out — if I have an accident — you know, get too close and cave the house in a little — well, I might get a couple of dollars. And my youngest kid never had no shoes yet."

"I built it with my hands. Straightened old nails to put the sheathing on. Rafters are wired to the stringers with baling wire. It's mine. I built it. You bump it down — I'll be in the window with a rifle. You even come too close and I'll pot you like a rabbit."

"It's not me. There's nothing I can do. I'll lose my job if I don't do it. And look — suppose you kill me? They'll just hang you, but long before you're hung there'll be another guy on the tractor, and he'll bump the house down. You're not killing the right guy."

"That's so," the tenant said. "Who gave you orders? I'll go after him. He's the one to kill."

"You're wrong. He got his orders from the bank. The bank told him, 'Clear those people out or it's your job.'"

860

"Well, there's a president of the bank. There's a board of directors. I'll fill up the magazine of the rifle and go into the bank."

The driver said, "Fellow was telling me the bank gets orders from the East. The orders were, 'Make the land show profit or we'll close you up.'"

"But where does it stop? Who can we shoot? I don't aim to starve to death before I kill the man that's starving me."

"I don't know. Maybe there's nobody to shoot. Maybe the thing isn't men at all. Maybe, like you said, the property's doing it. Anyway I told you my orders."

"I got to figure," the tenant said. "We all got to figure. There's some way to stop this. It's not like lightning or earthquakes. We've got a bad thing made by men, and by God that's something we can change." The tenant sat in his doorway, and the driver thundered his engine and started off, tracks falling and curving, harrows combing, and the phalli of the seeder slipping into the ground. Across the dooryard the tractor cut, and the hard, foot-beaten ground was seeded field, and the tractor cut through again; the uncut space was ten feet wide. And back he came. The iron guard bit into the house-corner, crumbled the wall, and wrenched the little house from its foundation so that it fell sideways, crushed like a bug. And the driver was goggled and a rubber mask covered his nose and mouth. The tractor cut a straight line on, and the air and the ground vibrated with its thunder. The tenant man stared after it, his rifle in his hand. His wife was beside him, and the quiet children behind. And all of them stared after the tractor.

Along 66. . . . The transport truck, a driver and relief. How 'bout stoppin' for a cup a Java? I know this dump.

How's the schedule?

Oh, we're ahead!

Pull up, then. They's a ol' war horse in here that's a kick. Good Java, too.

The truck pulls up. Two men in khaki riding trousers, boots, short jackets, and shiny-visored military caps. Screen door — slam.

H'ya, Mae?

Well, if it ain't Big Bill the Rat! When'd you get back on this run? Week ago.

The other man puts a nickel in the phonograph, watches the disk slip free and the turntable rise up under it. Bing Crosby's voice — golden.

"Thanks for the memory, of sunburn at the shore — You might have been a headache, but you never were a bore —" And the truck driver sings for Mae's ears, you might have been a haddock but you never was a whore —

Mae laughs. Who's ya frien', Bill? New on this run, ain't he?

The other puts a nickel in the slot machine, wins four slugs, and puts them back. Walks to the counter.

Well, what's it gonna be?

Oh, cup a Java. Kinda pie ya got?

Banana cream, pineapple cream, chocolate cream — an' apple.

Make it apple. Wait — Kind is that big thick one?

Mae lifts it out and sniffs it. Banana cream.

Cut off a hunk; make it a big hunk.

Man at the slot machine says, Two all around.

Two it is. Seen any new etchin's lately, Bill?

Well, here's one.

Now, you be careful front of a lady.

Oh, this ain't bad. Little kid comes in late ta school. Teacher says, "Why ya late?" Kid says, "Had a take a heifer down — get 'er bred." Teacher says, "Couldn't your ol' man do it?" Kid says, "Sure he could, but not as good as the bull."

Mae squeaks with laughter, harsh screeching laughter. Al, slicing onions carefully on a board, looks up and smiles, and then looks down again. Truck drivers, that's the stuff. Gonna leave a quarter each for Mae. Fifteen cents for pie an' coffee an' a dime for Mae. An' they ain't tryin' to make her, neither.

Sitting together on the stools, spoons sticking up out of the coffee mugs. Passing the time of day. And Al, rubbing down his griddle, listening but making no comment. Bing Crosby's voice stops. The turntable drops down and the record swings into its place in the pile. The purple light goes off. The nickel, which has caused all this mechanism to work, has caused Crosby to sing and an orchestra to play — this nickel drops from between the contact points into the box where the profits go. This nickel, unlike most money, has actually done a job of work, has been physically responsible for a reaction.

Steam spurts from the valve of the coffee urn. The compressor of the ice machine chugs softly for a time and then stops. The electric fan in the corner waves its head slowly back and forth, sweeping the room with a warm breeze. On the highway, on 66, the cars whiz by.

They was a Massachusetts car stopped a while ago, said Mae.

Big Bill grasped his cup around the top so that the spoon stuck up between his first and second fingers. He drew in a snort of air with the coffee, to cool it. " You ought to be out on 66. Cars from all over the country. All headin' west. Never seen so many before. Sure some honeys on the road."

" We seen a wreck this mornin'," his companion said. " Big car. Big Cad', a special job and a honey, low, cream-color, special job. Hit a truck. Folded the radiator right back into the driver. Must a been doin' ninety. Steerin' wheel went right on through the guy an' lef' him a-wigglin' like a frog on a hook. Peach of a car. A honey. You can have her for peanuts now. Drivin' alone, the guy was."

Al looked up from his work. " Hurt the truck? "

" Oh, Jesus Christ! Wasn't a truck. One of them cut-down cars full a stoves an' pans an' mattresses an' kids an' chickens. Goin' west, you know. This guy come by us doin' ninety — r'ared up on two wheels just to pass us, an' a car's comin' so he cuts in an' whangs this here truck. Drove like he's blin' drunk. Jesus, the air was full a bed clothes an' chickens an' kids. Killed one kid. Never seen such a mess. We pulled up. Ol' man that's drivin' the truck, he jus' stan's there lookin' at that dead kid. Can't get a word out of 'im. Jus' rum-dumb. God Almighty, the road is full a them families goin' west. Never seen so many. Gets worse all a time. Wonder where the hell they all come from? "

" Wonder where they all go to," said Mae. " Come here for gas some-times, but they don't hardly never buy nothin' else. People says they steal. We ain't got nothin' layin' around. They never stole nothin' from us."

Big Bill, munching his pie, looked up the road through the screened window. " Better tie your stuff down. I think you got some of 'em comin' now."

A 1926 Nash sedan pulled wearily off the highway. The back seat was piled nearly to the ceiling with sacks, with pots and pans, and on the very top, right up against the ceiling, two boys rode. On the top of the car, a mattress and a folded tent; tent poles tied along the running board. The car pulled up to the gas pumps. A dark-haired, hatchet-faced man got slowly out. And the two boys slid down from the load and hit the ground.

Mae walked around the counter and stood in the door. The man was dressed in gray wool trousers and a blue shirt, dark blue with

sweat on the back and under the arms. The boys in overalls and nothing else, ragged patched overalls. Their hair was light, and it stood up
evenly all over their heads, for it had been roached. Their faces were
streaked with dust. They went directly to the mud puddle under the
hose and dug their toes into the mud.

The man asked, "Can we git some water, ma'am?"

A look of annoyance crossed Mae's face. "Sure, go ahead." She
said softly over her shoulder, "I'll keep my eye on the hose." She
watched while the man slowly unscrewed the radiator cap and ran
the hose in.

A woman in the car, a flaxen-haired woman, said, "See if you can't
git it here."

The man turned off the hose and screwed on the cap again. The
little boys took the hose from him and they upended it and drank
thirstily. The man took off his dark, stained hat and stood with a curious
humility in front of the screen. "Could you see your way to sell us
a loaf of bread, ma'am?"

Mae said, "This ain't a grocery store. We got bread to make
san'widges."

"I know, ma'am." His humility was insistent. "We need bread and
there ain't nothin' for quite a piece, they say."

"'F we sell bread we gonna run out." Mae's tone was faltering.

"We're hungry," the man said.

"Whyn't you buy a san'widge? We got nice san'widges, hamburgs."

"We'd sure admire to do that, ma'am. But we can't. We got to make
a dime do all of us." And he said embarrassedly, "We ain't got but a
little."

Mae said, "You can't get no loaf a bread for a dime. We only got
fifteen-cent loafs."

From behind her Al growled, "God Almighty, Mae, give 'em bread."

"We'll run out 'fore the bread truck comes."

"Run out, then, goddamn it," said Al. And he looked sullenly down
at the potato salad he was mixing.

Mae shrugged her plump shoulders and looked to the truck drivers
to show them what she was up against.

She held the screen door open and the man came in, bringing a smell
of sweat with him. The boys edged in behind him and they went immediately to the candy case and stared in — not with craving or with

hope or even with desire, but just with a kind of wonder that such things could be. They were alike in size and their faces were alike. One scratched his dusty ankle with the toe nails of his other foot. The other whispered some soft message and then they straightened their arms so that their clenched fists in the overall pockets showed through the thin blue cloth.

Mae opened a drawer and took out a long waxpaper-wrapped loaf. "This here is a fifteen-cent loaf."

The man put his hat back on his head. He answered with inflexible humility, "Won't you — can't you see your way to cut off ten cents' worth?"

Al said snarlingly, "Goddamn it, Mae. Give 'em the loaf."

The man turned toward Al. "No, we want ta buy ten cents' worth of it. We got it figgered awful close, mister, to get to California."

Mae said resignedly, "You can have this for ten cents."

"That'd be robbin' you, ma'am."

"Go ahead — Al says to take it." She pushed the wax-papered loaf across the counter. The man took a deep leather pouch from his rear pocket, untied the strings, and spread it open. It was heavy with silver and with greasy bills.

"May soun' funny to be so tight," he apologized. "We got a thousan' miles to go, an' we don' know if we'll make it." He dug in the pouch with a forefinger, located a dime, and pinched in for it. When he put it down on the counter he had a penny with it. He was about to drop the penny back into the pouch when his eye fell on the boys frozen before the candy counter. He moved slowly down to them. He pointed in the case at big long sticks of striped peppermint. "Is them penny candy, ma'am?"

Mae moved down and looked in. "Which ones?"

"There, them stripy ones."

The little boys raised their eyes to her face and they stopped breathing; their mouths were partly opened, their half-naked bodies were rigid.

"Oh — them. Well, no — them's two for a penny."

"Well, gimme two then, ma'am." He placed the copper cent carefully on the counter. The boys expelled their held breath softly. Mae held the big sticks out.

"Take 'em," said the man.

They reached timidly, each took a stick, and they held them down at their sides and did not look at them. But they looked at each other, and their mouth corners smiled rigidly with embarrassment.

"Thank you, ma'am." The man picked up the bread and went out the door, and the little boys marched stiffly behind him, the red-striped sticks held tightly against their legs. They leaped like chipmunks over the front seat and onto the top of the load, and they burrowed back out of sight like chipmunks.

The man got in and started his car, and with a roaring motor and a cloud of blue oily smoke the ancient Nash climbed up on the highway and went on its way to the west.

From inside the restaurant the truck drivers and Mae and Al stared after them.

Big Bill wheeled back. "Them wasn't two-for-a-cent candy," he said.

"What's that to you?" Mae said fiercely.

"Them was nickel apiece candy," said Bill.

"We got to get goin'," said the other man. "We're droppin' time." They reached in their pockets. Bill put a coin on the counter and the other man looked at it and reached again and put down a coin. They swung around and walked to the door.

"So long," said Bill.

Mae called, "Hey! Wait a minute. You got change."

"You go to hell," said Bill, and the screen door slammed.

Mae watched them get into the great truck, watched it lumber off in low gear, and heard the shift of the whining gears to cruising ratio. "Al —" she said softly.

He looked up from the hamburger he was patting thin and stacking between waxed papers. "What ya want?"

"Look there." She pointed at the coins beside the cups — two half-dollars. Al walked near and looked, and then he went back to his work.

"Truck drivers," Mae said reverently. . . .

[*1939*]

LEWIS MUMFORD

[1895–   ]

HE WAS born in Flushing, Long Island, and educated in the schools and colleges of New York City. From early boyhood he was interested in science, and to this he soon added interests in sociology, architecture, and literature. During the First World War he was a radio operator in the United States Navy. After the war he began to write for the *Dial*, the *Freeman*, the *New Republic*, and various architectural magazines. His first book was *The Story of Utopias* (1922) and his second was *Sticks and Stones* (1924), a study of American architecture. These volumes indicated the wide range of his inquiries. Since then he has published such well-known works as *The Golden Day* (1926), *The Brown Decades* (1931), *Technics and Civilization* (1934), *The Culture of Cities* (1938), and *Faith for Living* (1940). Through these works he has become known as one of our foremost liberals — as a student of civilization from the standpoint of an emotional antagonism toward strictly materialistic philosophies and an almost poetic appreciation of a voluntarily collective society. Since the outbreak of the Second World War he became an active advocate of American participation, believing that only thus could his concept of a liberal civilization survive.

---

from

FAITH FOR LIVING

Man's chief purpose . . . is the creation and preservation of values: that is what gives meaning to our civilization, and the participation in this is what gives significance, ultimately, to the individual human life.

Only in so far as values are fostered — through art and religion and science and love and domestic life — can men effectively use the machines and powers that have enabled them to tame nature and secure human existence from the worst outrages and accidents that forever threaten it. Civilization, our very capacity to be human, rests on that

867

perpetual effort. If any nation or group thinks that the job is finished, or if man puts his confidence solely in the instruments and forgets the ends and ideals and metaphysical purposes — then the structure crumbles away: then man himself is finished.

Thought, social relations, economic practices, biological activities, cosmic backgrounds — all these are organically united and call for co-operations that reach out beyond the borders of any single community, even as they reach out, beyond our limited present, into the past and future. That which exists by itself has, indeed, no real existence at all; it is a phantasm, an aberration of the mind. The finer life becomes, the more complicated becomes the network of relationships, and the more invisible filaments bind part with part.

Goethe once put this truth admirably in a conversation with Eckermann. "People," he said, "are always talking about originality; but what do they mean? As soon as we are born, the world begins to work upon us, and keeps on to the end. What can we call ours except energy, strength, will? If I could give an account of what I owe to great predecessors and contemporaries, there would be but a small remainder." That does not merely hold for Goethe; it holds for every human group, every community, every person.

The individual who fancies he has made his own professional career, or the inventor who believes he has the sole right to his invention, or the business man who thinks his own unaided efforts have brought him his fortune is merely ignorant of his debts. Like Bounderby, whom Dickens portrayed in "Hard Times," he is a monster of ingratitude. Darwin formulated his "Origin of Species" with the sense that he was making a completely unique personal discovery. Before he was finished the similar hypothesis of another young naturalist, Wallace, was brought to his attention: it turned out that they had both got their clue from Malthus's "Essay on Population." By the time Darwin published his second edition, he had at last become aware of a whole line of predecessors and partial anticipators, extending back to the Greeks.

The individual contribution, the work of any single generation, is infinitesimal: the power and glory belong to human society at large, and are the long result of selection, conservation, sacrifice, creation, and renewal — the outcome of endless brave efforts to conserve values and ideas, and to hand them on to posterity, along with physical life itself. Each person is a temporary focus of forces, vitalities, and values that carry back into an immemorial past and that reach forward into an unthinkable future. The best consolation for the dying is the thought that others, equally good, will carry on their work: that is the comfort the father and mother derive from their children, that the teacher derives from his student, that comrades and colleagues pass on to each other. . . .

This . . . is the philosophic justification for every form of social justice: not merely for a sharing of material goods and animal satisfactions, sufficient to sustain life on its humblest levels — though this is important — but also for that degree of cultivation and leisure which makes possible a fuller sharing of all the higher goods of life.

In America we have an historic tradition that recognizes both needs. The Land Grant act that was passed during the Civil War was an attempt to give to every able and willing family that would stake out a homestead a generous share in the land of our Republic. In another period of crisis, the distribution of work by the W.P.A. was a recognition of the same principle. Embedded still deeper in our traditions is the free elementary school education, now extending even through high school and college, which we have taken to be the inalienable right of every member of the community; as a very means of ensuring his fitness to be an intelligent and responsible member of that community.

Within very definite limits, differentiation of talent must be recognized and differentiation of reward may be serviceable; but never to such an extent as to continue the gross inequalities, the grotesque specialisms, the unpardonable parasitisms that have grown up in the United States — as in the whole Western World — during the past century.

Differentiated tasks, individual preferences, special incentives, intense interests, must all be taken into account in allowing for the full growth of the human personality. But this can happen with justice only after the continuity and security of the person and the community itself are secured. Every attempt to depart from the rule of justice, and to put first, not that which all men must have, but that which a few are able to seize, must defeat the permanent interests of human society. When justice is flouted, in order to give precedence to large holders of capital or landed property, to create a fixed caste with special privileges, or to preserve property itself without respect for its social functions and its duties to the whole community, the result is an evil one.

It often ends in the very downfall of the protected caste, through inanition, failure of nerve, sheer laziness.

The first move in the direction of justice is to remove, by example, the false scheme of values that has so long prevailed in Western society. Bread and circuses are no substitute for justice: they lower both the giver and the receiver. Profits and power and special privilege cannot remain as the main motive force of a society that seeks to preserve democratic values and personal liberties: for it is ultimately the one-sided concern with these values that has vitiated and corrupted and now desperately endangered our whole civilization.

The fundamental values of a true community are elsewhere: in love, poetry, disinterested thought, the free use of the imagination, the pursuit of non-utilitarian activities, the production of non-profitmaking goods, the enjoyment of non-consumable wealth — here are the sustaining values of a living culture. To be alive is to hear, to see, to feel, to touch, to shape, to manipulate, to think, and create: then to intensify all these experiences through an organized system of recording and preserving and reproducing them, through the church and the art museum and the concert hall and the laboratory and the school. This is the head-water and reservoir of social life: the Grand Coulee Dam of our whole culture which will finally create a lake from which energy and life will flow into even the most arid spots of human existence.

A community whose life is not irrigated by art and science, by religion and philosophy, day upon day, is a community that exists half alive. A personality who has not entered into this realm has not yet reached the human estate. The very means and instruments of daily routine, our houses and our clothes, our motor cars and our factories, are conditioned by the existence of these other needs that spring out of the needs of the personality: otherwise those who use them are barbarians — or robots — or at best children playing vacantly with toys. . . .

Our economic activities, during the era that boasted so loudly of industrial progress, failed to achieve their full potentialities for life. This was in no small part because the goods that the machine could produce so plentifully were not justly shared. Hence poverty, secondary starvation, crime, theft, sordid and battered environments, occupied by depressed and battered people: the industrial environment of the larger part of Western civilization.

Our society was divided against itself. It sought progress and it found itself faced with a dead end: economic crises and wars. It boasted of wealth, and its vast mass of tenant farmers, unemployed workers and underfed children proclaimed its poverty. So we had dearth in the midst of plenty, war in the midst of peace, riches atop of squalor, and, finally, a growing wave of irrationality and superstition and man-worship in a period when exact scientific research had even entered industry.

Human culture, plainly, cannot be sustained unless values enter into every activity. Otherwise we are cursed with a Sunday morality, in which decency and brotherhood and justice are flouted for six days and then piously reinstated on the seventh: a system under which our deeds never by any accident coincide with our professions.

The Athenians were right in believing that the ultimate goods of life could be enjoyed only by free men; they meant by this that they can not be fully enjoyed if they are offered to people who are forced to spend their days in some spiritually deadening or physically exhausting task, whether in the market, the mine, or the workshop. Human development requires both periods of activity and periods of leisure, in which the results of this activity may be meditated upon, absorbed, digested. One of the reasons that country folk, with limited experience, are nevertheless so much better companions for an artist or a thinker than city people of the same class, is that the former have always kept for themselves a little free time to sit still and brood, whittling wood around a winter fire, or bent impassively over a fishing pole, watching the trout's canny flirtations. The city worker may be better read; but the countryman is more reflective: such experience as he has encountered he has salted down.

But it is equally true — and the intellectual tends always to forget this — that spiritual life suffers by complete divorce from the vivid experiences and the salutary restraints of practical activity. The Athenians, fortunately, before they became engrossed in imperialist ambitions, managed to retain in some measure their hold upon the fundamental manual and operative realities of sport and war. They had tough muscles and well-tempered bodies and eyes quick to note how the grapes were ripening or how the potter molded his clay on the wheel. That sense distinguished Plato from every philosopher down to Descartes. So it is possibly no accident that the most original mind among the Athenians was a stone-cutter by trade and the son of

871

a midwife, or that perhaps the greatest tragic dramatist was also a general. Nor was it an accident, in our own American Golden Day, that Henry Thoreau was a pencil maker and a surveyor, that Herman Melville was a sailor, that Walt Whitman was a carpenter and a printer good enough to set up his own "Leaves of Grass"; or that Abe Lincoln was a rail-splitter who retained to the end of his life a solid confidence in himself that was based on his sure axmanship and shoulders that could carry a heavier burden than his neighbor's.

The segregation of the spiritual life from the practical life is a curse that falls impartially upon both sides of our existence. A society that gives to one class all the opportunities for leisure, and to another all the burdens of work, dooms both classes to spiritual sterility. The first will make busy work for itself: games, fox hunts, parties, organized inanities; while the other will make work itself empty, and even go the forces that make it empty one better, by reducing work to "as little as you can get away with" — only to lose self-respect as well as craftsmanlike pleasure in that very act. One of the main tasks of a purposive intelligence is to keep the inner world and the outer, the spiritual and the practical, the personal and the mechanical or automatic, in constant interaction. They form a dynamic unity.

The moral to be drawn from this is that servile labor — even if it produces social necessities — should be minimized to the utmost. The problem is not entirely solved by the invention of automatic machines; because, if pushed too far, the routine of mechanized production robs those engaged in it, and even more those displaced by it, of the opportunities for educative, person-satisfying activities. Such work as remains servile or dangerous in our society — whether on the assembly line or on the battlefield — should be shared by the entire adult community.

In short, justice demands either equality of life-sustenance and leisure, in times of plenty and peace, or equality of sacrifice in times of hardship and war. The principle is the same in both cases; and if we introduce the element of sacrifice into our economic system now, where it will affect principally the middle classes and those above them, we may as a country have some guarantee for fruitful and refined leisure — for the good life itself — when at long last we emerge from this murky period.

[*1940*]

LILLIAN HELLMAN

[1905–   ]

MISS HELLMAN was born in New Orleans, Louisiana. She studied at New York University and Columbia, and at nineteen joined the staff of Horace Liveright, who was then a brilliantly successful book-publisher. Shortly afterwards she began to write book reviews for the New York *Herald Tribune*. From 1927 to 1930 she was a play-reader — and the experience obviously was instructive, for when her first play, *The Children's Hour* (1934), was produced, it was a model of craftsmanship. This was followed by *Days to Come* (1936), *The Little Foxes* (1939), and *Watch on the Rhine* (1941). Three of these four plays were " smash hits," the exception being *Days to Come*. The portrayal of people who have been hurt, corrupted, or embittered by greed or malice has been considered her special talent, but in *Watch on the Rhine* she has proved that she can write warmly and humanely and that she can deal effectively with political issues.

---

from

WATCH ON THE RHINE

[*Kurt Mueller, a German anti-fascist fighter, arrives with his American wife, Sara, and their three children, Joshua, Bodo, and Babette, at the home of his wife's mother and brother, Fanny and David Farrelly. It is an aristocratic home in Washington, D.C. After years of poverty, struggle, and dangerous living, the Muellers are happy in this sanctuary surrounded by peace and plenty. Ten days later, however, news comes of the arrest in Germany of two of Kurt Mueller's associates, and it is his duty to go back — secretly, of course — to rescue them. But his identity has been discovered by a blackmailer who threatens to denounce him to the Nazis. The Farrellys agree to pay for silence and go out to get the money, leaving Kurt and Sara Mueller and the blackmailer in the living-room. . . . A few minutes later . . .*]

[FANNY *comes in from hall. After a second,* DAVID *comes in from library. Stops, looks around room.*]

DAVID: Where is he? Upstairs?

SARA: No. They went outside.

873

FANNY: Outside? They went outside. What are they doing, picking a bouquet together?

SARA [*without turning*]: They just went outside.

DAVID [*looks at her*]: What's the matter, Sara?

[SARA *shakes her head. Goes to the desk, opens the telephone book, looks at a number, begins to dial the telephone.*]

FANNY: Eleven hundred, eleven hundred and fifty, twelve, twelve-fifty —

DAVID: For God's sake, stop counting that money.

FANNY: All right. I'm nervous. And I don't like to think of giving him too much.

SARA: It's very nice of you and Mama. All that money — [*Into the telephone*] Hello. What time is your next plane? Oh. To — South. To El Paso, or — Brownsville. Yes.

DAVID [*to* FANNY]: Is Joseph ready?

FANNY: I don't know. I told him I'd call him.

SARA: To Brownsville? Yes. Yes. That's all right. At what time? Yes. No. The ticket will be picked up at the airport. [DAVID *begins to cross to the bell cord. She looks up.*] No. David. Don't call Joseph. *David! Please!* [*He draws back, stares at her. Looking at him, she goes on with the conversation.*] Ritter. R-I-T-T-E-R. From Chicago. Yes. Yes. [*She hangs up, walks away.*]

DAVID: Sara! What's happening? What is all this? [*She does not answer.*] Where is Kurt? What — [*He starts for the terrace door.*]

SARA: David. *Don't go out.*

FANNY [*rises*]: Sara! What's happening —

SARA: For seven years now, day in, day out, men have crossed the German border. They are always in danger. They always may be going in to die. Did you ever see the face of a man who never knows if this day will be the last day? [*Softly*] Don't go out on the terrace, David. Leave Kurt alone.

FANNY [*softly*]: Sara! What is —

SARA [*quietly*]: For them, it may be torture, and it may be death. Some day, when it's all over, maybe there'll be a few of them left to celebrate. There aren't many of Kurt's age left. He couldn't take a chance on them. They wouldn't have liked it. [*Suddenly, violently*] He'd have had a bad time trying to explain to them that because of this house and this nice town and my mother and my brother, he took chances with their work and with their lives. [*Quietly*] Sit down,

Mama. I think it's all over now. [*To* DAVID] There's nothing you can do about it. It's the way it had to be.

DAVID: Sara —

FANNY: Do you mean what I think you — [*Sinks slowly into her chair.*]

SARA [*She turns, looks out toward the doors. After a pause*]: He's going away tonight and he's never coming back any more. [*In a sing-song*] Never, never, never. [*She looks down at her hands, as if she were very interested in them.*] I don't like to be alone at night. I guess every-body in the world's got a time in the day they don't like. Me, it's right before I go to sleep. And now it's going to be for always. All the rest of my life. [*She looks up as* KURT *comes in from the terrace.*] I've told them. There is an eight-thirty plane going as far south as Brownsville. I've made you a reservation. In the name of Ritter.

KURT [*stands looking at her*]: Liebe Sara! [*Then he goes to the table at which* FANNY *is sitting. To* FANNY]: It is hard for you, eh? [*He pats her hand.*] I am sorry.

FANNY [*without knowing why, she takes her hand away*]: Hard? I don't know. I — I don't — I don't know what I want to say.

KURT [*looks at the hand she has touched, then turns to look at* DAVID]: Before I come in, I stand and think. I say, I will make Fanny and David understand. I say, how can I? Does one understand a killing? No. To hell with it, I say. I do what must be done. I have long sickened of words when I see the men who live by them. What do you wish to make them understand, I ask myself. Wait. Stand here. Just stand here. What are you thinking? Say it to them just as it comes to you. And this is what came to me. When you kill in a war, it is not so lonely; and I remember a cousin I have not seen for many years; and a melody comes back and I begin to make it with my fingers; a staircase in a house in Bonn years ago; an old dog who used to live in our town; Sara in a hundred places — Shame on us. Thousands of years and we cannot yet make a world. Like a child I am. I have stopped a man's life. [*Points to the place on the couch where he had been sitting opposite* TECK.] I sit here. I listen to him. You will not believe — but I pray that I will not have to touch him. Then I know I will have to. I know that if I do not, it is only that I pamper myself, and risk the lives of others. I want you from the room. I know what I must do. [*Loudly.*] All right. Do I now pretend sorrow? Do I now pretend it is not I who act thus? No. I do it. I have done it. I will do it again. And I will keep my hope that we may make a world in which all men can die in bed. I have a great hate for the violent. They are the sick of the world. [*Softly.*] Maybe I am sick now, too.

SARA: You aren't sick. Stop that. It's late. You must go soon.

KURT [*looks up at her*]: Maybe all that I have ever wanted is a land that would let me have you. [*Then without looking away from her, he puts out his hands, she touches them.*] I am going to say good-bye now to my children. Then I am going to take your car — [*Motions with his head.*] I will take him with me. After that, it is up to you. Two ways: You can let me go and keep silent. I believe I can hide him and the car. At the end of two days, if they have not been found, you will tell as much of the truth as is safe for you to say. Tell them the last time you saw us we were on our way to Washington. You did not worry at the absence, we might have rested there. Two crazy foreigners fight, one gets killed, you know nothing of the reason. I will have left the gun, there will be no doubt who did the killing. If you will give me those two days, I think I will be far enough away from here. If the car is found before then — [*Shrugs.*] I will still try to move with speed. And all that will make you, for yourselves, part of a murder. For the world, I do not think you will be in bad trouble. [*He pauses.*] There is another way. You can call your police. You can tell them the truth. I will not get home. [*To* SARA] I wish to see the children now.

[*She goes out into the hall and up the stairs. There is silence.*]

FANNY: What are you thinking, David?

DAVID: I don't know. What are you thinking?

FANNY: Me? Oh, I was thinking about my Joshua. I was thinking that a few months before he died, we were sitting out there. [*Points to terrace.*] He said, "Fanny, the Renaissance American is dying, the Renaissance man is dying." I said what do you mean, although I knew what he meant, I always knew. "A Renaissance man," he said, "is a man who wants to know. He wants to know how fast a bird will fly, how thick is the crust of the earth, what made Iago evil, how to plow a field. He knows there is no dignity to a mountain, if there is no dignity to man. You can't put that in a man, but when it's *really* there, and he will fight for it, put your trust in him."

DAVID [*gets up, smiles, looks at* FANNY]: You're a smart woman sometimes. [SARA *enters with* JOSHUA. *To* KURT] Don't worry about things here. My soul doesn't have to be so nice and clean. I'll take care of it. You'll have your two days. And good luck to you.

876

FANNY: You go with my blessing, too. I like you.

[BODO *enters.*]

SARA: See? I come from good stock.

[KURT *looks at* DAVID. *Then he begins to smile. Nods to* DAVID. *Turns, smiles at* FANNY.]

FANNY: Do you like me?

KURT: I like you, Madame, very much.

FANNY: Would you be able to cash that check?

KURT [*laughs*]: Oh, no.

FANNY: Then take the cash. I, too, would like to contribute to your work.

KURT [*slowly*]: All right. Thank you. [*He takes the money from the table, puts it in his pocket.*]

BODO [*to* KURT]: You like Grandma? I thought you would, with time. I like her, too. Sometimes she dilates with screaming, but — Dilates is correct?

[BABETTE *enters.* JOSHUA *stands away from the others, looking at his father.* KURT *turns to look at him.*]

JOSHUA: Alles in Ordnung?

KURT: Alles in Ordnung.

BODO: What? What does that mean, all is well?

[*There is an awkward silence.*]

BABETTE [*as if she sensed it*]: We are all clean for dinner. But nobody else is clean. And I have on Grandma's dress to me —

FANNY [*very nervously*]: Of course. And you look very pretty. You're a pretty little girl, Babbie.

BODO [*looks around the room*]: What is the matter? Everybody is acting like such a ninny. I got that word from Grandma.

KURT: Come here. [*They look at him. Then slowly* BABETTE *comes toward him, followed by* BODO. JOSHUA *comes more slowly, to stand at the side of* KURT's *chair.*] We have said many good-byes to each other, eh? We must now say another. [*As they stare at him, he smiles, slowly, as if it were difficult.*] This time, I leave you with good people to whom I believe you also will be good. [*Half playfully*] Would you allow me to give away my share in you, until I come back?

BABETTE [*slowly*]: If you would like it.

KURT: Good. To your mother, her share. My share, to Fanny and David. It is all and it is the most I have to give. [*Laughs.*] There. I have made a will, eh? Now. We will not joke. I have something to say to you. It is important for me to say it.

JOSHUA [*softly*]: You are talking to us as if we were children.

KURT [*turns to look at him*]: Am I, Joshua? I wish you were children. I wish I could say love your mother, do not eat too many sweets, clean your teeth — [*Draws* BODO *to him.*] I cannot say these things. You are not children. I took it all away from you.

BABETTE: We have had a most enjoyable life, Papa.

KURT [*smiles*]: You are a gallant little liar. And I thank you for it. I have done something bad today —

FANNY [*shocked, sharply*]: Kurt —

SARA: Don't, Mama.

[BODO *and* BABETTE *have looked at* FANNY *and* SARA, *puzzled. Then they have turned again to look at* KURT.]

KURT: It is not to frighten you. In a few days, your mother and David will tell you.

BODO: You could not do a bad thing.

BABETTE [*proudly*]: You could not.

KURT [*shakes his head*]: Now let us get straight together. The four of us. Do you remember when we read about " Les Misérables "? Do you remember that we talked about it afterwards and Bodo got candy on Mama's bed?

BODO: I remember.

KURT: Well. He stole bread. The world is out of shape we said, when there are hungry men. And until it gets in shape, men will steal and lie and — [*A little more slowly*] — kill. But for whatever reason it is done, and whoever does it — you understand me — it is all bad. I want you to remember that. Whoever does it, it is bad. [*Then very gaily*] But you will live to see the day when it will not have to be. All over the world, in every place and every town, there are men who are going to make sure it will not have to be. They want what I want: a childhood for every child. For my children, and I for theirs. [*He picks* BODO *up, rises.*] Think of that. It will make you happy. In every town and every village and every mud hut in the world, there is always a man who loves children and who will fight to make a good world for them. And now good-bye. Wait for me. I shall try to come back for you. [*He moves toward the hall, followed by* BABETTE, *and more slowly, by* JOSHUA.] Or you shall come to me. At Hamburg, the boat will come in. It will be a fine, safe land — I will be waiting on the dock. And there will be the three of you and Mama and Fanny and David. And I will have ordered an extra big dinner and we will show them what our Germany can be like — [*He has put* BODO *down. He leans down, presses his face in* BABETTE's *hair. Tenderly, as her mother has done earlier, she touches his hair.*]

JOSHUA: Of course. That is the way it will be. Of course. But — but if you should find yourself delayed — [*Very slowly*] Then I will come to you. Mama.

SARA [*she has turned away*]: I heard you, Joshua.

KURT [*he kisses* BABETTE]: Gute Nacht, Liebling!

BABETTE: Gute Nacht, Papa. Mach's gut!

KURT [*leans to kiss* BODO]: Good night, baby.

BODO: Good night, Papa. Mach's gut!

[BABETTE *runs up the steps. Slowly* BODO *follows her.*]

KURT [*kisses* JOSHUA]: Good night, son.

JOSHUA: Good night, Papa. Mach's gut! [*He begins to climb the steps.* KURT *stands watching them, smiling. When they disappear, he turns to* DAVID.]

KURT: Good-bye, and thank you.

DAVID: Good-bye, and good luck.

KURT [*he moves to* FANNY]: Good-bye. I have good children, eh?

FANNY: Yes, you have. [KURT *kisses her hand.*]

KURT [*slowly, he turns toward* SARA]: Men who wish to live have the best chance to live. I wish to live. I wish to live with you. [*She comes toward him.*]

SARA: For twenty years. It is as much for me today — [*Takes his arms.*] Just once, and for all my life. [*He pulls her toward him.*] Come back for me, darling. If you can. [*Takes briefcase from table and gives it to him.*]

KURT [*simply*]: I will try. [*He turns.*] Good-bye, to you all. [*He exits. After a second, there is the sound of a car starting. They sit listening to it. Gradually the noise begins to go off into the distance. A second later,* JOSHUA *appears.*]

JOSHUA: Mama — [*She looks up. He is very tense.*] Bodo cries. Babette looks very queer. I think you should come.

SARA [*gets up, slowly*]: I'm coming.

JOSHUA [*to* FANNY *and* DAVID. *Still very tense*]: Bodo talks so fancy, we forget sometimes he is a baby. [*He waits for* SARA *to come up to him. When she reaches him, she takes his hand, goes up the steps, disappears.* FANNY *and* DAVID *watch them.*]

FANNY [*after a minute*]: Well, here we are. We're shaken out of the magnolias, eh?

DAVID: Yes. So we are.

FANNY: Tomorrow will be a hard day. But we'll have Babbie's birthday dinner. And we'll have music afterwards. You can be the audience. I think you'd better go up to Marthe now. Be as careful as you can. She'd better stay here for a while. I daresay I can stand it.

DAVID [*turns, smiles*]: Even your graciousness is ungracious, Mama.

FANNY: I do my best. Well, I think I shall go and talk to Anise. I like Anise best when I don't feel well. [*She begins to move off.*]

DAVID: Mama. [*She turns.*] We are going to be in for trouble. You understand that?

FANNY: I understand it very well. We will manage. You and I. I'm not put together with flour paste. And neither are you — I am happy to learn.

DAVID: Good night, Mama. [*As she moves out, the curtain falls.*]

[*1941*]

FRANKLIN D. ROOSEVELT

[1882–   ]

THE THIRTY-SECOND President of the United States, who is regarded by the majority of the American people as the leader of the democratic movement of our day, is a descendant of an admittedly aristocratic family. The Roosevelts have been landowners, merchants, and capitalists since colonial days, and have intermarried with other aristocratic Dutch and English families. President Roosevelt was born in Hyde Park, New York, and was educated at Groton and Harvard, receiving his A.B. in 1904. He studied law at Columbia, was graduated in 1907, and practiced until 1910, when he entered politics and was elected to the New York State Senate. From 1913 to 1920 he was Assistant Secretary of the Navy. For some years afterwards he was inactive because of illness, then began again to practice his profession. In 1929 he was elected Governor of New York, and was re-elected in 1931. In 1932 he was nominated for the presidency by the Democratic Party and was swept into office by the revolt of the electorate against the Hoover administration. His first four years in office, marked by liberal reforms in labor, banking, and social legislation, earned him the love of the masses. The peak of his campaign for re-election was the great speech which follows — a most eloquent statement of progressive politics and a most damning attack upon reactionary cliques. He won the election. In 1940 he became the first President to be elected for a third term. It was inevitable that he should align America against the Axis and that war should follow. Once in the war it was characteristic that he should devise a formula for a liberal post-war program. His formula, now popularly known as " the four freedoms," is a very general but essentially democratic statement of our war aims and is thus one of the significant documents of our time.

ADDRESS AT MADISON SQUARE GARDEN, NEW YORK, 1936

On the eve of a national election, it is well for us to stop for a moment and analyze calmly and without prejudice the effect on our Nation of a victory by either of the major political parties.

The problem of the electorate is far deeper, far more vital than the continuance in the Presidency of an individual. For the greater issue goes beyond units of humanity — it goes to humanity itself.

In 1932 the issue was the restoration of American democracy; and the American people were in a mood to win. They did win. In 1936 the issue is the preservation of their victory. Again they are in a mood to win. Again they will win.

More than four years ago in accepting the Democratic nomination in Chicago, I said: " Give me your help not to win votes alone, but to win in this crusade to restore America to its own people."

The banners of that crusade still fly in the van of a Nation that is on the march.

It is needless to repeat the details of the program which this Administration has been hammering out on the anvils of experience. No amount of misrepresentation or statistical contortion can conceal or blur or smear that record. Neither the attacks of unscrupulous enemies nor the exaggerations of over-zealous friends will serve to mislead the American people.

What was our hope in 1932? Above all other things the American people wanted peace. They wanted peace of mind instead of gnawing fear.

First, they sought escape from the personal terror which had stalked them for three years. They wanted the peace that comes from security in their homes: safety for their savings, permanence in their jobs, a fair profit from their enterprise.

Next, they wanted peace in the community, the peace that springs from the ability to meet the needs of community life: schools, playgrounds, parks, sanitation, highways — those things which are expected of solvent local government. They sought escape from disintegration and bankruptcy in local and state affairs.

They also sought peace within the Nation: protection of their currency, fairer wages, the ending of long hours of toil, the abolition of child labor, the elimination of wild-cat speculation, the safety of their children from kidnappers.

And, finally, they sought peace with other Nations — peace in a world of unrest. The Nation knows that I hate war, and I know that the Nation hates war.

I submit to you a record of peace; and on that record a well-founded expectation for future peace — peace for the individual, peace for the community, peace for the Nation, and peace with the world.

Tonight I call the roll — the roll of honor of those who stood with us in 1932 and still stand with us today.

Written on it are the names of millions who never had a chance — men at starvation wages, women in sweatshops, children at looms.

Written on it are the names of those who despaired, young men and young women for whom opportunity had become a will-o'-the-wisp.

Written on it are the names of farmers whose acres yielded only bitterness, business men whose books were portents of disaster, home owners who were faced with eviction, frugal citizens whose savings were insecure.

Written there in large letters are the names of countless other Americans of all parties and all faiths, Americans who had eyes to see and hearts to understand, whose consciences were burdened because too many of their fellows were burdened, who looked on these things four years ago and said, " This can be changed. We will change it."

We still lead that army in 1936. They stood with us then because in 1932 they believed. They stand with us today because in 1936 they know. And with them stand millions of new recruits who have come to know.

Their hopes have become our record.

We have not come this far without a struggle and I assure you we cannot go further without a struggle.

For twelve years this Nation was afflicted with hear-nothing, see-nothing, do-nothing Government. The Nation looked to Government but the Government looked away. Nine mocking years with the golden calf and three long years of the scourge! Nine crazy years at the ticker and three long years in the breadlines! Nine mad years of mirage and three long years of despair! Powerful influences strive today to restore that kind of government with its doctrine that that Government is best which is most indifferent.

For nearly four years you have had an Administration which instead of twirling its thumbs has rolled up its sleeves. We will keep our sleeves rolled up.

We had to struggle with the old enemies of peace — business and financial monopoly, speculation, reckless banking, class antagonism, sectionalism, war profiteering.

They had begun to consider the Government of the United States as a mere appendage to their own affairs. We know now that Government by organized money is just as dangerous as Government by organized mob.

Never before in all our history have these forces been so united against one candidate as they stand today. They are unanimous in their hate for me — and I welcome their hatred.

I should like to have it said of my first Administration that in it the forces of selfishness and of lust for power met their match. I should like to have it said of my second Administration that in it these forces met their master.

The American people know from a four-year record that today there is only one entrance to the White House — by the front door. Since March 4, 1933, there has been only one pass-key to the White House. I have carried that key in my pocket. It is there tonight. So long as I am President, it will remain in my pocket.

Those who used to have pass-keys are not happy. Some of them are desperate. Only desperate men with their backs to the wall would descend so far below the level of decent citizenship as to foster the current pay-envelope campaign against America's working people. Only reckless men, heedless of consequences, would risk the disruption of the hope for a new peace between worker and employer by returning to the tactics of the labor spy.

Here is an amazing paradox! The very employers and politicians and publishers who talk most loudly of class antagonism and the destruction of the American system now undermine that system by this attempt to coerce the votes of the wage earners of this country. It is the 1936 version of the old threat to close down the factory or the office if a particular candidate does not win. It is an old strategy of tyrants to delude their victims into fighting their battles for them.

Every message in a pay envelope, even if it is the truth, is a command to vote according to the will of the employer. But this propaganda is worse — it is deceit.

They tell the worker his wage will be reduced by a contribution to some vague form of old-age insurance. They carefully conceal from him the fact that for every dollar of premium he pays for that insurance, the employer pays another dollar. That omission is deceit.

They carefully conceal from him the fact that under the federal law, he receives another insurance policy to help him if he loses his job, and that the premium of that policy is paid 100 percent by the employer and not one cent by the worker. They do not tell him that the insurance policy that is bought for him is far more favorable to him than any policy that any private insurance company could afford to issue. That omission is deceit.

They imply to him that he pays all the cost of both forms of insurance. They carefully conceal from him the fact that for every dollar put up by him his employer puts up three dollars — three for one. And that omission is deceit.

But they are guilty of more than deceit. When they imply that the reserves thus created against both these policies will be stolen by some future Congress, diverted to some wholly foreign purpose, they attack the integrity and honor of American Government itself. Those who suggest that, are already aliens to the spirit of American democracy. Let them emigrate and try their lot under some foreign flag in which they have more confidence.

The fraudulent nature of this attempt is well shown by the record of votes on the passage of the Social Security Act. In addition to an overwhelming majority of Democrats in both Houses, seventy-seven Republican Representatives voted for it and only eighteen against it and fifteen Republican Senators voted for it and only five against it. Where does this last-minute drive of the Republican leadership leave these Republican Representatives and Senators who helped enact this law?

I am sure the vast majority of law-abiding business men who are not parties to this propaganda fully appreciate the extent of the threat to honest business contained in this coercion.

I have expressed indignation at this form of campaigning and I am confident that the overwhelming majority of employers, workers and the general public share that indignation and will show it at the polls on Tuesday next.

Aside from this phase of it, I prefer to remember this campaign not as bitter but only as hard-fought. There should be no bitterness or hate where the sole thought is the welfare of the United States of America. No man can occupy the office of President without realizing that he is President of all the people.

It is because I have sought to think in terms of the whole Nation that I am confident that today, just as four years ago, the people want more than promises.

Our vision for the future contains more than promises.

This is our answer to those who, silent about their own plans, ask us to state our objectives.

Of course we will continue to seek to improve working conditions for the workers of America — to reduce hours over-long, to increase wages that spell starvation, to end the labor of children, to wipe out sweatshops. Of course we will continue every effort to end monopoly in business, to support collective bargaining, to stop unfair competition, to abolish dishonorable trade practices. For all these we have only just begun to fight.

Of course we will continue to work for cheaper electricity in the homes and on the farms of America, for better and cheaper transportation, for low interest rates, for sounder home financing, for better banking, for the regulation of security issues, for reciprocal trade among nations, for the wiping out of slums. For all these we have only just begun to fight.

Of course we will continue our efforts in behalf of the farmers of America. With their continued cooperation we will do all in our power to end the piling up of huge surpluses which spelled ruinous prices for their crops. We will persist in successful action for better land use, for reforestation, for the conservation of water all the way from its source to the sea, for drought and flood control, for better marketing facilities for farm commodities, for a definite reduction of farm tenancy, for encouragement of farmer cooperatives, for crop insurance and a stable food supply. For all these we have only just begun to fight.

Of course we will provide useful work for the needy unemployed; we prefer useful work to the pauperism of a dole.

Here and now I want to make myself clear about those who disparage their fellow citizens on the relief rolls. They say that those on relief are not merely jobless — that they are worthless. Their solution for the relief problem is to end relief — to purge the rolls by starvation. To use the language of the stock broker, our needy unemployed would be cared for when, as, and if some fairy godmother should happen on the scene.

You and I will continue to refuse to accept that estimate of our unemployed fellow Americans. Your Government is still on the same side of the street with the Good Samaritan and not with those who pass by on the other side.

Again — what of our objectives?

Of course we will continue our efforts for young men and women so that they may obtain an education and an opportunity to put it to use.

Of course we will continue our help for the crippled, for the blind, for the mothers, our insurance for the unemployed, our security for the aged. Of course we will continue to protect the consumer against unnecessary price spreads, against the costs that are added by monopoly and speculation. We will continue our successful efforts to increase his purchasing power and to keep it constant.

For these things, too, and for a multitude of others like them, we have only just begun to fight.

All this — all these objectives — spell peace at home. All our actions, all our ideals, spell also peace with other nations.

Today there is war and rumor of war. We want none of it. But while we guard our shores against threats of war, we will continue to remove the causes of unrest and antagonism at home which might make our people easier victims to those for whom foreign war is profitable. You know well that those who stand to profit by war are not on our side in this campaign.

" Peace on earth, good will toward men " — democracy must cling to that message. For it is my deep conviction that democracy cannot live without that true religion which gives a nation a sense of justice and of moral purpose. Above our political forums, above our market places stand the altars of our faith — altars on which burn the fires of devotion that maintain all that is best in us and all that is best in our Nation.

We have need of that devotion today. It is that which makes it possible for government to persuade those who are mentally prepared to fight each other to go on instead, to work for and to sacrifice for each other. That is why we need to say with the Prophet: "What doth the Lord require of thee — but to do justly, to love mercy and to walk humbly with thy God?" That is why the recovery we seek, the recovery we are winning, is more than economic. In it are included justice and love and humility, not for ourselves as individuals alone, but for our Nation.

That is the road to peace.

[*1936*]

SPEECH TO CONGRESS ON THE
FOUR FREEDOMS

In fulfilling my duty to report upon the state of the Union, I am proud to say to you that the spirit of the American people was never higher than it is today — the Union was never more closely knit together — this country was never more deeply determined to face the solemn tasks before it.

The response of the American people has been instantaneous. It will be sustained until our security is assured.

Exactly one year ago today I said to this Congress:

"When the dictators are ready to make war upon us, they will not wait for an act of war on our part. . . . They — not we — will choose the time and the place and the method of their attack."

We now know their choice of the time: a peaceful Sunday morning — December 7th, 1941. We know their choice of the place: an American outpost in the Pacific. We know their choice of the method: the method of Hitler himself.

Japan's scheme of conquest goes back half a century. It was not merely a policy of seeking living room: it was a plan which included the subjugation of all the peoples in the Far East and in the Islands of the Pacific, and the domination of that ocean by Japanese military and naval control of the western coasts of North, Central, and South America.

The development of this ambitious conspiracy was marked by the war against China in 1894; the subsequent occupation of Korea; the war against Russia in 1904; the illegal fortification of the mandated Pacific Islands following 1920; the seizure of Manchuria in 1931; and the invasion of China in 1937.

A similar policy of criminal conquest was adopted by Italy. The Fascists first revealed their imperial designs in Libya and Tripoli. In 1935 they seized Abyssinia. Their goal was the domination of all North Africa, Egypt, parts of France, and the entire Mediterranean world.

But the dreams of empire of the Japanese and Fascist leaders were modest in comparison with the gargantuan aspirations of Hitler and his

888

Nazis. Even before they came to power in 1933, their plans for conquest had been drawn. Those plans provided for ultimate domination, not of any one section of the world, but of the whole earth and all the oceans on it.

With Hitler's formation of the Berlin-Rome-Tokyo alliance, all these plans of conquest became a single plan. Under this, in addition to her own schemes of conquest, Japan's role was to cut off our supply of weapons of war to Britain, Russia, and China — weapons which increasingly were speeding the day of Hitler's doom. The act of Japan at Pearl Harbor was intended to stun us — to terrify us to such an extent that we would divert our industrial and military strength to the Pacific area, or even to our own, continental defense.

The plan failed in its purpose. We have not been stunned. We have not been terrified or confused. This re-assembling of the Seventy-seventh Congress is proof of that; for the mood of quiet, grim resolution which here prevails, bodes ill for those who conspired and collaborated to murder world peace.

That mood is stronger than any mere desire for revenge. It expresses the will of the American people to make very certain that the world will never so suffer again.

Admittedly, we have been faced with hard choices. It was bitter, for example, not to be able to relieve the heroic and historic defenders of Wake Island. It was bitter for us not to be able to land a million men and a thousand ships in the Philippine Islands.

But this adds only to our determination to see to it that the Stars and Stripes will fly again over Wake and Guam; and that the brave people of the Philippines will be rid of Japanese imperialism, and will live in freedom, security, and independence.

Powerful and offensive actions must and will be taken in proper time. The consolidation of the United Nations' total war effort against our common enemies is being achieved.

That is the purpose of conferences which have been held during the past two weeks in Washington, in Moscow, and in Chungking. That is the primary objective of the declaration of solidarity signed in Washington on January 1, 1942, by twenty-six nations united against the Axis powers.

Difficult choices may have to be made in the months to come. We will not shrink from such decisions. We and those united with us will make those decisions with courage and determination.

Plans have been laid here and in the other capitals for co-ordinated and co-operative action by all the United Nations — military action and economic action. Already we have established unified command of land, sea, and air forces in the southwestern Pacific theater of war. There will be a continuation of conferences and consultations among military staffs, so that the plans and operations of each will fit into a general strategy designed to crush the enemy. We shall not fight isolated wars — each nation going its own way. These twenty-six nations are united — not in spirit and determination alone, but in the broad conduct of the war in all its phases.

For the first time since the Japanese and the Fascists and the Nazis started along their blood-stained course of conquest they now face the fact that superior forces are assembling against them. Gone forever are the days when the aggressors could attack and destroy their victims one by one without unity of resistance. We of the United Nations will so dispose our forces that we can strike at the common enemy wherever the greatest damage can be done.

The militarists in Berlin and Tokyo started this war. But the massed, angered forces of common humanity will finish it.

Destruction of the material and spiritual centers of civilization — this has been and still is the purpose of Hitler and his Italian and Japanese chessmen. They would wreck the power of the British Commonwealth and Russia and China and the Netherlands — and then combine all their forces to achieve their ultimate goal, the conquest of the United States.

They know that victory for us means victory for freedom.

They know that victory for us means victory for the institution of democracy — the ideal of the family, the simple principles of common decency and humanity.

They know that victory for us means victory for religion.

And they could not tolerate that. The world is too small to provide adequate " living room " for both Hitler and God. In proof of that, the Nazis have now announced their plan for enforcing their new German, pagan religion throughout the world — the plan by which the Holy Bible and the Cross of Mercy would be displaced by *Mein Kampf* and the Swastika and the naked sword.

Our own objectives are clear; the objective of smashing the militarism imposed by war lords upon their enslaved peoples — the objective of liberating subjugated nations — the objective of establishing and securing *freedom of speech, freedom of religion, freedom from want, and freedom from fear everywhere in the world.*

We shall not stop short of these objectives — nor shall we be satisfied merely to gain them and then call it a day. I know that I speak for the American people — and I have good reason to believe I speak also for all the other peoples who fight with us — when I say that this time we are determined not only to win the war, but also to maintain the security of the peace which will follow. . . .

As the United States goes into its full stride, we must always be on guard against misconceptions which will arise naturally or which will be planted among us by our enemies.

We must guard against complacency. We must not underrate the enemy. He is powerful and cunning — and cruel and ruthless. He will stop at nothing which gives him a chance to kill and to destroy. He has trained his people to believe that their highest perfection is conflict — planning, plotting, training, arming, fighting. We have already tasted defeat. We may suffer further setbacks. We must face the fact of a hard war, a long war, a bloody war, a costly war.

We must, on the other hand, guard against defeatism. That has been one of the chief weapons of Hitler's propaganda machine — used time and again with deadly results. It will not be used successfully on the American people.

We must guard against divisions among ourselves and among all the other United Nations. We must be particularly vigilant against racial discrimination in any of its ugly forms. Hitler will try again to breed mistrust and suspicion between one individual and another, one group and another, one race and another, one government and another. He will try to use the same technique of falsehood and rumor-mongering with which he divided France from Britain. He is trying to do this with us even now. But he will find a unity of will and purpose against him, which will persevere until the destruction of all his black designs upon the freedom and safety of the people of the world.

We cannot wage this war in a defensive spirit. As our power and our resources are fully mobilized, we shall carry the attack against the enemy — we shall hit him and hit him again wherever and whenever we can reach him.

We must keep him far from our shores, for we intend to bring this battle to him on his own home grounds.

American armed forces must be used at any place in all the world where it seems advisable to engage the forces of the enemy. In some cases these operations will be defensive, in order to protect key positions. In other cases, these operations will be offensive, in order to strike at the common enemy, with a view to his complete encirclement and eventual total defeat.

American armed forces will operate at many points in the Far East.

American armed forces will be on all the oceans — helping to guard the essential communications which are vital to the United Nations.

American land and air and sea forces will take stations in the British Isles — which constitute an essential fortress in this world struggle.

American armed forces will help to protect this Hemisphere — and also bases outside this Hemisphere, which could be used for an attack on the Americas.

If any of our enemies, from Europe or from Asia, attempt long-range raids by " suicide " squadrons of bombing planes, they will do so only in the hope of terrorizing our people and disrupting our morale. Our people are not afraid of that. We know that we may have to pay a heavy price for freedom. We will pay this price with a will. Whatever the price, it is a thousand times worth it. No matter what our enemies in their desperation, may attempt to do to us — we will say, as the people of London have said, "We can take it." And what's more, we can give it back — and we will give it back — with compound interest.

When our enemies challenged our country to stand up and fight, they challenged each and every one of us. And each and every one of us has accepted the challenge — for himself and for the nation.

There were only some four hundred United States Marines who in the heroic and historic defense of Wake Island inflicted such great losses on the enemy. Some of those men were killed in action; and others are now prisoners of war. When the survivors of that great fight are liberated and restored to their homes, they will learn that a hundred and thirty million of their fellow citizens have been inspired to render their own full share of service and sacrifice.

Our men on the fighting fronts have already proved that Americans today are just as rugged and just as tough as any of the heroes whose exploits we celebrate on the Fourth of July.

Many people ask, "When will this war end? " There is only one answer to that. It will end just as soon as we make it end, by our combined efforts, our combined strength, our combined determination to fight through and work through until the end — and the end of militarism in Germany and Italy and Japan. Most certainly we shall not settle for less.

That is the spirit in which discussions have been conducted during the visit of the British Prime Minister to Washington. Mr. Churchill and I understand each other, our motives and our purposes. Together, during the past two weeks, we have faced squarely the major military and economic problems of this greatest world war.

All in our nation have been cheered by Mr. Churchill's visit. We have been deeply stirred by his great message to us. We wish him a safe return to his home. He is welcome in our midst, now and in days to come.

We are fighting on the same side with the British people, who fought alone for long, terrible months, and withstood the enemy with fortitude and tenacity and skill.

We are fighting on the same side with the Russian people, who have seen the Nazi hordes swarm up to the very gates of Moscow, and who with almost superhuman will and courage have forced the invaders back into retreat.

We are fighting on the same side as the brave people of China, who for four and a half long years have withstood bombs and starvation and have whipped the invaders time and again in spite of superior Japanese equipment and arms.

We are fighting on the same side as the indomitable Dutch.

We are fighting on the same side as all the other governments in exile, whom Hitler and all his armies and all his Gestapo have not been able to conquer.

But we of the United Nations are not making all this sacrifice of human effort and human lives to return to the kind of world we had after the last world war.

We are fighting today for security, for progress, and for peace, not only for ourselves, but for all men, not only for one generation but for all generations. We are fighting to cleanse the world of ancient evils, ancient ills.

Our enemies are guided by brutal cynicism, by unholy contempt for the human race. We are inspired by a faith which goes back through all the years to the first chapter of the Book of Genesis: " God created man in His own image."

We on our side are striving to be true to that divine heritage. We are fighting, as our fathers have fought, to uphold the doctrine that all men are equal in the sight of God. Those on the other side are striving to destroy this deep belief and to create a world in their own image — a world of tyranny and cruelty and serfdom.

That is the conflict that day and night now pervades our lives. No compromise can end that conflict. There never has been — there never can be — successful compromise between good and evil. Only total victory can reward the champions of tolerance, and decency, and freedom, and faith.

[*1942*]

WENDELL L. WILLKIE

[1892–   ]

BORN in Elwood, Indiana, of a middle-class family of German origin, he was
educated at the University of Indiana and admitted to the Indiana bar in
1916. He began the practice of law in his native town, moved on to Akron,
Ohio, and eventually to New York City. His was the typical story of a small-
town American youth who made good in the business world. He was able
enough as a corporation lawyer to become, in 1933, president of the Commonwealth and Southern Corporation, a Morgan company controlling utility
stocks. In 1940 he was nominated by the Republican party for the presidency
of the United States. His unsuccessful campaign became a sort of crusade
of all camps of right-wing opinion, and by liberals he was then regarded as
the apostle of Wall Street and Park Avenue. Within two years he had lost
the friendship of many of the people who had originally backed him and had
become one of America's most articulate liberals — a champion of the underdog, of internationalism, and of a progressive economy; a foe of imperialism
and isolation. There is no more remarkable transition in our time. The
speech which follows has been one of the notable expressions of democratic
opinion in this period. Perhaps the most significant thing about it is that
fundamentally it coincides with the views of Roosevelt and Wallace, and it
is therefore an eloquent testimonial to the essential unity of the best minds
of this country in a time of crisis.

---

from

REPORT TO THE NATION ON GLOBAL
WAR AND PEACE

Several months ago it occurred to me that perhaps I could make a contribution to the war by visiting the world's people who have a stake in
it. I wanted to see them. I wanted to talk to them at their fighting
fronts. I also wanted frank discussion with both leaders and people in
countries which have not yet decided on their course of action. . . .

If I ever had any doubts that the world has become small and completely interdependent, this trip would have dispelled them altogether. I traveled a total of 31,000 miles, which sounds very far. The net impression of my trip, however, is not one of distance from other peoples, but of closeness to them.

The new world that has been opened up by modern inventions was never more vividly illustrated, I think, than on our last lap home. We left Chengtu on Oct. 9, traveled almost a thousand miles in China, crossed the vast expanse of the Gobi Desert and the Mongolian Republic, crossed thousands of miles of Siberia, crossed the Bering Sea, the full length of Alaska and the full width of Canada and arrived in the United States four days later on Oct. 13.

I say to you: there are no distant points in the world any longer. The myriad millions of human beings of the Far East are as close to us as Los Angeles is to New York by the fastest railroad trains. I cannot escape the conviction that in the future what concerns them must concern us, almost as much as the problems of the people of California concern the people of New York.

Our thinking and planning in the future must be global.

Now this world we live in has become small not only on the map but also in the minds of men. All around the world, there are some ideas which millions and millions of men hold in common, almost as much as if they lived in the same town. One of these ideas, and one which I can report without hesitation, has tremendous significance for us in America; it is the mixture of respect and hope with which the world looks to this country. . . .

The people of every land, whether industrialized or not, admire the aspirations and accomplishments of American labor, which they have heard about, and which they long to emulate. Also they are impressed by American business and industry. In nearly every country I went to, there is some great dam or irrigation project, some harbor or factory, which has been built by Americans. People like our works, I found, not only because they help to make life easier and richer, but also because we have shown that American business enterprise, unlike that of most other industrial nations, does not necessarily lead to political control or imperialism.

I found this dread of imperialism everywhere. The fact that we are not associated with it in men's minds has caused people to go much farther in their approval of us than I had dared to imagine. I was amazed to discover how keenly the world is aware of the fact that we do not seek — anywhere, in any region — to impose our rule upon others or to exact special privileges.

All the people of the earth know that we have no sinister designs upon them, that even when we have in the past withdrawn from international affairs into a false self-sufficiency, it was without sinister purpose. And they know that, now we are in the war, we are not fighting for profit, or loot, or territory, or mandatory power over the lives or the governments of other people. That, I think, is the single most important reason for the existence of our reservoir of good-will around the world.

Now, as I see it, the existence of this reservoir is the biggest political fact of our time. No other nation has such a reservoir. Ours must be used to unify the peoples of the earth in the human quest for freedom and justice. It must be maintained so that, with confidence, they may fight and work with us against the gigantic evil forces that are seeking to destroy all that we stand for, all that they hope for. The preservation of this reservoir of good-will is a sacred responsibility, not alone toward the aspiring peoples of the earth, but toward our own sons who are fighting this battle on every continent. For the water in this reservoir is the clean, invigorating water of freedom.

I bring you the assurance that this reservoir exists. I also bring you the warning that it is leaking. It is leaking dangerously. It is leaking at a thousand points. It is leaking through steadily spreading cracks and holes. These holes have not been punched in it by Hitler. They have been punched by us. All the leaks in this priceless reservoir are of our making. For the very existence of this reservoir is built on confidence in us, in our integrity of purpose, our honesty in dealing, our ability in performance. We have made great promises. How have these promises been fulfilled?

Take the vital matter of our production of war materials. Here we are, supposedly the biggest industrial nation on earth. But the flow of war materials out of this country to some of the nations I visited is not only small in itself, but as compared to the immensity of this global war we are engaged in, it is tragically small. . . . If I were to tell you how few bombers China has received from us you simply would not believe me. If I were to tell you how far Russia feels we are from fulfilling our commitments, you would agree with me that we have little reason to boast about our performance. . . .

I tell you that if we continue to fail to deliver to our Allies what they are entitled to expect of us or what we have promised them, our reservoir of good-will will turn into one of resentment. We cannot laugh this off or shrug it away or hide it behind censorship. Five million Russians and five million Chinese have given their lives in this struggle. Each of these countries has lost as many men as we have in our entire Army. We owe them more than boasts and broken promises.

We are also punching holes in our reservoir of good-will every day by failing to define clearly our war aims. Besides giving our Allies in Asia and Eastern Europe something to fight with, we have got to give them assurance of what we are fighting for. The two hundred million people of Russia and the 450,000,000 people of China — people like you and me — are bewildered and anxious. They know what they are fighting for. They are not so sure of us. Many of them have read the Atlantic Charter. Rightly or wrongly, they are not satisfied. They ask: what about a Pacific Charter; what about a World Charter?

Their doubts were expressed to me in simple, unmistakable, and direct questions. "Is there to be a charter only for the millions of the Western Hemisphere?" they asked. "Is there to be no charter of freedom for the billion people of the East? Is freedom supposed to be priceless for the white man, or for the western world, but of no account to us in the East?"

Many of them asked me the question which has become almost a symbol all through Asia: what about India? Now I did not go to India. I do not propose to discuss that tangled question tonight. But it has one aspect, in the East, which I should report to you. From Cairo on, it confronted me at every turn. The wisest man in China said to me: "When the aspiration of India for freedom was put aside to some future date, it was not Great Britain that suffered in public esteem in the Far East. It was the United States."

This wise man was not quarrelling with British imperialism in India when he said this — a benevolent imperialism, if you like. He does not happen to believe in it, but he was not even talking about it. He was telling me, and through me, you, that by our silence on India we have already drawn heavily on our reservoir of good-will in the Far East. People of the East who would like to count on us are doubtful. They cannot ascertain from our Government's wishy-washy attitude towards the problem of India what we are likely to feel at the end of the war about all the other hundreds of millions of Eastern peoples. They cannot tell from our vague and vacillating talk whether or not we really do stand for freedom, or what we mean by freedom.

In Africa, in the Middle East, throughout the Arab world, as well as in China and the whole Far East, freedom means the orderly but scheduled abolition of the colonial system. I can assure you that this is true. I can assure you that the rule of people by other peoples is not freedom, and not what we must fight to preserve. . . .

There will be lots of tough problems. And they will differ in different mandates, different colonies. Not all the peoples of the world are ready for freedom, or can defend it, the day after tomorrow. But today they all want some date to work toward, some guarantee that the date will be kept. For the future, they do not ask that we solve their problems for them. They are neither so foolish nor so fainthearted. They ask only for the chance to solve their own problems with economic as well as political co-operation. For the peoples of the world intend to be free not only for their political satisfaction, but, also, for their economic advancement. . . .

There is one more leak in our reservoir of good-will which I must report to you. It can be plugged, I believe, by resolute and aggressive action by the people of democratic nations, and especially of the United States. This is the atrophy of intelligence which is produced by stupid, arbitrary or undemocratic censorship.

It has been suggested much of late, for example, that private citizens, particularly those not expert in military affairs or those unconnected with Government, should refrain from making suggestions about the conduct of the war — military, industrial, economic or political. It is said that we must remain silent and allow our leaders and the experts to solve these problems unmolested.

This position threatens, I believe, to become a tight wall which will keep the truth out and lock misrepresentation and false security within. It is plain that to win this war we must make it our war, the war of all of us. In order to do this we must all know as much about it as possible. subject only to the needs of military security. A misdirected censorship will not accomplish this. . . .

The record of this war to date is not such as to inspire in us any sublime faith in the infallibility of our military and naval experts. Let's have no more of this nonsense. Military experts, as well as our leaders, must be constantly exposed to democracy's greatest driving power — the whip-lash of public opinion, developed from honest, free discussion. Men with great power usually like to live free of criticism. But when they get that way, that's the time to increase the criticism. . . .

I believe that in a military sense we can win this war. I believe we have the resources, the manpower, and the courage to do so. But a victory from a military standpoint as such, will not be enough. . . . We must fight our war through not alone to the destruction of our enemies but to a new world idea. We must win the peace.

To win that peace three things seem to me necessary — first, we must plan now for peace on a global basis; second, the world must be free, economically and politically, for nations and for men that peace may exist in it; third, America must play an active, constructive part in freeing it and keeping its peace.

When I say that peace must be planned on a global basis, I mean quite literally that it must embrace the earth. Continents and oceans are plainly only parts of a whole, seen, as I have just seen them, from the air. Russia and China, Egypt, Syria and Turkey, Iraq and Iran are also parts. And it is inescapable that there can be no peace for any part of the world unless the foundations of peace are made secure throughout all parts of the world.

When I say that in order to have peace this world must be free, I am only reporting that a great process has started which no man — certainly not Hitler — can stop. Men and women all over the world are on the march, physically, intellectually and spiritually. After centuries of ignorant and dull compliance, hundreds of millions of people in eastern Europe and Asia have opened the books. Old fears no longer frighten them. They are no longer willing to be Eastern slaves for Western profits. They are beginning to know that men's welfare throughout the world is interdependent. They are resolved, as we must be, that there is no more place for imperialism within their own society than in the society of nations. The big house on the hill surrounded by mud huts has lost its awesome charm.

Our western world and our presumed supremacy are now on trial. Our boasting and our big talk leave Asia cold. Men and women in Russia and China and in the Middle East are conscious now of their own potential strength. They are coming to know that many of the decisions about the future of the world lie in their hands.

Finally, when I say that this world demands the full participation of a self-confident America, I am only passing on an invitation which these peoples of the East have given us. They would like the United States to be one of their partners in this grand adventure. They want us to join them in creating a new society, global in scope, free alike of the economic injustices of the West and the political malpractices of the East. But as a partner in that great new combination they want us neither hesitant, incompetent nor afraid. They want a partner who will not hesitate to speak out for the correction of injustice anywhere in the world.

Our Allies in the East know that we intend to pour out our resources in this war. But they expect us now — not after the war — to use the enormous power of our giving to promote liberty and justice. Other peoples, not yet fighting, are waiting no less eagerly, for us to accept the most challenging opportunity of all history — the chance to help create a new society in which men and women the globe around can live and grow invigorated by freedom.

[*1942*]

HENRY A. WALLACE

[1888–   ]

HE WAS born in the farming country of Iowa and educated at Iowa State
College. On graduating he joined the staff of his father's periodical, *Wallaces'
Farmer,* becoming editor-in-chief in 1924. Thus he became an influential and
prominent figure in agrarian thought and politics. He became Secretary of
Agriculture in Franklin D. Roosevelt's cabinet in 1933, remaining in that
position until 1940, when he ran for the vice-presidency of the United States
and was carried into that office when Roosevelt won his third campaign. In
recent years Mr. Wallace has occupied an extraordinary position in our government. The vice-presidency is traditionally an office of minor importance,
and its occupant is usually obscured and forgotten. But Mr. Wallace's writings and speeches have been so forthrightly and vigorously democratic and
progressive that he has come to be regarded as a sort of official voice for the
most idealistic tendencies in the New Deal. As a consequence he has naturally been vilified by conservatives and revered by liberals. The speech
which follows is commonly regarded as an expression of the war aims — or
rather the war hopes and aspirations — of the left wing of the Roosevelt
administration. It was delivered in New York City at a dinner of the Free
World Association.

THE CENTURY OF THE COMMON MAN

We, who in a formal or an informal way represent most of the free
peoples of the world, are met here tonight in the interests of the millions
in all the nations who have freedom in their souls. To my mind this
meeting has just one purpose — to let those millions in other countries
know that here in the United States are 130 million men, women, and
children who are in this war to the finish. Our American people are utterly resolved to go on until they can strike the relentless blows that
will asssure a complete victory, and with it win a new day for the lovers of freedom, everywhere on this earth.

This is a fight between a slave world and a free world. Just as the

United States in 1862 could not remain half slave and half free, so in 1942 the world must make its decision for a complete victory one way or the other.

As we begin the final stages of this fight to the death between the free world and the slave world, it is worth while to refresh our minds about the march of freedom for the common man. The idea of freedom — the freedom that we in the United States know and love so well — is derived from the Bible with its extraordinary emphasis on the dignity of the individual. Democracy is the only true political expression of Christianity.

The prophets of the Old Testament were the first to preach social justice. But that which was sensed by the prophets many centuries before Christ was not given complete and powerful political expression until our nation was formed as a Federal Union a century and a half ago. Even then, the march of the common people had just begun. Most of them did not yet know how to read and write. There were no public schools to which all children could go. Men and women cannot be really free until they have plenty to eat, and time and ability to read and think and talk things over. Down the years, the people of the United States have moved steadily forward in the practice of democracy. Through universal education, they now can read and write and form opinions of their own. They have learned, and are still learning, the art of production — that is, how to make a living. They have learned, and are still learning, the art of self-government.

If we were to measure freedom by standards of nutrition, education, and self-government, we might rank the United States and certain nations of Western Europe very high. But this would not be fair to other nations where education has become widespread only in the last twenty years. In many nations, a generation ago, nine out of ten of the people could not read or write. Russia, for example, was changed from an illiterate to a literate nation within one generation and, in the process, Russia's appreciation of freedom was enormously enhanced. In China, the increase during the past thirty years in the ability of the people to read and write has been matched by their increased interest in real liberty.

Everywhere, reading and writing are accompanied by industrial progress, and industrial progress sooner or later inevitably brings a strong labor movement. From a long-time and fundamental point of view, there are no backward peoples which are lacking in mechanical sense. Russians, Chinese, and the Indians both of India and the Americas all learn to read and write and operate machines just as well as your children and my children. Everywhere the common people are on the march. Thousands of them are learning to read and write, learning to think together, learning to use tools. These people are learning to think and work together in labor movements, some of which may be extreme or impractical at first, but which eventually will settle down to serve effectively the interests of the common man.

When the freedom-loving people march — when the farmers have an opportunity to buy land at reasonable prices and to sell the produce of their land through their own organizations, when workers have the opportunity to form unions and bargain through them collectively, and when the children of all the people have an opportunity to attend schools which teach them truths of the real world in which they live — when these opportunities are open to everyone, then the world moves straight ahead.

But in countries where the ability to read and write has been recently acquired or where the people have had no long experience in governing themselves on the basis of their own thinking, it is easy for demagogues to arise and prostitute the mind of the common man to their own base ends. Such a demagogue may get financial help from some person of wealth who is unaware of what the end result will be. With this backing, the demagogue may dominate the minds of the people, and, from whatever degree of freedom they have, lead them backward into slavery. Herr Thyssen, the wealthy German steel man, little realized what he was doing when he gave Hitler enough money to enable him to play on the minds of the German people. The demagogue is the curse of the modern world, and of all the demagogues, the worst are those financed by well-meaning wealthy men who sincerely believe that their wealth is likely to be safer if they can hire men with political " it " to change the sign posts and lure the people back into slavery of the most degraded kind. Unfortunately for the wealthy men who finance movements of this sort, as well as for the people themselves, the successful demagogue is a powerful genie who, when once let out of his bottle, refuses to obey anyone's command. As long as his spell holds, he defies God Himself, and Satan is turned loose upon the world.

Through the leaders of the Nazi revolution, Satan now is trying to lead the common man of the whole world back into slavery and darkness. For the stark truth is that the violence preached by the Nazis is the devil's own religion of darkness. So also is the doctrine that one race or one class is by heredity superior and that all other races or classes are supposed to be slaves. The belief in one Satan-inspired Fuehrer, with his Quislings, his Lavals, and his Mussolinis — his " gauleiters " in every nation in the world — is the last and ultimate darkness. Is there any hell hotter than that of being a Quisling, unless it is that of being a Laval or a Mussolini?

In a twisted sense, there is something almost great in the figure of the Supreme Devil operating through a human form, in a Hitler who has the daring to spit straight into the eye of God and man. But the Nazi system has a heroic position for only one leader. By definition only one person is allowed to retain full sovereignty over his own soul. All the rest are stooges — they are stooges who have been mentally and politically degraded, and who feel that they can get square with the world only by mentally and politically degrading other people. These stooges are really psychopathic cases. Satan has turned loose upon us the insane.

The march of freedom of the past 150 years has been a long-drawn-out people's revolution. In this Great Revolution of the people, there were the American Revolution of 1775, the French Revolution of 1792, the Latin-American revolutions of the Bolivarian era, the German revolution of 1848, and the Russian Revolution of 1918. Each spoke for the common man in terms of blood on the battlefield. Some went to excess. But the significant thing is that the people groped their way to the light. More of them learned to think and work together.

The people's revolution aims at peace and not at violence, but if the rights of the common man are attacked, it unleashes the ferocity of a she-bear who has lost a cub. When the Nazi psychologists tell their master Hitler that we in the United States may be able to produce hundreds of thousands of planes, but that we have no will to fight, they are only fooling themselves and him. The truth is that when the rights of the American people are transgressed, as those rights have been transgressed, the American people will fight with a relentless fury which will drive the ancient Teutonic gods back cowering into their caves. The *Götterdämmerung* has come for Odin and his crew.

The people are on the march toward even fuller freedom than the most fortunate peoples of the earth have hitherto enjoyed. No Nazi counter-revolution will stop it. The common man will smoke the Hitler stooges out into the open in the United States, in Latin America, and in

India. He will destroy their influence. No Lavals, no Mussolinis will be tolerated in a free world.

The people, in their millennial and revolutionary march toward manifesting here on earth the dignity that is in every human soul, hold as their credo the Four Freedoms enunciated by President Roosevelt in his message to Congress on January 6, 1942. These Four Freedoms are the very core of the revolution for which the United Nations have taken their stand. We who live in the United States may think there is nothing very revolutionary about freedom of religion, freedom of expression, and freedom from the fear of secret police. But when we begin to think about the significance of freedom from want for the average man, then we know that the revolution of the past 150 years has not been complete, either here in the United States or in any other nation in the world. We know that this revolution cannot stop until freedom from want has actually been attained.

And now, as we move forward toward realizing the Four Freedoms of this people's revolution, I would like to speak about four duties. It is my belief that every freedom, every right, every privilege has its price, its corresponding duty without which it cannot be enjoyed. The four duties of the people's revolution, as I see them today, are these:

1. The duty to produce to the limit.
2. The duty to transport as rapidly as possible to the field of battle.
3. The duty to fight with all that is in us.
4. The duty to build a peace — just, charitable, and enduring.

The fourth duty is that which inspires the other three.

We failed in our job after World War No. 1. We did not know how to go about it to build an enduring world-wide peace. We did not have the nerve to follow through and prevent Germany from rearming. We did not insist that she " learn war no more." We did not build a peace treaty on the fundamental doctrine of the people's revolution. We did not strive whole-heartedly to create a world where there could be freedom from want for all the peoples. But by our very errors we learned much, and after this war we shall be in position to utilize our knowledge in building a world which is economically, politcially, and, I hope, spiritually sound.

Modern science, which is a by-product and an essential part of the people's revolution, has made it technologically possible to see that all of the people of the world get enough to eat. Half in fun and half seriously, I said the other day to Madame Litvinoff: "The object of this war is to make sure that everybody in the world has the privilege of drinking a quart of milk a day." She replied: "Yes, even half a pint." The peace must mean a better standard of living for the common man, not merely in the United States and England, but also in India, Russia, China, and Latin America — not merely in the United Nations, but also in Germany and Italy and Japan.

Some have spoken of the "American Century." I say that the century on which we are entering — the century which will come out of this war — can be and must be the century of the common man. Perhaps it will be America's opportunity to suggest the freedoms and duties by which the common man must live. Everywhere the common man must learn to build his own industries with his own hands in a practical fashion. Everywhere the common man must learn to increase his productivity so that he and his children can eventually pay to the world community all that they have received. No nation will have the God-given right to exploit other nations. Older nations will have the privilege to help younger nations get started on the path to industrialization, but there must be neither military nor economic imperialism. The methods of the nineteenth century will not work in the people's century which is now about to begin. India, China, and Latin America have a tremendous stake in the people's century. As their masses learn to read and write, and as they become productive mechanics, their standard of living will double and treble. Modern science, when devoted whole-heartedly to the general welfare, has in it potentialities of which we do not yet dream.

And modern science must be released from German slavery. International cartels that serve American greed and the German will to power must go. Cartels in the peace to come must be subjected to international control for the common man, as well as being under adequate control by the respective home governments. In this way, we can prevent the Germans from again building a war machine while we sleep. With international monopoly pools under control, it will be possible for inventions to serve all the people instead of only the few.

Yes, and when the time of peace comes, the citizen will again have a duty, the supreme duty of sacrificing the lesser interest for the greater interest of the general welfare. Those who write the peace must think of the whole world. There can be no privileged peoples. We ourselves in the United States are no more a master race than the Nazis. And we

907

cannot perpetuate economic warfare without planting the seeds of military warfare. We must use our power at the peace table to build an economic peace that is just, charitable, and enduring.

If we really believe that we are fighting for a people's peace, all the rest becomes easy. Production, yes — it will be easy to get production without either strikes or sabotage; production with the whole-hearted co-operation between willing arms and keen brains; enthusiasm, zip, energy geared to the tempo of keeping at it everlastingly day after day. Hitler knows as well as those of us who sit in on the War Production Board meetings that we here in the United States are winning the battle of production. He knows that both labor and business in the United States are doing a most remarkable job and that his only hope is to crash through to a complete victory some time during the next six months.

And then there is the task of transportation to the line of battle by truck, by railroad car, by ship. We shall joyously deny ourselves so that our transportation system is improved by at least 30 percent.

I need say little about the duty to fight. Some people declare, and Hitler believes, that the American people have grown soft in the last generation. Hitler agents continually preach in South America that we are cowards, unable to use, like the " brave " German soldiers, the weapons of modern war. It is true that American youth hates war with a holy hatred. But because of that fact and because Hitler and the German people stand as the very symbol of war, we shall fight with a tireless enthusiasm until the war and the possibility of war have been removed from this planet. We shall cleanse the plague spot of Europe, which is Hitler's Germany, and with it the hell-hole of Asia — Japan.

The American people have always had guts and always will have. You know the story of Bomber Pilot Dixon and Radioman Gene Aldrich and Ordnanceman Tony Pastula — the story which Americans will be telling their children for generations to illustrate man's ability to master any fate. These men lived for thirty-four days on the open sea in a rubber life raft, eight feet by four feet, with no food but that which they took from the sea and the air with one pocket knife and a pistol. And yet they lived it through and came at last to the beach of an island they did not know. In spite of their suffering and weakness, they stood like men, with no weapon left to protect themselves, and no shoes on their feet or clothes on their backs, and walked in military file because, they said, " if there were Japs, we didn't want to be crawling."

The American fighting men, and all the fighting men of the United Nations, will need to summon all their courage during the next few months. I am convinced that the summer and fall of 1942 will be a time of supreme crisis for us all. Hitler, like the prize-fiighter who realizes he is on the verge of being knocked out, is gathering all his remaining forces for one last desperate blow. There is abject fear in the heart of the madman and a growing discontent among his people as he prepares for his last all-out offensive. . . .

We must be especially prepared to stifle the fifth columnists in the United States who will try to sabotage not merely our war material plants but, even more important, our minds. We must be prepared for the worst kind of fifth column work in Latin America, much of it operating through the agency of governments with which the United States at present is at peace. When I say this, I recognize that the peoples, both of Latin America and of the nations supporting the agencies through which the fifth columnists work, are overwhelmingly on the side of the democracies. We must expect the offensive against us on the military, propaganda, and sabotage fronts, both in the United States and in Latin America, to reach its apex some time during the next few months. The convulsive efforts of the dying madman will be so great that some of us may be deceived into thinking that the situation is bad at a time when it is really getting better. But in the case of most of us, the events of the next few months, disturbing though they may be, will only increase our will to bring about complete victory in this war of liberation. Prepared in spirit, we cannot be surprised. Psychological terrorism will fall flat. As we nerve ourselves for the supreme effort in this hemisphere we must not forget the sublime heroism of the oppressed in Europe and Asia, whether it be in the mountains of Yugoslavia, the factories of Czechoslovakia and France, the farms of Poland, Denmark, Holland, and Belgium, among the seamen of Norway, or in the occupied areas of China and the Dutch East Indies. Everywhere the soul of man is letting the tyrant know that slavery of the body does not end resistance.

There can be no half measures. North, South, East, West, and Middlewest — the will of the American people is for complete victory.

No compromise with Satan is possible. We shall not rest until all the victims under the Nazi yoke are freed. We shall fight for a complete peace as well as a complete victory.

The people's revolution is on the march, and the devil and all his angels can not prevail against it. They cannot prevail, for on the side of the people is the Lord.

He giveth power to the faint; to them that have no might He increaseth strength. . . . They that wait upon the Lord shall mount up with wings as eagles; they shall run, and not be weary; they shall walk and not be faint.

Strong in the strength of the Lord, we who fight in the people's cause will never stop until that cause is won.

[1942]

CARL SANDBURG

[1878–   ]

HE WAS born of Swedish immigrant parents in Galesburg, Illinois. It was a working-class family and even as a young boy Sandburg had to do his share. He had few opportunities for schooling. At seventeen he went west, riding freight cars, to work in the wheat fields of Kansas and as a dishwasher in Omaha and Denver. When the Spanish-American War broke out, he enlisted and served for eight months in Puerto Rico. On his return he decided to acquire an education; he entered Lombard College and worked his way through. While at college he became interested in writing, edited the college paper. After being graduated he went into journalism and politics in Milwaukee, became a socialist organizer, finally went to Chicago to work for a magazine. In 1917 he joined the staff of the *Chicago Daily News*, eventually becoming an editorial writer. He was connected with this paper until 1933. Since his college days he had been writing poetry. In 1914 the magazine *Poetry* published some of his work and awarded him a prize; in 1916 his *Chicago Poems* was published and in 1918 his volume *Cornhuskers*. From that time on he has generally been ranked among the best of our contemporaries. What distinguished him above all else was his unwavering devotion to the common people. He has been the Walt Whitman of our age. *Smoke and Steel* (1922) and *Slabs of the Sunburnt West* (1922) increased his reputation. Other volumes followed, until at last came *The People, Yes* (1936), a poetic affirmation of democracy, of belief in the masses, which has already become a classic. Best known, however, is his six-volume biography of Lincoln, of which two volumes appeared in 1926 and four in 1939. This, too, is a pæan of praise to the plain people of America.

from

THE PEOPLE, YES

A

The people is Everyman, everybody.
Everybody is you and me and all others.
What everybody says is what we all say.
And what is it we all say?

Where did we get these languages?
Why is your baby-talk deep in your blood?
What is the cling of the tongue
To what it heard with its mother-milk?

They cross on the ether now.
They travel on high frequencies
Over the border-lines and barriers
Of mountain ranges and oceans.
When shall we all speak the same language?
And do we want to have all the same language?
Are we learning a few great signs and passwords?
Why should Everyman be lost for words?
The questions are put every day in every tongue:
    " Where you from, Stranger?
    Where were you born?
    Got any money?
    What do you work at?
    Where's your passport?
    Who are your people? "

Over the ether crash the languages.
    And the people listen.
As on the plain of Howdeehow they listen.
    They want to hear.
They will be told when the next war is ready.
The long wars and the short wars will come on the air,
How many got killed and how the war ended
And who got what and the price paid
And how there were tombs for the Unknown Soldier,
    The boy nobody knows the name of,
The boy whose great fame is that of the masses,
The millions of names too many to write on a tomb,
The heroes, the cannonfodder, the living targets,
The mutilated and sacred dead,
The people, yes.

Two countries with two flags
are nevertheless one land, one blood, one people —
    can this be so?

912

And the earth belongs to the family of man?
　can this be so?

The first world war came and its cost was laid on the people.
The second world war — the third — what will be the cost?
And will it repay the people for what they pay?

B

In the folded and quiet yesterdays
Put down in the book of the past
Is a scrawl of scrawny thumbs
And a smudge of clutching fingers
And the breath of hanged men,
Of thieves and vagabonds,
Of killers saying welcome as an ax fell,
Of traitors cut in four pieces
And their bowels thrust over their faces
According to the ancient Anglo-Saxon
Formula for the crime of treason,
Of persons covered with human filth
In due exaction of a penalty,
Of ears clipped, noses slit, fingers chopped
For the identification of vagrants,
Of loiterers and wanderers seared
" with a hot iron in the breast the mark V,"
Of violence as a motive lying deep
As the weather changes of the sea,
Of gang wars, tong wars, civil tumults,
Industrial strife, international mass murders,
Of agitators outlawed to live on thistles,
Of thongs for holding plainspoken men,
Of thought and speech being held a crime,
And a woman burned for saying,
" I listen to my Voices and obey them,"
And a thinker locked into stone and iron
For saying, " The earth moves,"
And the pity of men learning by shocks,
By pain and practice,
By plunges and struggles in a bitter pool.

913

In the folded and quiet yesterdays
how many times has it happened?
The leaders of the people estimated as to price
And bought with bribes signed and delivered
Or waylaid and shot or meshed by perjurers
Or hunted and sent into hiding
Or taken and paraded in garments of dung,
Fire applied to their footsoles:
　" Now will you talk? "
Their mouths basted with rubber hose:
　" Now will you talk? "
Thrown into solitary, fed on slops, hung by thumbs,
Till the mention of that uprising is casual, so-so,
As though the next revolt breeds somewhere
In the bowels of that mystic behemoth, the people.
" And when it comes again," say watchers, " we are ready."
　How many times
　in the folded and quiet yesterdays
　has it happened?

　" You may burn my flesh and bones
　and throw the ashes to the four winds,"
　smiled one of them,
　" Yet my voice shall linger on
　and in the years yet to come
　the young shall ask what was the idea
　for which you gave me death
　and what was I saying
　that I must die for what I said? "

C

Hunger and only hunger changes worlds?
The dictate of the belly
that gnawing under the navel,
this alone is the builder and the pathfinder
sending man into danger and fire
and death by struggle?
　Yes and no, no and yes.

The strong win against the weak.
The strong lose against the stronger.
And across the bitter years and the howling winters
    the deathless dream will be the stronger,
    the dream of equity will win.
There are shadows and bones shot with lights
    too strong to be lost.
    Can the wilderness be put behind?
    Shall man always go on dog-eat-dog?
    Who says so?
    The stronger?
    And who is the stronger?
And how long shall the stronger hold on as the stronger?
    What will tomorrow write?
    " Of the people by the people for the people? "
What mockers ever wrung a crop from a waiting soil
Or when did cold logic bring forth a child?
" What use is it? " they asked a kite-flying sky gazer
And he wished in return to know, " What use is a baby? "
The dreaming scholars who quested the useless,
who wanted to know merely for the sake of knowing,
they sought and harnessed electrodynamic volts
becoming in time thirty billion horses in one country
hauling with thirty-billion-horse-power
and this is an early glimpse, a dim beginning,
the first hill of a series of hills.

    What comes after the spectrum?
With what will the test-tubes be shaken tomorrow?
For what will the acetylene torch and pneumatic chisel be scrapped?
What will the international partnerships of the world laboratories
    track down next, what new fuels, amalgams, alloys, seeds, cross-
    breeds, unforeseen short cuts to power?
Whose guess is better than anybody else's on whether the breed of
    fire-bringers is run out, whether light rays, death rays, laugh rays,
    are now for us only in a dim beginning?
Across the bitter years and the howling winters
    the deathless dream will be the stronger
    the dream of equity will win.

D

The people will live on.
The learning and blundering people will live on.
They will be tricked and sold and again sold
And go back to the nourishing earth for rootholds,
The people so peculiar in renewal and comeback,
You can't laugh off their capacity to take it.
The mammoth rests between his cyclonic dramas.

The people so often sleepy, weary, enigmatic,
is a vast huddle with many units saying:
" I earn my living.
I make enough to get by
and it takes all my time.
If I had more time
I could do more for myself
and maybe for others.
I could read and study
and talk things over
and find out about things.
It takes time.
I wish I had the time."

The people is a tragic and comic two-face: hero and hoodlum:
phantom and gorilla twisting to moan with a gargoyle mouth:
" They buy me and sell me . . . it's a game . . .
sometime I'll break loose. . . ."

Once having marched
Over the margins of animal necessity,
Over the grim line of sheer subsistence
Then man came
To the deeper rituals of his bones,
To the lights lighter than any bones,
To the time for thinking things over,
To the dance, the song, the story,
Or the hours given over to dreaming,
Once having marched.

Between the finite limitations of the five senses
and the endless yearnings of man for the beyond
the people hold to the humdrum bidding of work and food
while reaching out when it comes their way
for lights beyond the prison of the five senses,
for keepsakes lasting beyond any hunger or death.
    This reaching is alive.
The panderers and liars have violated and smutted it.
    Yet this reaching is alive yet
    for lights and keepsakes.

        The people know the salt of the sea
        and the strength of the winds
        lashing the corners of the earth.
        The people take the earth
        as a tomb of rest and a cradle of hope.
        Who else speaks for the Family of Man?
        They are in tune and step
        with constellations of universal law.

    The people is a polychrome,
    a spectrum and a prism
    held in a moving monolith,
    a console organ of changing themes,
    a clavilux of color poems
    wherein the sea offers fog
    and the fog moves off in rain
    and the labrador sunset shortens
    to a nocturne of clear stars
    serene over the shot spray
    of northern lights.

    The steel mill sky is alive.
    The fire breaks white and zigzag
    shot on a gun-metal gloaming.
    Man is a long time coming.
    Man will yet win.
    Brother may yet line up with brother:

917

This old anvil laughs at many broken hammers.
    There are men who can't be bought.
    The fireborn are at home in fire.
    The stars make no noise.
    You can't hinder the wind from blowing.
    Time is a great teacher.
    Who can live without hope?

In the darkness with a great bundle of grief the people march.
In the night, and overhead a shovel of stars for keeps, the people march:
                " Where to? what next? "

[*1936*]

BIBLIOGRAPHICAL NOTE

☼

As supplements to this volume, I recommend the following four anthologies of American writings:

The Oxford Anthology of American Literature, edited by William Rose Benét and Norman Holmes Pearson. Oxford University Press, 1938.

The Heritage of America, edited by Henry Steele Commager and Allan Nevins. Little, Brown and Company, 1939.

The Puritans, edited by Perry Miller and Thomas H. Johnson. American Book Company, 1938.

The American Mind, edited by Harry R. Warfel, Ralph H. Gabriel, and Stanley T. Williams. American Book Company, 1937.

For general literary background, the following are recommended:

The Flowering of New England, by Van Wyck Brooks. E. P. Dutton and Company, 1936.

A History of American Literature, by W. B. Cairns. Oxford University Press, 1930 (revised edition).

Main Currents in American Thought, by Vernon Louis Parrington. 3 volumes. Harcourt, Brace and Company, 1927–30.

Forces in American Criticism, by Bernard Smith. Harcourt, Brace and Company, 1939.

The Cambridge History of American Literature, edited by W. P. Trent, John Erskine, Stuart P. Sherman, and Carl Van Doren. 4 volumes. G. P. Putnam's Sons, 1917–21.

The Literary History of the American Revolution, by Moses Coit Tyler. 2 volumes. G. P. Putnam's Sons, 1897.

For general historical background, the following are recommended:

Founding of New England, by James Truslow Adams. Little, Brown and Company, 1921.

Revolutionary New England, by James Truslow Adams. Little, Brown and Company, 1923.

919

American Faith, by Ernest Sutherland Bates. W. W. Norton and Company, 1940.

Let My People Go, by Henrietta Buckmaster. Harper and Brothers, 1941.

The Rise of American Civilization, by Charles A. and Mary R. Beard. 2 volumes. The Macmillan Company, 1927.

The Mind of the South, by W. J. Cash. Alfred A. Knopf, 1941.

History of Labor in the United States, by John R. Commons and others. 2 volumes. The Macmillan Company, 1918.

American Economic History, by Harold Underwood Faulkner. Harper and Brothers, 1935 (third edition).

Crusaders for American Liberalism, by Louis Filler. Harcourt, Brace and Company, 1939.

The Course of American Democratic Thought, by Ralph Henry Gabriel. The Ronald Press, 1940.

The United States since 1865, by Louis M. Hacker and Benjamin B. Kendrick. F. S. Crofts and Company, 1934 (revised edition).

The Growth of the American Republic, by Samuel Eliot Morison and Henry Steele Commager. 2 volumes. Oxford University Press, 1937.

History of the American Frontier, 1763–1893, by Frederic L. Paxson. Houghton Mifflin Company, 1924.

For biographical information the indispensable works are:

The Dictionary of American Biography, edited by Allen Johnson and Dumas Malone. 20 volumes. Charles Scribner's Sons, 1928–36.

Contemporary American Authors, by Fred B. Millett. Harcourt, Brace and Company, 1940.

ACKNOWLEDGMENTS

✲

The editor gratefully acknowledges the kindness of authors and publishers in giving permission to reproduce copyright material in *The Democratic Spirit* as follows:

STEPHEN VINCENT BENÉT: for " Ode to the Austrian Socialists " and the selection from " Ode to Walt Whitman," from *Burning City*, published by Farrar & Rinehart, Inc., copyright 1933, 1935, 1936 by Stephen Vincent Benét. Reprinted by permission.

THE JOHN DAY COMPANY: for the selection from *The Myth of Rugged American Individualism* by Charles A. Beard. Reprinted by permission of the John Day Company.

JOHN DOS PASSOS: for the selections from *U. S. A.* by John Dos Passos. Reprinted by permission.

DOUBLEDAY, DORAN AND COMPANY, INC.: for the selection from *The New Freedom* by Woodrow Wilson, copyright 1913, 1933 by Doubleday, Doran and Company, Inc.; for the selection from *It Can't Happen Here* by Sinclair Lewis, copyright 1935. Reprinted by permission of Doubleday, Doran and Company, Inc.

DUELL, SLOAN & PEARCE, INC.: for " Daughter," from *Jackpot* by Erskine Caldwell. Reprinted by permission of Duell, Sloan & Pearce, Inc.

E. P. DUTTON & CO., INC.: for the selection from " America's Coming-of-Age," from *Three Essays on America* by Van Wyck Brooks, copyright by E. P. Dutton & Co., Inc., New York. Reprinted by permission of E. P. Dutton & Co., Inc.

FARRAR & RINEHART, INC.: for " Pole Star for This Year " and " Speech to a Crowd," from *Public Speech* by Archibald MacLeish, copyright 1936. Reprinted by permission of Farrar & Rinehart, Inc., publishers.

HARCOURT, BRACE AND COMPANY, INC.: for the selection from *Main Currents in American Thought* by Vernon L. Parrington, copyright 1930 by Harcourt, Brace and Company, Inc.; for " The Miracle of Debs," " Sacco and Vanzetti," and " Two-Gun Crowley," from *It Seems to Me* by Heywood Broun, copyright 1935 by Harcourt, Brace and Company, Inc.; for the selection from *The Autobiography of Lincoln Steffens*, copyright 1931 by Harcourt, Brace and Company, Inc.; for the selections from *The People, Yes* by Carl Sandburg, copyright 1936 by Harcourt, Brace and Company, Inc.; for the selection from *Faith for Living* by Lewis Mumford, copyright 1940 by Lewis Mumford. Reprinted by permission of Harcourt, Brace and Company, Inc.

HARPER AND BROTHERS: for the selection from *A Connecticut Yankee in King Arthur's Court* by Mark Twain; for the selection from " To the Person Sitting in Darkness," from *Europe and Elsewhere* by Mark Twain; for " Incident " and " Yet Do I Marvel," from *Color* by Countee Cullen; for the

921

selection from *Native Son* by Richard Wright; for " Silence in Mallorca," from *Collected Poems* by Genevieve Taggard; for the selection from *You Can't Go Home Again* by Thomas Wolfe. Reprinted by permission of Harper and Brothers.

HOUGHTON MIFFLIN COMPANY: for the selection from *Looking Backward* by Edward Bellamy; for the selections from *Letters of Charles Eliot Norton;* for the selections from *The Poems of William Vaughn Moody*. Reprinted by permission of Houghton Mifflin Company.

MILDRED HOWELLS: for the selections from *A Hazard of New Fortunes* and *Criticism and Fiction* by William Dean Howells. Reprinted by permission of Mildred Howells.

LANGSTON HUGHES: for " Let America Be America Again." Reprinted by permission.

ALFRED A. KNOPF, INC.: for " Cross " and " I, Too, Sing America," from *The Weary Blues* by Langston Hughes. Reprinted by permission of Alfred A. Knopf, Inc.

LIVERIGHT PUBLISHING CORP.: for the selection from *Jews Without Money* by Michael Gold, published by Liveright Publishing Corp. Reprinted by permission.

CHARMIAN LONDON: for " What Life Means to Me," from *Revolution and Other Essays* by Jack London. Reprinted by permission of Charmian London.

A. C. McCLURG & Co.: for the selection from *The Souls of Black Folk* by W. E. B. DuBois. Reprinted by permission of A. C. McClurg & Co.

THE MACMILLAN COMPANY: for the selection from *A Son of the Middle Border* by Hamlin Garland; for the selection from *The Promise of American Life* by Herbert Croly; for " Factory Windows Are Always Broken," " Tolstoi Is Plowing Yet," " A Net to Snare the Moonlight," and " Bryan, Bryan, Bryan, Bryan," from *Collected Poems* by Vachel Lindsay; for the selection from *Democracy and Education* by John Dewey; for the selection from *A Southerner Discovers the South* by Jonathan Daniels. Reprinted by permission of The Macmillan Company, publishers.

VIRGIL MARKHAM: for " The Man With the Hoe " by Edwin Markham. Reprinted by permission of Virgil Markham.

EDGAR LEE MASTERS: for " English Thornton," " Harry Wilmans," and " John Wasson," from *Spoon River Anthology* by Edgar Lee Masters. Reprinted, by permission.

EDNA ST. VINCENT MILLAY: for " Justice Denied in Massachusetts," from *The Buck in the Snow,* published by Harper and Brothers, copyright 1928 by Edna St. Vincent Millay; for " Czecho-Slovakia " and " Say That We Saw Spain Die," from *Huntsman, What Quarry?* published by Harper and Brothers, copyright 1933, 1934, 1936, 1937, 1939 by Edna St. Vincent Millay. Reprinted by permission.

RANDOM HOUSE, INC.: for " Room in the World," from *Home Is Where You Hang Your Childhood* by Leane Zugsmith; for the selection from *Watch on the Rhine* by Lillian Hellman. Reprinted by permission of Random House, Inc.

CHARLES SCRIBNER'S SONS: for the selections from *Mr. Dooley at His Best* by Finley Peter Dunne; for the selection from *Of Time and the River* by Thomas Wolfe. Reprinted by permission of Charles Scribner's Sons.

SIMON AND SCHUSTER, INC.: for the selection from *A Book About Myself* by Theodore Dreiser. Reprinted by permission of Simon and Schuster, Inc.

GENEVIEVE TAGGARD: for "Long View," copyright by Genevieve Taggard. Reprinted by permission.

THE VIKING PRESS, INC.: for selections from "The War and the Intellectuals" and "Unfinished Fragment on the State," from *Untimely Papers* by Randolph Bourne, copyright 1919 by B. W. Huebsch; for "To America" and "The Black Mammy," from *St. Peter Relates an Incident* by James Weldon Johnson, copyright 1917, 1921, 1935 by James Weldon Johnson; for selections from *The Letters of Sacco and Vanzetti* edited by Marion D. Frankfurter and Gardner Jackson, copyright 1928; for "Soldiers of the Republic," from *Here Lies* by Dorothy Parker, copyright 1930, 1933, 1939 by Dorothy Parker; for the selections from *The Grapes of Wrath* by John Steinbeck, copyright 1939 by John Steinbeck. Reprinted by permission of the Viking Press, Inc., New York.

WENDELL L. WILLKIE: for selections from his "Report to the Nation on Global War and Peace." Reprinted by permission.

INDEX OF AUTHORS

✵

A NOTE ON THE TYPE

The text of this book is set in Caledonia, a Linotype face designed by W. A. DWIGGINS, the man responsible for so much that is good in contemporary book design and typography. Caledonia belongs to the family of printing types called "modern face" by printers — a term used to mark the change in style of type-letters that occurred about 1800. It has all the hard-working feet-on-the-ground qualities of the Scotch Modern face plus the liveliness and grace that is integral in every Dwiggins "product" whether it be a simple catalogue cover or an almost human puppet.

The book was composed, printed, and bound by THE PLIMPTON PRESS, Norwood, Mass. The typography and design were by S. R. JACOBS; the drawings for the binding, by OSCAR OGG.

Date Due

MAR 28 '50			
NOV 27 '50			
DEC 18 '50			
DEC 15 '51			
DEC 18 '51			
MAY 2 2 1951			
OCT 2 4 '62			